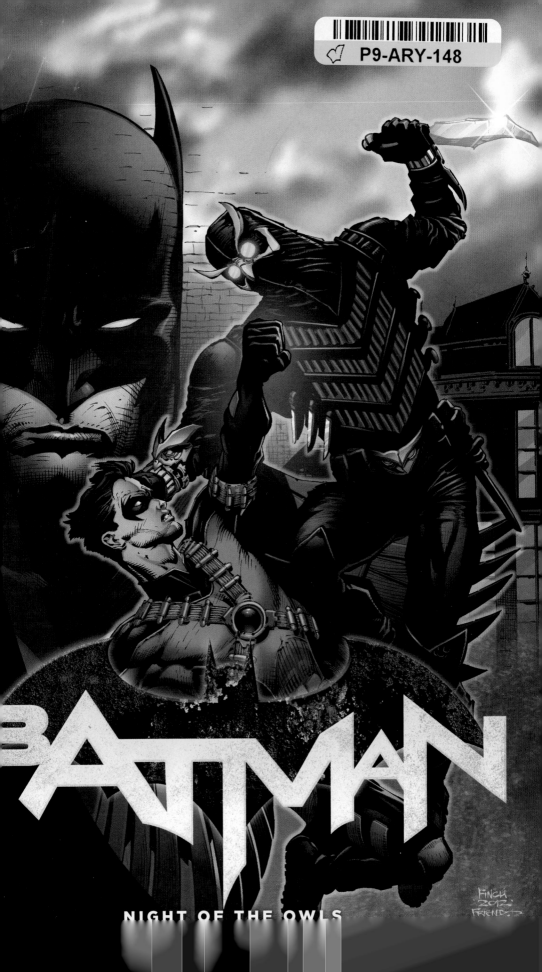

BATMAN

NIGHT OF THE OWLS

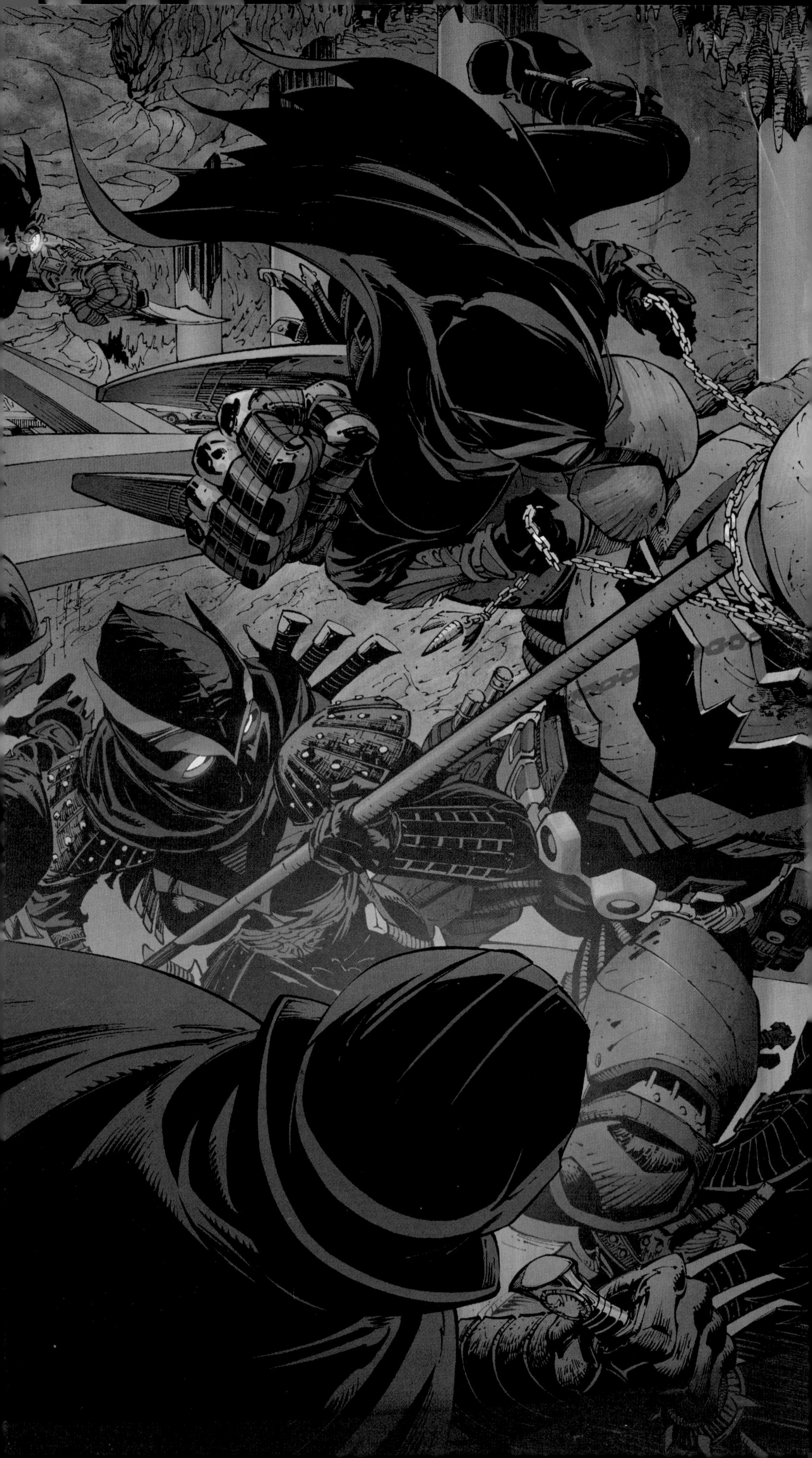

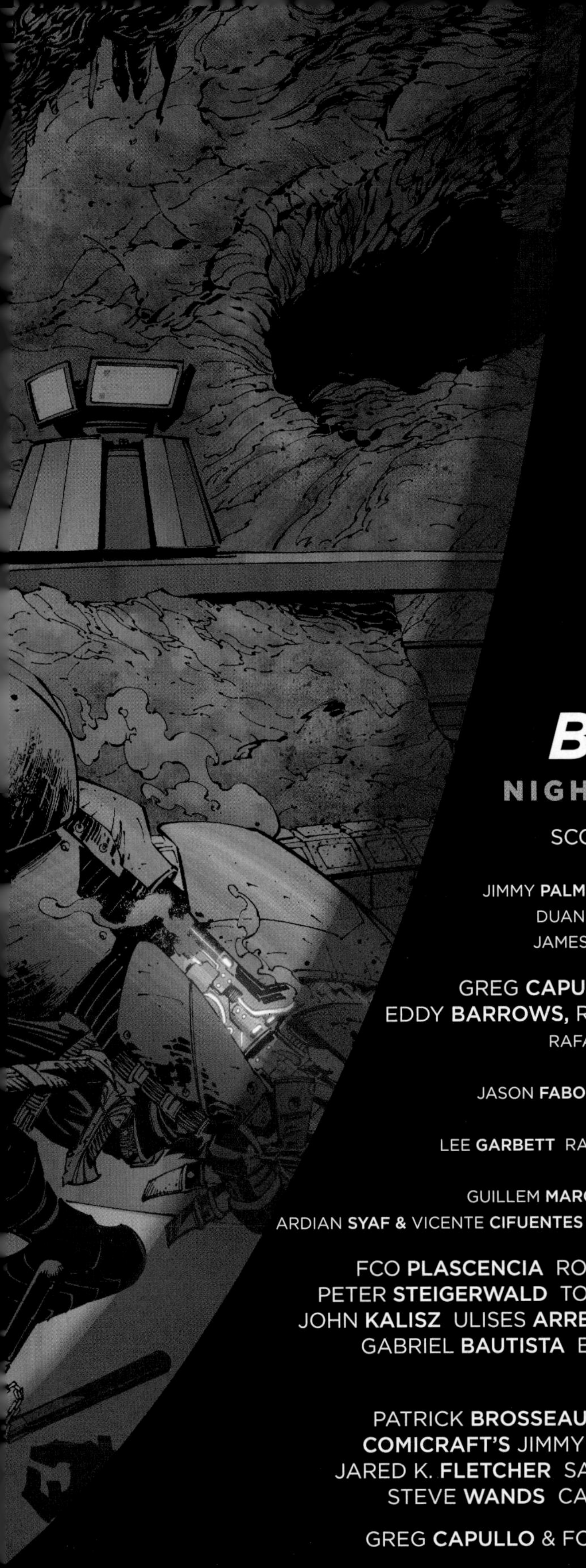

BATMAN

NIGHT OF THE OWLS

SCOTT **SNYDER** KYLE **HIGGINS**
TONY S. **DANIEL** SCOTT **LOBDELL**
JIMMY **PALMIOTTI** & JUSTIN **GRAY** GAIL **SIMONE**
DUANE **SWIERCZYNSKI** PETER J. **TOMASI**
JAMES **TYNION IV** JUDD **WINICK** writers

GREG **CAPULLO &** JONATHAN **GLAPION**
EDDY **BARROWS,** RUY JÓSE & EBER **FERREIRA**
RAFAEL **ALBUQUERQUE** ANDY **CLARKE**
TONY S. **DANIEL &** SANDU **FLOREA**
JASON **FABOK** DAVID **FINCH &** RICHARD **FRIEND**
TRAVEL **FOREMAN &** JEFF **HUET**
LEE **GARBETT** RAY **MCCARTHY &** KEITH **CHAMPAGNE**
ANDRES **GUINALDO &** MARK **IRWIN**
GUILLEM **MARCH** **MORITAT** KENNETH **ROCAFORT**
ARDIAN **SYAF &** VICENTE **CIFUENTES** MARCUS **TO &** RYAN **WINN** artists

FCO **PLASCENCIA** ROD **REIS** NATHAN **FAIRBAIRN**
PETER **STEIGERWALD** TOMEU **MOREY** SONIA **OBACK**
JOHN **KALISZ** ULISES **ARREOLA** **BLOND** GABE **ELTAEB**
GABRIEL **BAUTISTA** BRIAN **REBER** DAVE **MCCAIG**
PETER **PANTAZIS** colorists

PATRICK **BROSSEAU** RICHARD **STARKINGS** AND
COMICRAFT'S JIMMY B ROB **LEIGH** DEZI **SIENTY**
JARED K. **FLETCHER** SAL **CIPRIANO** DAVE **SHARPE**
STEVE **WANDS** CARLOS M. **MANGUAL** letterers

GREG **CAPULLO** & FCO **PLASCENCIA** cover artists

BATMAN created by BOB **KANE**

NIGHTWING created by MARV **WOLFMAN** & GEORGE **PÉREZ**

MIKE MARTS JOEY CAVALIERI BOBBIE CHASE BRIAN CUNNINGHAM RACHEL GLUCKSTERN HARVEY RICHARDS Editors – Orig
KATIE KUBERT RICKEY PURDIN KATE STEWART Assistant Editors – Original Series PETER HAMBOUSSI Editor
ROBBIN BROSTERMAN Design Director – Books ROBBIE BIEDERMAN Publication Design

BOB HARRAS Senior VP – Editor-in-Chief, DC Comics

DIANE NELSON President DAN DIDIO and JIM LEE Co-Publishers
GEOFF JOHNS Chief Creative Officer
JOHN ROOD Executive VP – Sales, Marketing and Business Development
AMY GENKINS Senior VP – Business and Legal Affairs NAIRI GARDINER Senior VP – Finance
JEFF BOISON VP – Publishing Planning MARK CHIARELLO VP – Art Direction and Design
JOHN CUNNINGHAM VP – Marketing TERRI CUNNINGHAM VP – Editorial Administration
ALISON GILL Senior VP – Manufacturing and Operations HANK KANALZ Senior VP – Vertigo and Integrated Publishing
JAY KOGAN VP – Business and Legal Affairs, Publishing JACK MAHAN VP – Business Affairs, Talent
NICK NAPOLITANO VP – Manufacturing Administration SUE POHJA VP – Book Sales
COURTNEY SIMMONS Senior VP – Publicity BOB WAYNE Senior VP – Sales

BATMAN: NIGHT OF THE OWLS

Originally published in single magazine form in ALL-STAR WESTERN 9, BATMAN 8-9, BATMAN ANNUAL 1,
BATMAN: THE DARK KNIGHT 9, BATMAN: DETECTIVE COMICS 9, BATGIRL 9, BATWING 9, BIRDS OF PREY 9,
NIGHTWING 8-9, BATMAN AND ROBIN 9, CATWOMAN 9 and RED HOOD AND THE OUTLAWS 9 Copyright © 2012 DC Com
All Rights Reserved. All characters, their distinctive likenesses and related elements featured in this publication
are trademarks of DC Comics. The stories, characters and incidents featured in this publication are entirely fictional.
DC Comics does not read or accept unsolicited ideas, stories or artwork.

DC Comics, 1700 Broadway, New York, NY 10019
A Warner Bros. Entertainment Company.
Printed by RR Donnelley, Willard, OH, USA. 10/4/13. First Printing.

HC ISBN: 978-1-4012-3773-8
SC ISBN: 978-1-4012-4252-7

SUSTAINABLE Certified Chain of Custody
FORESTRY   At Least 20% Certified Forest Content
INITIATIVE www.sfiprogram.org
SFI-01042
APPLIES TO TEXT STOCK ONLY

Library of Congress Cataloging-in-Publication Data

Snyder, Scott.
Batman : night of the owls / Scott Snyder, Kyle Higgins, Greg Capullo, Eddy Barrows.
p. cm.
"Originally published in single magazine form in Batman 8-11, Nightwing 8-9, All-Star Western 9, Catwoman 9, Batgirl 9, Batman:
Knight 9, Batman and Robin 9, Batwing 9, Birds Of Prey 9, Red Hood and The Outlaws 9, Batman Annual 1."
ISBN 978-1-4012-3773-8
1. Graphic novels. I. Higgins, Kyle, 1985- II. Capullo, Greg. III. Barrows, Eddy. IV. Title. V. Title: Night of the owls.
PN6728.B36S666 2012
741.5'973—dc23
2012040574

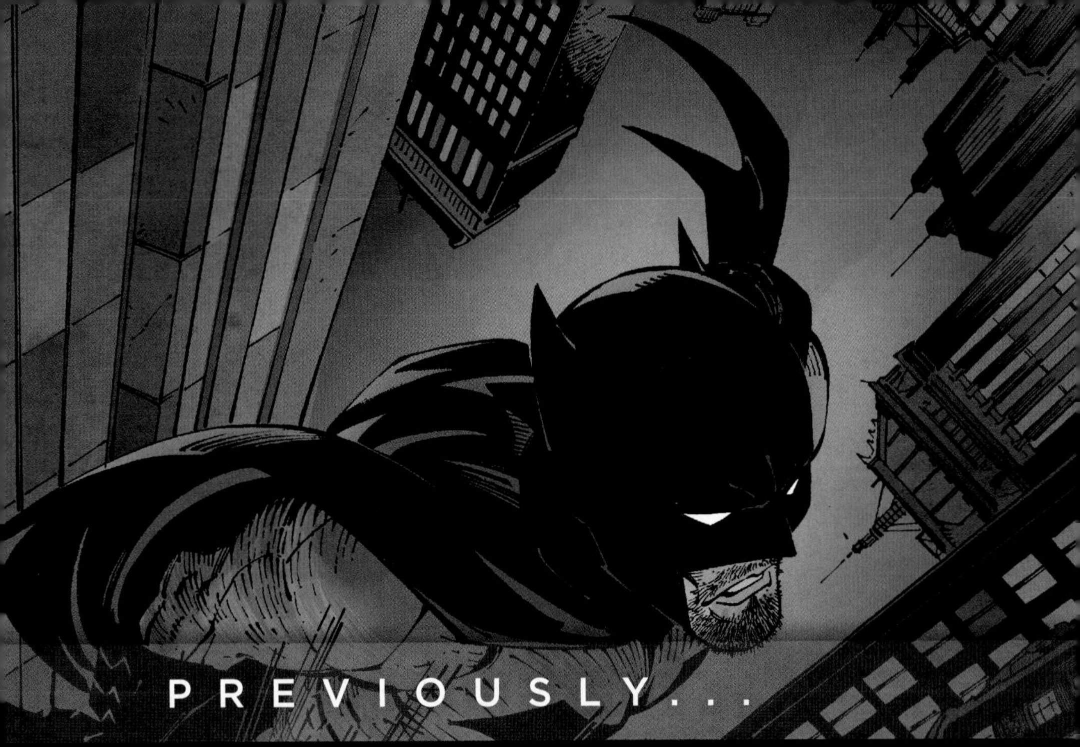

PREVIOUSLY...

Batman had believed the Court of Owls was just a nursery rhyme. As a young boy, he'd even honed his detective skills trying to prove that they existed, but despite careful investigation, he never found any proof that a secret, owl-obsessed cabal ruled Gotham City.

That was before the Talon, the Court's legendary assassin, tried to kill Bruce Wayne in the middle of his meeting with mayoral candidate Lincoln March. It took all of his wits and skills as the Dark Knight to survive the deadly plummet from the top of Old Wayne Tower.

Batman uncovered the Court's nests, hidden in secret floors of Wayne-constructed buildings, dating as far back as the 19th century. The Talon ambushed the Caped Crusader while he was investigating a lead, thereby capturing him—and proceeded to hunt the Dark Knight through a labyrinth for the Court's sadistic amusement!

While trapped in the Court's maze, he discovered evidence of a longstanding rivalry between the Owls and the Wayne family... even proof that they were responsible for the death of his great-great-grandfather, the architect Alan Wayne. After a strenuous battle with the Talon, only Batman's incredible perseverance allowed him to make a harrowing escape—almost at the cost of his own life.

In defeat, the Court abandoned their champion. Upon examining his bested enemy, Batman made several shocking discoveries. The Talon he'd fought was William Cobb, Dick Grayson's great-grandfather—the Court recruited their killers from Haly's Circus—and they had intended to make Dick their next executioner! Even more worrisome was the fact that the process by which Cobb had been reanimated endowed him with metahuman regenerative abilities, which only extreme cold could suppress.

The Court unleashed their ultimate offensive. They awakened all of the Talons from previous generations who, like William Cobb, had been kept in suspended animation—and set them all loose on Gotham City! Against a plague of nearly undying assassins, Batman and his allies are in for one LONG night...

THE NIGHT OF THE OWLS HAS BEGUN!

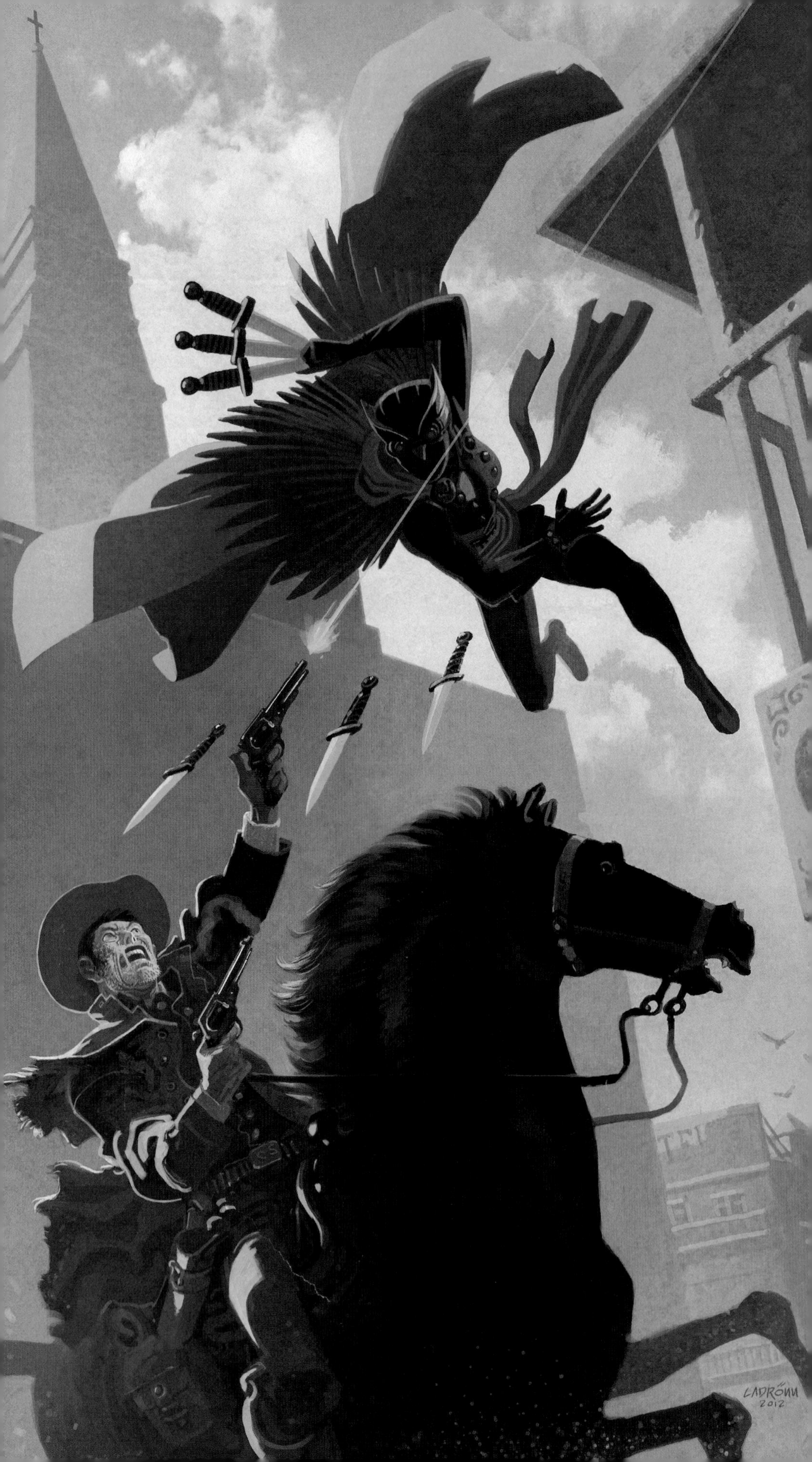
LADRÖNN
2012

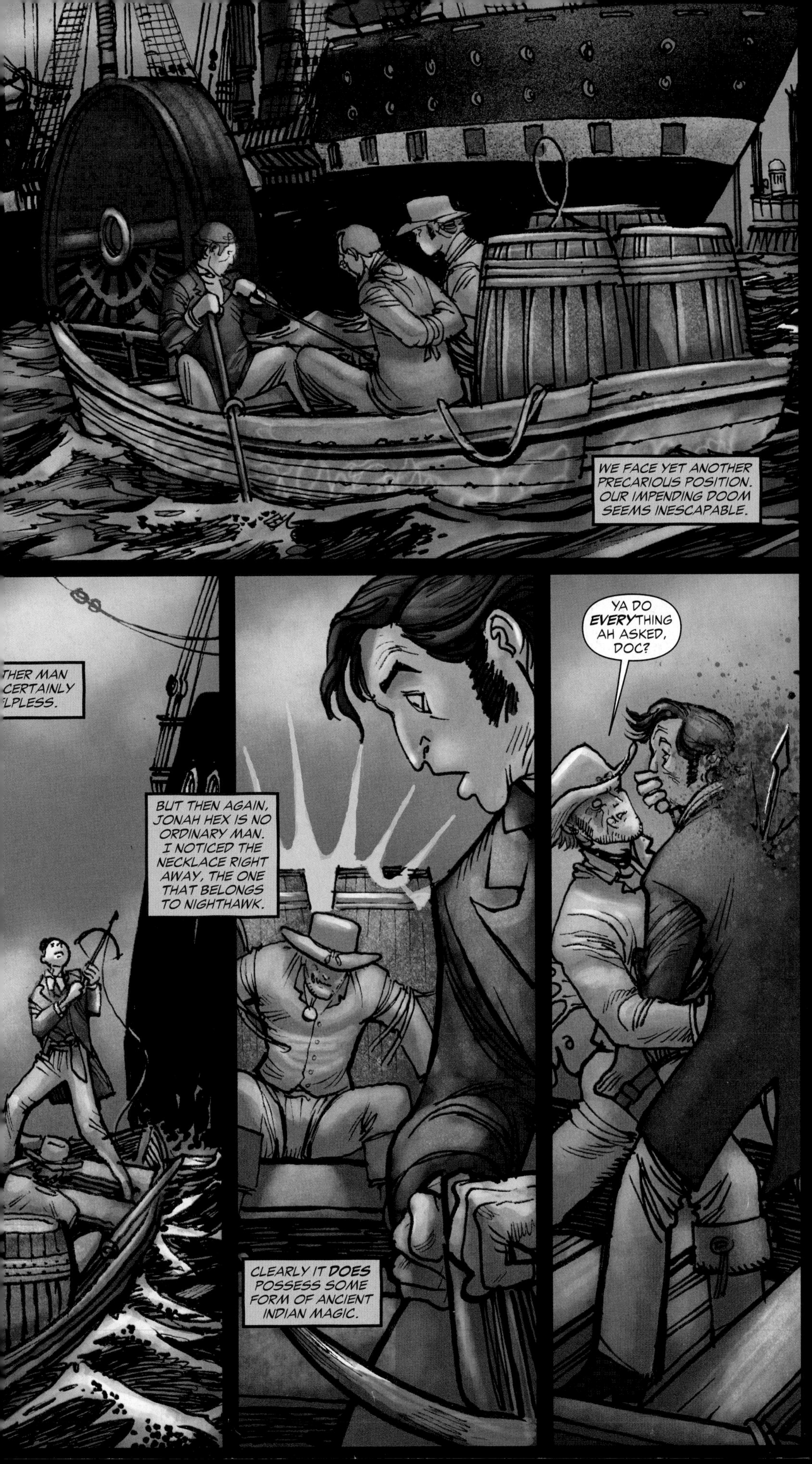
WE FACE YET ANOTHER PRECARIOUS POSITION. OUR IMPENDING DOOM SEEMS INESCAPABLE.
THER MAN CERTAINLY LPLESS.
BUT THEN AGAIN, JONAH HEX IS NO ORDINARY MAN. I NOTICED THE NECKLACE RIGHT AWAY, THE ONE THAT BELONGS TO NIGHTHAWK.
CLEARLY IT **DOES** POSSESS SOME FORM OF ANCIENT INDIAN MAGIC.
YA DO **EVERY**THING AH ASKED, DOC?

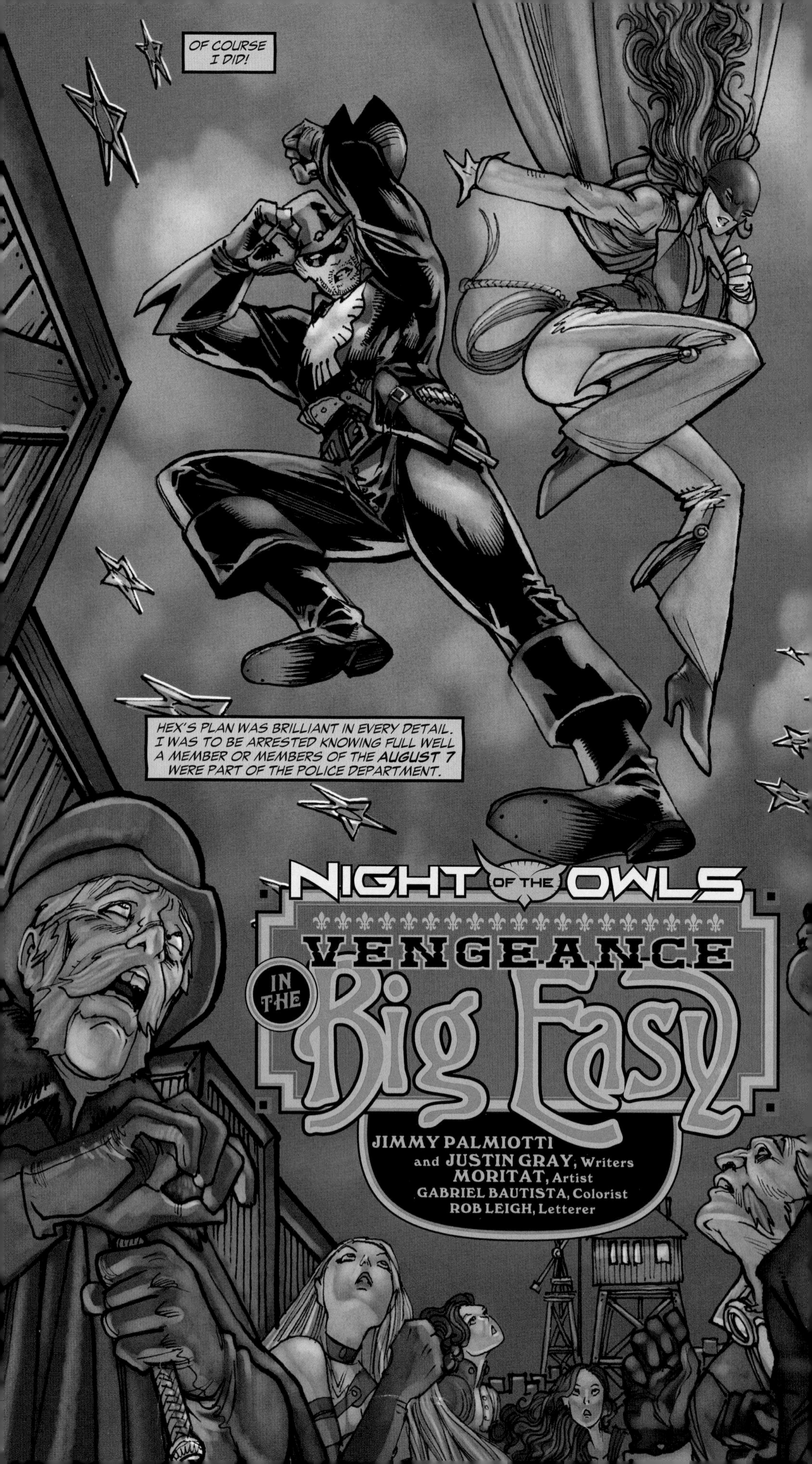

OF COURSE I DID!
HEX'S PLAN WAS BRILLIANT IN EVERY DETAIL. I WAS TO BE ARRESTED KNOWING FULL WELL A MEMBER OR MEMBERS OF THE AUGUST 7 WERE PART OF THE POLICE DEPARTMENT.
NIGHT OF THE OWLS
VENGEANCE IN THE Big Easy
JIMMY PALMIOTTI and JUSTIN GRAY, Writers
MORITAT, Artist
GABRIEL BAUTISTA, Colorist
ROB LEIGH, Letterer

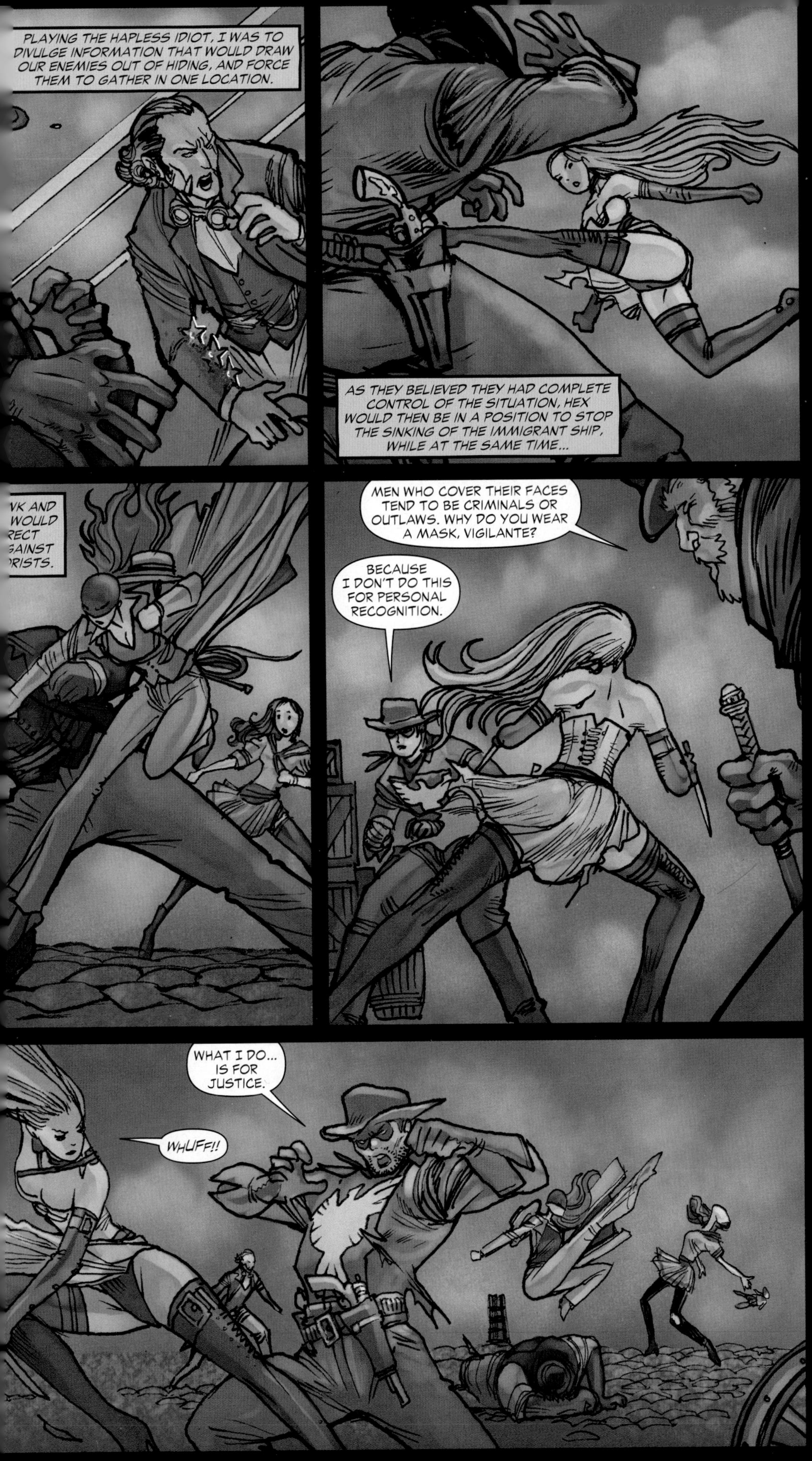
PLAYING THE HAPLESS IDIOT, I WAS TO DIVULGE INFORMATION THAT WOULD DRAW OUR ENEMIES OUT OF HIDING, AND FORCE THEM TO GATHER IN ONE LOCATION.
AS THEY BELIEVED THEY HAD COMPLETE CONTROL OF THE SITUATION, HEX WOULD THEN BE IN A POSITION TO STOP THE SINKING OF THE IMMIGRANT SHIP, WHILE AT THE SAME TIME...
NK AND WOULD RECT GAINST ORISTS.
MEN WHO COVER THEIR FACES TEND TO BE CRIMINALS OR OUTLAWS. WHY DO YOU WEAR A MASK, VIGILANTE?
BECAUSE I DON'T DO THIS FOR PERSONAL RECOGNITION.
WHAT I DO... IS FOR JUSTICE.
WHUFF!!

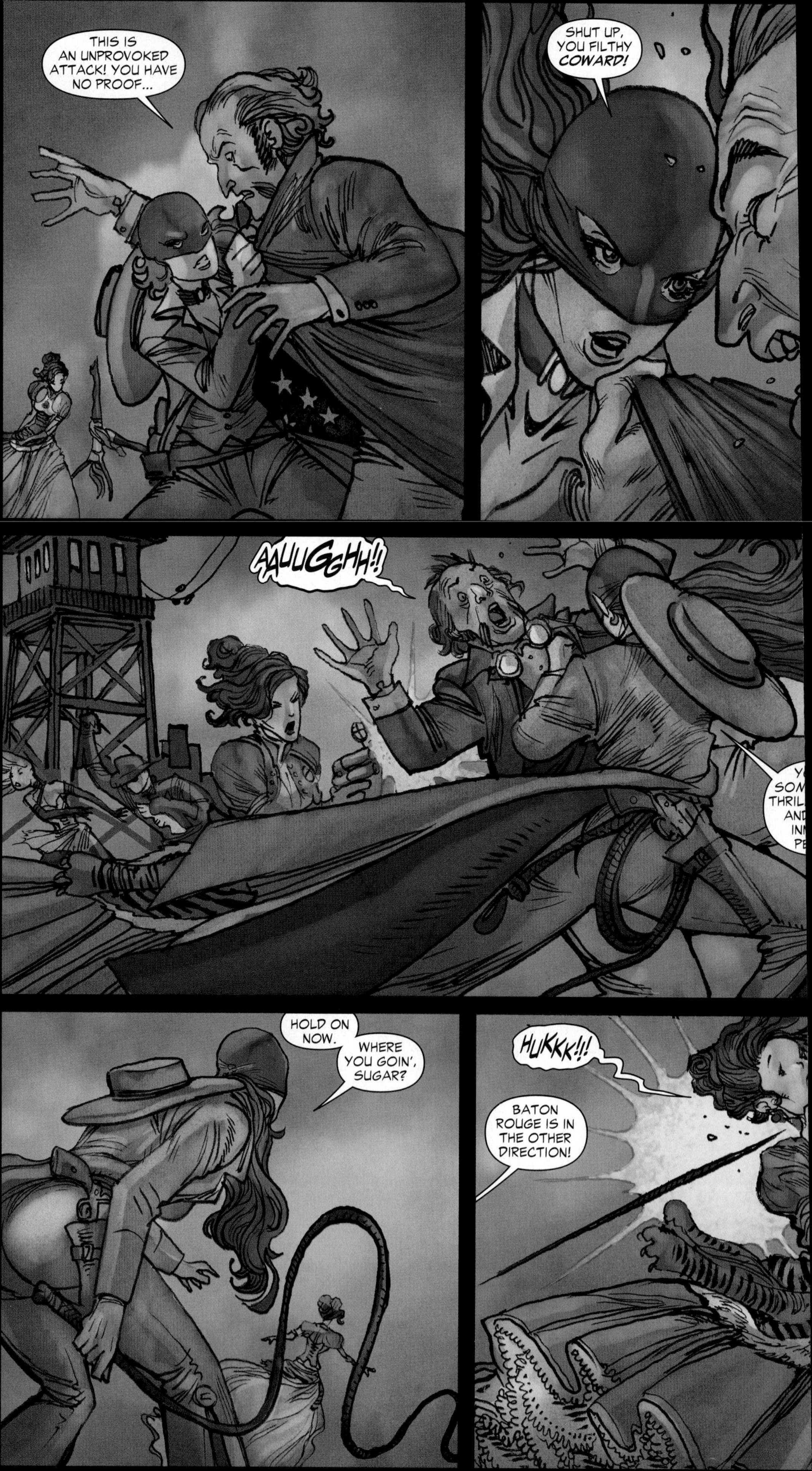
THIS IS AN UNPROVOKED ATTACK! YOU HAVE NO PROOF...
SHUT UP, YOU FILTHY COWARD!
AAUUGGHH!!
HOLD ON NOW.
WHERE YOU GOIN', SUGAR?
HUKKK!!!
BATON ROUGE IS IN THE OTHER DIRECTION!

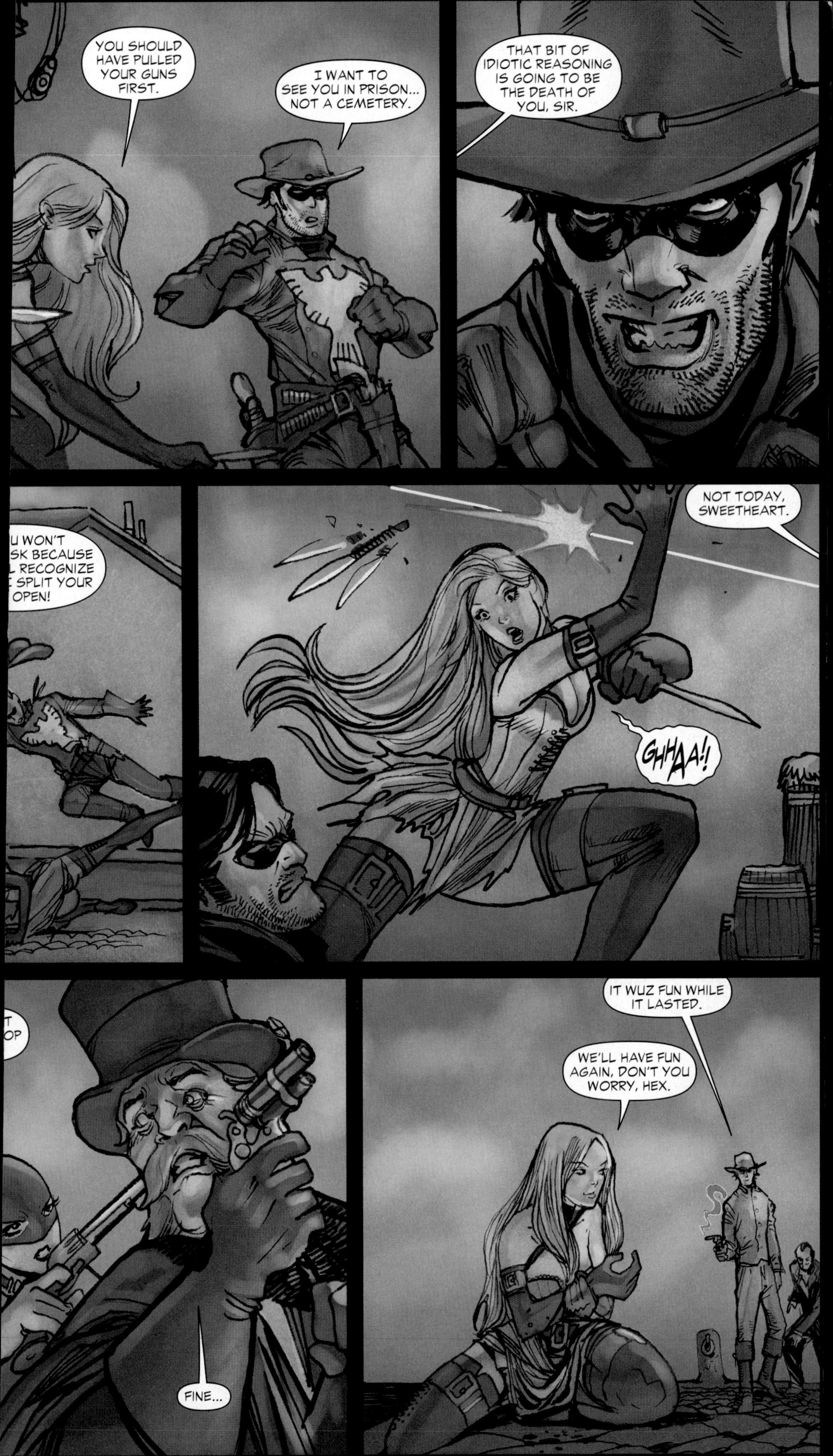
YOU SHOULD HAVE PULLED YOUR GUNS FIRST.
I WANT TO SEE YOU IN PRISON... NOT A CEMETERY.
THAT BIT OF IDIOTIC REASONING IS GOING TO BE THE DEATH OF YOU, SIR.
U WON'T SK BECAUSE L RECOGNIZE SPLIT YOUR OPEN!
NOT TODAY, SWEETHEART.
GHHAA!!
FINE...
IT WUZ FUN WHILE IT LASTED.
WE'LL HAVE FUN AGAIN, DON'T YOU WORRY, HEX.

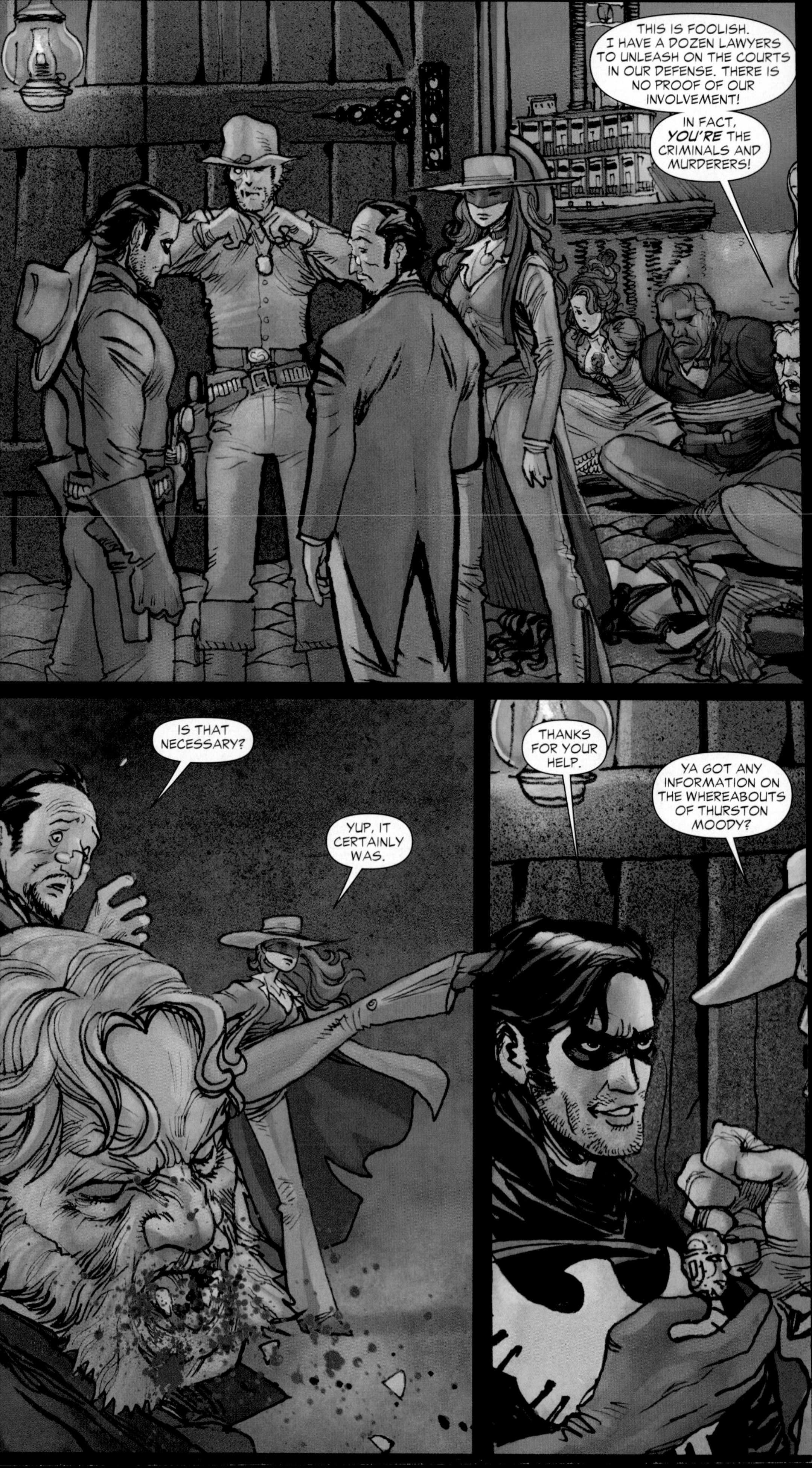
THIS IS FOOLISH. I HAVE A DOZEN LAWYERS TO UNLEASH ON THE COURTS IN OUR DEFENSE. THERE IS NO PROOF OF OUR INVOLVEMENT!
IN FACT, ***YOU'RE*** THE CRIMINALS AND MURDERERS!
IS THAT NECESSARY?
YUP, IT CERTAINLY WAS.
THANKS FOR YOUR HELP.
YA GOT ANY INFORMATION ON THE WHEREABOUTS OF THURSTON MOODY?

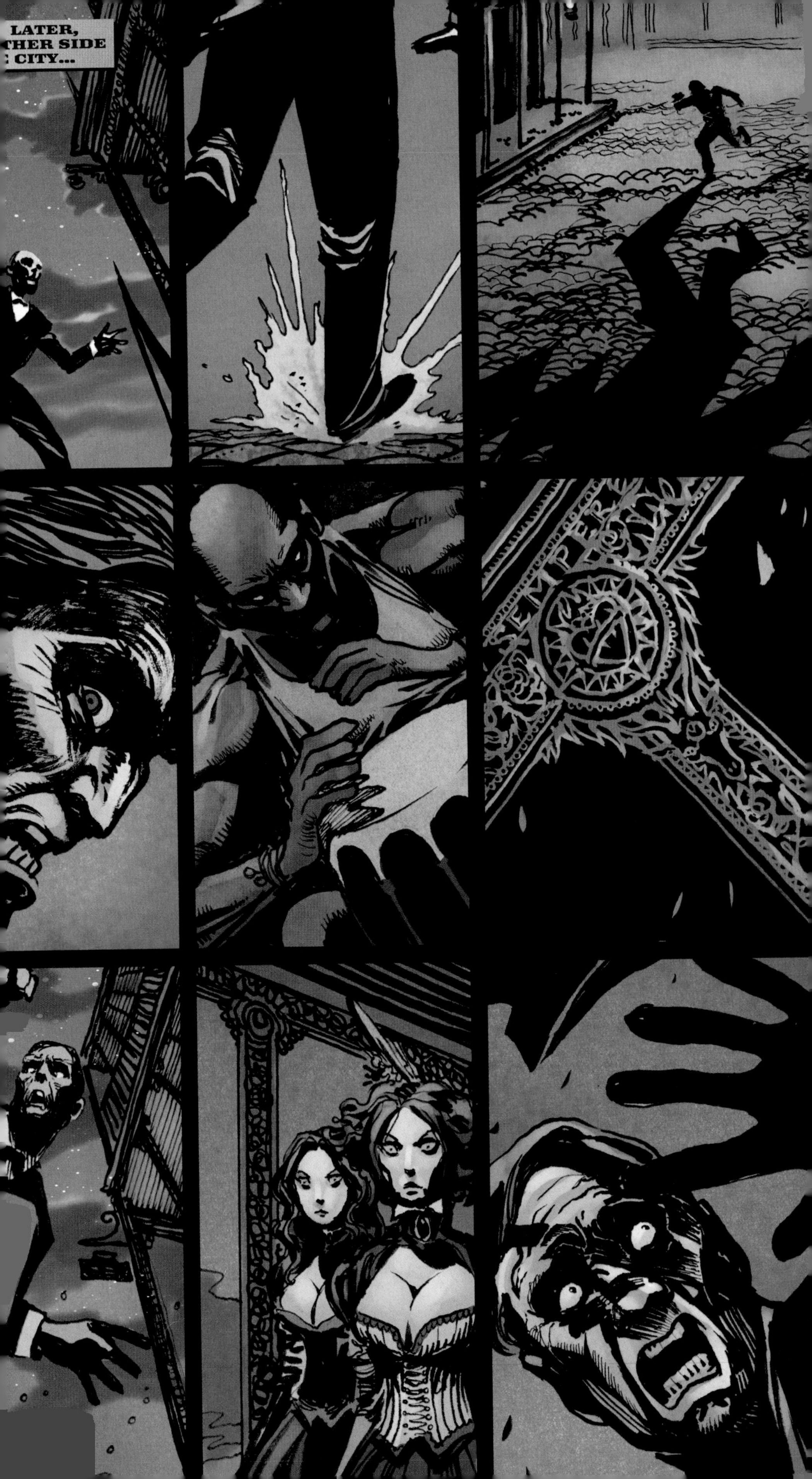
LATER,
THER SIDE
CITY...

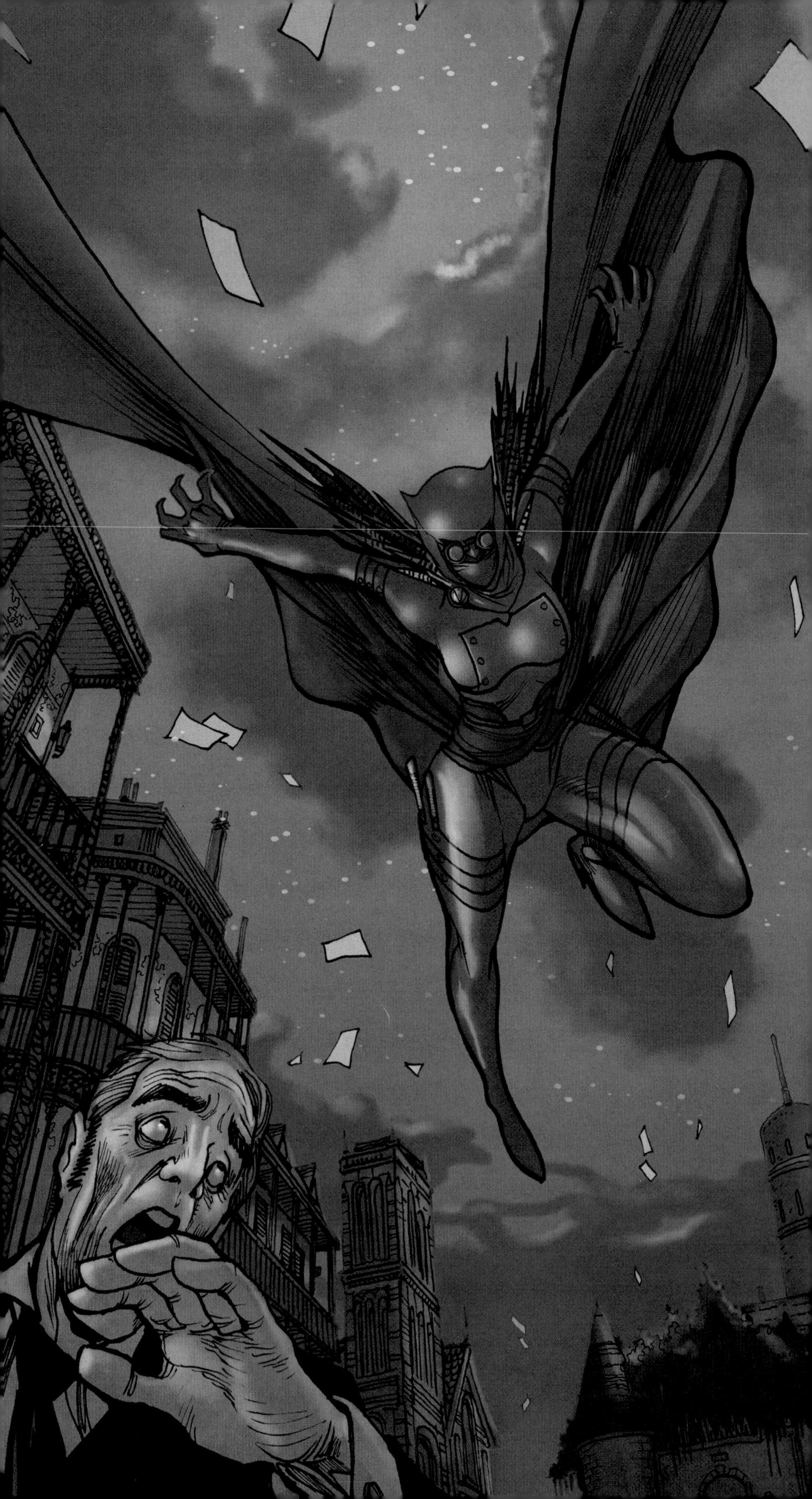

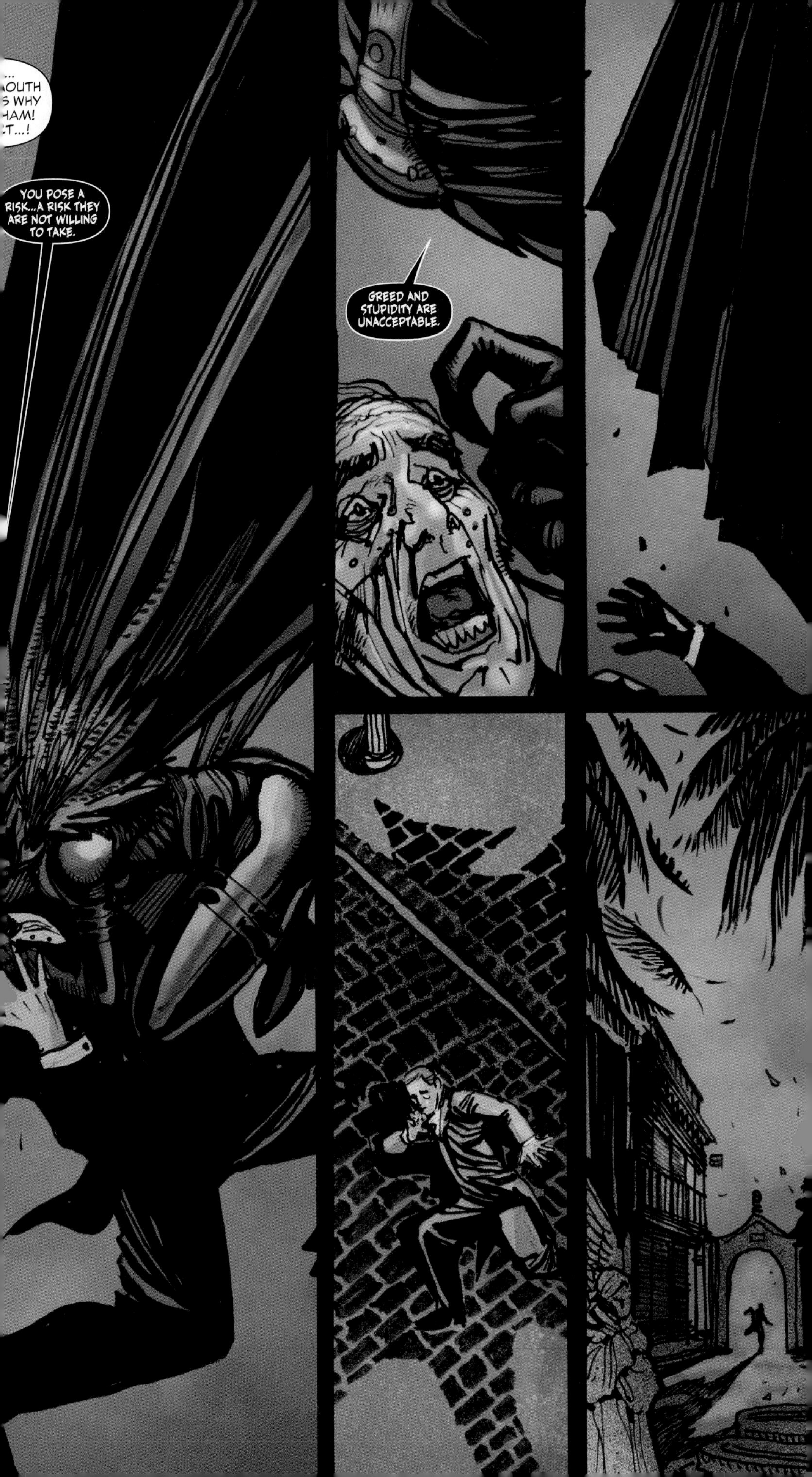
YOU POSE A RISK...A RISK THEY ARE NOT WILLING TO TAKE.
GREED AND STUPIDITY ARE UNACCEPTABLE.

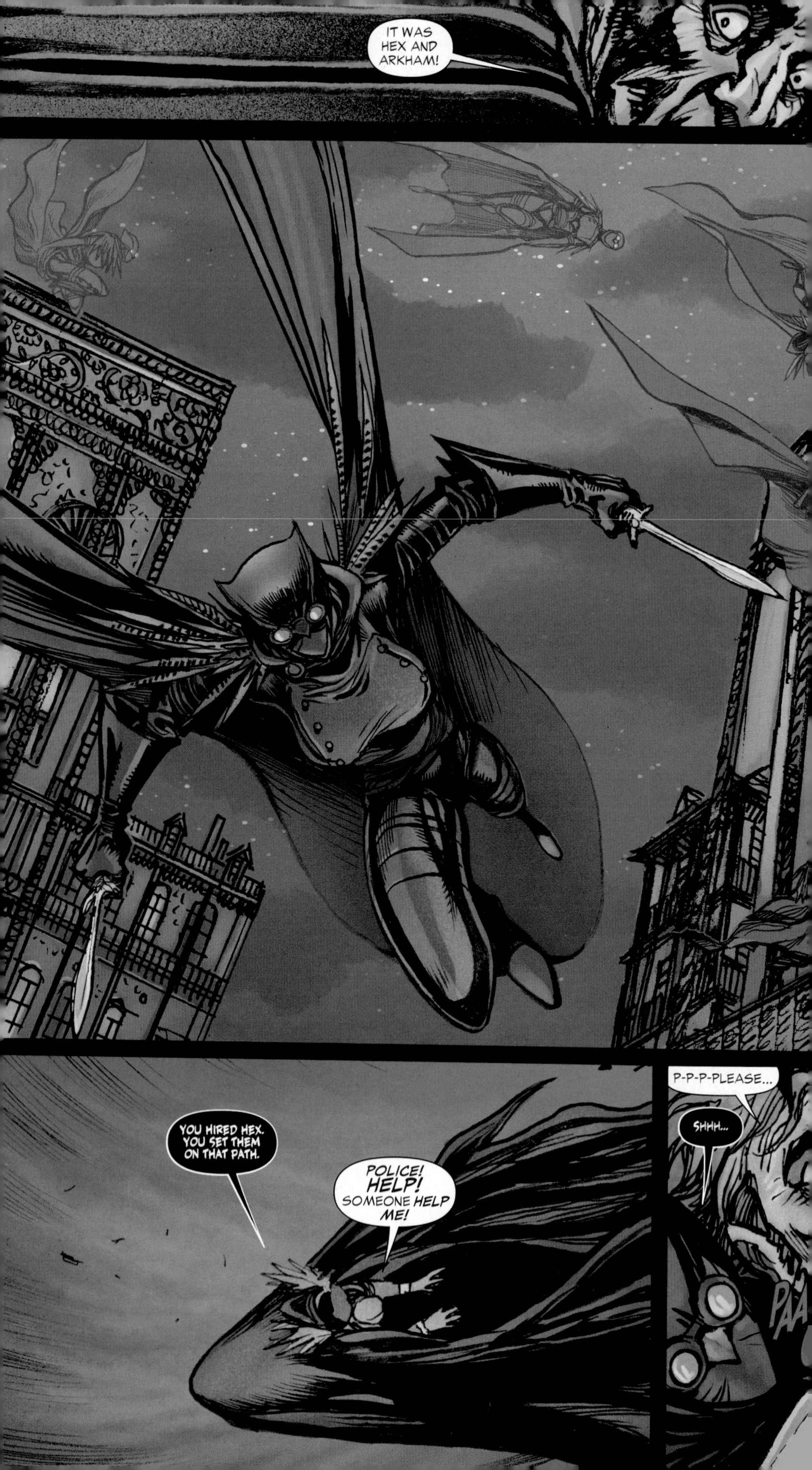
IT WAS HEX AND ARKHAM!
YOU HIRED HEX. YOU SET THEM ON THAT PATH.
POLICE! HELP! SOMEONE HELP ME!
P-P-P-PLEASE...
SHHH...

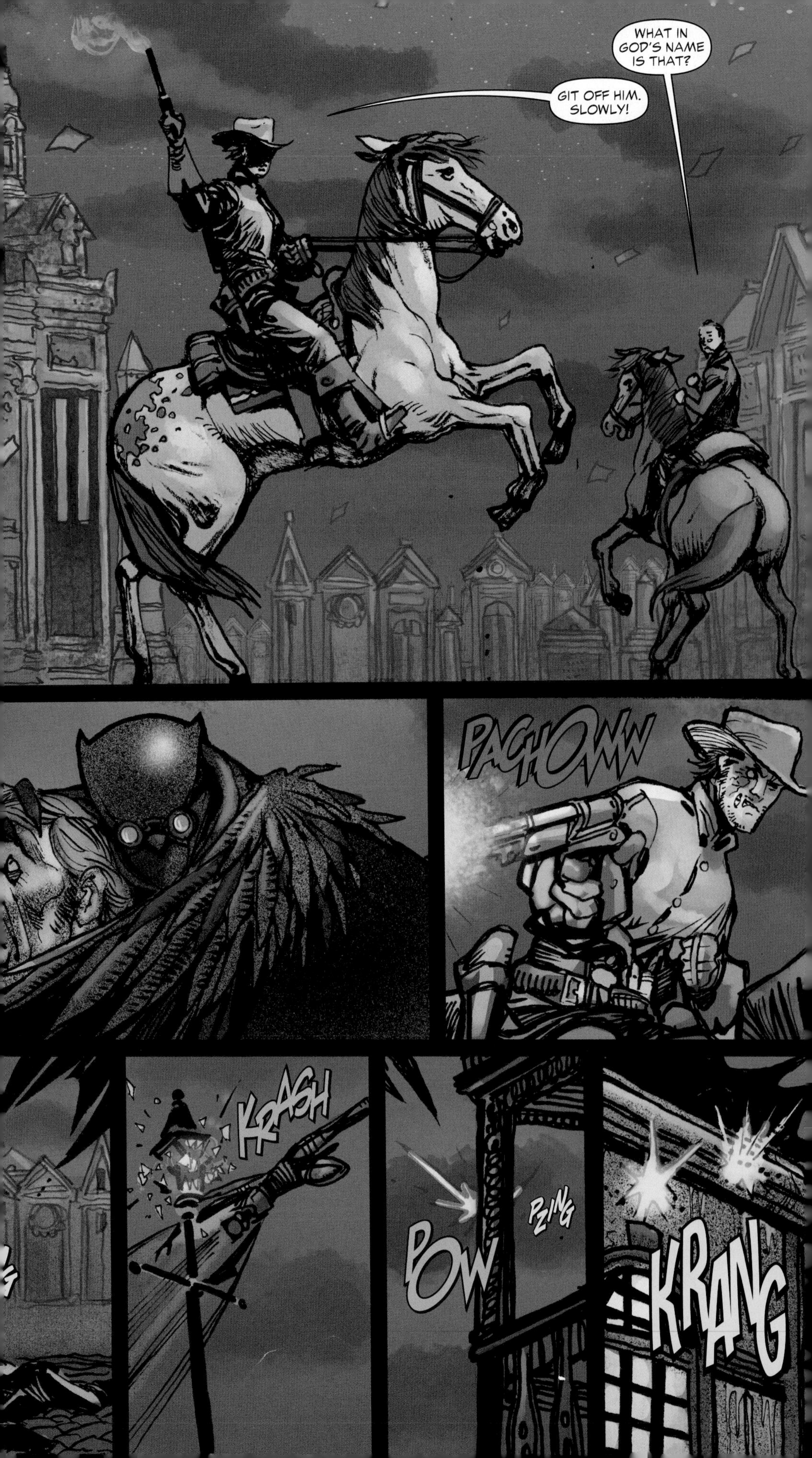
GIT OFF HIM. SLOWLY!
WHAT IN GOD'S NAME IS THAT?
PACHOWW
KRASH
POW
PZING
KRANG

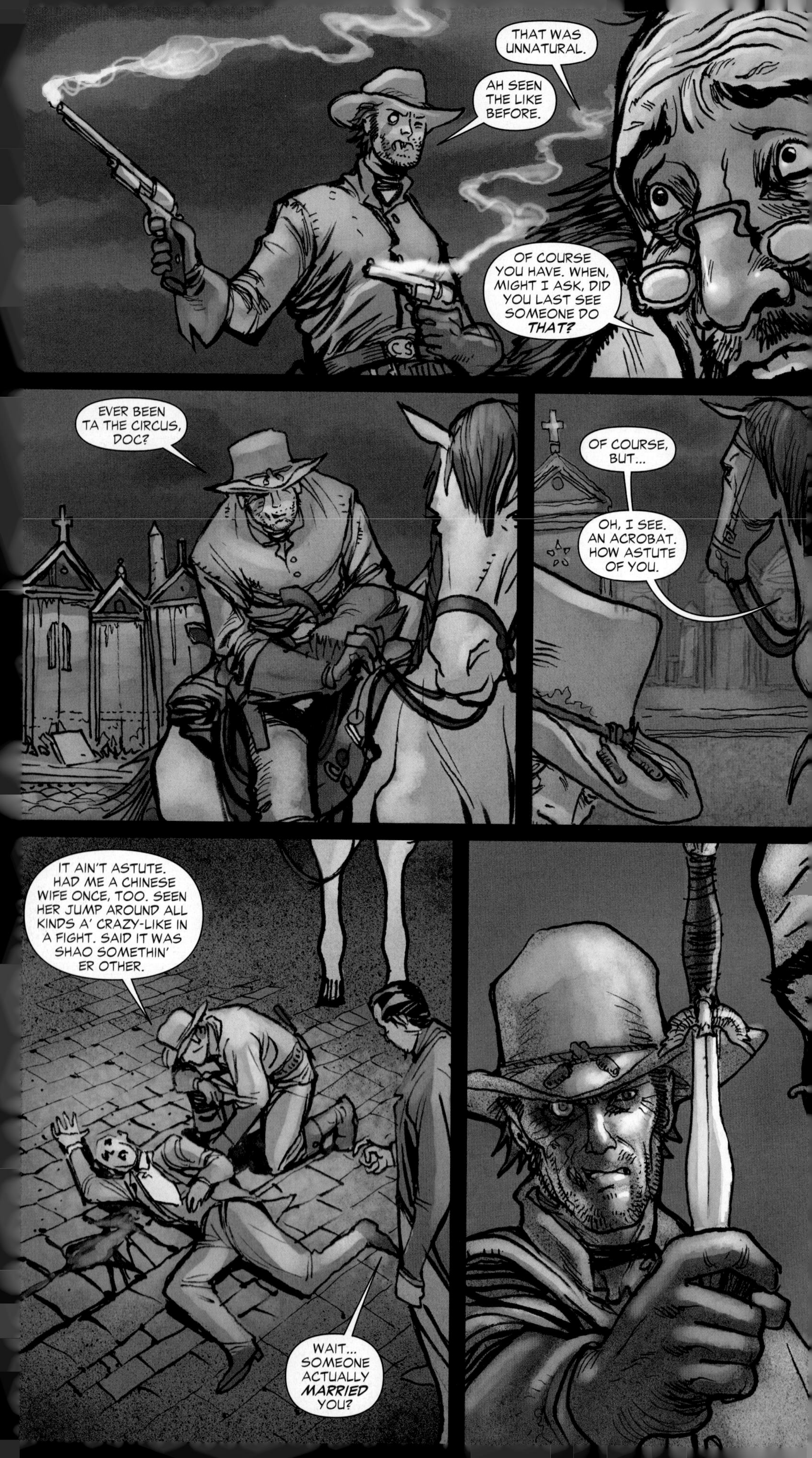
THAT WAS UNNATURAL.
AH SEEN THE LIKE BEFORE.
OF COURSE YOU HAVE. WHEN, MIGHT I ASK, DID YOU LAST SEE SOMEONE DO *THAT?*
EVER BEEN TA THE CIRCUS, DOC?
OF COURSE, BUT...
OH, I SEE. AN ACROBAT. HOW ASTUTE OF YOU.
IT AIN'T ASTUTE. HAD ME A CHINESE WIFE ONCE, TOO. SEEN HER JUMP AROUND ALL KINDS A' CRAZY-LIKE IN A FIGHT. SAID IT WAS SHAO SOMETHIN' ER OTHER.
WAIT... SOMEONE ACTUALLY *MARRIED* YOU?

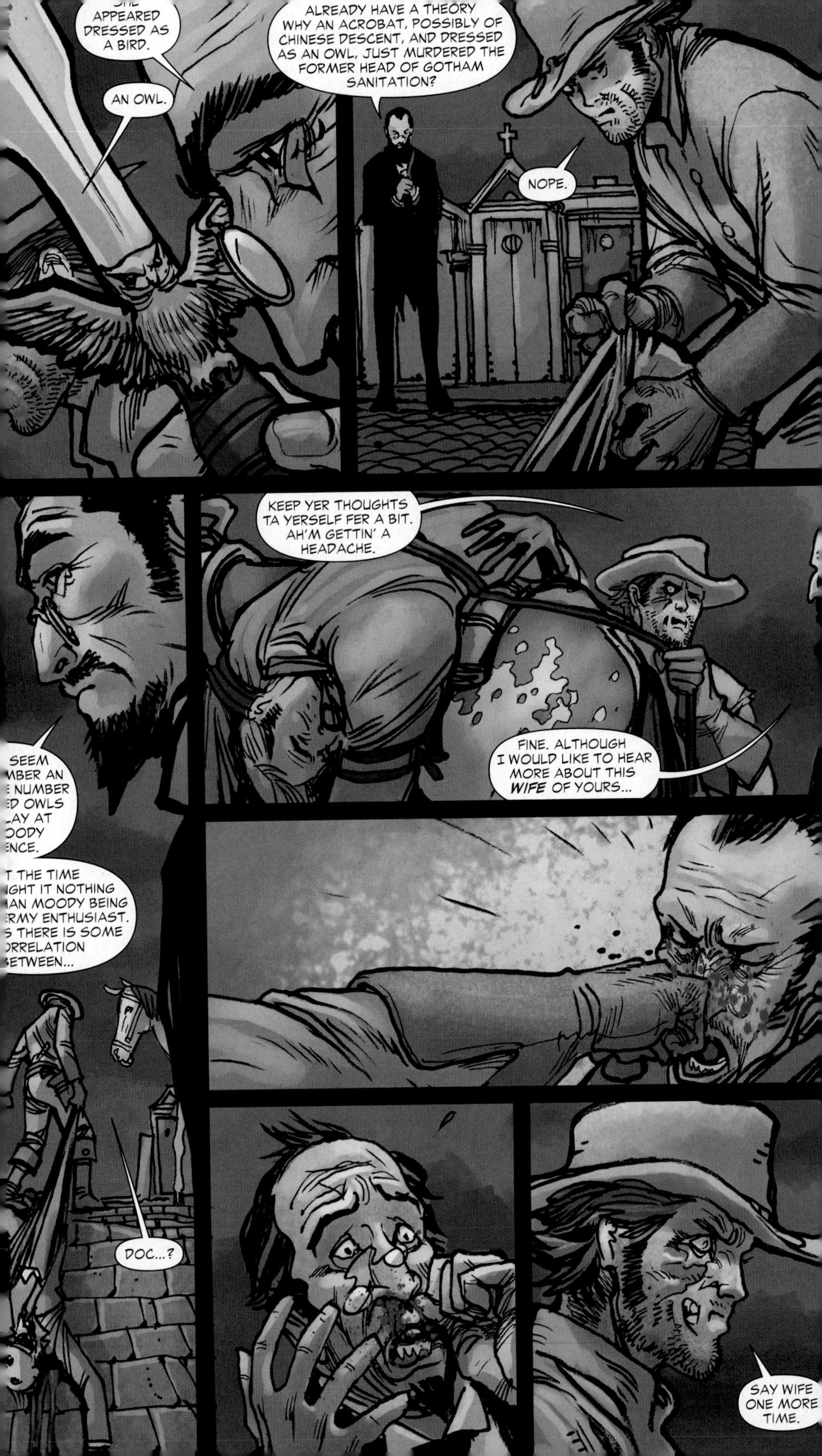
APPEARED DRESSED AS A BIRD.
AN OWL.
ALREADY HAVE A THEORY WHY AN ACROBAT, POSSIBLY OF CHINESE DESCENT, AND DRESSED AS AN OWL, JUST MURDERED THE FORMER HEAD OF GOTHAM SANITATION?
NOPE.
SEEM
MBER AN
E NUMBER
ED OWLS
LAY AT
OODY
ENCE.
T THE TIME
IGHT IT NOTHING
HAN MOODY BEING
ERMY ENTHUSIAST.
S THERE IS SOME
ORRELATION
BETWEEN...
KEEP YER THOUGHTS TA YERSELF FER A BIT. AH'M GETTIN' A HEADACHE.
FINE. ALTHOUGH I WOULD LIKE TO HEAR MORE ABOUT THIS *WIFE* OF YOURS...
DOC...?
SAY WIFE ONE MORE TIME.

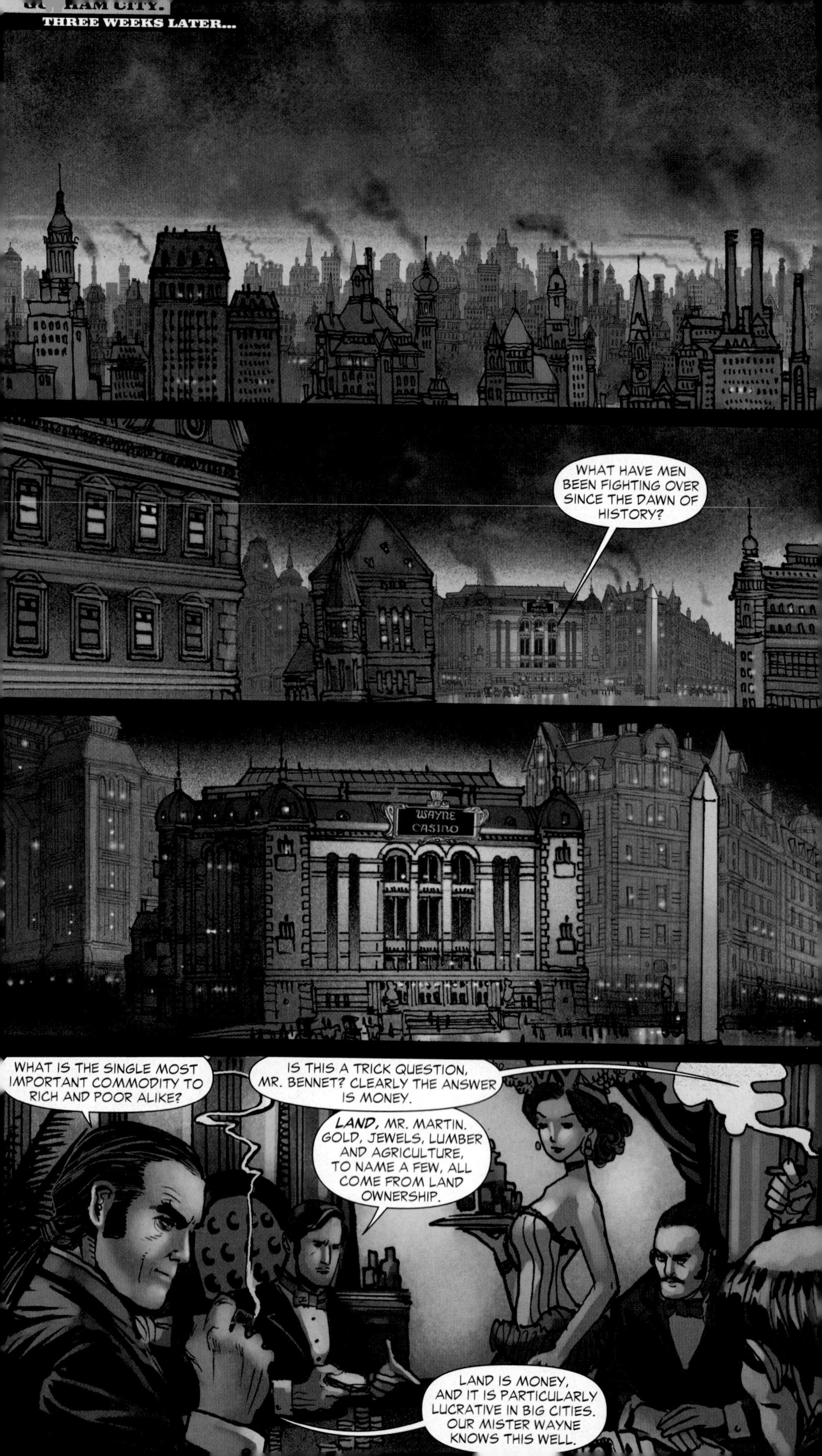
THREE WEEKS LATER...
WHAT HAVE MEN BEEN FIGHTING OVER SINCE THE DAWN OF HISTORY?
WAYNE CASINO
WHAT IS THE SINGLE MOST IMPORTANT COMMODITY TO RICH AND POOR ALIKE?
IS THIS A TRICK QUESTION, MR. BENNET? CLEARLY THE ANSWER IS MONEY.
LAND, MR. MARTIN. GOLD, JEWELS, LUMBER AND AGRICULTURE, TO NAME A FEW, ALL COME FROM LAND OWNERSHIP.
LAND IS MONEY, AND IT IS PARTICULARLY LUCRATIVE IN BIG CITIES. OUR MISTER WAYNE KNOWS THIS WELL.

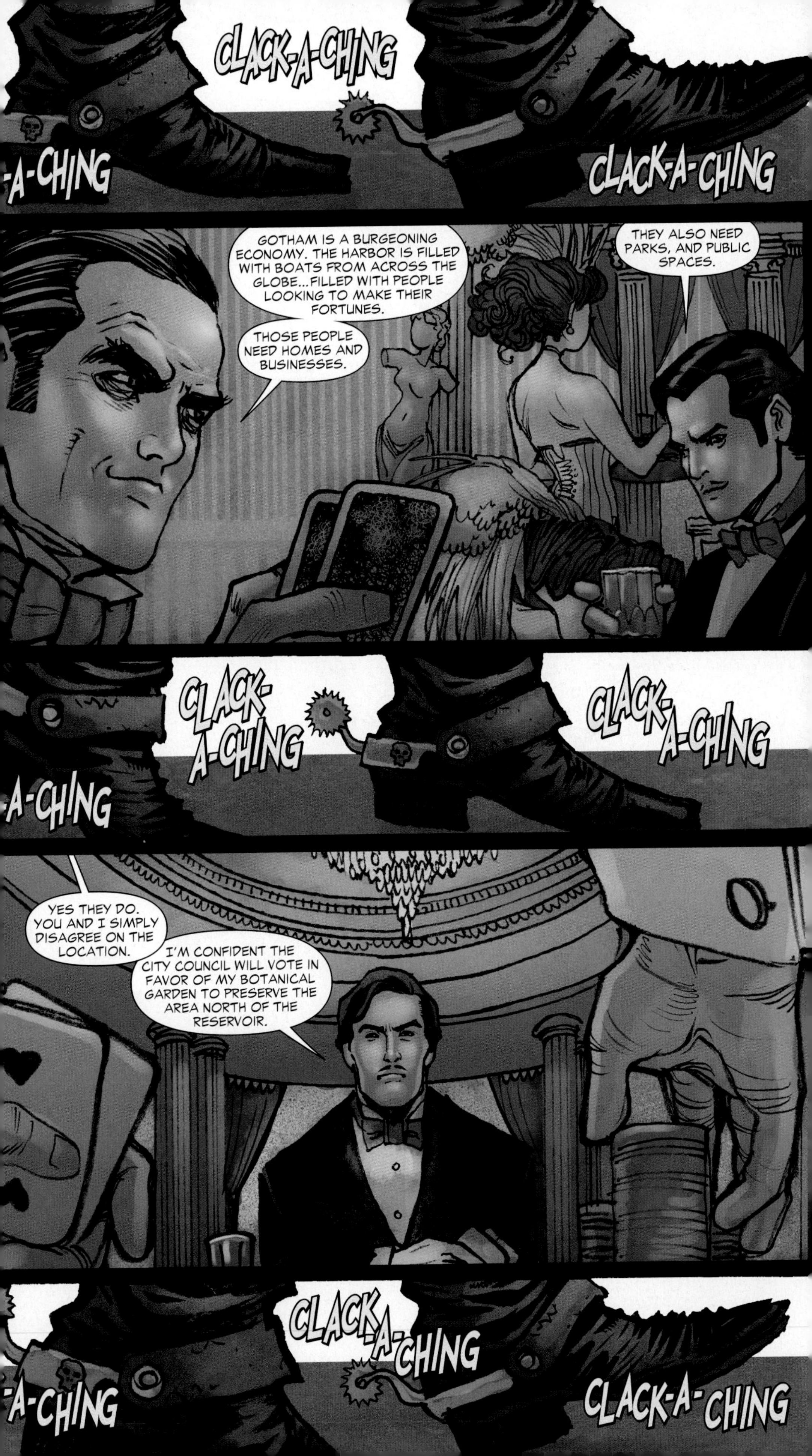
CLACK-A-CHING
-A-CHING
CLACK-A-CHING
GOTHAM IS A BURGEONING ECONOMY. THE HARBOR IS FILLED WITH BOATS FROM ACROSS THE GLOBE...FILLED WITH PEOPLE LOOKING TO MAKE THEIR FORTUNES.
THOSE PEOPLE NEED HOMES AND BUSINESSES.
THEY ALSO NEED PARKS, AND PUBLIC SPACES.
CLACK-A-CHING
-A-CHING
CLACK-A-CHING
YES THEY DO. YOU AND I SIMPLY DISAGREE ON THE LOCATION.
I'M CONFIDENT THE CITY COUNCIL WILL VOTE IN FAVOR OF MY BOTANICAL GARDEN TO PRESERVE THE AREA NORTH OF THE RESERVOIR.
CLACK-A-CHING
-A-CHING
CLACK-A-CHING

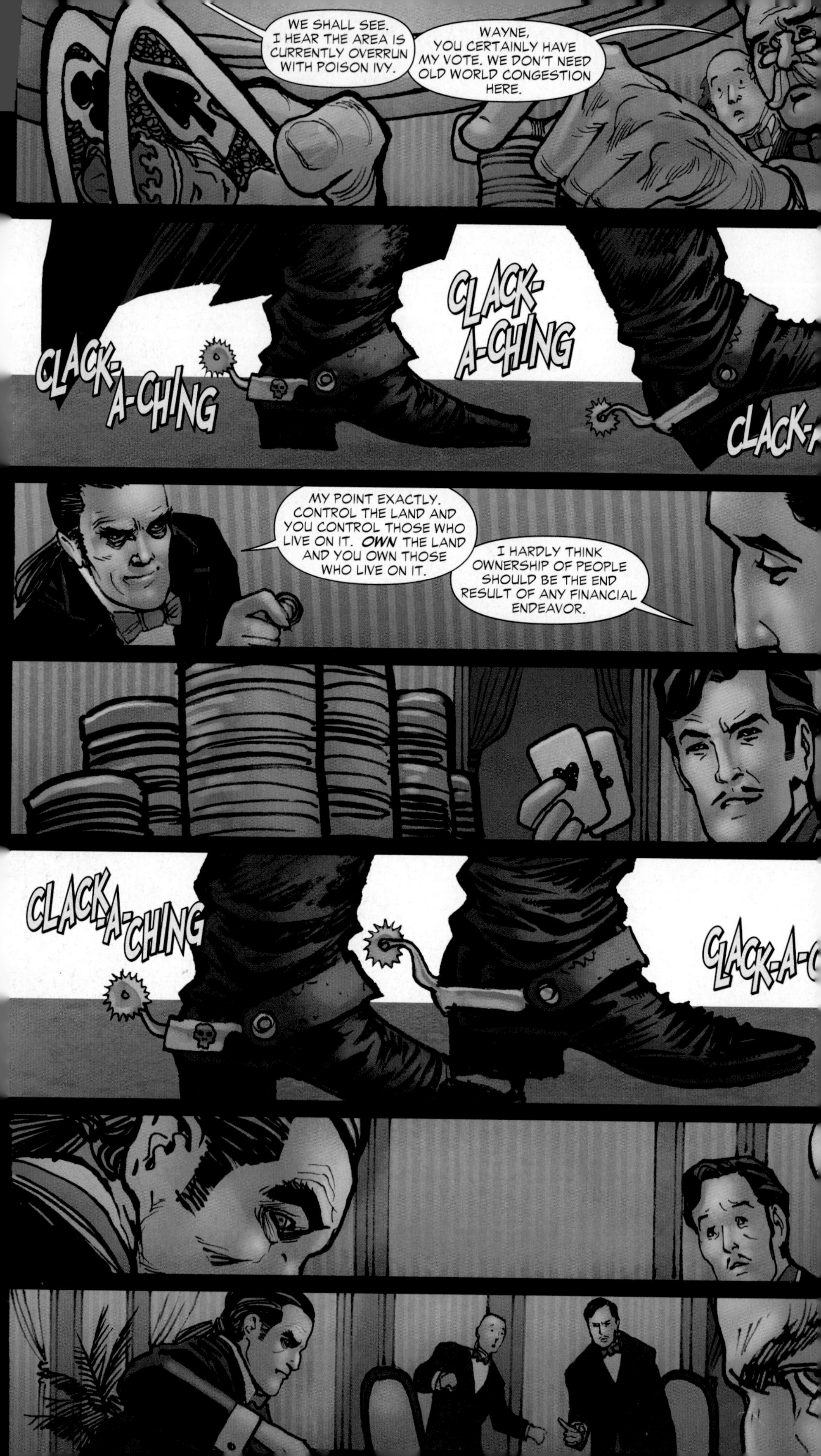
WE SHALL SEE. I HEAR THE AREA IS CURRENTLY OVERRUN WITH POISON IVY.
WAYNE, YOU CERTAINLY HAVE MY VOTE. WE DON'T NEED OLD WORLD CONGESTION HERE.
CLACK-A-CHING
CLACK-A-CHING
MY POINT EXACTLY. CONTROL THE LAND AND YOU CONTROL THOSE WHO LIVE ON IT. *OWN* THE LAND AND YOU OWN THOSE WHO LIVE ON IT.
I HARDLY THINK OWNERSHIP OF PEOPLE SHOULD BE THE END RESULT OF ANY FINANCIAL ENDEAVOR.
CLACK-A-CHING

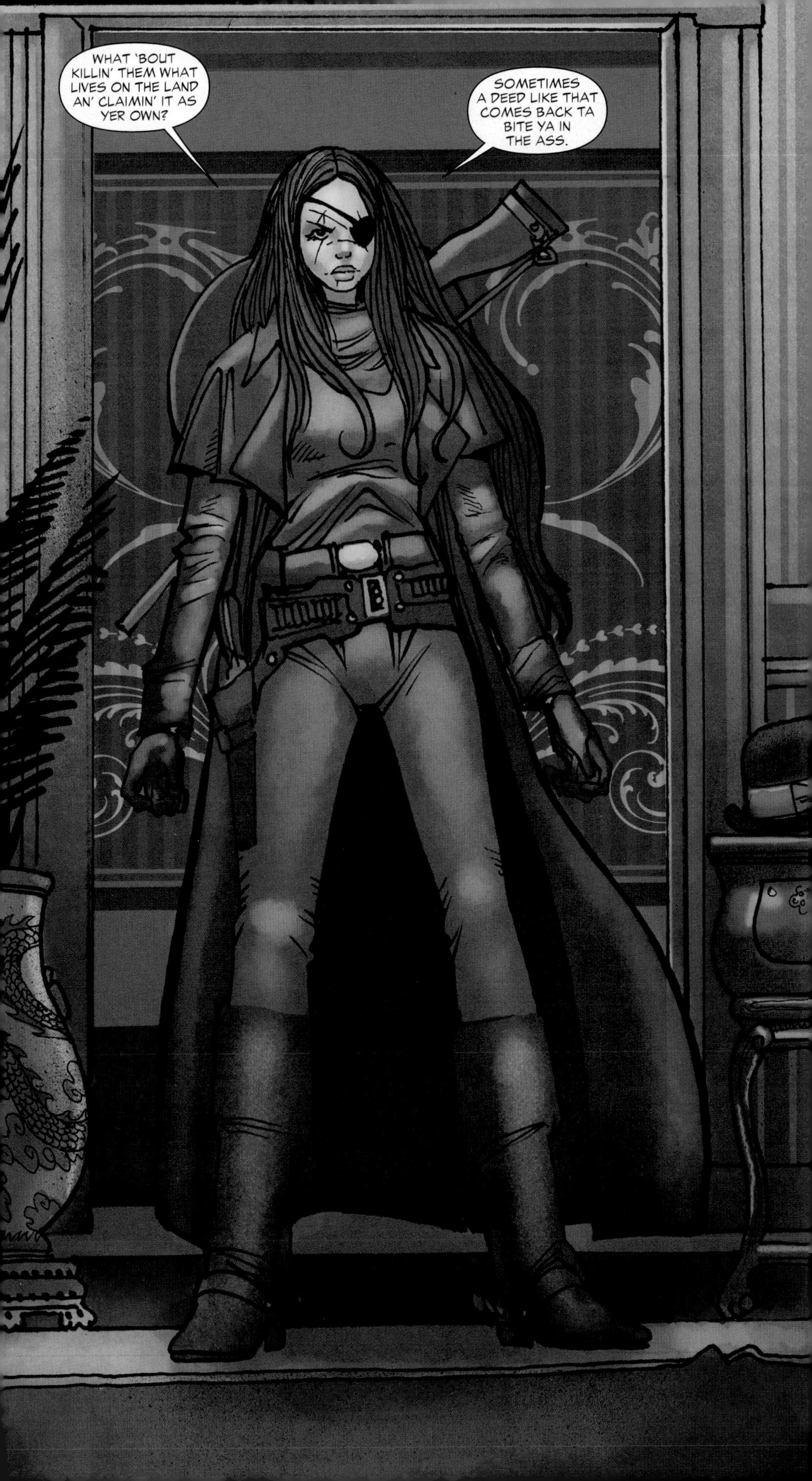
WHAT 'BOUT KILLIN' THEM WHAT LIVES ON THE LAND AN' CLAIMIN' IT AS YER OWN?
SOMETIMES A DEED LIKE THAT COMES BACK TA BITE YA IN THE ASS.

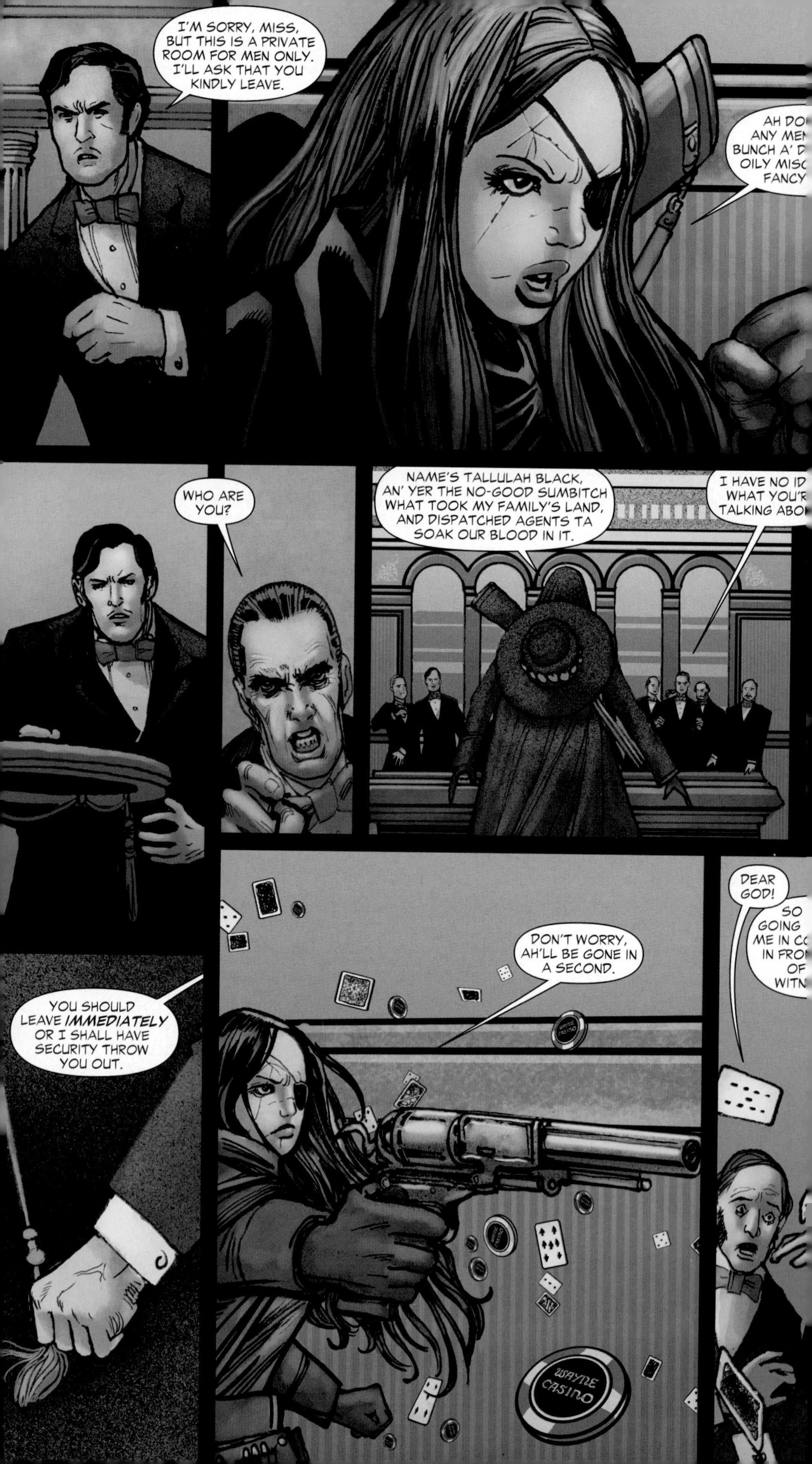
I'M SORRY, MISS, BUT THIS IS A PRIVATE ROOM FOR MEN ONLY. I'LL ASK THAT YOU KINDLY LEAVE.
AH DO ANY ME BUNCH A' D OILY MISC FANCY
WHO ARE YOU?
NAME'S TALLULAH BLACK, AN' YER THE NO-GOOD SUMBITCH WHAT TOOK MY FAMILY'S LAND, AND DISPATCHED AGENTS TA SOAK OUR BLOOD IN IT.
I HAVE NO ID WHAT YOU'R TALKING ABO
YOU SHOULD LEAVE *IMMEDIATELY* OR I SHALL HAVE SECURITY THROW YOU OUT.
DON'T WORRY, AH'LL BE GONE IN A SECOND.
DEAR GOD!
SO GOING ME IN C IN FRO OF WITN
WAYNE CASINO

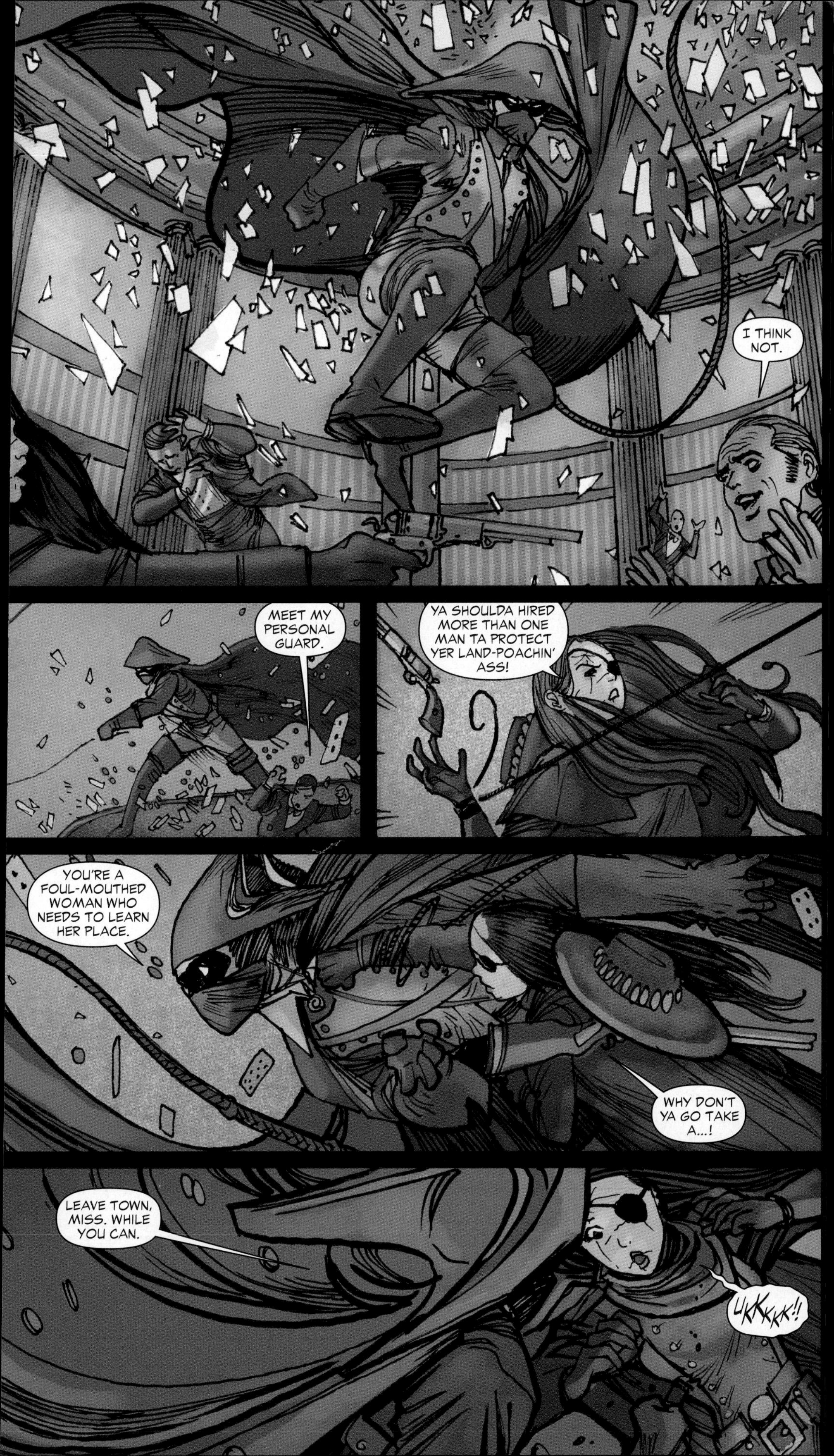
I THINK NOT.
MEET MY PERSONAL GUARD.
YA SHOULDA HIRED MORE THAN ONE MAN TA PROTECT YER LAND-POACHIN' ASS!
YOU'RE A FOUL-MOUTHED WOMAN WHO NEEDS TO LEARN HER PLACE.
WHY DON'T YA GO TAKE A...!
LEAVE TOWN, MISS. WHILE YOU CAN.
UKKKKK!!

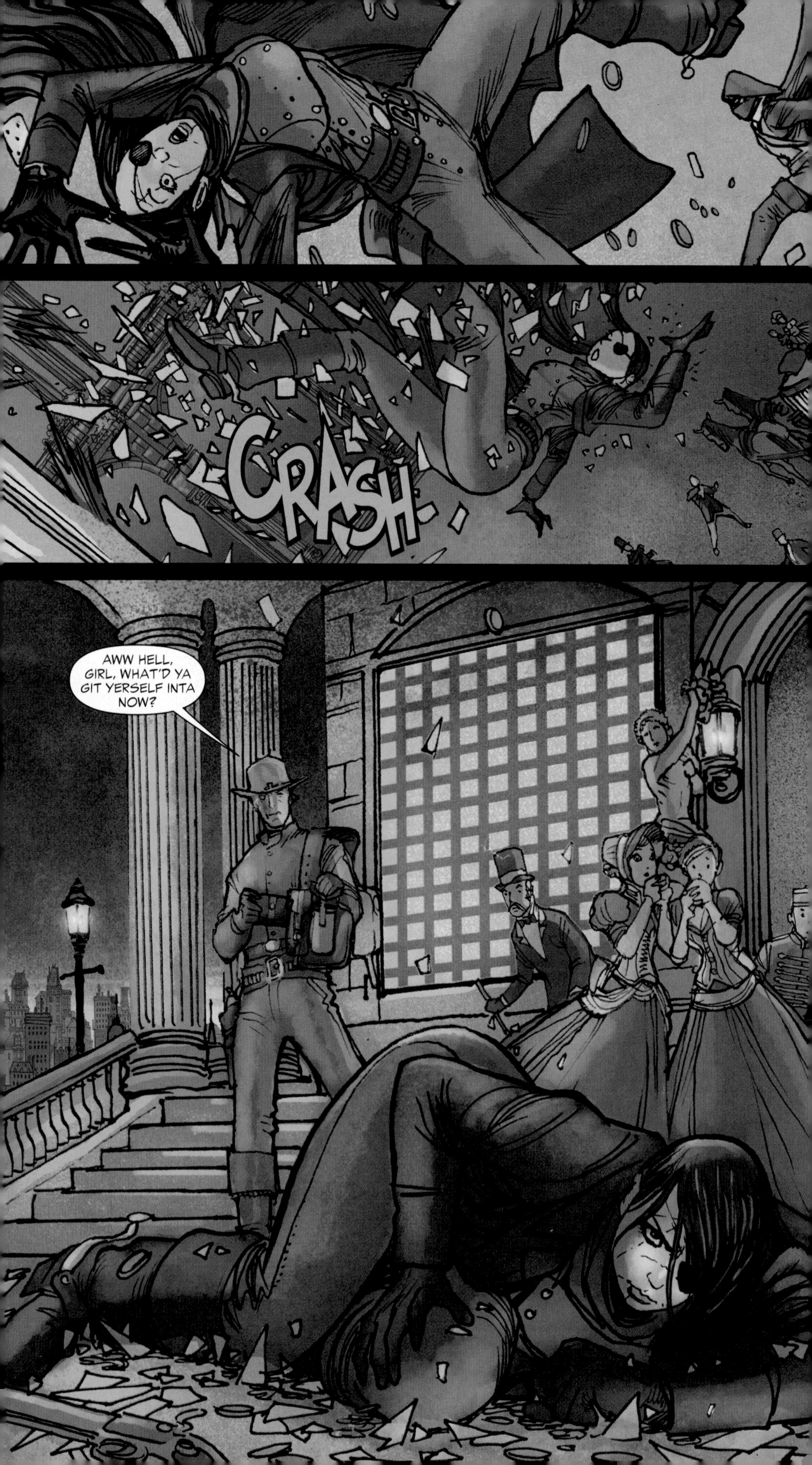
CRASH
AWW HELL, GIRL, WHAT'D YA GIT YERSELF INTA NOW?

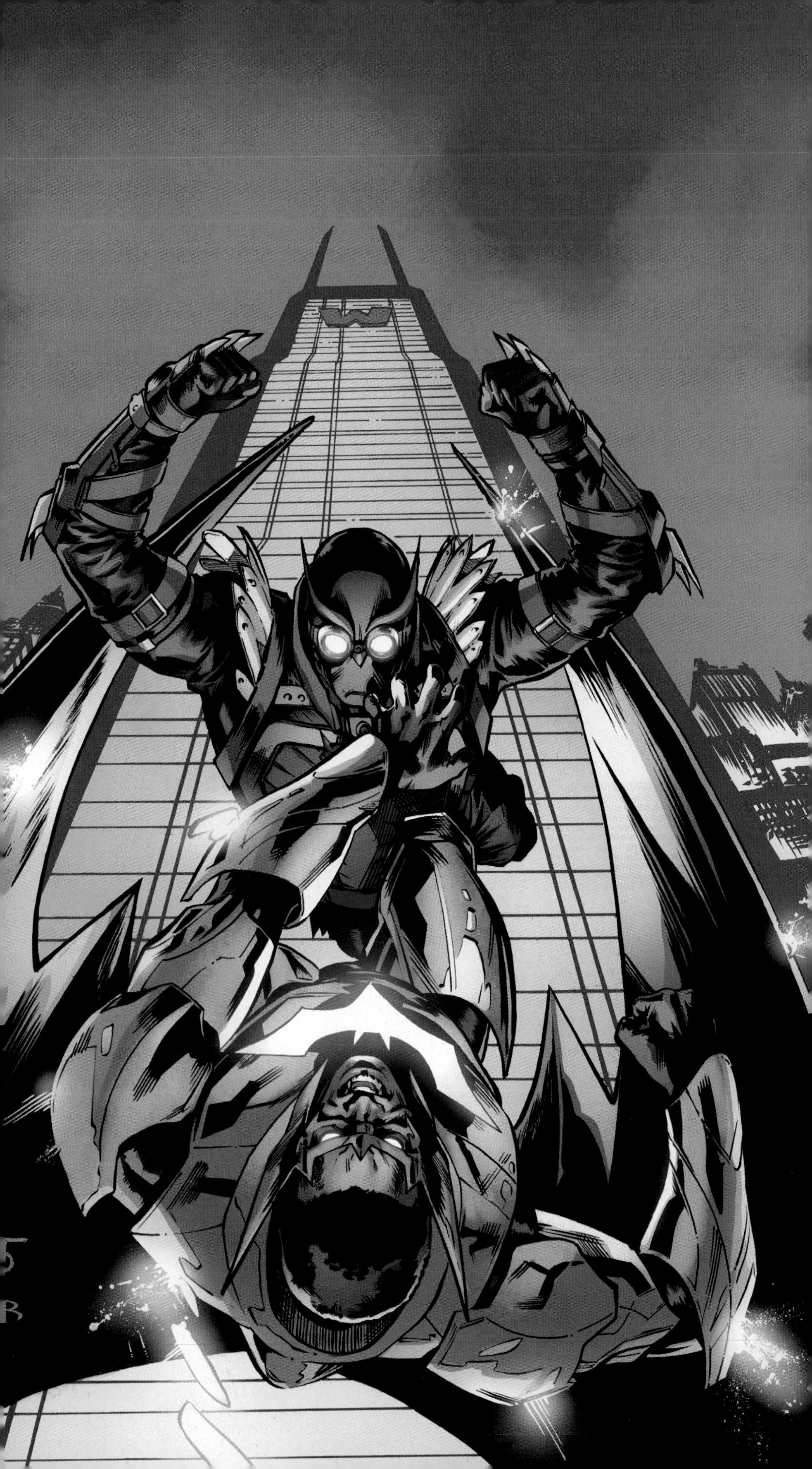

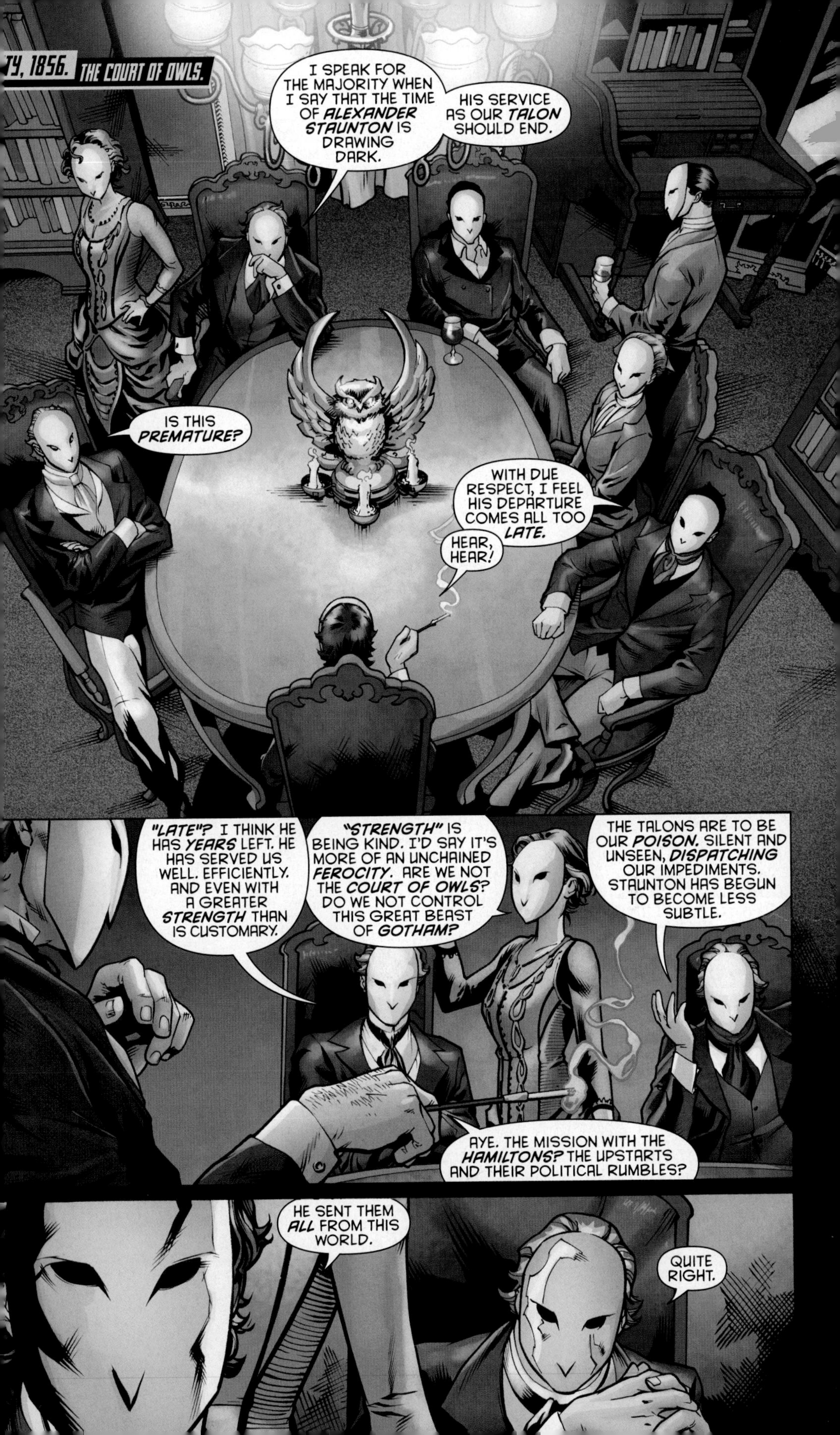
TY, 1856. THE COURT OF OWLS.
I SPEAK FOR THE MAJORITY WHEN I SAY THAT THE TIME OF ALEXANDER STAUNTON IS DRAWING DARK.
HIS SERVICE AS OUR TALON SHOULD END.
IS THIS PREMATURE?
WITH DUE RESPECT, I FEEL HIS DEPARTURE COMES ALL TOO LATE.
HEAR, HEAR!
"LATE"? I THINK HE HAS YEARS LEFT. HE HAS SERVED US WELL. EFFICIENTLY. AND EVEN WITH A GREATER STRENGTH THAN IS CUSTOMARY.
"STRENGTH" IS BEING KIND. I'D SAY IT'S MORE OF AN UNCHAINED FEROCITY. ARE WE NOT THE COURT OF OWLS? DO WE NOT CONTROL THIS GREAT BEAST OF GOTHAM?
THE TALONS ARE TO BE OUR POISON. SILENT AND UNSEEN, DISPATCHING OUR IMPEDIMENTS. STAUNTON HAS BEGUN TO BECOME LESS SUBTLE.
AYE. THE MISSION WITH THE HAMILTONS? THE UPSTARTS AND THEIR POLITICAL RUMBLES?
HE SENT THEM ALL FROM THIS WORLD.
QUITE RIGHT.

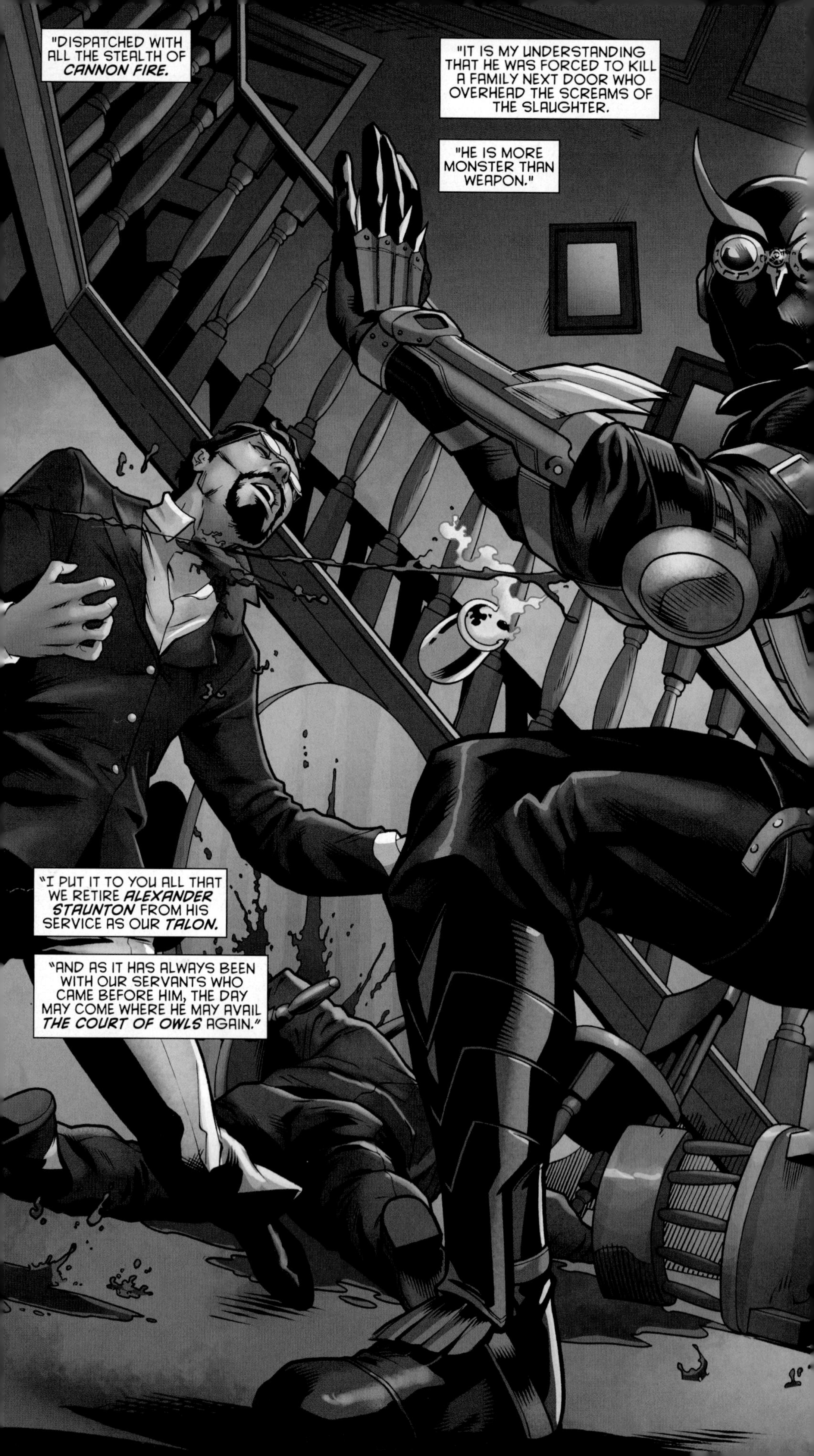
"DISPATCHED WITH ALL THE STEALTH OF *CANNON FIRE.*
"IT IS MY UNDERSTANDING THAT HE WAS FORCED TO KILL A FAMILY NEXT DOOR WHO OVERHEAD THE SCREAMS OF THE SLAUGHTER.
"HE IS MORE MONSTER THAN WEAPON."
"I PUT IT TO YOU ALL THAT WE RETIRE *ALEXANDER STAUNTON* FROM HIS SERVICE AS OUR *TALON.*
"AND AS IT HAS ALWAYS BEEN WITH OUR SERVANTS WHO CAME BEFORE HIM, THE DAY MAY COME WHERE HE MAY AVAIL *THE COURT OF OWLS* AGAIN."

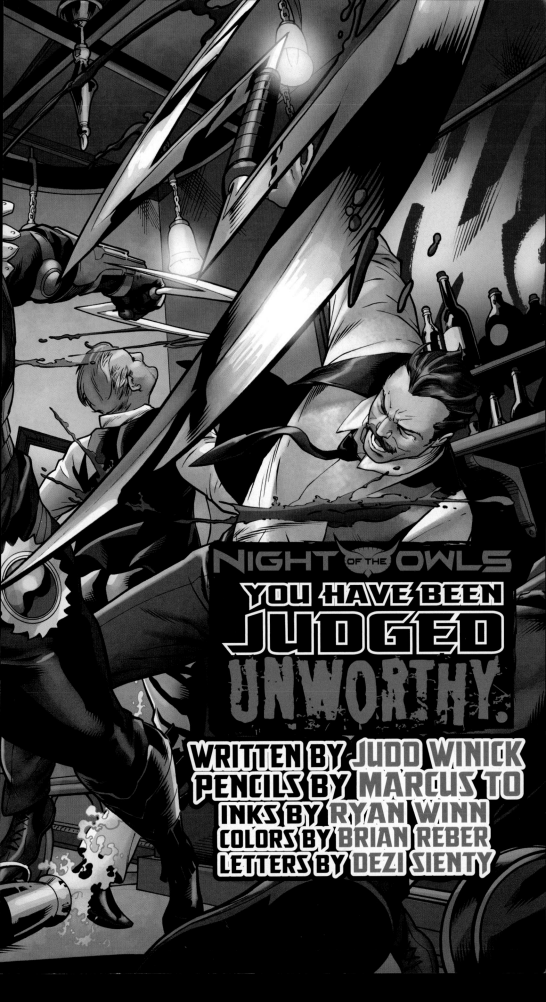

NIGHT OF THE OWLS
YOU HAVE BEEN JUDGED UNWORTHY.

WRITTEN BY JUDD WINICK
PENCILS BY MARCUS TO
INKS BY RYAN WINN
COLORS BY BRIAN REBER
LETTERS BY DEZI SIENTY

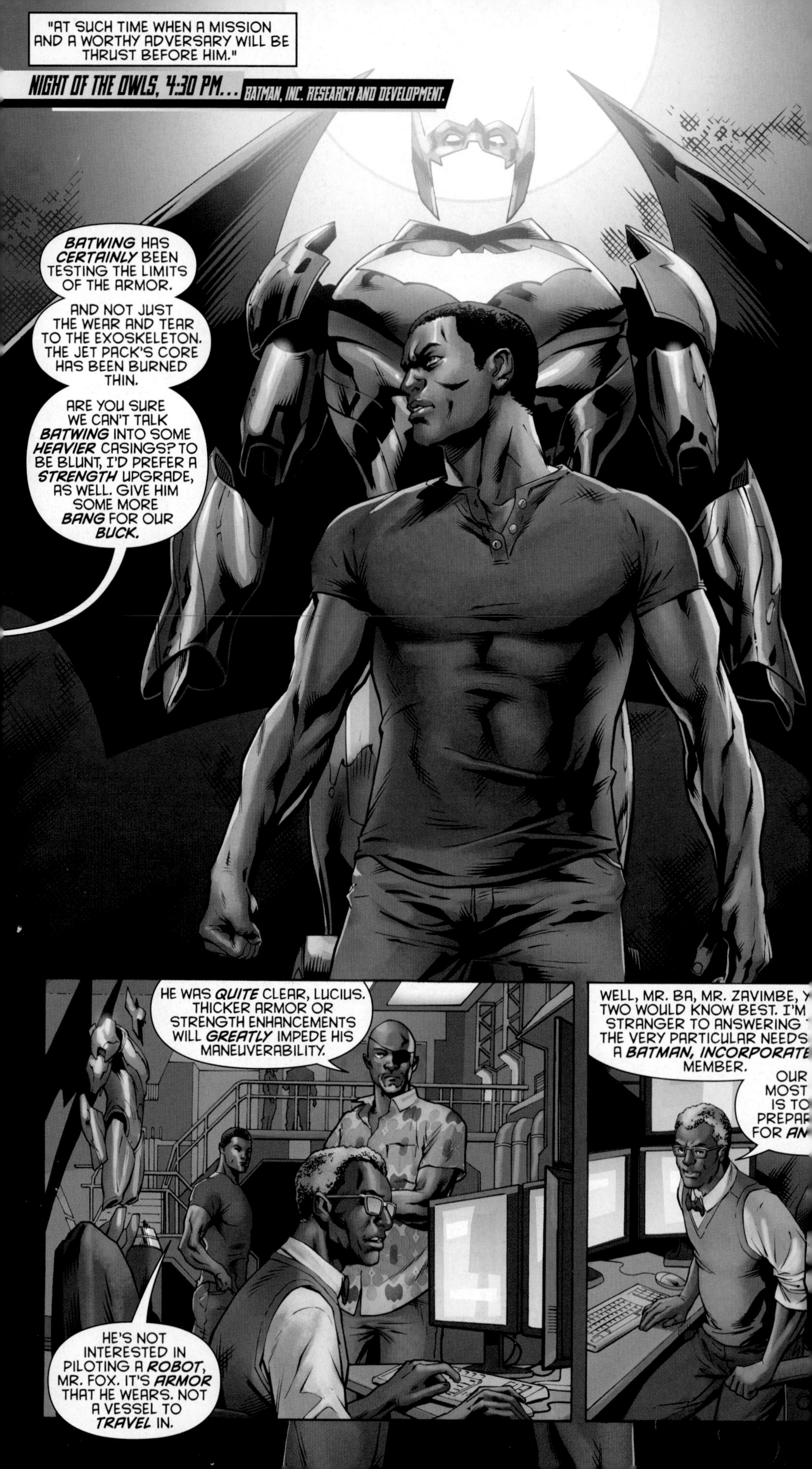
"AT SUCH TIME WHEN A MISSION AND A WORTHY ADVERSARY WILL BE THRUST BEFORE HIM."
NIGHT OF THE OWLS, 4:30 PM... BATMAN, INC. RESEARCH AND DEVELOPMENT.
BATWING HAS CERTAINLY BEEN TESTING THE LIMITS OF THE ARMOR.
AND NOT JUST THE WEAR AND TEAR TO THE EXOSKELETON. THE JET PACK'S CORE HAS BEEN BURNED THIN.
ARE YOU SURE WE CAN'T TALK BATWING INTO SOME HEAVIER CASINGS? TO BE BLUNT, I'D PREFER A STRENGTH UPGRADE, AS WELL. GIVE HIM SOME MORE BANG FOR OUR BUCK.
HE WAS QUITE CLEAR, LUCIUS. THICKER ARMOR OR STRENGTH ENHANCEMENTS WILL GREATLY IMPEDE HIS MANEUVERABILITY.
HE'S NOT INTERESTED IN PILOTING A ROBOT, MR. FOX. IT'S ARMOR THAT HE WEARS. NOT A VESSEL TO TRAVEL IN.
WELL, MR. BA, MR. ZAVIMBE, Y TWO WOULD KNOW BEST. I'M STRANGER TO ANSWERING THE VERY PARTICULAR NEEDS A BATMAN, INCORPORATE MEMBER.
OUR MOST IS TO PREPAR FOR AN

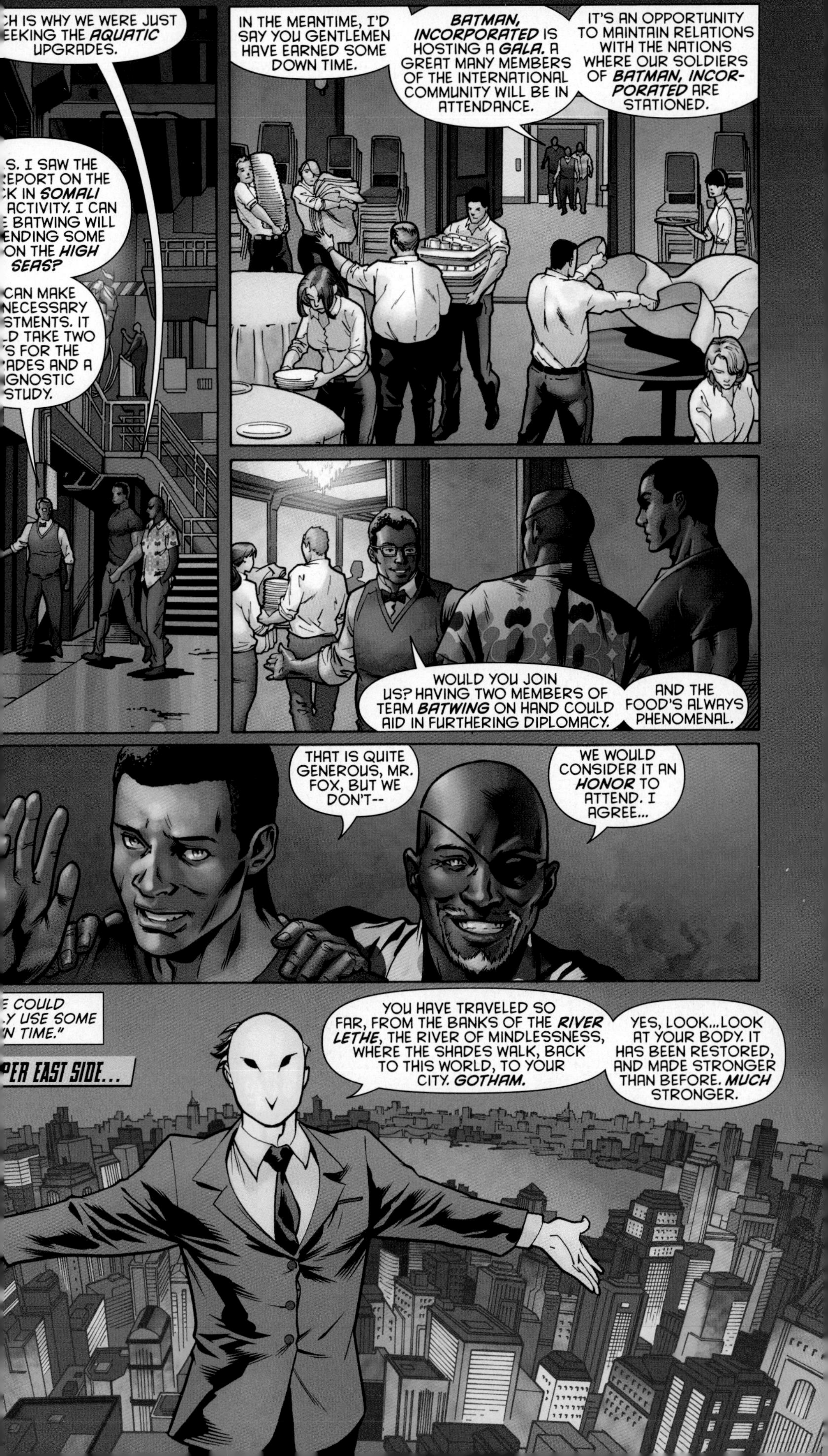

CH IS WHY WE WERE JUST EEKING THE AQUATIC UPGRADES.
S. I SAW THE REPORT ON THE CK IN SOMALI ACTIVITY. I CAN E BATWING WILL ENDING SOME ON THE HIGH SEAS?
CAN MAKE NECESSARY STMENTS. IT LD TAKE TWO 'S FOR THE ADES AND A GNOSTIC STUDY.
IN THE MEANTIME, I'D SAY YOU GENTLEMEN HAVE EARNED SOME DOWN TIME.
BATMAN, INCORPORATED IS HOSTING A GALA. A GREAT MANY MEMBERS OF THE INTERNATIONAL COMMUNITY WILL BE IN ATTENDANCE.
IT'S AN OPPORTUNITY TO MAINTAIN RELATIONS WITH THE NATIONS WHERE OUR SOLDIERS OF BATMAN, INCORPORATED ARE STATIONED.
WOULD YOU JOIN US? HAVING TWO MEMBERS OF TEAM BATWING ON HAND COULD AID IN FURTHERING DIPLOMACY.
AND THE FOOD'S ALWAYS PHENOMENAL.
THAT IS QUITE GENEROUS, MR. FOX, BUT WE DON'T--
WE WOULD CONSIDER IT AN HONOR TO ATTEND. I AGREE...
E COULD Y USE SOME N TIME."
PER EAST SIDE...
YOU HAVE TRAVELED SO FAR, FROM THE BANKS OF THE RIVER LETHE, THE RIVER OF MINDLESSNESS, WHERE THE SHADES WALK, BACK TO THIS WORLD, TO YOUR CITY. GOTHAM.
YES, LOOK...LOOK AT YOUR BODY. IT HAS BEEN RESTORED, AND MADE STRONGER THAN BEFORE. MUCH STRONGER.

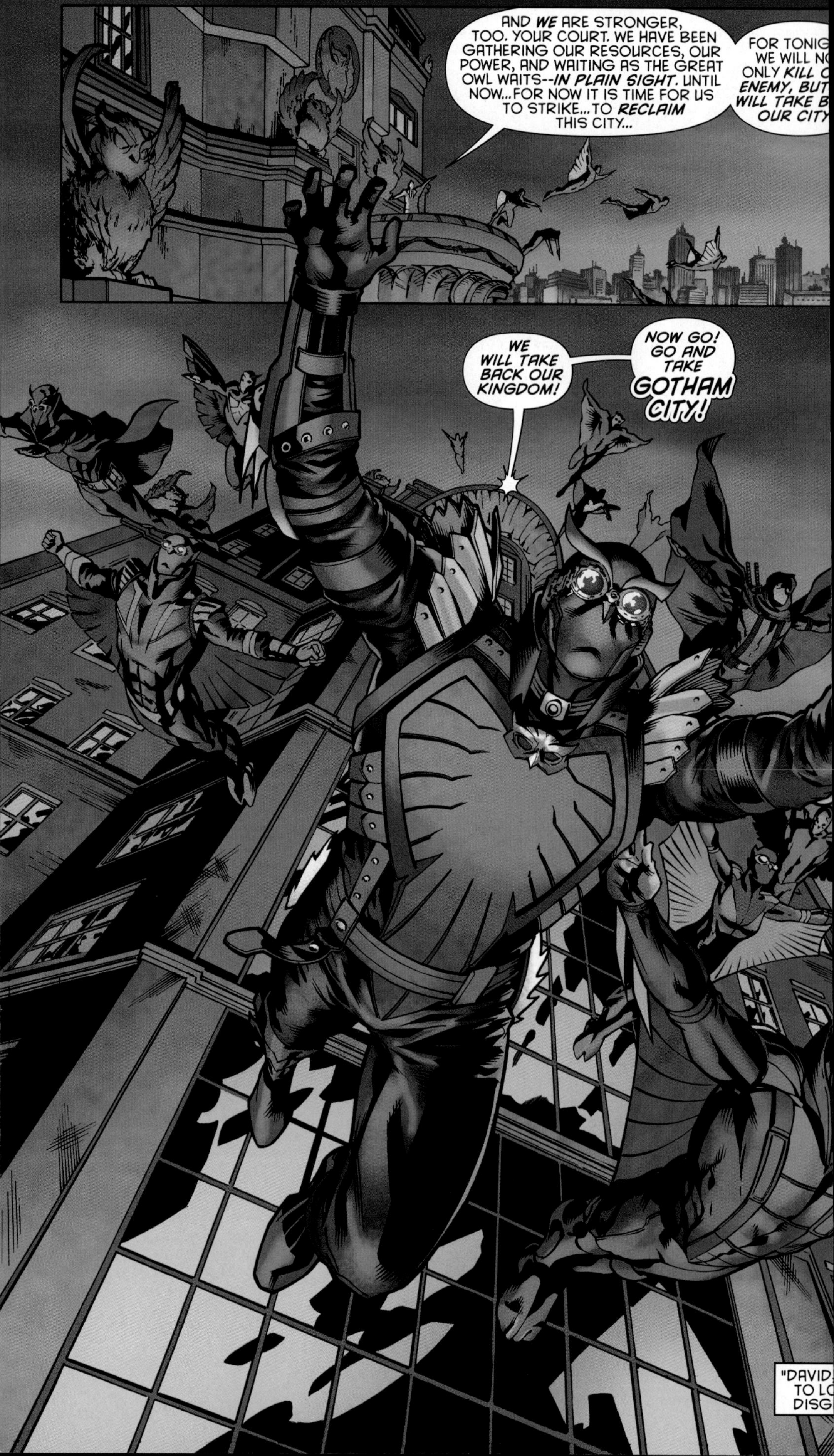

AND WE ARE STRONGER, TOO. YOUR COURT. WE HAVE BEEN GATHERING OUR RESOURCES, OUR POWER, AND WAITING AS THE GREAT OWL WAITS--IN PLAIN SIGHT. UNTIL NOW...FOR NOW IT IS TIME FOR US TO STRIKE...TO RECLAIM THIS CITY...
FOR TONIG WE WILL NO ONLY KILL O ENEMY, BUT WILL TAKE B OUR CITY
WE WILL TAKE BACK OUR KINGDOM!
NOW GO! GO AND TAKE GOTHAM CITY!
"DAVID, TO LO DISG

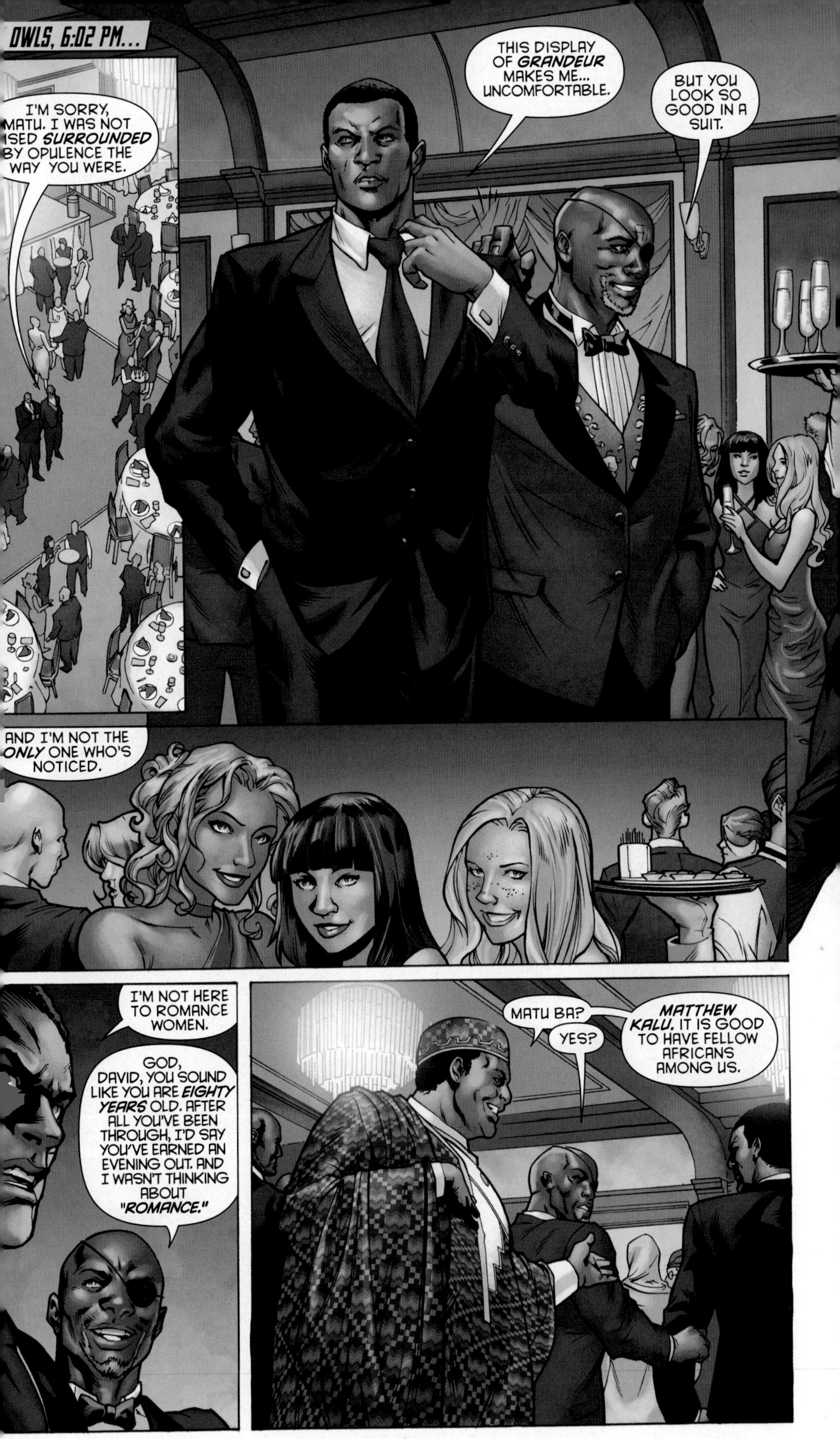

OWLS, 6:02 PM...
I'M SORRY, MATU. I WAS NOT ISED SURROUNDED BY OPULENCE THE WAY YOU WERE.
THIS DISPLAY OF GRANDEUR MAKES ME... UNCOMFORTABLE.
BUT YOU LOOK SO GOOD IN A SUIT.
AND I'M NOT THE ONLY ONE WHO'S NOTICED.
I'M NOT HERE TO ROMANCE WOMEN.
GOD, DAVID, YOU SOUND LIKE YOU ARE EIGHTY YEARS OLD. AFTER ALL YOU'VE BEEN THROUGH, I'D SAY YOU'VE EARNED AN EVENING OUT. AND I WASN'T THINKING ABOUT "ROMANCE."
MATU BA?
YES?
MATTHEW KALU. IT IS GOOD TO HAVE FELLOW AFRICANS AMONG US.

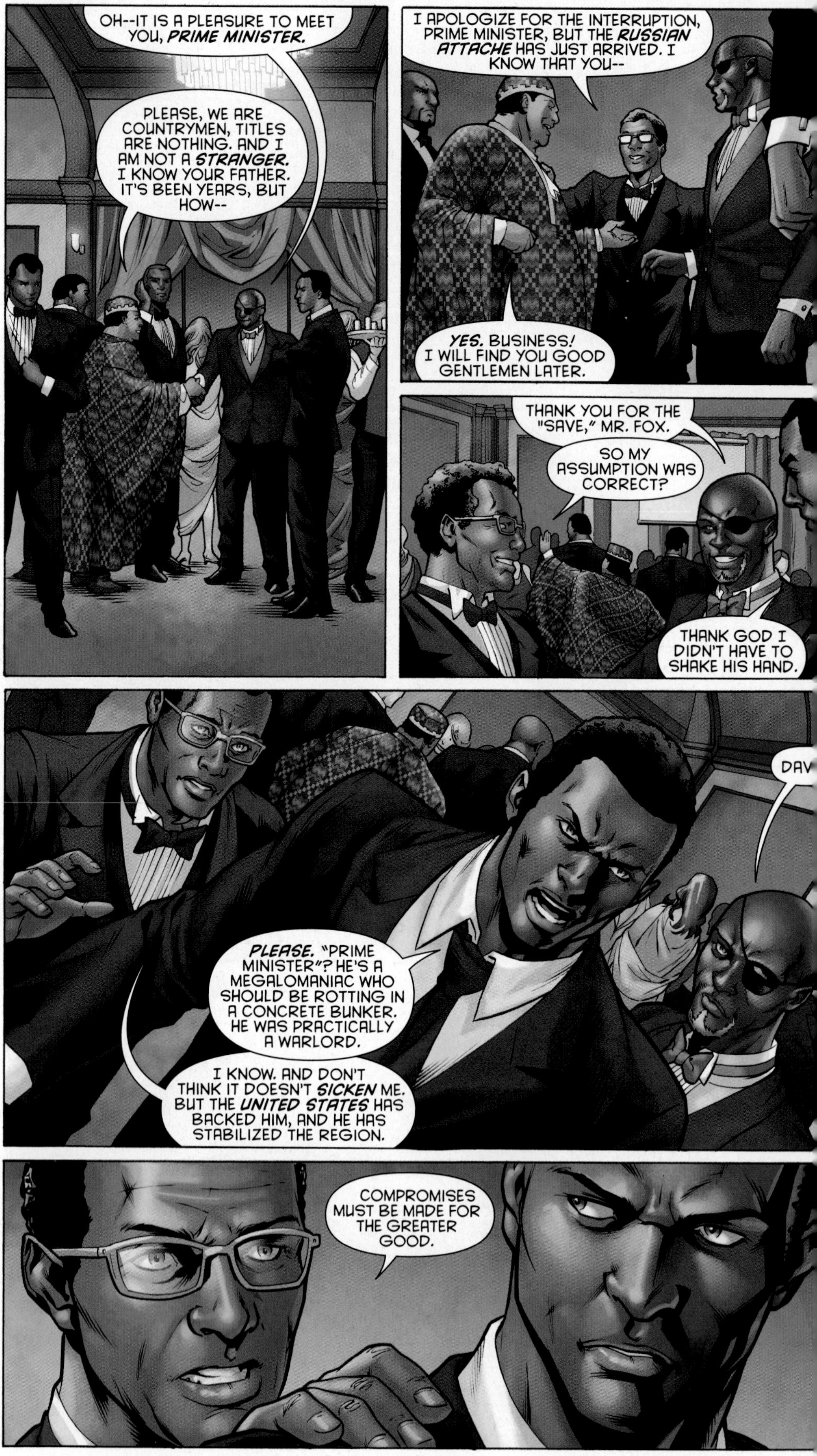
OH--IT IS A PLEASURE TO MEET YOU, PRIME MINISTER.
PLEASE, WE ARE COUNTRYMEN, TITLES ARE NOTHING. AND I AM NOT A STRANGER. I KNOW YOUR FATHER. IT'S BEEN YEARS, BUT HOW--
I APOLOGIZE FOR THE INTERRUPTION, PRIME MINISTER, BUT THE RUSSIAN ATTACHE HAS JUST ARRIVED. I KNOW THAT YOU--
YES. BUSINESS! I WILL FIND YOU GOOD GENTLEMEN LATER.
THANK YOU FOR THE "SAVE," MR. FOX.
SO MY ASSUMPTION WAS CORRECT?
THANK GOD I DIDN'T HAVE TO SHAKE HIS HAND.
DAV
PLEASE. "PRIME MINISTER"? HE'S A MEGALOMANIAC WHO SHOULD BE ROTTING IN A CONCRETE BUNKER. HE WAS PRACTICALLY A WARLORD.
I KNOW. AND DON'T THINK IT DOESN'T SICKEN ME. BUT THE UNITED STATES HAS BACKED HIM, AND HE HAS STABILIZED THE REGION.
COMPROMISES MUST BE MADE FOR THE GREATER GOOD.

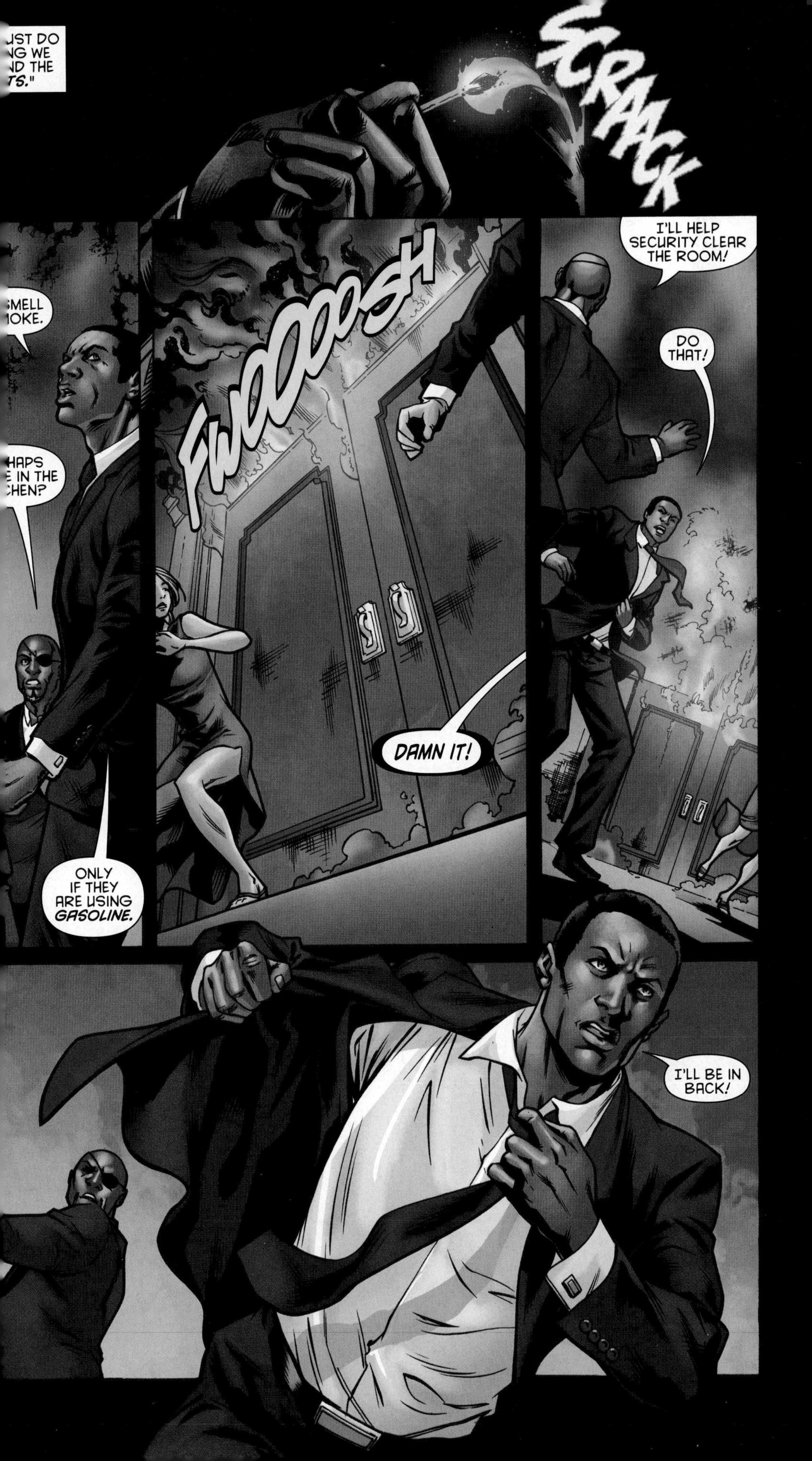
UST DO
NG WE
ND THE
TS."
SCRACK
SMELL
IOKE.
HAPS
E IN THE
CHEN?
ONLY IF THEY ARE USING GASOLINE.
FWOOOOSH
DAMN IT!
I'LL HELP SECURITY CLEAR THE ROOM!
DO THAT!
I'LL BE IN BACK!

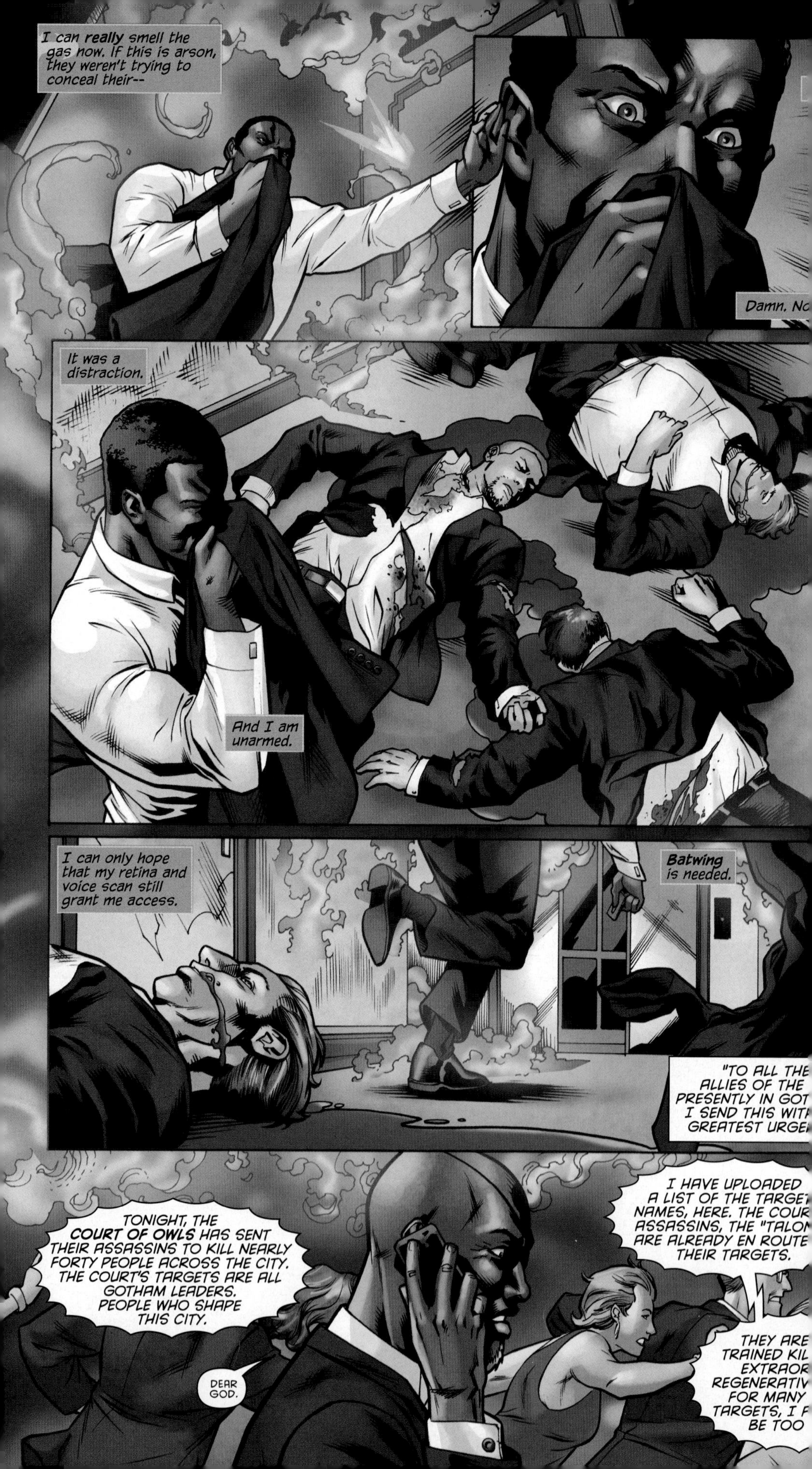
I can really smell the gas now. If this is arson, they weren't trying to conceal their--
Damn. No
It was a distraction.
And I am unarmed.
I can only hope that my retina and voice scan still grant me access.
Batwing is needed.
"TO ALL THE
ALLIES OF THE
PRESENTLY IN GOT
I SEND THIS WIT
GREATEST URGE
TONIGHT, THE COURT OF OWLS HAS SENT THEIR ASSASSINS TO KILL NEARLY FORTY PEOPLE ACROSS THE CITY. THE COURT'S TARGETS ARE ALL GOTHAM LEADERS. PEOPLE WHO SHAPE THIS CITY.
I HAVE UPLOADED A LIST OF THE TARGE NAMES, HERE. THE COUR ASSASSINS, THE "TALON ARE ALREADY EN ROUTE THEIR TARGETS.
DEAR GOD.
THEY ARE TRAINED KIL EXTRAOR REGENERATIV FOR MANY TARGETS, I F BE TOO

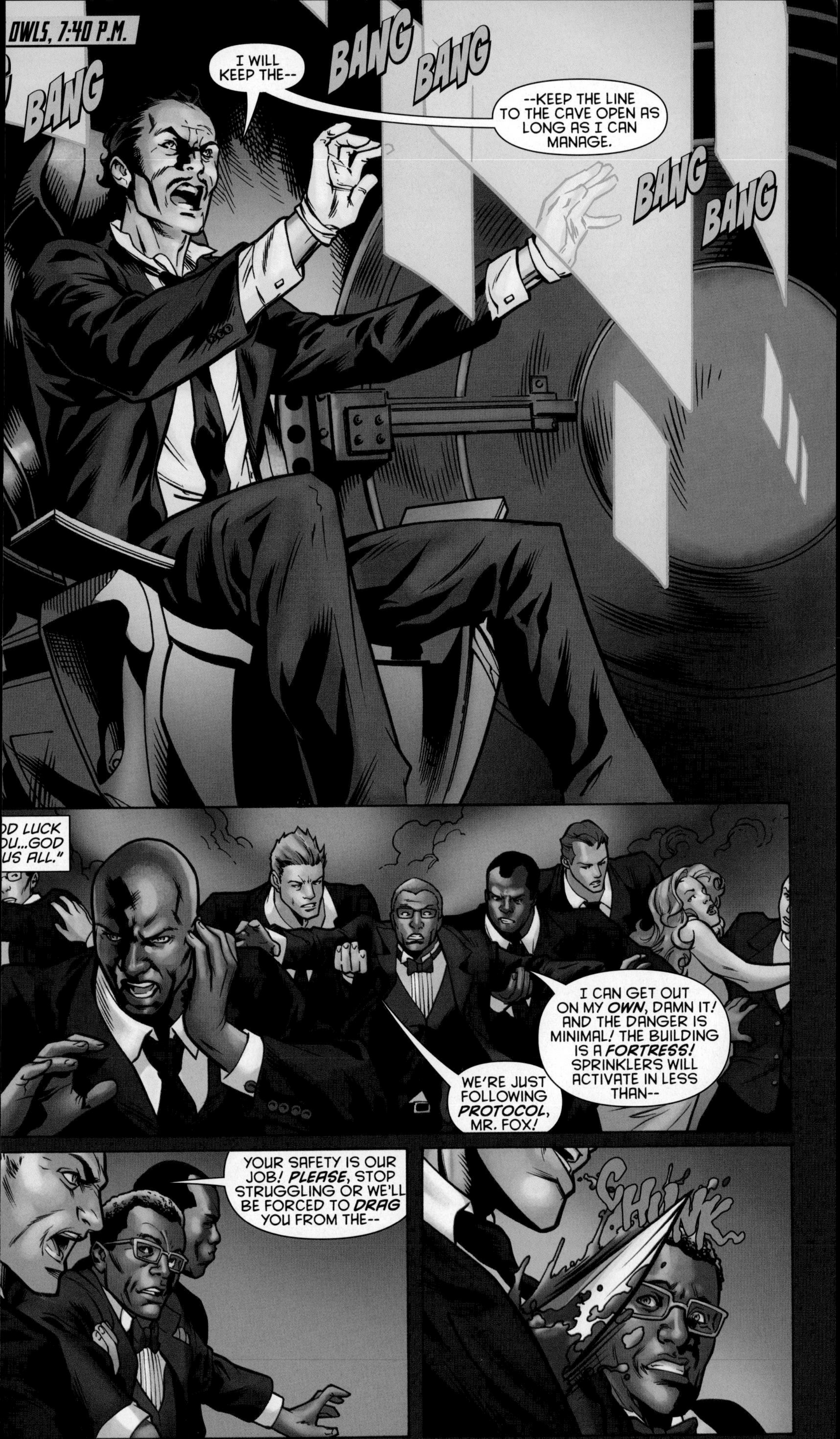
OWLS, 7:40 P.M.
BANG
I WILL KEEP THE--
BANG
BANG
--KEEP THE LINE TO THE CAVE OPEN AS LONG AS I CAN MANAGE.
BANG
BANG
OD LUCK OU...GOD US ALL."
I CAN GET OUT ON MY OWN, DAMN IT! AND THE DANGER IS MINIMAL! THE BUILDING IS A FORTRESS! SPRINKLERS WILL ACTIVATE IN LESS THAN--
WE'RE JUST FOLLOWING PROTOCOL, MR. FOX!
YOUR SAFETY IS OUR JOB! PLEASE, STOP STRUGGLING OR WE'LL BE FORCED TO DRAG YOU FROM THE--
CHUNK

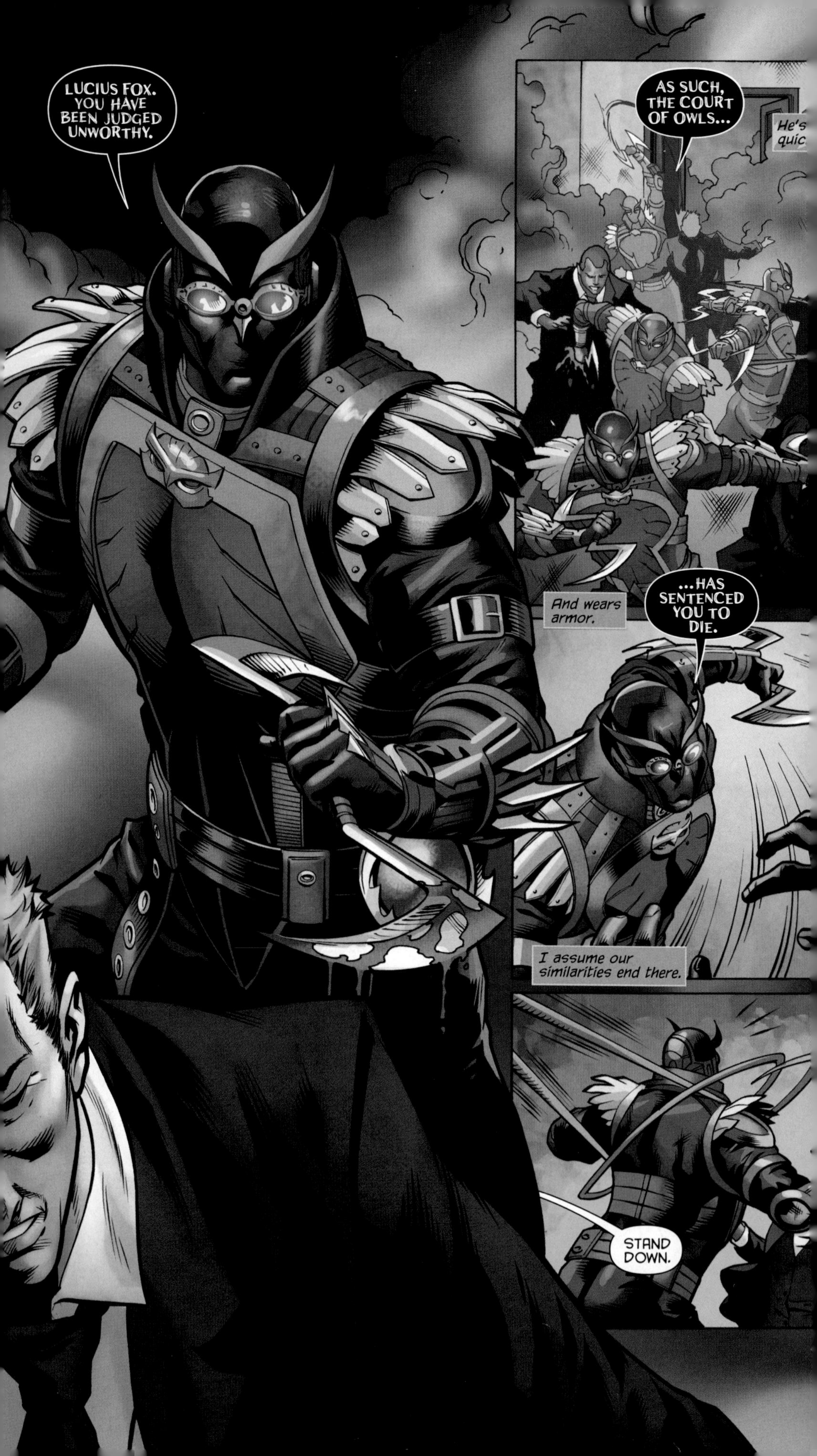
LUCIUS FOX. YOU HAVE BEEN JUDGED UNWORTHY.
AS SUCH, THE COURT OF OWLS...
And wears armor.
...HAS SENTENCED YOU TO DIE.
I assume our similarities end there.
STAND DOWN.

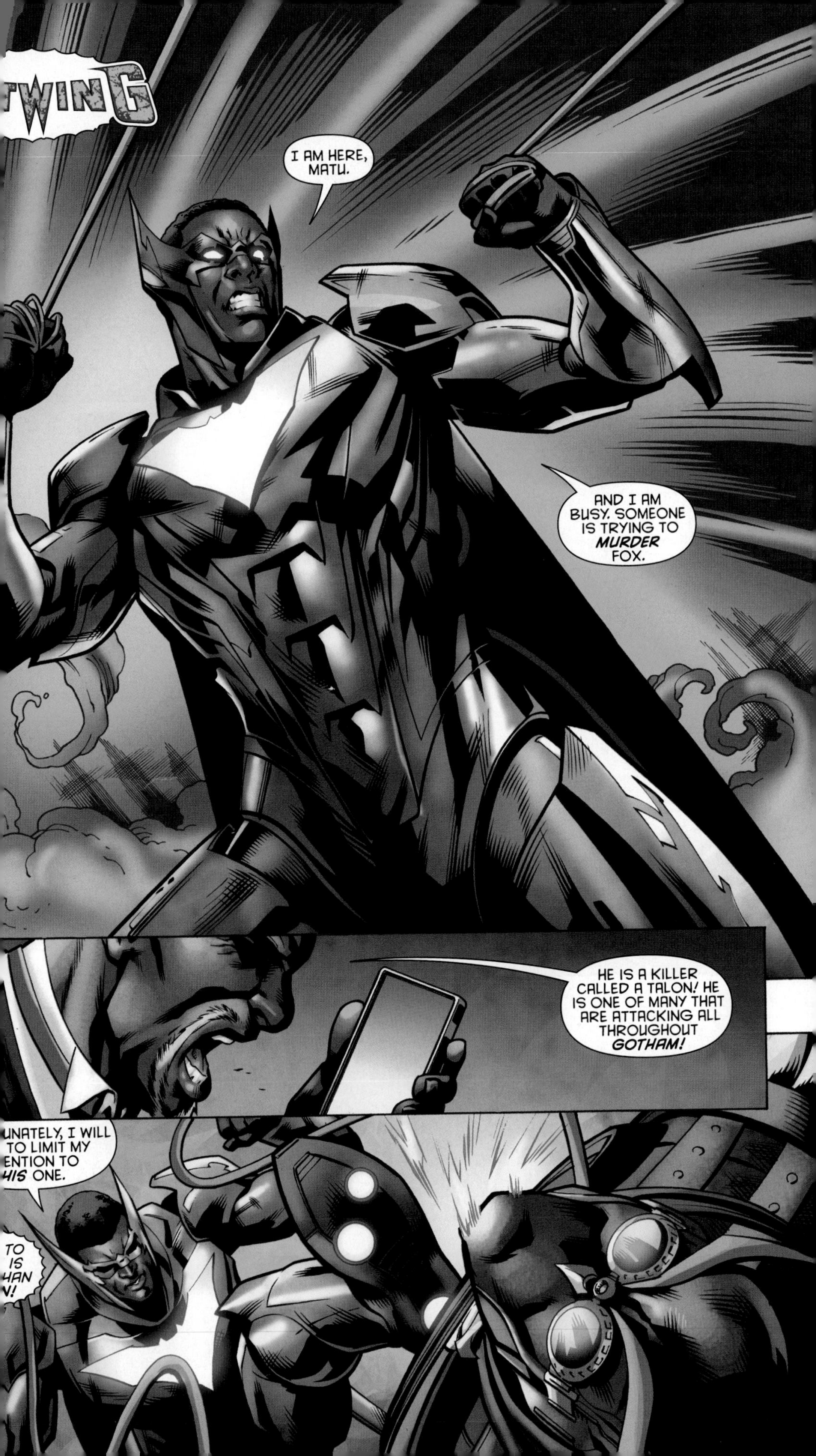
TWING
I AM HERE, MATU.
AND I AM BUSY. SOMEONE IS TRYING TO MURDER FOX.
HE IS A KILLER CALLED A TALON! HE IS ONE OF MANY THAT ARE ATTACKING ALL THROUGHOUT GOTHAM!
UNATELY, I WILL TO LIMIT MY ENTION TO HIS ONE.

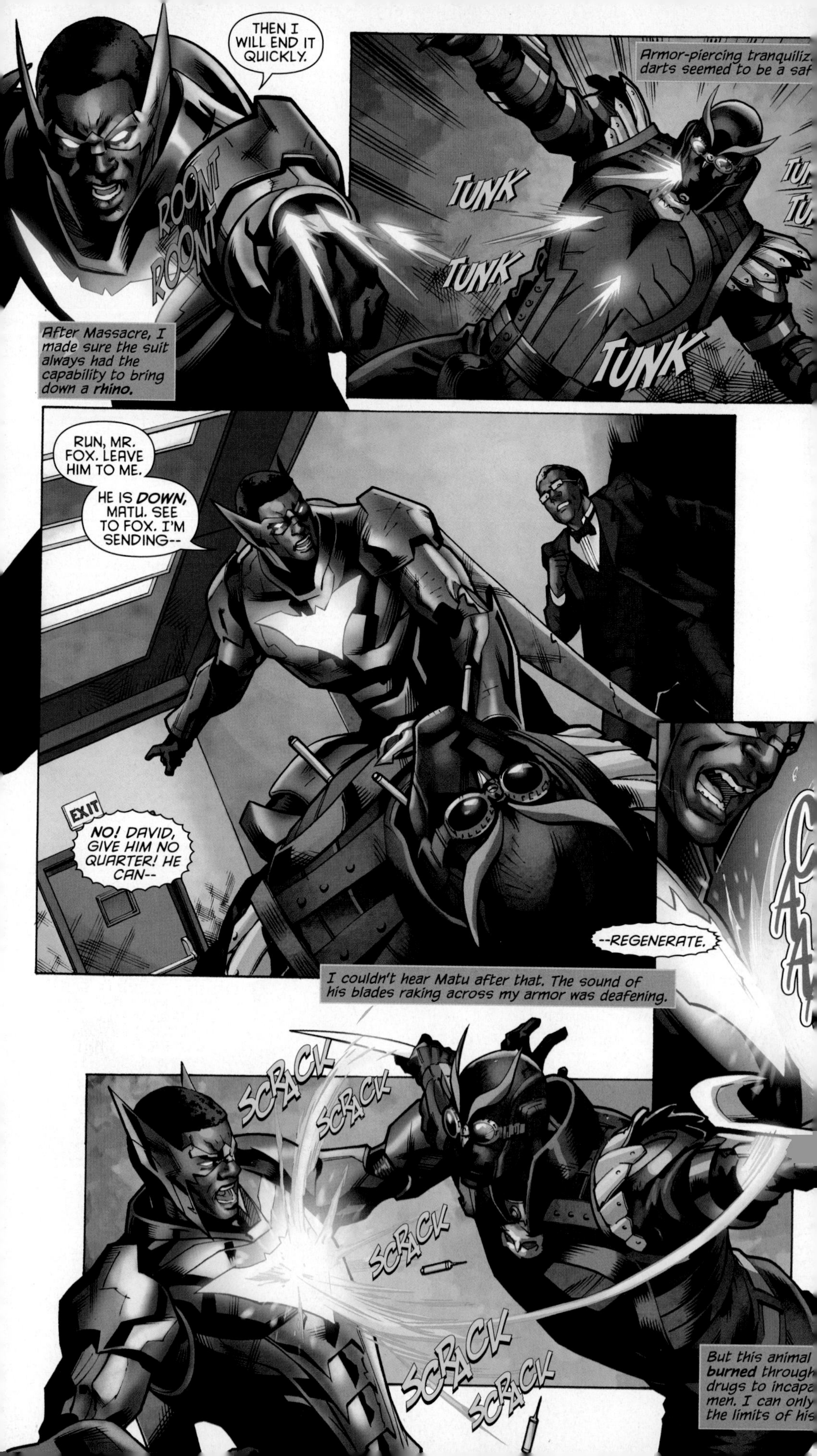
THEN I WILL END IT QUICKLY.
ROONT ROONT
After Massacre, I made sure the suit always had the capability to bring down a rhino.
Armor-piercing tranquiliz darts seemed to be a saf
TUNK
TUNK
TUNK
RUN, MR. FOX. LEAVE HIM TO ME.
HE IS DOWN, MATU. SEE TO FOX. I'M SENDING--
EXIT
NO! DAVID, GIVE HIM NO QUARTER! HE CAN--
--REGENERATE.
I couldn't hear Matu after that. The sound of his blades raking across my armor was deafening.
SCRACK
SCRACK
SCRACK
SCRACK
SCRACK
But this animal burned through drugs to incapa men. I can only the limits of his

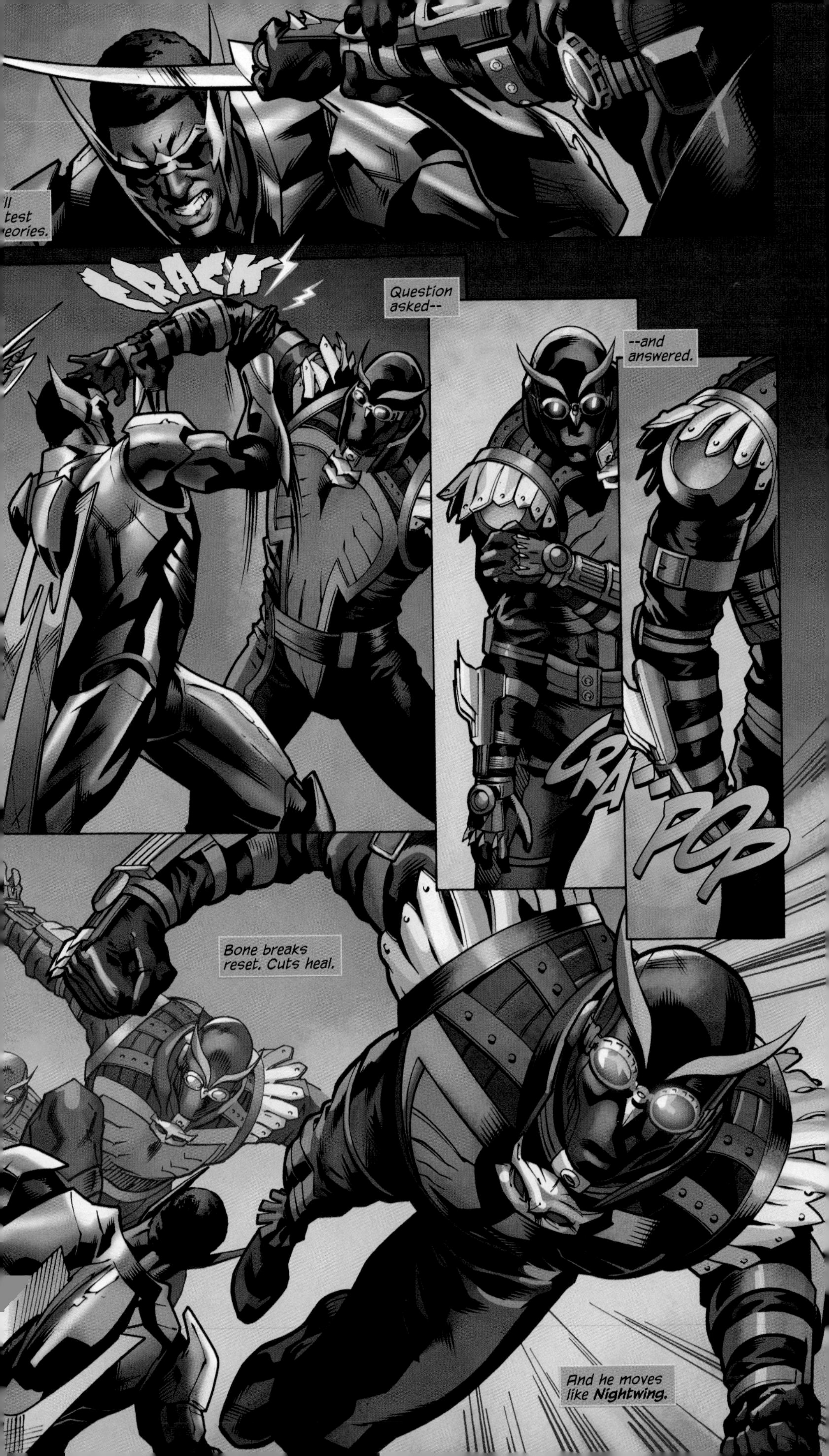

'll test eories.
CRACK
Question asked--
--and answered.
CRA-POP
Bone breaks reset. Cuts heal.
And he moves like **Nightwing**.

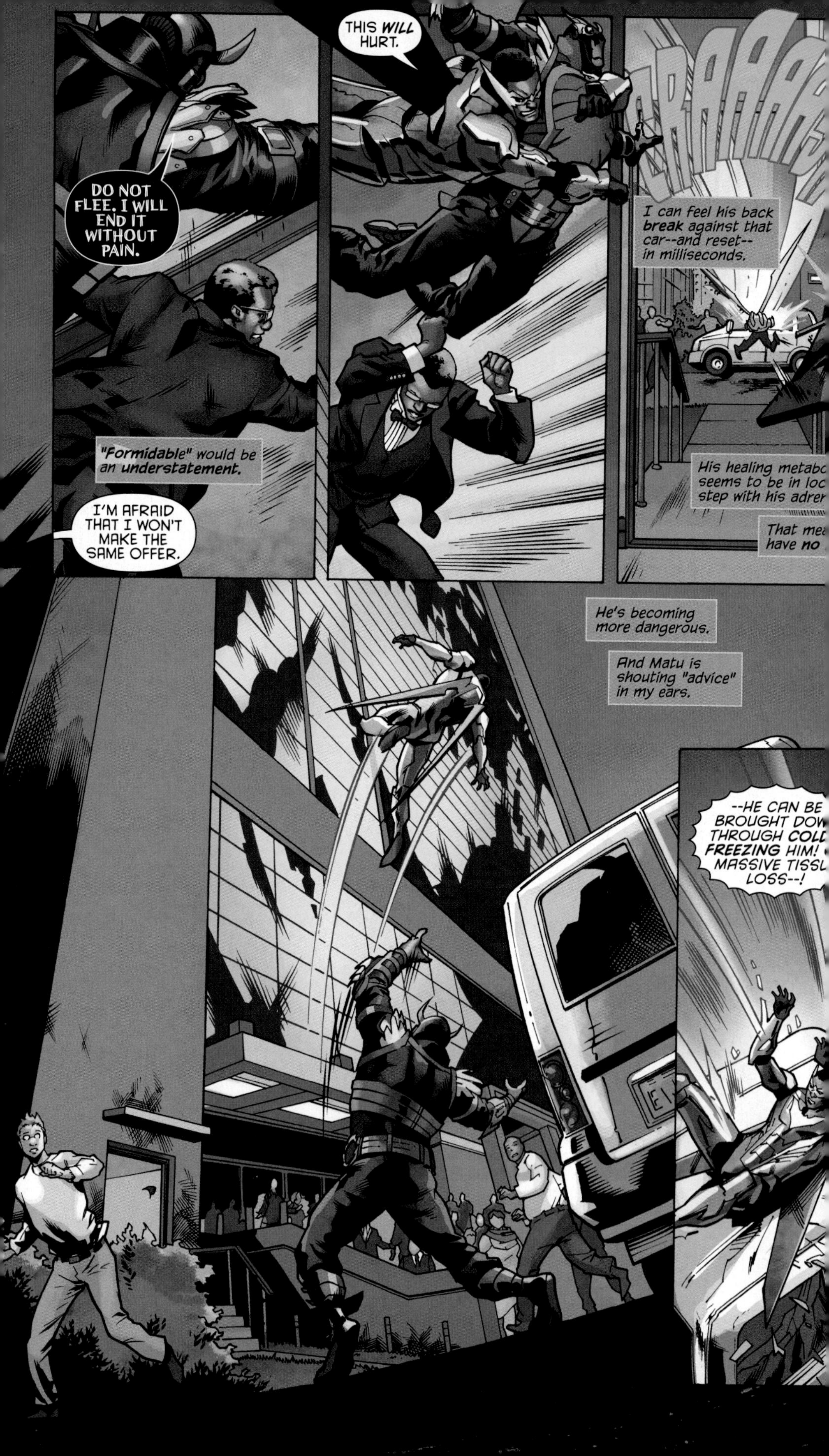
DO NOT FLEE. I WILL END IT WITHOUT PAIN.
"Formidable" would be an understatement.
I'M AFRAID THAT I WON'T MAKE THE SAME OFFER.
THIS WILL HURT.
I can feel his back break against that car--and reset--in milliseconds.
His healing metabo seems to be in loc step with his adrer
That mea have no
He's becoming more dangerous.
And Matu is shouting "advice" in my ears.
--HE CAN BE BROUGHT DOW THROUGH COLD FREEZING HIM! MASSIVE TISSU LOSS--!

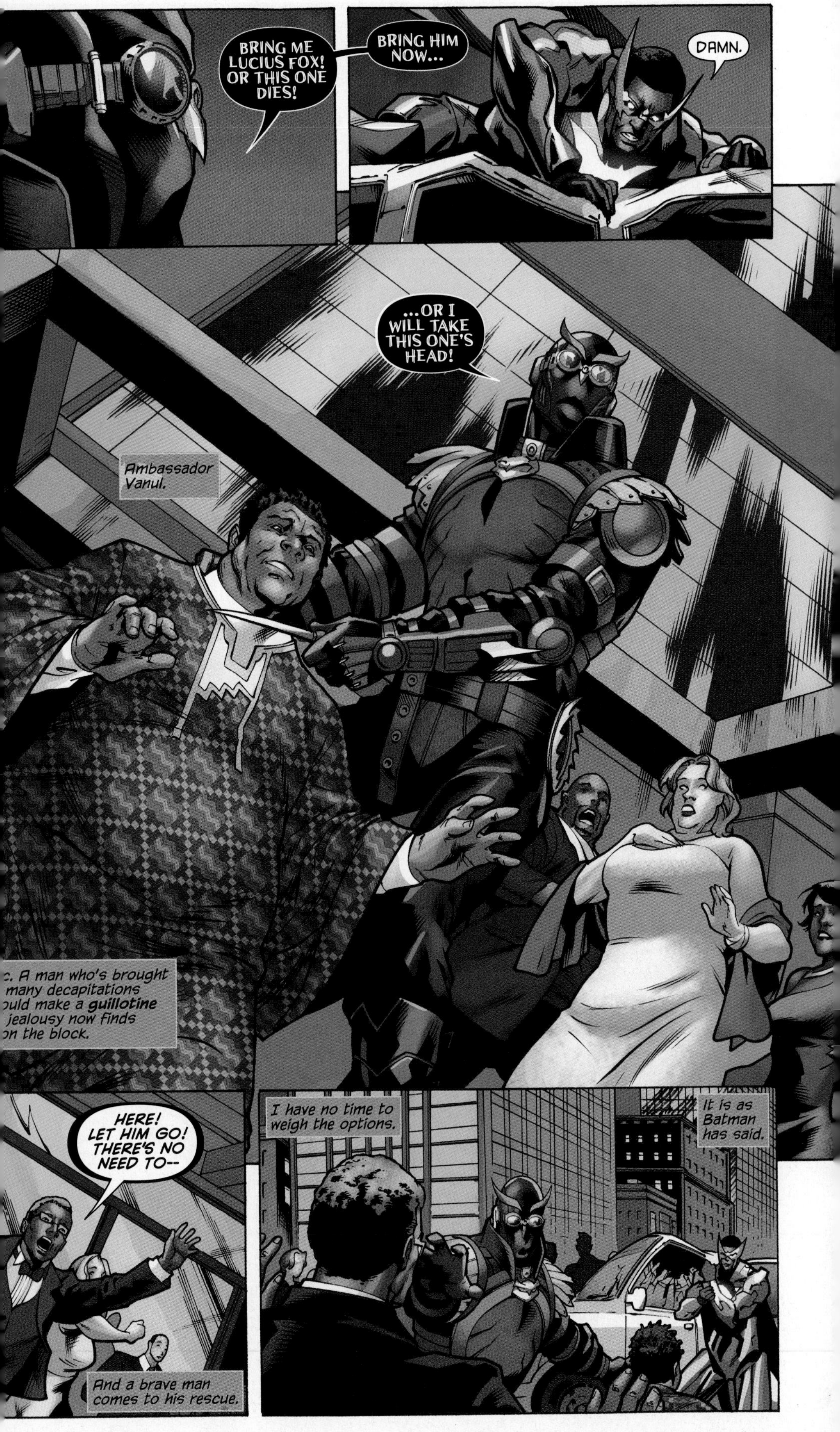
BRING ME LUCIUS FOX! OR THIS ONE DIES!
BRING HIM NOW...
DAMN.
...OR I WILL TAKE THIS ONE'S HEAD!
Ambassador Vanul.
c. A man who's brought many decapitations ould make a guillotine jealousy now finds on the block.
HERE! LET HIM GO! THERE'S NO NEED TO--
And a brave man comes to his rescue.
I have no time to weigh the options.
It is as Batman has said.

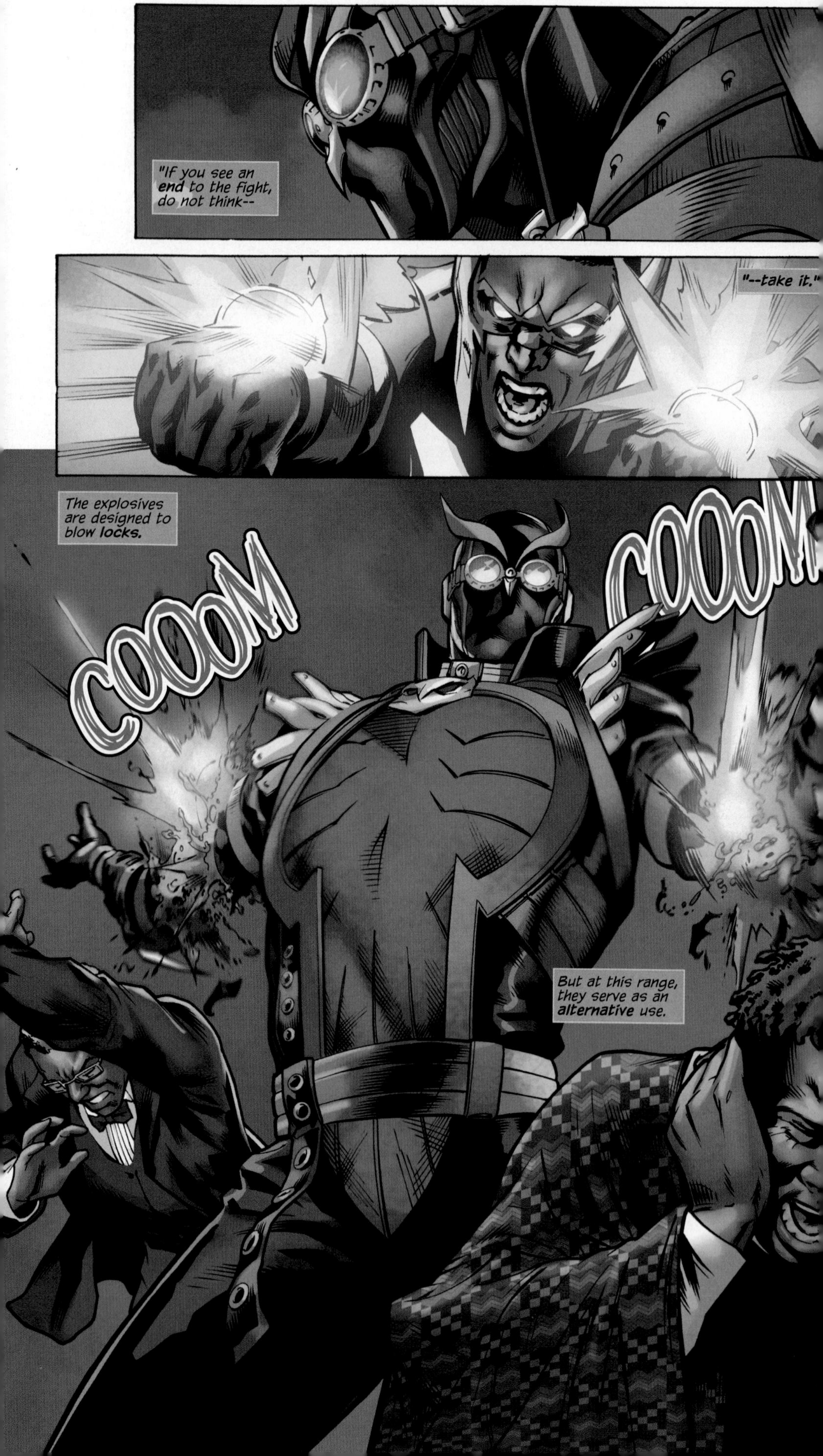
"If you see an end to the fight, do not think--
"--take it."
The explosives are designed to blow locks.
COOOM
COOOM
But at this range, they serve as an alternative use.

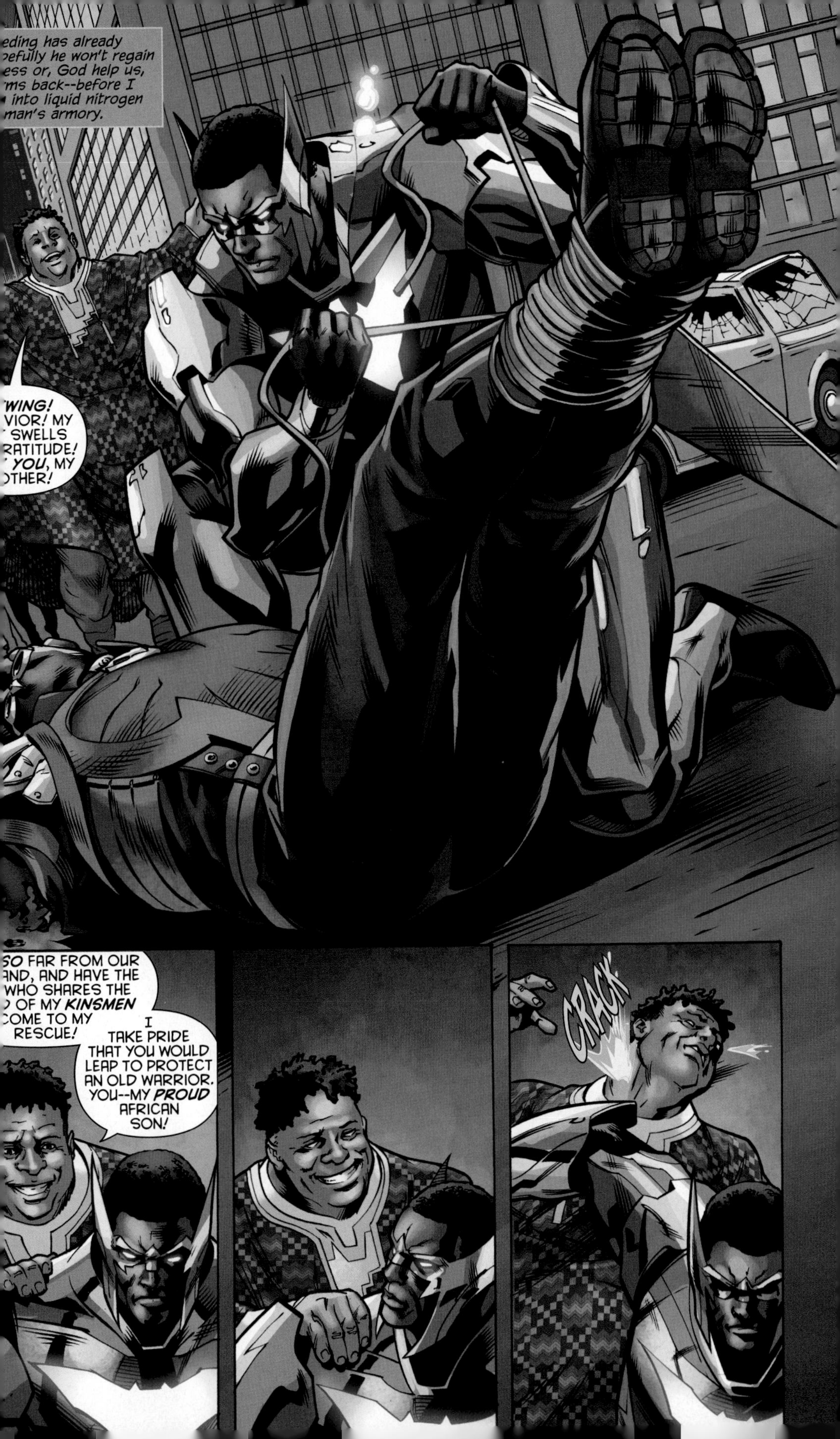
eding has already
pefully he won't regain
ess or, God help us,
rms back--before I
into liquid nitrogen
man's armory.
WING!
VIOR! MY
SWELLS
RATITUDE!
YOU, MY
OTHER!
SO FAR FROM OUR
AND, AND HAVE THE
WHO SHARES THE
OF MY KINSMEN
COME TO MY
RESCUE!
I TAKE PRIDE THAT YOU WOULD LEAP TO PROTECT AN OLD WARRIOR. YOU--MY PROUD AFRICAN SON!
CRACK

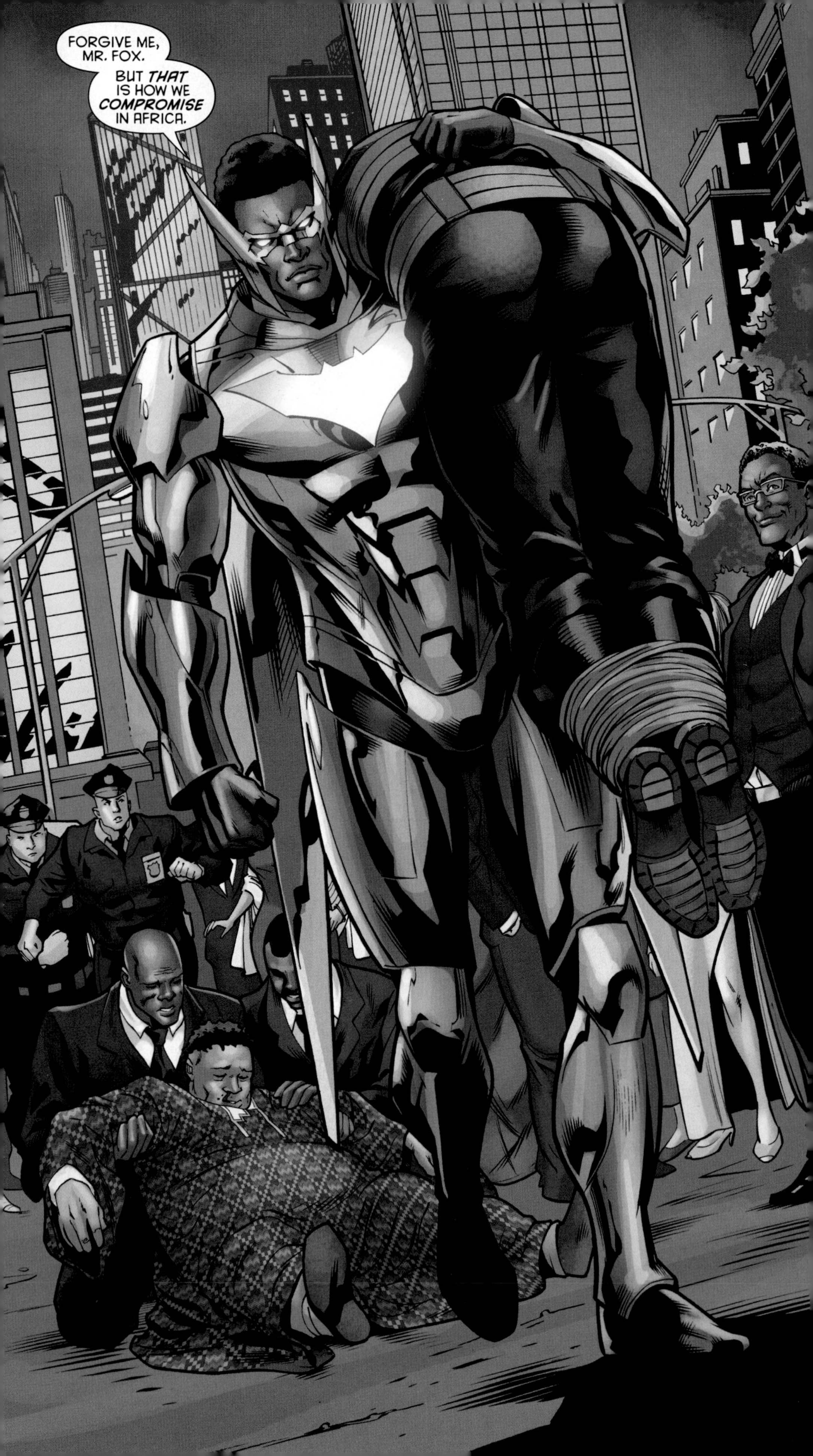
FORGIVE ME, MR. FOX.
BUT *THAT* IS HOW WE ***COMPROMISE*** IN AFRICA.

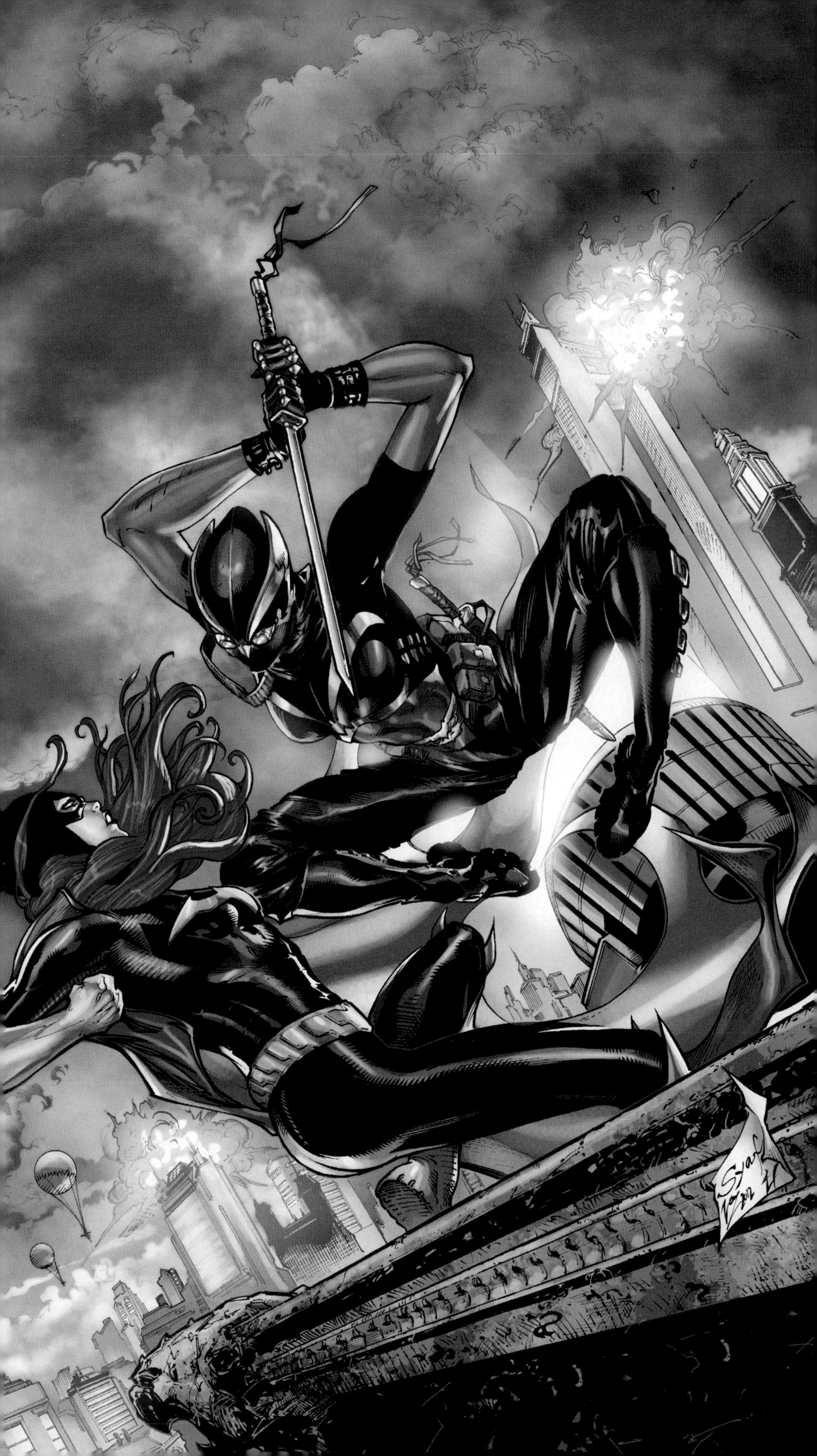

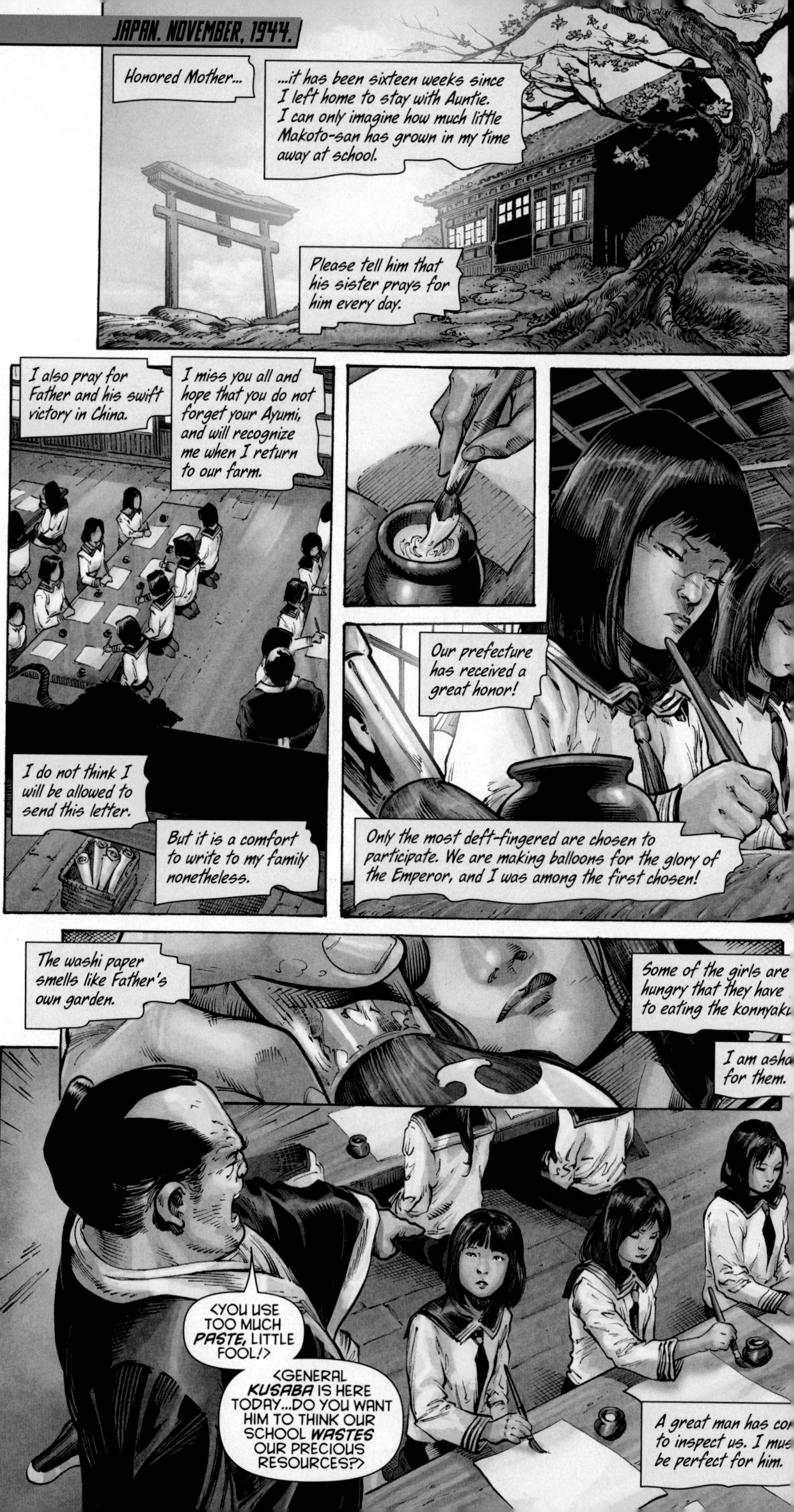
JAPAN. NOVEMBER, 1944.
Honored Mother...
...it has been sixteen weeks since I left home to stay with Auntie. I can only imagine how much little Makoto-san has grown in my time away at school.
Please tell him that his sister prays for him every day.
I also pray for Father and his swift victory in China.
I miss you all and hope that you do not forget your Ayumi, and will recognize me when I return to our farm.
I do not think I will be allowed to send this letter.
But it is a comfort to write to my family nonetheless.
Our prefecture has received a great honor!
Only the most deft-fingered are chosen to participate. We are making balloons for the glory of the Emperor, and I was among the first chosen!
The washi paper smells like Father's own garden.
Some of the girls are hungry that they have to eating the konnyaku
I am ash for them.
<YOU USE TOO MUCH PASTE, LITTLE FOOL!>
<GENERAL KUSABA IS HERE TODAY...DO YOU WANT HIM TO THINK OUR SCHOOL WASTES OUR PRECIOUS RESOURCES?>
A great man has co to inspect us. I mus be perfect for him.

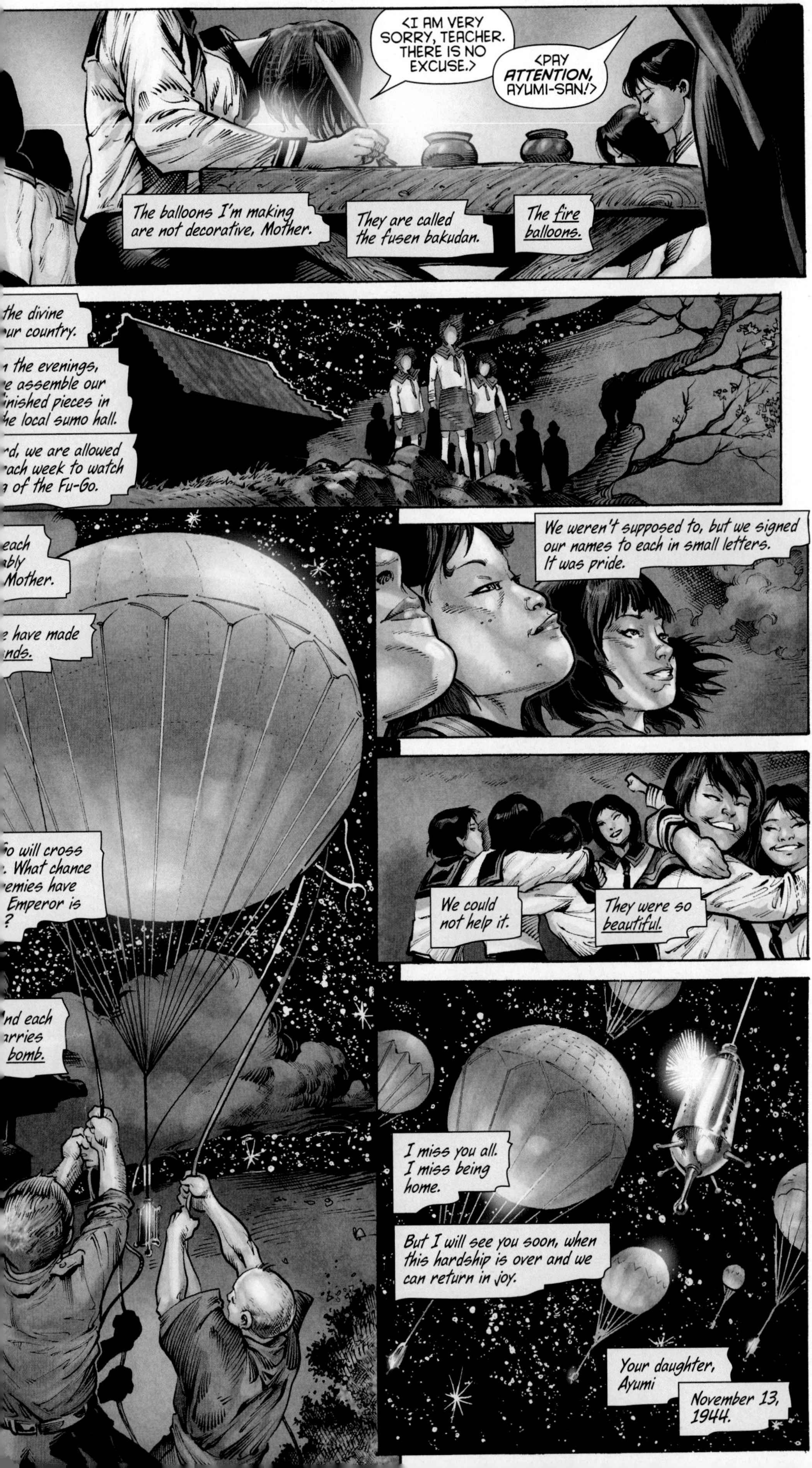
<I AM VERY SORRY, TEACHER. THERE IS NO EXCUSE.>
<PAY **ATTENTION,** AYUMI-SAN!>
The balloons I'm making are not decorative, Mother.
They are called the fusen bakudan.
The fire balloons.
the divine
ur country.
n the evenings,
e assemble our
inished pieces in
he local sumo hall.
rd, we are allowed
each week to watch
n of the Fu-Go.
each
ably
Mother.
e have made
nds.
o will cross
. What chance
emies have
Emperor is
?
nd each
arries
bomb.
We weren't supposed to, but we signed our names to each in small letters. It was pride.
We could not help it.
They were so beautiful.
I miss you all. I miss being home.
But I will see you soon, when this hardship is over and we can return in joy.
Your daughter, Ayumi
November 13, 1944.

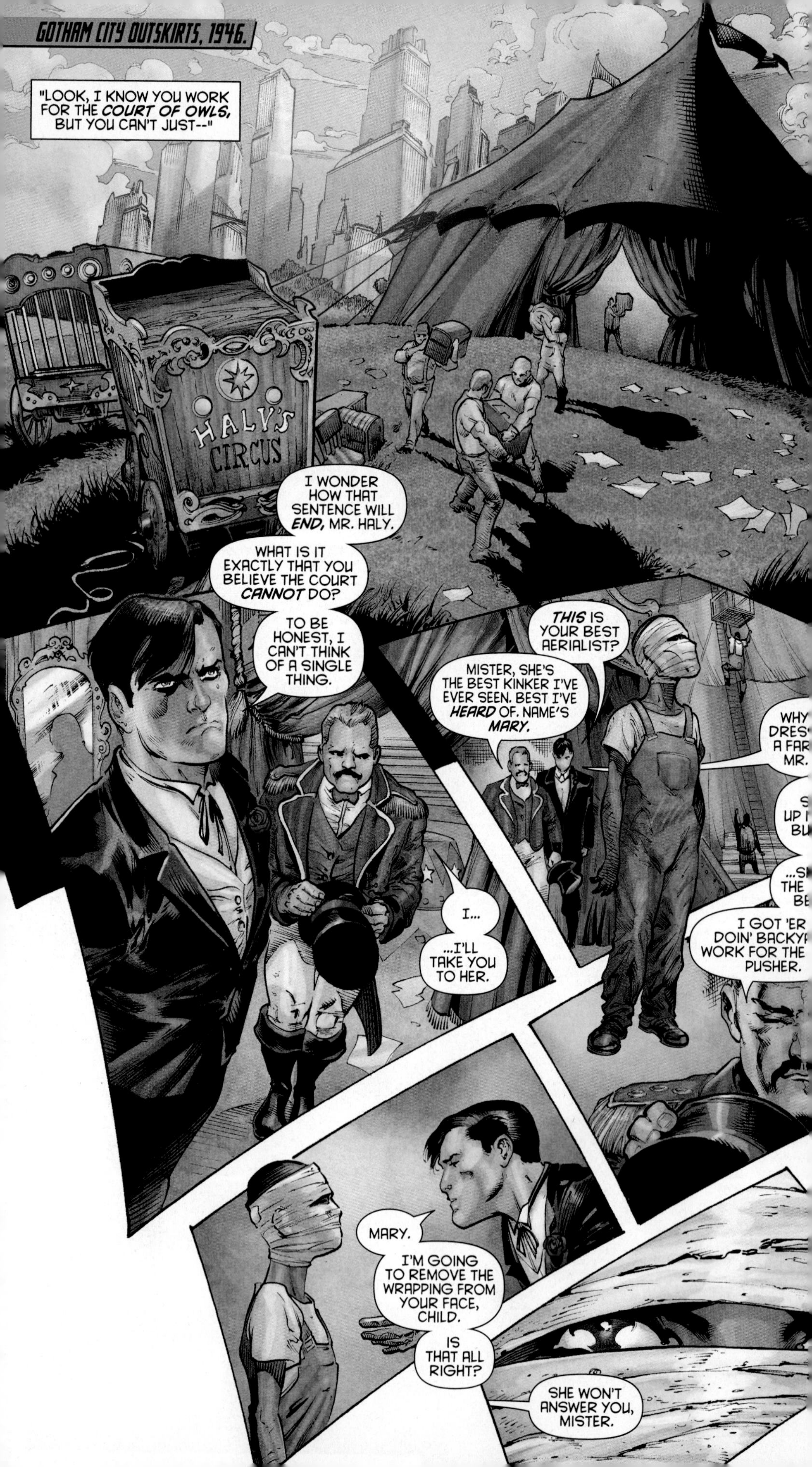
GOTHAM CITY OUTSKIRTS, 1946.
"LOOK, I KNOW YOU WORK FOR THE *COURT OF OWLS,* BUT YOU CAN'T JUST--"
HALY'S CIRCUS
I WONDER HOW THAT SENTENCE WILL *END,* MR. HALY.
WHAT IS IT EXACTLY THAT YOU BELIEVE THE COURT *CANNOT* DO?
TO BE HONEST, I CAN'T THINK OF A SINGLE THING.
I...
...I'LL TAKE YOU TO HER.
THIS IS YOUR BEST AERIALIST?
MISTER, SHE'S THE BEST KINKER I'VE EVER SEEN. BEST I'VE *HEARD* OF. NAME'S *MARY.*
I GOT 'ER DOIN' BACKY WORK FOR THE PUSHER.
MARY.
I'M GOING TO REMOVE THE WRAPPING FROM YOUR FACE, CHILD.
IS THAT ALL RIGHT?
SHE WON'T ANSWER YOU, MISTER.

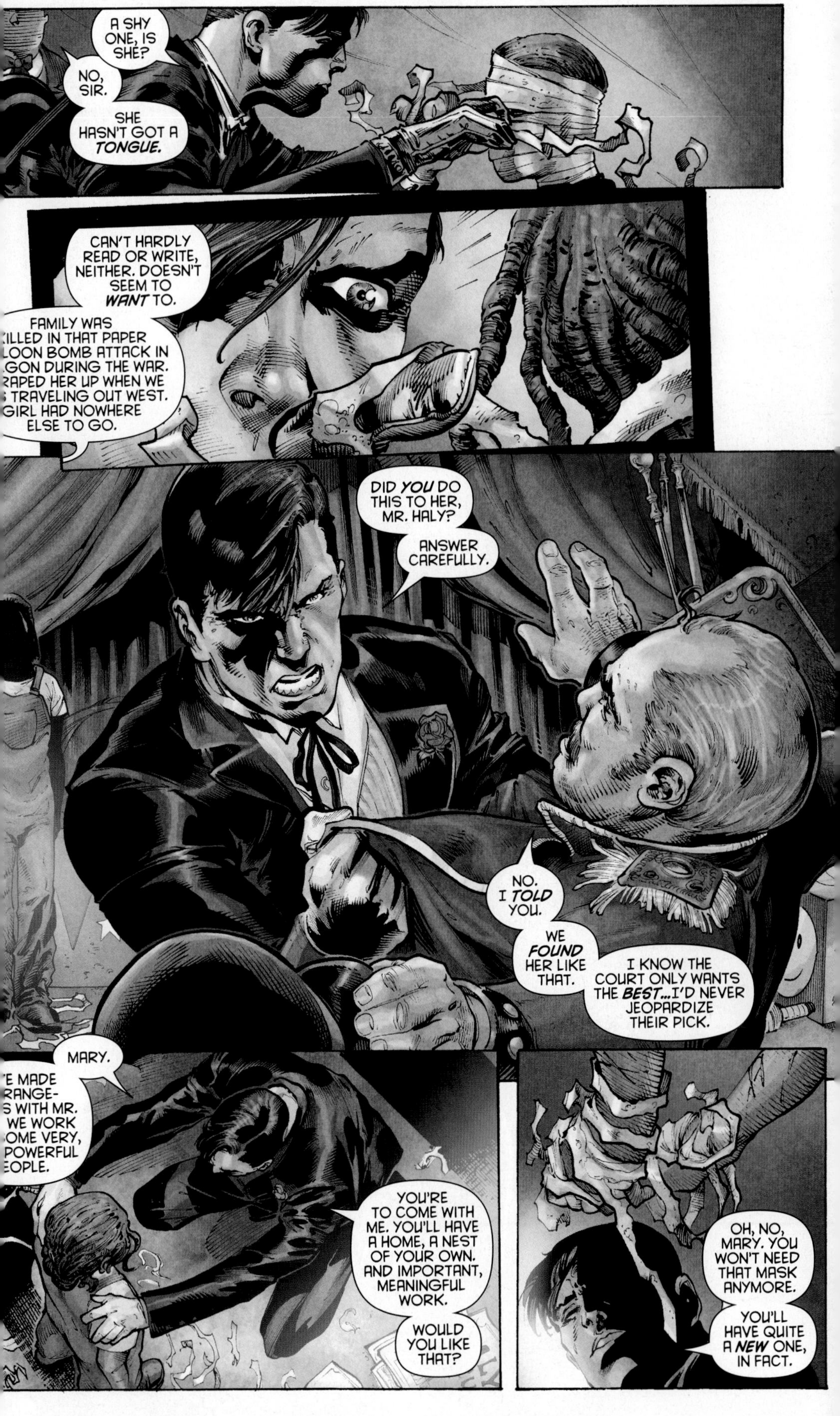
A SHY ONE, IS SHE?
NO, SIR.
SHE HASN'T GOT A *TONGUE.*
CAN'T HARDLY READ OR WRITE, NEITHER. DOESN'T SEEM TO *WANT* TO.
FAMILY WAS KILLED IN THAT PAPER LOON BOMB ATTACK IN GON DURING THE WAR. RAPED HER UP WHEN WE S TRAVELING OUT WEST. GIRL HAD NOWHERE ELSE TO GO.
DID *YOU* DO THIS TO HER, MR. HALY?
ANSWER CAREFULLY.
NO. I *TOLD* YOU.
WE *FOUND* HER LIKE THAT.
I KNOW THE COURT ONLY WANTS THE *BEST*...I'D NEVER JEOPARDIZE THEIR PICK.
MARY.
E MADE RANGE- S WITH MR. WE WORK OME VERY, POWERFUL EOPLE.
YOU'RE TO COME WITH ME. YOU'LL HAVE A HOME, A NEST OF YOUR OWN. AND IMPORTANT, MEANINGFUL WORK.
WOULD YOU LIKE THAT?
OH, NO, MARY. YOU WON'T NEED THAT MASK ANYMORE.
YOU'LL HAVE QUITE A *NEW* ONE, IN FACT.

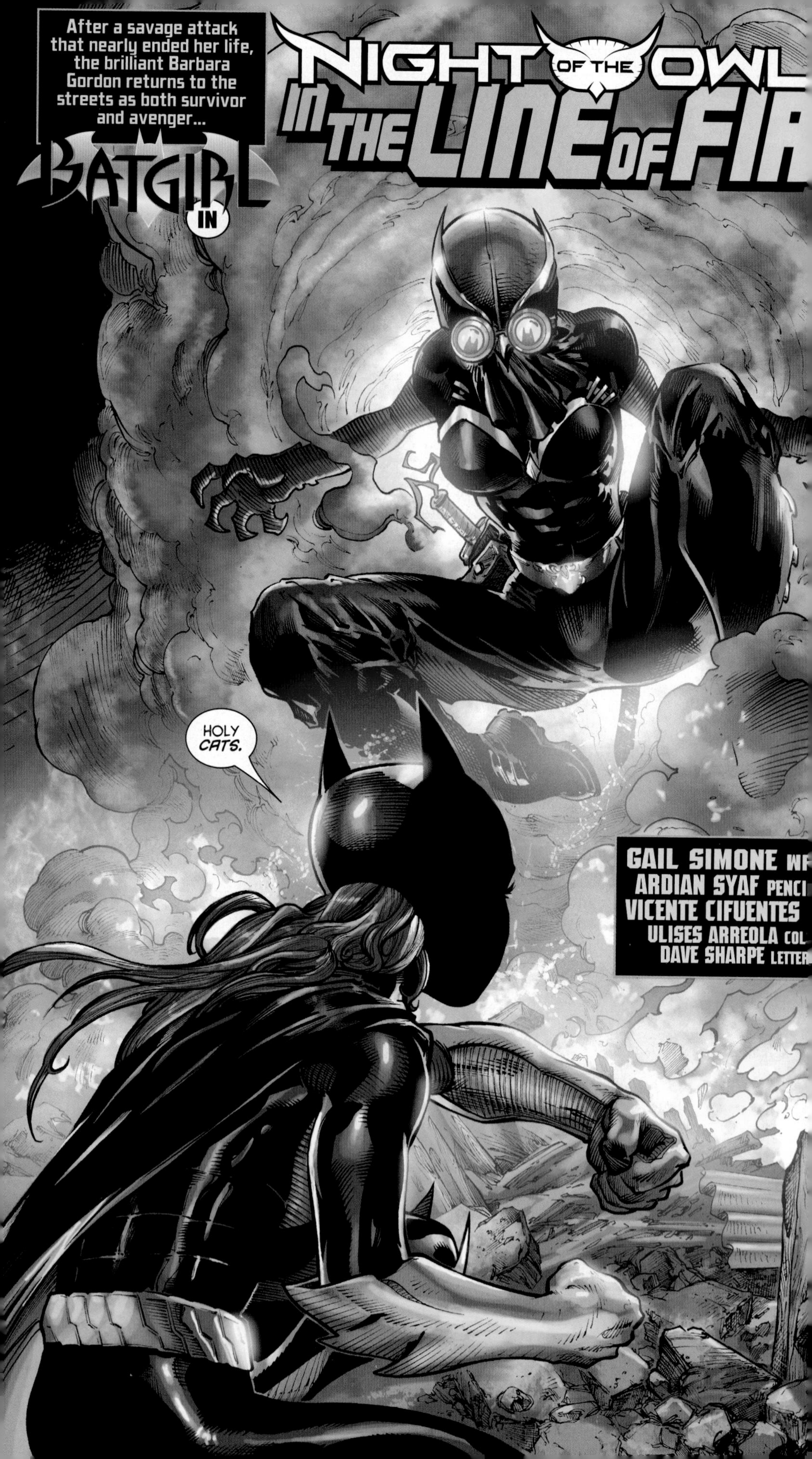
After a savage attack that nearly ended her life, the brilliant Barbara Gordon returns to the streets as both survivor and avenger...
BATGIRL IN
NIGHT OF THE OWL
IN THE LINE OF FIR
HOLY CATS.
GAIL SIMONE
ARDIAN SYAF
VICENTE CIFUENTES
ULISES ARREOLA
DAVE SHARPE

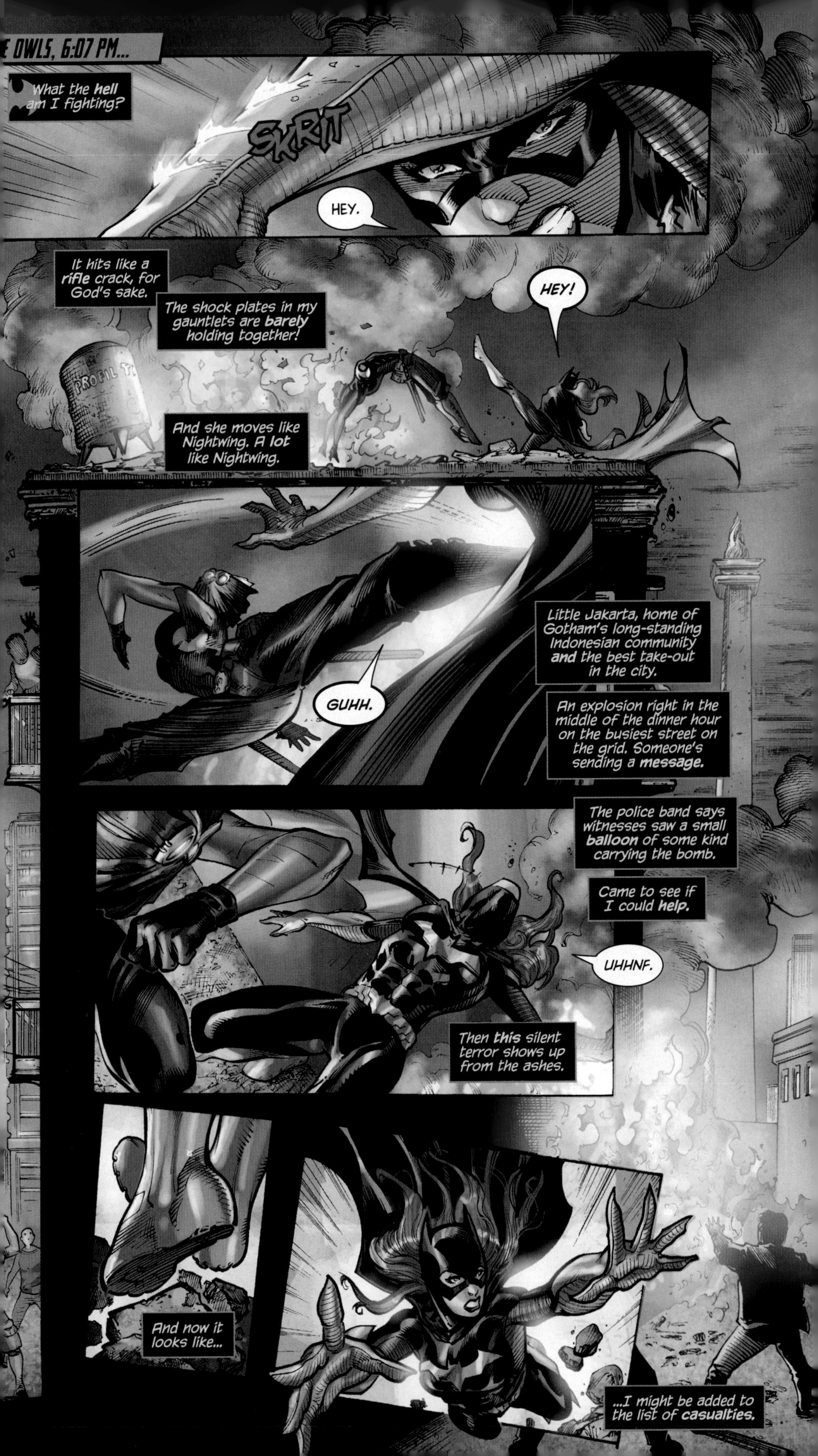
E OWLS, 6:07 PM...
What the hell am I fighting?
SKRIT
HEY.
It hits like a rifle crack, for God's sake.
The shock plates in my gauntlets are barely holding together!
HEY!
PROFIL
And she moves like Nightwing. A lot like Nightwing.
Little Jakarta, home of Gotham's long-standing Indonesian community and the best take-out in the city.
GUHH.
An explosion right in the middle of the dinner hour on the busiest street on the grid. Someone's sending a message.
The police band says witnesses saw a small balloon of some kind carrying the bomb.
Came to see if I could help.
UHHNF.
Then this silent terror shows up from the ashes.
And now it looks like...
...I might be added to the list of casualties.

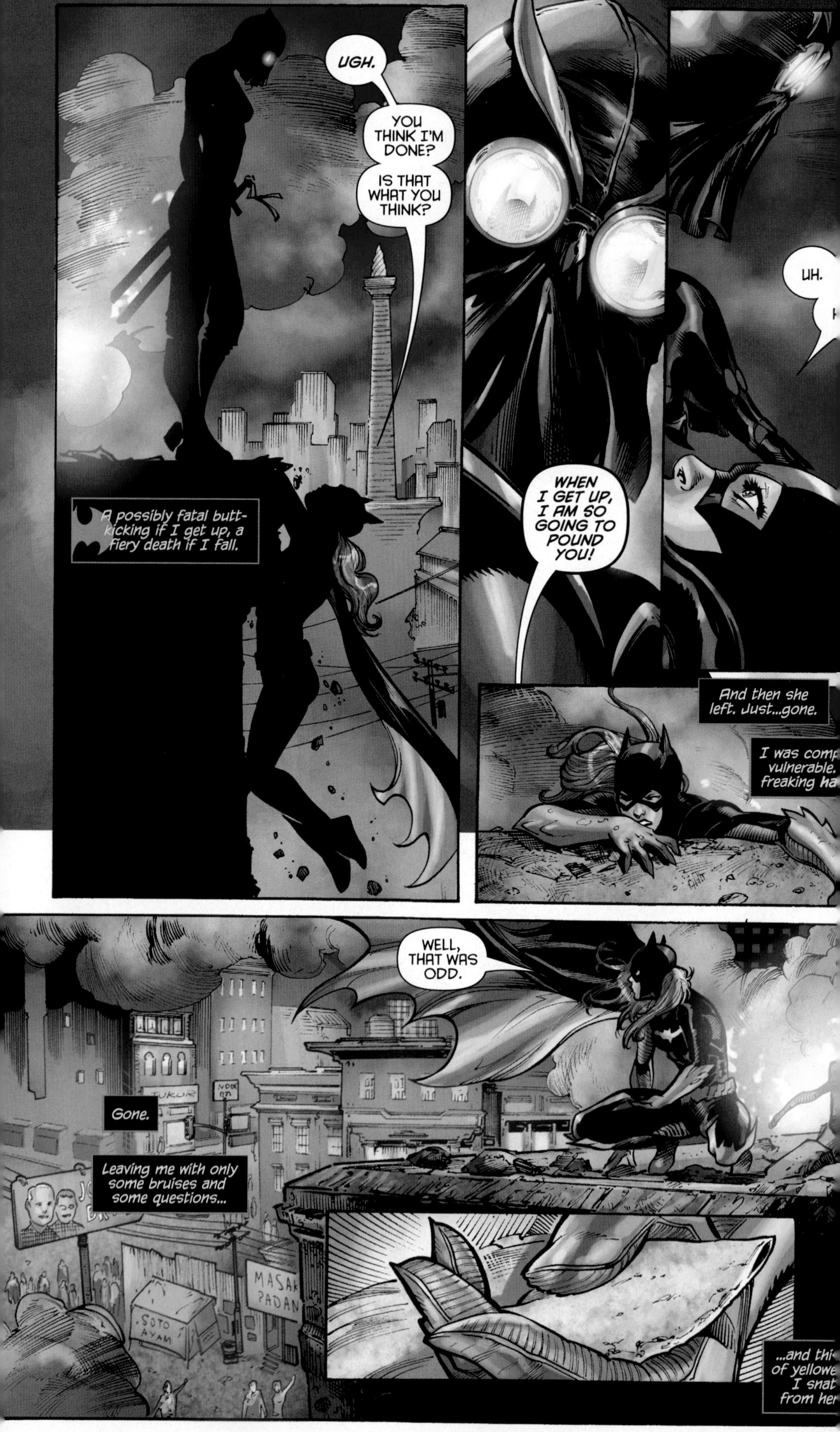

UGH.
YOU THINK I'M DONE?
IS THAT WHAT YOU THINK?
A possibly fatal butt-kicking if I get up, a fiery death if I fall.
WHEN I GET UP, I AM SO GOING TO POUND YOU!
UH.
And then she left. Just...gone.
I was comp
vulnerable.
freaking ha
WELL, THAT WAS ODD.
Gone.
Leaving me with only some bruises and some questions...
MASAK PADAN
SOTO AYAM
...and thi
of yellowe
I snat
from her

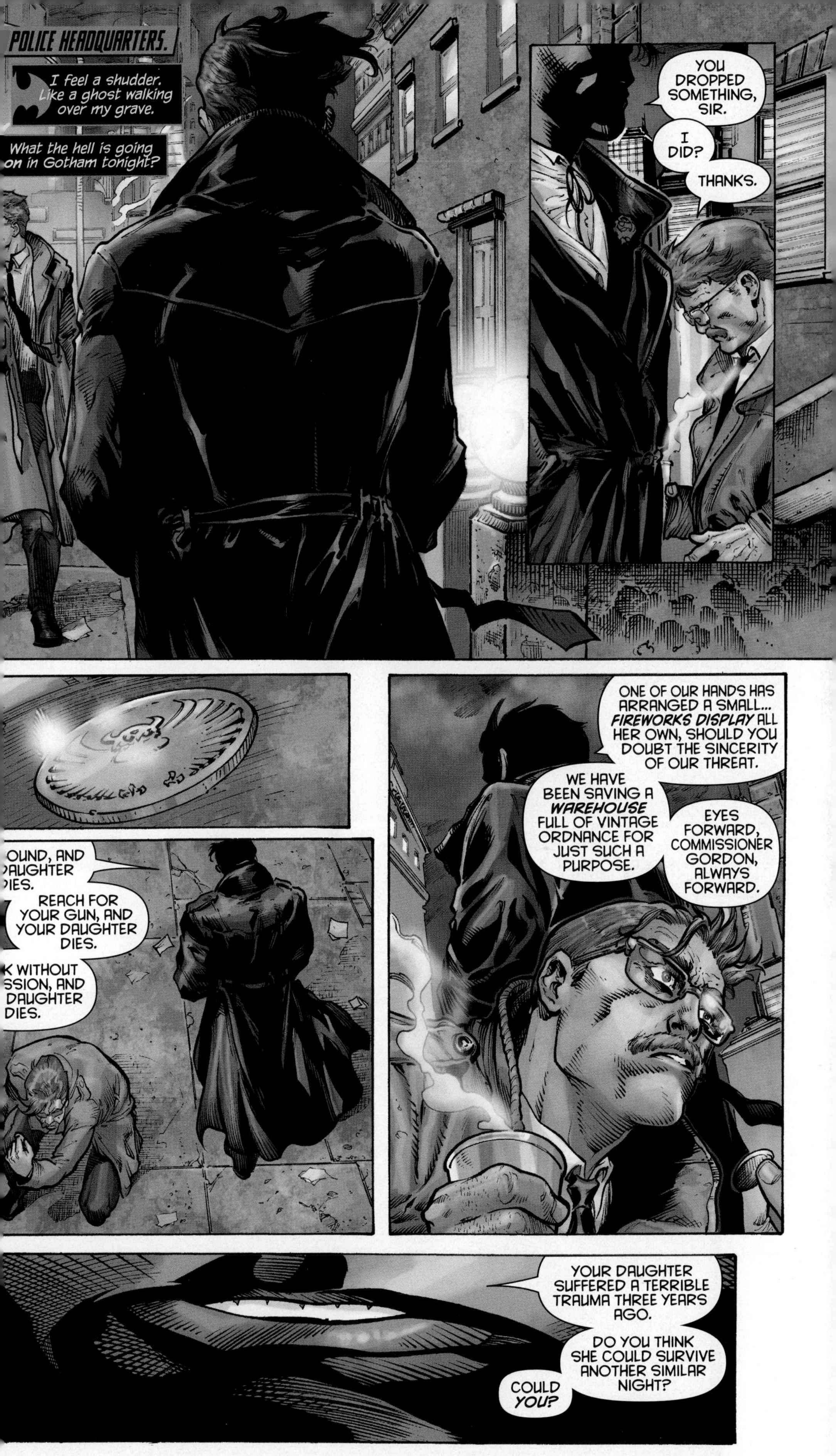
POLICE HEADQUARTERS.
I feel a shudder. Like a ghost walking over my grave.
What the hell is going on in Gotham tonight?
YOU DROPPED SOMETHING, SIR.
I DID?
THANKS.
OUND, AND DAUGHTER DIES.
REACH FOR YOUR GUN, AND YOUR DAUGHTER DIES.
K WITHOUT SSION, AND DAUGHTER DIES.
ONE OF OUR HANDS HAS ARRANGED A SMALL... FIREWORKS DISPLAY ALL HER OWN, SHOULD YOU DOUBT THE SINCERITY OF OUR THREAT.
WE HAVE BEEN SAVING A WAREHOUSE FULL OF VINTAGE ORDNANCE FOR JUST SUCH A PURPOSE.
EYES FORWARD, COMMISSIONER GORDON, ALWAYS FORWARD.
YOUR DAUGHTER SUFFERED A TERRIBLE TRAUMA THREE YEARS AGO.
DO YOU THINK SHE COULD SURVIVE ANOTHER SIMILAR NIGHT?
COULD YOU?

SEVERAL PROMINENT GOTHAM CITIZENS WILL *DIE* TONIGHT, COMMISSIONER. THERE'S NOTHING YOU CAN DO TO PREVENT THAT.

YOUR EFFORTS AND OPINIONS ON THE MATTER ARE IRRELEVANT.

IT IS VITAL THAT THE CITIZENS OF GOTHAM UNDER-STAND THIS--

--THERE IS *NO* SAVIOR.

YOU WILL SOON FEEL THE NEED, PERHAPS THE COMPULSION, TO LIGHT THE SIGNAL FOR *THE BATMAN*, JAMES. DO NOT GIVE IN.

THE RABBLE MUST NEVER BE ALLOWED TO BELIEVE *ONE MAN* OWNS WHAT GOTHAM IS AT NIGHT.

GO UPSTAI DRINK YO COFFEE. D WARN *AN* WE'LL E *WATCH*

BE A *FATHER*.

OR EVERYTHING CLOSE TO YOU *BURNS*.

HEY...HEY, COMMISSIONER! WE'VE GOT AN *EXPLOSION* UP IN THE INDONESIA GRID. NO CASUALTIES, THANK GOD, BUT WHAT A *MESS*.

...

I'LL BE IN MY OFFICE, RENNY.

TEN MINUTES LA

HEY? YOO HOO?

A

Huh. She shou be home by no

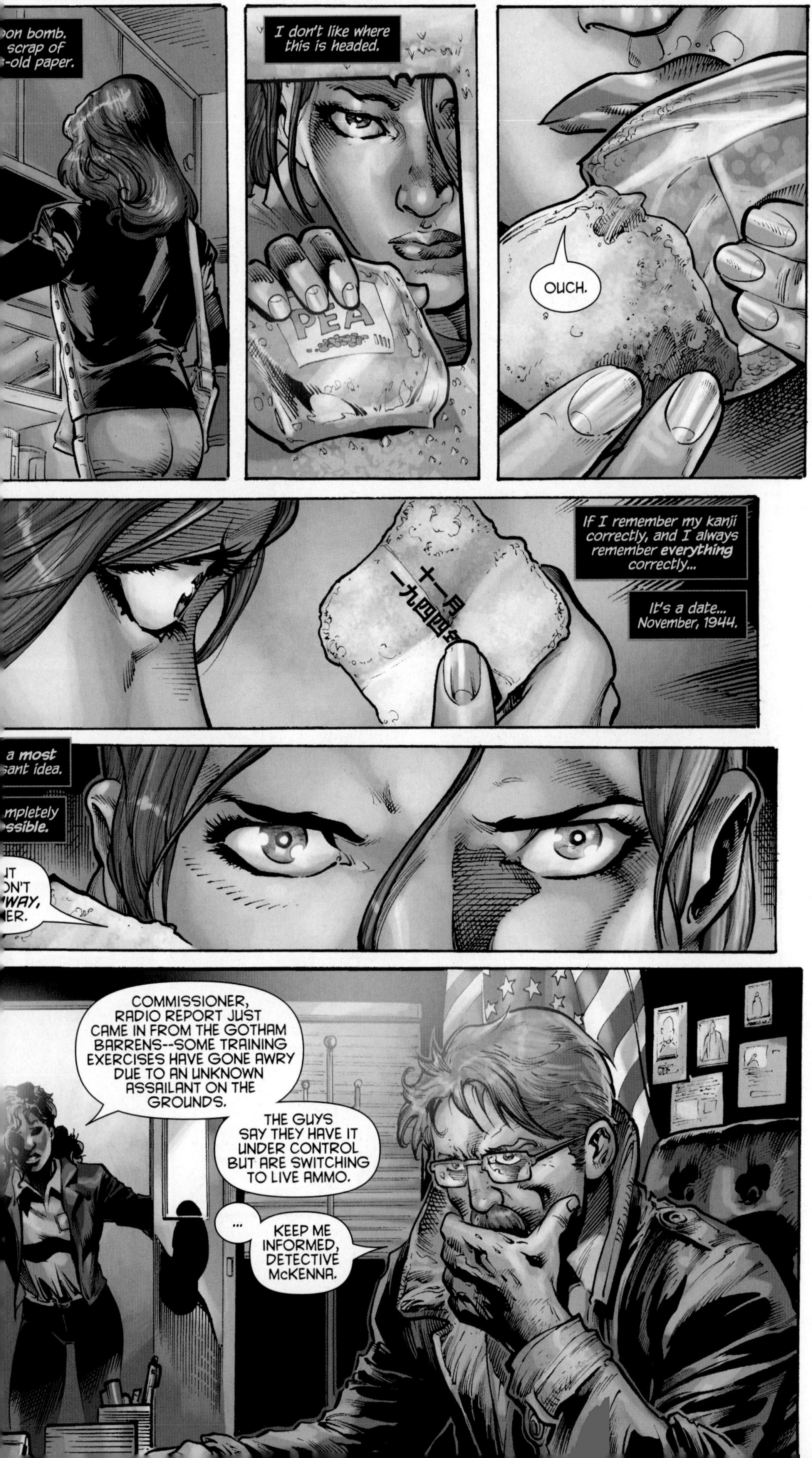
oon bomb.
scrap of
-old paper.
I don't like where this is headed.
OUCH.
If I remember my kanji correctly, and I always remember everything correctly...
十一月
一九四四年
It's a date... November, 1944.
a most
sant idea.
mpletely
ssible.
IT
ON'T
WAY,
ER.
COMMISSIONER, RADIO REPORT JUST CAME IN FROM THE GOTHAM BARRENS--SOME TRAINING EXERCISES HAVE GONE AWRY DUE TO AN UNKNOWN ASSAILANT ON THE GROUNDS.
THE GUYS SAY THEY HAVE IT UNDER CONTROL BUT ARE SWITCHING TO LIVE AMMO.
...
KEEP ME INFORMED, DETECTIVE McKENNA.

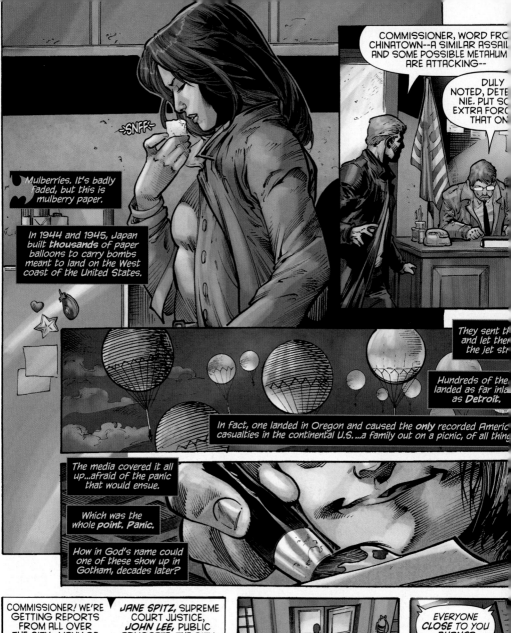

-SNFF-

Mulberries. It's badly faded, but this is mulberry paper.

*In 1944 and 1945, Japan built **thousands** of paper balloons to carry bombs meant to land on the West coast of the United States.*

COMMISSIONER, WORD FRO[M] CHINATOWN--A SIMILAR ASSAIL[T] AND SOME POSSIBLE METAHUM[AN] ARE ATTACKING--

DULY NOTED, DETE[C] NIE. PUT SO[ME] EXTRA FOR[CE] THAT ON[E]

They sent th[em] and let the[m] the jet str[eam]

*Hundreds of the[m] landed as far inla[nd] as **Detroit**.*

*In fact, one landed in Oregon and caused the **only** recorded Americ[an] casualties in the continental U.S....a family out on a picnic, of all thing[s]*

The media covered it all up...afraid of the panic that would ensue.

*Which was the whole **point. Panic.***

How in God's name could one of these show up in Gotham, decades later?

COMMISSIONER! WE'RE GETTING REPORTS FROM ALL OVER THE CITY--MANY OF GOTHAM'S LEADERS ARE WINDING UP DEAD!

JANE SPITZ, SUPREME COURT JUSTICE, JOHN LEE, PUBLIC ADVOCATE, THE CITY COMPTROLLER, THEY'VE ALL BEEN FOUND MURDERED--

GOD HELP ME.

GET ME A CELL PHONE. ANY PHONE BUT MINE.

BARBARA? IT'S YOUR FATHER...

OH, COMMISSIONER. WE DID GIVE YOU A WARNING, DIDN'T WE?

REMEMBER WHAT WE SAID?

EVERYONE CLOSE TO YOU BURNS?

R[...]

DON'T OPEN THE DOOR!

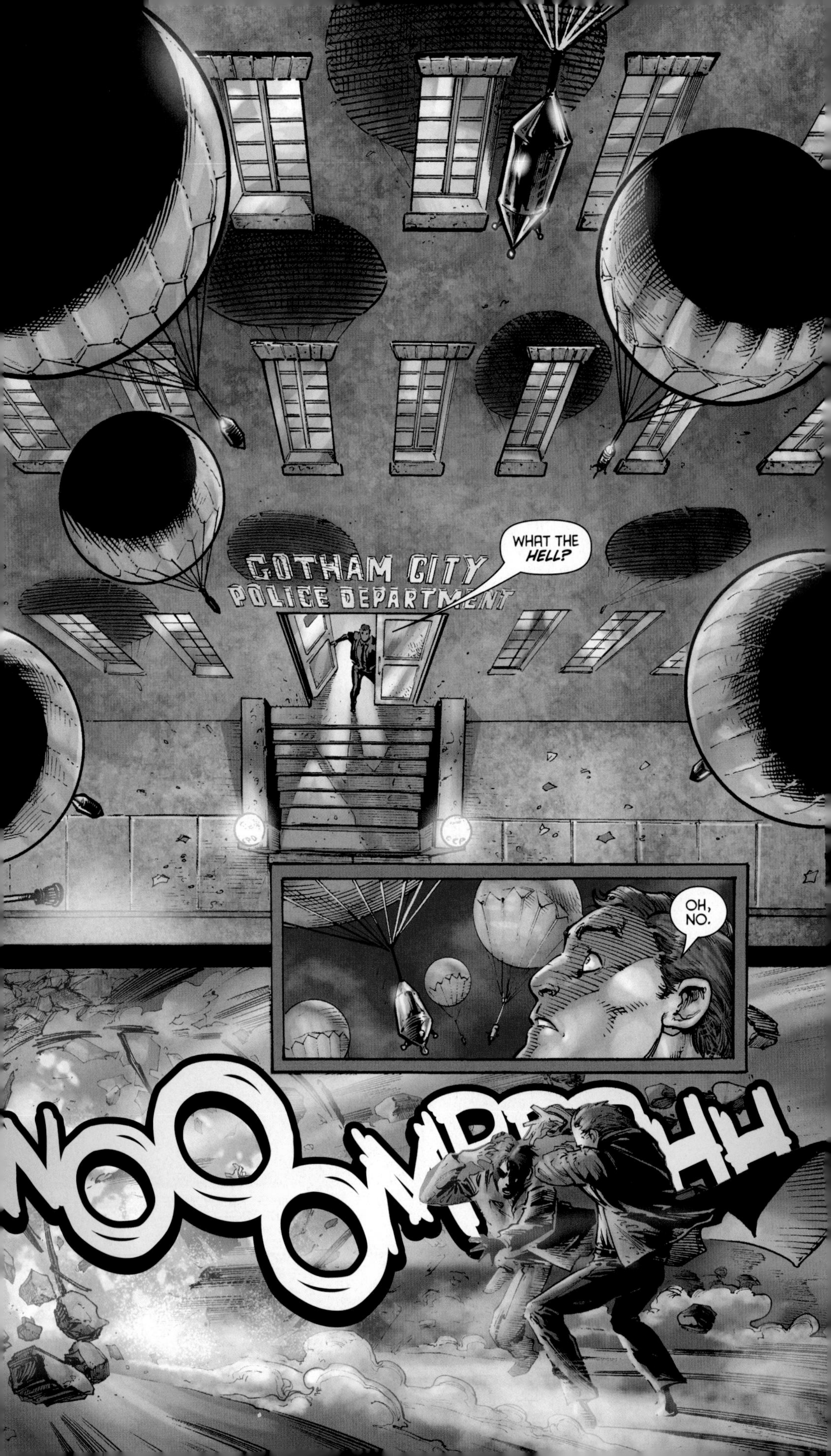
GOTHAM CITY
POLICE DEPARTMENT
WHAT THE *HELL?*
OH, NO.

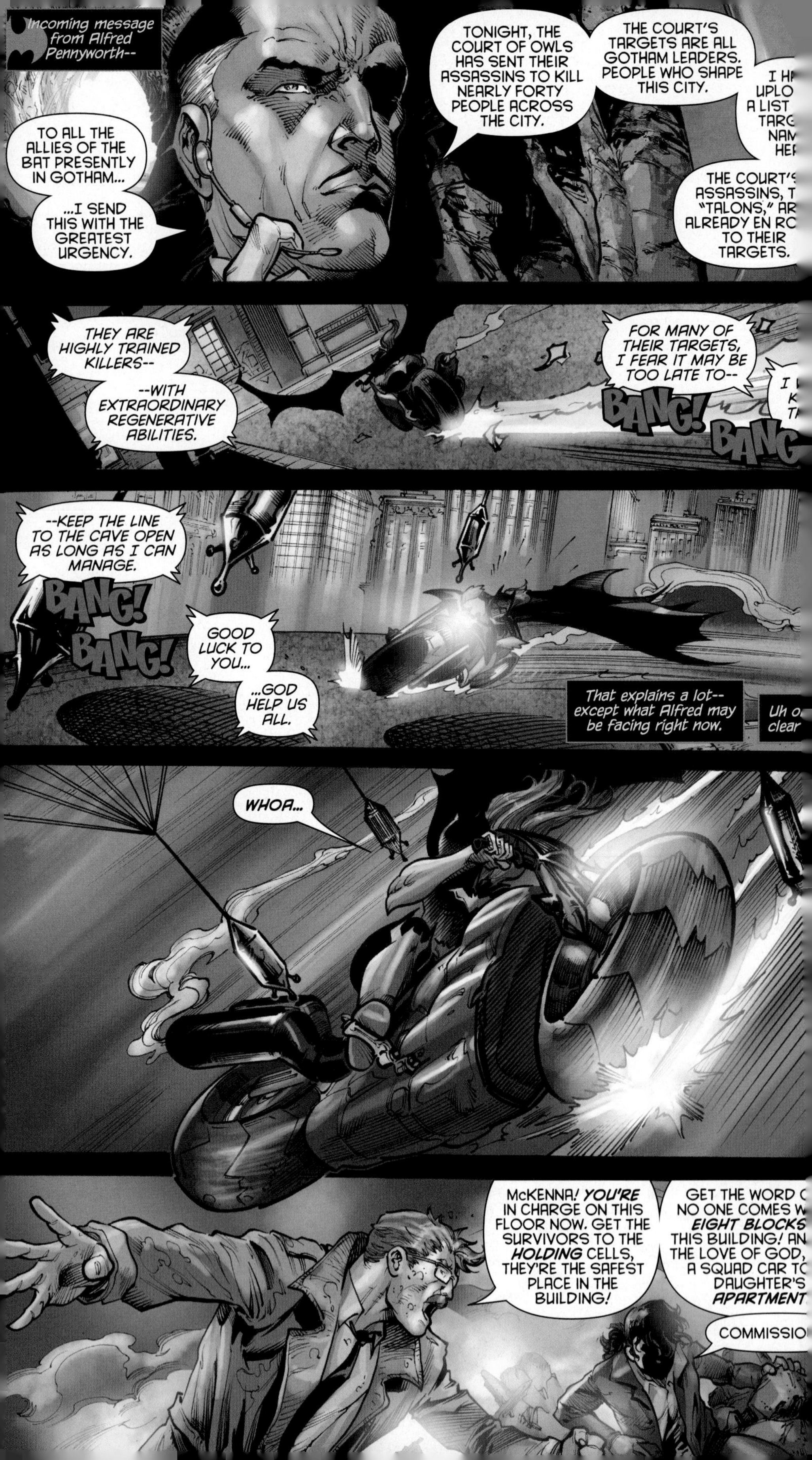
Incoming message from Alfred Pennyworth--
TO ALL THE ALLIES OF THE BAT PRESENTLY IN GOTHAM...
...I SEND THIS WITH THE GREATEST URGENCY.
TONIGHT, THE COURT OF OWLS HAS SENT THEIR ASSASSINS TO KILL NEARLY FORTY PEOPLE ACROSS THE CITY.
THE COURT'S TARGETS ARE ALL GOTHAM LEADERS. PEOPLE WHO SHAPE THIS CITY.
THE COURT'S ASSASSINS, THE "TALONS," ARE ALREADY EN RO... TO THEIR TARGETS.
THEY ARE HIGHLY TRAINED KILLERS--
--WITH EXTRAORDINARY REGENERATIVE ABILITIES.
FOR MANY OF THEIR TARGETS, I FEAR IT MAY BE TOO LATE TO--
BANG!
BANG
--KEEP THE LINE TO THE CAVE OPEN AS LONG AS I CAN MANAGE.
BANG!
BANG!
GOOD LUCK TO YOU...
...GOD HELP US ALL.
That explains a lot--except what Alfred may be facing right now.
WHOA...
McKENNA! YOU'RE IN CHARGE ON THIS FLOOR NOW. GET THE SURVIVORS TO THE HOLDING CELLS, THEY'RE THE SAFEST PLACE IN THE BUILDING!
COMMISSIO

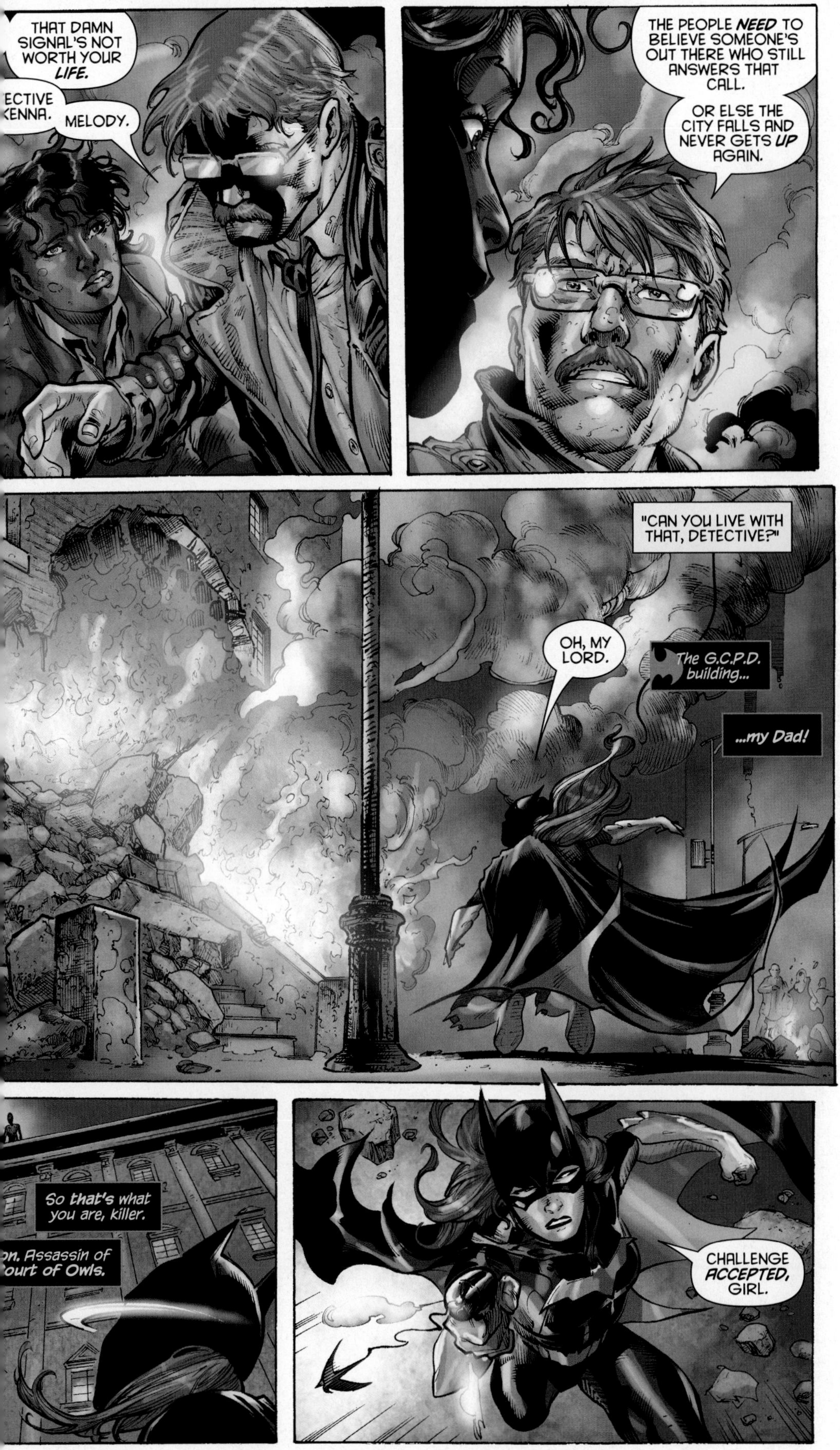
THAT DAMN SIGNAL'S NOT WORTH YOUR LIFE.
ECTIVE KENNA.
MELODY.
THE PEOPLE NEED TO BELIEVE SOMEONE'S OUT THERE WHO STILL ANSWERS THAT CALL.
OR ELSE THE CITY FALLS AND NEVER GETS UP AGAIN.
"CAN YOU LIVE WITH THAT, DETECTIVE?"
OH, MY LORD.
The G.C.P.D. building...
...my Dad!
So that's what you are, killer.
on. Assassin of ourt of Owls.
CHALLENGE ACCEPTED, GIRL.

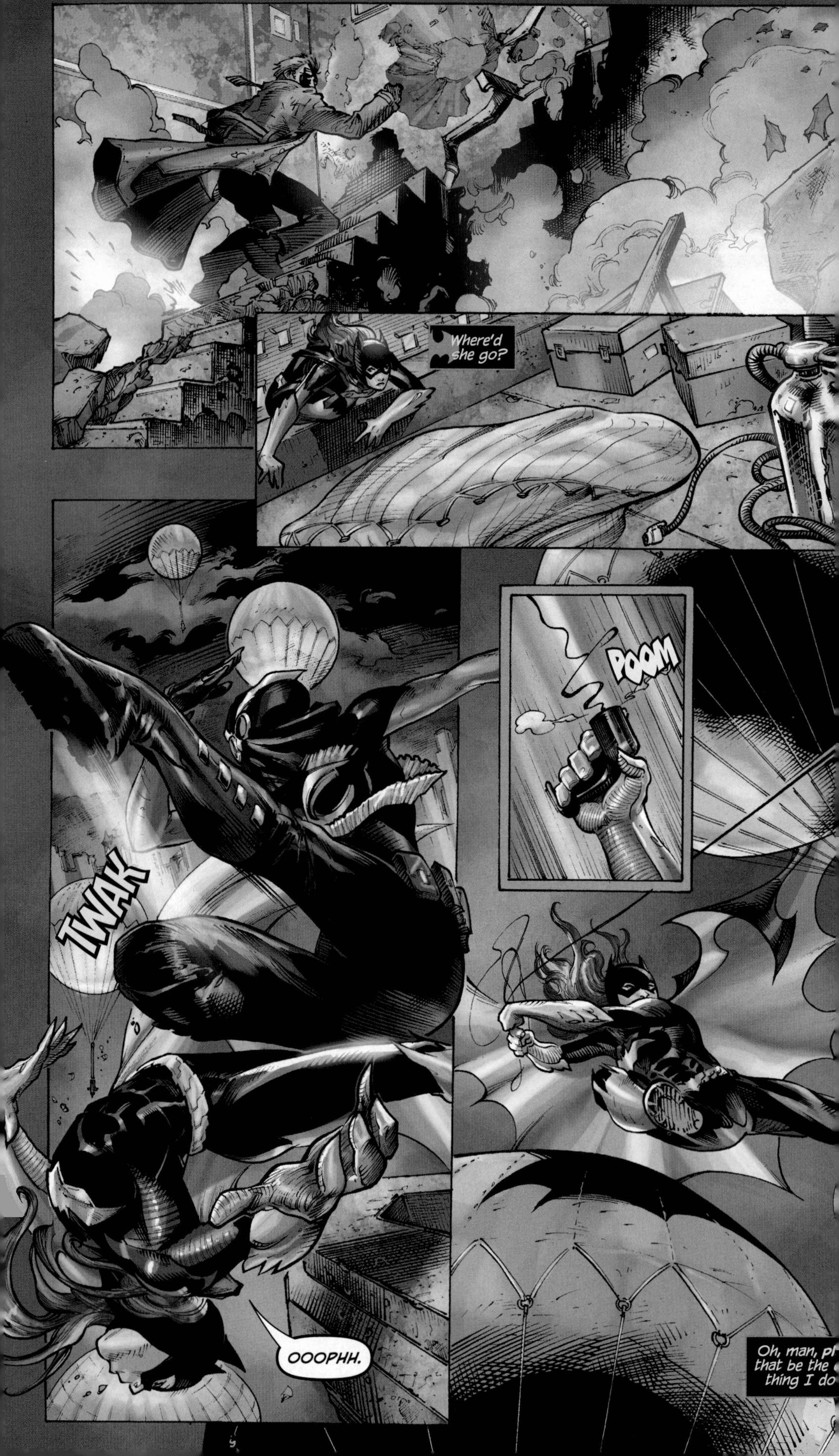

Where'd she go?
TWAK
OOOPHH.
POOM
Oh, man, pl
that be the
thing I do

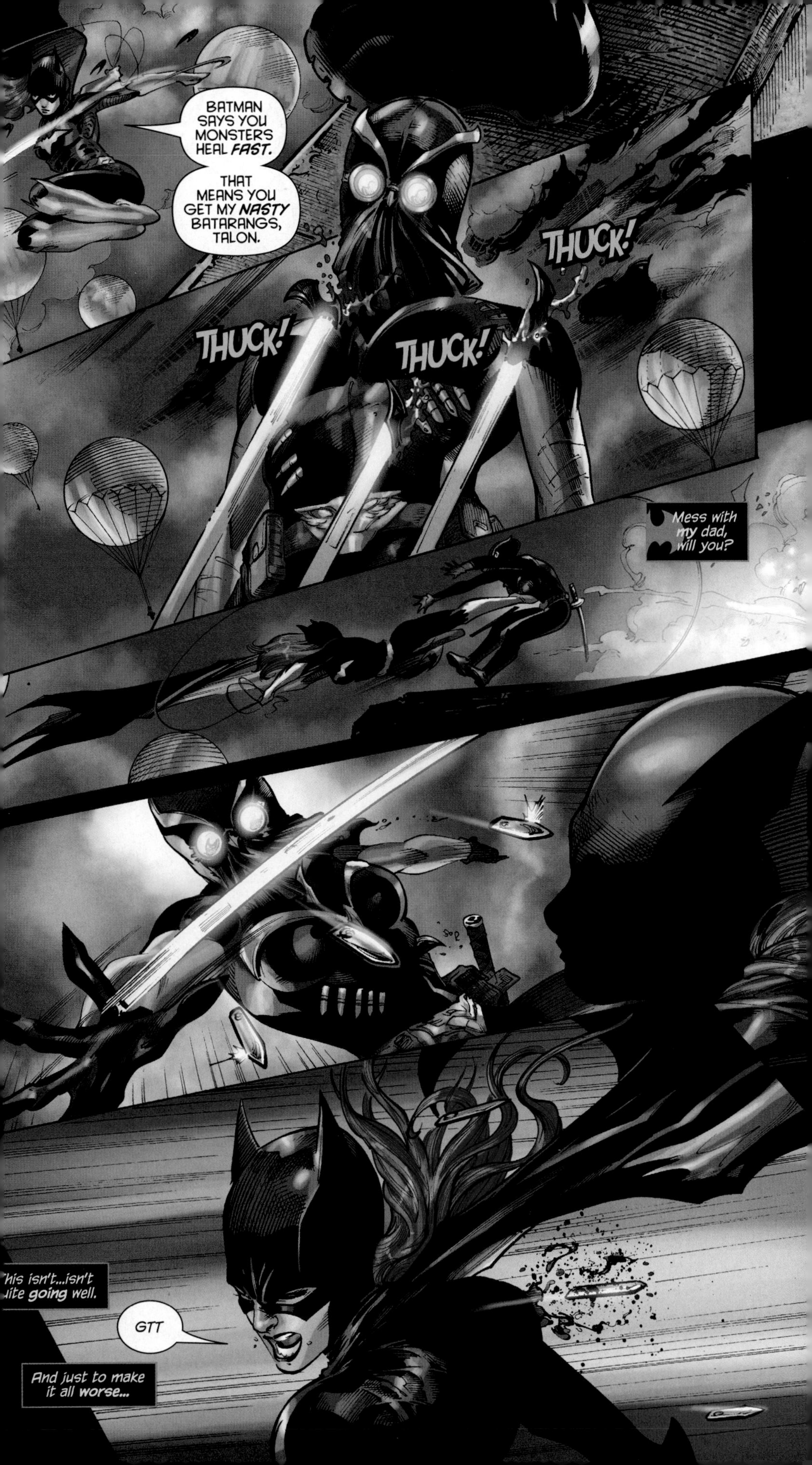

BATMAN SAYS YOU MONSTERS HEAL FAST.
THAT MEANS YOU GET MY NASTY BATARANGS, TALON.
THUCK!
THUCK!
THUCK!
Mess with my dad, will you?
This isn't...isn't quite going well.
GTT
And just to make it all worse...

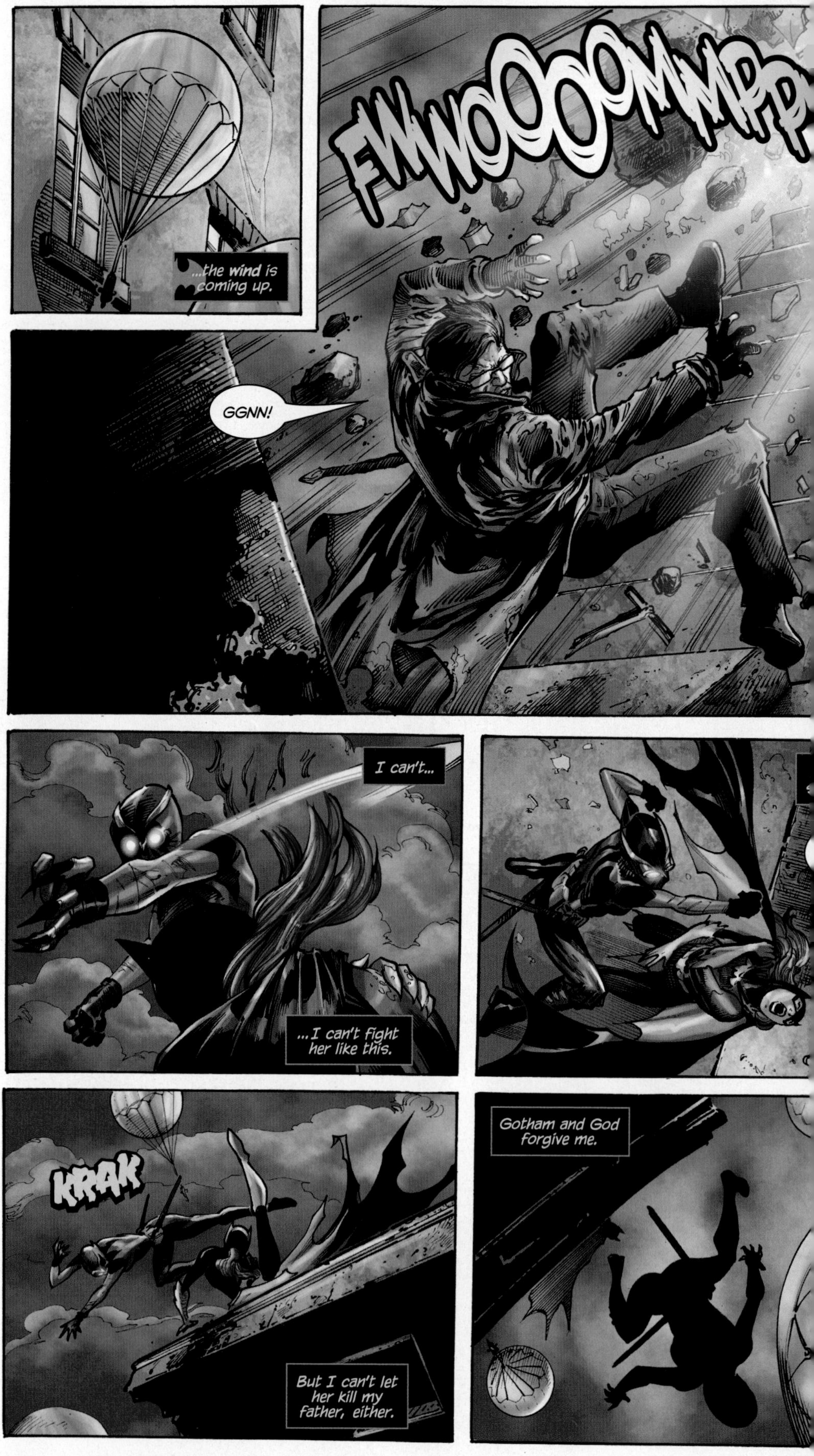
...the wind is coming up.
FWWOOOOMMPP
GGNN!
I can't...
...I can't fight her like this.
KRAK
But I can't let her kill my father, either.
Gotham and God forgive me.

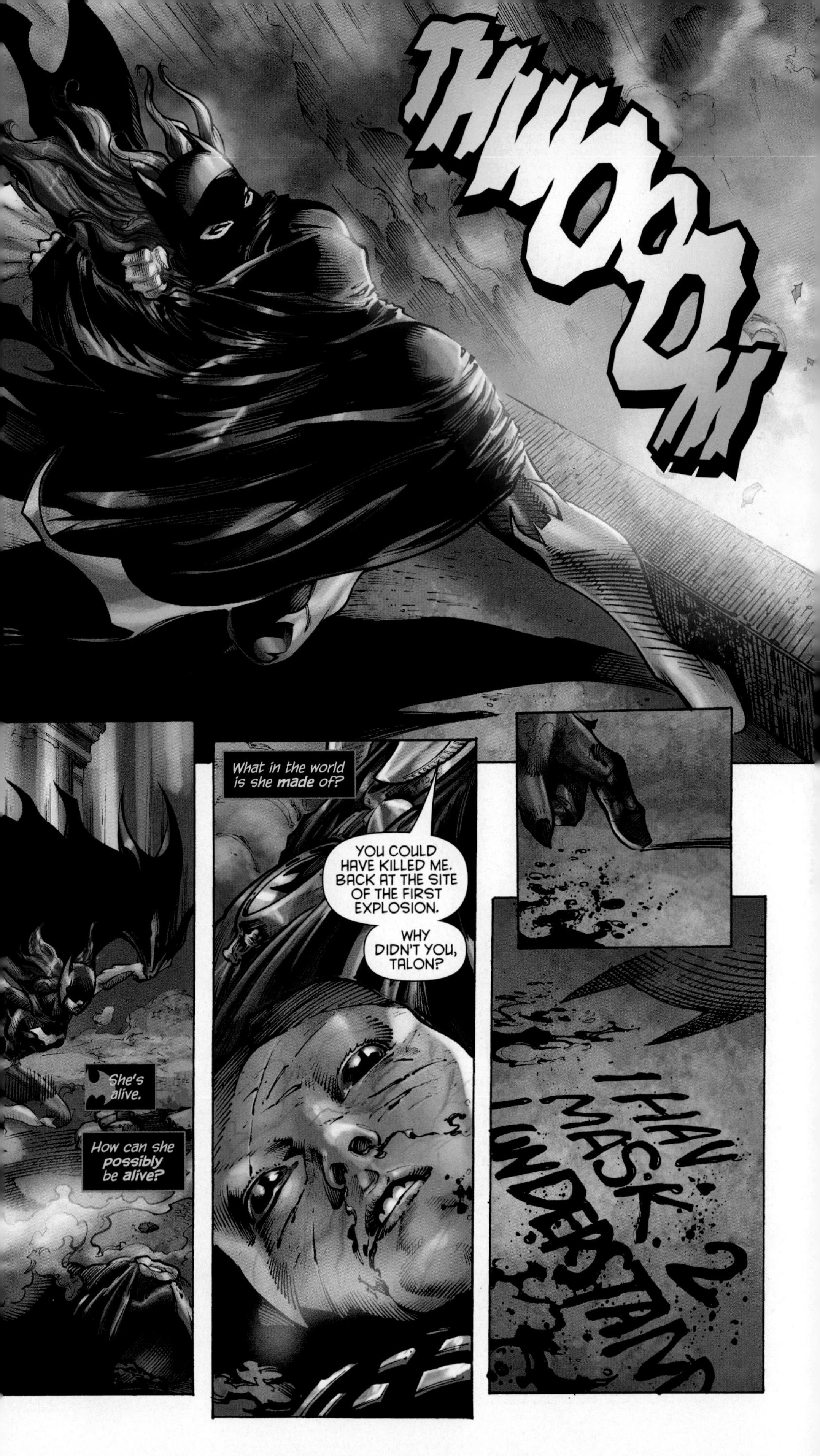
THHOOOOM
She's alive.
How can she possibly be alive?
What in the world is she made of?
YOU COULD HAVE KILLED ME. BACK AT THE SITE OF THE FIRST EXPLOSION.
WHY DIDN'T YOU, TALON?
I HAV MASK. UNDERSTAN?

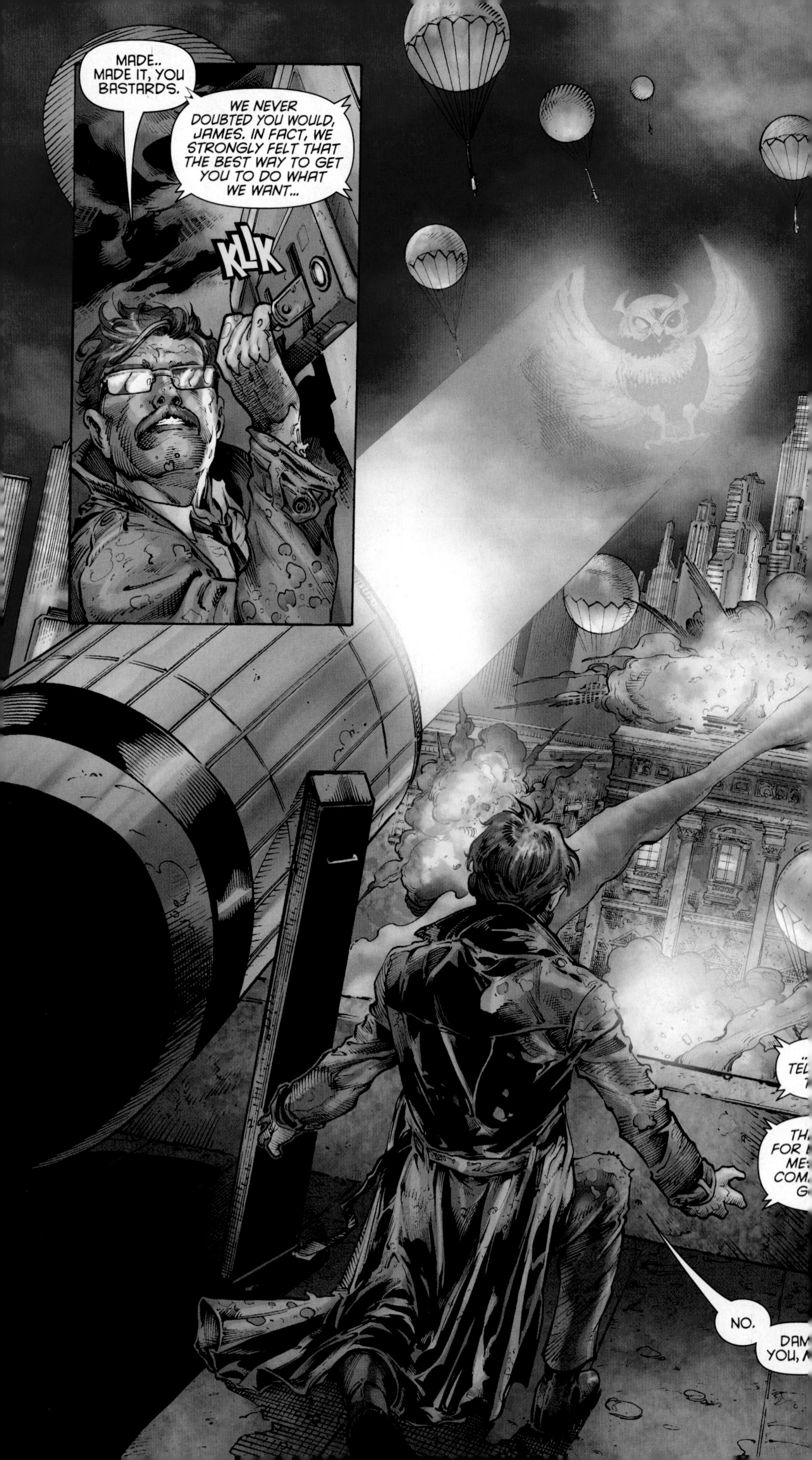
MADE.. MADE IT, YOU BASTARDS.
WE NEVER DOUBTED YOU WOULD, JAMES. IN FACT, WE STRONGLY FELT THAT THE BEST WAY TO GET YOU TO DO WHAT WE WANT...
KLIK
NO.

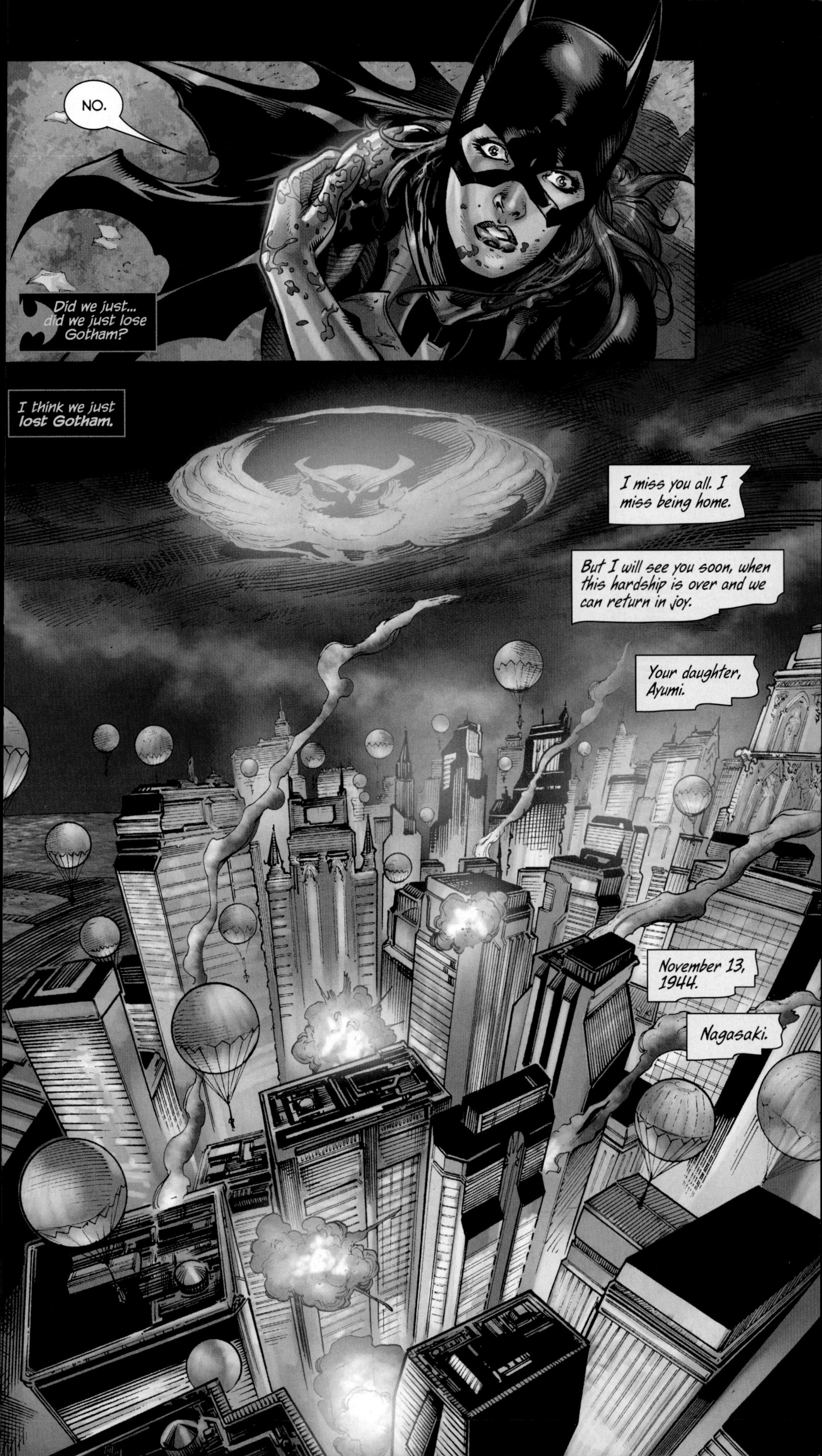

NO.
Did we just... did we just lose Gotham?
I think we just lost Gotham.
I miss you all. I miss being home.
But I will see you soon, when this hardship is over and we can return in joy.
Your daughter, Ayumi.
November 13, 1944.
Nagasaki.

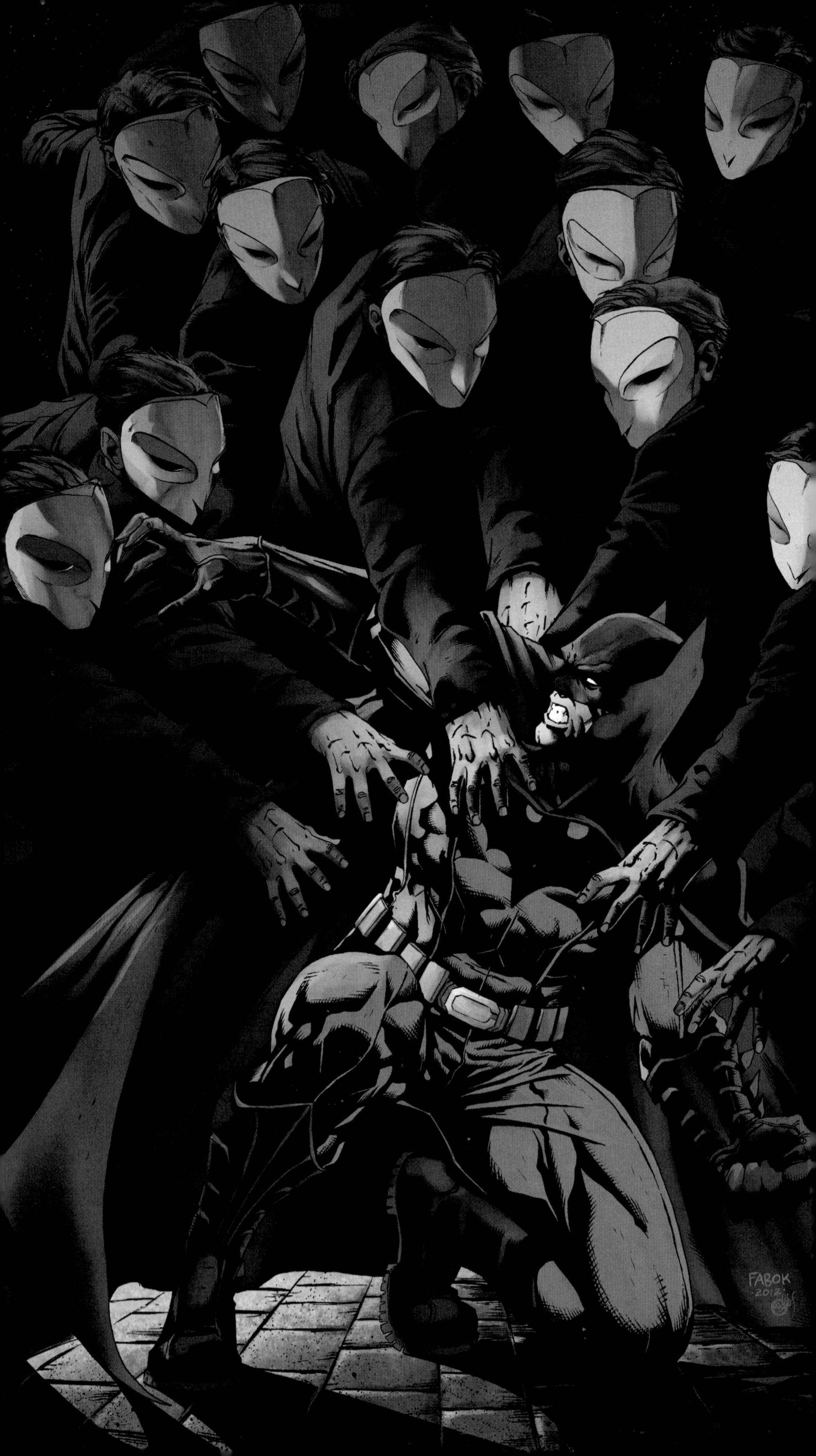
FABOK
2012

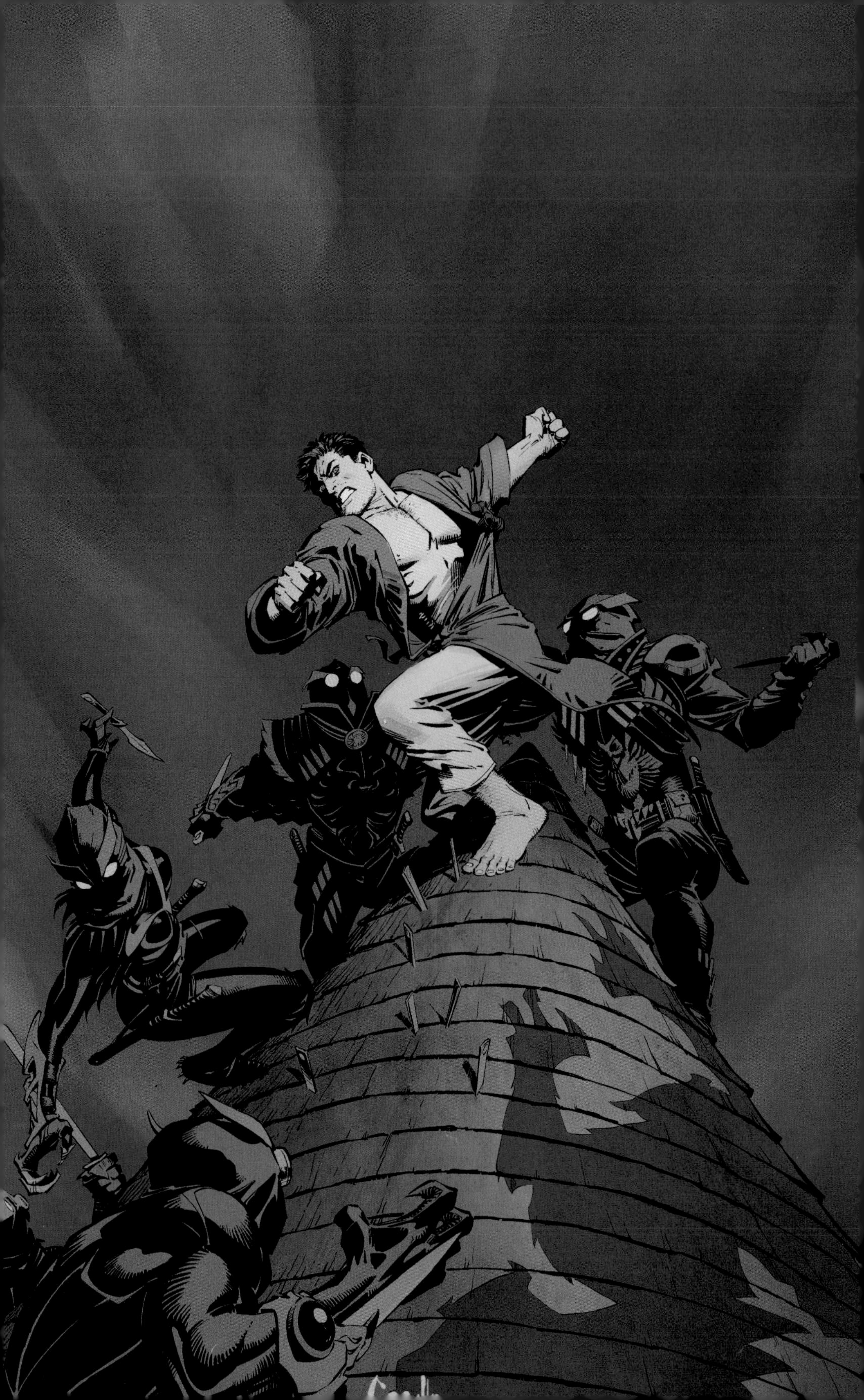

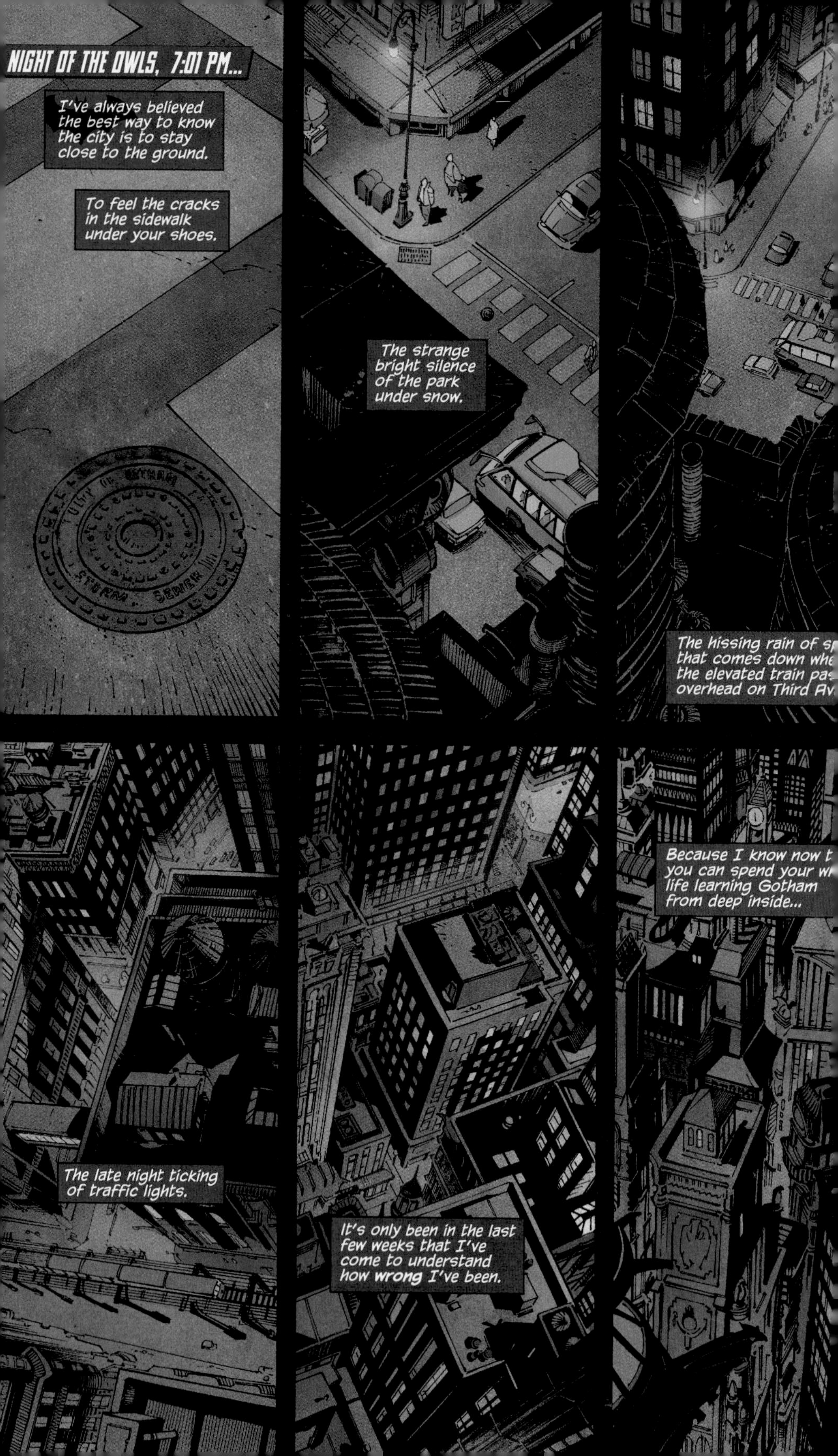
NIGHT OF THE OWLS, 7:01 PM...
I've always believed the best way to know the city is to stay close to the ground.
To feel the cracks in the sidewalk under your shoes.
CITY OF GOTHAM
STORM SEWER
The strange bright silence of the park under snow.
The hissing rain of s
that comes down whe
the elevated train pa
overhead on Third Av
The late night ticking of traffic lights.
It's only been in the last few weeks that I've come to understand how **wrong** I've been.
Because I know now t
you can spend your w
life learning Gotham from deep inside...

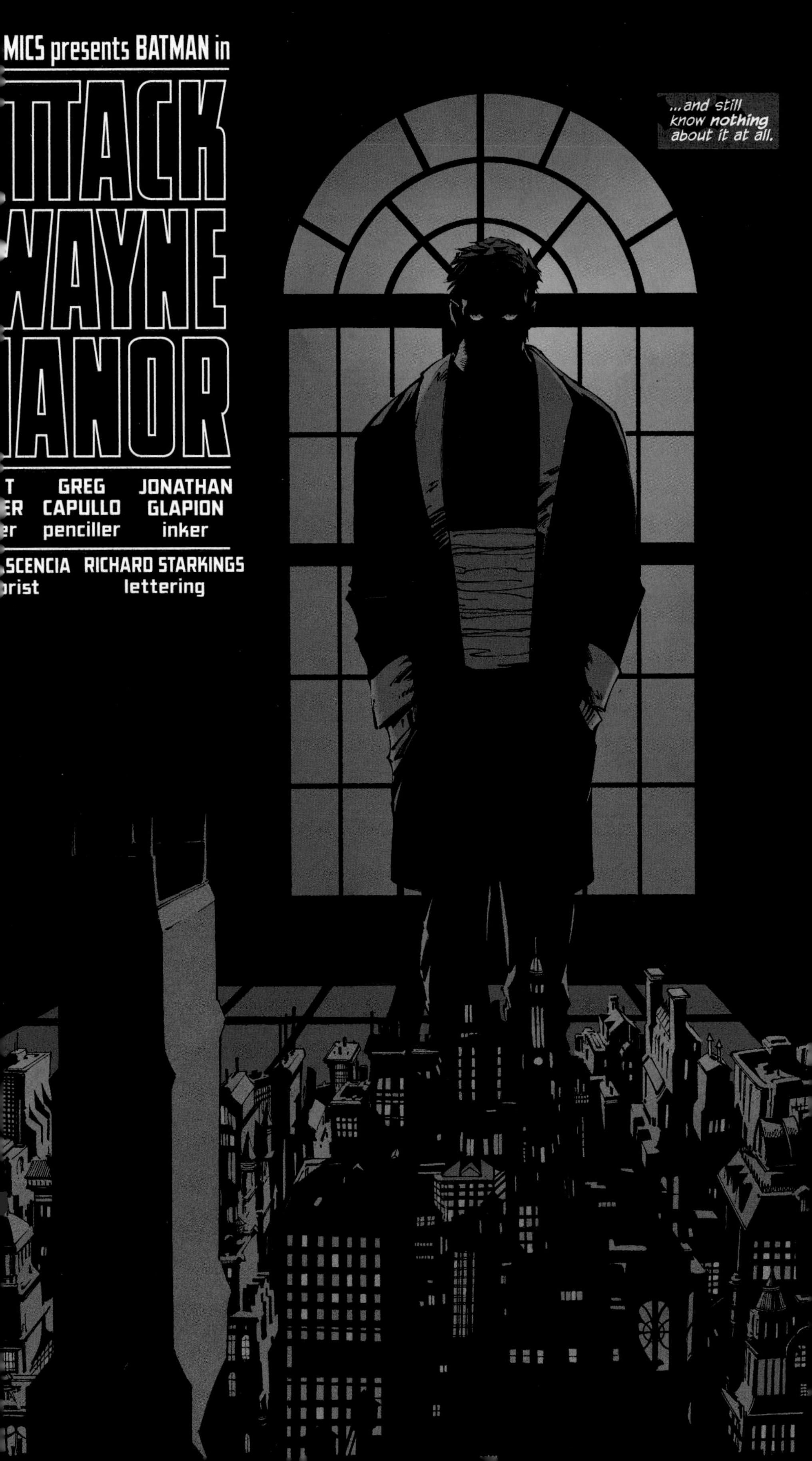
MICS presents BATMAN in
TTACK
WAYNE
IANOR
T
ER
er
GREG
CAPULLO
penciller
JONATHAN
GLAPION
inker
SCENCIA
orist
RICHARD STARKINGS
lettering
...and still know nothing about it at all.

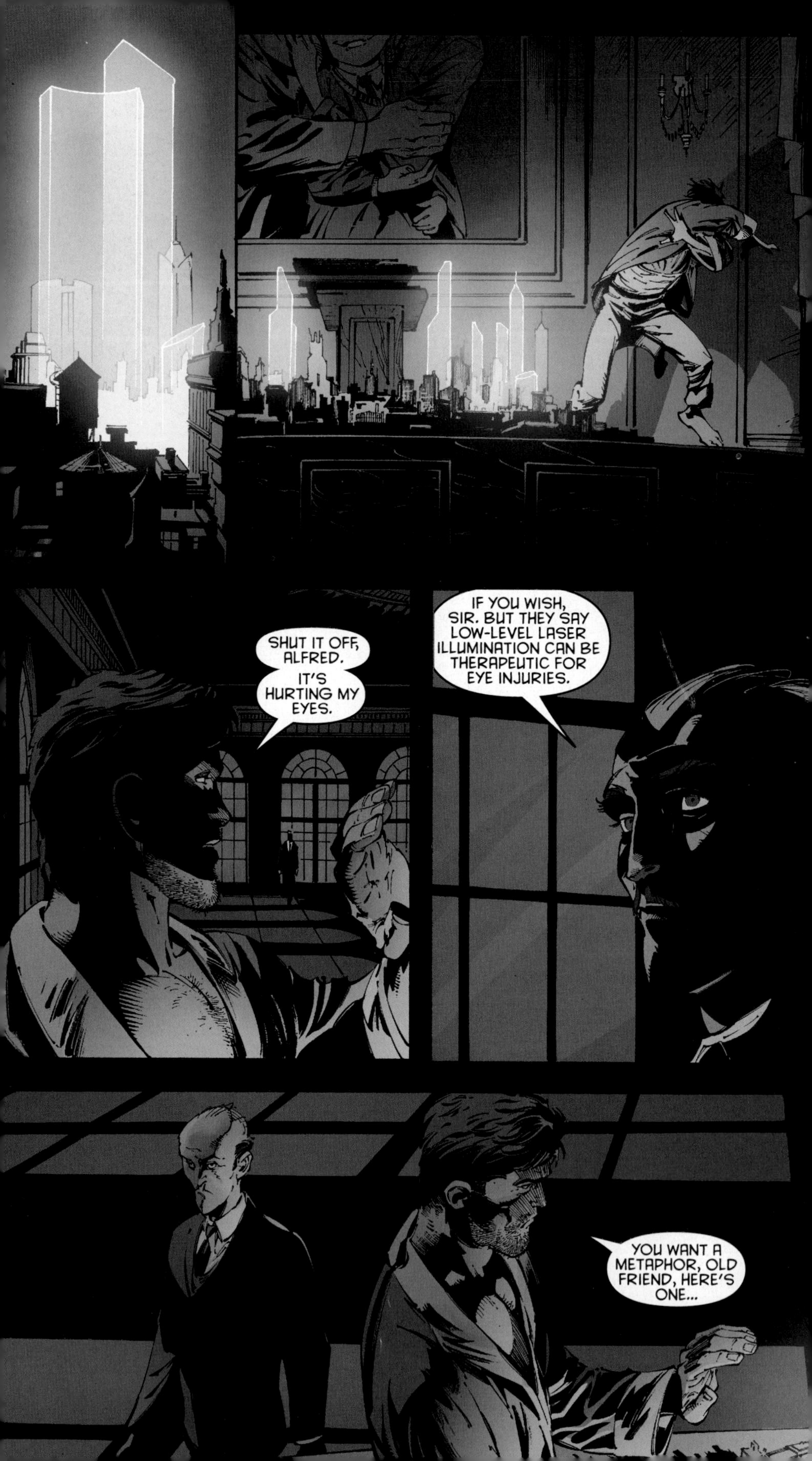
SHUT IT OFF, ALFRED.
IT'S HURTING MY EYES.
IF YOU WISH, SIR. BUT THEY SAY LOW-LEVEL LASER ILLUMINATION CAN BE THERAPEUTIC FOR EYE INJURIES.
YOU WANT A METAPHOR, OLD FRIEND, HERE'S ONE...

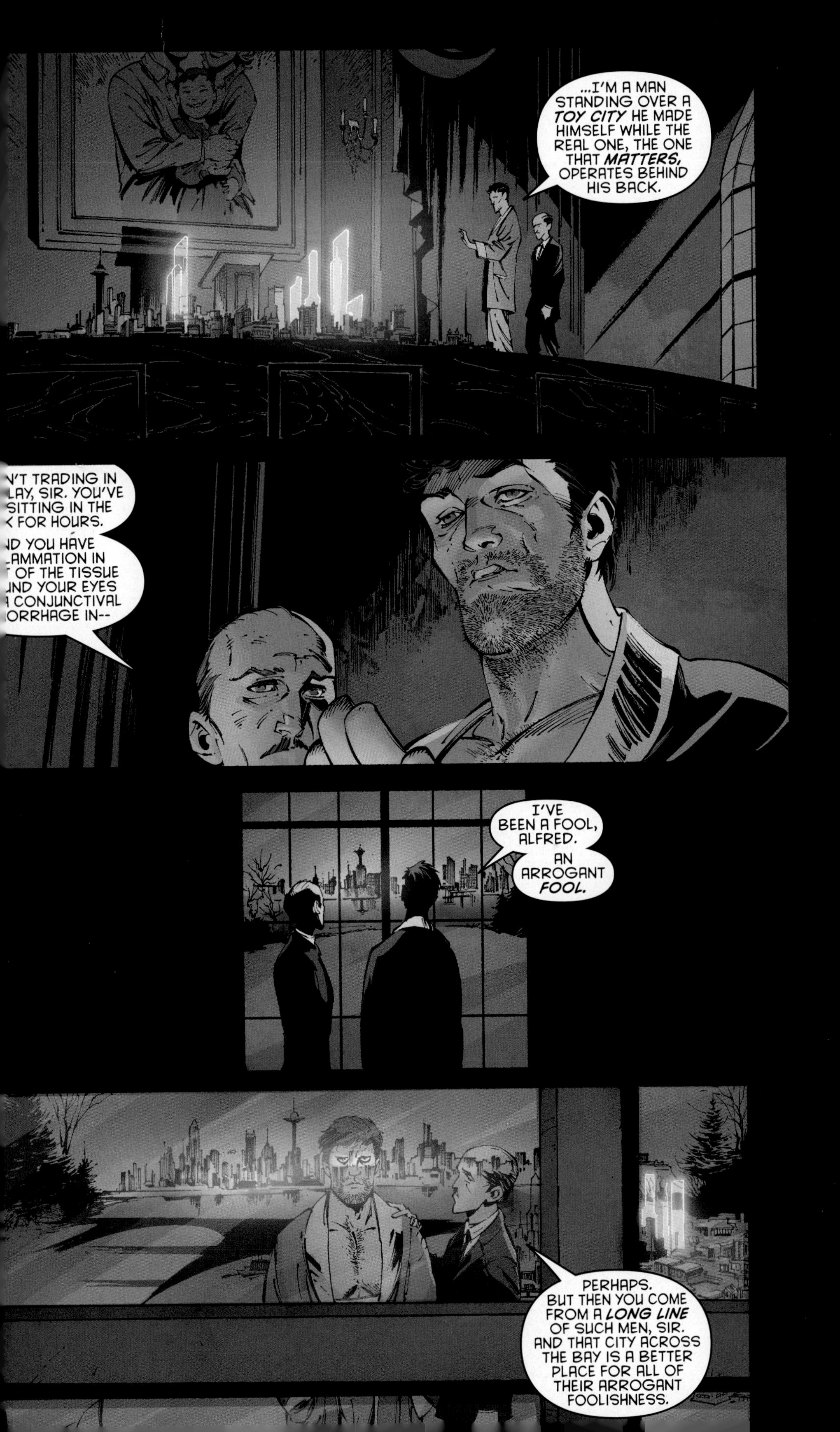
...I'M A MAN STANDING OVER A TOY CITY HE MADE HIMSELF WHILE THE REAL ONE, THE ONE THAT MATTERS, OPERATES BEHIND HIS BACK.
N'T TRADING IN LAY, SIR. YOU'VE SITTING IN THE K FOR HOURS.
ND YOU HAVE LAMMATION IN T OF THE TISSUE UND YOUR EYES A CONJUNCTIVAL ORRHAGE IN--
I'VE BEEN A FOOL, ALFRED.
AN ARROGANT FOOL.
PERHAPS. BUT THEN YOU COME FROM A LONG LINE OF SUCH MEN, SIR. AND THAT CITY ACROSS THE BAY IS A BETTER PLACE FOR ALL OF THEIR ARROGANT FOOLISHNESS.

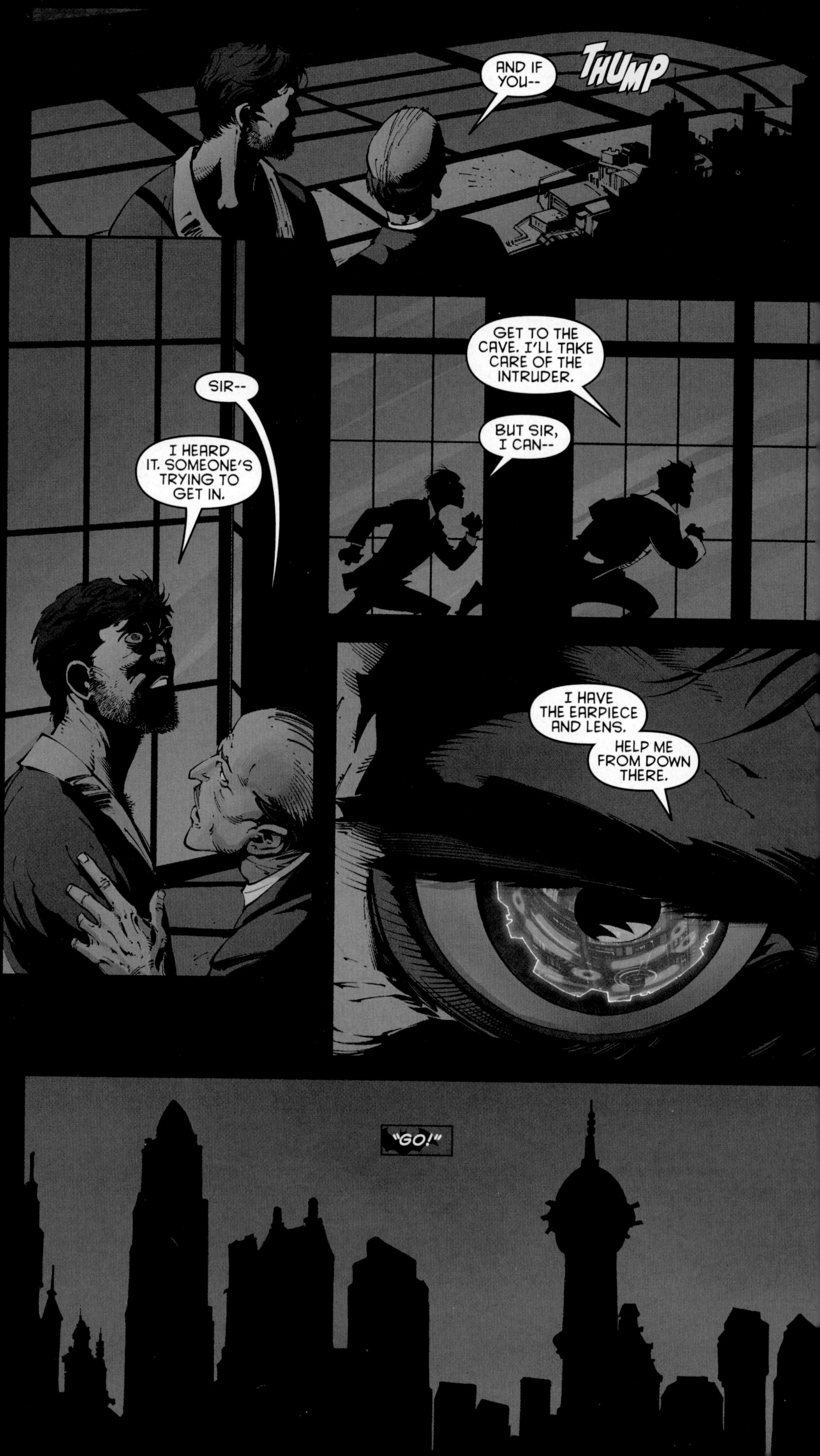
AND IF YOU--
THUMP
SIR--
I HEARD IT. SOMEONE'S TRYING TO GET IN.
GET TO THE CAVE. I'LL TAKE CARE OF THE INTRUDER.
BUT SIR, I CAN--
I HAVE THE EARPIECE AND LENS.
HELP ME FROM DOWN THERE.
"GO!"

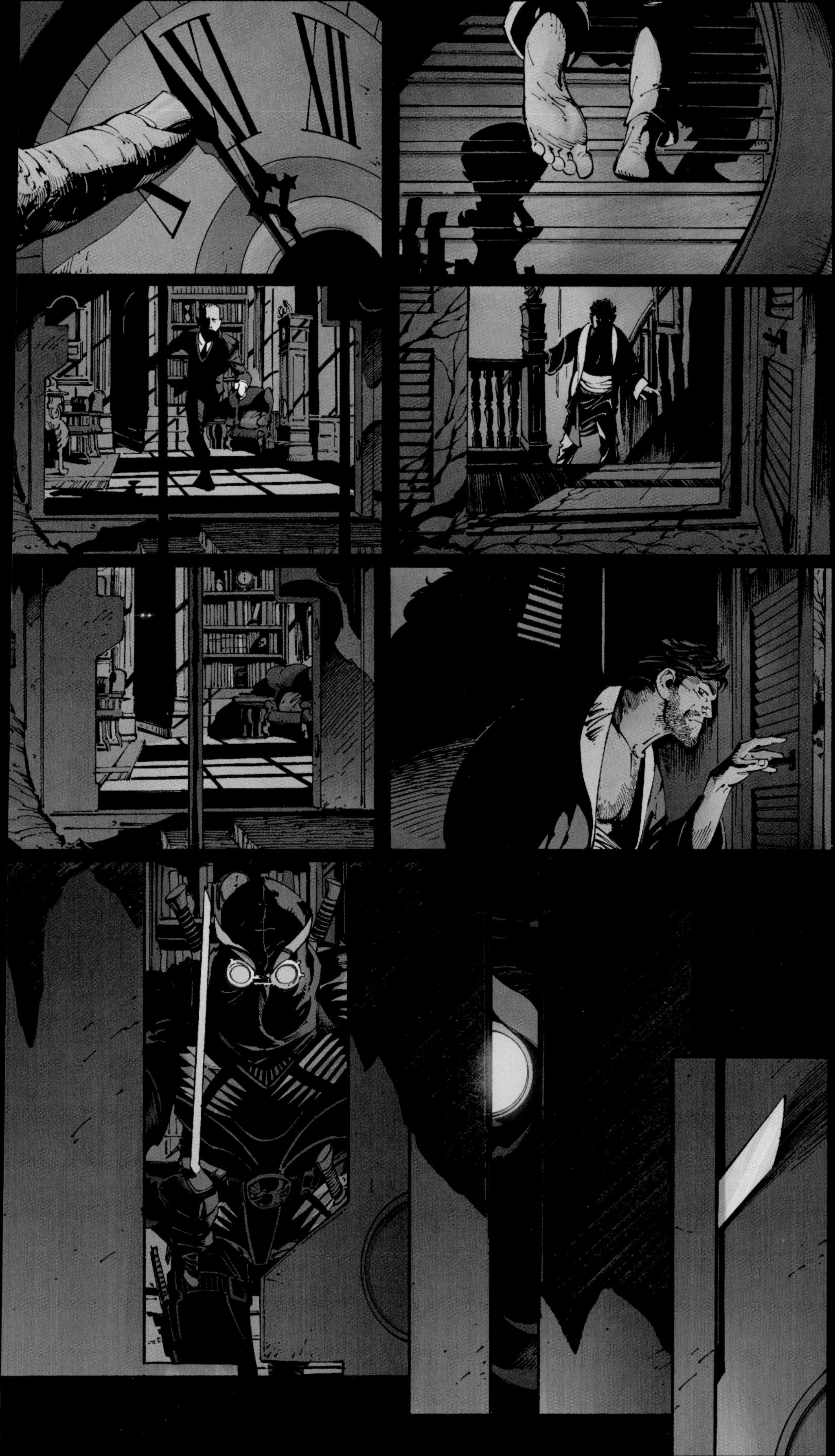

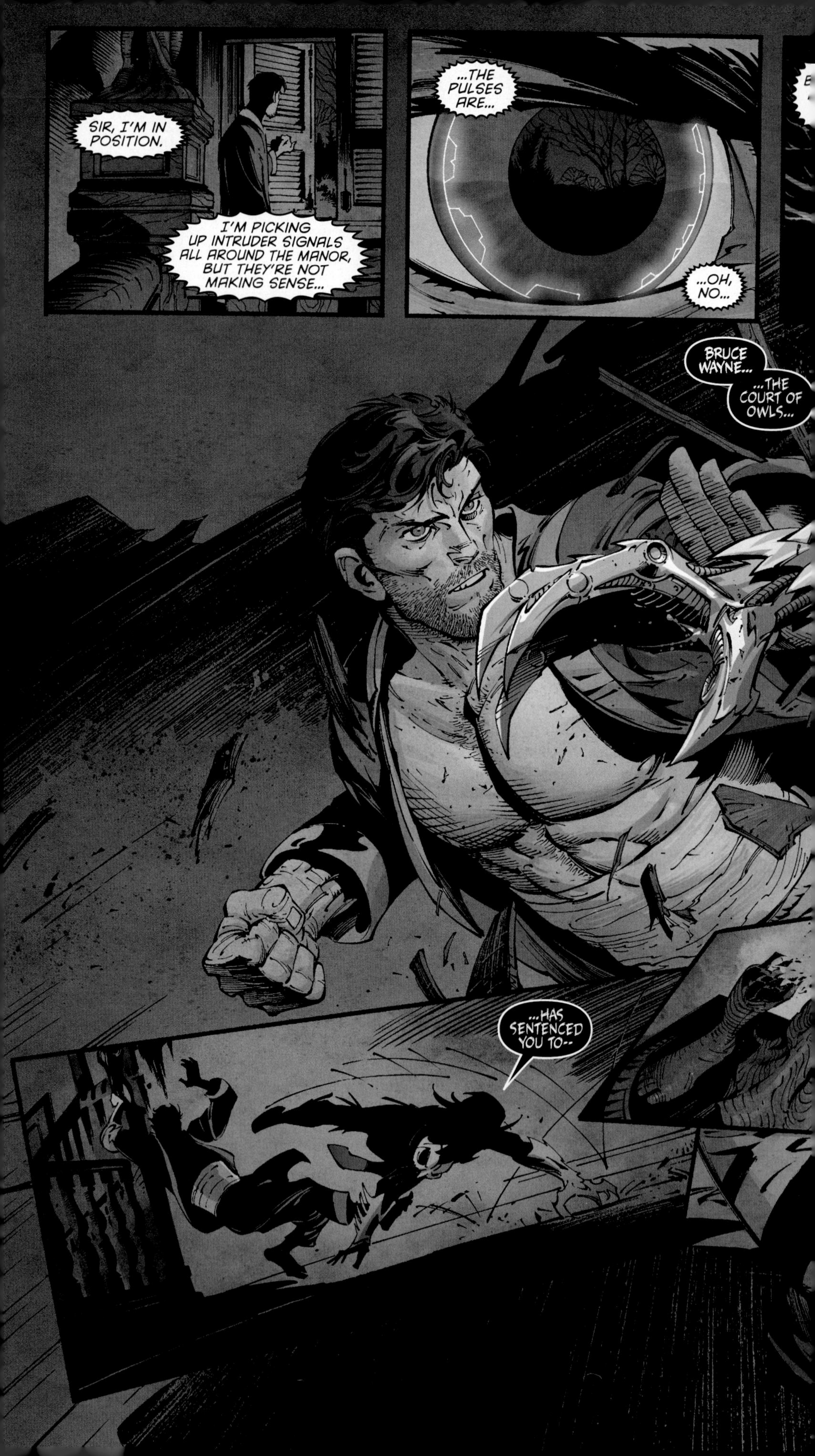
SIR, I'M IN POSITION.
I'M PICKING UP INTRUDER SIGNALS ALL AROUND THE MANOR, BUT THEY'RE NOT MAKING SENSE...
...THE PULSES ARE...
...OH, NO...
BRUCE WAYNE...
...THE COURT OF OWLS...
...HAS SENTENCED YOU TO--

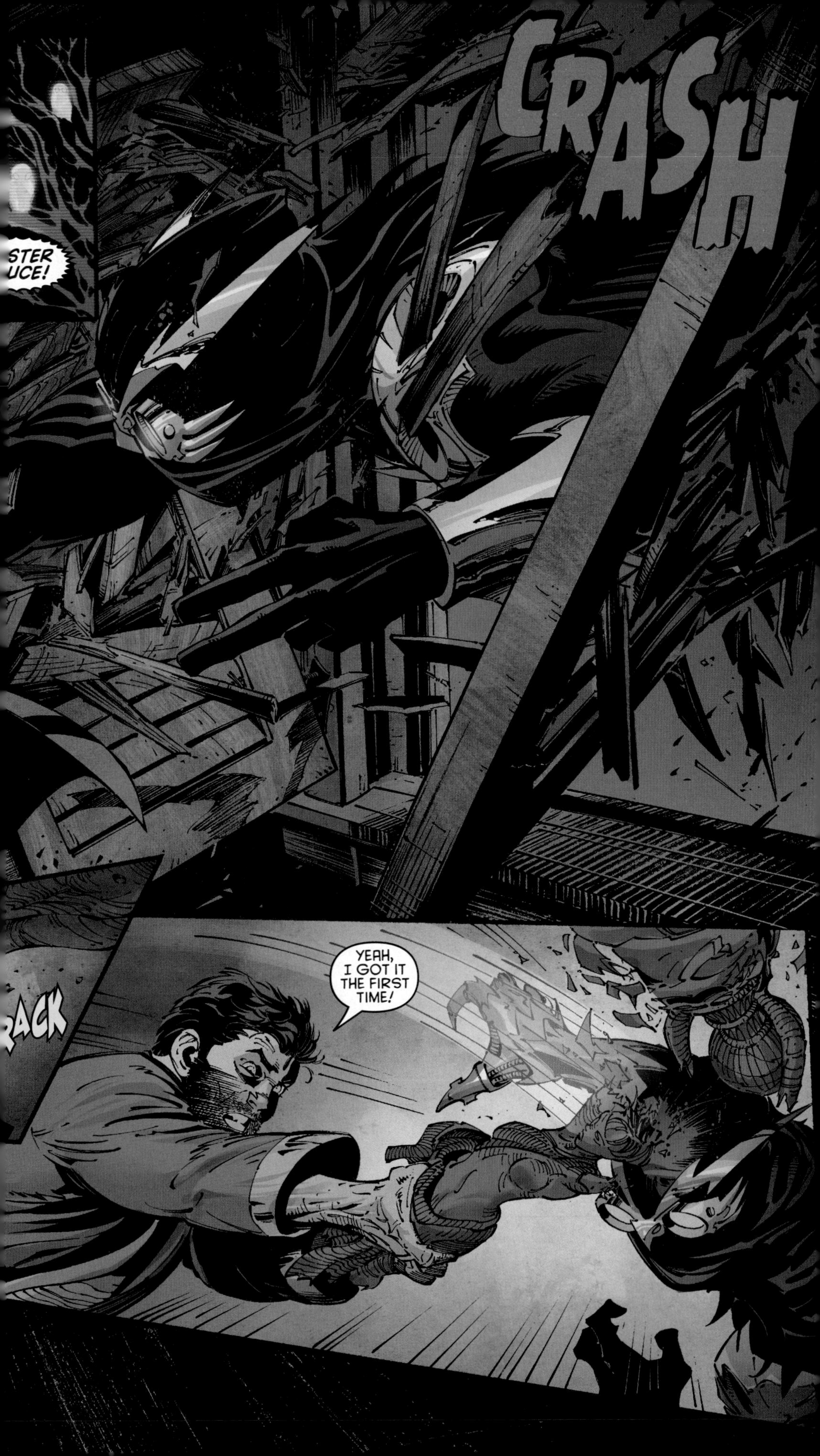

STER
UCE!
CRASH
RACK
YEAH, I GOT IT THE FIRST TIME!

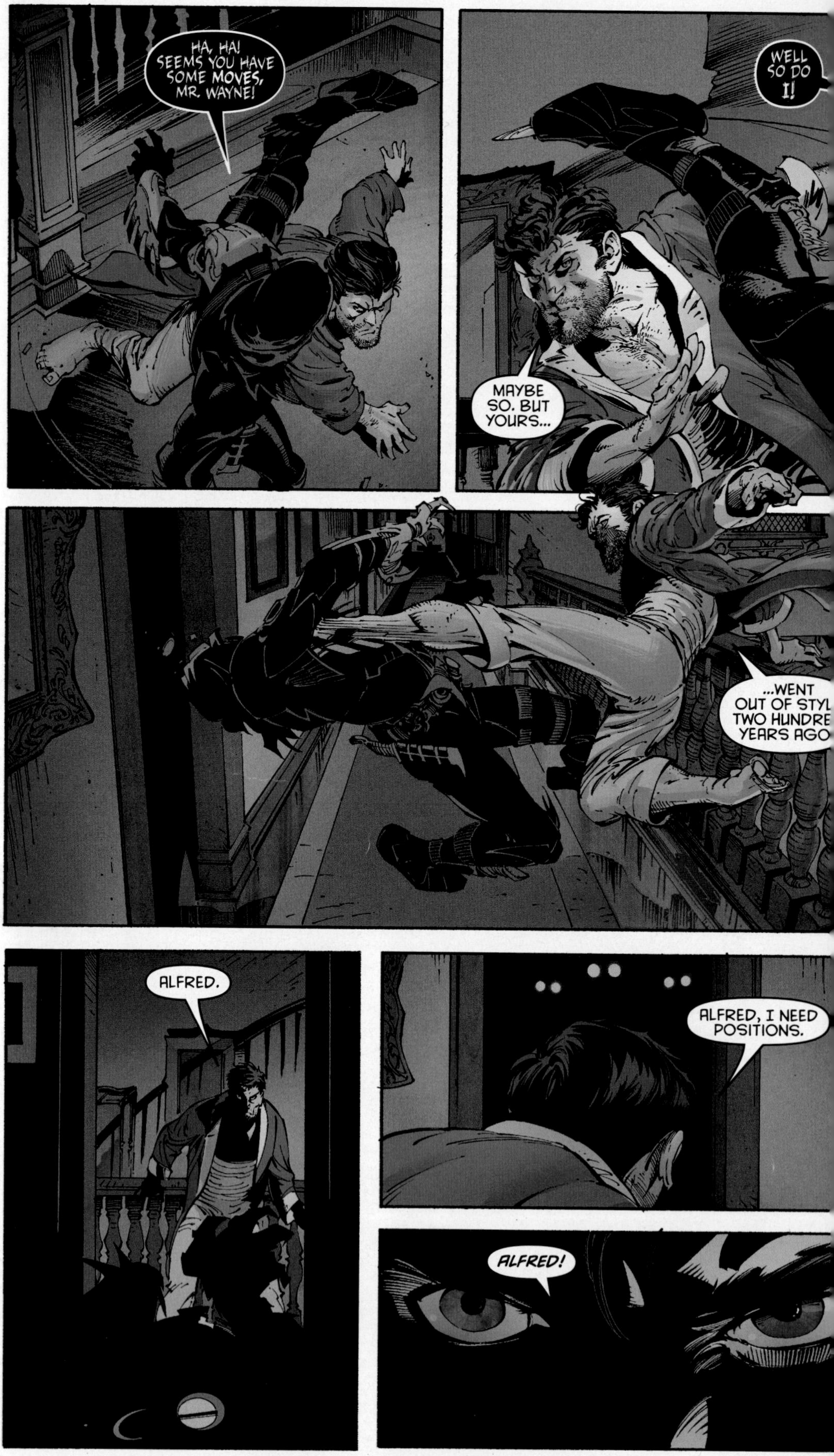
HA, HA! SEEMS YOU HAVE SOME MOVES, MR. WAYNE!
WELL SO DO I!
MAYBE SO. BUT YOURS...
...WENT OUT OF STYL TWO HUNDRE YEARS AGO
ALFRED.
ALFRED, I NEED POSITIONS.
ALFRED!

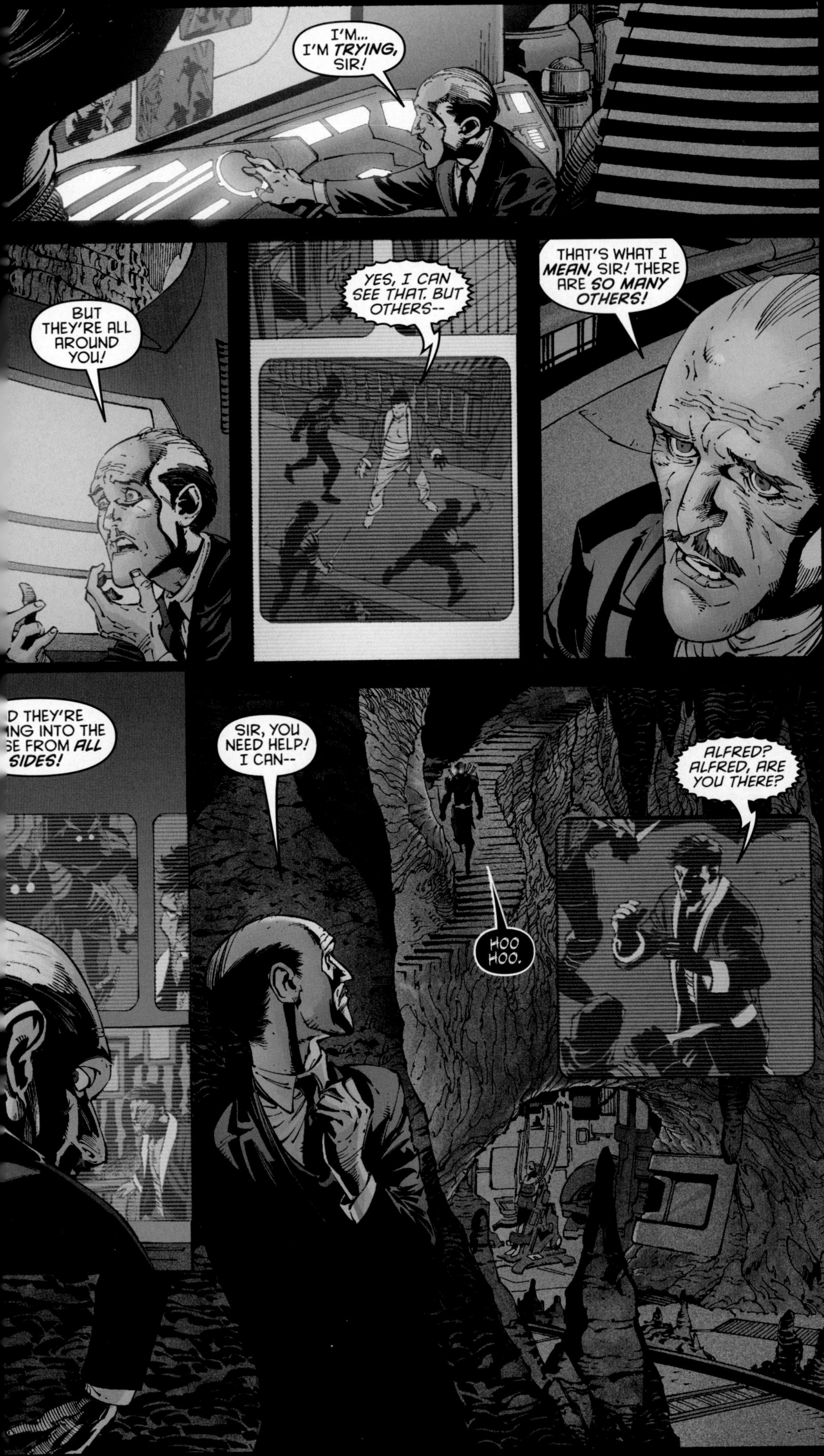
I'M... I'M TRYING, SIR!
BUT THEY'RE ALL AROUND YOU!
YES, I CAN SEE THAT. BUT OTHERS--
THAT'S WHAT I MEAN, SIR! THERE ARE SO MANY OTHERS!
D THEY'RE NG INTO THE SE FROM ALL SIDES!
SIR, YOU NEED HELP! I CAN--
HOO HOO.
ALFRED? ALFRED, ARE YOU THERE?

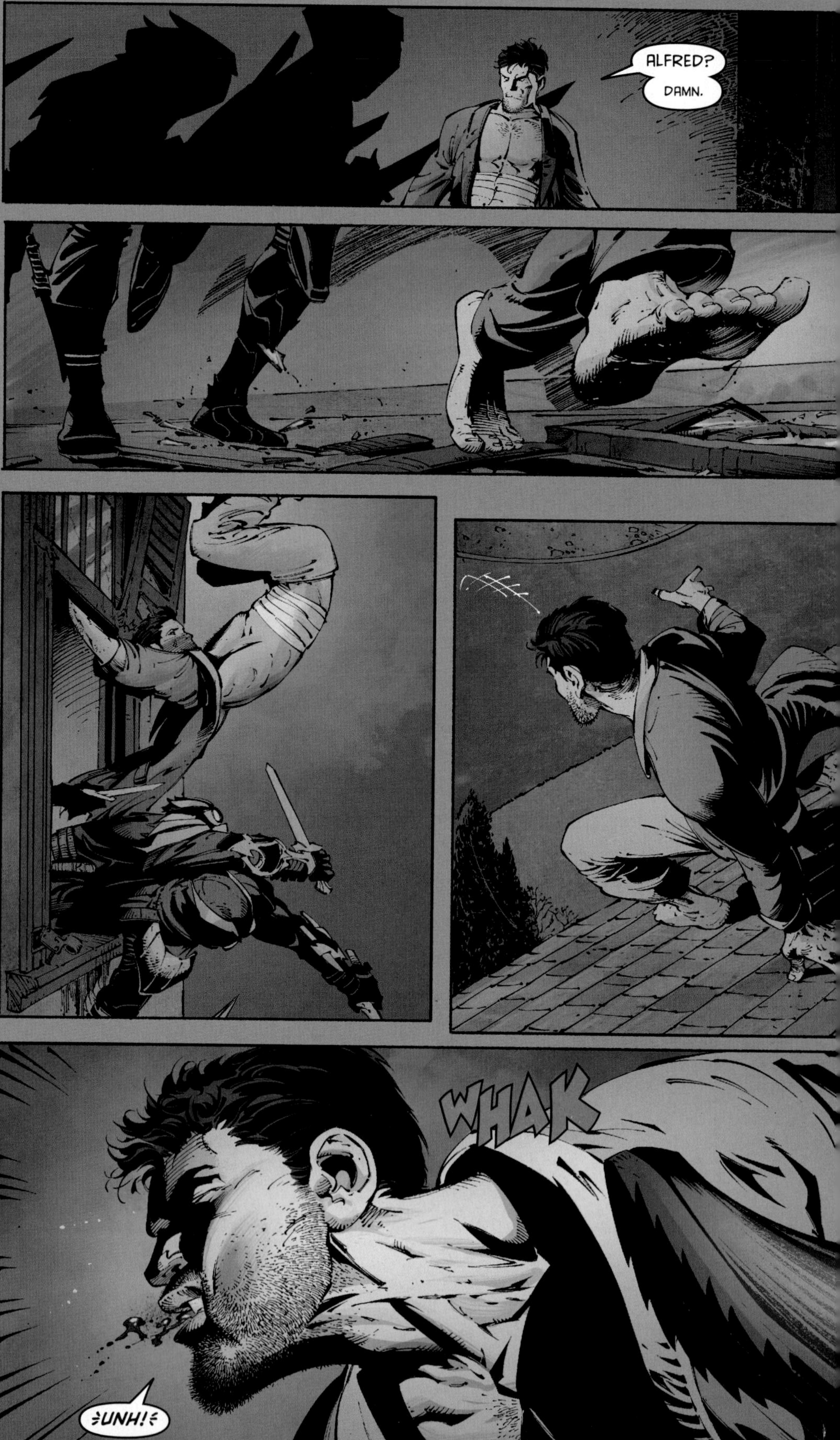
ALFRED?
DAMN.
WHAK
UNH!

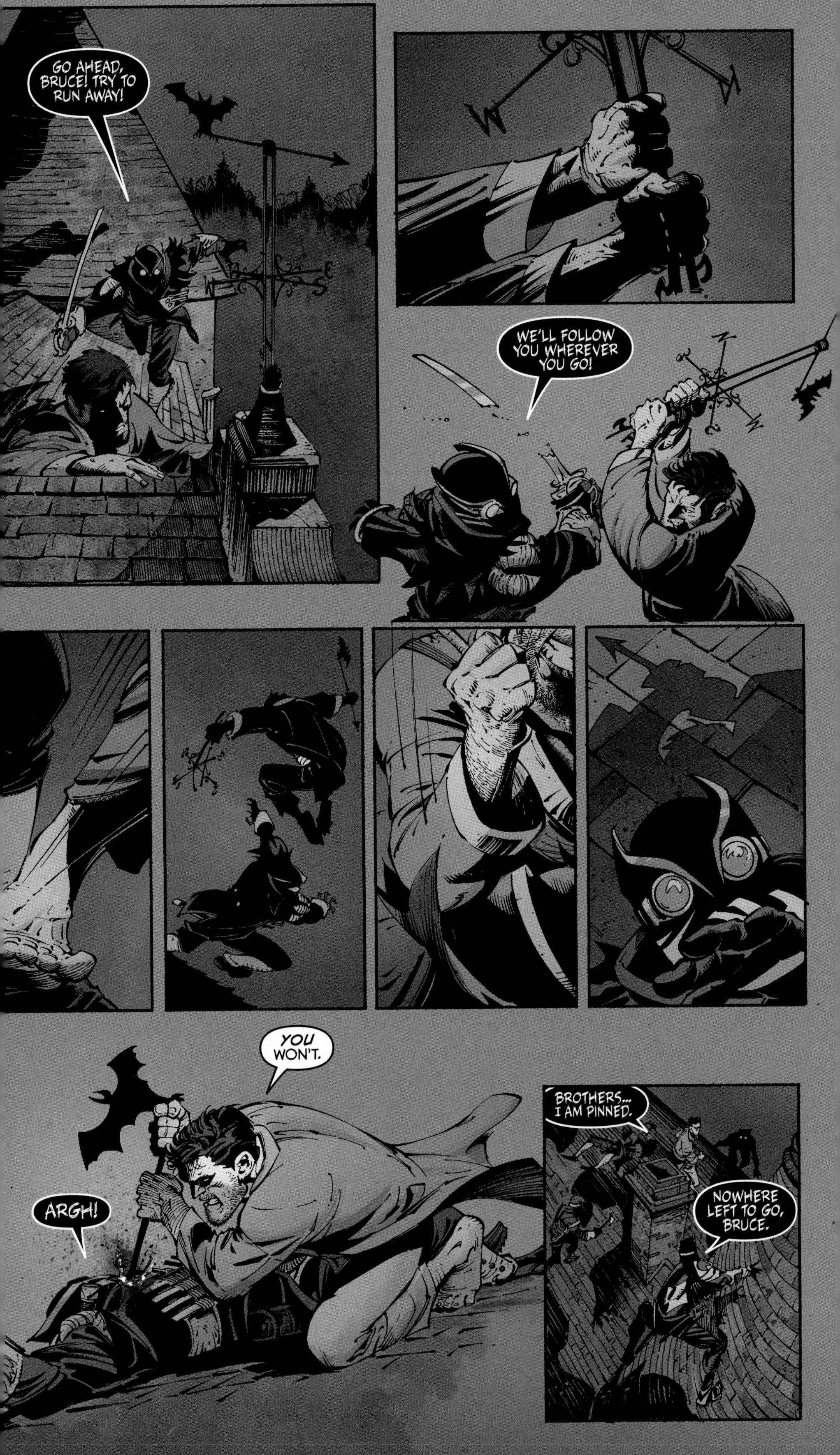

GO AHEAD, BRUCE! TRY TO RUN AWAY!
WE'LL FOLLOW YOU WHEREVER YOU GO!
YOU WON'T.
ARGH!
BROTHERS... I AM PINNED.
NOWHERE LEFT TO GO, BRUCE.

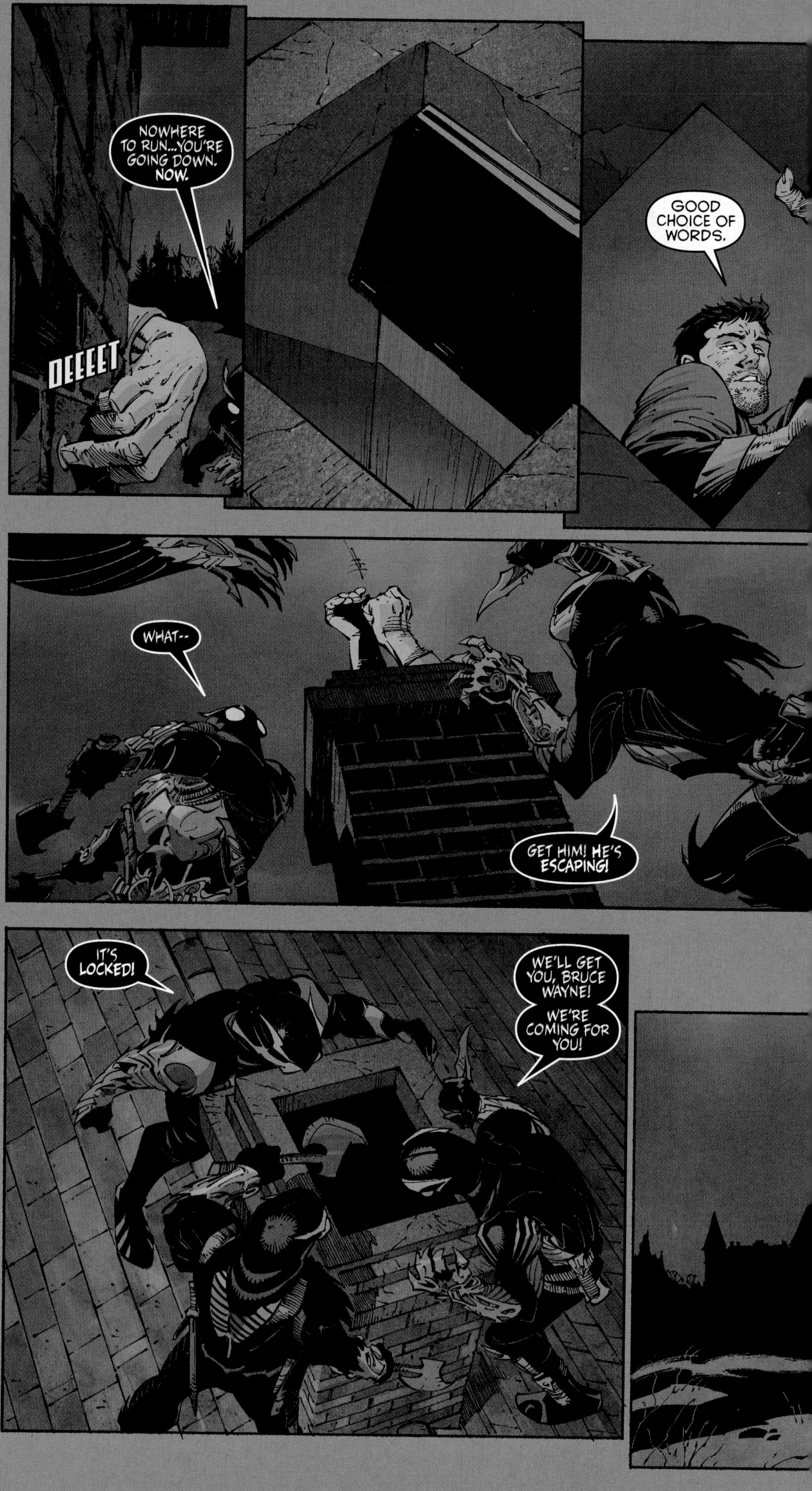
NOWHERE TO RUN...YOU'RE GOING DOWN. NOW.
DEEEET
GOOD CHOICE OF WORDS.
WHAT--
GET HIM! HE'S ESCAPING!
IT'S LOCKED!
WE'LL GET YOU, BRUCE WAYNE!
WE'RE COMING FOR YOU!

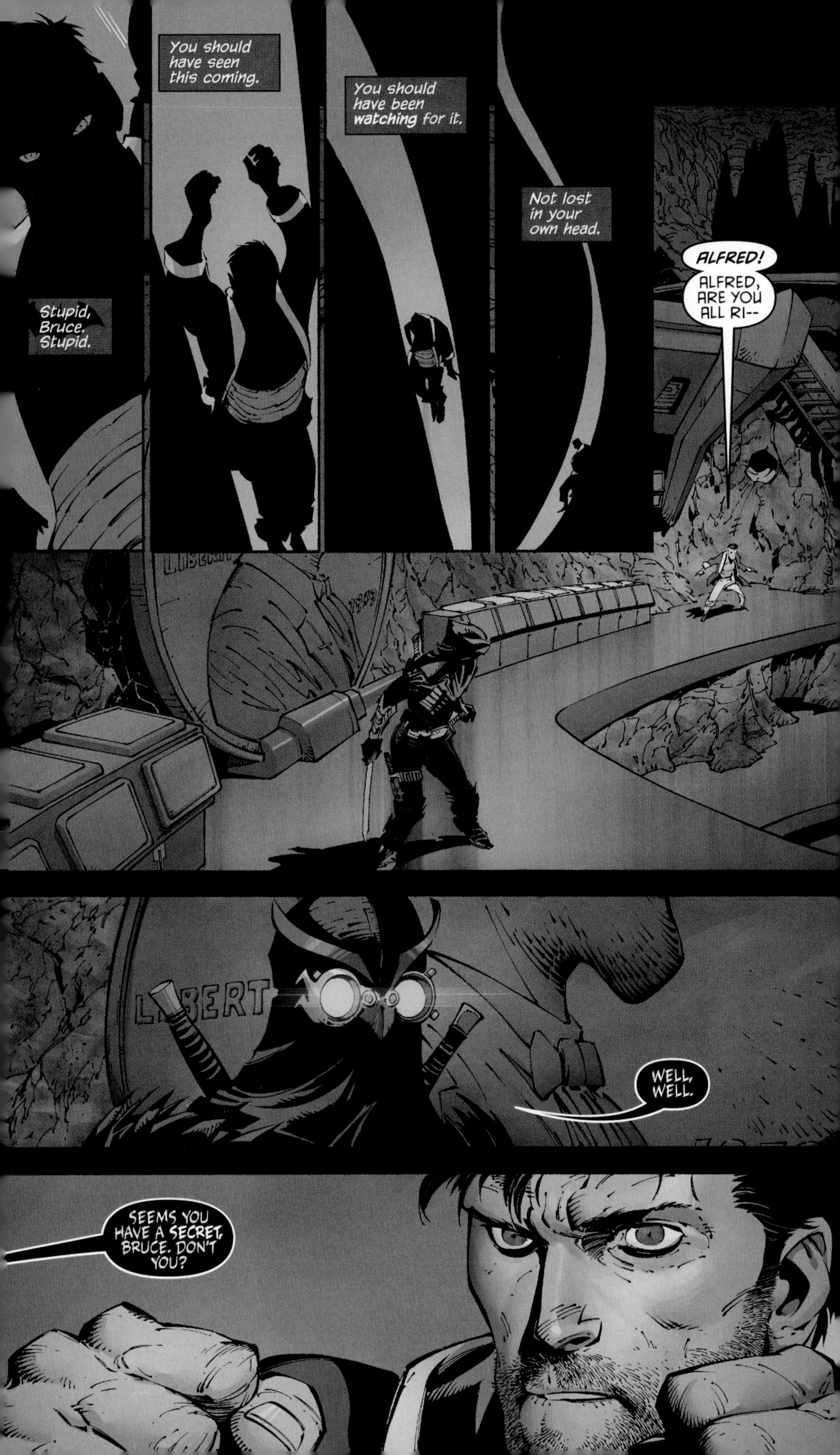

Stupid, Bruce. Stupid.
You should have seen this coming.
You should have been **watching** for it.
Not lost in your own head.
ALFRED!
ALFRED, ARE YOU ALL RI--
WELL, WELL.
SEEMS YOU HAVE A **SECRET**, BRUCE. DON'T YOU?

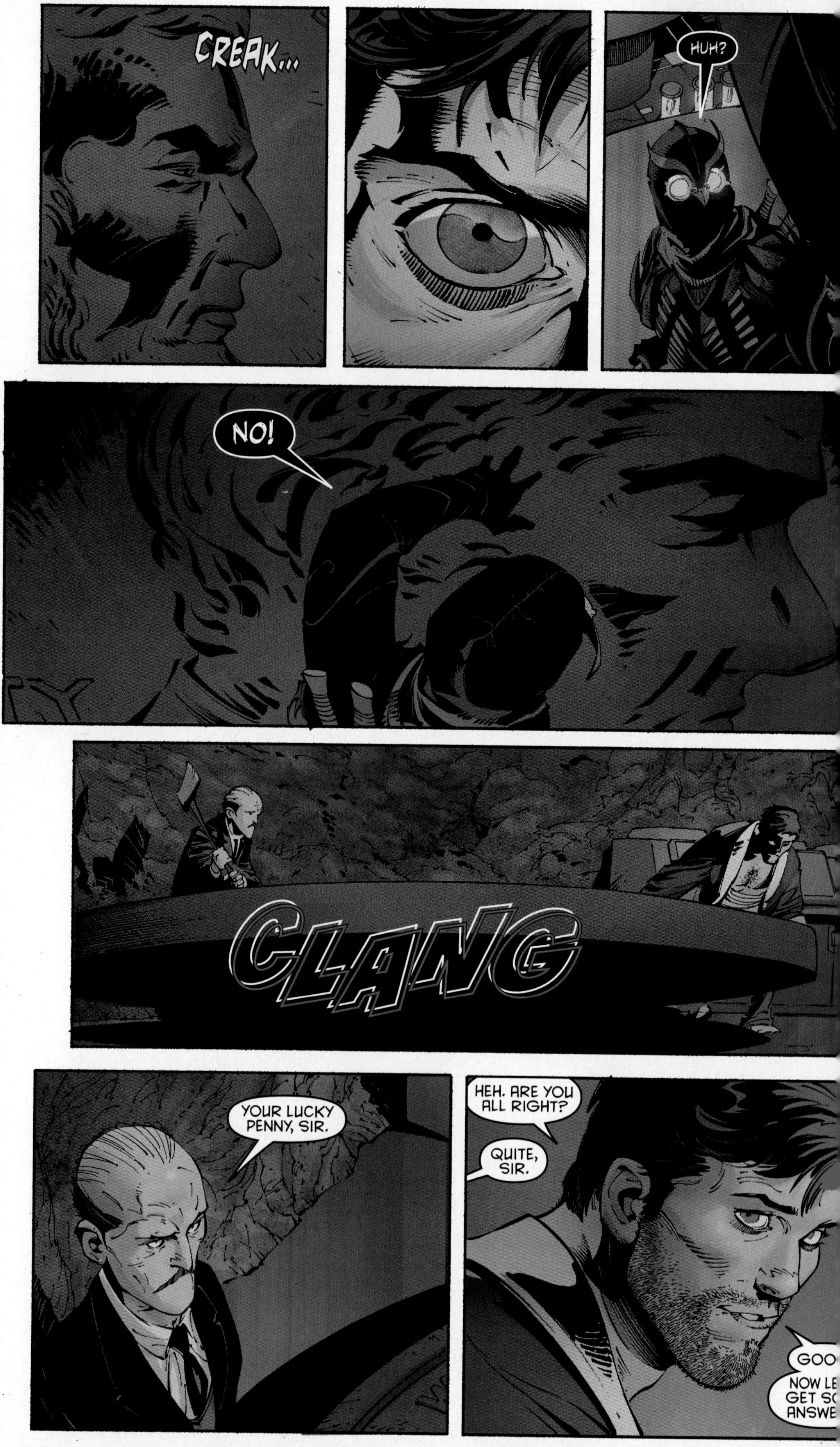
CREAK...
HUH?
NO!
CLANG
YOUR LUCKY PENNY, SIR.
HEH. ARE YOU ALL RIGHT?
QUITE, SIR.

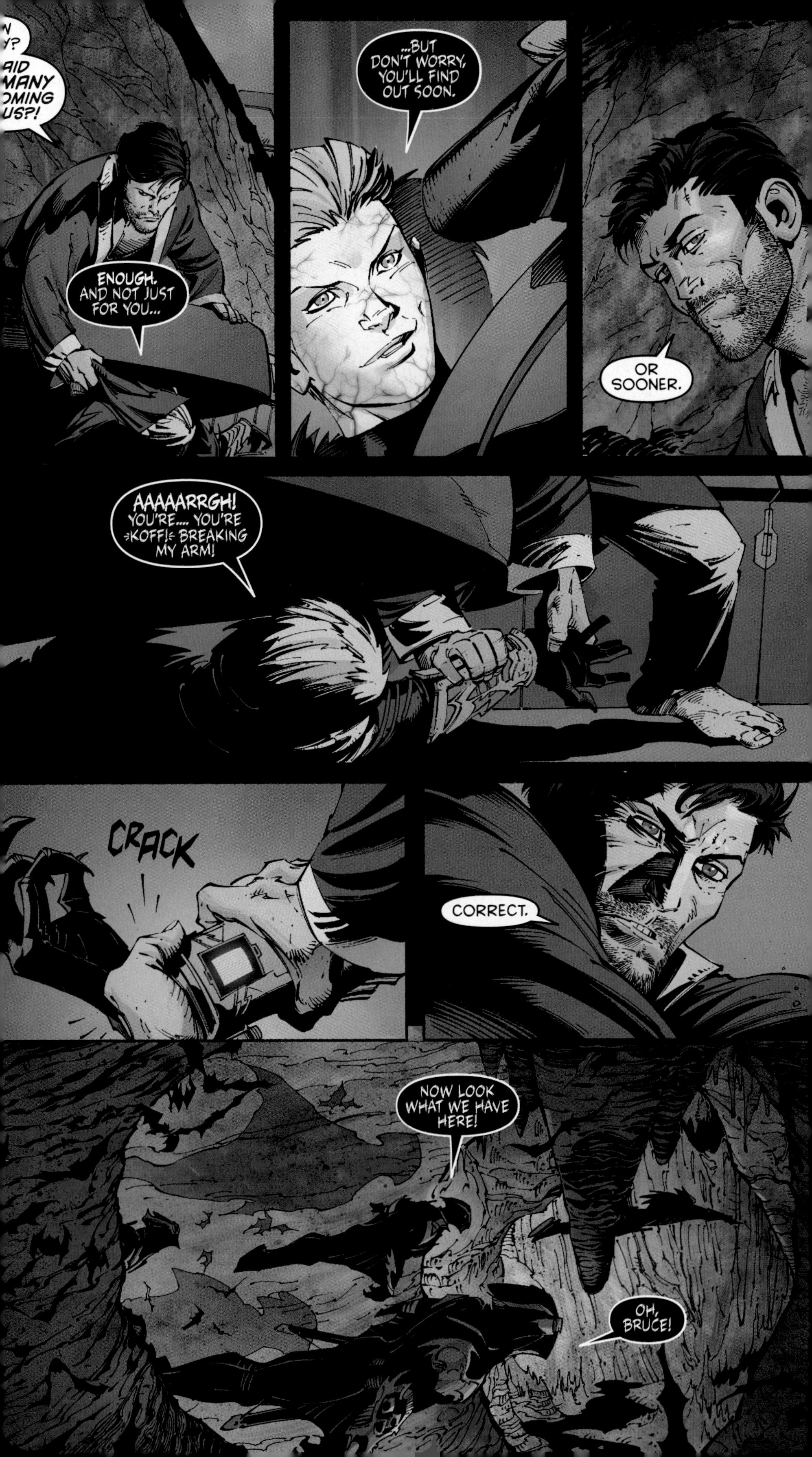
ENOUGH. AND NOT JUST FOR YOU...
...BUT DON'T WORRY, YOU'LL FIND OUT SOON.
OR SOONER.
AAAAARRGH! YOU'RE... YOU'RE -KOFF!- BREAKING MY ARM!
CRACK
CORRECT.
NOW LOOK WHAT WE HAVE HERE!
OH, BRUCE!

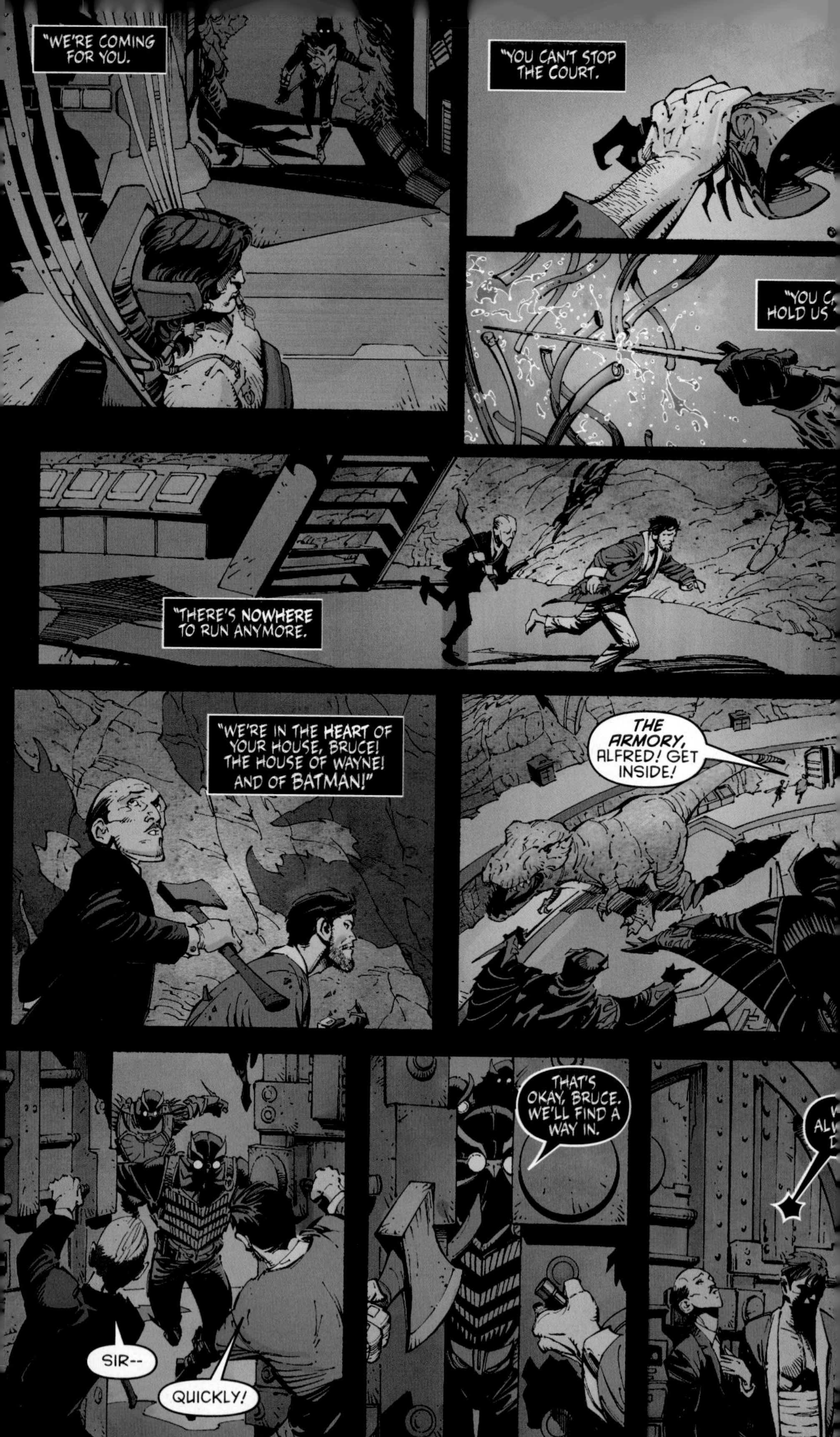

“WE'RE COMING FOR YOU.
“YOU CAN'T STOP THE COURT.
“YOU C HOLD US
“THERE'S NOWHERE TO RUN ANYMORE.
“WE'RE IN THE HEART OF YOUR HOUSE, BRUCE! THE HOUSE OF WAYNE! AND OF BATMAN!”
THE ARMORY, ALFRED! GET INSIDE!
SIR--
QUICKLY!
THAT'S OKAY, BRUCE. WE'LL FIND A WAY IN.

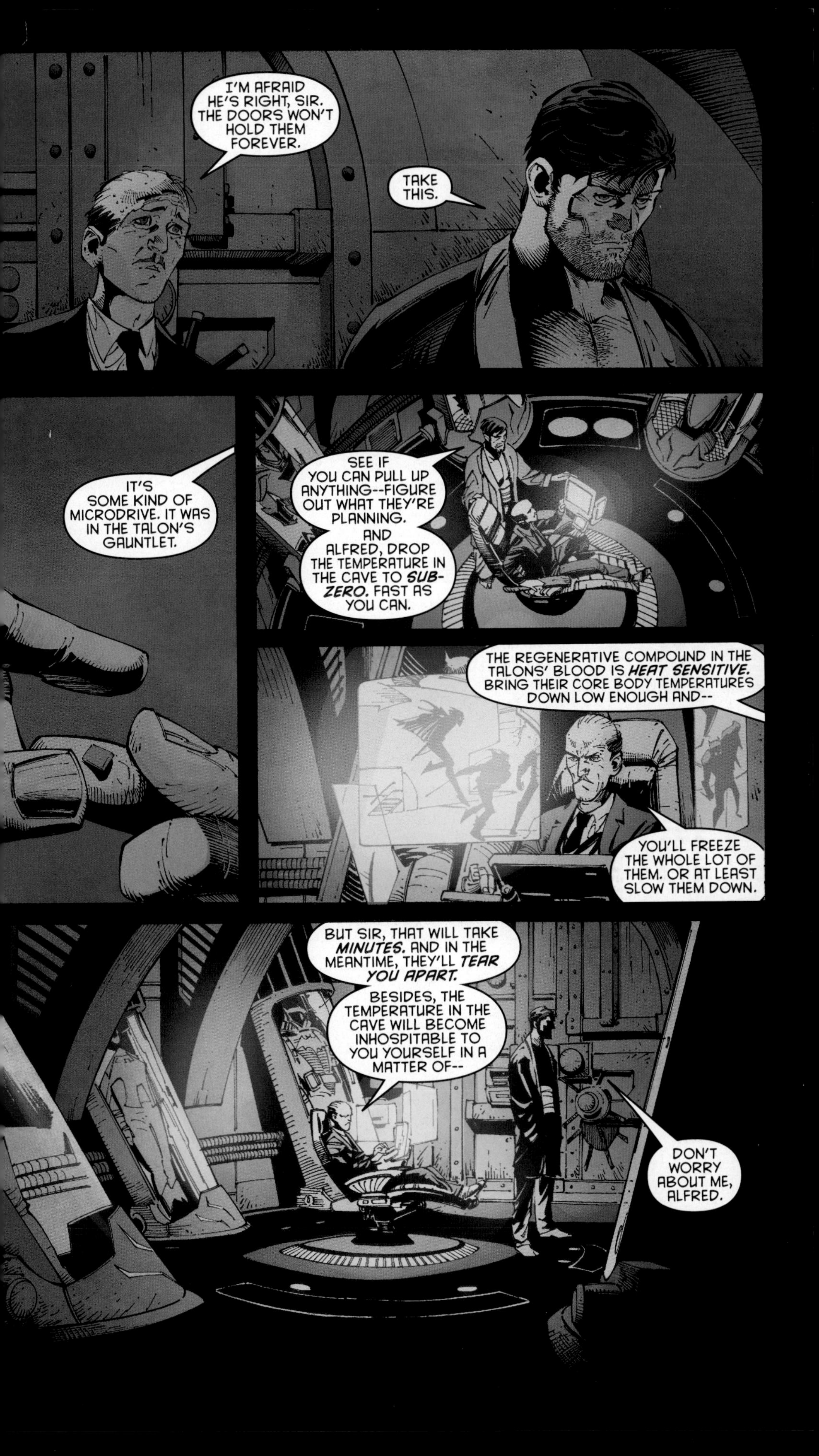
I'M AFRAID HE'S RIGHT, SIR. THE DOORS WON'T HOLD THEM FOREVER.
TAKE THIS.
IT'S SOME KIND OF MICRODRIVE. IT WAS IN THE TALON'S GAUNTLET.
SEE IF YOU CAN PULL UP ANYTHING--FIGURE OUT WHAT THEY'RE PLANNING.
AND ALFRED, DROP THE TEMPERATURE IN THE CAVE TO *SUB-ZERO.* FAST AS YOU CAN.
THE REGENERATIVE COMPOUND IN THE TALONS' BLOOD IS *HEAT SENSITIVE.* BRING THEIR CORE BODY TEMPERATURES DOWN LOW ENOUGH AND--
YOU'LL FREEZE THE WHOLE LOT OF THEM. OR AT LEAST SLOW THEM DOWN.
BUT SIR, THAT WILL TAKE *MINUTES.* AND IN THE MEANTIME, THEY'LL *TEAR YOU APART.*
BESIDES, THE TEMPERATURE IN THE CAVE WILL BECOME INHOSPITABLE TO YOU YOURSELF IN A MATTER OF--
DON'T WORRY ABOUT ME, ALFRED.

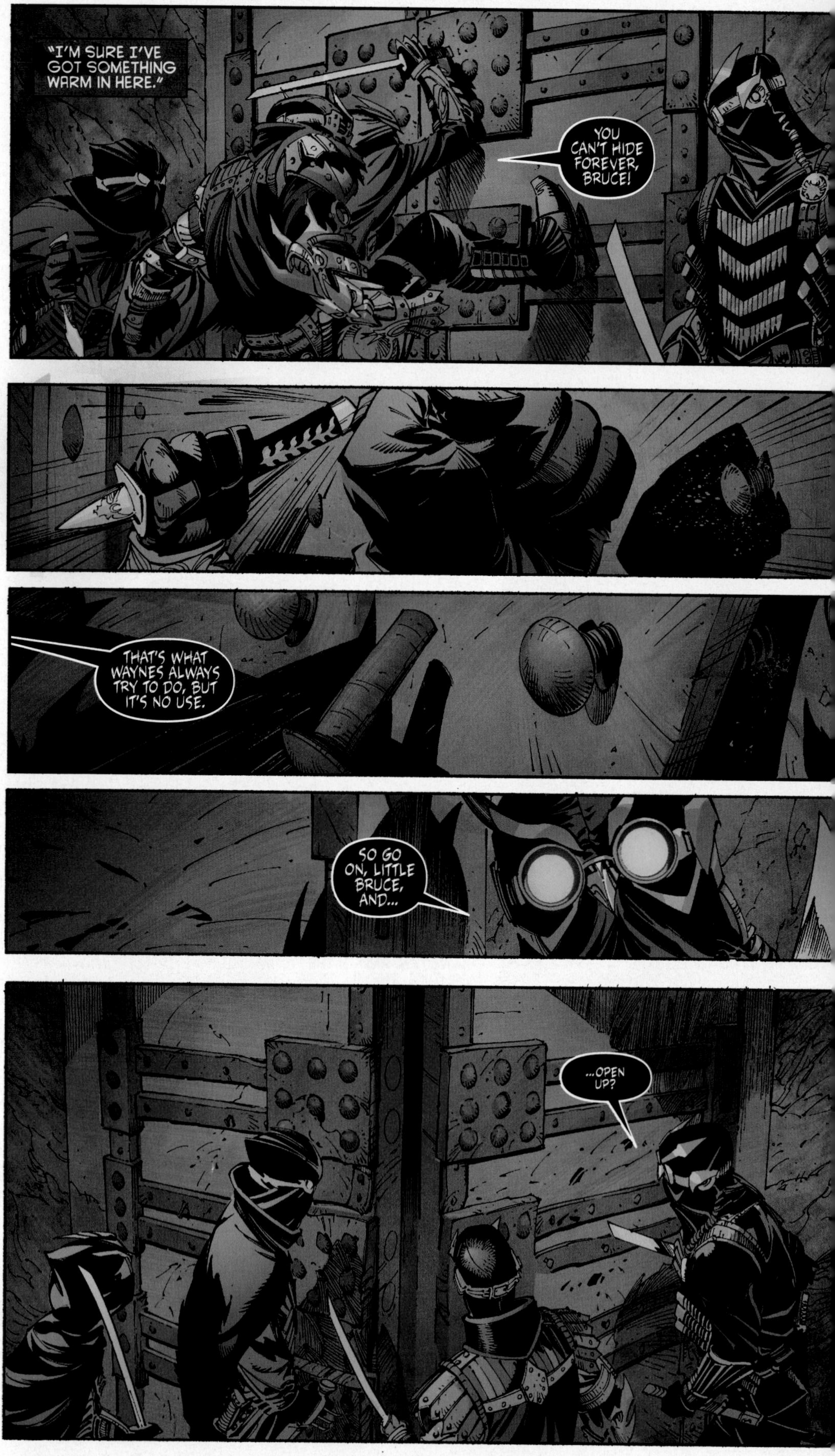
"I'M SURE I'VE GOT SOMETHING WARM IN HERE."
YOU CAN'T HIDE FOREVER, BRUCE!
THAT'S WHAT WAYNES ALWAYS TRY TO DO, BUT IT'S NO USE.
SO GO ON, LITTLE BRUCE, AND...
...OPEN UP?

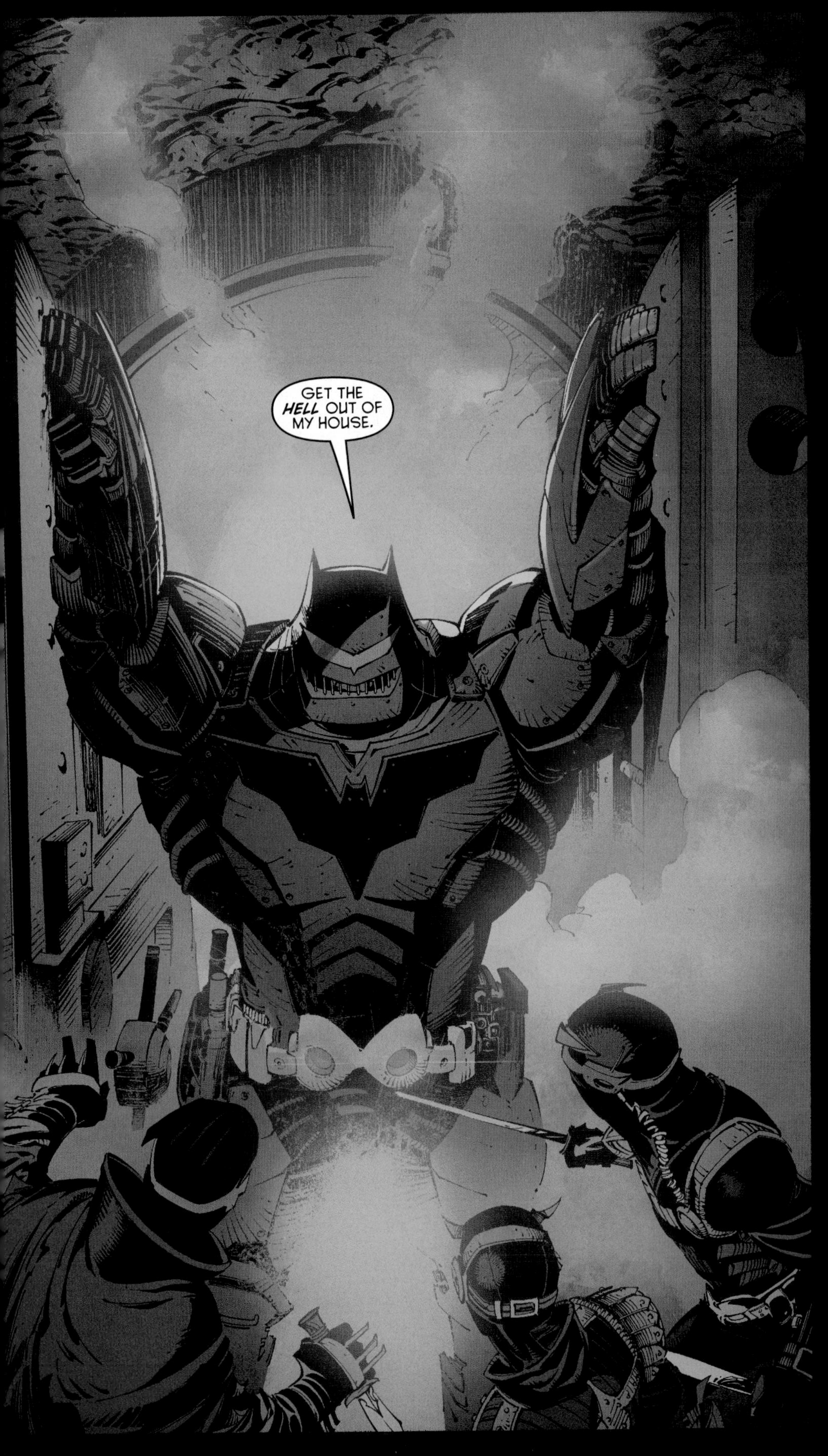
GET THE *HELL* OUT OF MY HOUSE.

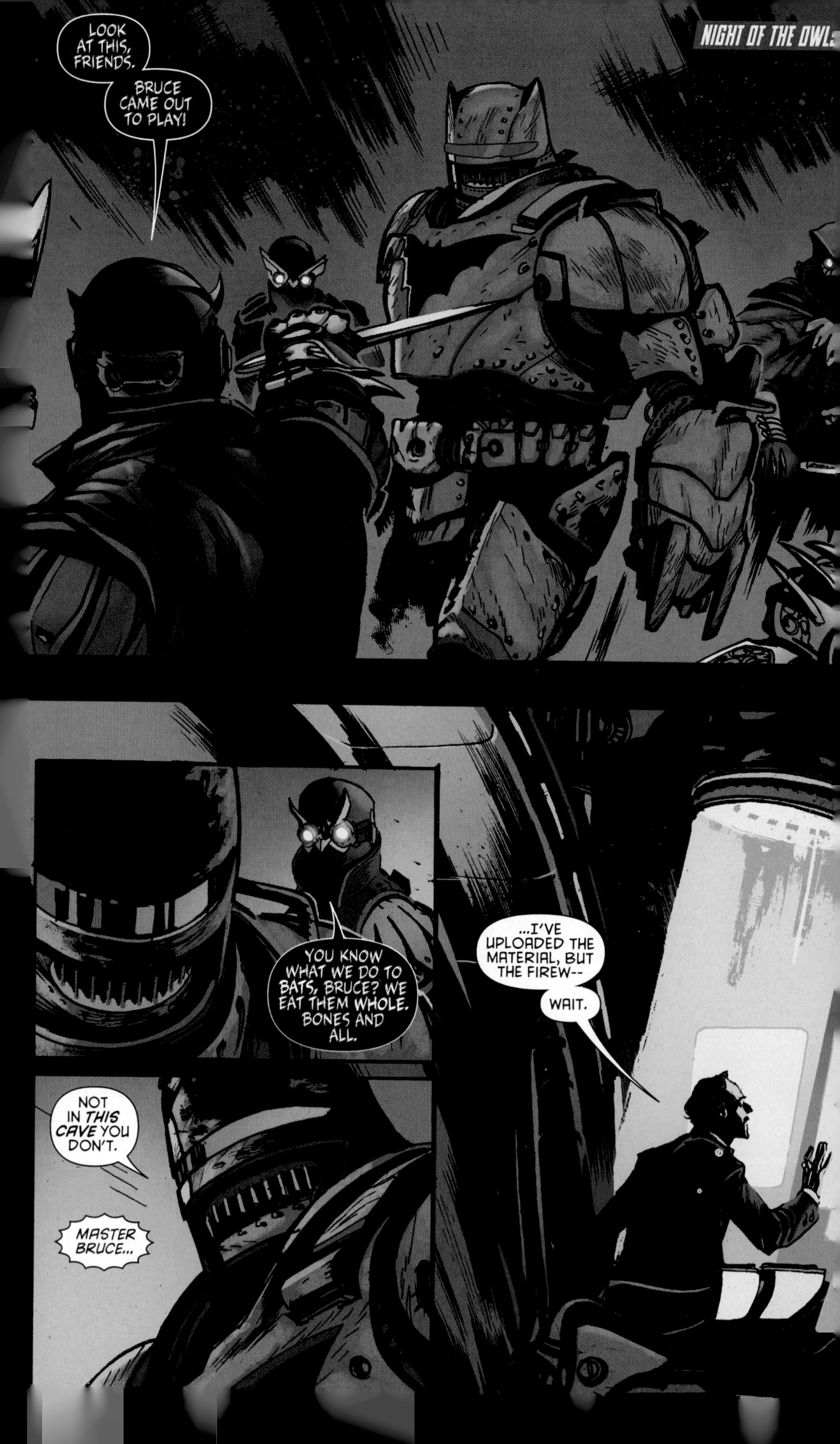
LOOK AT THIS, FRIENDS.
BRUCE CAME OUT TO PLAY!
YOU KNOW WHAT WE DO TO BATS, BRUCE? WE EAT THEM WHOLE. BONES AND ALL.
...I'VE UPLOADED THE MATERIAL, BUT THE FIREW--
WAIT.
NOT IN *THIS CAVE* YOU DON'T.
MASTER BRUCE...

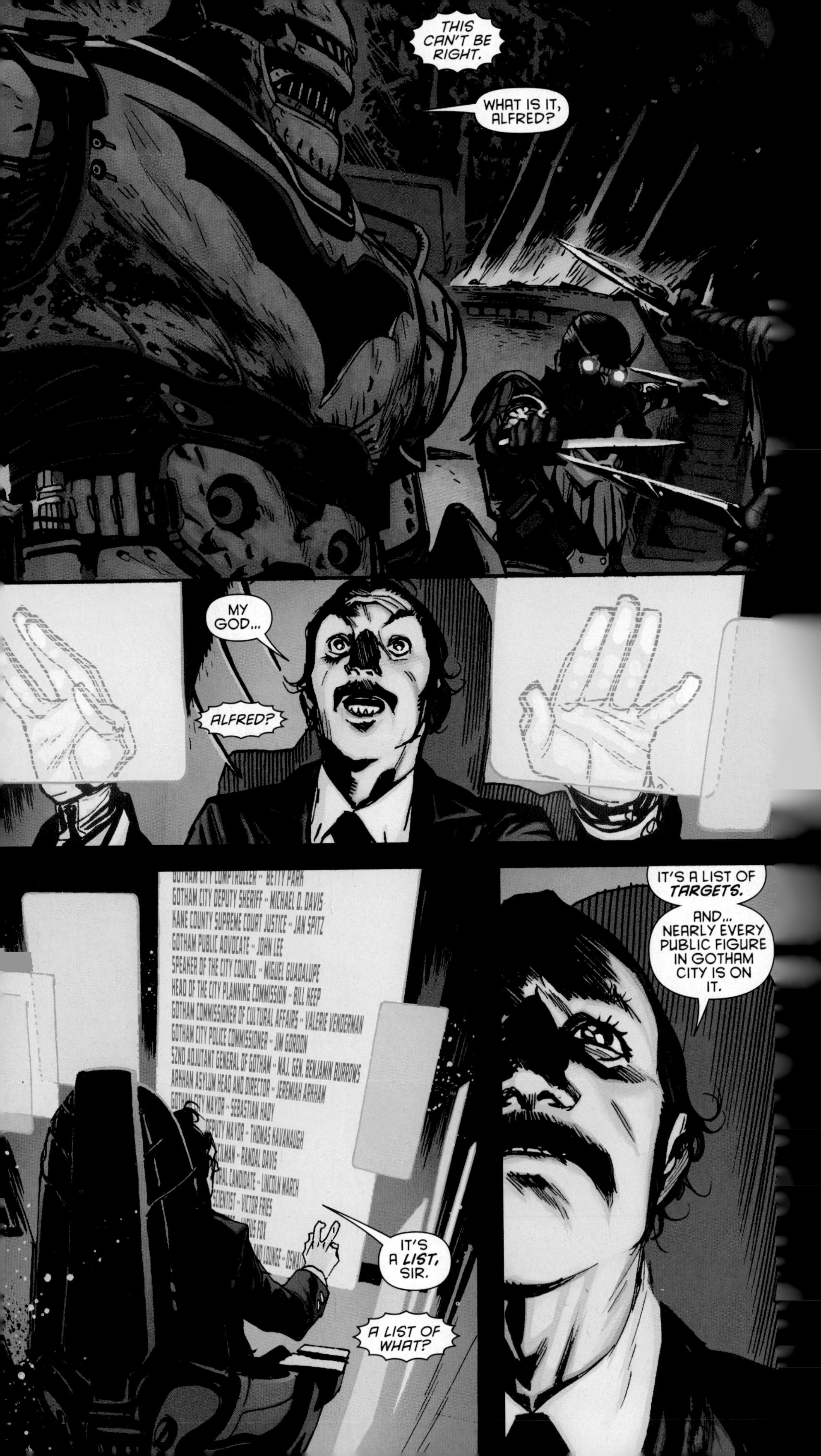

THIS CAN'T BE RIGHT.
WHAT IS IT, ALFRED?
MY GOD...
ALFRED?
GOTHAM CITY DEPUTY SHERIFF -- MICHAEL D. DAVIS
KANE COUNTY SUPREME COURT JUSTICE -- JAN SPITZ
GOTHAM PUBLIC ADVOCATE -- JOHN LEE
SPEAKER OF THE CITY COUNCIL -- MIGUEL GUADALUPE
HEAD OF THE CITY PLANNING COMMISSION -- BILL KEEP
GOTHAM COMMISSIONER OF CULTURAL AFFAIRS -- VALERIE VENDERMAN
GOTHAM CITY POLICE COMMISSIONER -- JIM GORDON
52ND ADJUTANT GENERAL OF GOTHAM -- MAJ. GEN. BENJAMIN BURROWS
ARKHAM ASYLUM HEAD AND DIRECTOR -- JEREMIAH ARKHAM
GOTHAM CITY MAYOR -- SEBASTIAN HADY
IT'S A LIST, SIR.
A LIST OF WHAT?
IT'S A LIST OF TARGETS.
AND... NEARLY EVERY PUBLIC FIGURE IN GOTHAM CITY IS ON IT.

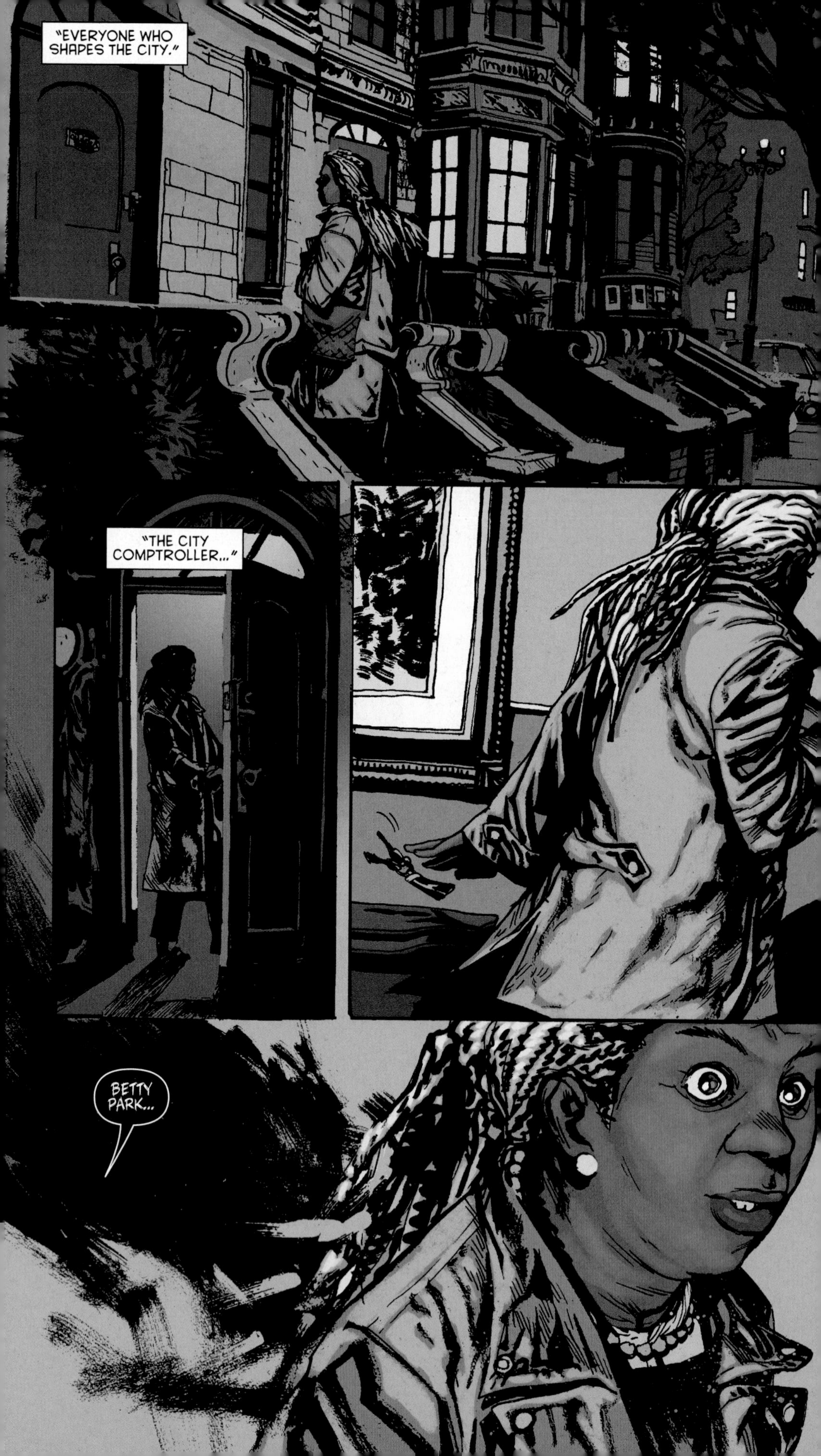
"EVERYONE WHO SHAPES THE CITY."
"THE CITY COMPTROLLER..."
BETTY PARK...

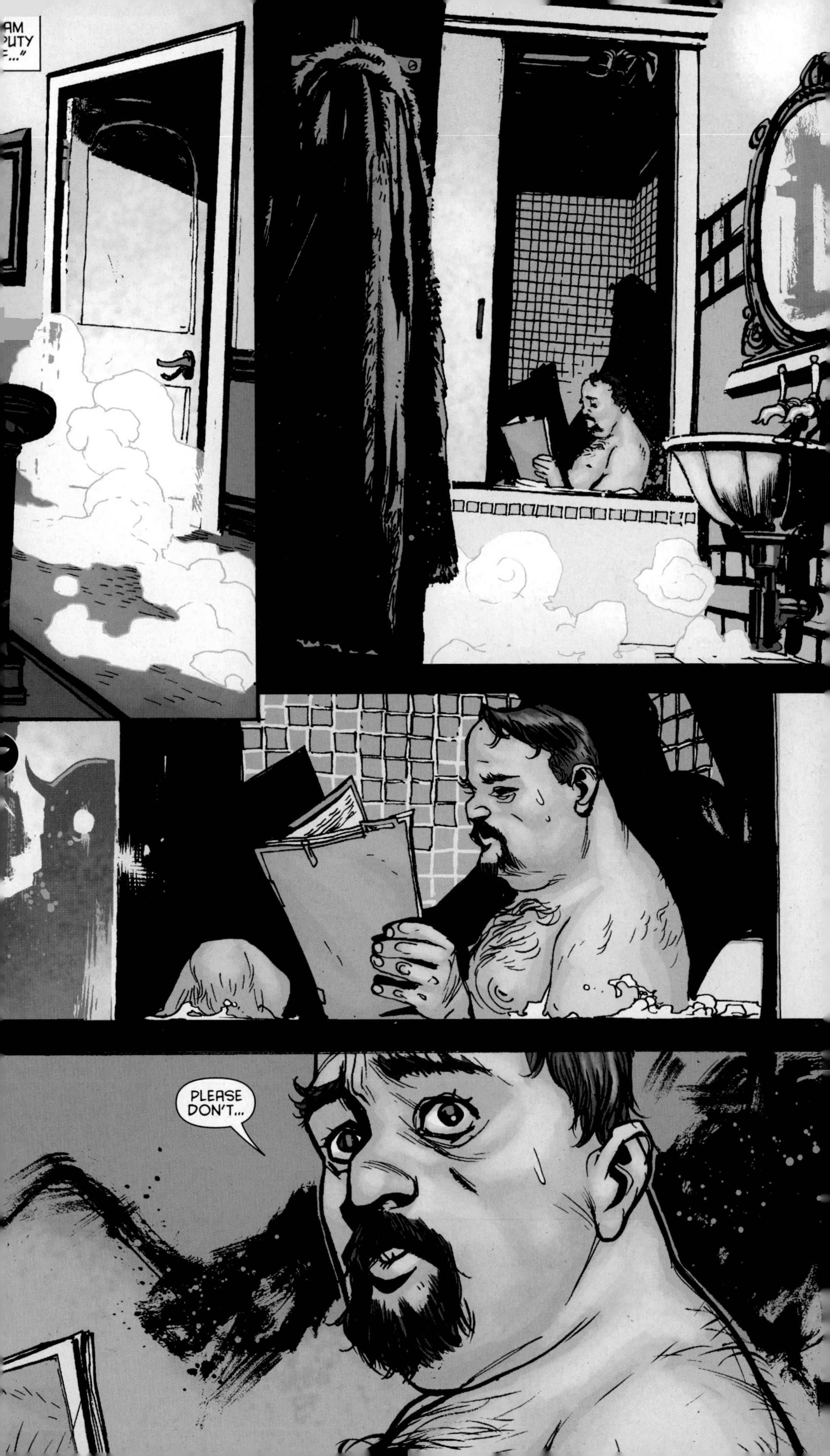

AM
PUTY
F..."
PLEASE DON'T...

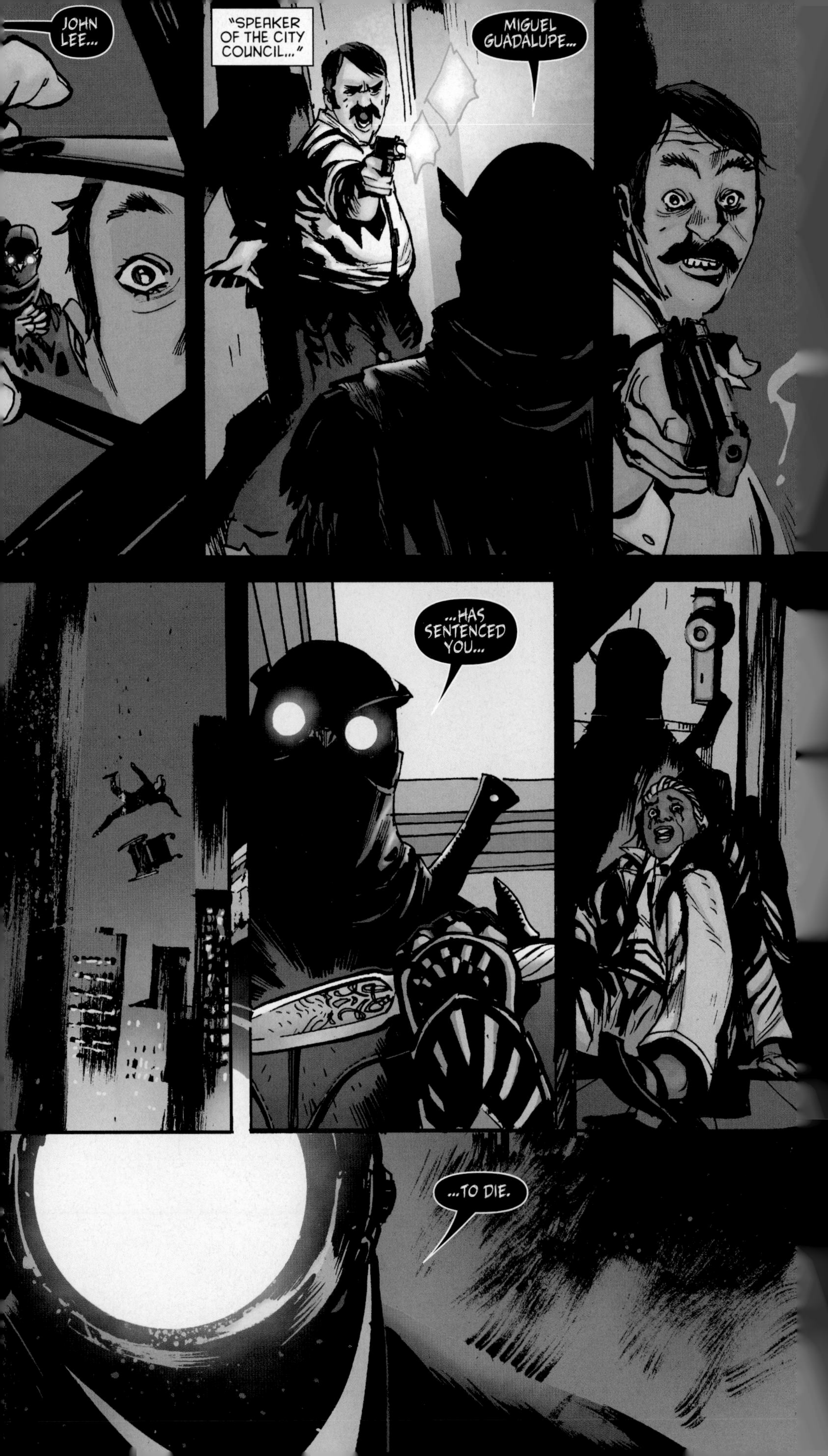
JOHN LEE...
"SPEAKER OF THE CITY COUNCIL..."
MIGUEL GUADALUPE...
...HAS SENTENCED YOU...
...TO DIE.

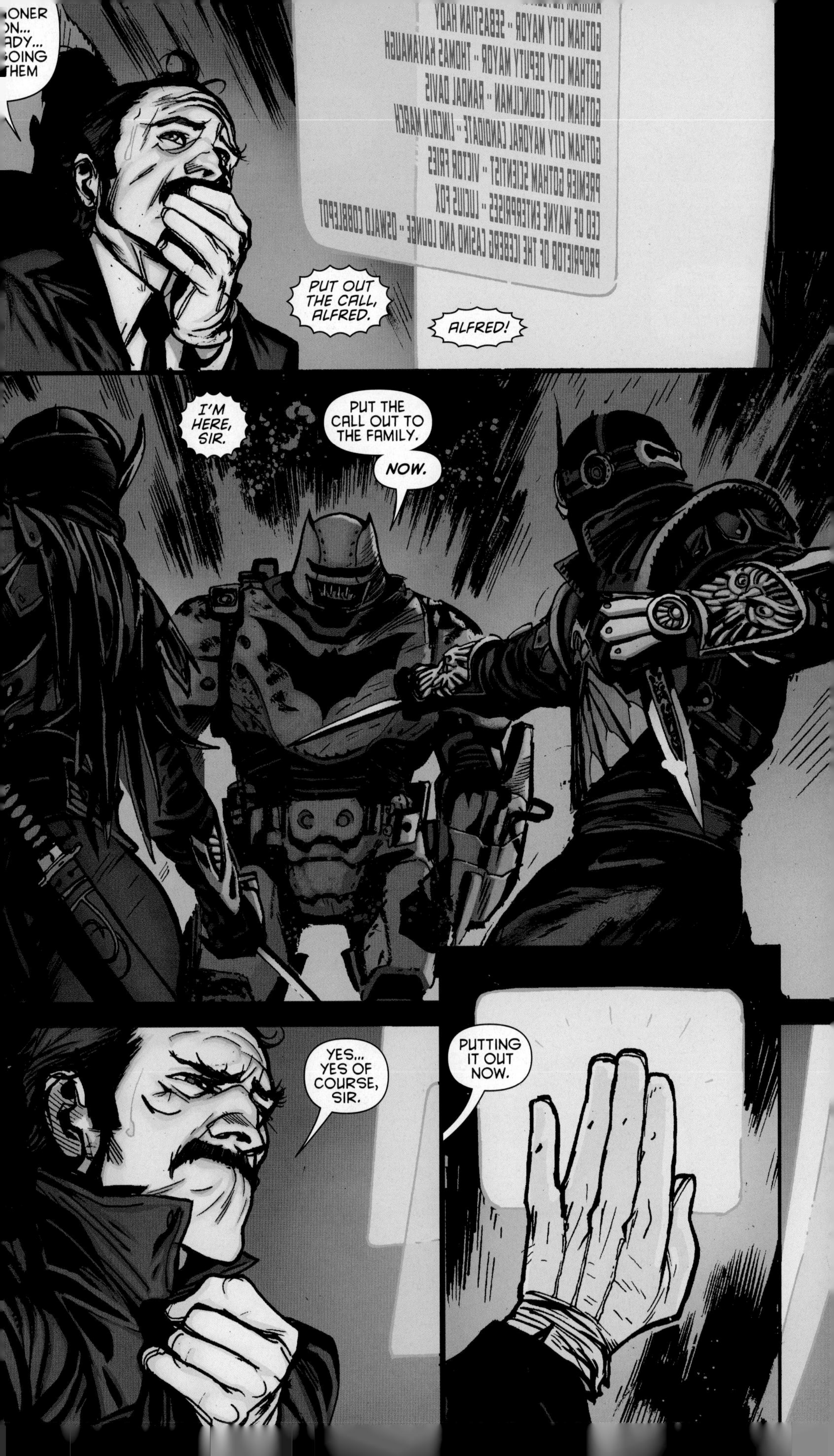
GOTHAM CITY MAYOR -- SEBASTIAN HADY
GOTHAM CITY DEPUTY MAYOR -- THOMAS KAVANAUGH
GOTHAM CITY COUNCILMAN -- RANDAL DAVIS
GOTHAM CITY MAYORAL CANDIDATE -- LINCOLN MARCH
PREMIER GOTHAM SCIENTIST -- VICTOR FRIES
CEO OF WAYNE ENTERPRISES -- LUCIUS FOX
PROPRIETOR OF THE ICEBERG CASINO AND LOUNGE -- OSWALD COBBLEPOT
PUT OUT THE CALL, ALFRED.
ALFRED!
I'M HERE, SIR.
PUT THE CALL OUT TO THE FAMILY.
NOW.
YES... YES OF COURSE, SIR.
PUTTING IT OUT NOW.

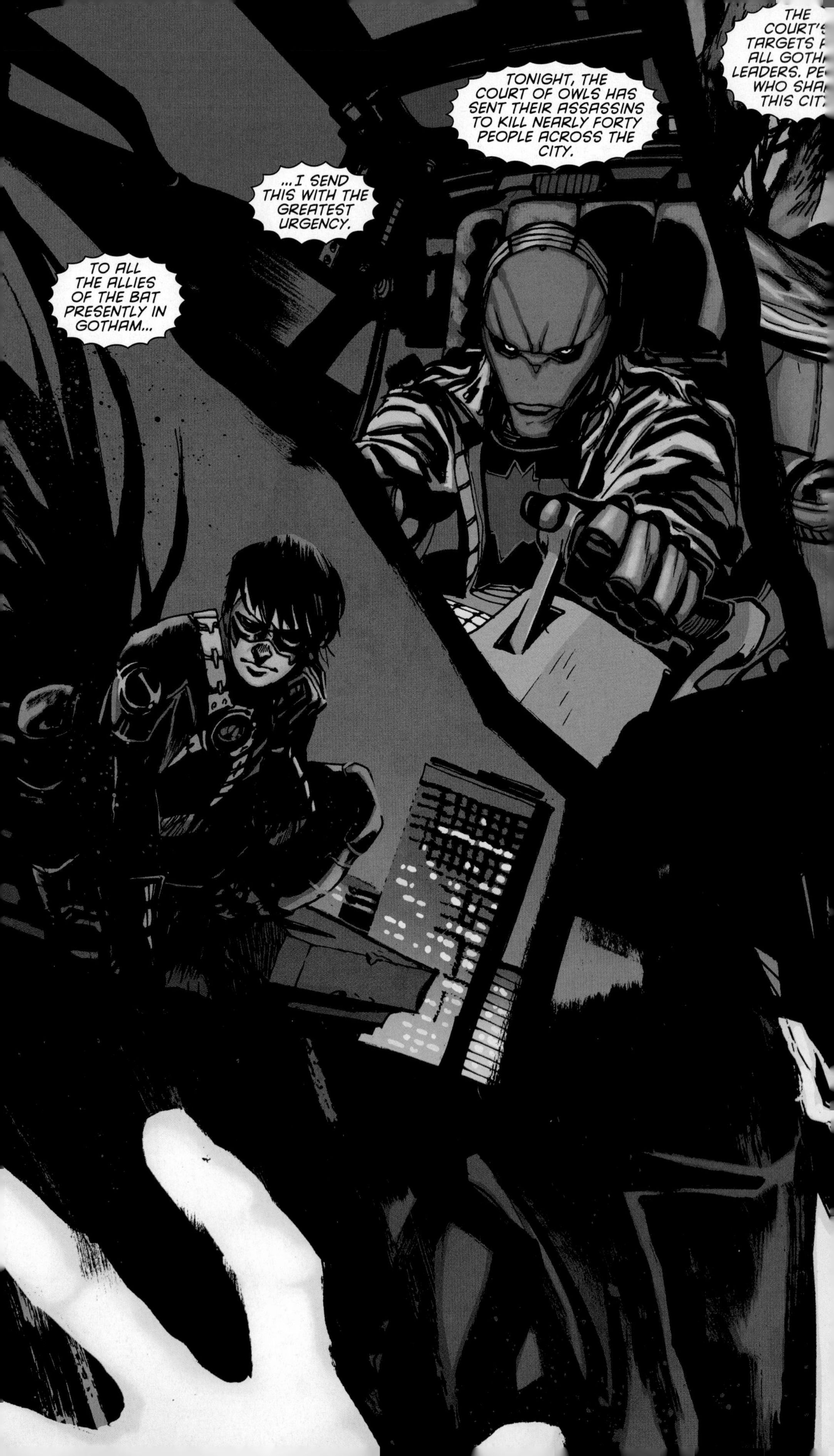
TO ALL THE ALLIES OF THE BAT PRESENTLY IN GOTHAM...
...I SEND THIS WITH THE GREATEST URGENCY.
TONIGHT, THE COURT OF OWLS HAS SENT THEIR ASSASSINS TO KILL NEARLY FORTY PEOPLE ACROSS THE CITY.
THE COURT'S TARGETS

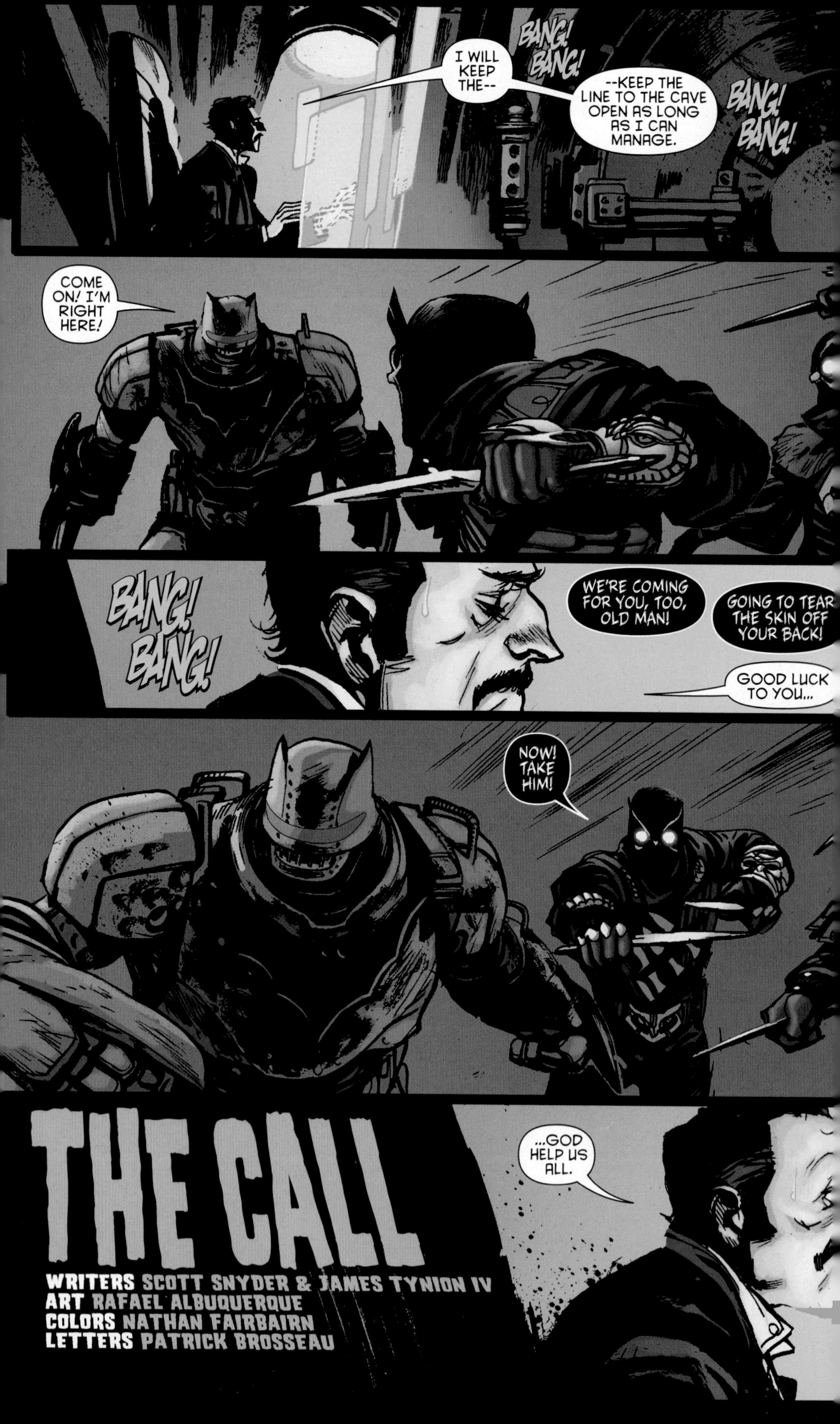
I WILL KEEP THE--
BANG! BANG!
--KEEP THE LINE TO THE CAVE OPEN AS LONG AS I CAN MANAGE.
BANG! BANG!
COME ON! I'M RIGHT HERE!
BANG! BANG!
WE'RE COMING FOR YOU, TOO, OLD MAN!
GOING TO TEAR THE SKIN OFF YOUR BACK!
GOOD LUCK TO YOU...
NOW! TAKE HIM!
THE CALL
...GOD HELP US ALL.
WRITERS SCOTT SNYDER & JAMES TYNION IV
ART RAFAEL ALBUQUERQUE
COLORS NATHAN FAIRBAIRN
LETTERS PATRICK BROSSEAU

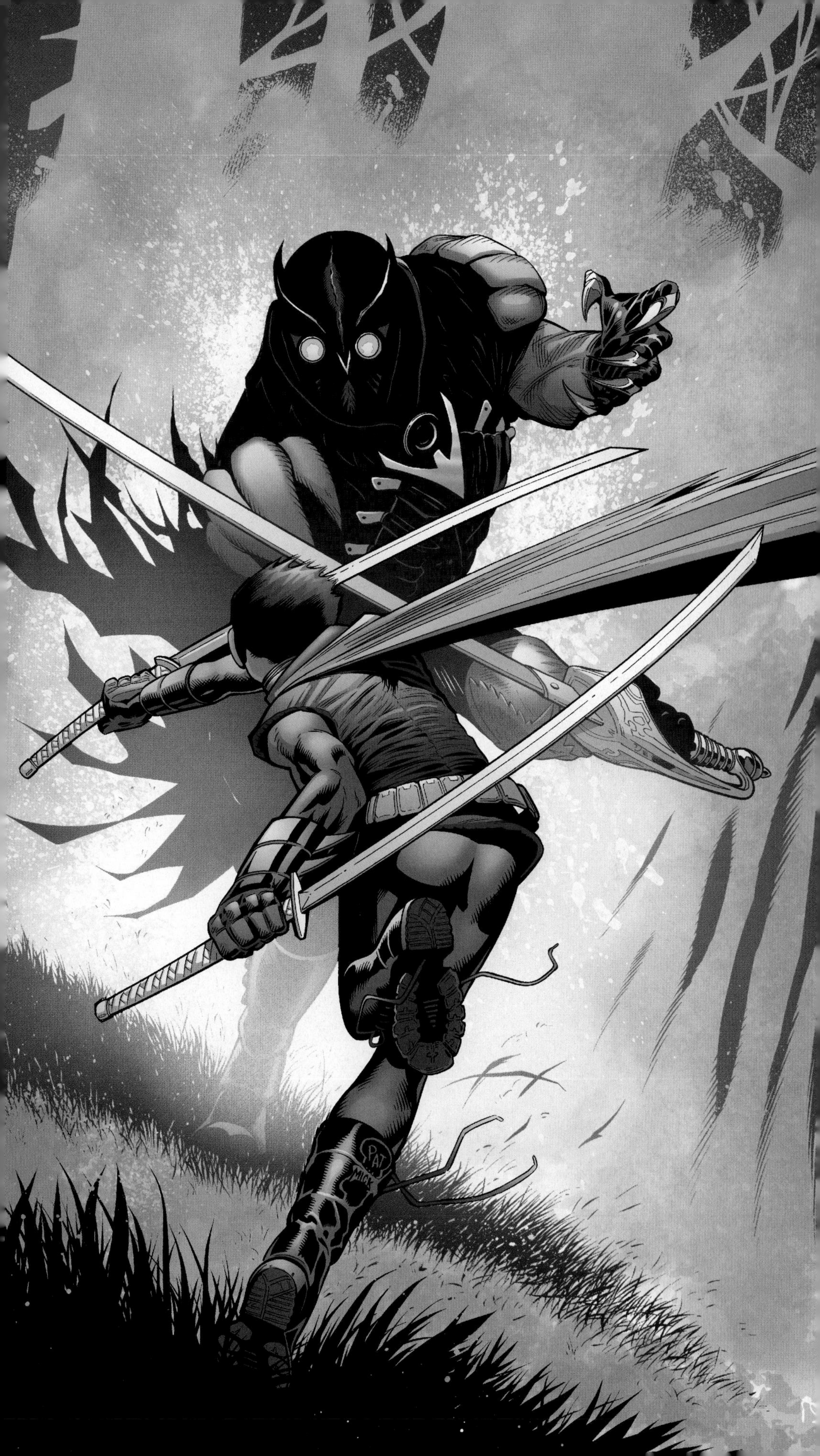
PAT
MICK

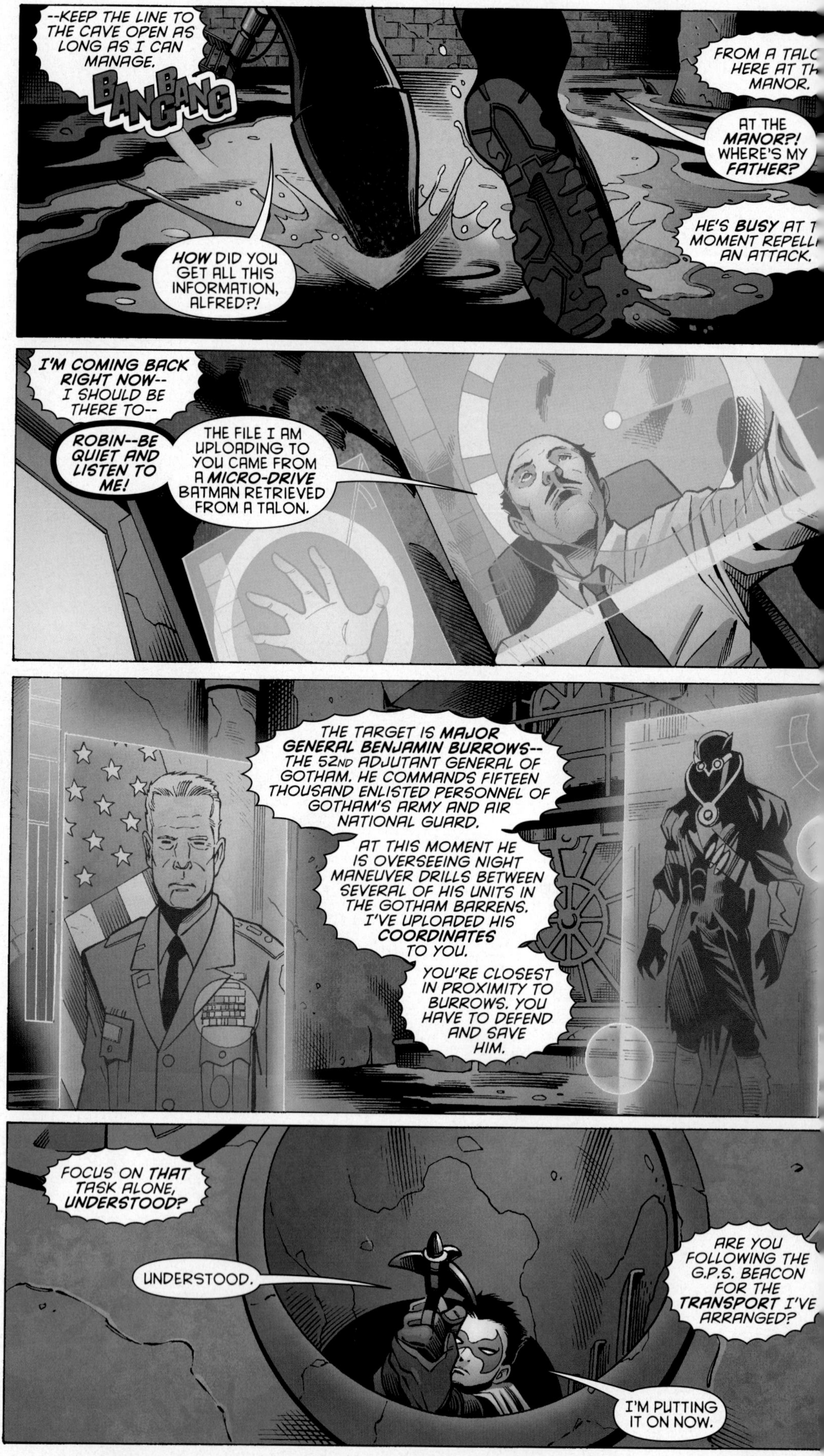
--KEEP THE LINE TO THE CAVE OPEN AS LONG AS I CAN MANAGE.
BANG BANG
FROM A TALC HERE AT TH MANOR.
HOW DID YOU GET ALL THIS INFORMATION, ALFRED?!
AT THE MANOR?! WHERE'S MY FATHER?
HE'S BUSY AT T MOMENT REPELLI AN ATTACK.
I'M COMING BACK RIGHT NOW-- I SHOULD BE THERE TO--
ROBIN--BE QUIET AND LISTEN TO ME!
THE FILE I AM UPLOADING TO YOU CAME FROM A MICRO-DRIVE BATMAN RETRIEVED FROM A TALON.
THE TARGET IS MAJOR GENERAL BENJAMIN BURROWS-- THE 52ND ADJUTANT GENERAL OF GOTHAM. HE COMMANDS FIFTEEN THOUSAND ENLISTED PERSONNEL OF GOTHAM'S ARMY AND AIR NATIONAL GUARD.
AT THIS MOMENT HE IS OVERSEEING NIGHT MANEUVER DRILLS BETWEEN SEVERAL OF HIS UNITS IN THE GOTHAM BARRENS. I'VE UPLOADED HIS COORDINATES TO YOU.
YOU'RE CLOSEST IN PROXIMITY TO BURROWS. YOU HAVE TO DEFEND AND SAVE HIM.
FOCUS ON THAT TASK ALONE, UNDERSTOOD?
UNDERSTOOD.
ARE YOU FOLLOWING THE G.P.S. BEACON FOR THE TRANSPORT I'VE ARRANGED?
I'M PUTTING IT ON NOW.

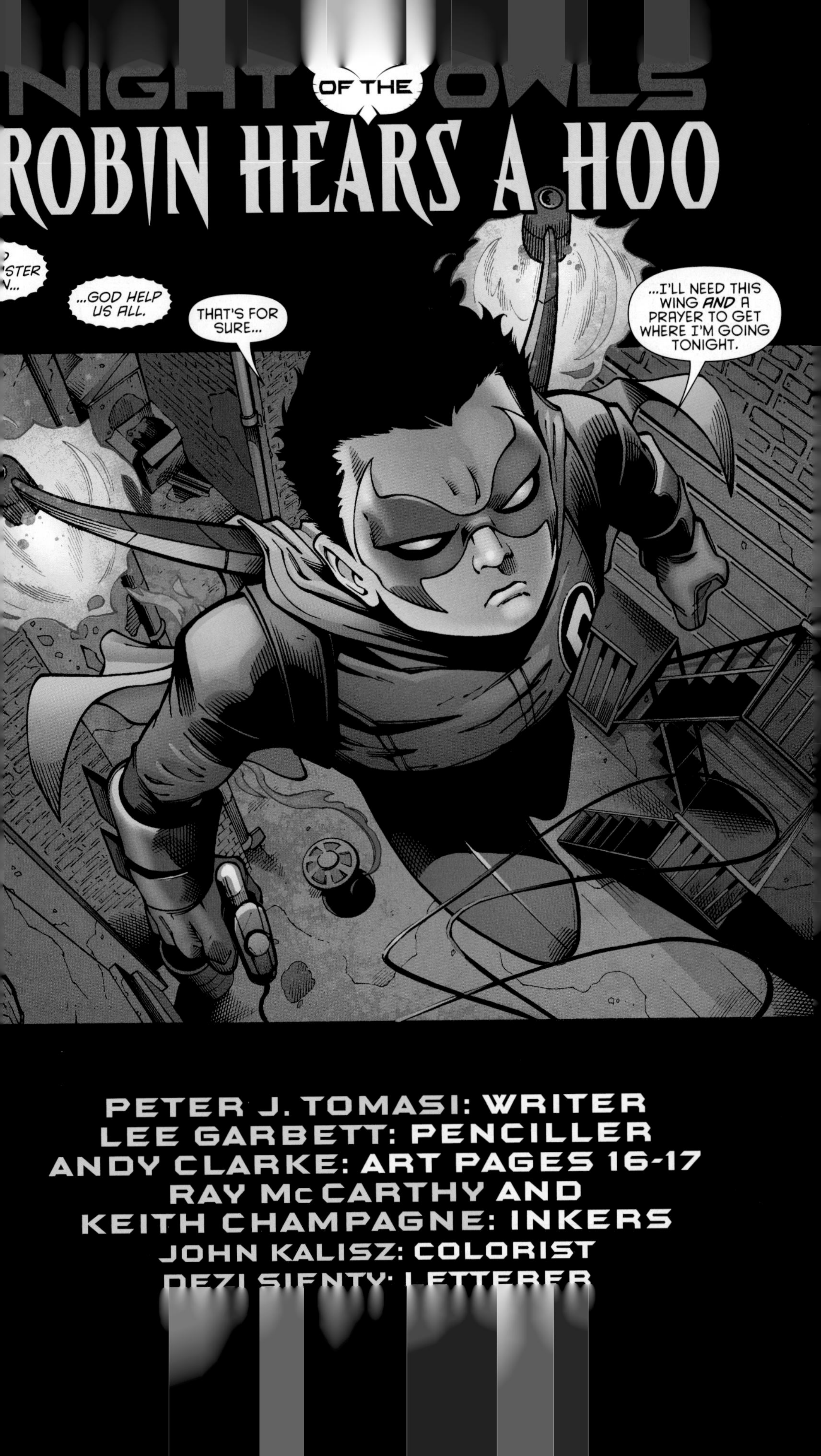
NIGHT OF THE OWLS
ROBIN HEARS A HOO
...GOD HELP US ALL.
THAT'S FOR SURE...
...I'LL NEED THIS WING AND A PRAYER TO GET WHERE I'M GOING TONIGHT.
PETER J. TOMASI: WRITER
LEE GARBETT: PENCILLER
ANDY CLARKE: ART PAGES 16-17
RAY McCARTHY AND
KEITH CHAMPAGNE: INKERS
JOHN KALISZ: COLORIST

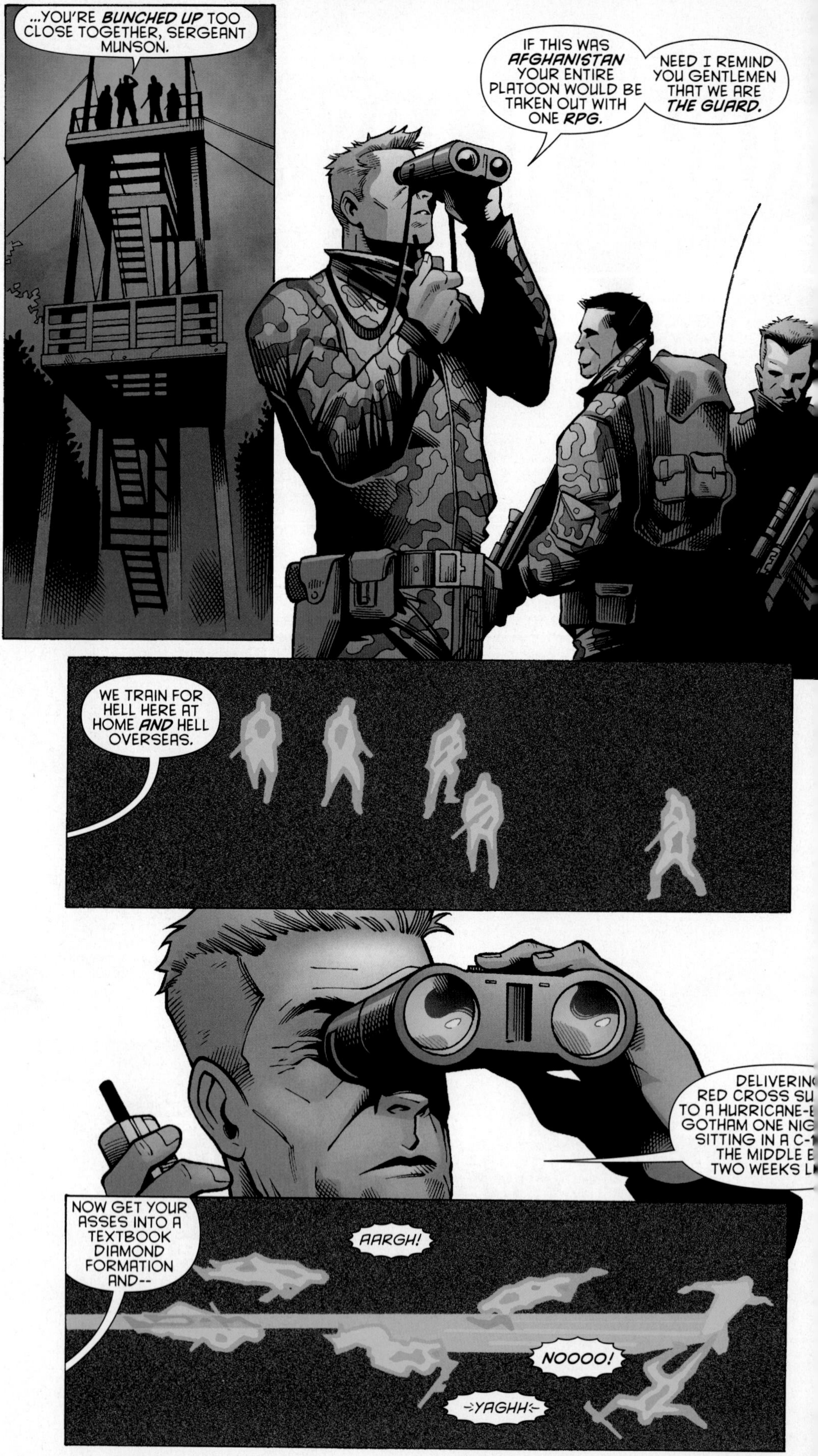
...YOU'RE BUNCHED UP TOO CLOSE TOGETHER, SERGEANT MUNSON.
IF THIS WAS AFGHANISTAN YOUR ENTIRE PLATOON WOULD BE TAKEN OUT WITH ONE RPG.
NEED I REMIND YOU GENTLEMEN THAT WE ARE THE GUARD.
WE TRAIN FOR HELL HERE AT HOME AND HELL OVERSEAS.
DELIVERIN
RED CROSS SU
TO A HURRICANE-
GOTHAM ONE NIG
SITTING IN A C-
THE MIDDLE
TWO WEEKS L
NOW GET YOUR ASSES INTO A TEXTBOOK DIAMOND FORMATION AND--
AARGH!
NOOOO!
YAGHH

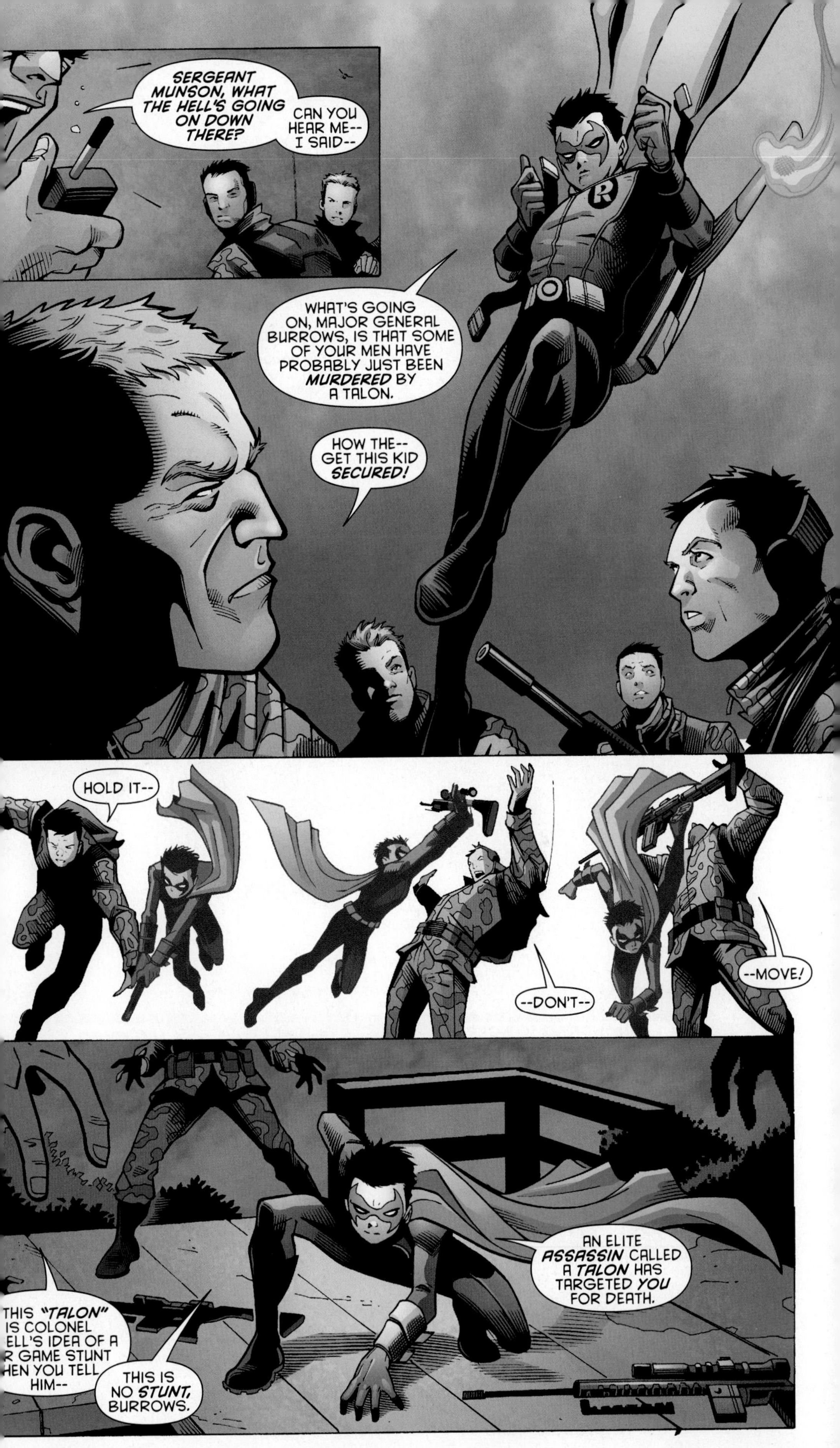
SERGEANT MUNSON, WHAT THE HELL'S GOING ON DOWN THERE?
CAN YOU HEAR ME-- I SAID--
WHAT'S GOING ON, MAJOR GENERAL BURROWS, IS THAT SOME OF YOUR MEN HAVE PROBABLY JUST BEEN MURDERED BY A TALON.
HOW THE-- GET THIS KID SECURED!
HOLD IT--
--DON'T--
--MOVE!
AN ELITE ASSASSIN CALLED A TALON HAS TARGETED YOU FOR DEATH.
THIS "TALON" IS COLONEL
THIS IS NO STUNT, BURROWS.

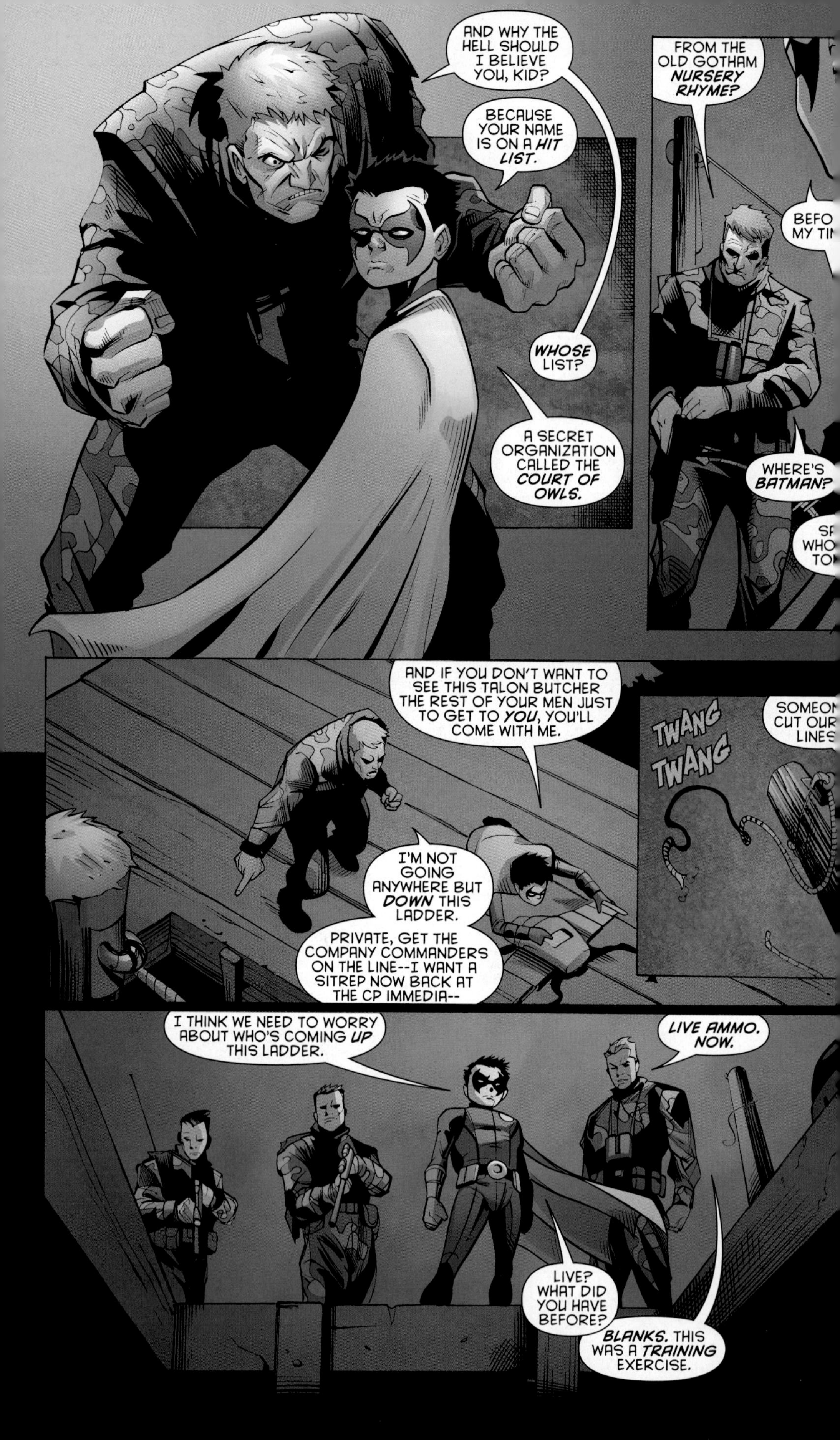
AND WHY THE HELL SHOULD I BELIEVE YOU, KID?
BECAUSE YOUR NAME IS ON A HIT LIST.
WHOSE LIST?
A SECRET ORGANIZATION CALLED THE COURT OF OWLS.
FROM THE OLD GOTHAM NURSERY RHYME?
WHERE'S BATMAN?
AND IF YOU DON'T WANT TO SEE THIS TALON BUTCHER THE REST OF YOUR MEN JUST TO GET TO YOU, YOU'LL COME WITH ME.
I'M NOT GOING ANYWHERE BUT DOWN THIS LADDER.
PRIVATE, GET THE COMPANY COMMANDERS ON THE LINE--I WANT A SITREP NOW BACK AT THE CP IMMEDIA--
TWANG
TWANG
I THINK WE NEED TO WORRY ABOUT WHO'S COMING UP THIS LADDER.
LIVE AMMO. NOW.
LIVE? WHAT DID YOU HAVE BEFORE?
BLANKS. THIS WAS A TRAINING EXERCISE.

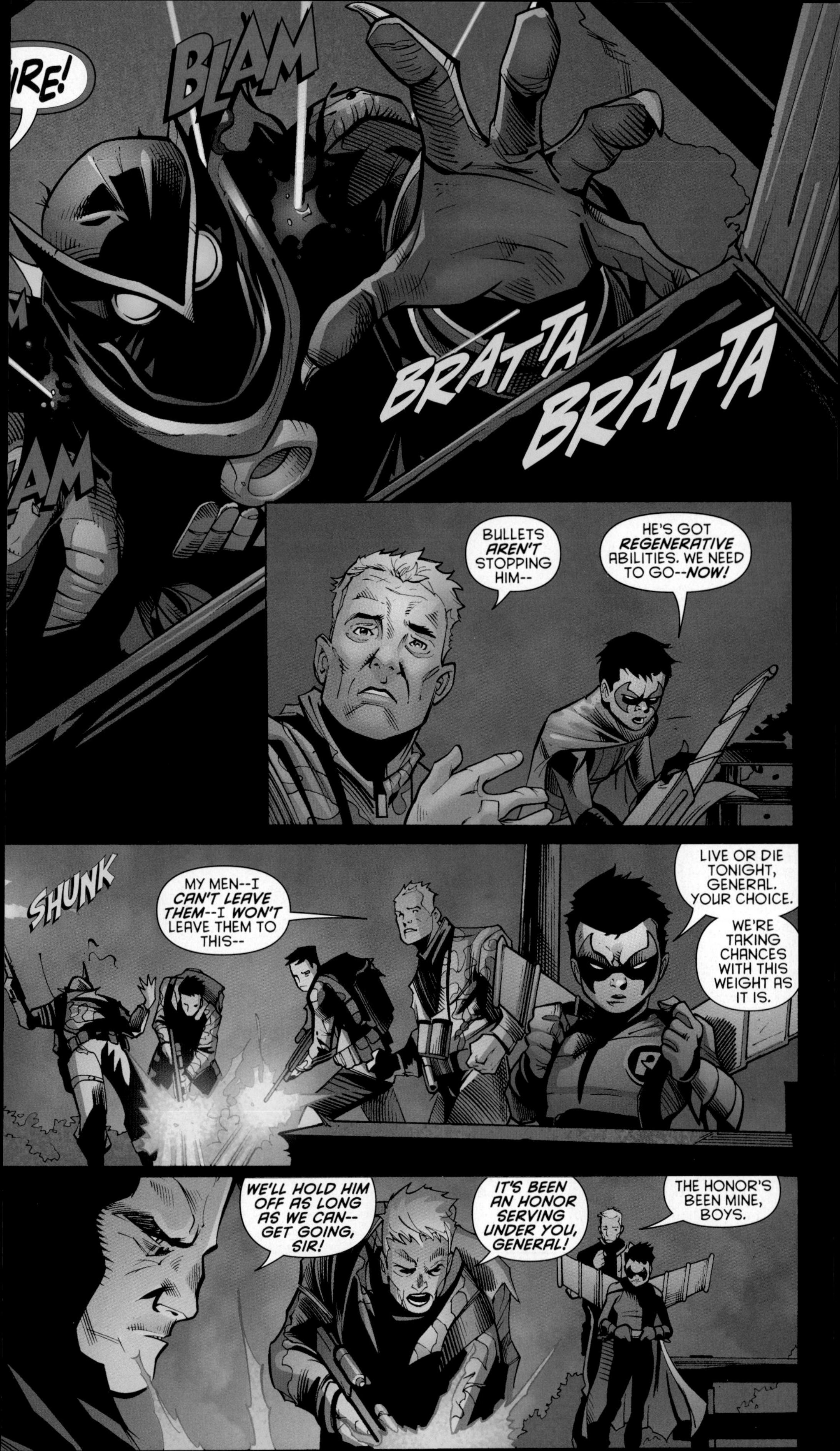
IRE!
BLAM
BRATTA BRATTA
BULLETS AREN'T STOPPING HIM--
HE'S GOT REGENERATIVE ABILITIES. WE NEED TO GO--NOW!
SHUNK
MY MEN--I CAN'T LEAVE THEM--I WON'T LEAVE THEM TO THIS--
LIVE OR DIE TONIGHT, GENERAL. YOUR CHOICE.
WE'RE TAKING CHANCES WITH THIS WEIGHT AS IT IS.
WE'LL HOLD HIM OFF AS LONG AS WE CAN-- GET GOING, SIR!
IT'S BEEN AN HONOR SERVING UNDER YOU, GENERAL!
THE HONOR'S BEEN MINE, BOYS.

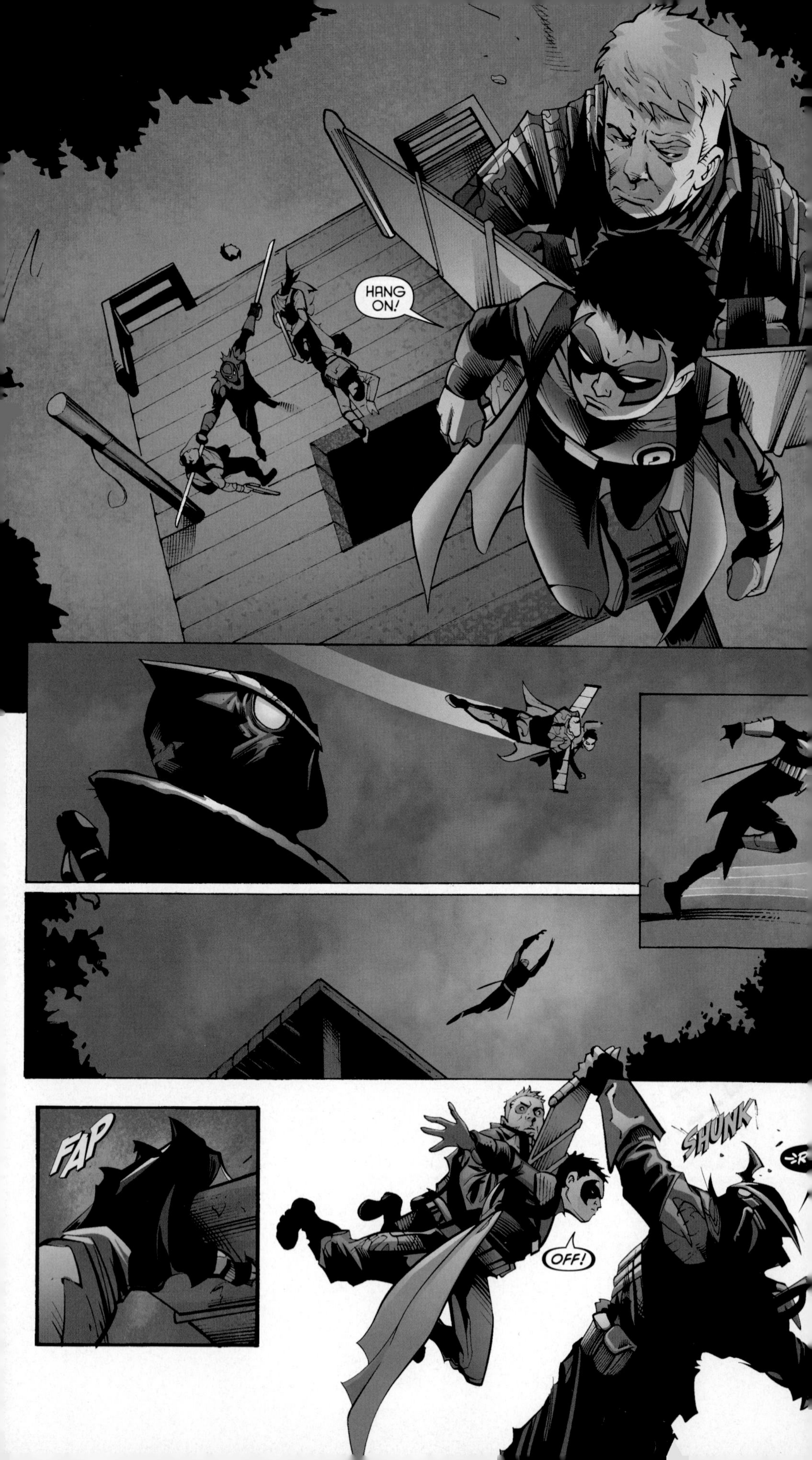
HANG ON!
FAP
SHUNK
OFF!

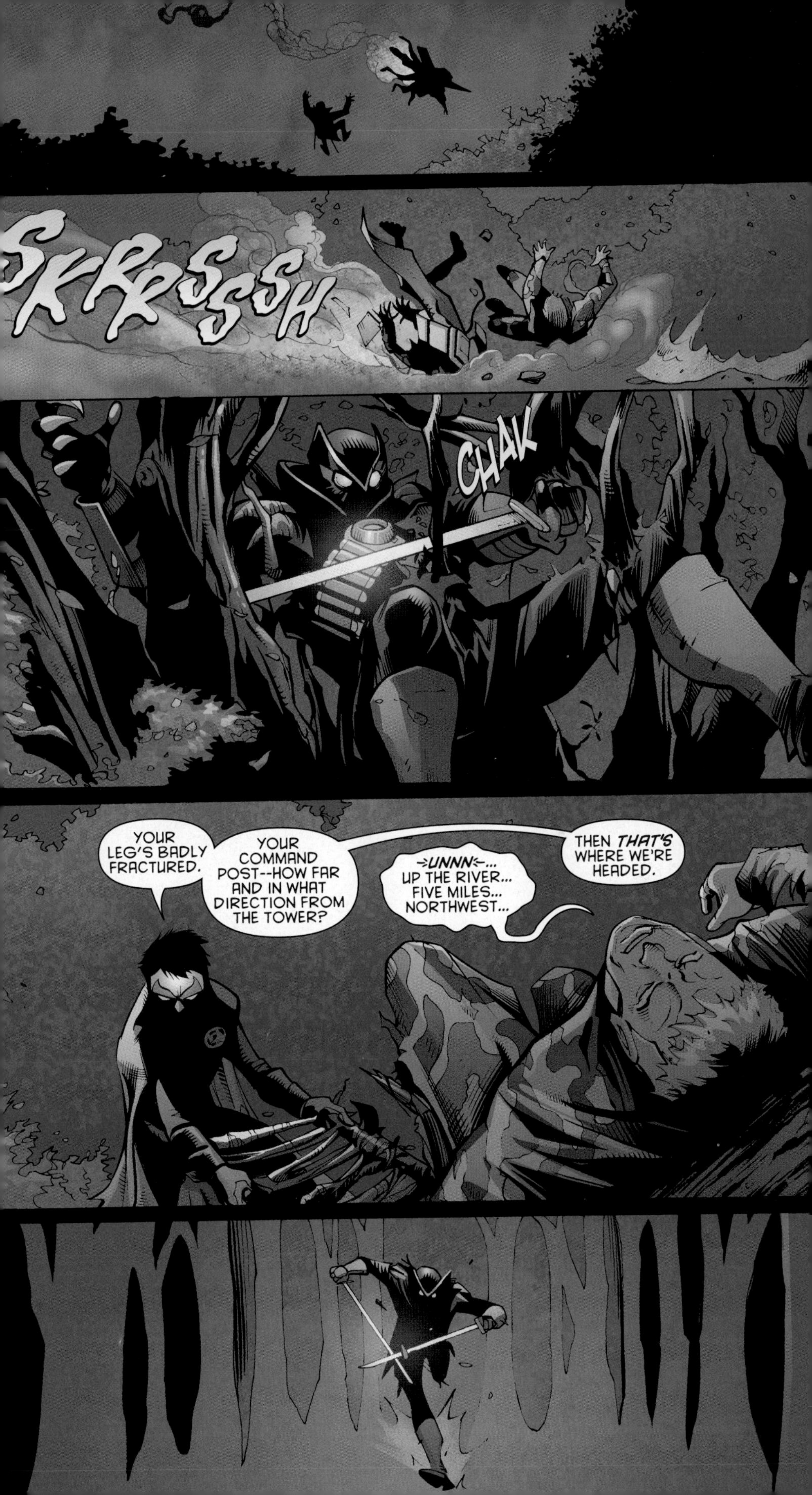
SKRSSSH
CHAK
YOUR LEG'S BADLY FRACTURED.
YOUR COMMAND POST--HOW FAR AND IN WHAT DIRECTION FROM THE TOWER?
-UNNN-... UP THE RIVER... FIVE MILES... NORTHWEST...
THEN *THAT'S* WHERE WE'RE HEADED.

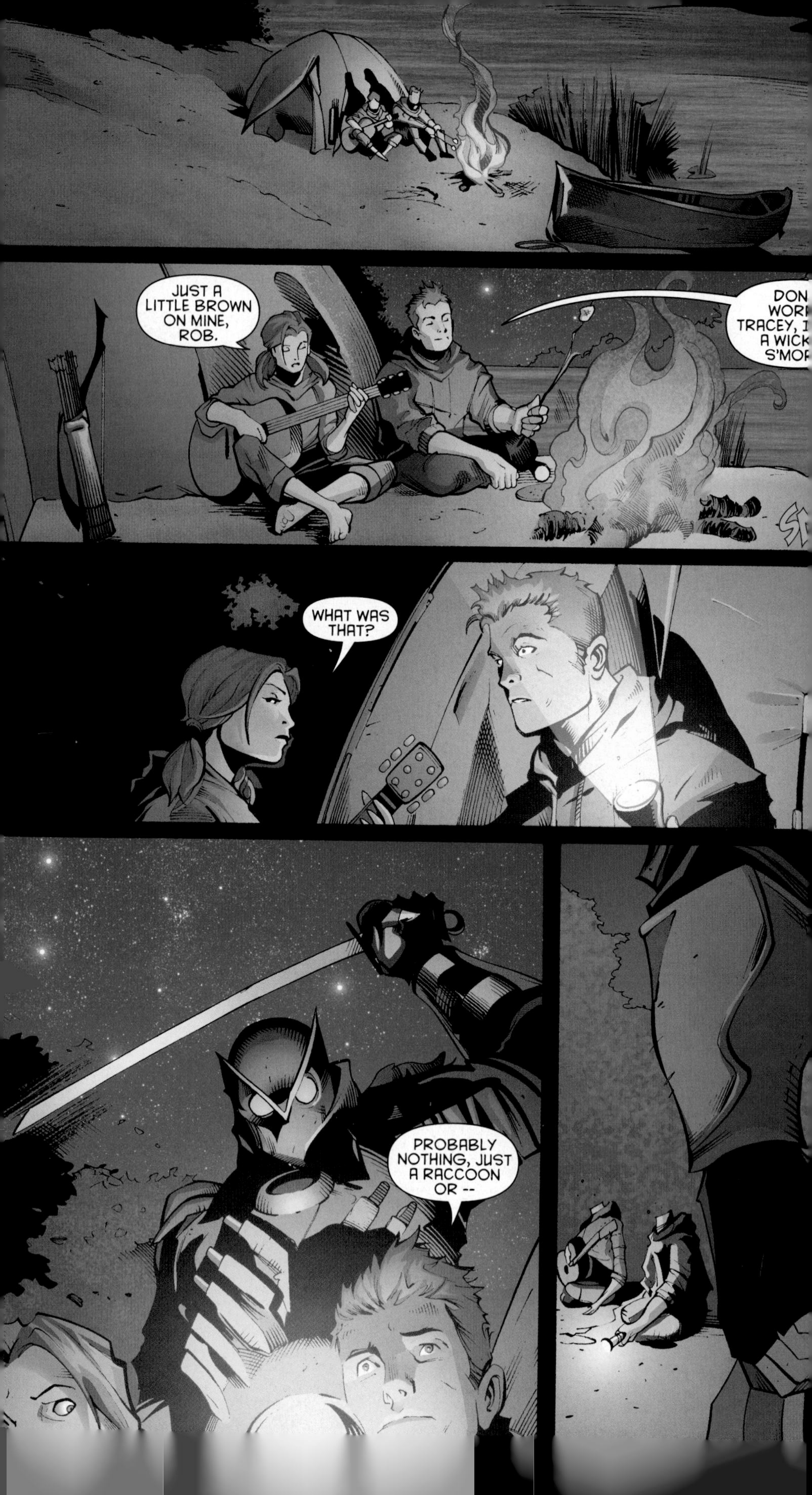
JUST A LITTLE BROWN ON MINE, ROB.
WHAT WAS THAT?
PROBABLY NOTHING, JUST A RACCOON OR --

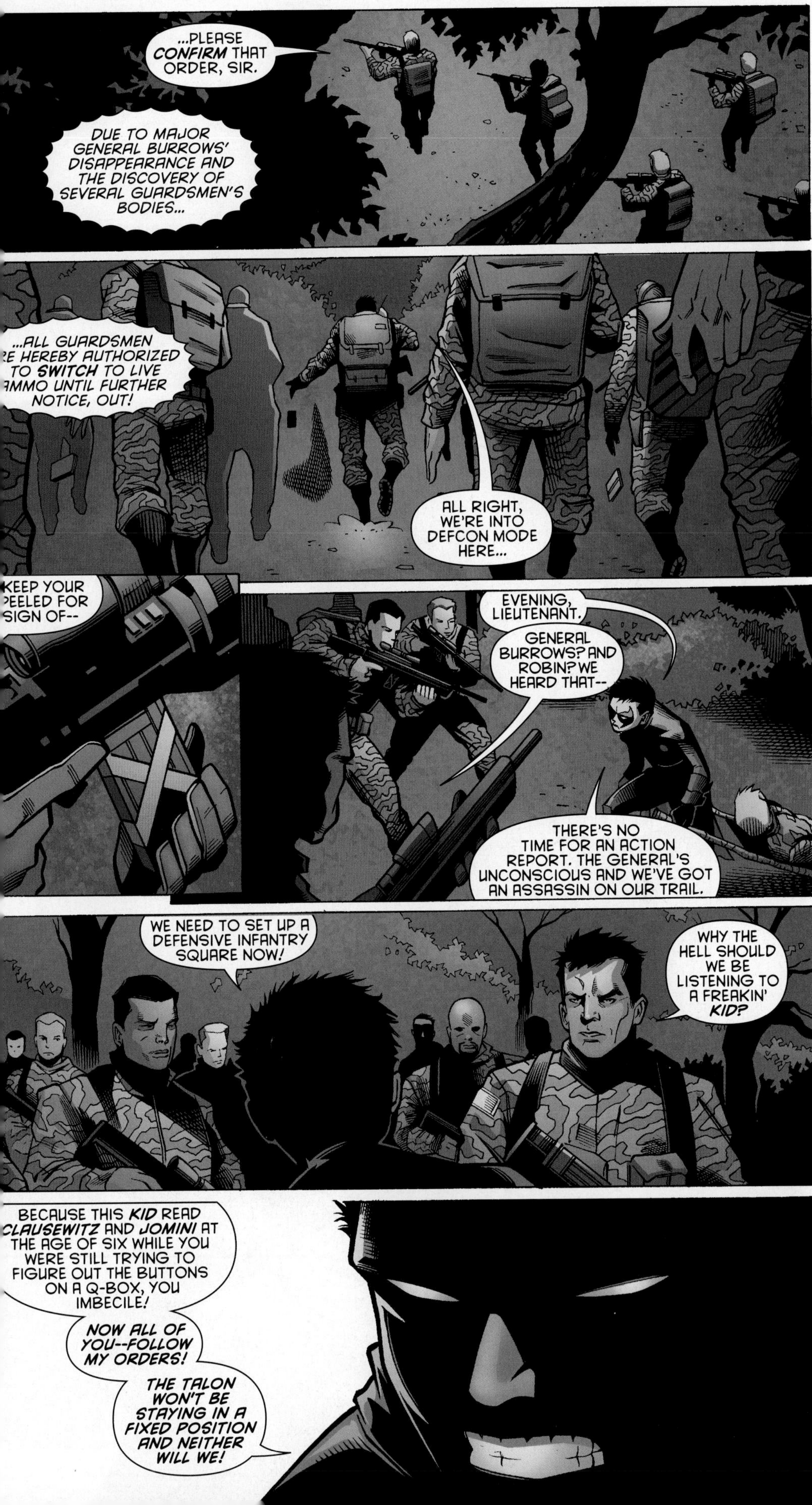
...PLEASE CONFIRM THAT ORDER, SIR.
DUE TO MAJOR GENERAL BURROWS' DISAPPEARANCE AND THE DISCOVERY OF SEVERAL GUARDSMEN'S BODIES...
...ALL GUARDSMEN ARE HEREBY AUTHORIZED TO SWITCH TO LIVE AMMO UNTIL FURTHER NOTICE, OUT!
ALL RIGHT, WE'RE INTO DEFCON MODE HERE...
KEEP YOUR PEELED FOR SIGN OF--
EVENING, LIEUTENANT.
GENERAL BURROWS? AND ROBIN? WE HEARD THAT--
THERE'S NO TIME FOR AN ACTION REPORT. THE GENERAL'S UNCONSCIOUS AND WE'VE GOT AN ASSASSIN ON OUR TRAIL.
WE NEED TO SET UP A DEFENSIVE INFANTRY SQUARE NOW!
WHY THE HELL SHOULD WE BE LISTENING TO A FREAKIN' KID?
BECAUSE THIS KID READ CLAUSEWITZ AND JOMINI AT THE AGE OF SIX WHILE YOU WERE STILL TRYING TO FIGURE OUT THE BUTTONS ON A Q-BOX, YOU IMBECILE!
NOW ALL OF YOU--FOLLOW MY ORDERS!
THE TALON WON'T BE STAYING IN A FIXED POSITION AND NEITHER WILL WE!

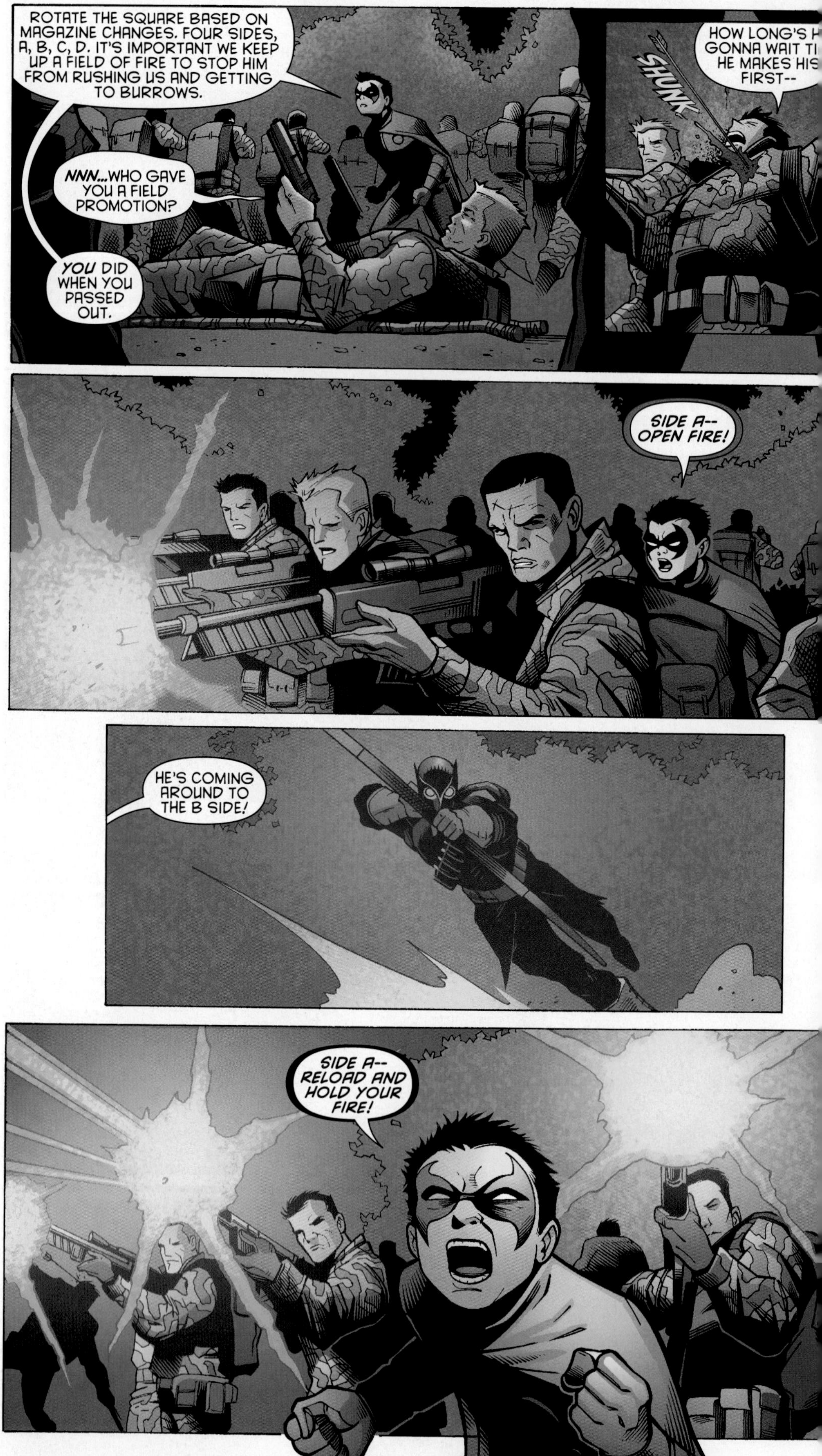
ROTATE THE SQUARE BASED ON MAGAZINE CHANGES. FOUR SIDES, A, B, C, D. IT'S IMPORTANT WE KEEP UP A FIELD OF FIRE TO STOP HIM FROM RUSHING US AND GETTING TO BURROWS.
NNN...WHO GAVE YOU A FIELD PROMOTION?
YOU DID WHEN YOU PASSED OUT.
SHUNK
SIDE A-- OPEN FIRE!
HE'S COMING AROUND TO THE B SIDE!
SIDE A-- RELOAD AND HOLD YOUR FIRE!

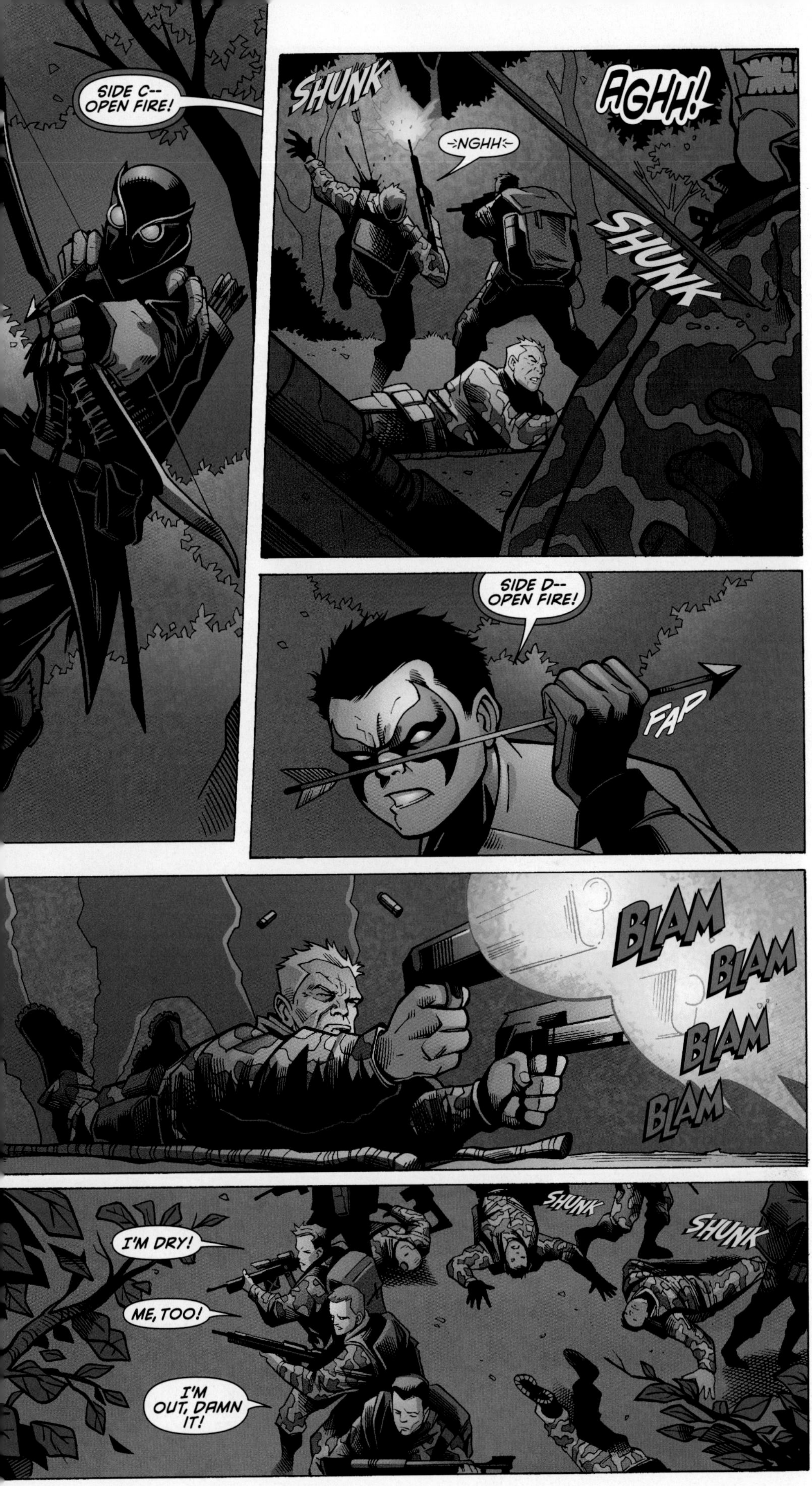
SIDE C-- OPEN FIRE!
SHUNK
-NGHH-
AGHH!
SHUNK
SIDE D-- OPEN FIRE!
FAP
BLAM
BLAM
BLAM
BLAM
I'M DRY!
ME, TOO!
I'M OUT, DAMN IT!
SHUNK
SHUNK

THERE'S ONLY ONE THING LEFT WHEN THE AMMO RUNS OUT, KID.
I KNOW.
FIX BAYONETS.
CHARGE!
HOW PERFECTLY PROPER.

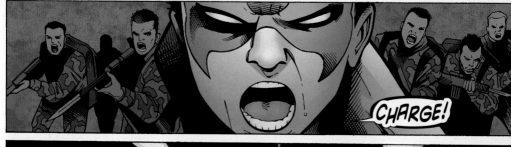

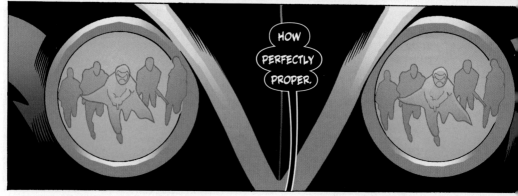

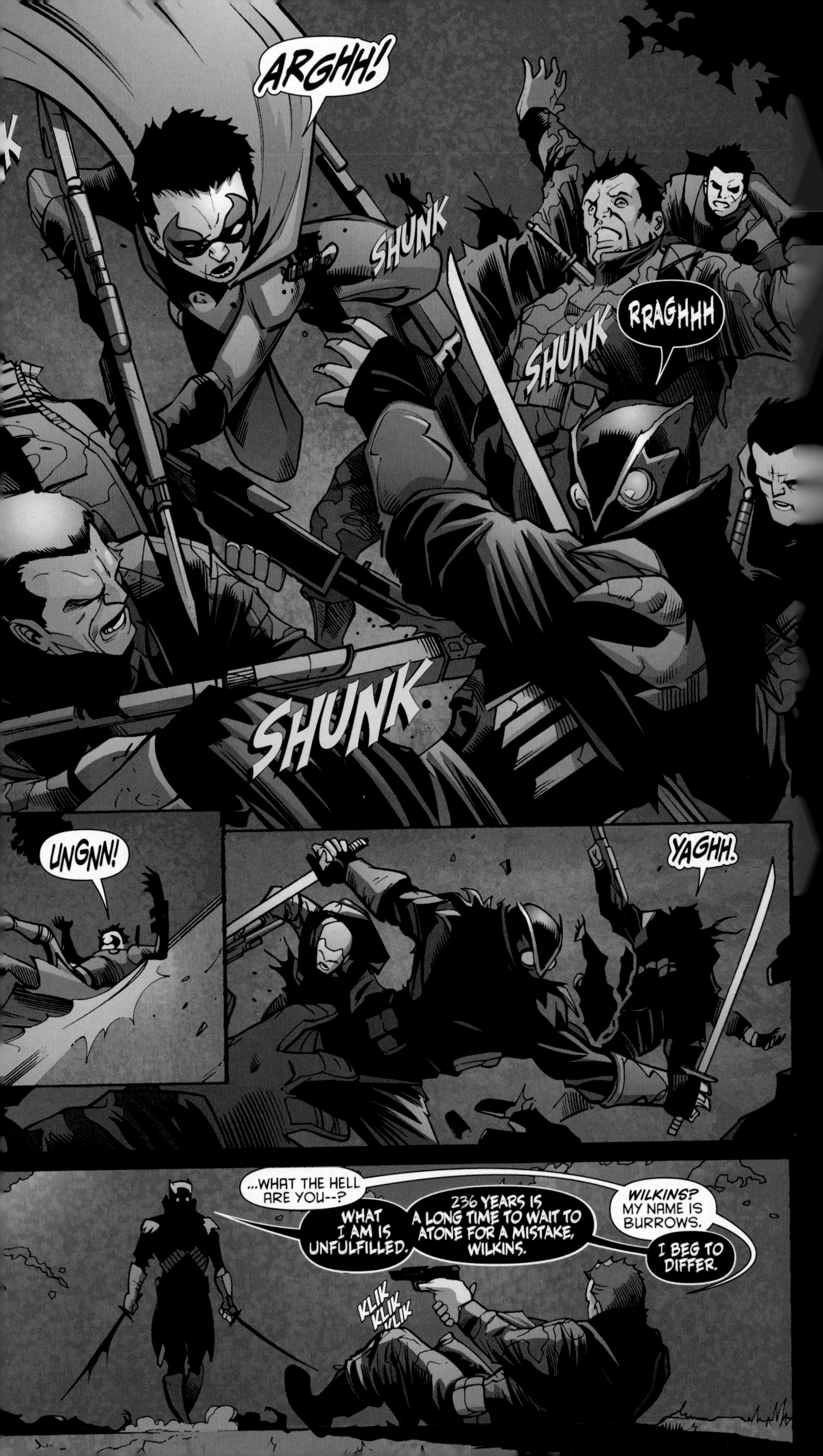
ARGHH!
SHUNK
SHUNK
RRAGHHH
SHUNK
UNGNN!
YAGHH.
...WHAT THE HELL ARE YOU--?
WHAT I AM IS UNFULFILLED.
236 YEARS IS A LONG TIME TO WAIT TO ATONE FOR A MISTAKE, WILKINS.
WILKINS? MY NAME IS BURROWS.
I BEG TO DIFFER.
KLIK KLIK KLIK

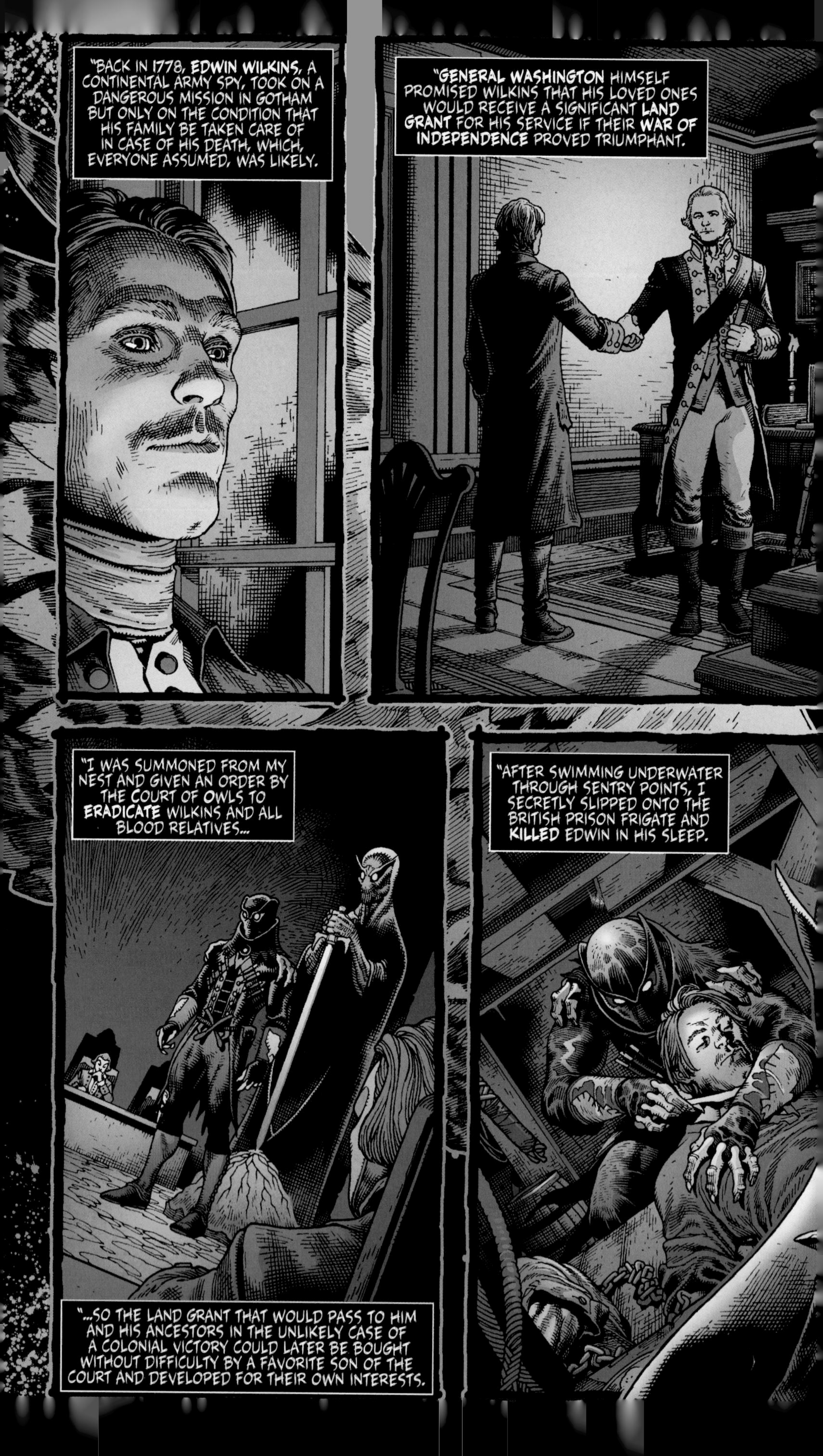
"BACK IN 1778, EDWIN WILKINS, A CONTINENTAL ARMY SPY, TOOK ON A DANGEROUS MISSION IN GOTHAM BUT ONLY ON THE CONDITION THAT HIS FAMILY BE TAKEN CARE OF IN CASE OF HIS DEATH, WHICH, EVERYONE ASSUMED, WAS LIKELY.
"GENERAL WASHINGTON HIMSELF PROMISED WILKINS THAT HIS LOVED ONES WOULD RECEIVE A SIGNIFICANT LAND GRANT FOR HIS SERVICE IF THEIR WAR OF INDEPENDENCE PROVED TRIUMPHANT.
"I WAS SUMMONED FROM MY NEST AND GIVEN AN ORDER BY THE COURT OF OWLS TO ERADICATE WILKINS AND ALL BLOOD RELATIVES...
"...SO THE LAND GRANT THAT WOULD PASS TO HIM AND HIS ANCESTORS IN THE UNLIKELY CASE OF A COLONIAL VICTORY COULD LATER BE BOUGHT WITHOUT DIFFICULTY BY A FAVORITE SON OF THE COURT AND DEVELOPED FOR THEIR OWN INTERESTS.
"AFTER SWIMMING UNDERWATER THROUGH SENTRY POINTS, I SECRETLY SLIPPED ONTO THE BRITISH PRISON FRIGATE AND KILLED EDWIN IN HIS SLEEP.

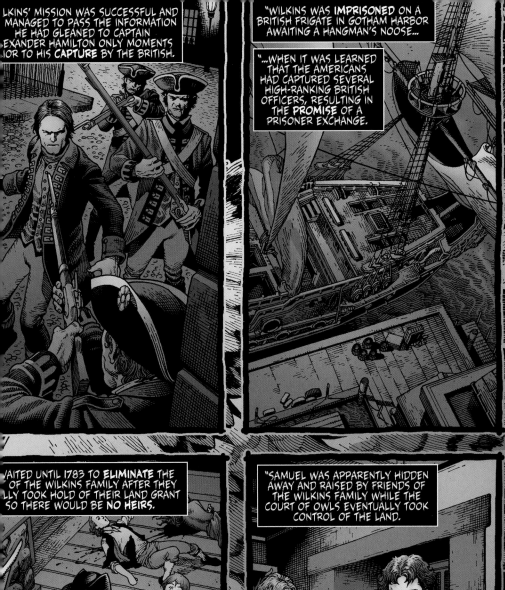

[W]ILKINS' MISSION WAS SUCCESSFUL AND MANAGED TO PASS THE INFORMATION HE HAD GLEANED TO CAPTAIN [AL]EXANDER HAMILTON ONLY MOMENTS [PR]IOR TO HIS **CAPTURE** BY THE BRITISH.

"WILKINS WAS **IMPRISONED** ON A BRITISH FRIGATE IN GOTHAM HARBOR AWAITING A HANGMAN'S NOOSE...

"...WHEN IT WAS LEARNED THAT THE AMERICANS HAD CAPTURED SEVERAL HIGH-RANKING BRITISH OFFICERS, RESULTING IN THE **PROMISE** OF A PRISONER EXCHANGE.

[W]AITED UNTIL 1783 TO **ELIMINATE** THE [REST] OF THE WILKINS FAMILY AFTER THEY [FINA]LLY TOOK HOLD OF THEIR LAND GRANT [SO] THERE WOULD BE **NO HEIRS.**

"EDWIN WILKINS' YOUNGEST SON, SAMUEL, SOMEHOW **SURVIVED** THE GRIEVOUS WOUNDS I INFLICTED UPON HIM.

"SAMUEL WAS APPARENTLY HIDDEN AWAY AND RAISED BY FRIENDS OF THE WILKINS FAMILY WHILE THE COURT OF OWLS EVENTUALLY TOOK CONTROL OF THE LAND.

"THIS FAMILY'S SURNAME WAS BURROWS."

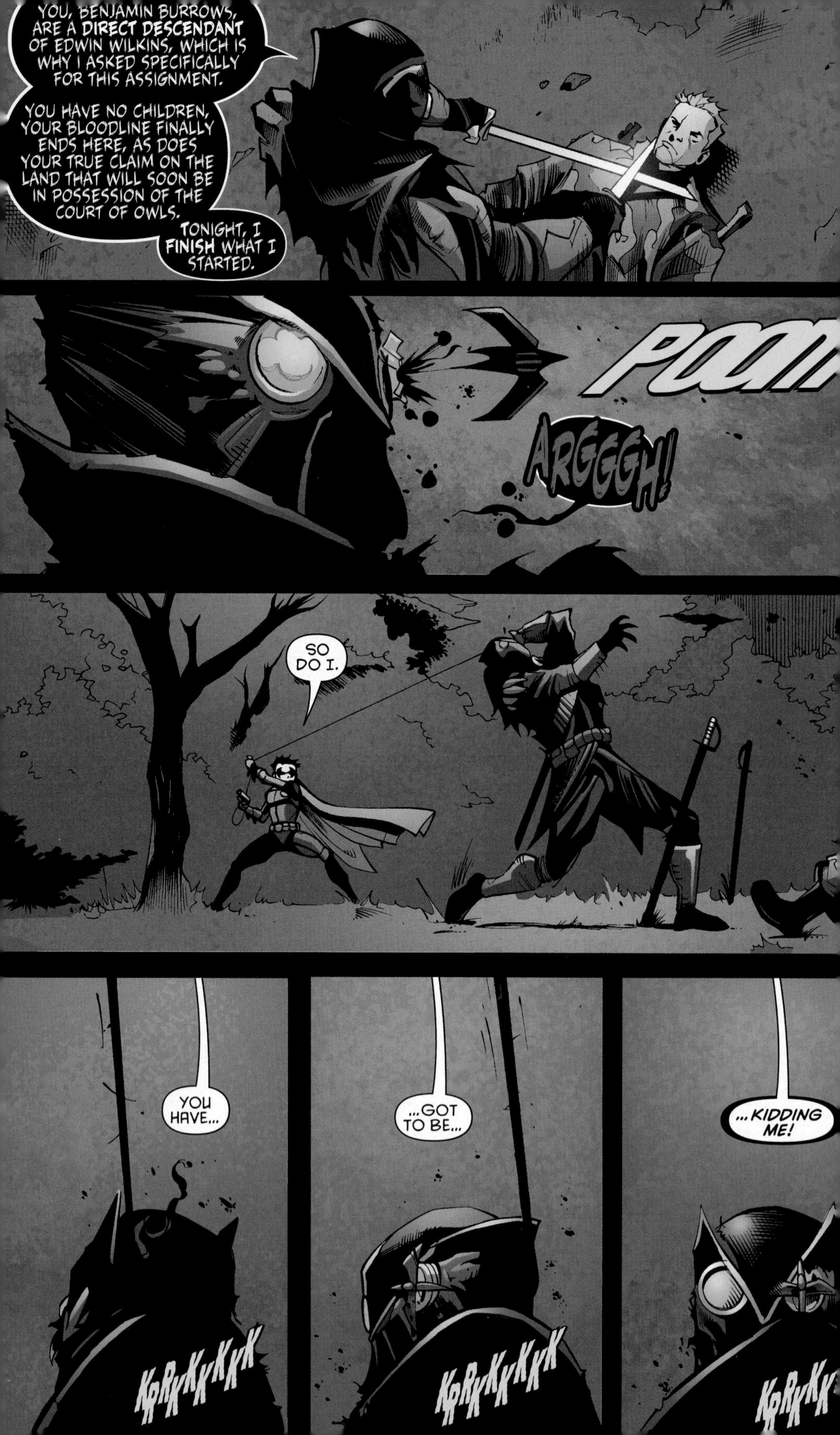

YOU, BENJAMIN BURROWS, ARE A DIRECT DESCENDANT OF EDWIN WILKINS, WHICH IS WHY I ASKED SPECIFICALLY FOR THIS ASSIGNMENT.
YOU HAVE NO CHILDREN, YOUR BLOODLINE FINALLY ENDS HERE, AS DOES YOUR TRUE CLAIM ON THE LAND THAT WILL SOON BE IN POSSESSION OF THE COURT OF OWLS.
TONIGHT, I FINISH WHAT I STARTED.
POOM
ARGGGH!
SO DO I.
YOU HAVE...
KRRKKKKKK
...GOT TO BE...
KRRKKKKKK
...KIDDING ME!
KRRKK

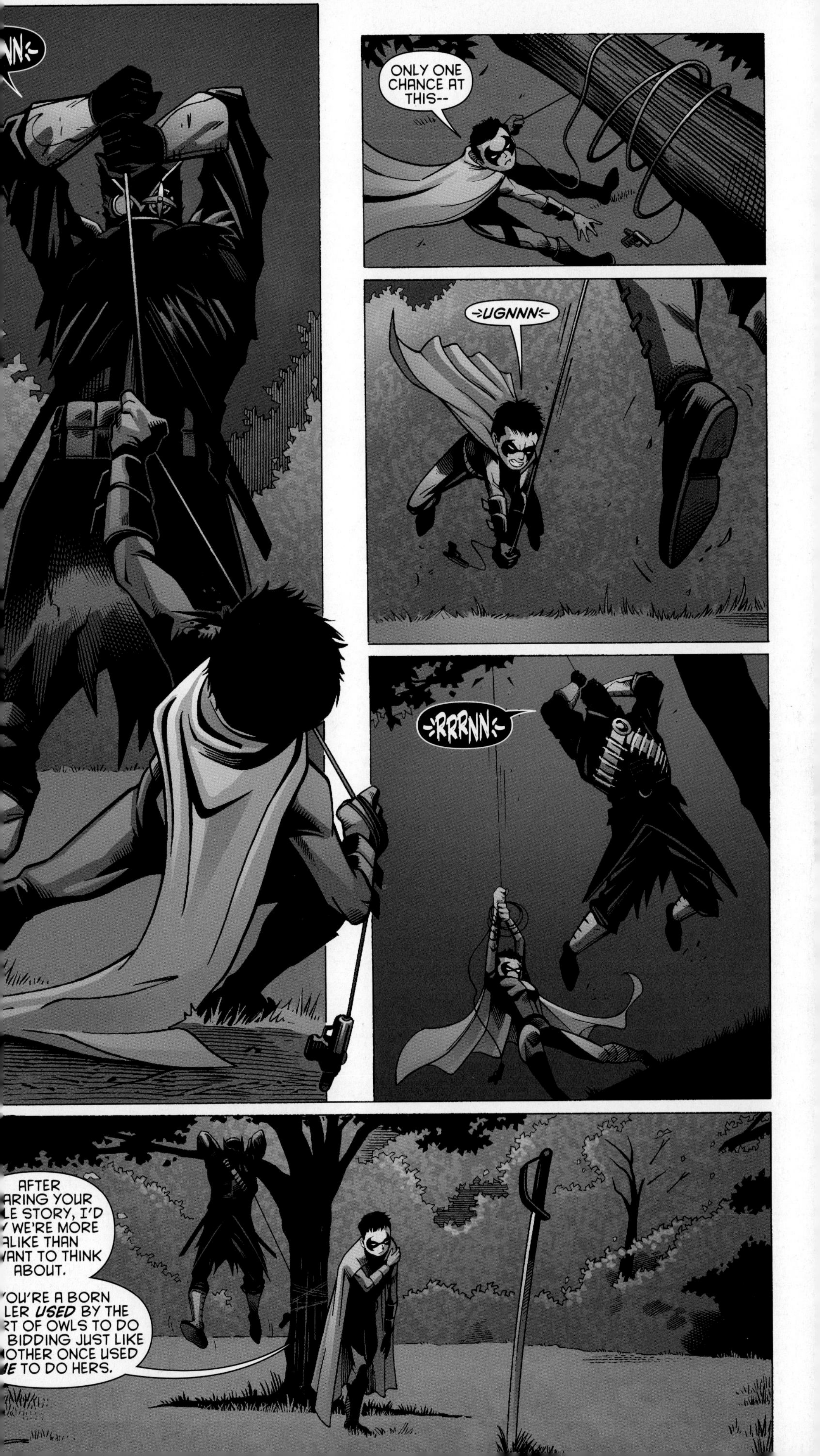

NN
ONLY ONE CHANCE AT THIS--
UGNNN
RRRNN
AFTER
ARING YOUR
LE STORY, I'D
WE'RE MORE
ALIKE THAN
WANT TO THINK
ABOUT.
YOU'RE A BORN
LER USED BY THE
RT OF OWLS TO DO
BIDDING JUST LIKE
OTHER ONCE USED
E TO DO HERS.

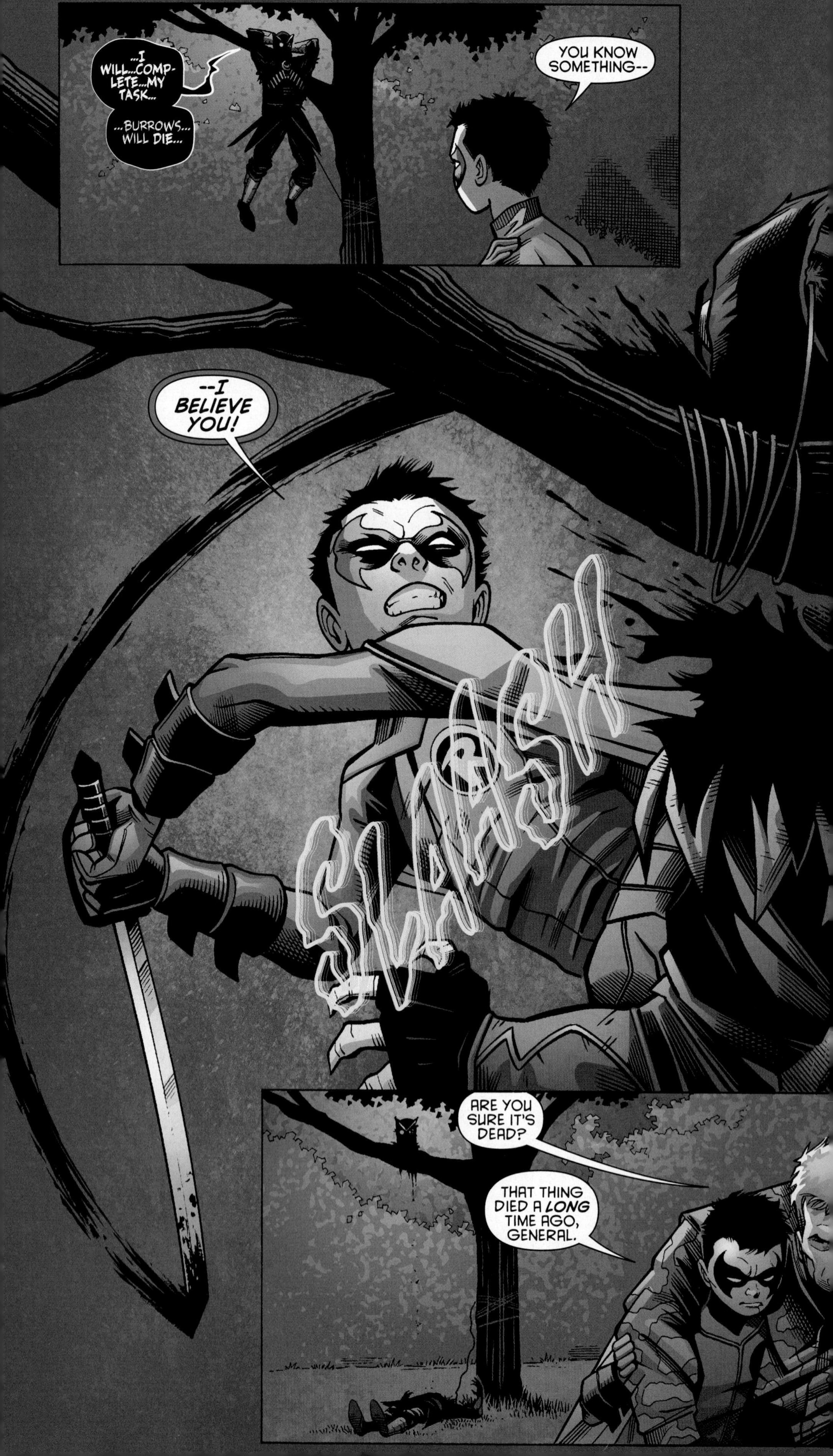

...I WILL...COMP-LETE...MY TASK...
...BURROWS... WILL DIE...
YOU KNOW SOMETHING--
--I BELIEVE YOU!
SLASH
ARE YOU SURE IT'S DEAD?
THAT THING DIED A LONG TIME AGO, GENERAL.

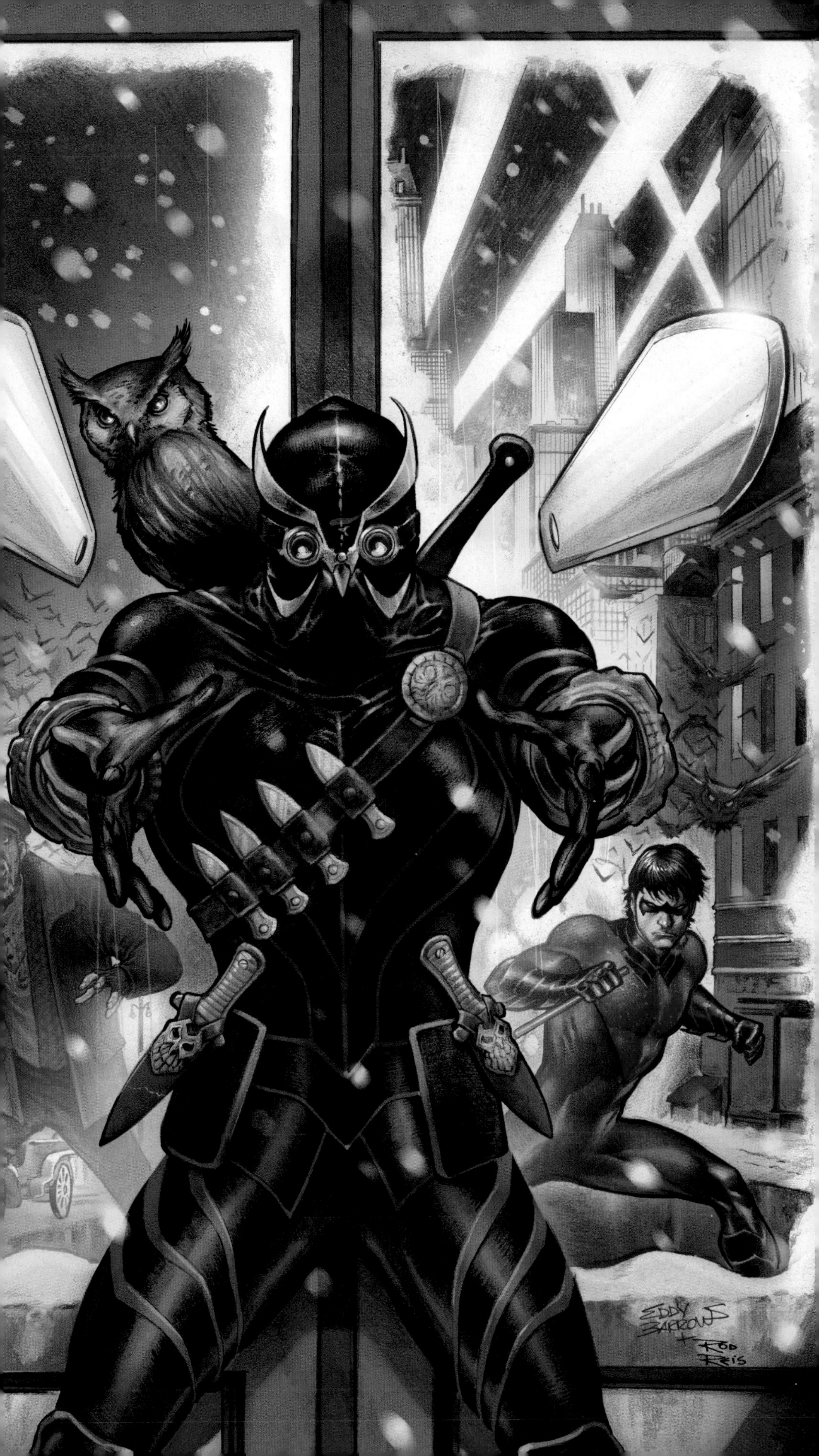
EDDY BARROWS
+ ROD REIS

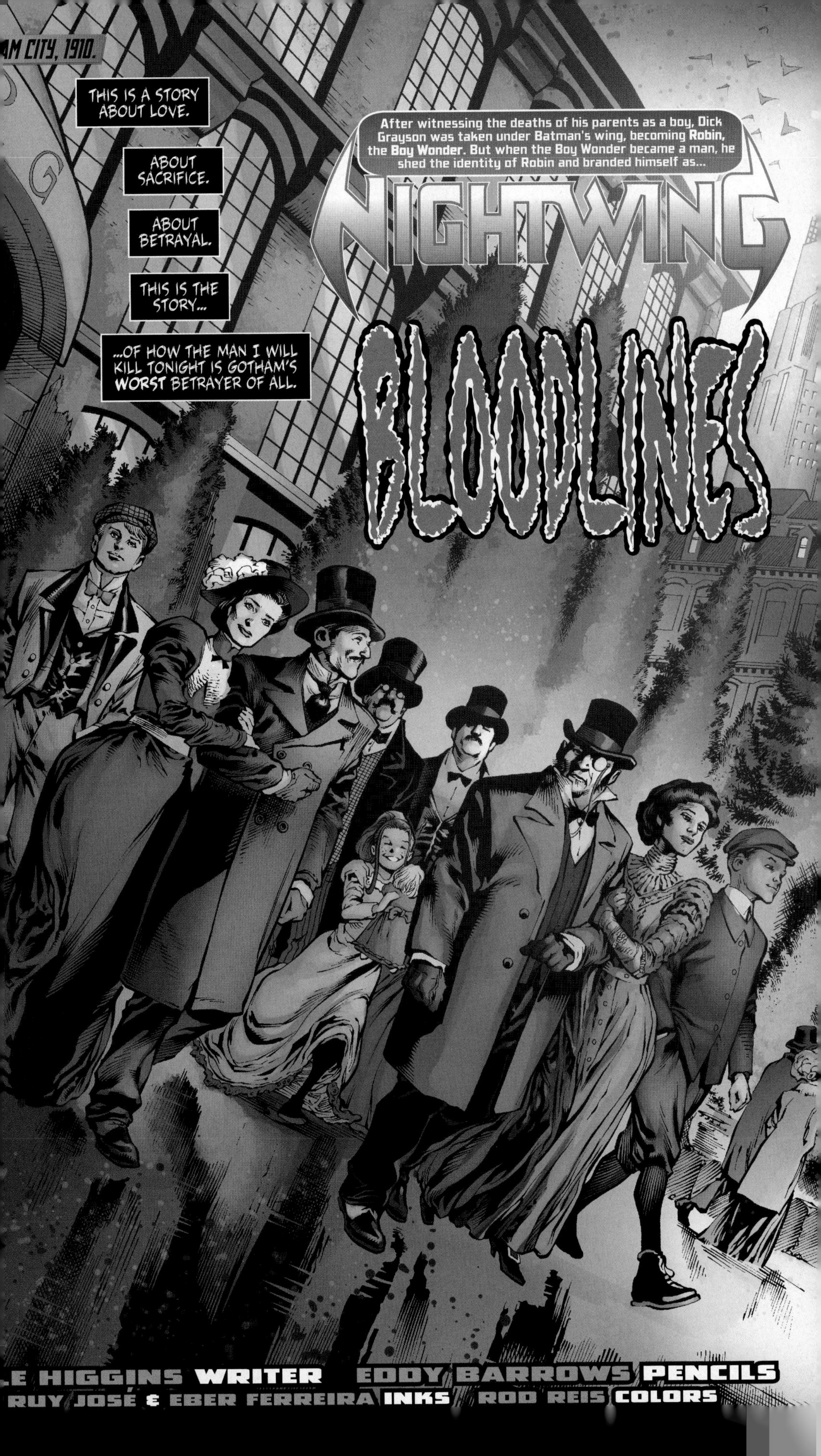
AM CITY, 1910.
THIS IS A STORY ABOUT LOVE.
ABOUT SACRIFICE.
ABOUT BETRAYAL.
THIS IS THE STORY...
...OF HOW THE MAN I WILL KILL TONIGHT IS GOTHAM'S WORST BETRAYER OF ALL.
After witnessing the deaths of his parents as a boy, Dick Grayson was taken under Batman's wing, becoming Robin, the Boy Wonder. But when the Boy Wonder became a man, he shed the identity of Robin and branded himself as...
NIGHTWING
BLOODLINES
LE HIGGINS WRITER EDDY BARROWS PENCILS
RUY JOSÉ & EBER FERREIRA INKS ROD REIS COLORS

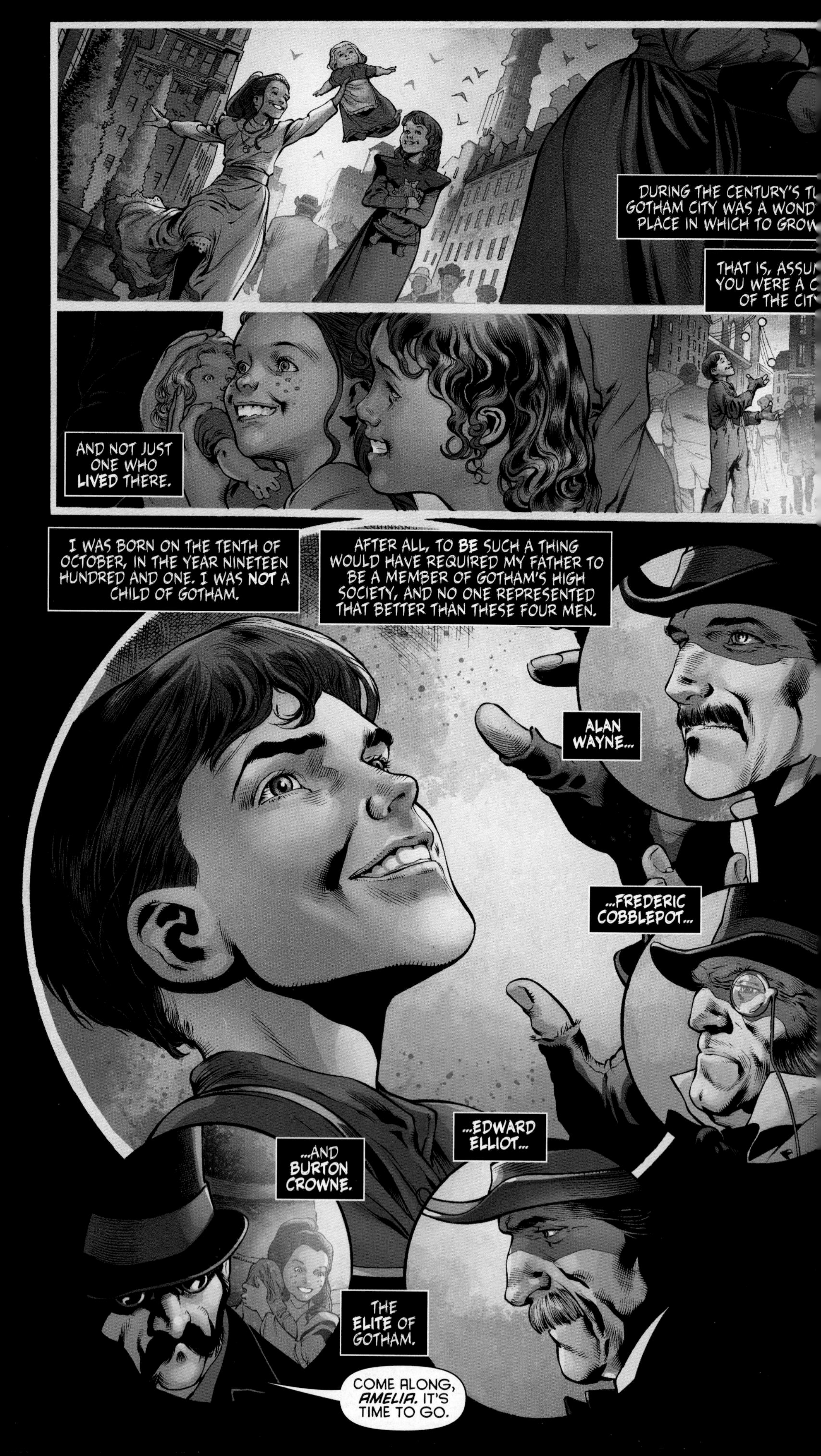

DURING THE CENTURY'S TU
GOTHAM CITY WAS A WOND
PLACE IN WHICH TO GROW
THAT IS, ASSUM
YOU WERE A C
OF THE CITY
AND NOT JUST ONE WHO LIVED THERE.
I WAS BORN ON THE TENTH OF OCTOBER, IN THE YEAR NINETEEN HUNDRED AND ONE. I WAS NOT A CHILD OF GOTHAM.
AFTER ALL, TO BE SUCH A THING WOULD HAVE REQUIRED MY FATHER TO BE A MEMBER OF GOTHAM'S HIGH SOCIETY, AND NO ONE REPRESENTED THAT BETTER THAN THESE FOUR MEN.
ALAN WAYNE...
...FREDERIC COBBLEPOT...
...EDWARD ELLIOT...
...AND BURTON CROWNE.
THE ELITE OF GOTHAM.
COME ALONG, AMELIA. IT'S TIME TO GO.

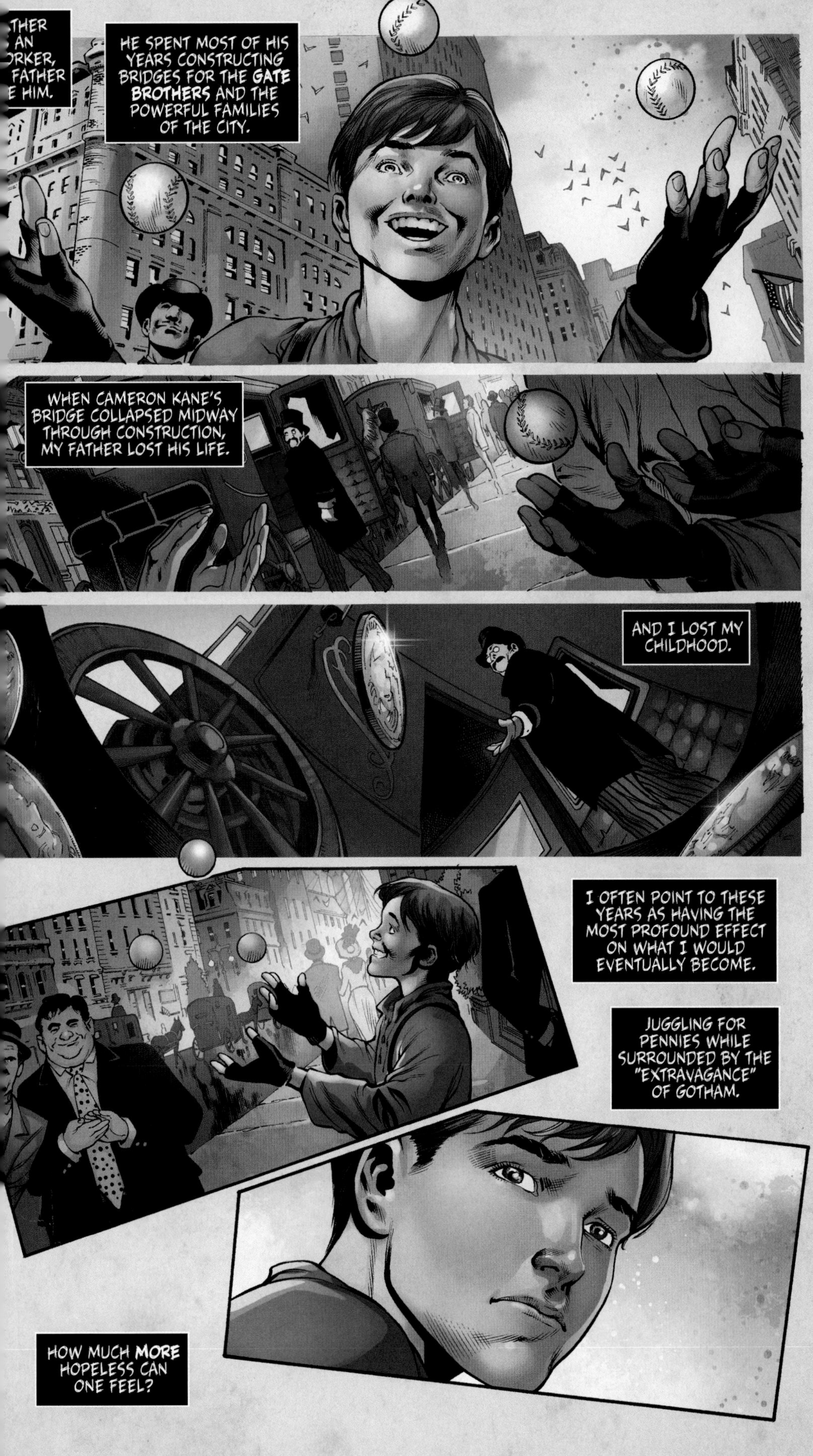
THER AN ORKER, FATHER E HIM.
HE SPENT MOST OF HIS YEARS CONSTRUCTING BRIDGES FOR THE **GATE BROTHERS** AND THE POWERFUL FAMILIES OF THE CITY.
WHEN CAMERON KANE'S BRIDGE COLLAPSED MIDWAY THROUGH CONSTRUCTION, MY FATHER LOST HIS LIFE.
AND I LOST MY CHILDHOOD.
I OFTEN POINT TO THESE YEARS AS HAVING THE MOST PROFOUND EFFECT ON WHAT I WOULD EVENTUALLY BECOME.
JUGGLING FOR PENNIES WHILE SURROUNDED BY THE "EXTRAVAGANCE" OF GOTHAM.
HOW MUCH **MORE** HOPELESS CAN ONE FEEL?

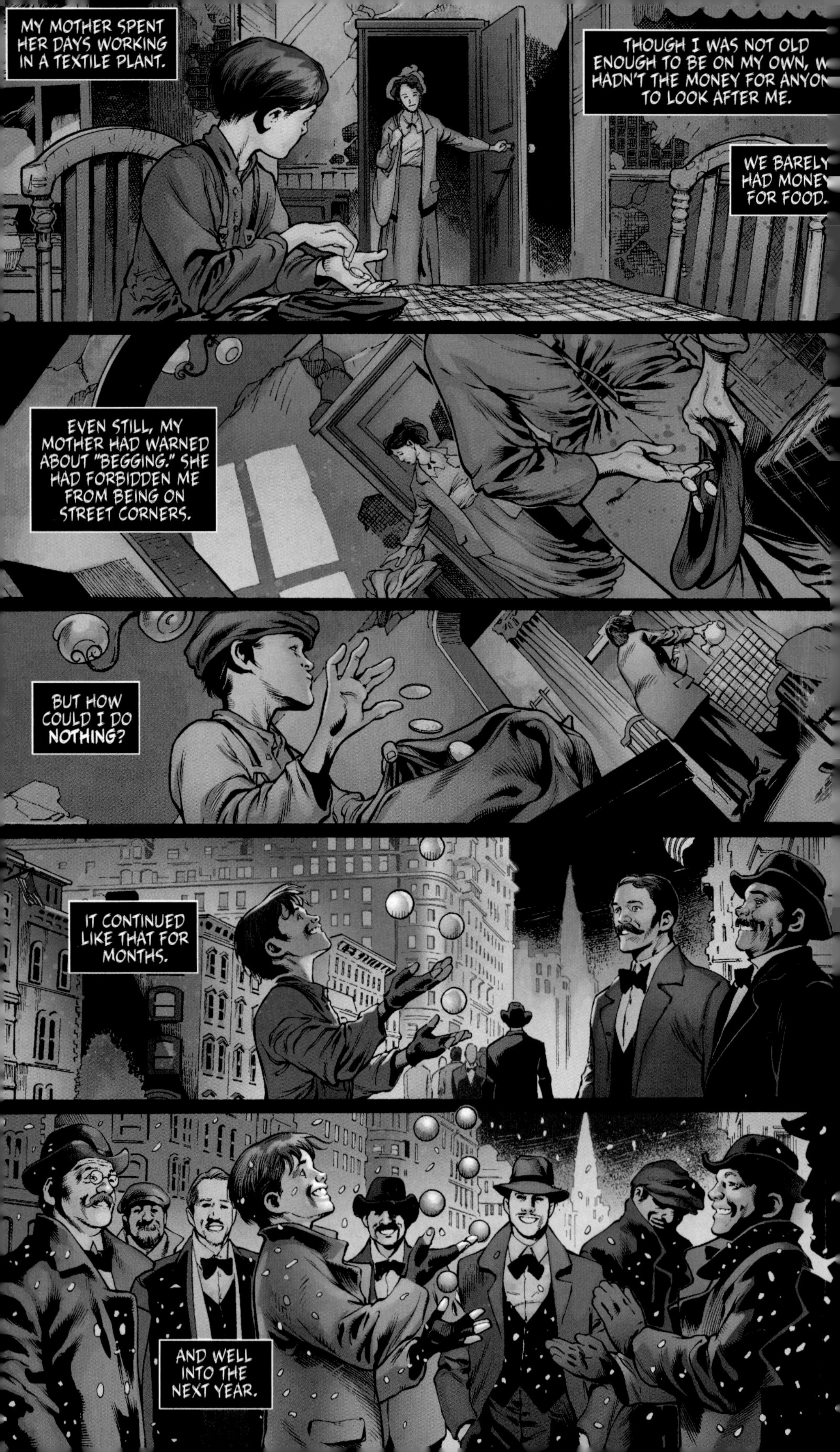
MY MOTHER SPENT HER DAYS WORKING IN A TEXTILE PLANT.
THOUGH I WAS NOT OLD ENOUGH TO BE ON MY OWN, W HADN'T THE MONEY FOR ANYON TO LOOK AFTER ME.
WE BARELY HAD MONEY FOR FOOD.
EVEN STILL, MY MOTHER HAD WARNED ABOUT "BEGGING." SHE HAD FORBIDDEN ME FROM BEING ON STREET CORNERS.
BUT HOW COULD I DO **NOTHING**?
IT CONTINUED LIKE THAT FOR MONTHS.
AND WELL INTO THE NEXT YEAR.

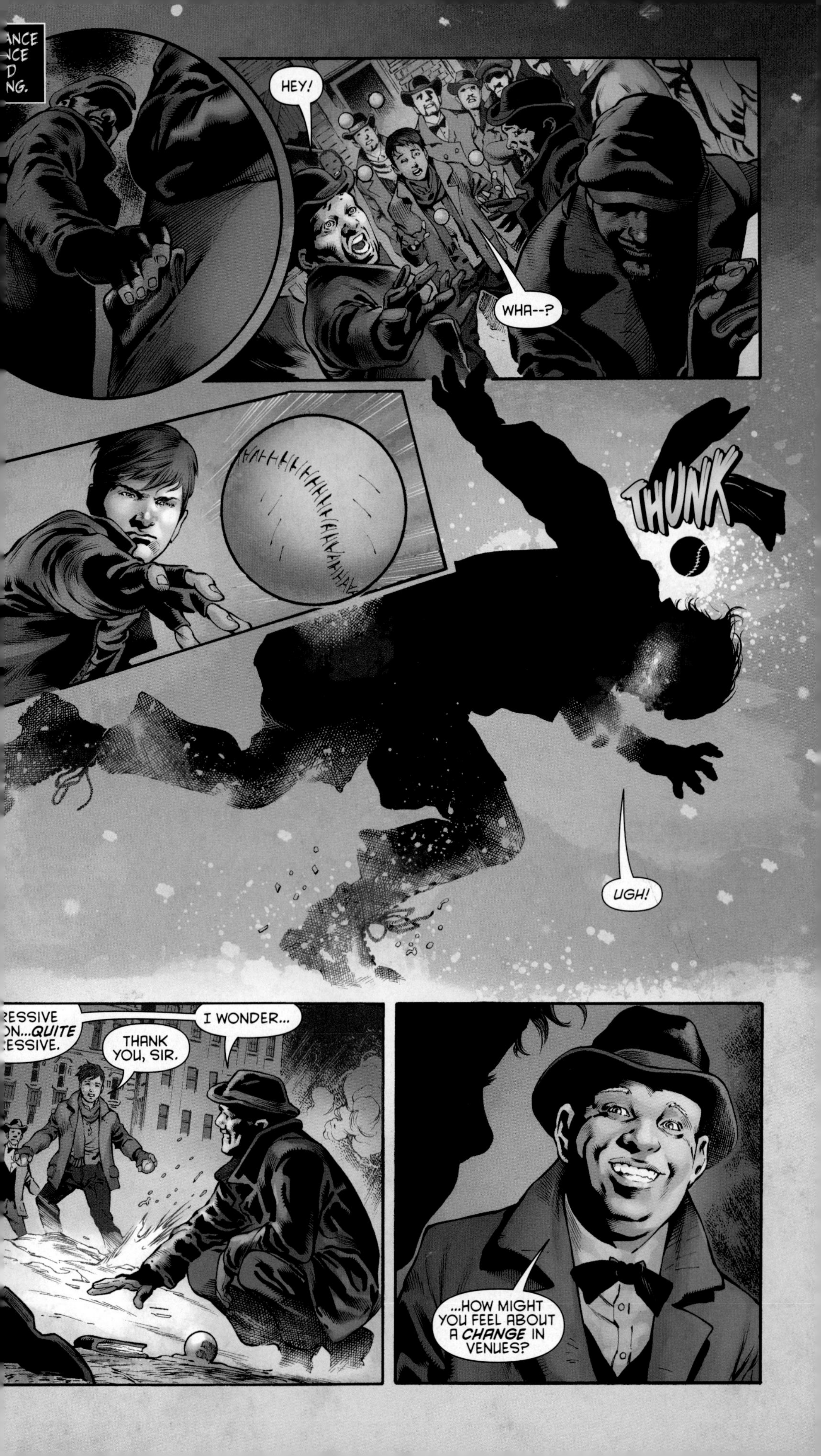

HEY!
WHA--?
THUNK
UGH!
I WONDER...
THANK YOU, SIR.
...HOW MIGHT YOU FEEL ABOUT A *CHANGE* IN VENUES?

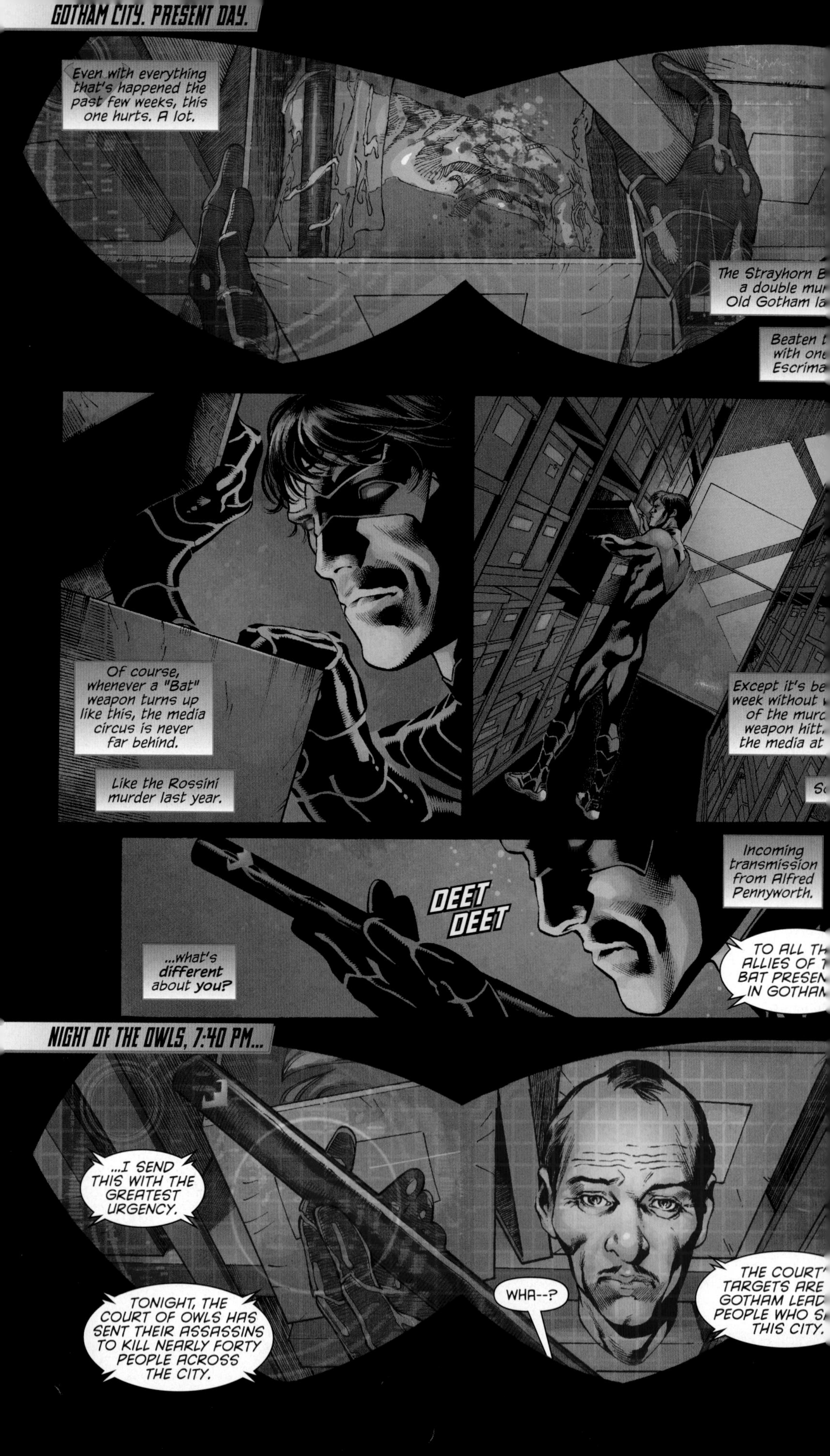
GOTHAM CITY. PRESENT DAY.
Even with everything that's happened the past few weeks, this one hurts. A lot.
The Strayhorn B
a double mu
Old Gotham la
Beaten t
with one
Escrima
Of course, whenever a "Bat" weapon turns up like this, the media circus is never far behind.
Like the Rossini murder last year.
Except it's be
week without
of the murd
weapon hitt
the media at
Incoming transmission from Alfred Pennyworth.
DEET DEET
...what's different about you?
TO ALL TH
ALLIES OF
BAT PRESEN
IN GOTHAM
NIGHT OF THE OWLS, 7:40 PM...
...I SEND THIS WITH THE GREATEST URGENCY.
TONIGHT, THE COURT OF OWLS HAS SENT THEIR ASSASSINS TO KILL NEARLY FORTY PEOPLE ACROSS THE CITY.
WHA--?
THE COURT'
TARGETS ARE
GOTHAM LEAD
PEOPLE WHO S
THIS CITY.

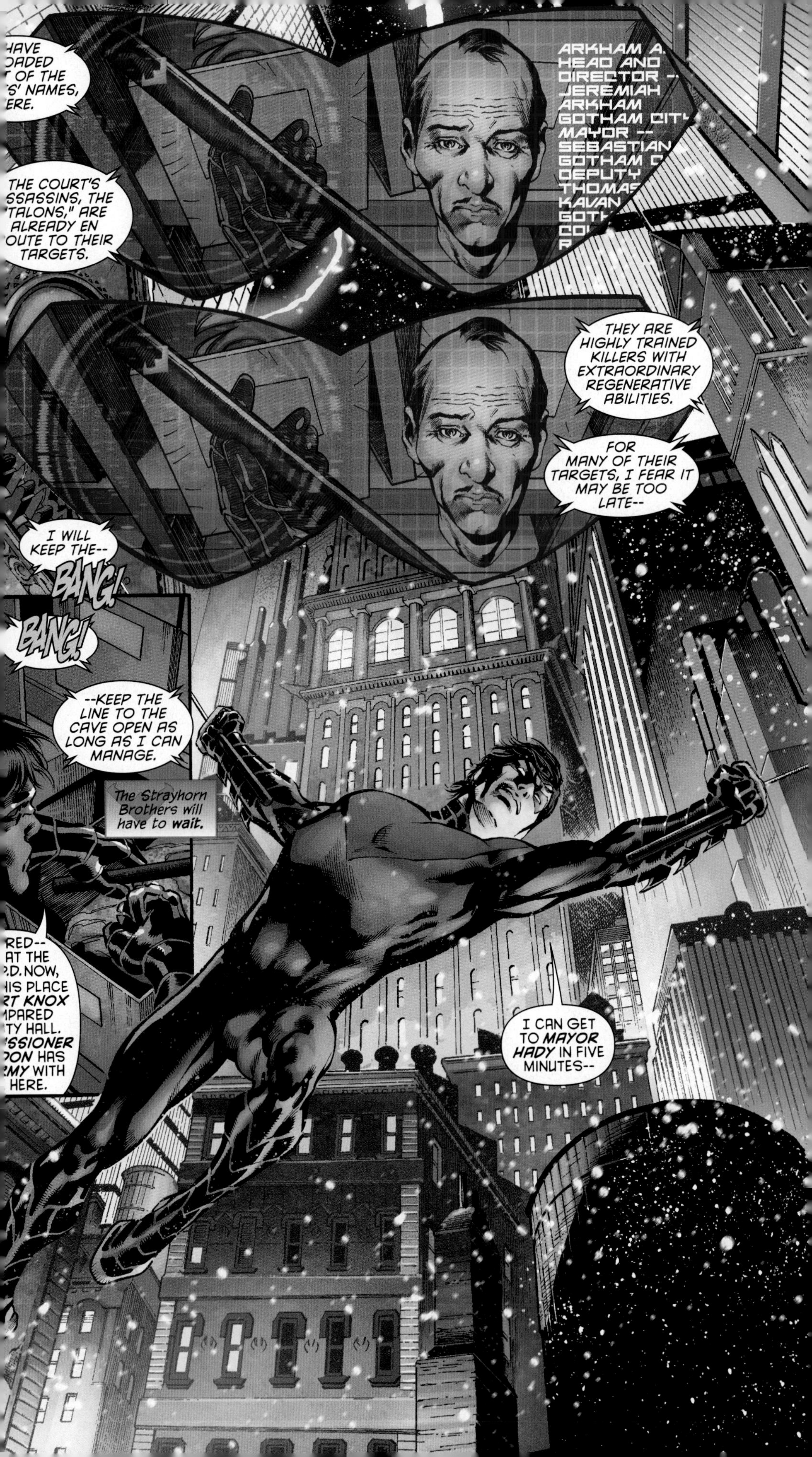

HAVE
OADED
T OF THE
S' NAMES,
ERE.
THE COURT'S
SSASSINS, THE
"TALONS," ARE
ALREADY EN
OUTE TO THEIR
TARGETS.
ARKHAM A.
HEAD AND
DIRECTOR --
JEREMIAH
ARKHAM
GOTHAM CIT
MAYOR --
SEBASTIAN
GOTHAM C
DEPUTY
THOMAS
KAVAN
THEY ARE HIGHLY TRAINED KILLERS WITH EXTRAORDINARY REGENERATIVE ABILITIES.
FOR MANY OF THEIR TARGETS, I FEAR IT MAY BE TOO LATE--
I WILL KEEP THE--
BANG!
BANG!
--KEEP THE LINE TO THE CAVE OPEN AS LONG AS I CAN MANAGE.
The Strayhorn Brothers will have to wait.
RED--
AT THE
P.D. NOW,
HIS PLACE
RT KNOX
MPARED
TY HALL.
SSIONER
DON HAS
RMY WITH
HERE.
I CAN GET TO MAYOR HADY IN FIVE MINUTES--

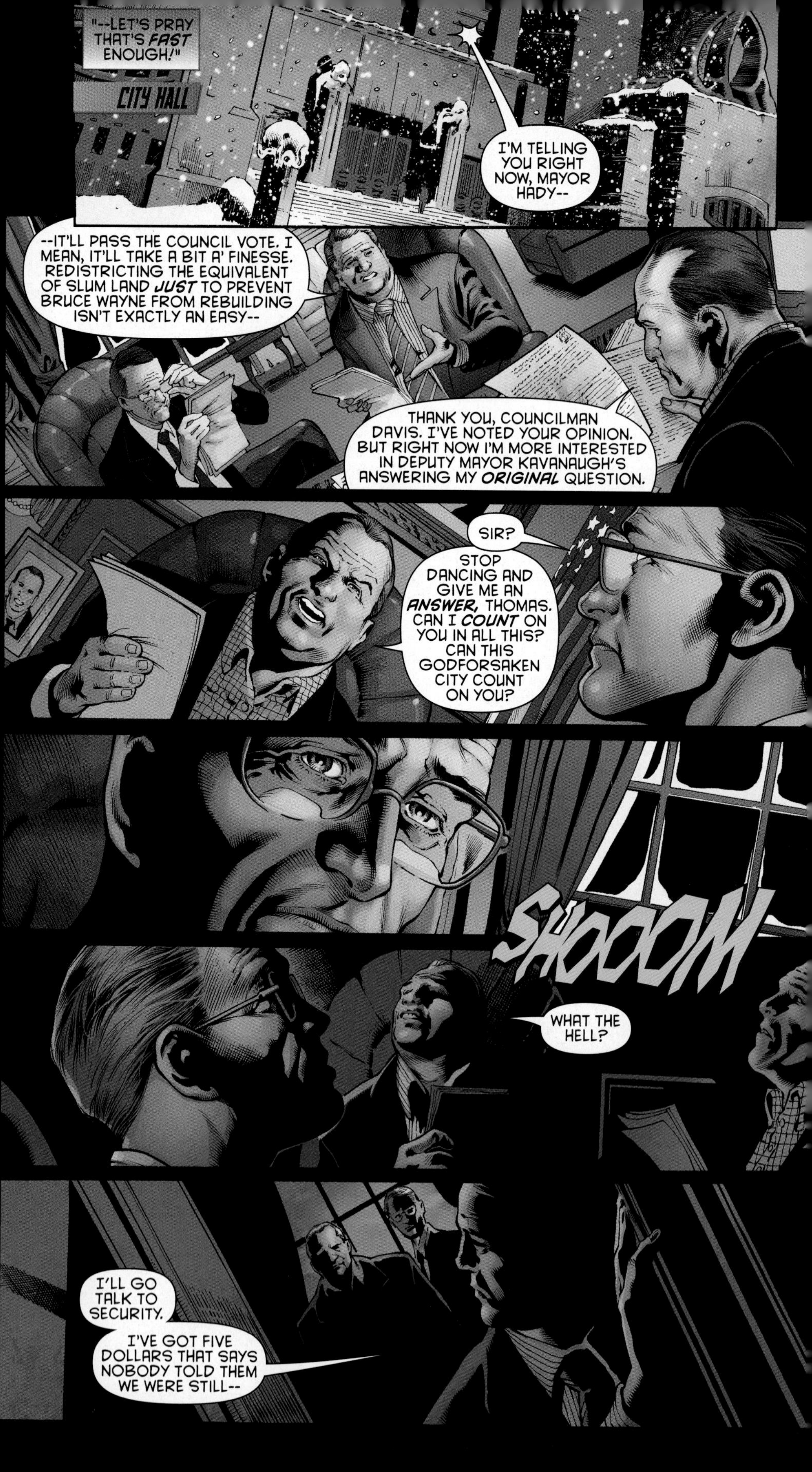
"--LET'S PRAY THAT'S FAST ENOUGH!"
CITY HALL
I'M TELLING YOU RIGHT NOW, MAYOR HADY--
--IT'LL PASS THE COUNCIL VOTE. I MEAN, IT'LL TAKE A BIT A' FINESSE. REDISTRICTING THE EQUIVALENT OF SLUM LAND JUST TO PREVENT BRUCE WAYNE FROM REBUILDING ISN'T EXACTLY AN EASY--
THANK YOU, COUNCILMAN DAVIS. I'VE NOTED YOUR OPINION. BUT RIGHT NOW I'M MORE INTERESTED IN DEPUTY MAYOR KAVANAUGH'S ANSWERING MY ORIGINAL QUESTION.
SIR?
STOP DANCING AND GIVE ME AN ANSWER, THOMAS. CAN I COUNT ON YOU IN ALL THIS? CAN THIS GODFORSAKEN CITY COUNT ON YOU?
SHOOOM
WHAT THE HELL?
I'LL GO TALK TO SECURITY.
I'VE GOT FIVE DOLLARS THAT SAYS NOBODY TOLD THEM WE WERE STILL--

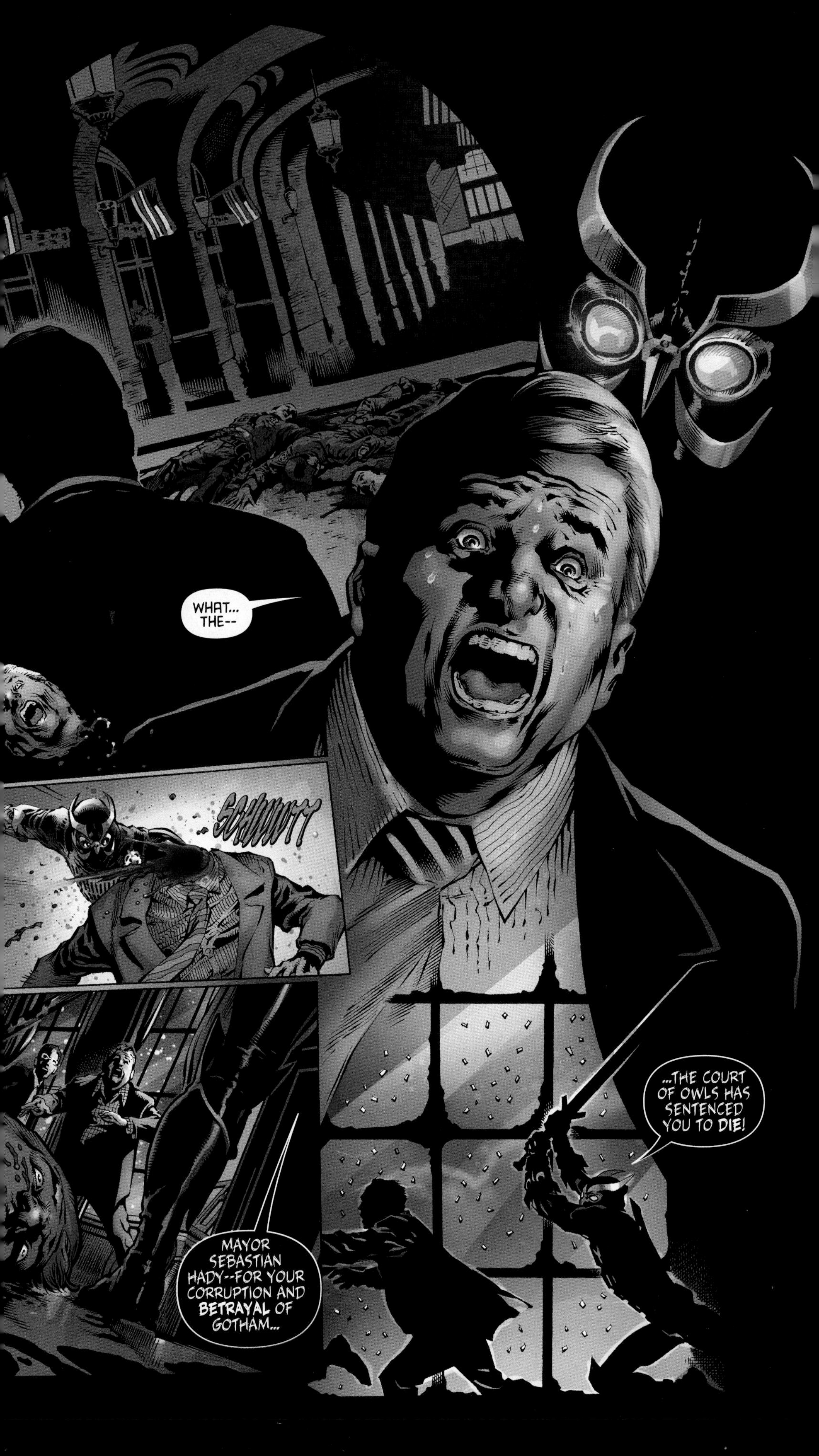
WHAT... THE--
SCHWWTT
MAYOR SEBASTIAN HADY--FOR YOUR CORRUPTION AND **BETRAYAL** OF GOTHAM...
...THE COURT OF OWLS HAS SENTENCED YOU TO **DIE**!

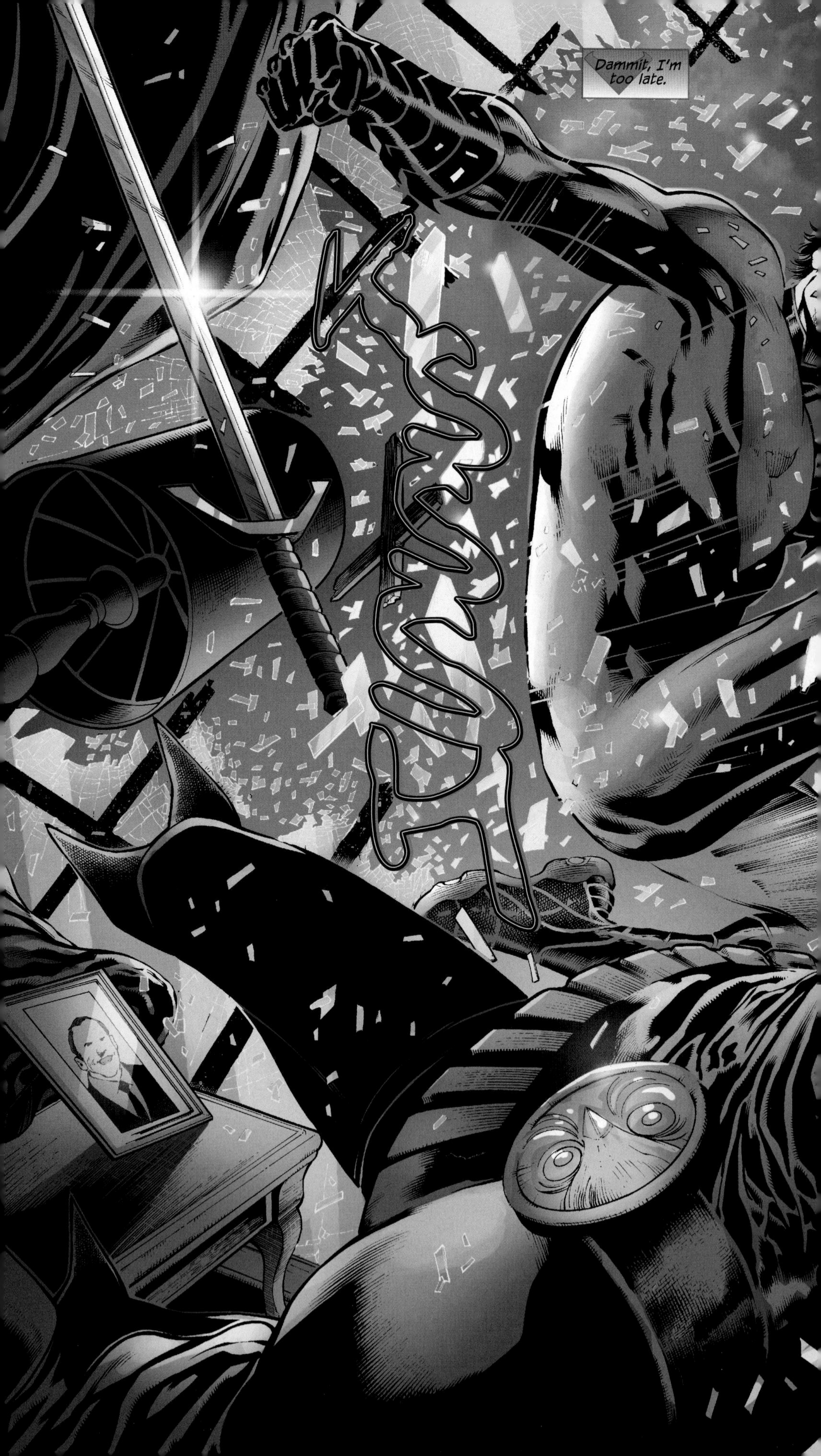
Dammit, I'm too late.

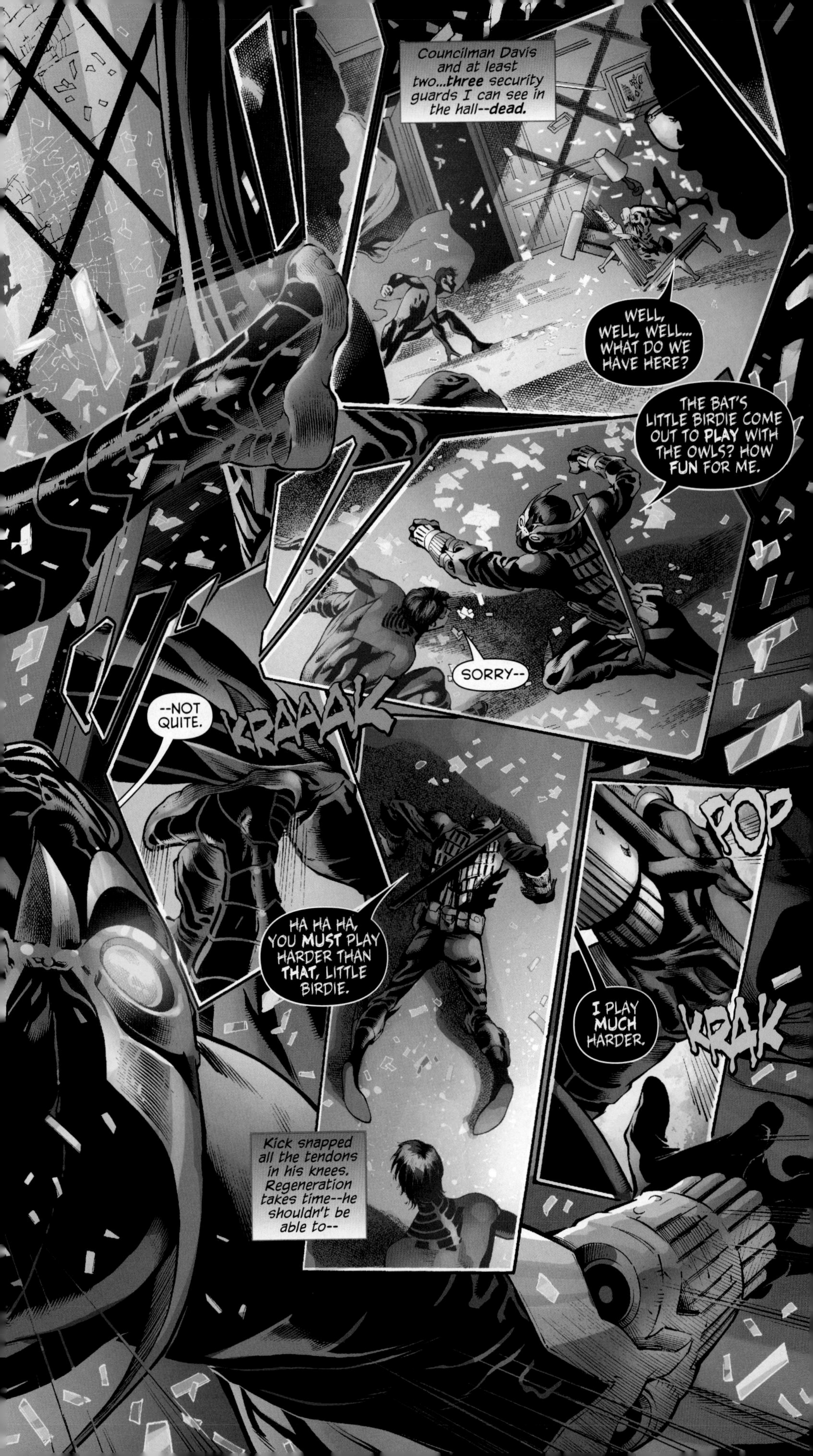
Councilman Davis and at least two...three security guards I can see in the hall--dead.
WELL, WELL, WELL... WHAT DO WE HAVE HERE?
THE BAT'S LITTLE BIRDIE COME OUT TO PLAY WITH THE OWLS? HOW FUN FOR ME.
SORRY--
--NOT QUITE.
KRAAAK
HA HA HA, YOU MUST PLAY HARDER THAN THAT, LITTLE BIRDIE.
POP
I PLAY MUCH HARDER.
KRAK
Kick snapped all the tendons in his knees. Regeneration takes time--he shouldn't be able to--

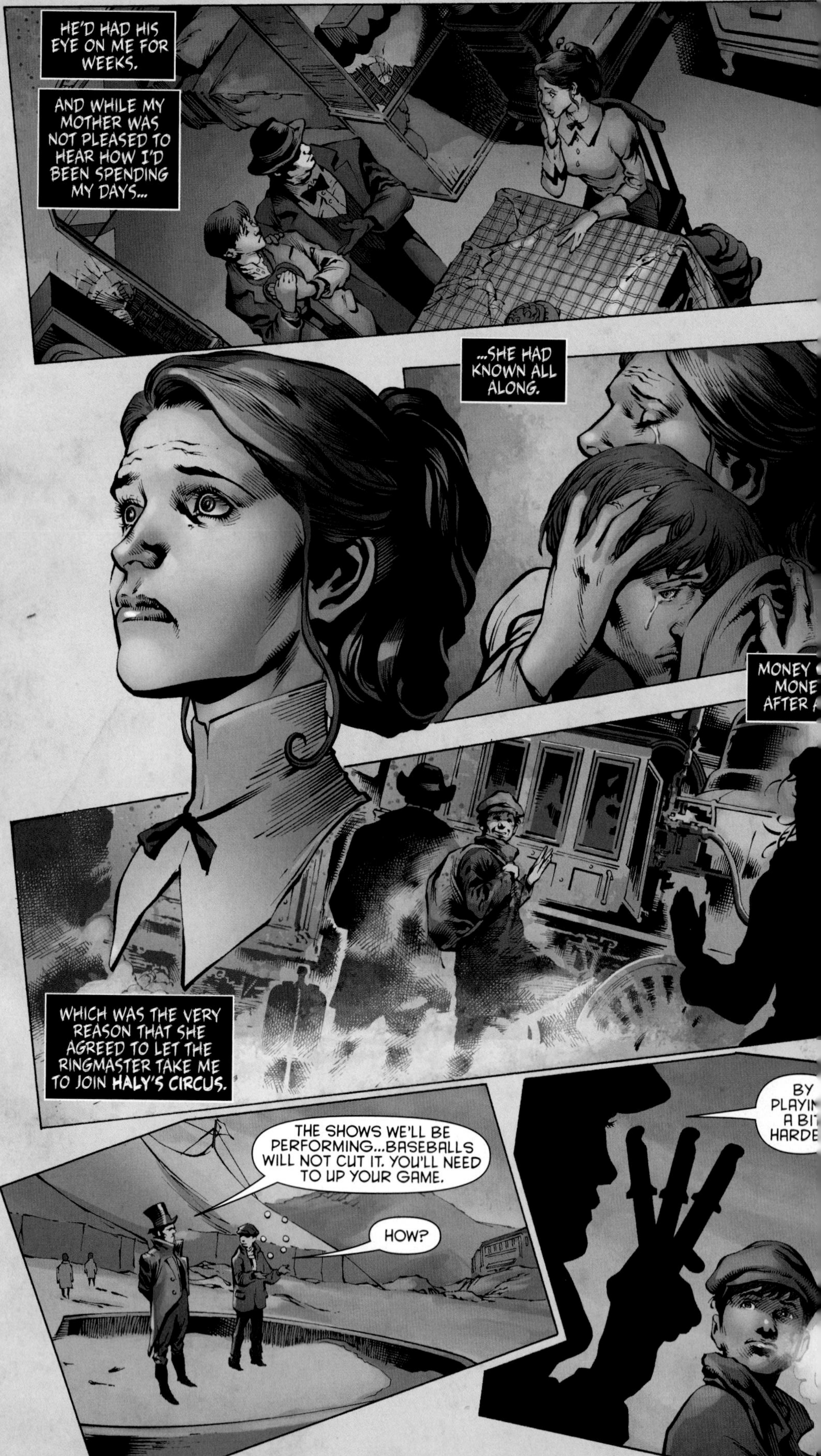
HE'D HAD HIS EYE ON ME FOR WEEKS.
AND WHILE MY MOTHER WAS NOT PLEASED TO HEAR HOW I'D BEEN SPENDING MY DAYS...
...SHE HAD KNOWN ALL ALONG.
MONEY
MONE
AFTER A
WHICH WAS THE VERY REASON THAT SHE AGREED TO LET THE RINGMASTER TAKE ME TO JOIN HALY'S CIRCUS.
THE SHOWS WE'LL BE PERFORMING...BASEBALLS WILL NOT CUT IT. YOU'LL NEED TO UP YOUR GAME.
HOW?
BY
PLAYIN
A BIT
HARDE

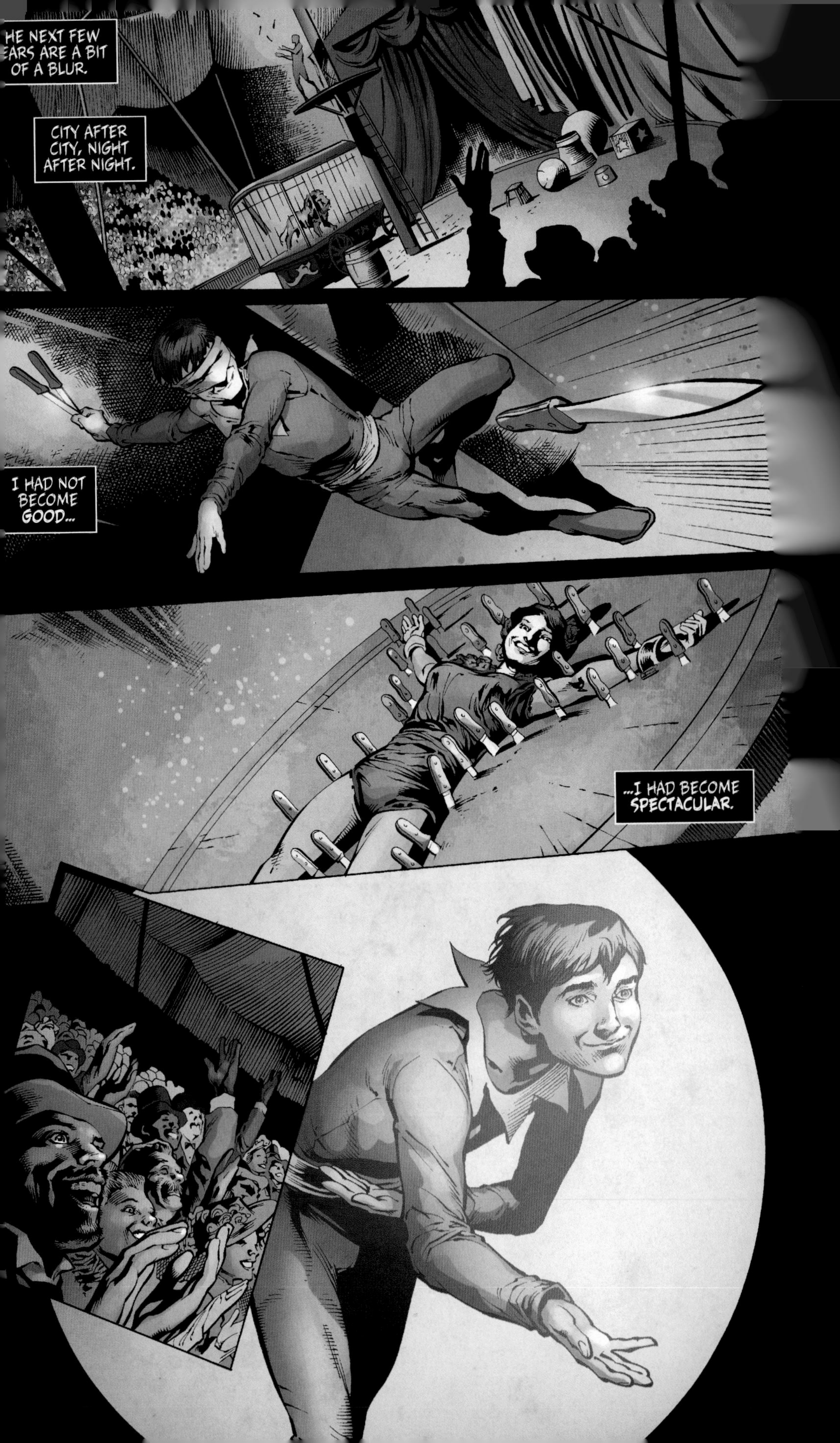
HE NEXT FEW
EARS ARE A BIT
OF A BLUR.
CITY AFTER
CITY, NIGHT
AFTER NIGHT.
I HAD NOT
BECOME
GOOD...
...I HAD BECOME
SPECTACULAR.

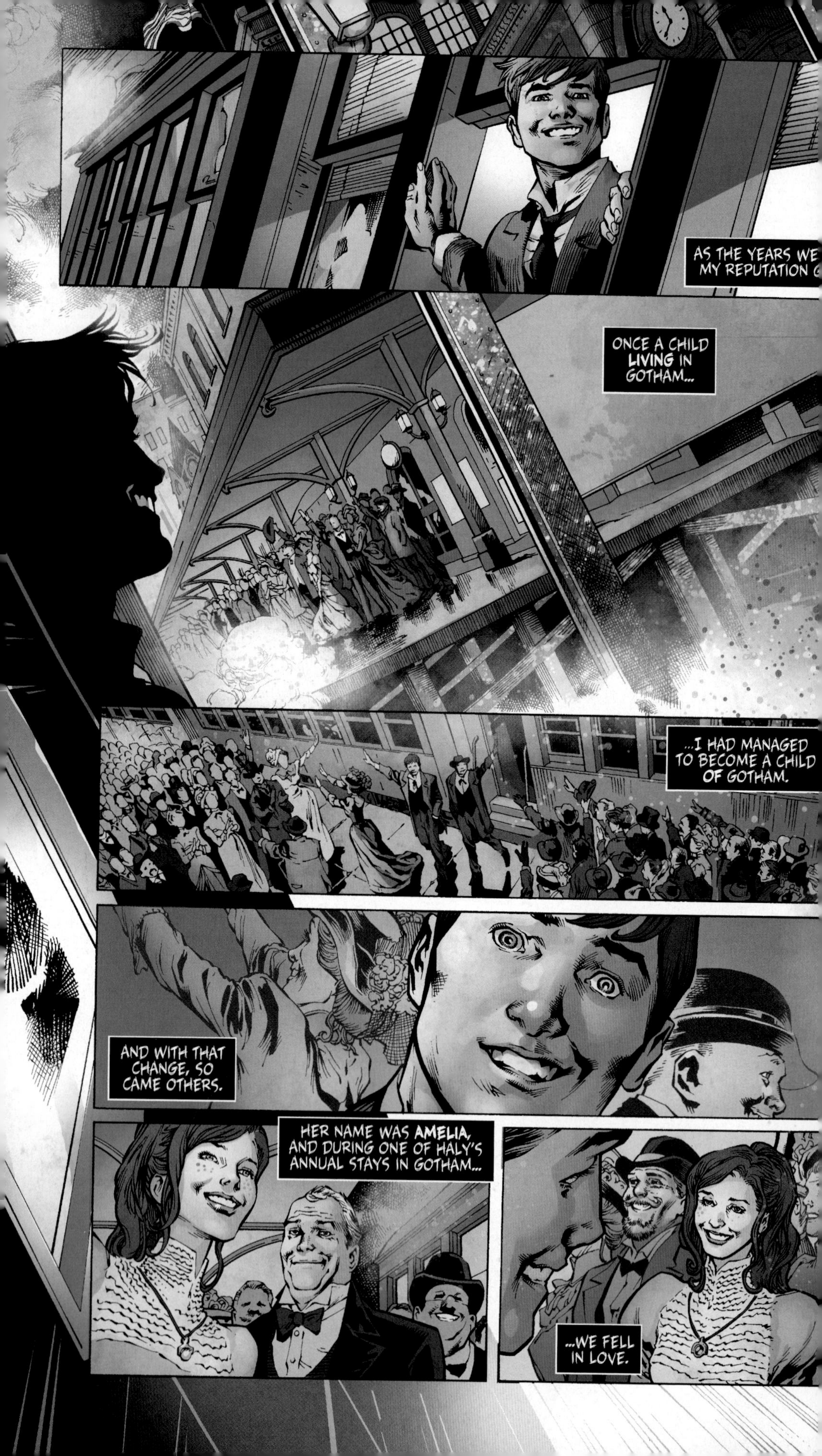
AS THE YEARS WE
MY REPUTATION G
ONCE A CHILD **LIVING** IN GOTHAM...
...I HAD MANAGED TO BECOME A CHILD **OF** GOTHAM.
AND WITH THAT CHANGE, SO CAME OTHERS.
HER NAME WAS **AMELIA**, AND DURING ONE OF HALY'S ANNUAL STAYS IN GOTHAM...
...WE FELL IN LOVE.

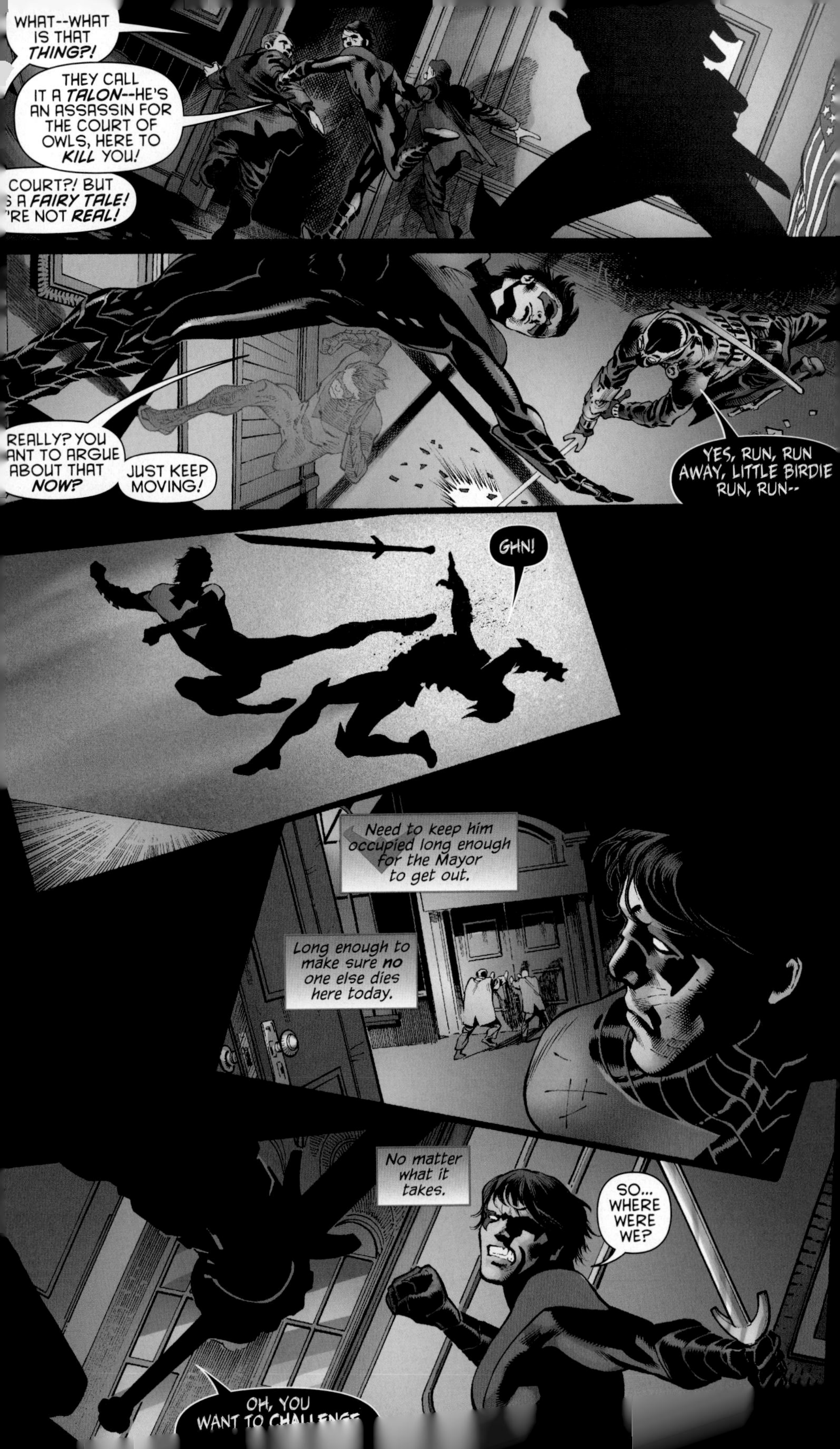

WHAT--WHAT IS THAT THING?!
THEY CALL IT A TALON--HE'S AN ASSASSIN FOR THE COURT OF OWLS, HERE TO KILL YOU!
COURT?! BUT S A FAIRY TALE! 'RE NOT REAL!
REALLY? YOU ANT TO ARGUE ABOUT THAT NOW?
JUST KEEP MOVING!
YES, RUN, RUN AWAY, LITTLE BIRDIE RUN, RUN--
GHN!
Need to keep him occupied long enough for the Mayor to get out.
Long enough to make sure no one else dies here today.
No matter what it takes.
SO... WHERE WERE WE?
OH, YOU WANT TO

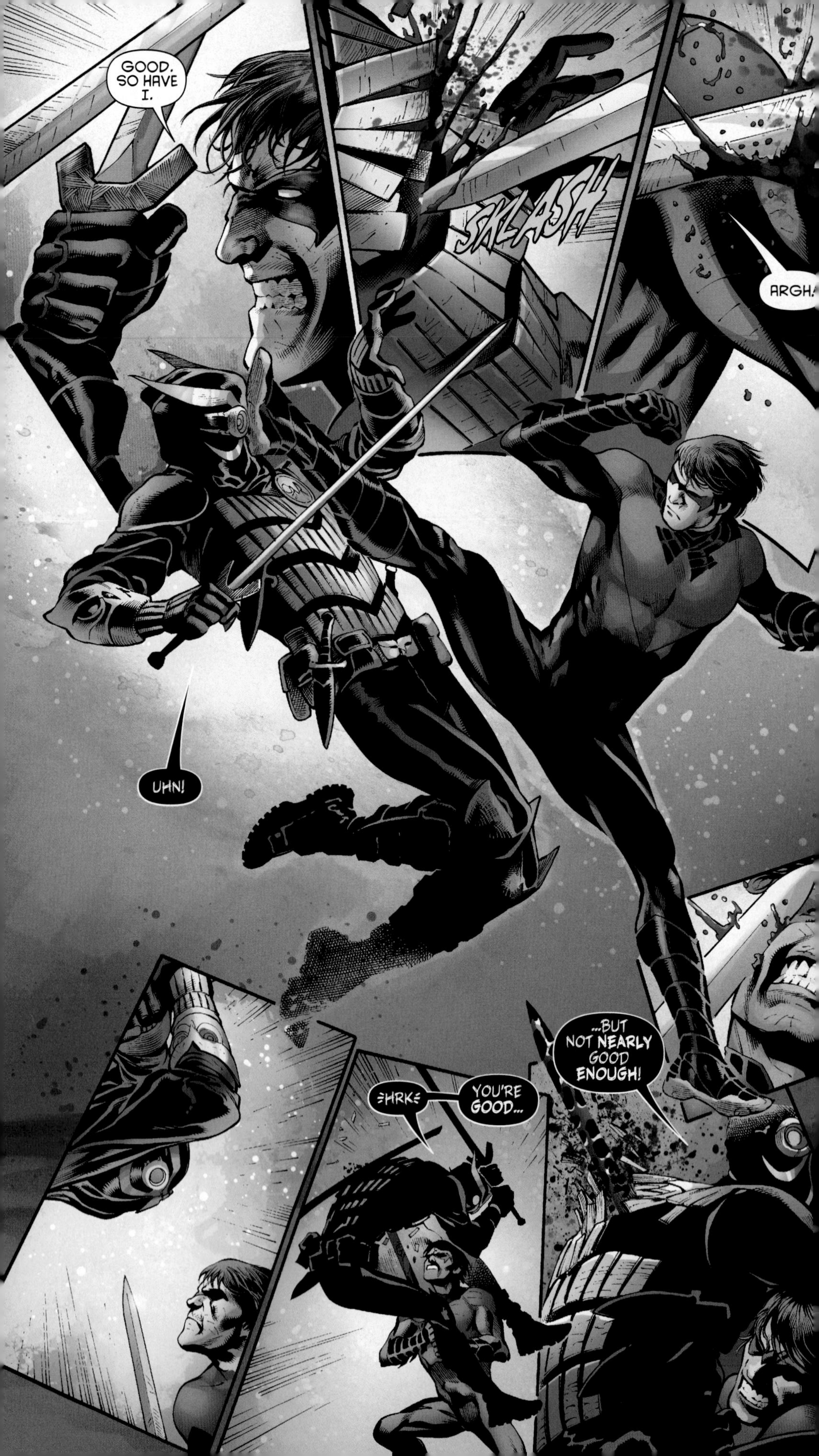
GOOD. SO HAVE I.
SKLASH
ARGH!
UHN!
HRK
YOU'RE GOOD...
...BUT NOT NEARLY GOOD ENOUGH!

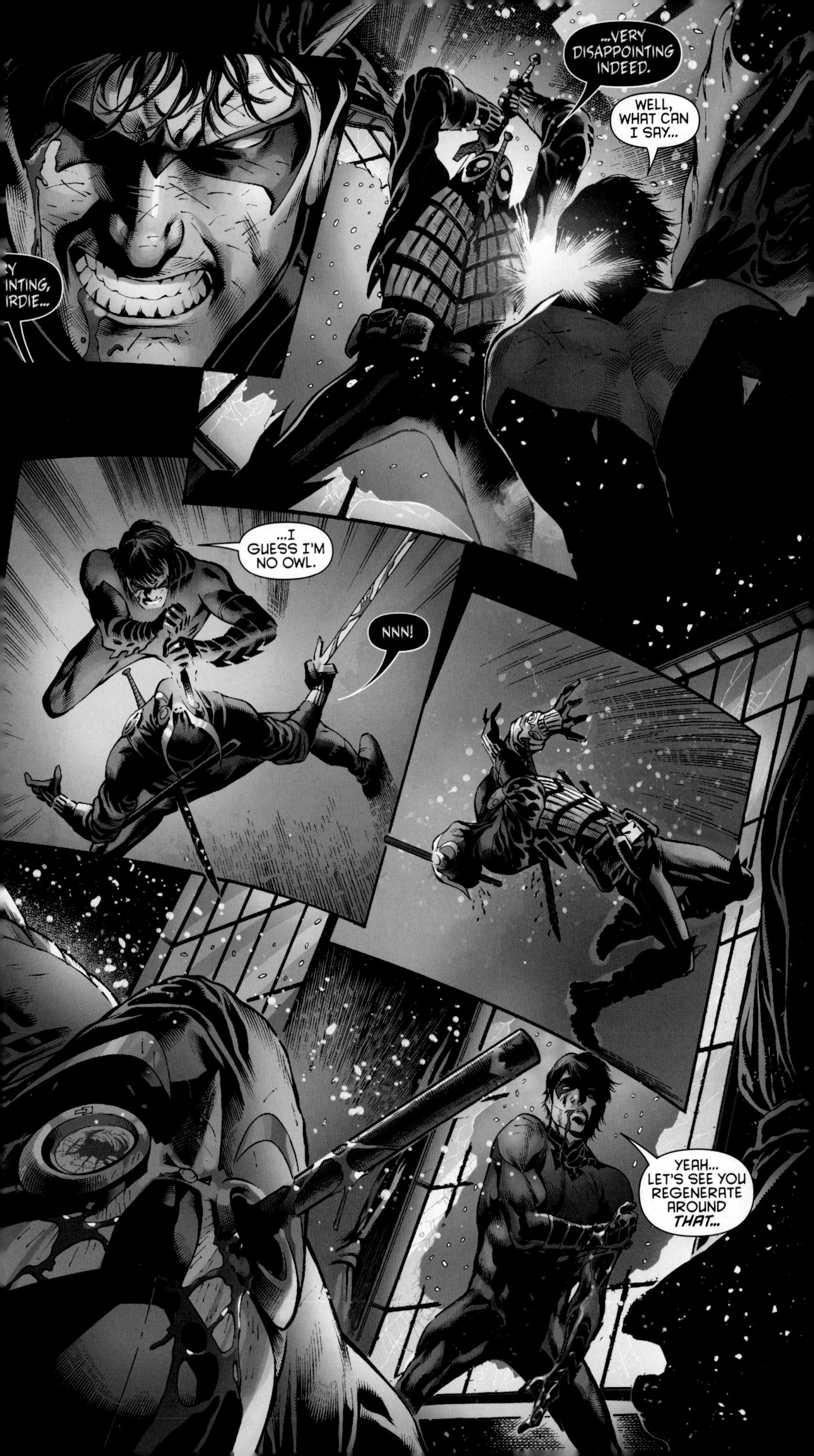
Y
INTING,
IRDIE...
...VERY DISAPPOINTING INDEED.
WELL, WHAT CAN I SAY...
...I GUESS I'M NO OWL.
NNN!
YEAH... LET'S SEE YOU REGENERATE AROUND *THAT*...

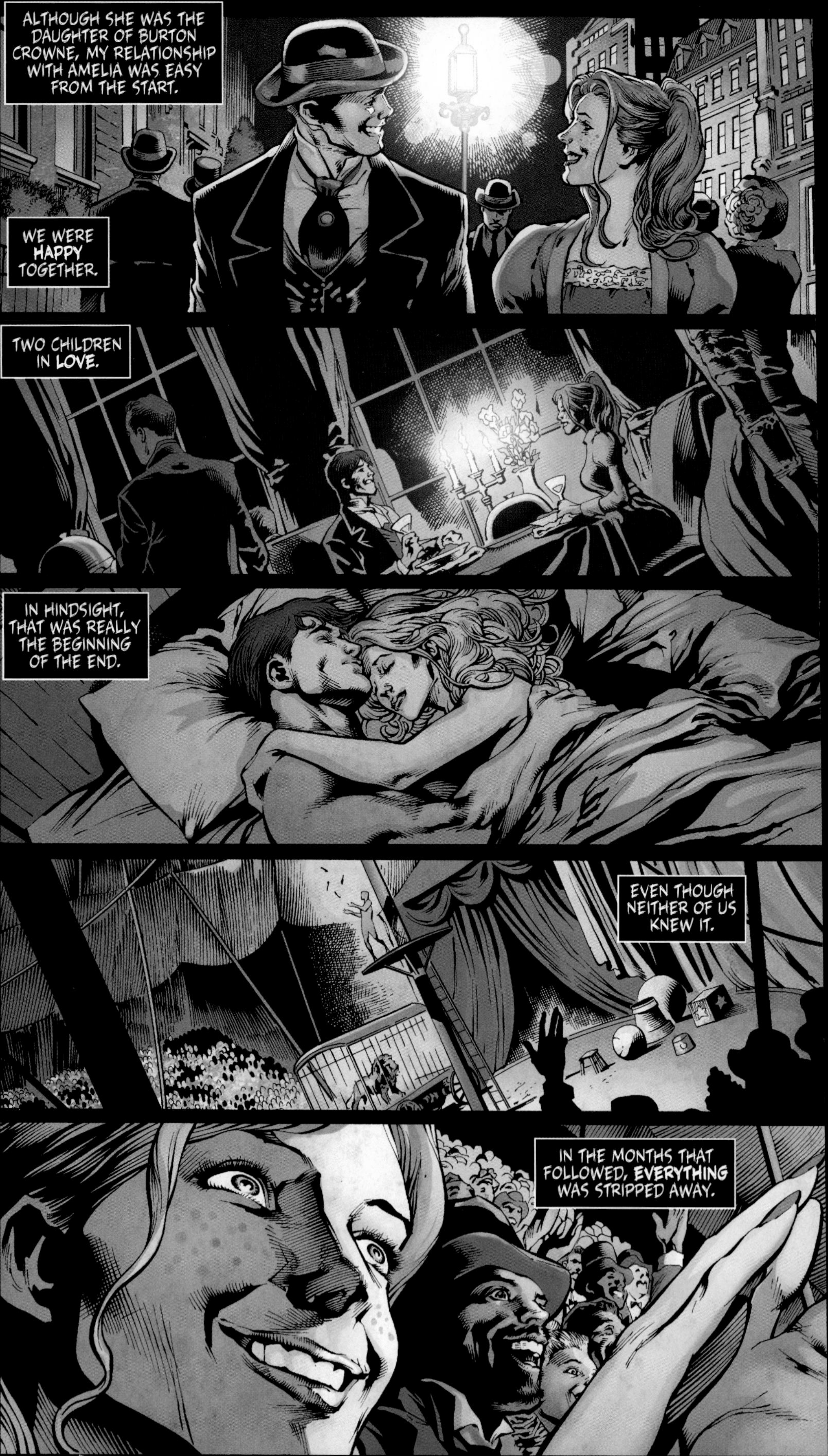
ALTHOUGH SHE WAS THE DAUGHTER OF BURTON CROWNE, MY RELATIONSHIP WITH AMELIA WAS EASY FROM THE START.
WE WERE HAPPY TOGETHER.
TWO CHILDREN IN LOVE.
IN HINDSIGHT, THAT WAS REALLY THE BEGINNING OF THE END.
EVEN THOUGH NEITHER OF US KNEW IT.
IN THE MONTHS THAT FOLLOWED, EVERYTHING WAS STRIPPED AWAY.

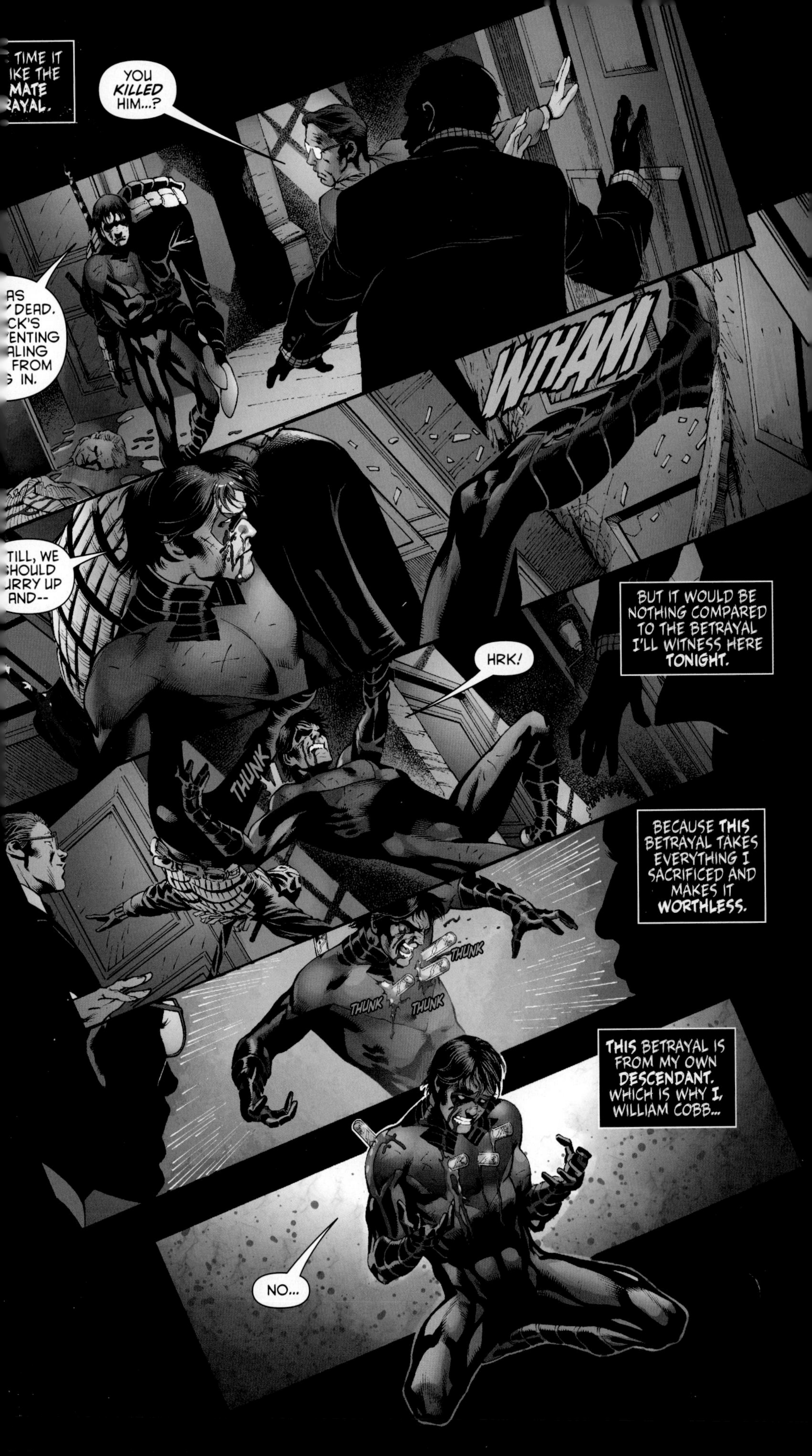

TIME IT
IKE THE
MATE
RAYAL.
YOU KILLED HIM...?
AS
DEAD.
CK'S
VENTING
ALING
FROM
IN.
WHAM
TILL, WE
SHOULD
URRY UP
AND--
BUT IT WOULD BE NOTHING COMPARED TO THE BETRAYAL I'LL WITNESS HERE TONIGHT.
HRK!
THUNK
BECAUSE THIS BETRAYAL TAKES EVERYTHING I SACRIFICED AND MAKES IT WORTHLESS.
THUNK
THUNK
THUNK
THIS BETRAYAL IS FROM MY OWN DESCENDANT. WHICH IS WHY I, WILLIAM COBB...
NO...

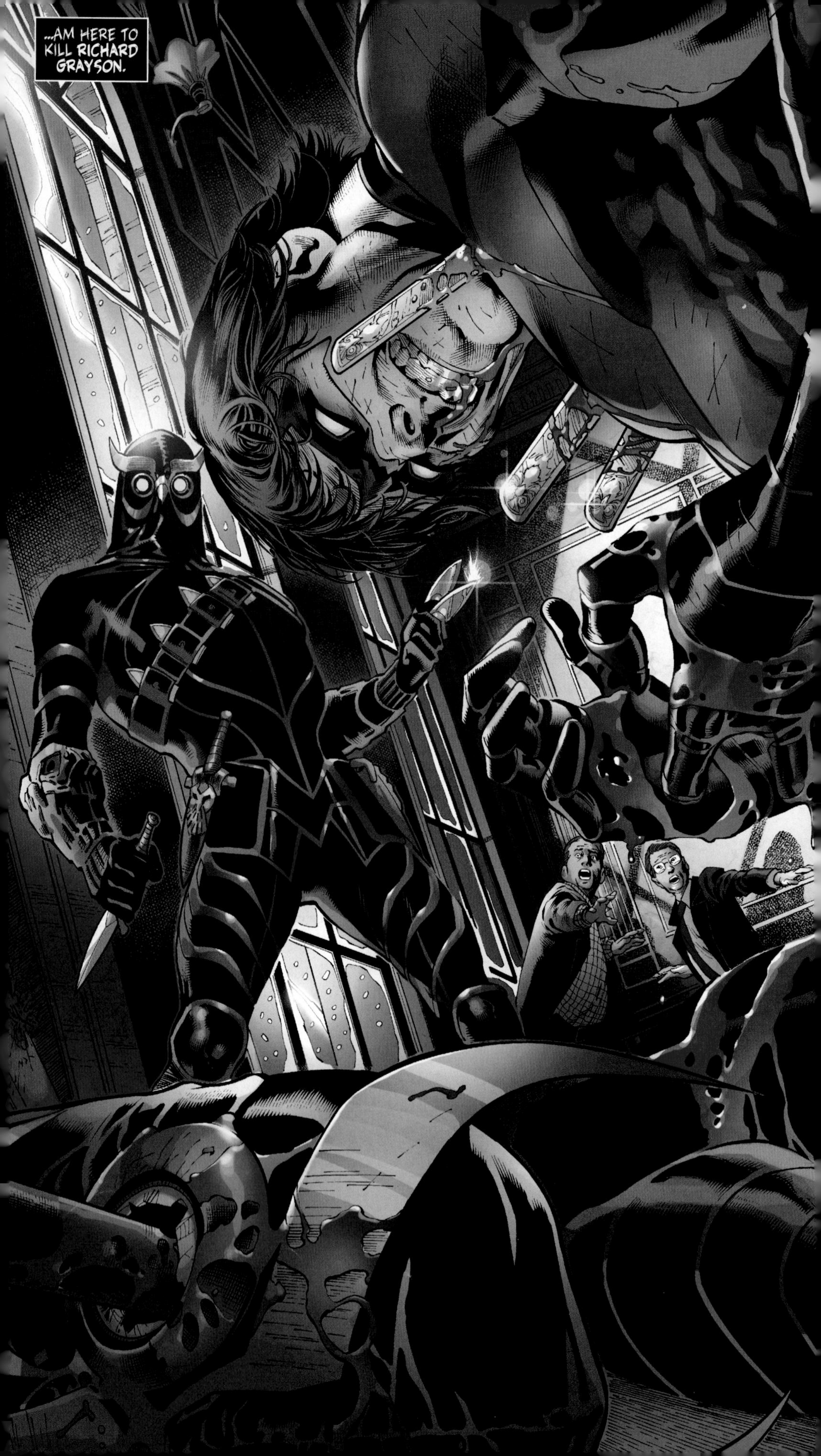
...AM HERE TO KILL RICHARD GRAYSON.

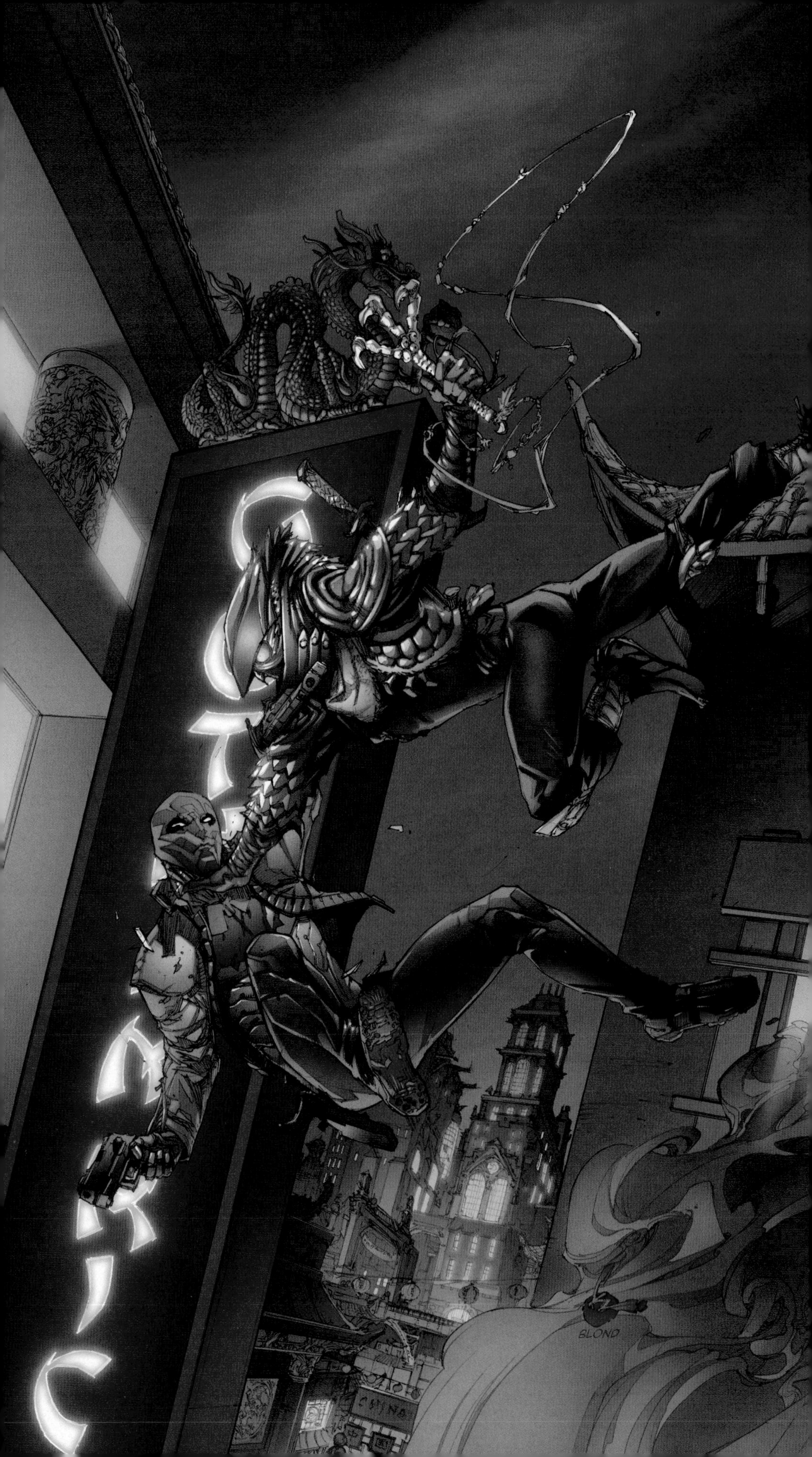
BLOND

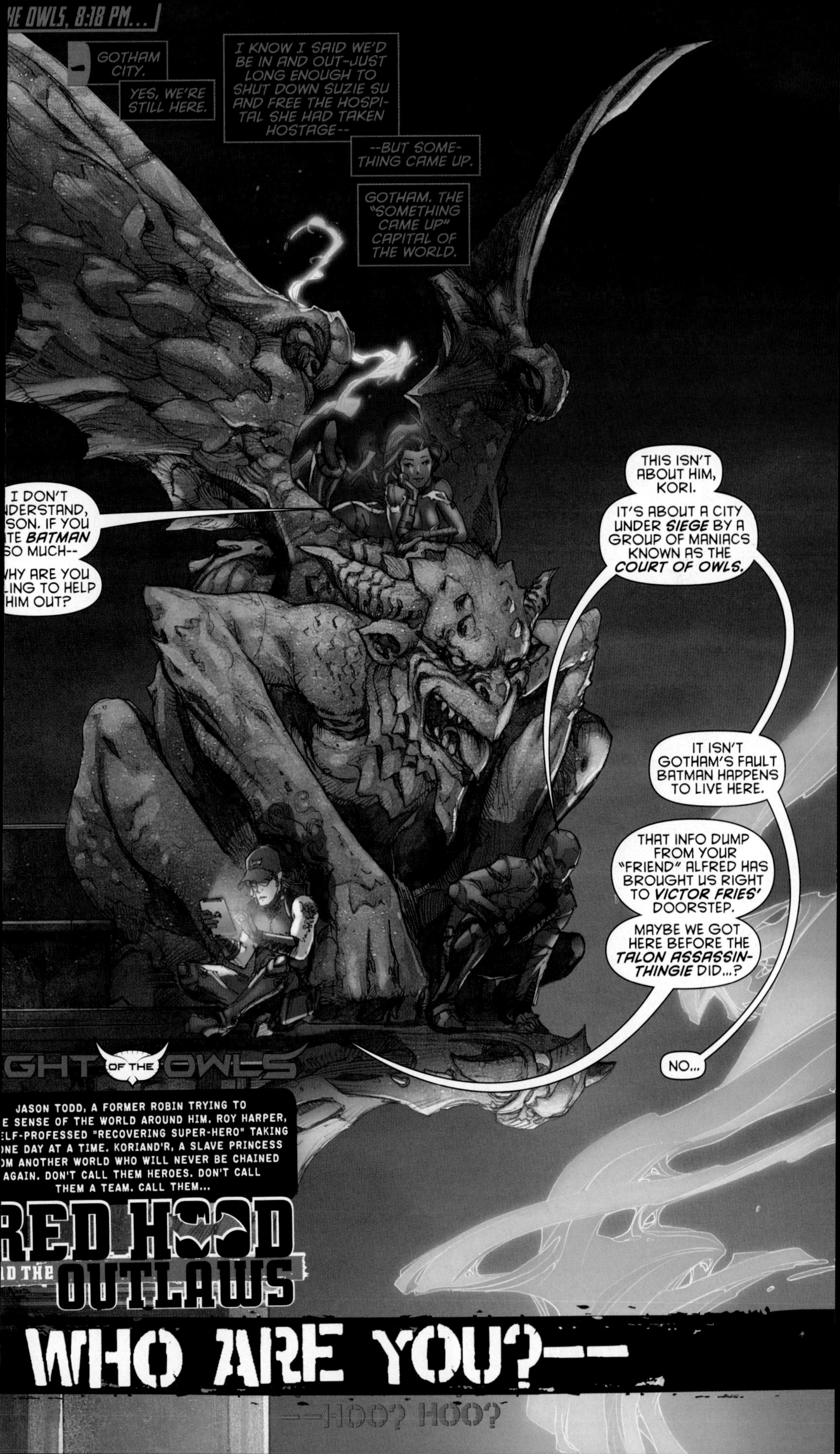

HE OWLS, 8:18 PM...
GOTHAM CITY.
YES, WE'RE STILL HERE.
I KNOW I SAID WE'D BE IN AND OUT-JUST LONG ENOUGH TO SHUT DOWN SUZIE SU AND FREE THE HOSPITAL SHE HAD TAKEN HOSTAGE--
--BUT SOMETHING CAME UP.
GOTHAM. THE "SOMETHING CAME UP" CAPITAL OF THE WORLD.
I DON'T NDERSTAND, SON. IF YOU TE BATMAN SO MUCH--
WHY ARE YOU LING TO HELP HIM OUT?
THIS ISN'T ABOUT HIM, KORI.
IT'S ABOUT A CITY UNDER SIEGE BY A GROUP OF MANIACS KNOWN AS THE COURT OF OWLS.
IT ISN'T GOTHAM'S FAULT BATMAN HAPPENS TO LIVE HERE.
THAT INFO DUMP FROM YOUR "FRIEND" ALFRED HAS BROUGHT US RIGHT TO VICTOR FRIES' DOORSTEP.
MAYBE WE GOT HERE BEFORE THE TALON ASSASSIN-THINGIE DID...?
NO...
GHT OF THE OWLS
JASON TODD, A FORMER ROBIN TRYING TO E SENSE OF THE WORLD AROUND HIM. ROY HARPER, ELF-PROFESSED "RECOVERING SUPER-HERO" TAKING ONE DAY AT A TIME. KORIAND'R, A SLAVE PRINCESS OM ANOTHER WORLD WHO WILL NEVER BE CHAINED AGAIN. DON'T CALL THEM HEROES. DON'T CALL THEM A TEAM. CALL THEM...
RED HOOD ND THE OUTLAWS
WHO ARE YOU?--
--HOO? HOO?

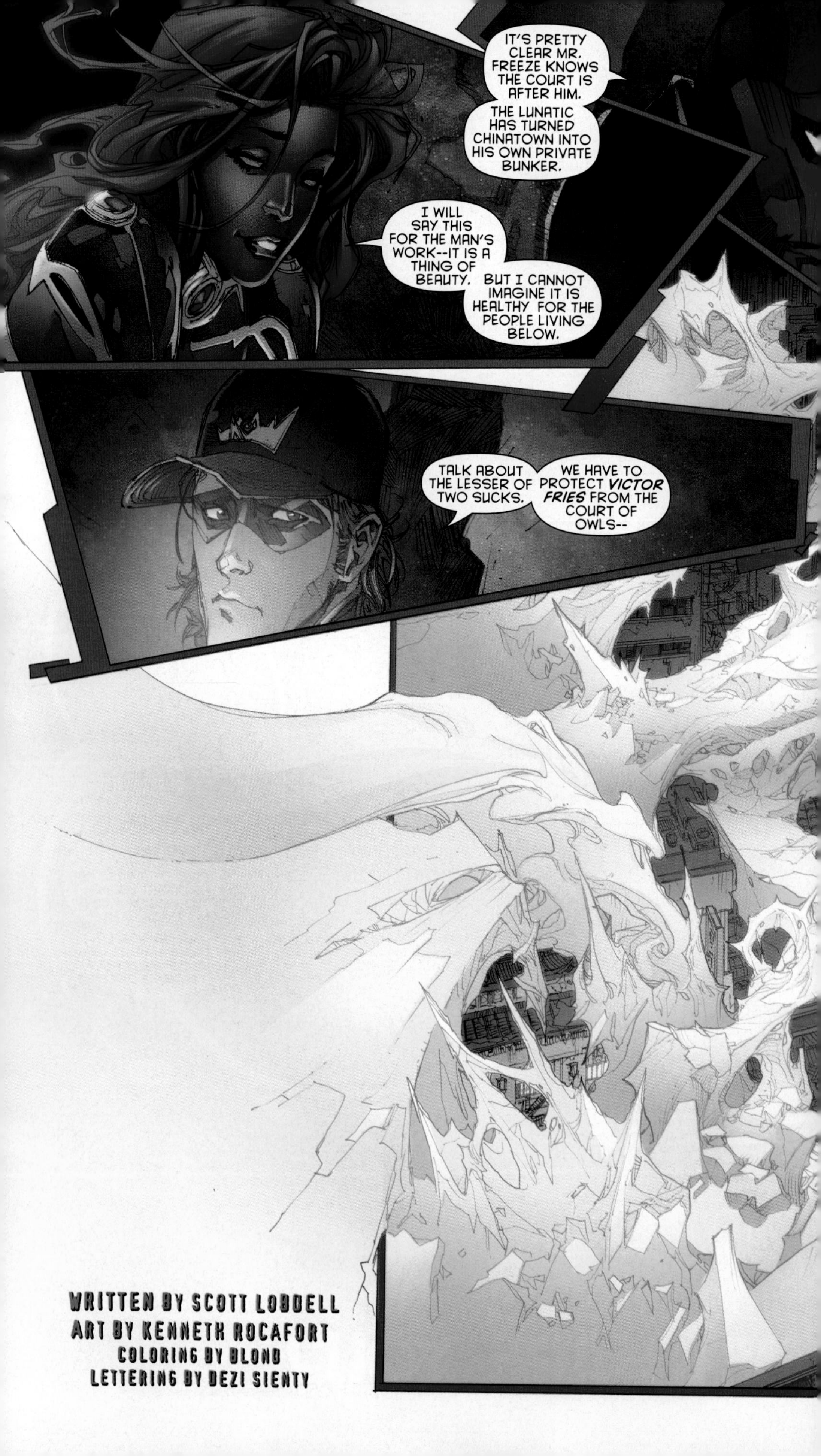

IT'S PRETTY CLEAR MR. FREEZE KNOWS THE COURT IS AFTER HIM.
THE LUNATIC HAS TURNED CHINATOWN INTO HIS OWN PRIVATE BUNKER.
I WILL SAY THIS FOR THE MAN'S WORK--IT IS A THING OF BEAUTY.
BUT I CANNOT IMAGINE IT IS HEALTHY FOR THE PEOPLE LIVING BELOW.
TALK ABOUT THE LESSER OF TWO SUCKS.
WE HAVE TO PROTECT *VICTOR FRIES* FROM THE COURT OF OWLS--
WRITTEN BY SCOTT LOBDELL
ART BY KENNETH ROCAFORT
COLORING BY BLOND
LETTERING BY DEZI SIENTY

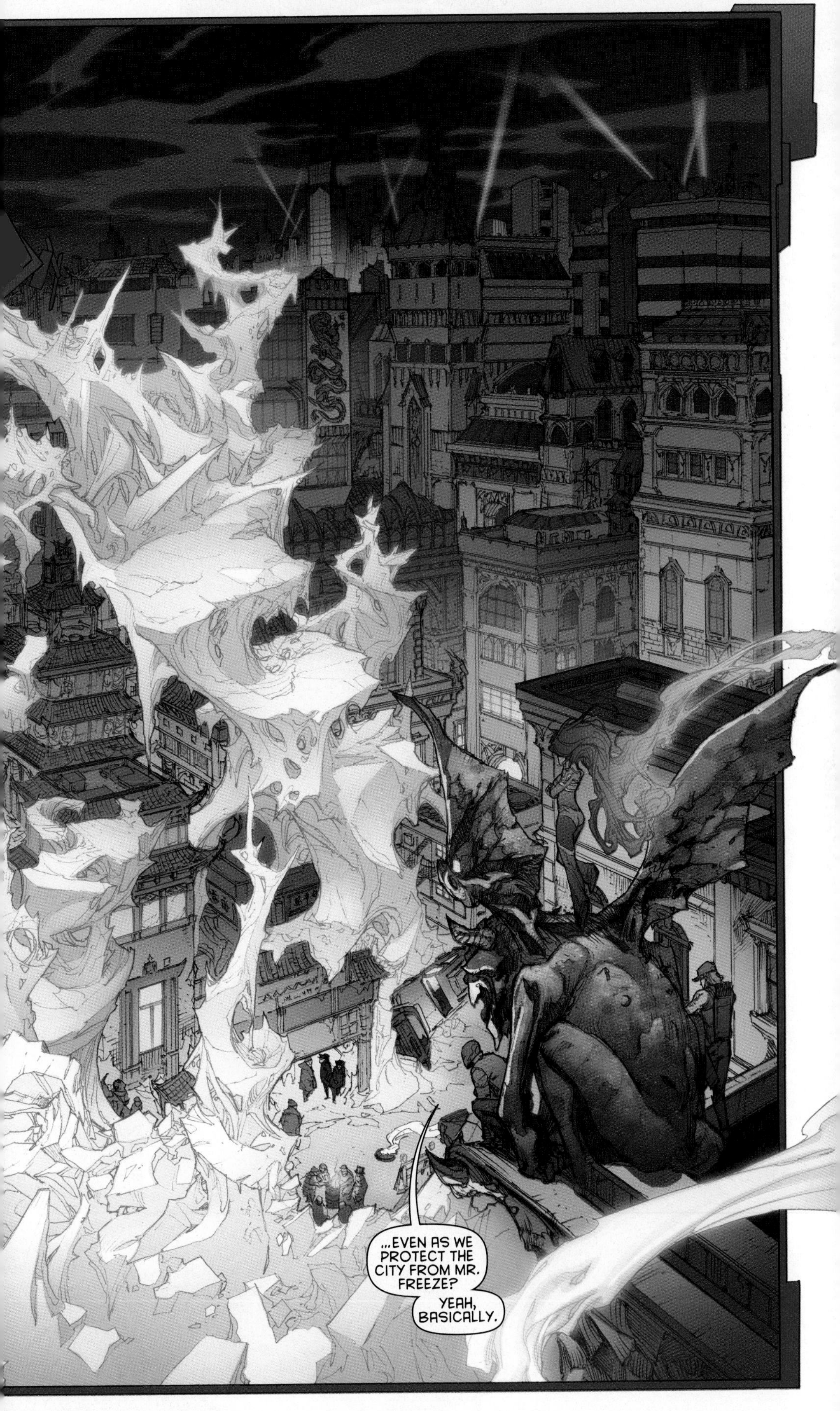
...EVEN AS WE PROTECT THE CITY FROM MR. FREEZE?
YEAH, BASICALLY.

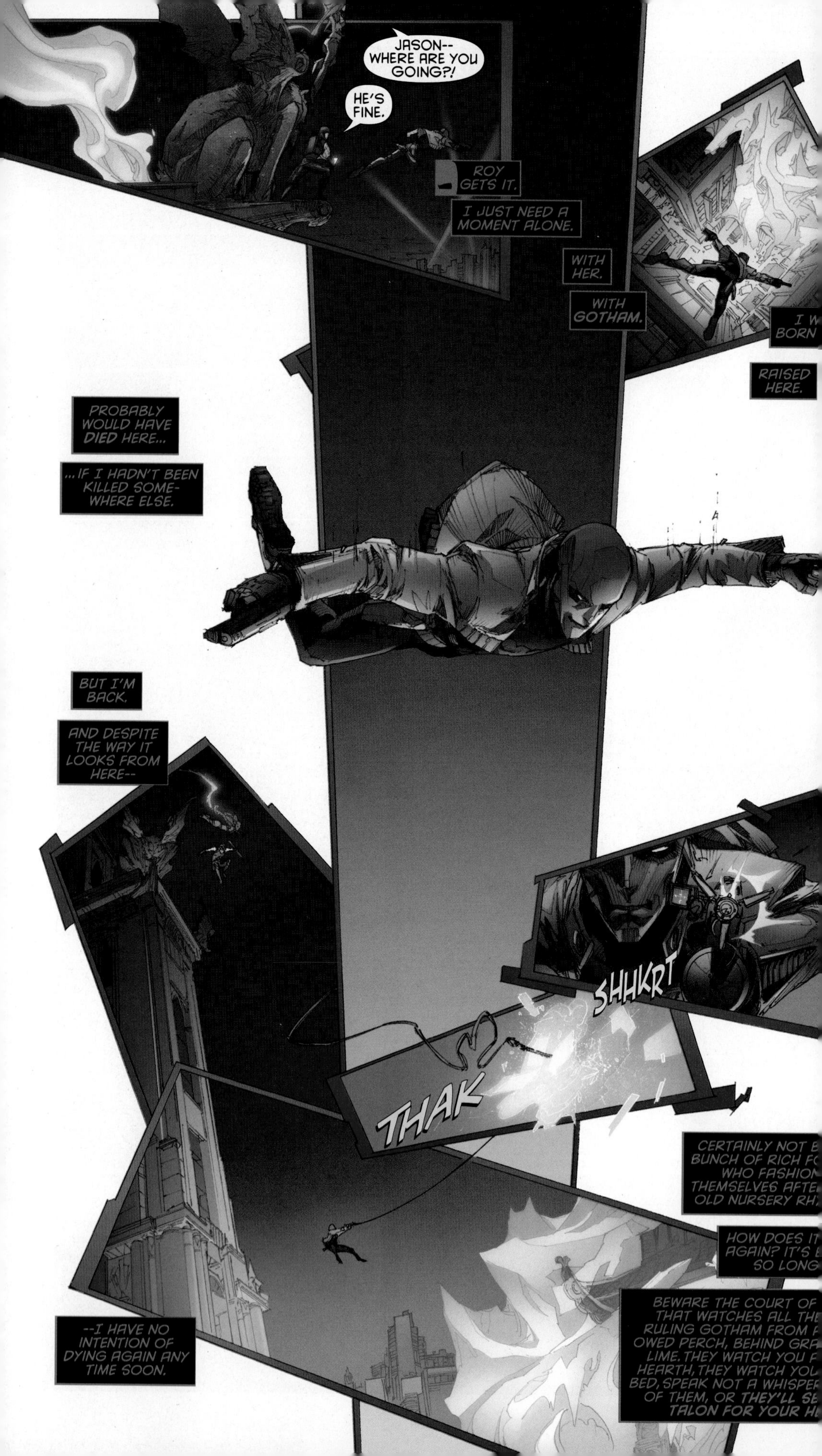
JASON-- WHERE ARE YOU GOING?!
HE'S FINE.
ROY GETS IT.
I JUST NEED A MOMENT ALONE.
WITH HER.
WITH GOTHAM.
I W
BORN
RAISED HERE.
PROBABLY WOULD HAVE DIED HERE...
...IF I HADN'T BEEN KILLED SOME-WHERE ELSE.
BUT I'M BACK.
AND DESPITE THE WAY IT LOOKS FROM HERE--
SHHKRT
THAK
--I HAVE NO INTENTION OF DYING AGAIN ANY TIME SOON.
CERTAINLY NOT B
BUNCH OF RICH F
WHO FASHION
THEMSELVES AFTE
OLD NURSERY RH
HOW DOES IT
AGAIN? IT'S
SO LONG
BEWARE THE COURT OF
THAT WATCHES ALL TH
RULING GOTHAM FROM
OWED PERCH, BEHIND GRA
LIME. THEY WATCH YOU A
HEARTH, THEY WATCH YOU
BED, SPEAK NOT A WHISPE
OF THEM, OR THEY'LL SE
TALON FOR YOUR H

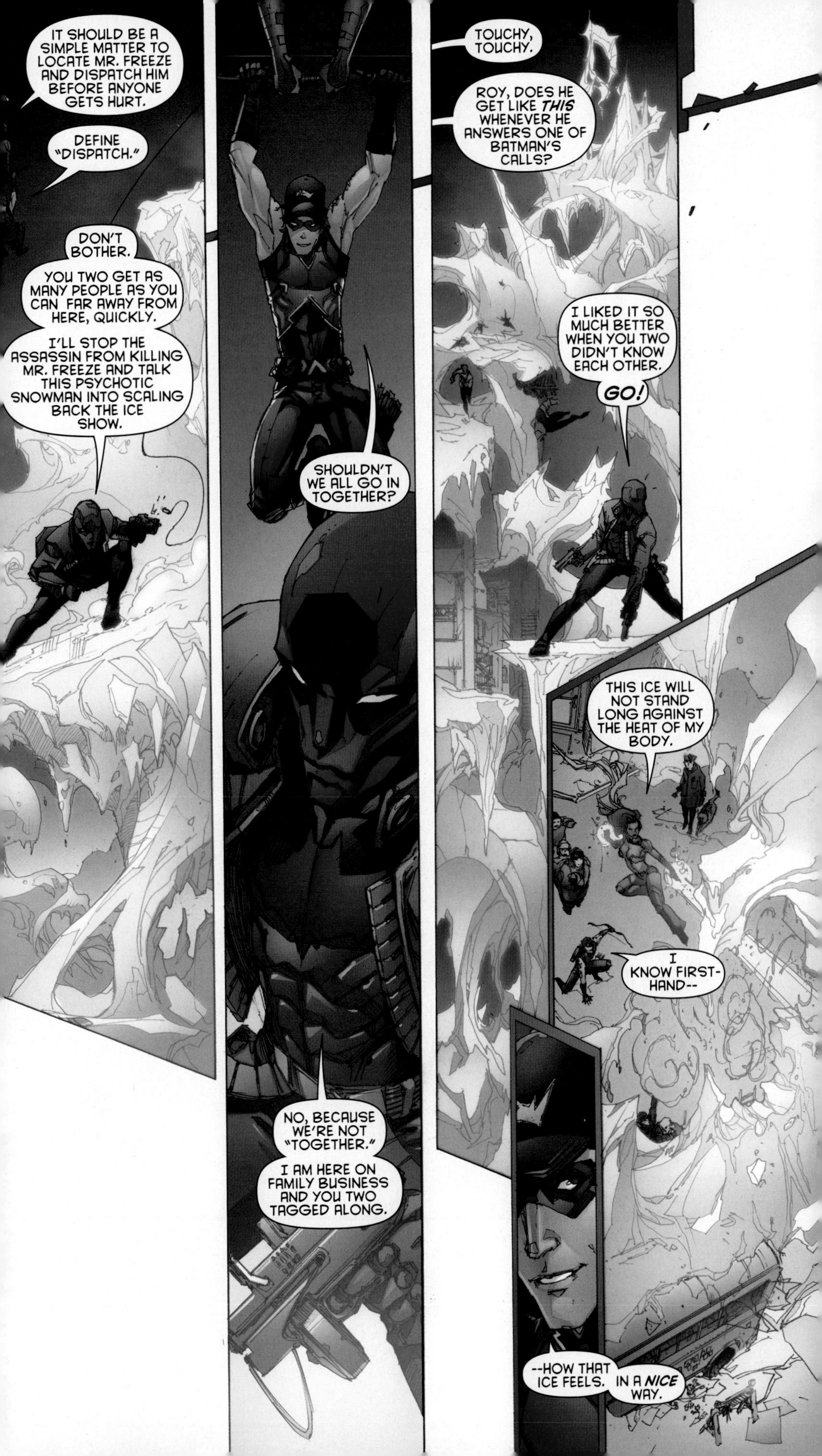

IT SHOULD BE A SIMPLE MATTER TO LOCATE MR. FREEZE AND DISPATCH HIM BEFORE ANYONE GETS HURT.
DEFINE "DISPATCH."
DON'T BOTHER.
YOU TWO GET AS MANY PEOPLE AS YOU CAN FAR AWAY FROM HERE, QUICKLY.
I'LL STOP THE ASSASSIN FROM KILLING MR. FREEZE AND TALK THIS PSYCHOTIC SNOWMAN INTO SCALING BACK THE ICE SHOW.
SHOULDN'T WE ALL GO IN TOGETHER?
NO, BECAUSE WE'RE NOT "TOGETHER."
I AM HERE ON FAMILY BUSINESS AND YOU TWO TAGGED ALONG.
TOUCHY, TOUCHY.
ROY, DOES HE GET LIKE *THIS* WHENEVER HE ANSWERS ONE OF BATMAN'S CALLS?
I LIKED IT SO MUCH BETTER WHEN YOU TWO DIDN'T KNOW EACH OTHER.
GO!
THIS ICE WILL NOT STAND LONG AGAINST THE HEAT OF MY BODY.
I KNOW FIRST-HAND--
--HOW THAT ICE FEELS.
IN A *NICE* WAY.

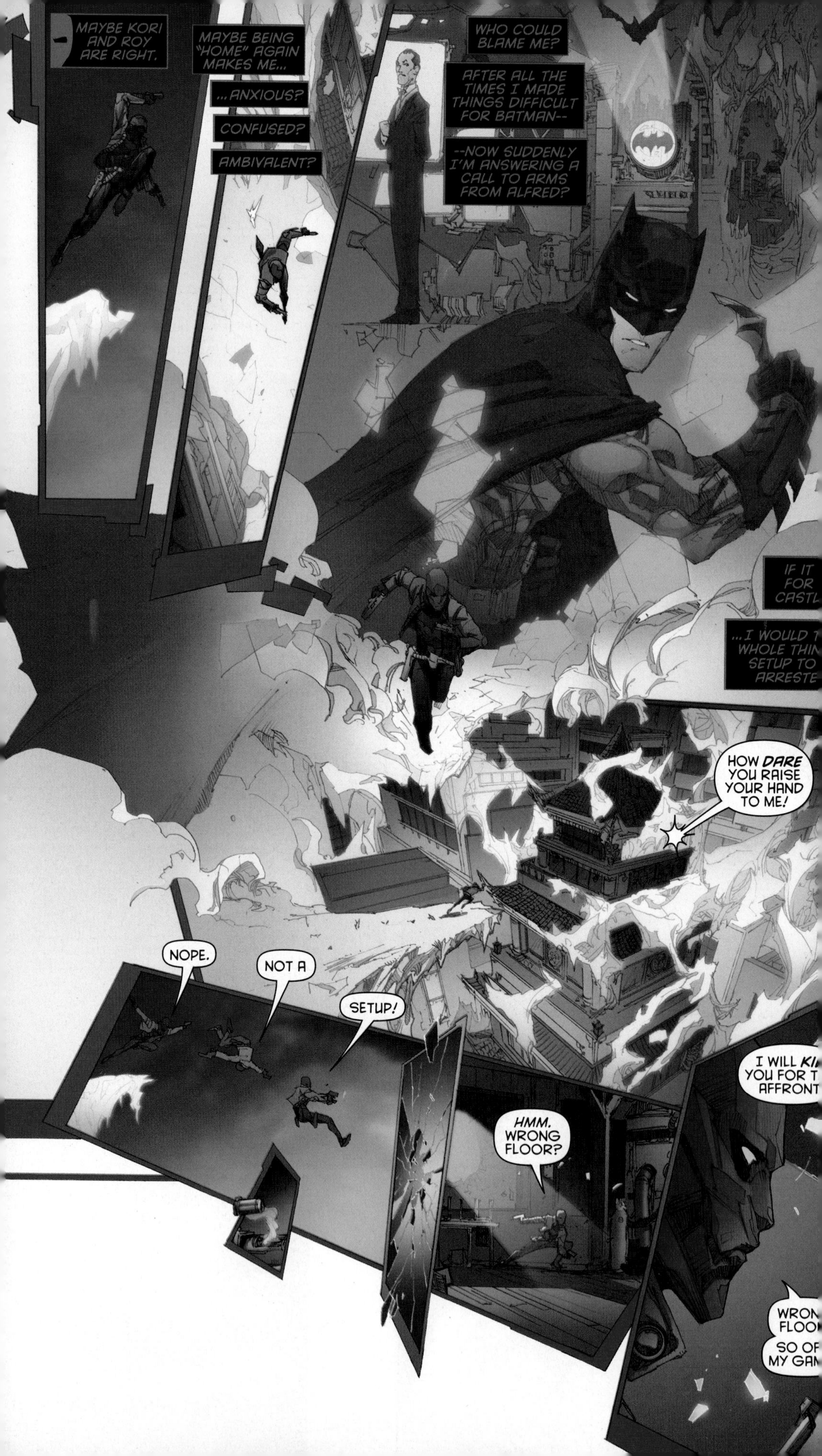
MAYBE KORI AND ROY ARE RIGHT.
MAYBE BEING "HOME" AGAIN MAKES ME...
...ANXIOUS?
CONFUSED?
AMBIVALENT?
WHO COULD BLAME ME?
AFTER ALL THE TIMES I MADE THINGS DIFFICULT FOR BATMAN--
--NOW SUDDENLY I'M ANSWERING A CALL TO ARMS FROM ALFRED?
IF IT FOR CASTL
...I WOULD WHOLE THIN SETUP TO ARRESTE
HOW DARE YOU RAISE YOUR HAND TO ME!
NOPE.
NOT A
SETUP!
HMM. WRONG FLOOR?
I WILL KI YOU FOR T AFFRONT
WRON FLOO
SO OF MY GAI

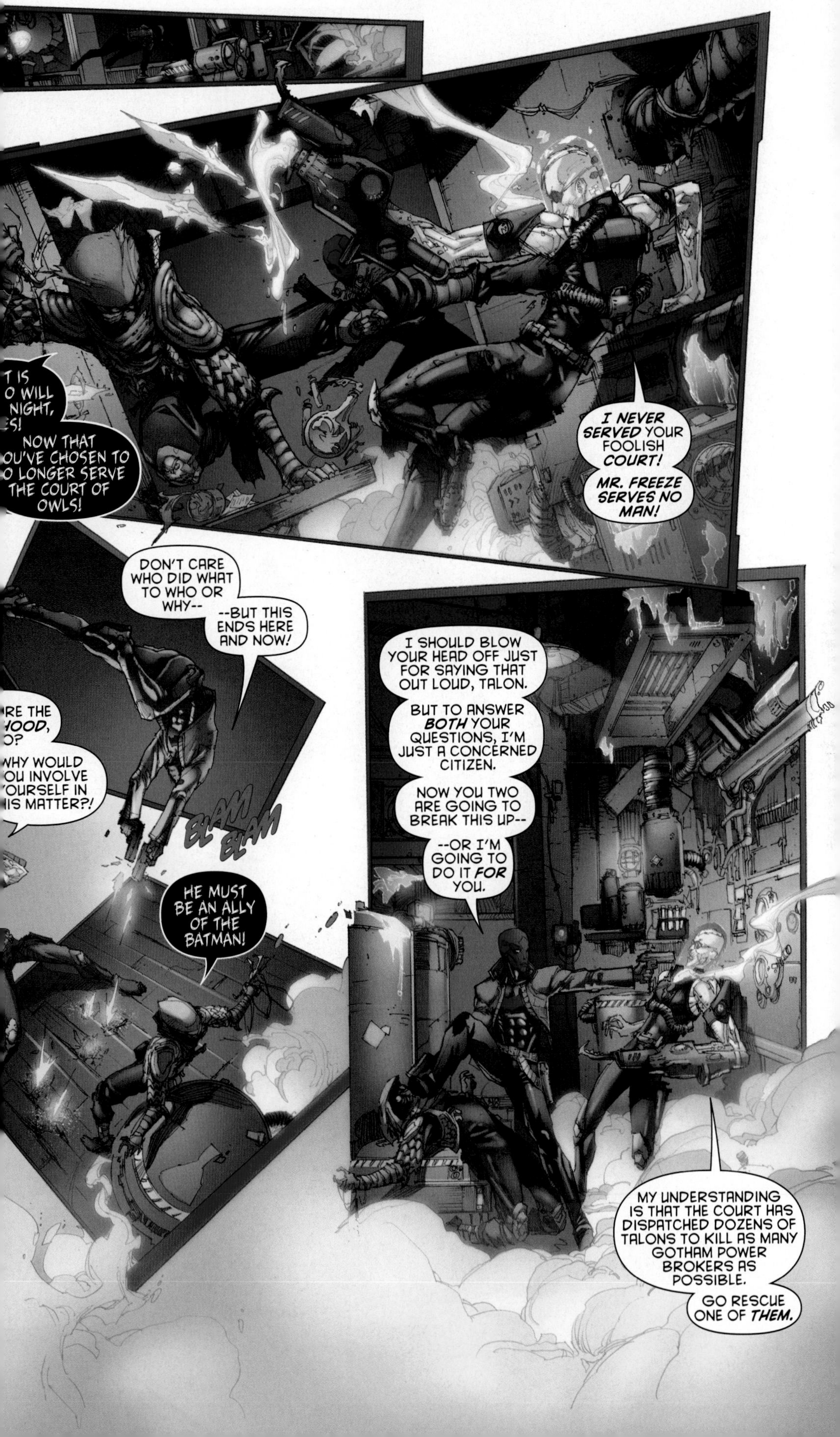

T IS
O WILL
NIGHT,
ES!
NOW THAT
OU'VE CHOSEN TO
O LONGER SERVE
THE COURT OF
OWLS!
I NEVER SERVED YOUR FOOLISH COURT!
MR. FREEZE SERVES NO MAN!
DON'T CARE WHO DID WHAT TO WHO OR WHY--
--BUT THIS ENDS HERE AND NOW!
RE THE
HOOD,
O?
WHY WOULD
OU INVOLVE
OURSELF IN
IS MATTER?!
BLAM BLAM
HE MUST BE AN ALLY OF THE BATMAN!
I SHOULD BLOW YOUR HEAD OFF JUST FOR SAYING THAT OUT LOUD, TALON.
BUT TO ANSWER BOTH YOUR QUESTIONS, I'M JUST A CONCERNED CITIZEN.
NOW YOU TWO ARE GOING TO BREAK THIS UP--
--OR I'M GOING TO DO IT FOR YOU.
MY UNDERSTANDING IS THAT THE COURT HAS DISPATCHED DOZENS OF TALONS TO KILL AS MANY GOTHAM POWER BROKERS AS POSSIBLE.
GO RESCUE ONE OF THEM.

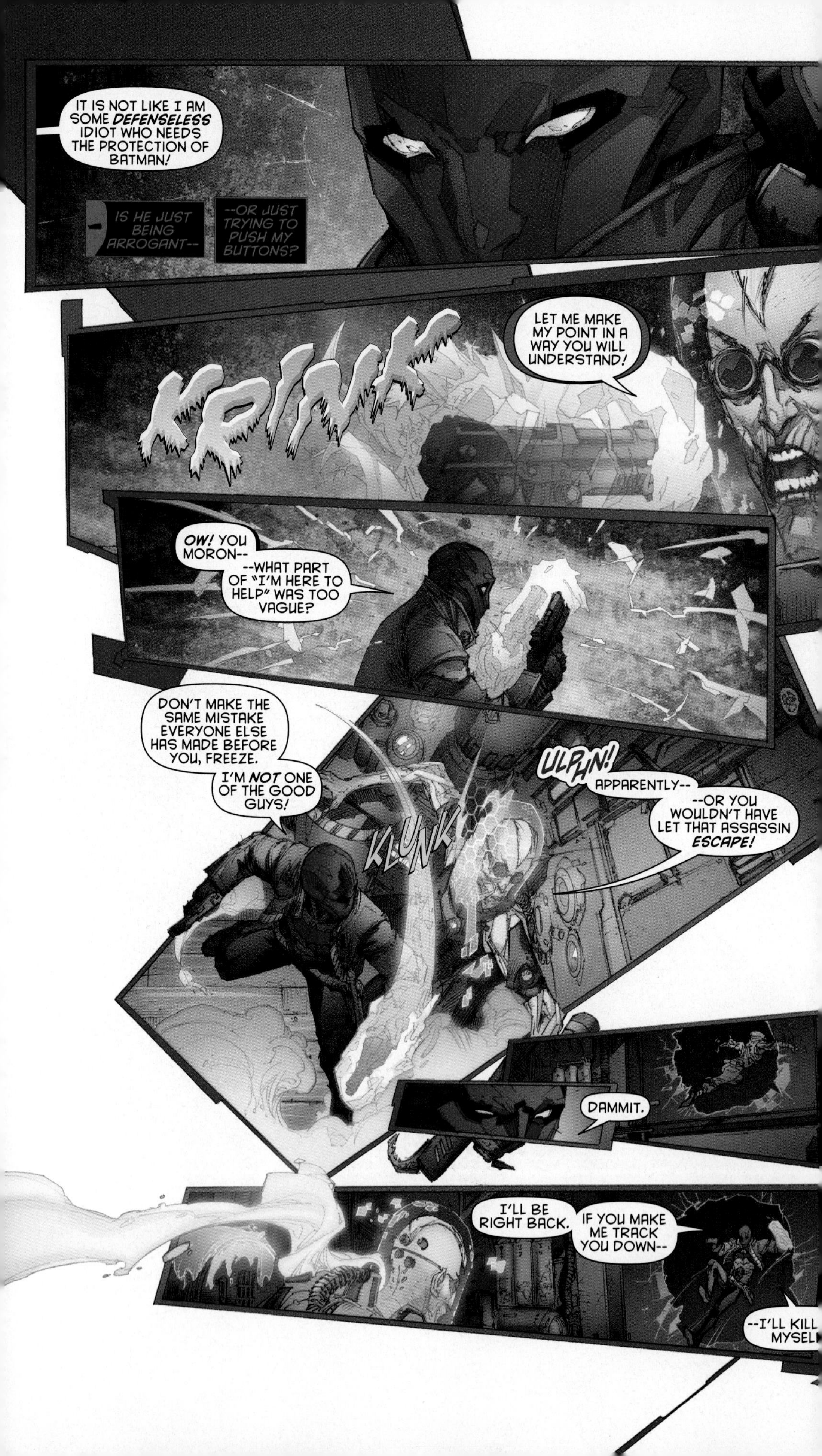

IT IS NOT LIKE I AM SOME DEFENSELESS IDIOT WHO NEEDS THE PROTECTION OF BATMAN!
IS HE JUST BEING ARROGANT--
--OR JUST TRYING TO PUSH MY BUTTONS?
KRINK
LET ME MAKE MY POINT IN A WAY YOU WILL UNDERSTAND!
OW! YOU MORON--
--WHAT PART OF "I'M HERE TO HELP" WAS TOO VAGUE?
DON'T MAKE THE SAME MISTAKE EVERYONE ELSE HAS MADE BEFORE YOU, FREEZE.
I'M NOT ONE OF THE GOOD GUYS!
ULPHN!
APPARENTLY--
--OR YOU WOULDN'T HAVE LET THAT ASSASSIN ESCAPE!
KLUNK
DAMMIT.
I'LL BE RIGHT BACK.
IF YOU MAKE ME TRACK YOU DOWN--
--I'LL KILL MYSEL

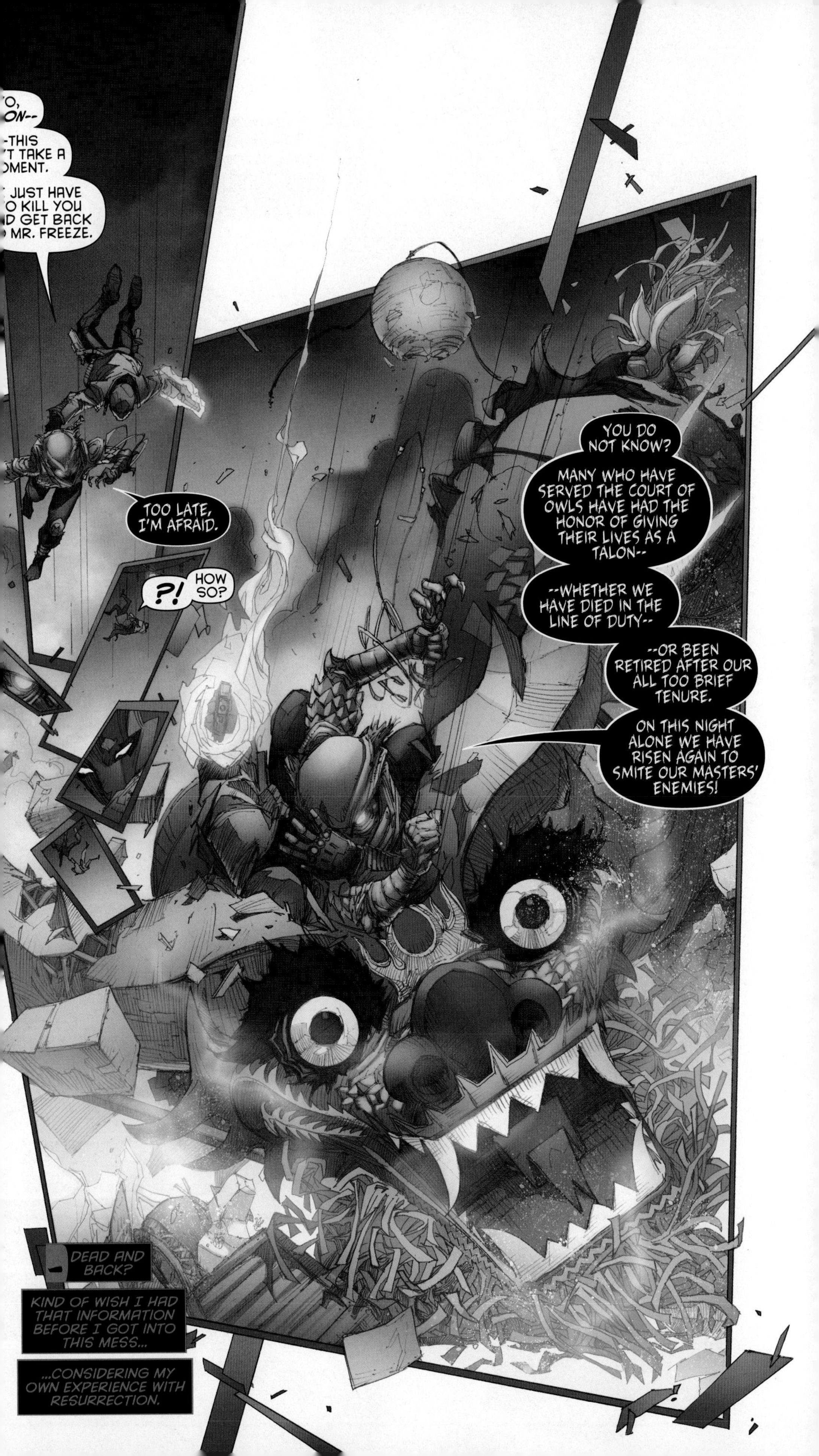

TOO LATE, I'M AFRAID.
?!
HOW SO?
YOU DO NOT KNOW?
MANY WHO HAVE SERVED THE COURT OF OWLS HAVE HAD THE HONOR OF GIVING THEIR LIVES AS A TALON--
--WHETHER WE HAVE DIED IN THE LINE OF DUTY--
--OR BEEN RETIRED AFTER OUR ALL TOO BRIEF TENURE.
ON THIS NIGHT ALONE WE HAVE RISEN AGAIN TO SMITE OUR MASTERS' ENEMIES!
DEAD AND BACK?
KIND OF WISH I HAD THAT INFORMATION BEFORE I GOT INTO THIS MESS...
...CONSIDERING MY OWN EXPERIENCE WITH RESURRECTION.

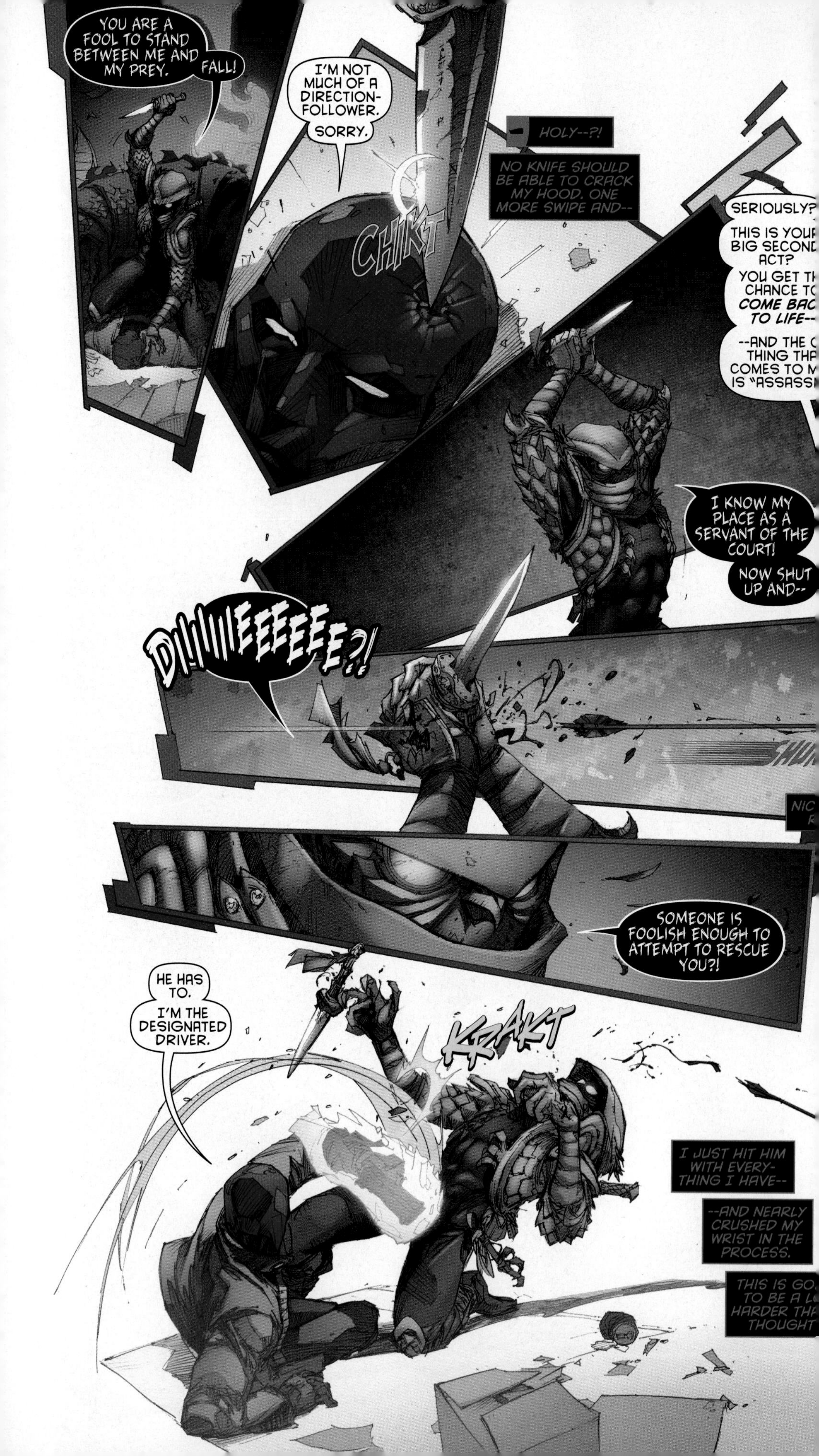
YOU ARE A FOOL TO STAND BETWEEN ME AND MY PREY.
FALL!
I'M NOT MUCH OF A DIRECTION-FOLLOWER.
SORRY.
CHIKT
HOLY--?!
NO KNIFE SHOULD BE ABLE TO CRACK MY HOOD. ONE MORE SWIPE AND--
SERIOUSLY?
THIS IS YOUR BIG SECOND ACT?
YOU GET TH CHANCE TO COME BAC TO LIFE--
--AND THE THING THA COMES TO M IS "ASSASS
I KNOW MY PLACE AS A SERVANT OF THE COURT!
NOW SHUT UP AND--
DIIIIIEEEEEE?!
SOMEONE IS FOOLISH ENOUGH TO ATTEMPT TO RESCUE YOU?!
HE HAS TO.
I'M THE DESIGNATED DRIVER.
KRAKT
I JUST HIT HIM WITH EVERY-THING I HAVE--
--AND NEARLY CRUSHED MY WRIST IN THE PROCESS.
THIS IS GO TO BE A L HARDER THA THOUGHT

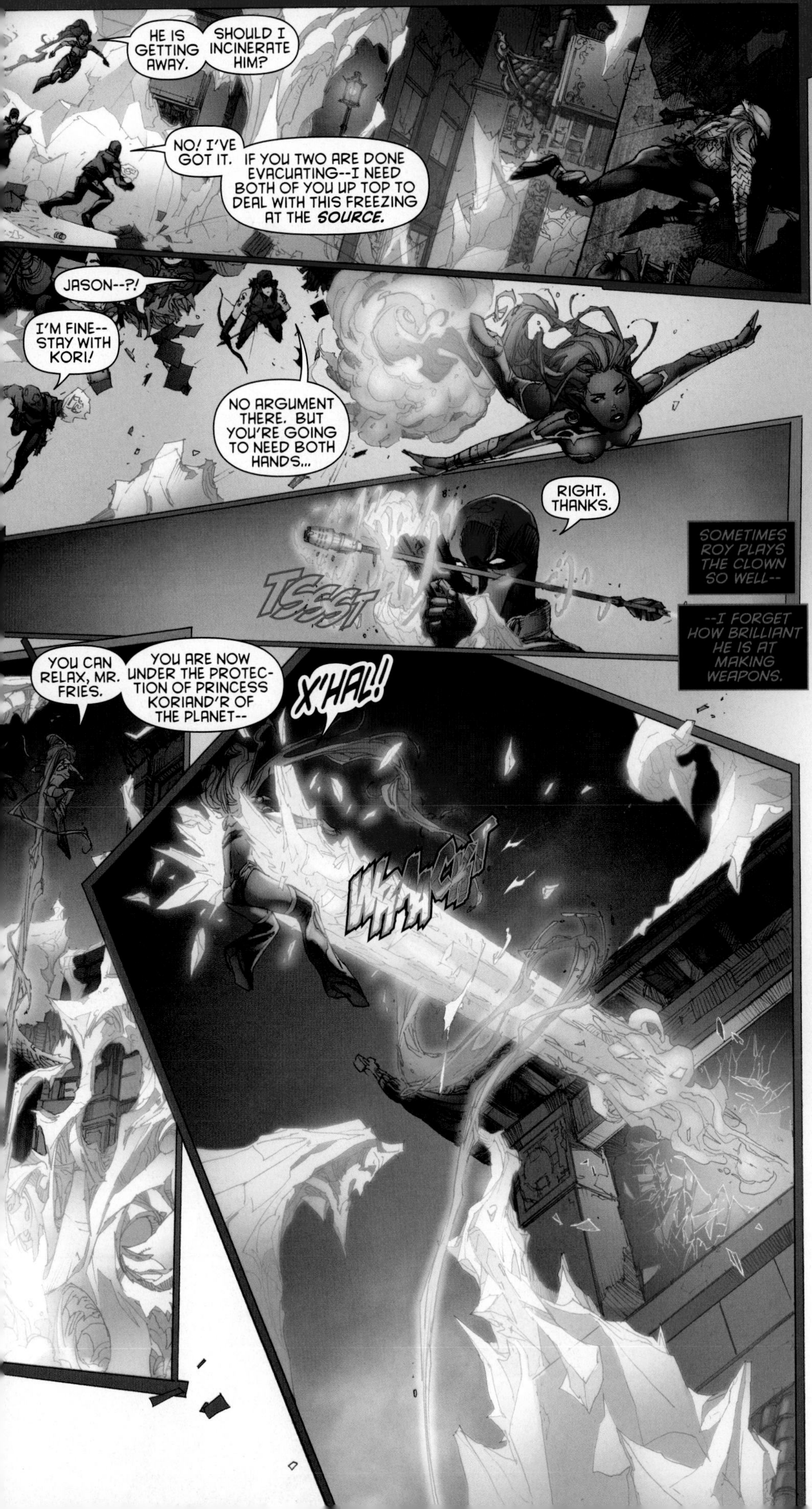
HE IS GETTING AWAY.
SHOULD I INCINERATE HIM?
NO! I'VE GOT IT.
IF YOU TWO ARE DONE EVACUATING--I NEED BOTH OF YOU UP TOP TO DEAL WITH THIS FREEZING AT THE SOURCE.
JASON--?!
I'M FINE--STAY WITH KORI!
NO ARGUMENT THERE. BUT YOU'RE GOING TO NEED BOTH HANDS...
RIGHT. THANKS.
TSSST
SOMETIMES ROY PLAYS THE CLOWN SO WELL--
--I FORGET HOW BRILLIANT HE IS AT MAKING WEAPONS.
YOU CAN RELAX, MR. FRIES.
YOU ARE NOW UNDER THE PROTECTION OF PRINCESS KORIAND'R OF THE PLANET--
X'HAL!
WHAAACK!

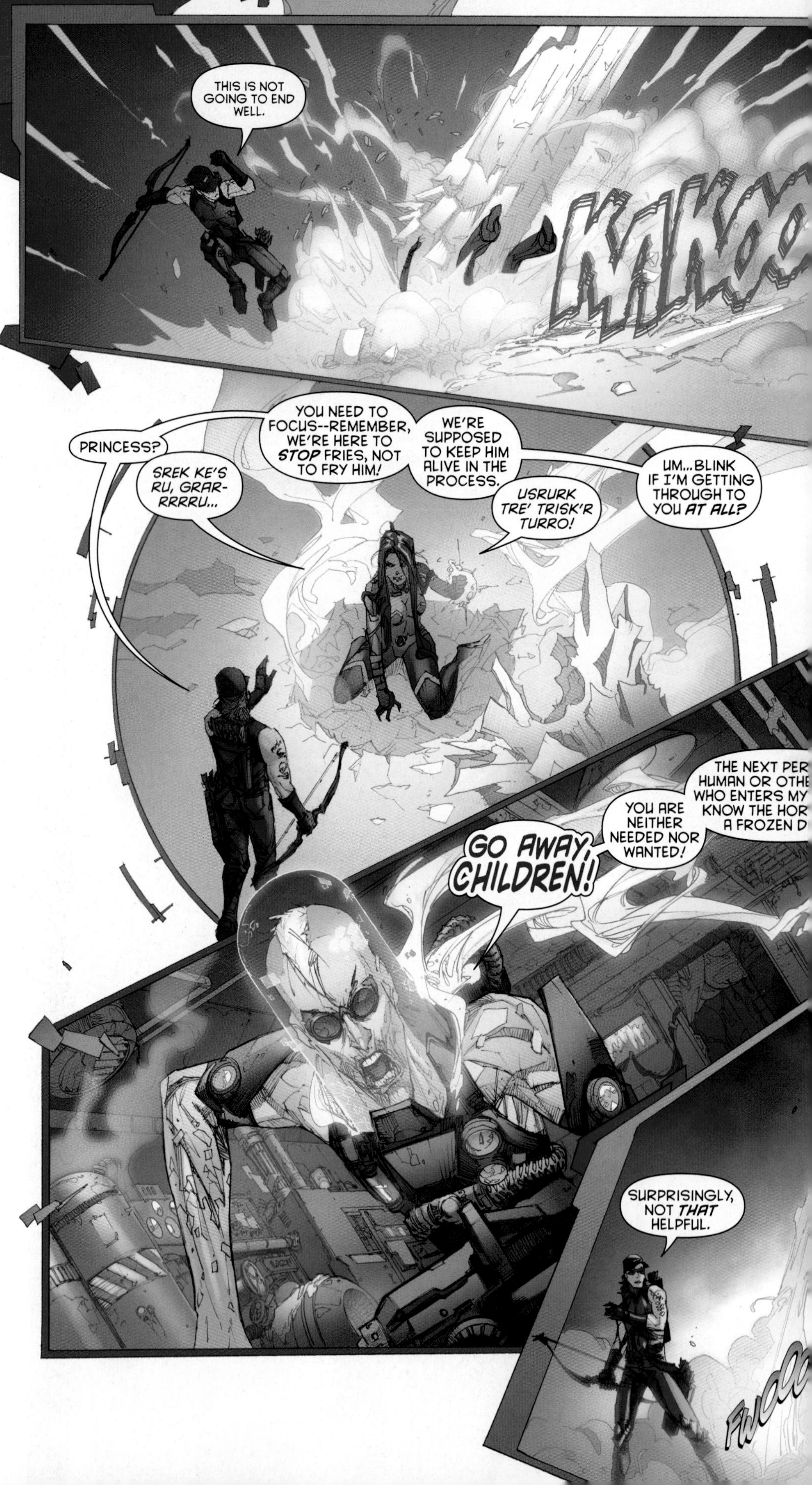
THIS IS NOT GOING TO END WELL.
PRINCESS?
SREK KE'S RU, GRAR-RRRRU...
YOU NEED TO FOCUS--REMEMBER, WE'RE HERE TO STOP FRIES, NOT TO FRY HIM!
WE'RE SUPPOSED TO KEEP HIM ALIVE IN THE PROCESS.
USRURK TRE' TRISK'R TURRO!
UM...BLINK IF I'M GETTING THROUGH TO YOU AT ALL?
THE NEXT PER HUMAN OR OTHE WHO ENTERS MY KNOW THE HOR A FROZEN D
YOU ARE NEITHER NEEDED NOR WANTED!
GO AWAY, CHILDREN!
SURPRISINGLY, NOT THAT HELPFUL.

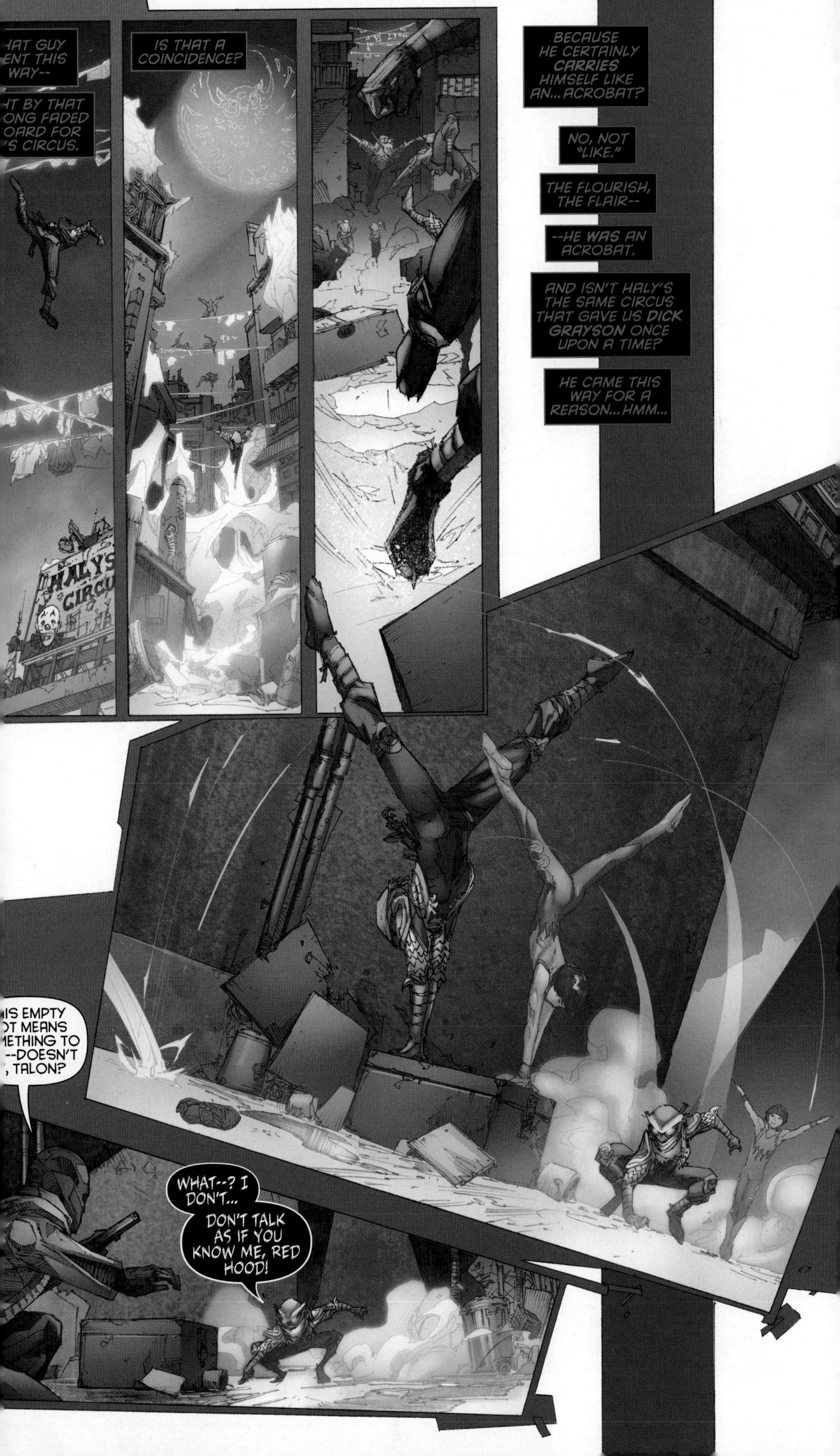

HAT GUY
ENT THIS
WAY--
HT BY THAT
ONG FADED
OARD FOR
'S CIRCUS.
IS THAT A COINCIDENCE?
BECAUSE HE CERTAINLY CARRIES HIMSELF LIKE AN... ACROBAT?
NO, NOT "LIKE."
THE FLOURISH, THE FLAIR--
--HE WAS AN ACROBAT.
AND ISN'T HALY'S THE SAME CIRCUS THAT GAVE US DICK GRAYSON ONCE UPON A TIME?
HE CAME THIS WAY FOR A REASON... HMM...
HALY'S
CIRCU
IS EMPTY
OT MEANS
METHING TO
--DOESN'T
, TALON?
WHAT--? I DON'T...
DON'T TALK AS IF YOU KNOW ME, RED HOOD!

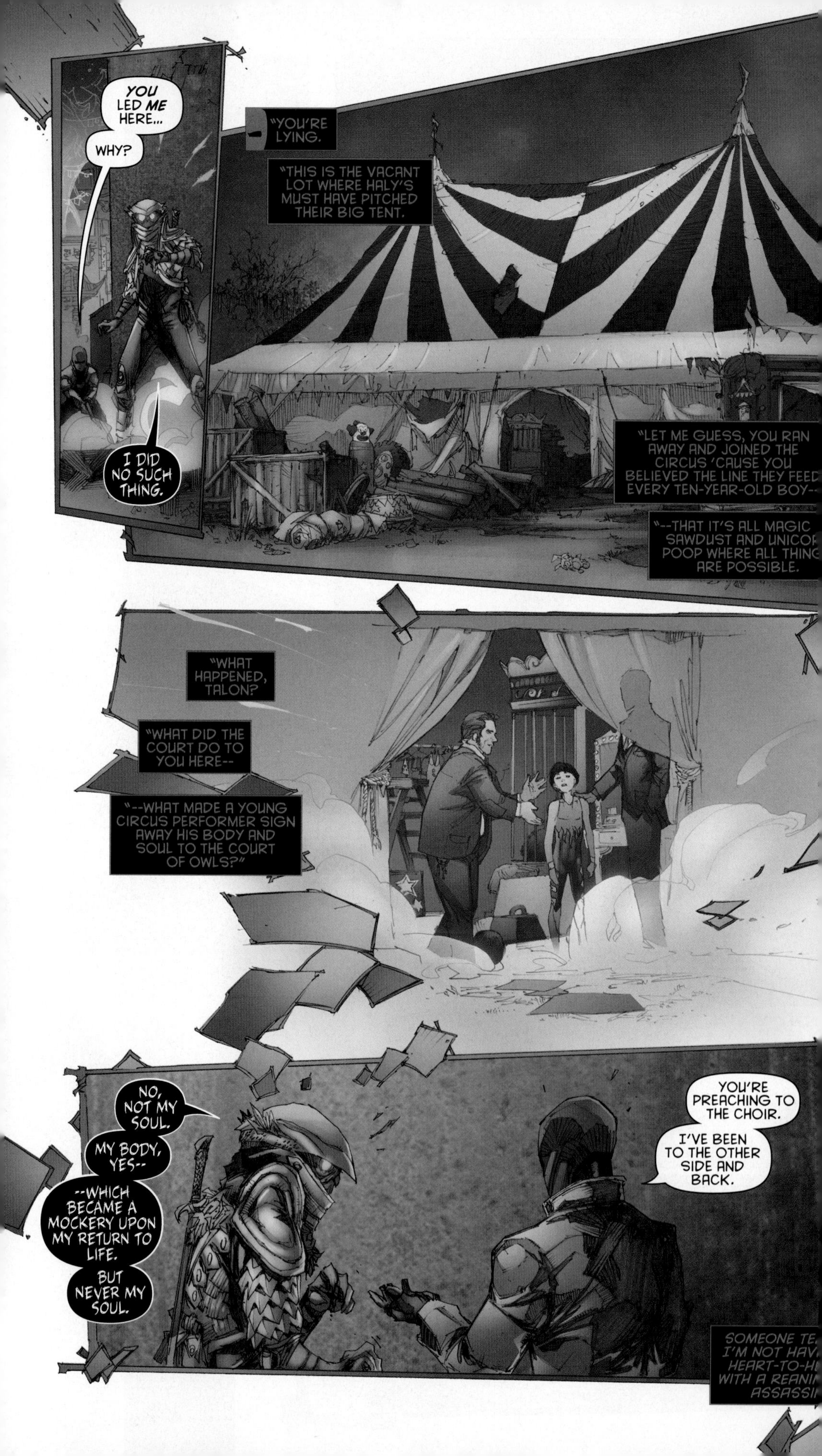

YOU LED ME HERE...
WHY?
I DID NO SUCH THING.
"YOU'RE LYING.
"THIS IS THE VACANT LOT WHERE HALY'S MUST HAVE PITCHED THEIR BIG TENT.
"LET ME GUESS, YOU RAN AWAY AND JOINED THE CIRCUS 'CAUSE YOU BELIEVED THE LINE THEY FEED EVERY TEN-YEAR-OLD BOY--
"--THAT IT'S ALL MAGIC SAWDUST AND UNICOR POOP WHERE ALL THING ARE POSSIBLE.
"WHAT HAPPENED, TALON?
"WHAT DID THE COURT DO TO YOU HERE--
"--WHAT MADE A YOUNG CIRCUS PERFORMER SIGN AWAY HIS BODY AND SOUL TO THE COURT OF OWLS?"
NO, NOT MY SOUL.
MY BODY, YES--
--WHICH BECAME A MOCKERY UPON MY RETURN TO LIFE.
BUT NEVER MY SOUL.
YOU'RE PREACHING TO THE CHOIR.
I'VE BEEN TO THE OTHER SIDE AND BACK.
SOMEONE TE I'M NOT HAV HEART-TO-H WITH A REANI ASSASSI

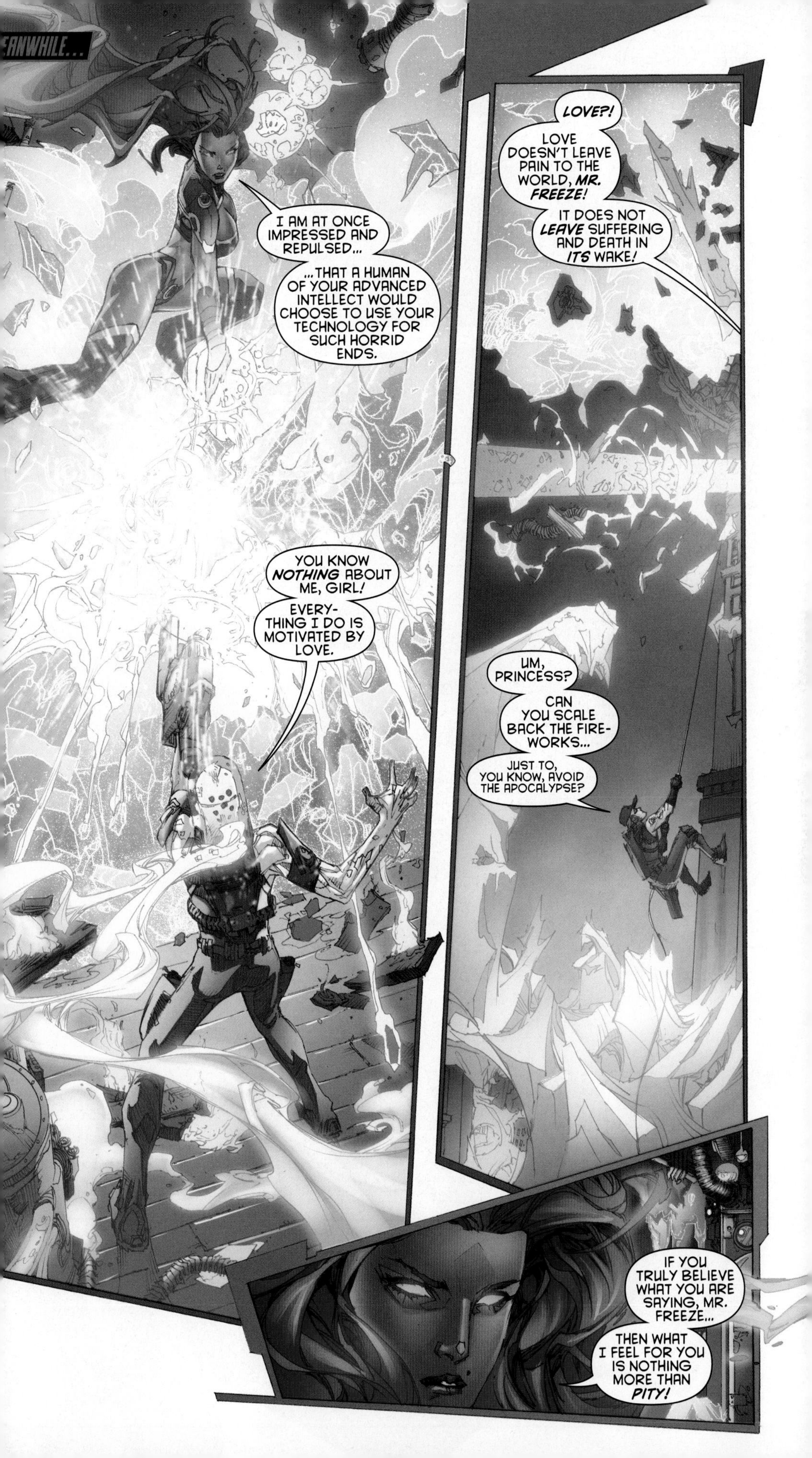

EANWHILE...
I AM AT ONCE IMPRESSED AND REPULSED...
...THAT A HUMAN OF YOUR ADVANCED INTELLECT WOULD CHOOSE TO USE YOUR TECHNOLOGY FOR SUCH HORRID ENDS.
YOU KNOW *NOTHING* ABOUT ME, GIRL!
EVERYTHING I DO IS MOTIVATED BY LOVE.
LOVE?!
LOVE DOESN'T LEAVE PAIN TO THE WORLD, *MR. FREEZE!*
IT DOES NOT *LEAVE* SUFFERING AND DEATH IN *ITS* WAKE!
UM, PRINCESS?
CAN YOU SCALE BACK THE FIREWORKS...
JUST TO, YOU KNOW, AVOID THE APOCALYPSE?
IF YOU TRULY BELIEVE WHAT YOU ARE SAYING, MR. FREEZE...
THEN WHAT I FEEL FOR YOU IS NOTHING MORE THAN *PITY!*

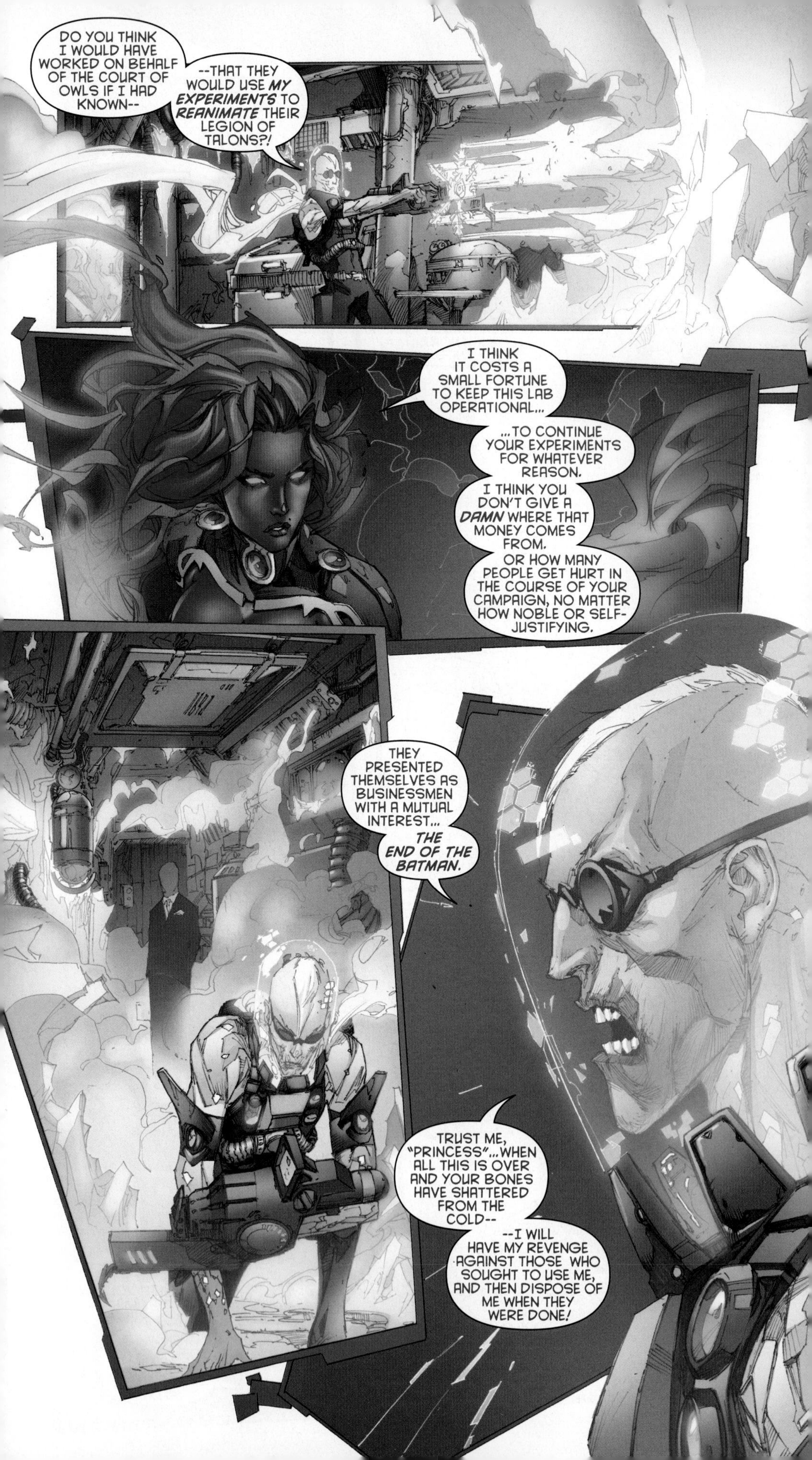
DO YOU THINK I WOULD HAVE WORKED ON BEHALF OF THE COURT OF OWLS IF I HAD KNOWN--
--THAT THEY WOULD USE *MY EXPERIMENTS* TO *REANIMATE* THEIR LEGION OF TALONS?!
I THINK IT COSTS A SMALL FORTUNE TO KEEP THIS LAB OPERATIONAL...
...TO CONTINUE YOUR EXPERIMENTS FOR WHATEVER REASON.
I THINK YOU DON'T GIVE A *DAMN* WHERE THAT MONEY COMES FROM.
OR HOW MANY PEOPLE GET HURT IN THE COURSE OF YOUR CAMPAIGN, NO MATTER HOW NOBLE OR SELF-JUSTIFYING.
THEY PRESENTED THEMSELVES AS BUSINESSMEN WITH A MUTUAL INTEREST... *THE END OF THE BATMAN.*
TRUST ME, "PRINCESS"...WHEN ALL THIS IS OVER AND YOUR BONES HAVE SHATTERED FROM THE COLD--
--I WILL HAVE MY REVENGE AGAINST THOSE WHO SOUGHT TO USE ME, AND THEN DISPOSE OF ME WHEN THEY WERE DONE!

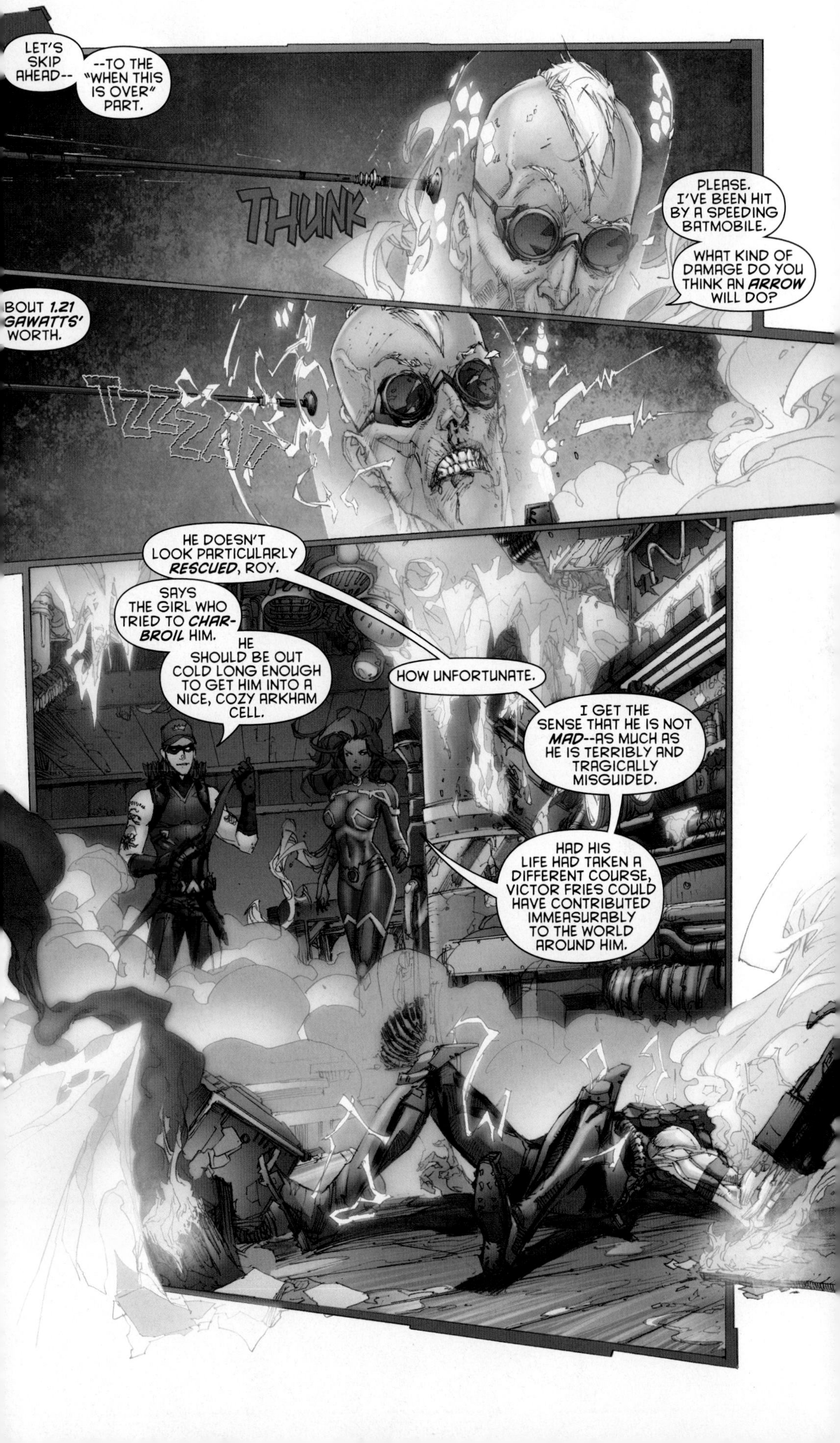
LET'S SKIP AHEAD--
--TO THE "WHEN THIS IS OVER" PART.
THUNK
PLEASE. I'VE BEEN HIT BY A SPEEDING BATMOBILE.
WHAT KIND OF DAMAGE DO YOU THINK AN ARROW WILL DO?
BOUT 1.21 GAWATTS' WORTH.
TZZZAT
HE DOESN'T LOOK PARTICULARLY RESCUED, ROY.
SAYS THE GIRL WHO TRIED TO CHAR-BROIL HIM.
HE SHOULD BE OUT COLD LONG ENOUGH TO GET HIM INTO A NICE, COZY ARKHAM CELL.
HOW UNFORTUNATE.
I GET THE SENSE THAT HE IS NOT MAD--AS MUCH AS HE IS TERRIBLY AND TRAGICALLY MISGUIDED.
HAD HIS LIFE HAD TAKEN A DIFFERENT COURSE, VICTOR FRIES COULD HAVE CONTRIBUTED IMMEASURABLY TO THE WORLD AROUND HIM.

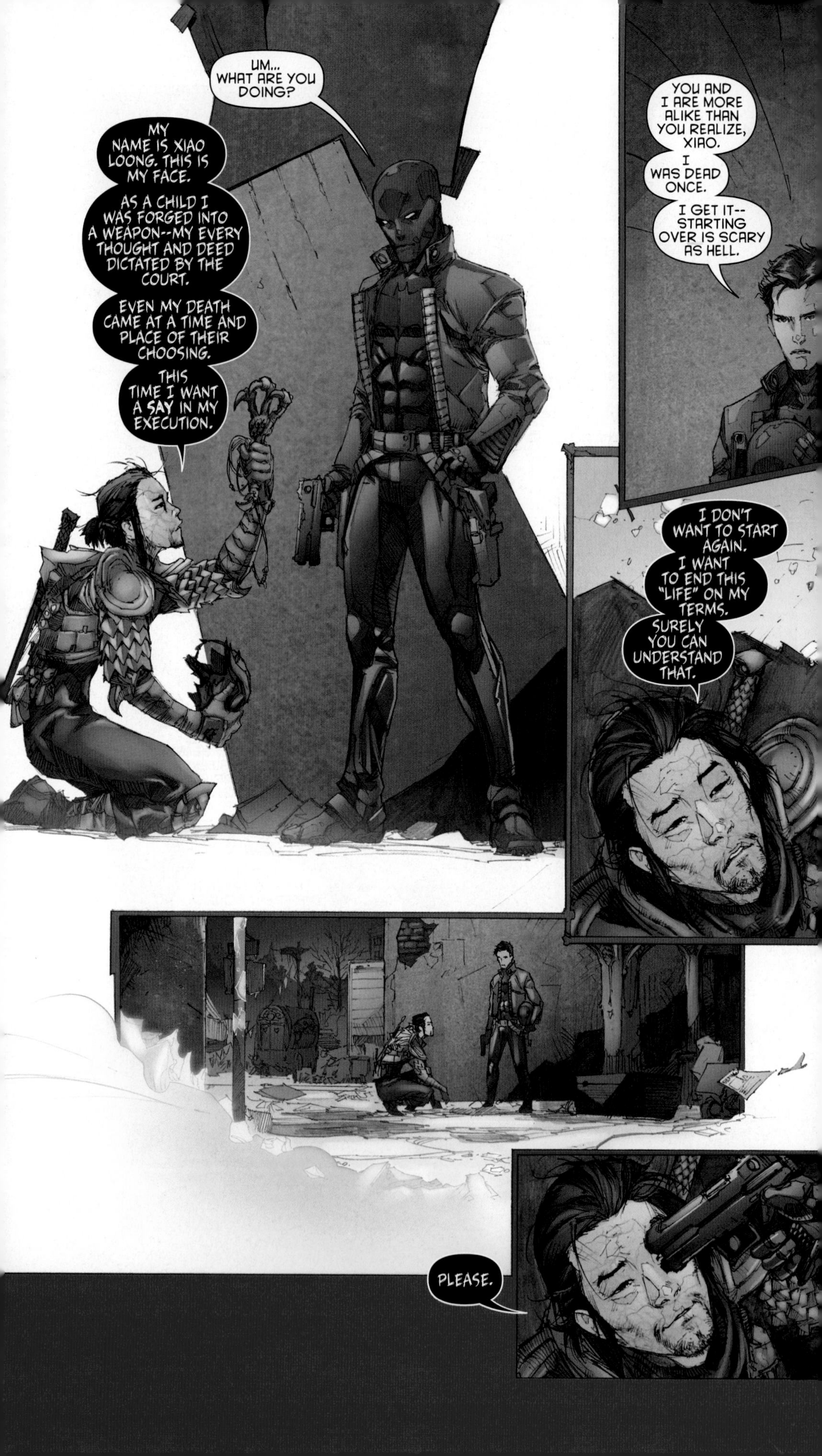
UM... WHAT ARE YOU DOING?
MY NAME IS XIAO LOONG. THIS IS MY FACE.
AS A CHILD I WAS FORGED INTO A WEAPON--MY EVERY THOUGHT AND DEED DICTATED BY THE COURT.
EVEN MY DEATH CAME AT A TIME AND PLACE OF THEIR CHOOSING.
THIS TIME I WANT A SAY IN MY EXECUTION.
YOU AND I ARE MORE ALIKE THAN YOU REALIZE, XIAO.
I WAS DEAD ONCE.
I GET IT-- STARTING OVER IS SCARY AS HELL.
I DON'T WANT TO START AGAIN.
I WANT TO END THIS "LIFE" ON MY TERMS.
SURELY YOU CAN UNDERSTAND THAT.
PLEASE.

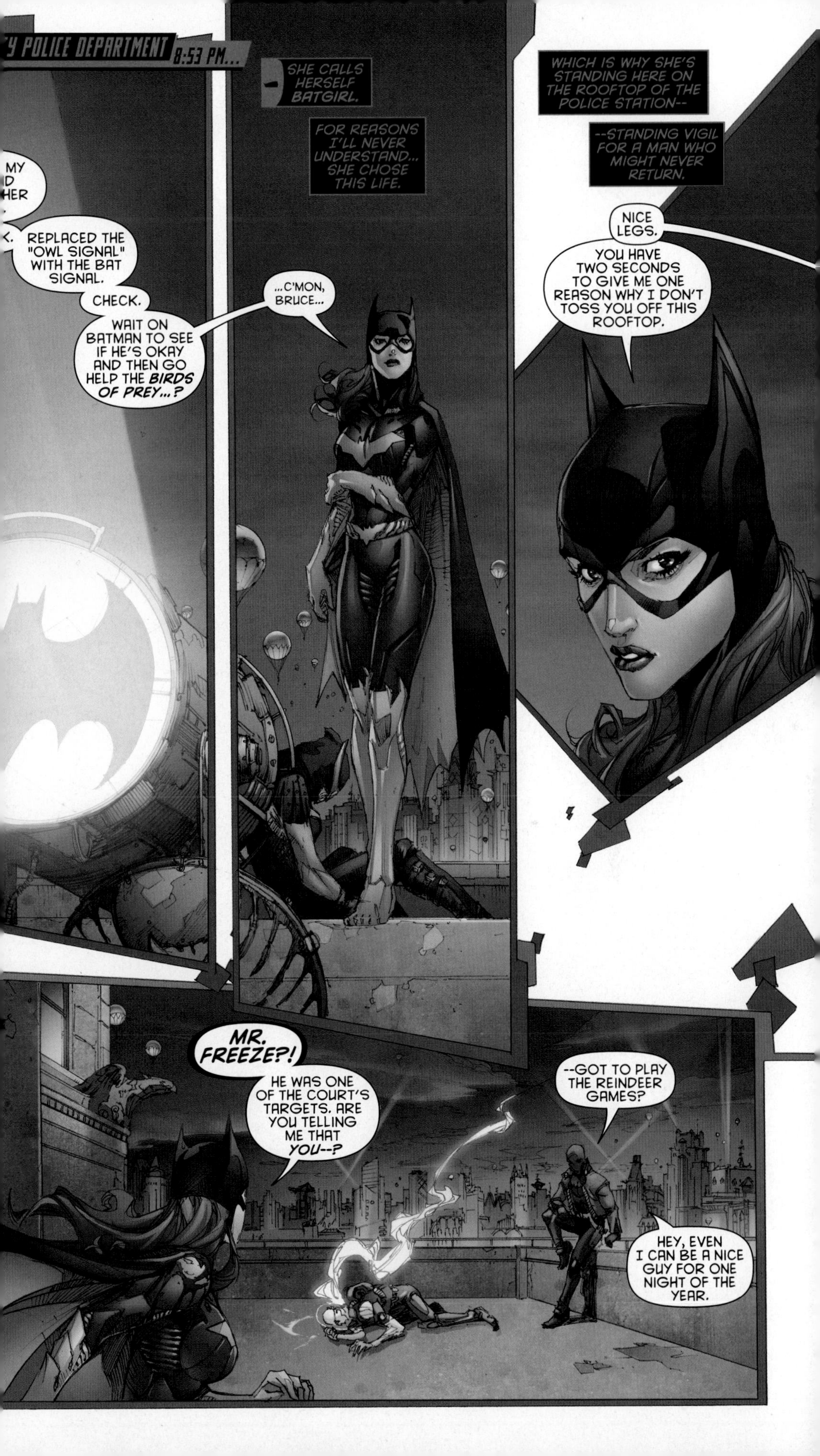

POLICE DEPARTMENT 8:53 PM...
MY
REPLACED THE "OWL SIGNAL" WITH THE BAT SIGNAL.
CHECK.
WAIT ON BATMAN TO SEE IF HE'S OKAY AND THEN GO HELP THE *BIRDS OF PREY*...?
SHE CALLS HERSELF BATGIRL.
FOR REASONS I'LL NEVER UNDERSTAND... SHE CHOSE THIS LIFE.
...C'MON, BRUCE...
WHICH IS WHY SHE'S STANDING HERE ON THE ROOFTOP OF THE POLICE STATION--
--STANDING VIGIL FOR A MAN WHO MIGHT NEVER RETURN.
NICE LEGS.
YOU HAVE TWO SECONDS TO GIVE ME ONE REASON WHY I DON'T TOSS YOU OFF THIS ROOFTOP.
--GOT TO PLAY THE REINDEER GAMES?
HEY, EVEN I CAN BE A NICE GUY FOR ONE NIGHT OF THE YEAR.
MR. FREEZE?!
HE WAS ONE OF THE COURT'S TARGETS. ARE YOU TELLING ME THAT *YOU*--?

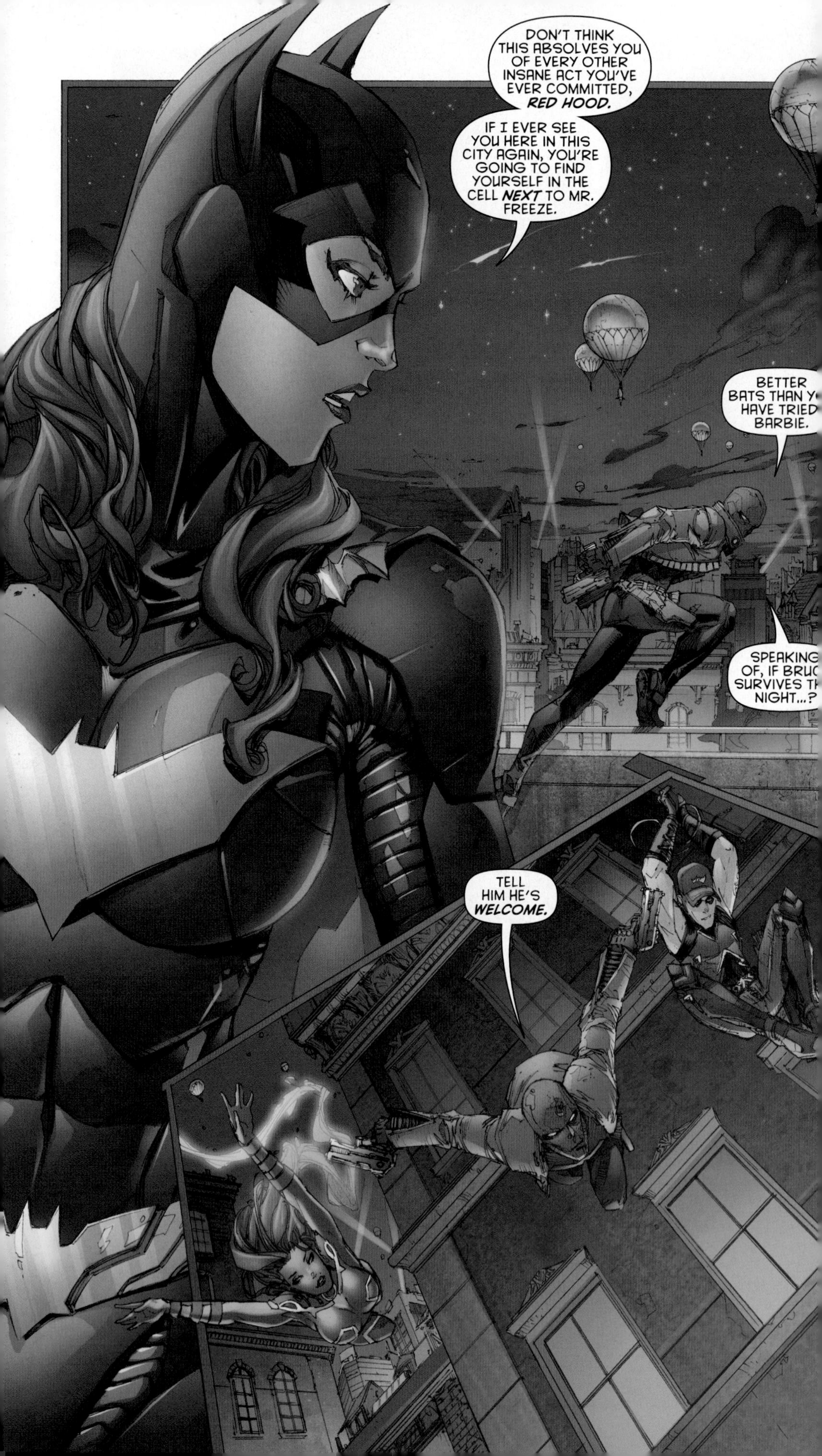
DON'T THINK THIS ABSOLVES YOU OF EVERY OTHER INSANE ACT YOU'VE EVER COMMITTED, RED HOOD.
IF I EVER SEE YOU HERE IN THIS CITY AGAIN, YOU'RE GOING TO FIND YOURSELF IN THE CELL NEXT TO MR. FREEZE.
BETTER BATS THAN Y HAVE TRIED BARBIE.
SPEAKING OF, IF BRUC SURVIVES T NIGHT...?
TELL HIM HE'S WELCOME.

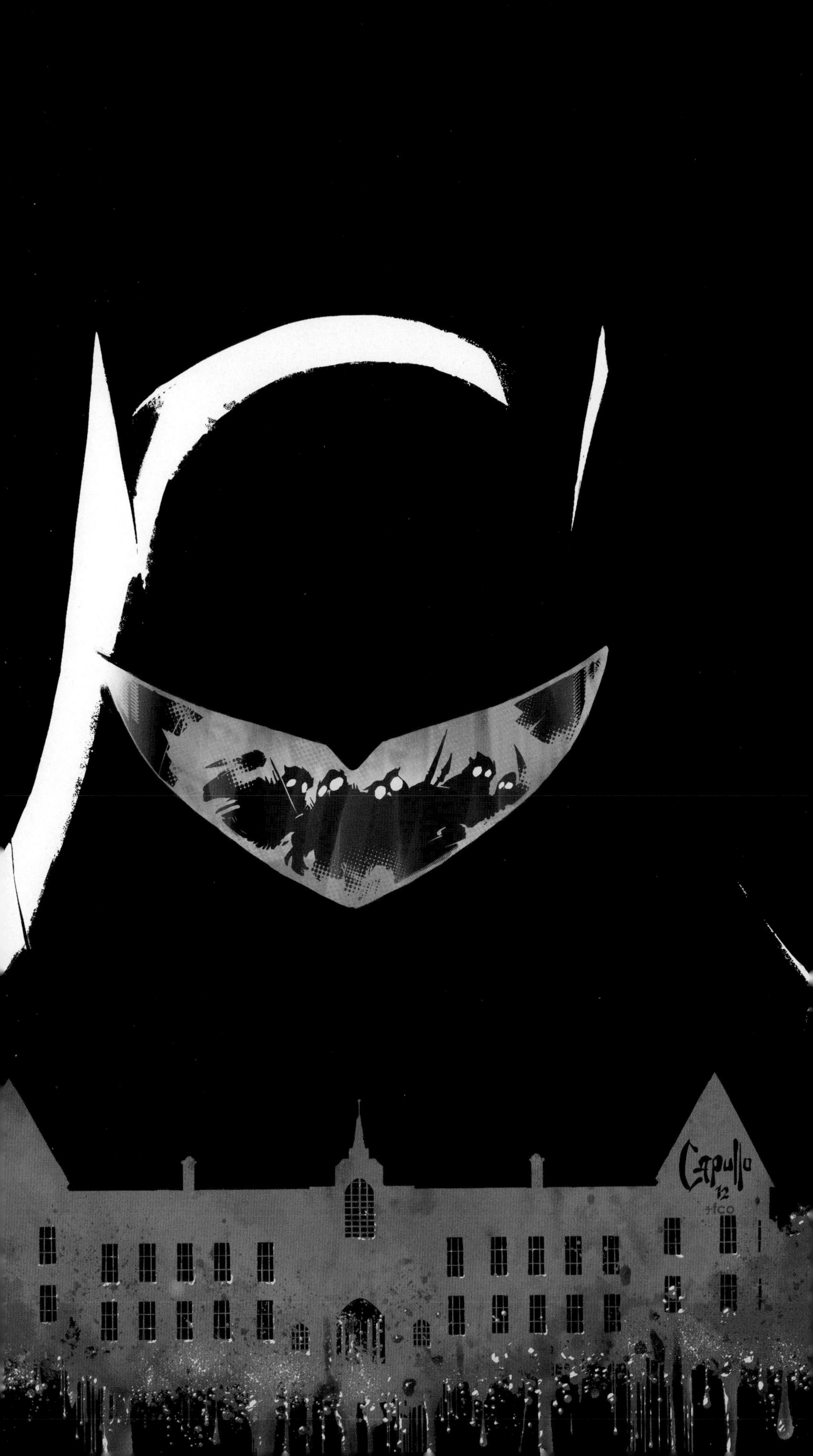
Capullo
'12
+fco

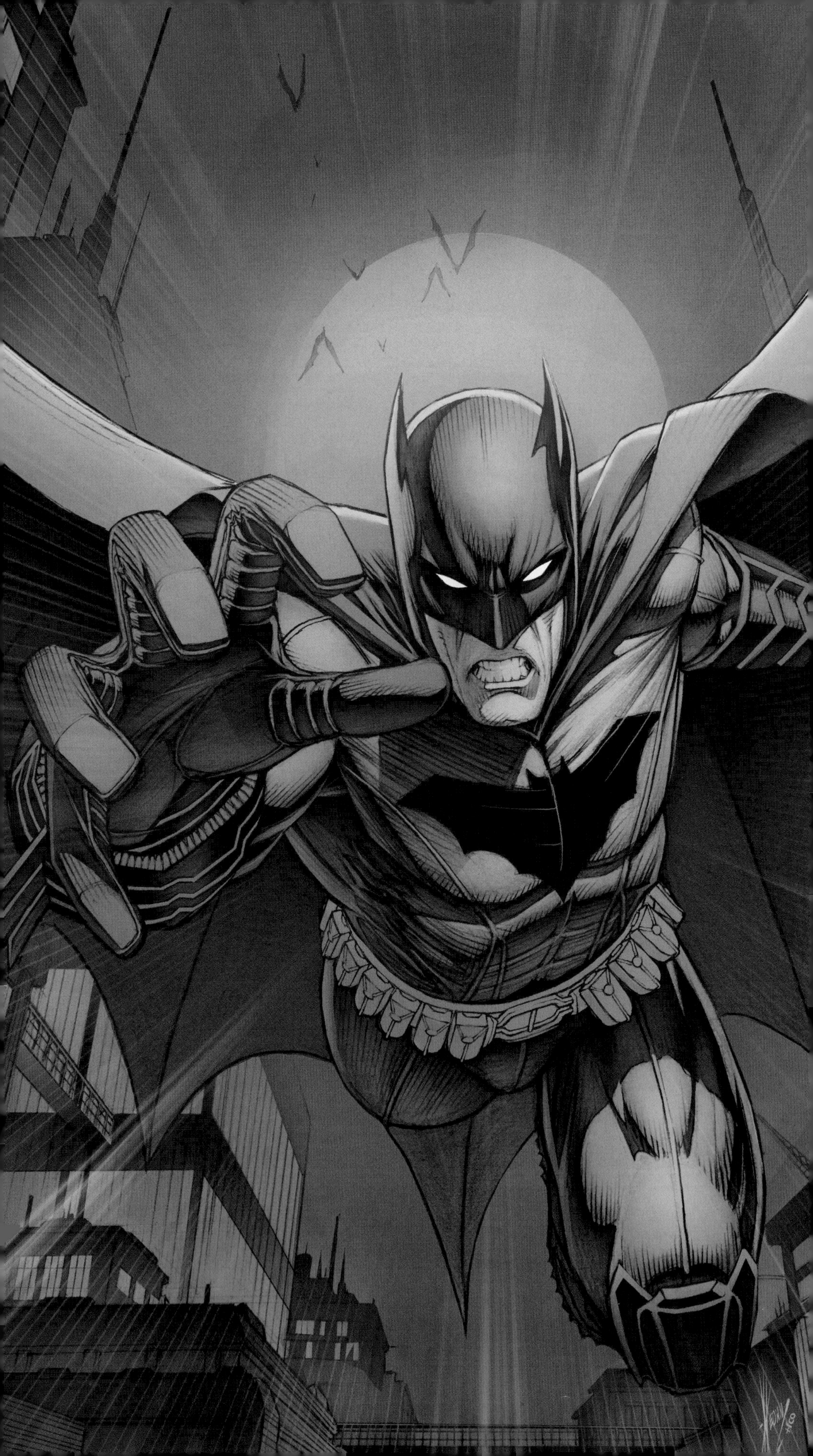

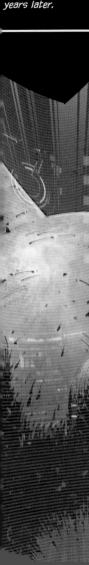

But they didn't
move in until two
years later.

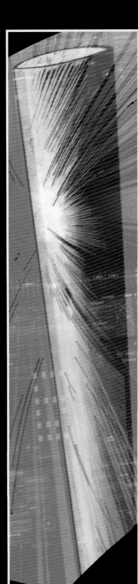

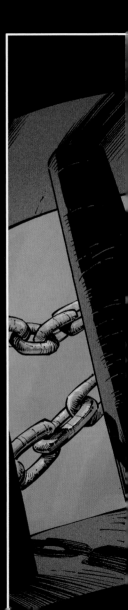

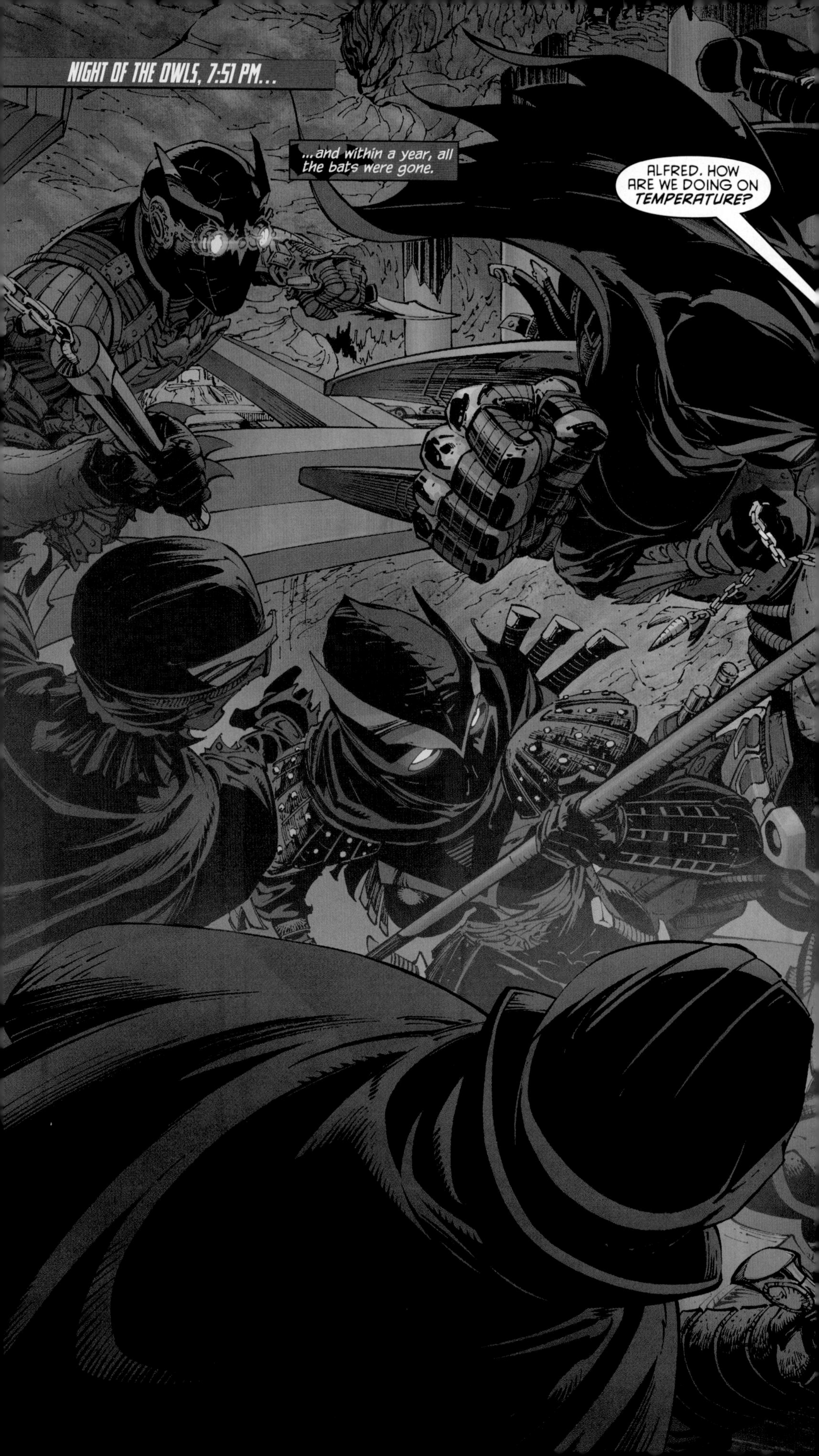
NIGHT OF THE OWLS, 7:51 PM...
...and within a year, all the bats were gone.
ALFRED. HOW ARE WE DOING ON TEMPERATURE?

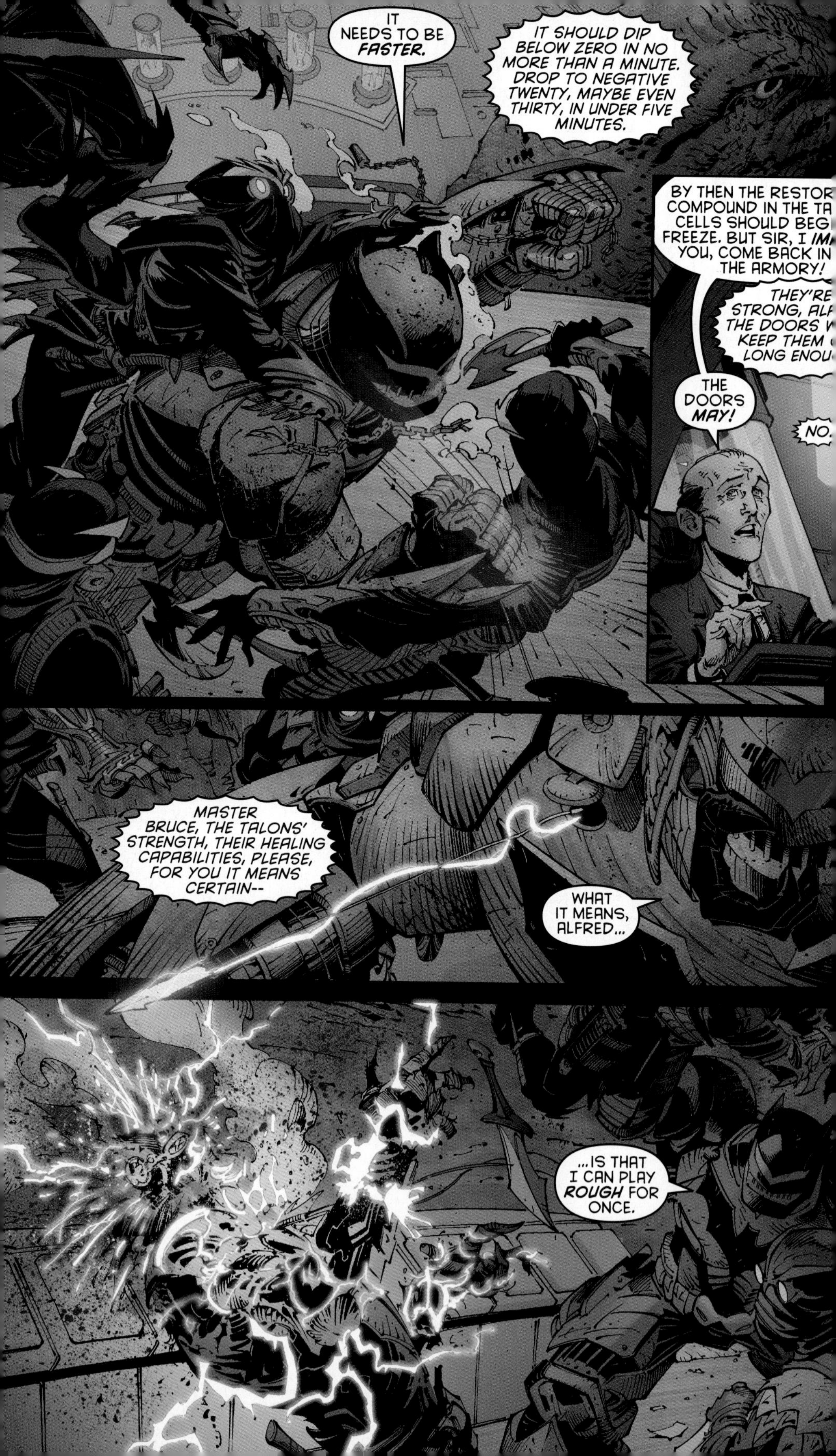
IT NEEDS TO BE FASTER.
IT SHOULD DIP BELOW ZERO IN NO MORE THAN A MINUTE. DROP TO NEGATIVE TWENTY, MAYBE EVEN THIRTY, IN UNDER FIVE MINUTES.
BY THEN THE RESTOR COMPOUND IN THE TA CELLS SHOULD BEG FREEZE. BUT SIR, I IM YOU, COME BACK IN THE ARMORY!
THEY'RE STRONG, AL THE DOORS KEEP THEM LONG ENOU
THE DOORS MAY!
NO.
MASTER BRUCE, THE TALONS' STRENGTH, THEIR HEALING CAPABILITIES, PLEASE, FOR YOU IT MEANS CERTAIN--
WHAT IT MEANS, ALFRED...
...IS THAT I CAN PLAY ROUGH FOR ONCE.

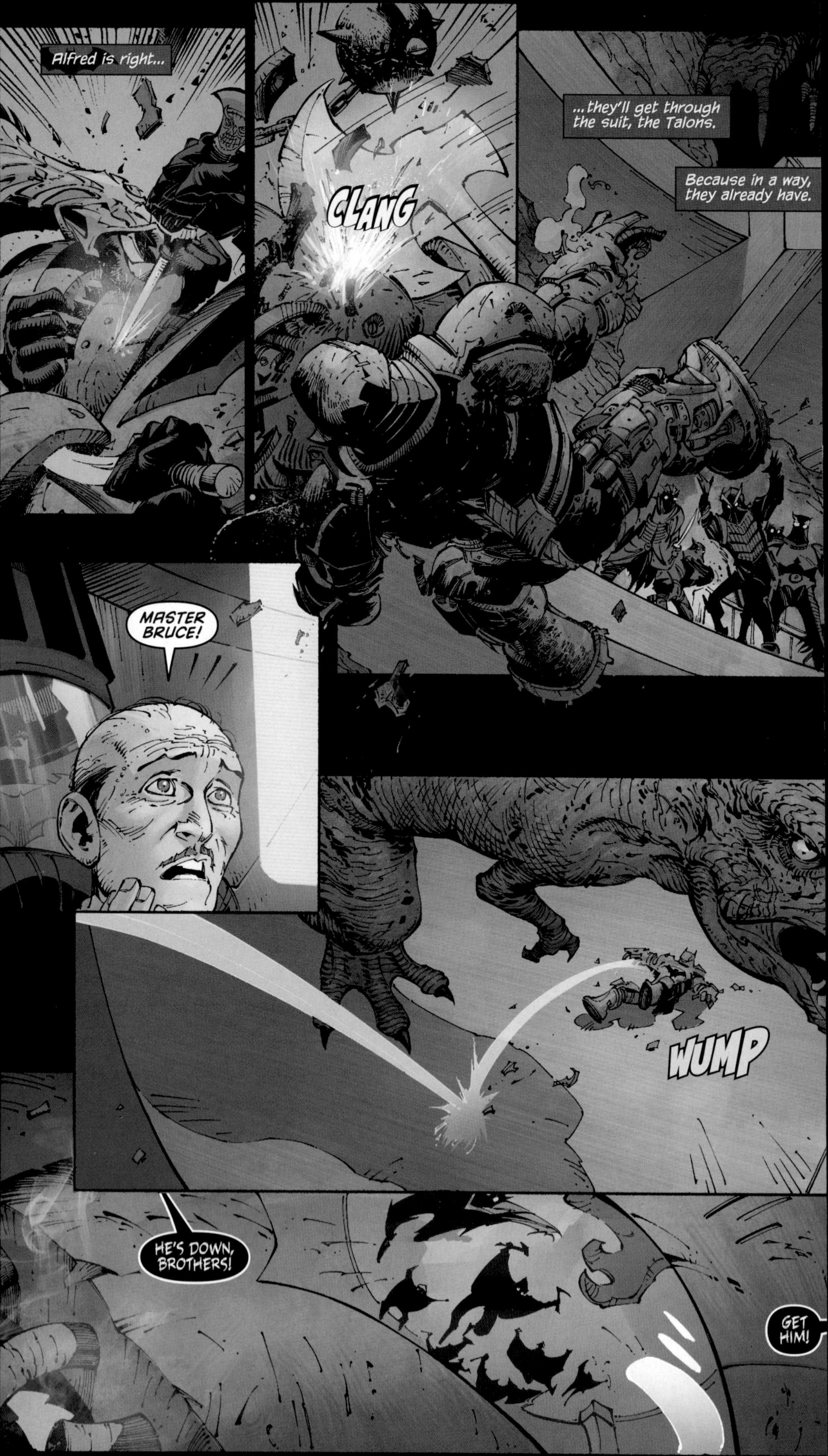
Alfred is right...
CLANG
...they'll get through the suit, the Talons.
Because in a way, they already have.
MASTER BRUCE!
WUMP
HE'S DOWN, BROTHERS!
GET HIM!

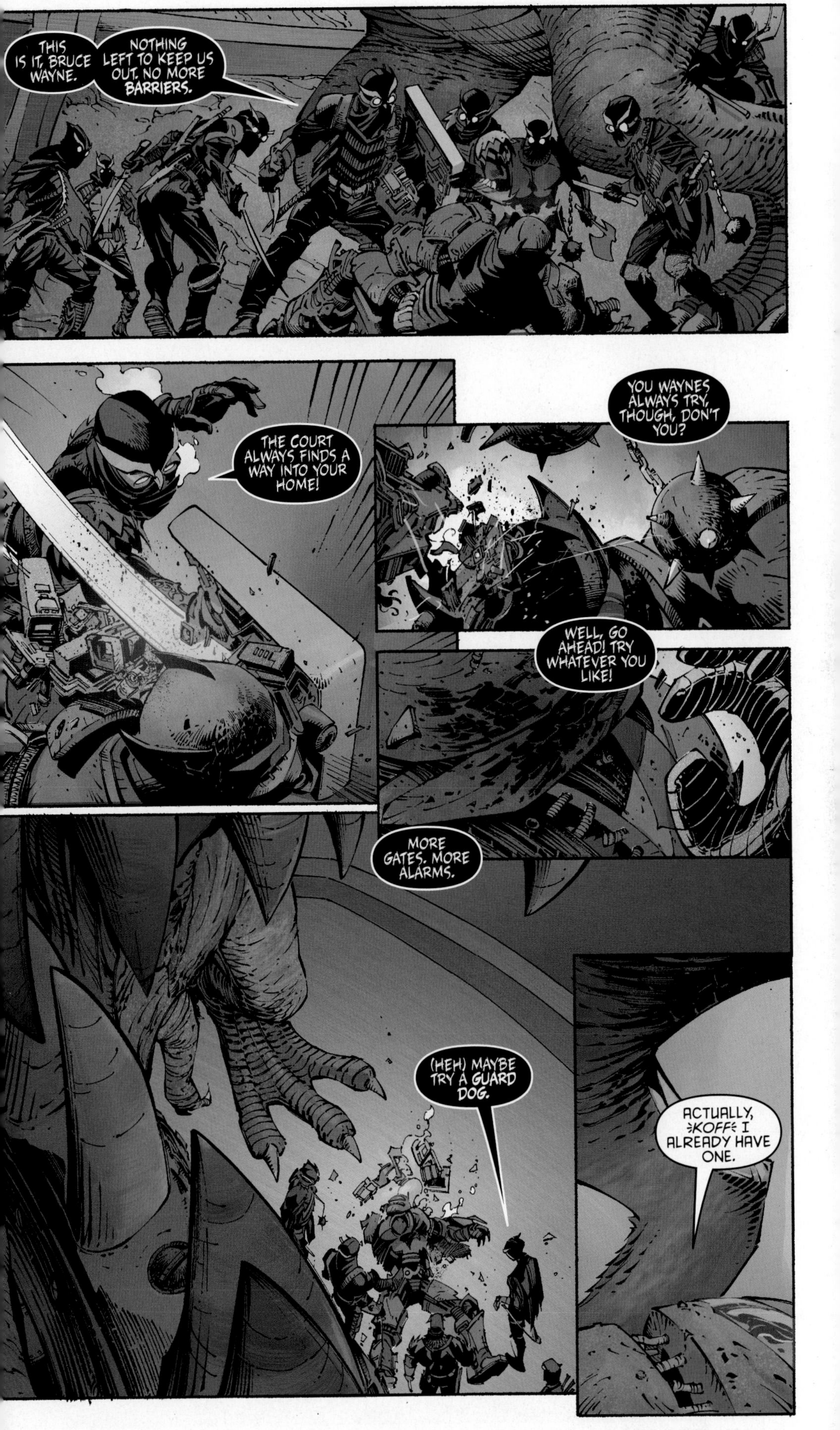
THIS IS IT, BRUCE WAYNE.
NOTHING LEFT TO KEEP US OUT. NO MORE BARRIERS.
THE COURT ALWAYS FINDS A WAY INTO YOUR HOME!
YOU WAYNES ALWAYS TRY, THOUGH, DON'T YOU?
WELL, GO AHEAD! TRY WHATEVER YOU LIKE!
MORE GATES. MORE ALARMS.
(HEH) MAYBE TRY A GUARD DOG.
ACTUALLY, *KOFF* I ALREADY HAVE ONE.

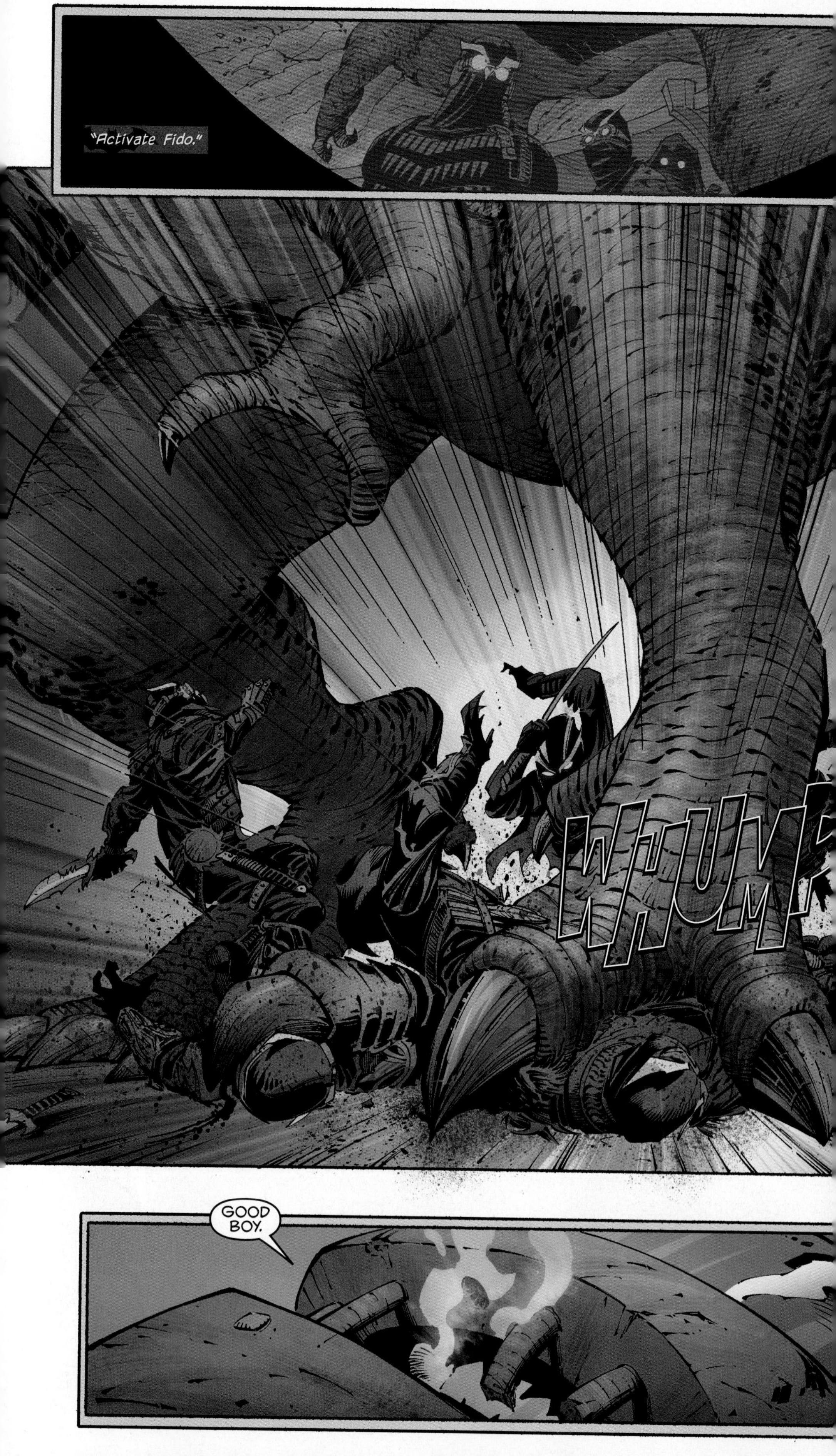
"Activate Fido."
WHUMP
GOOD BOY.

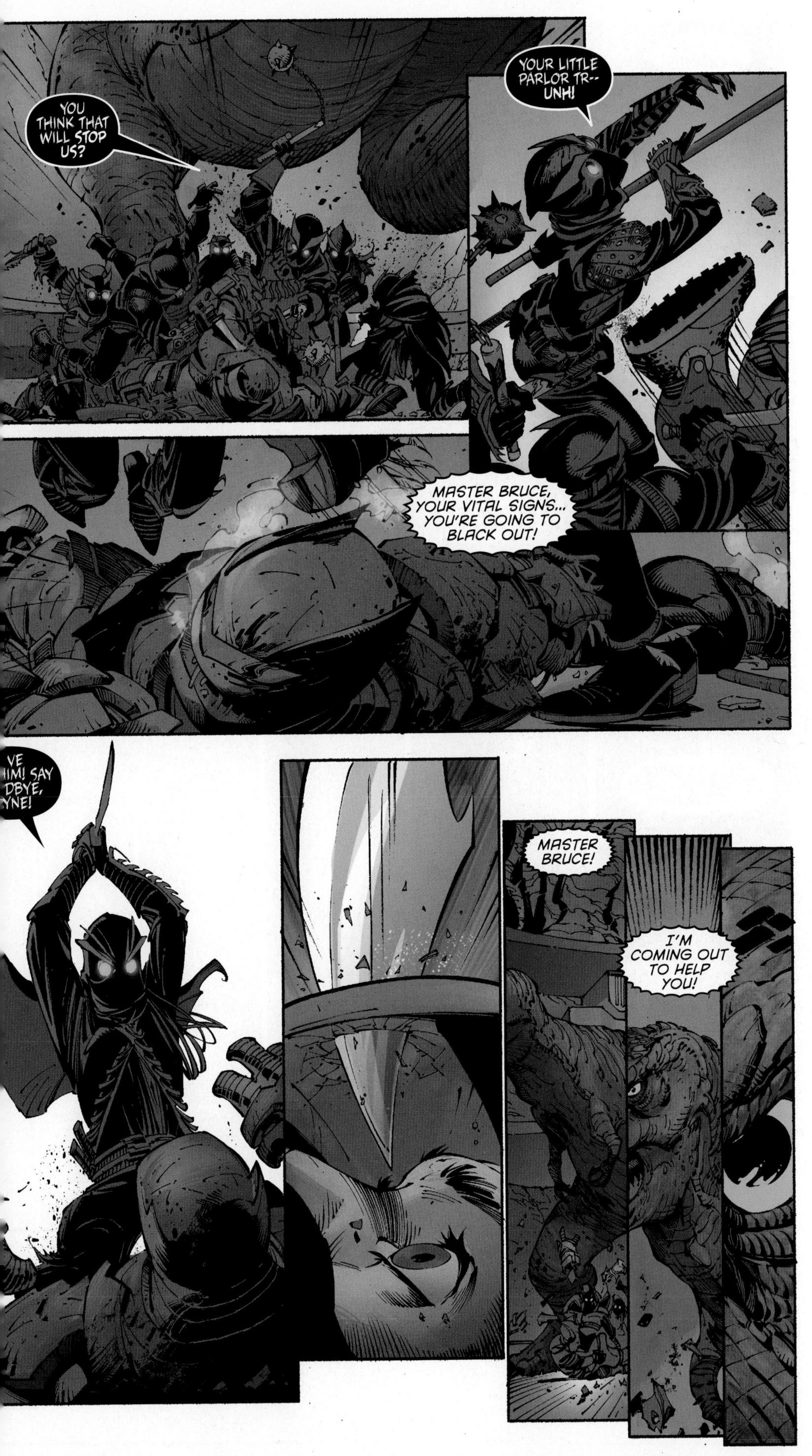
YOU THINK THAT WILL STOP US?
YOUR LITTLE PARLOR TR-- UNH!
MASTER BRUCE, YOUR VITAL SIGNS... YOU'RE GOING TO BLACK OUT!
VE HIM! SAY DBYE, YNE!
MASTER BRUCE!
I'M COMING OUT TO HELP YOU!

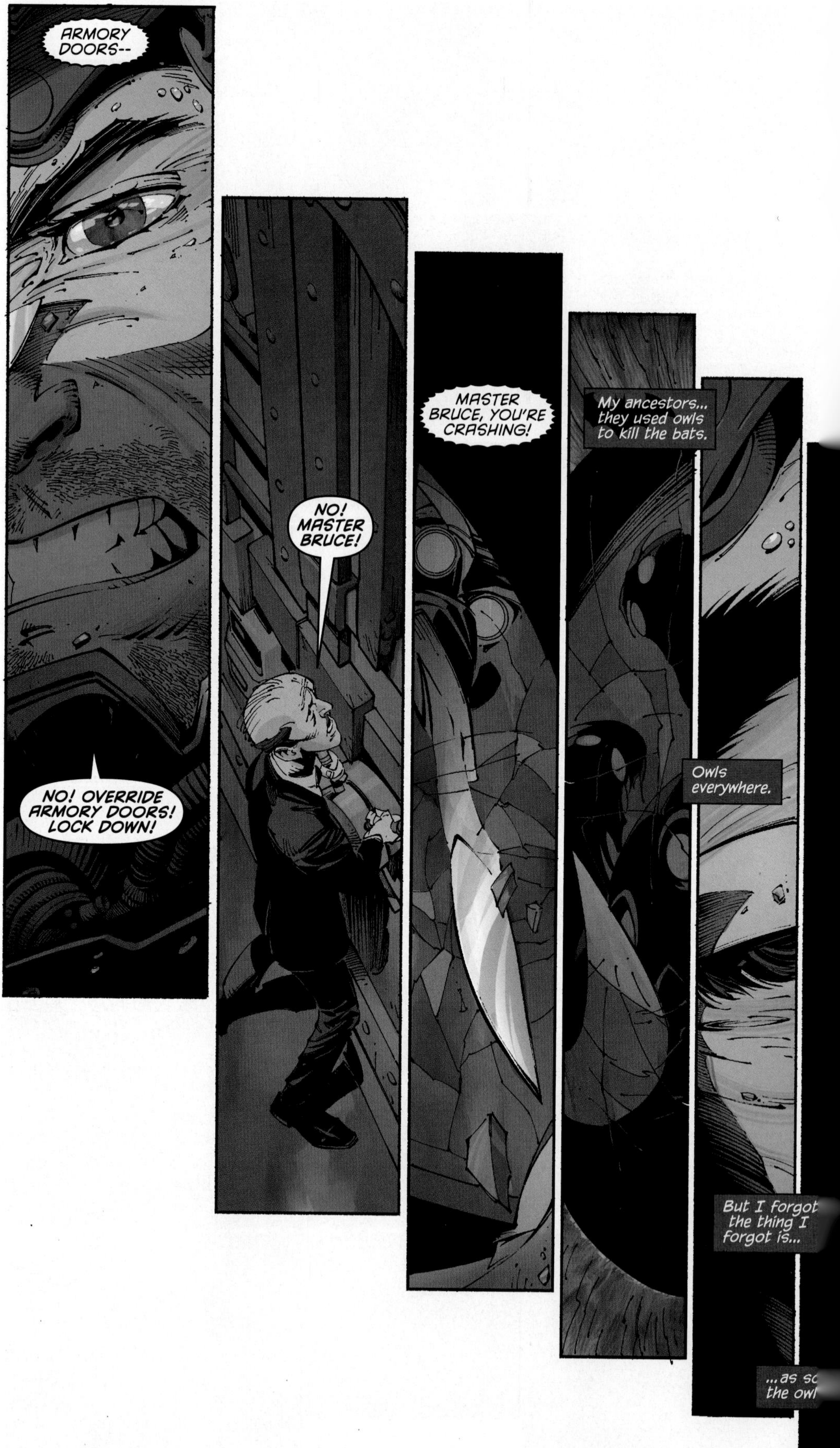

ARMORY DOORS--
NO! OVERRIDE ARMORY DOORS! LOCK DOWN!
NO! MASTER BRUCE!
MASTER BRUCE, YOU'RE CRASHING!
My ancestors... they used owls to kill the bats.
Owls everywhere.
But I forgot the thing I forgot is...

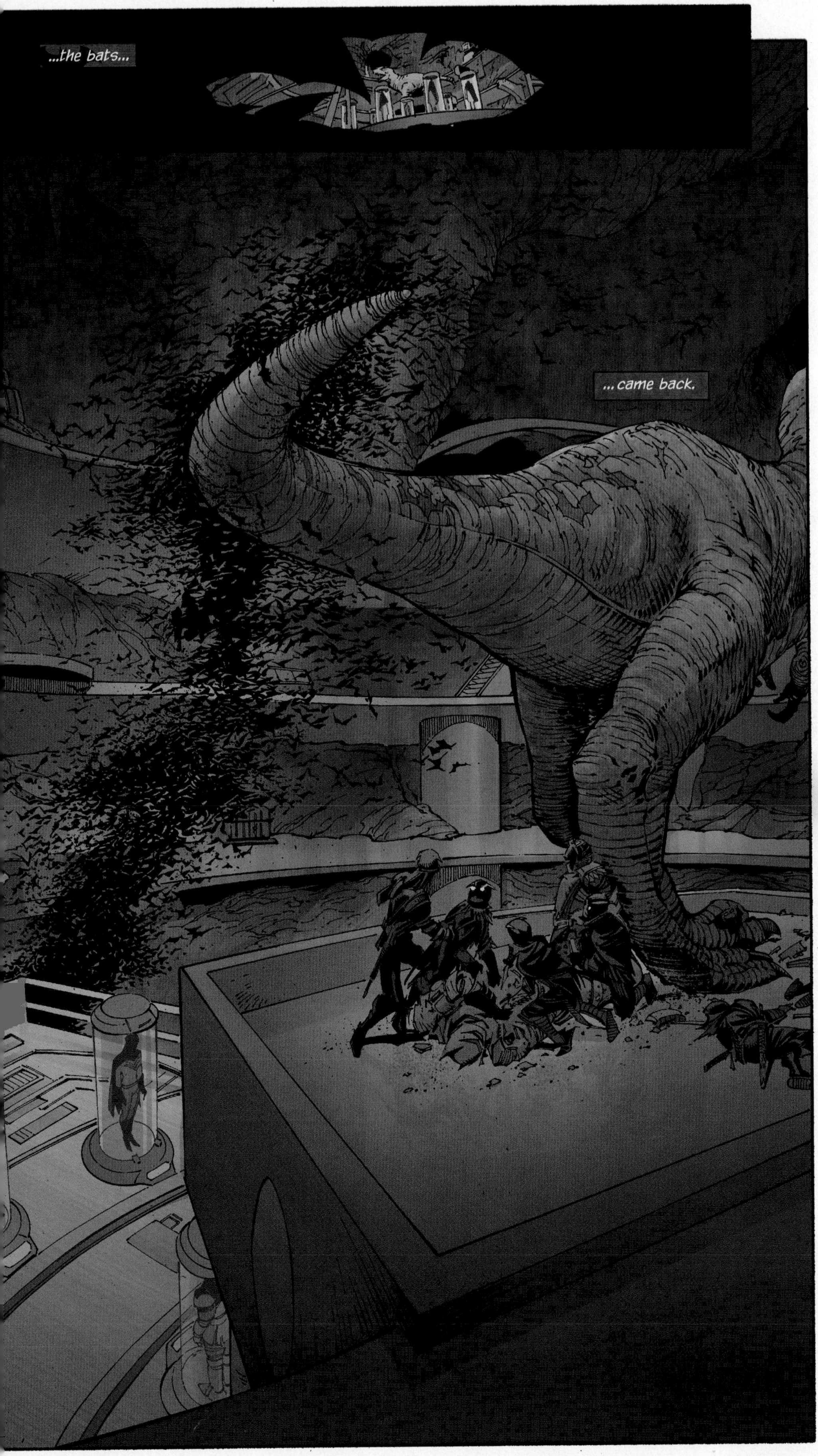
...the bats...
...came back.

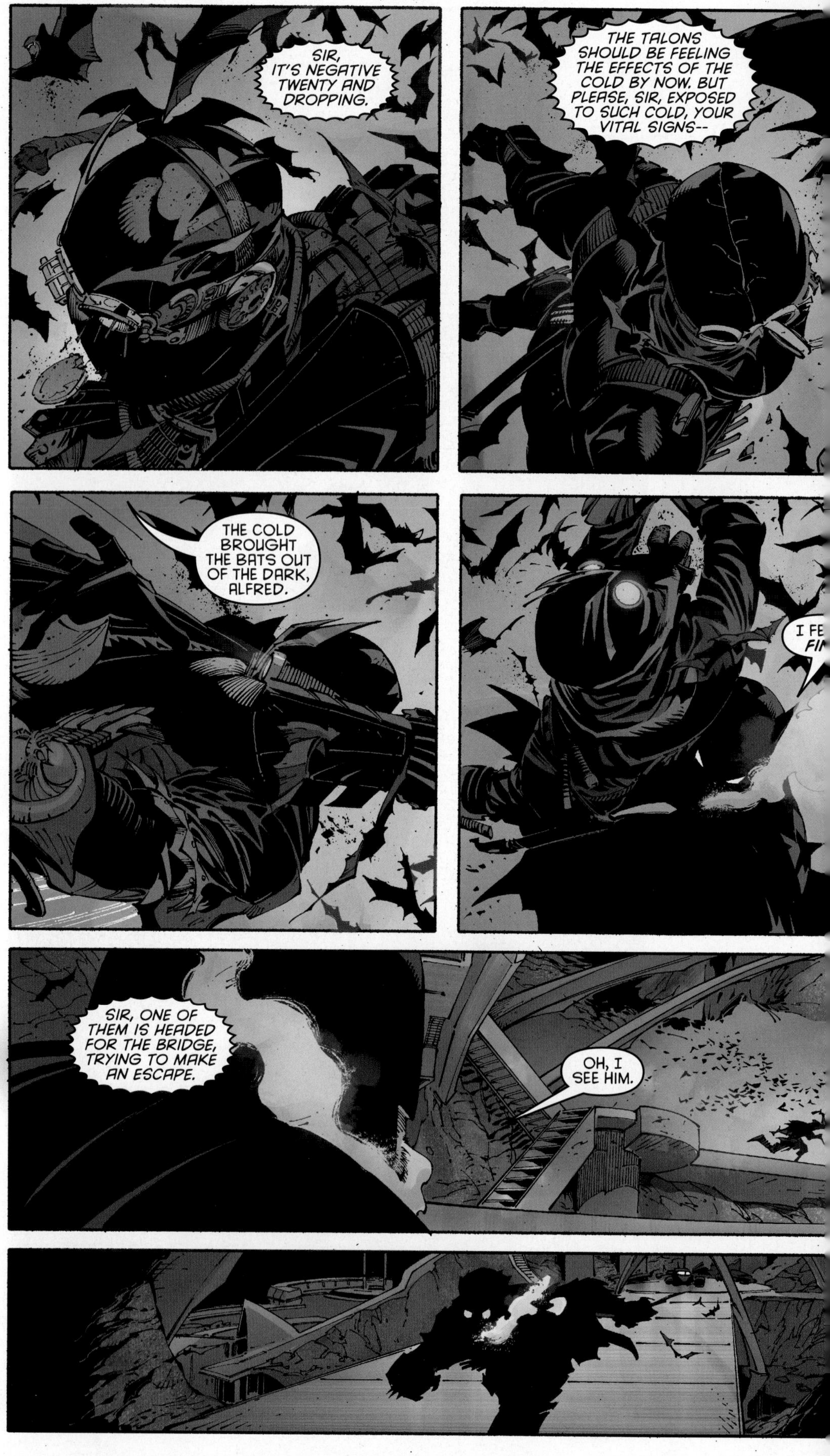
SIR, IT'S NEGATIVE TWENTY AND DROPPING.
THE TALONS SHOULD BE FEELING THE EFFECTS OF THE COLD BY NOW. BUT PLEASE, SIR, EXPOSED TO SUCH COLD, YOUR VITAL SIGNS--
THE COLD BROUGHT THE BATS OUT OF THE DARK, ALFRED.
SIR, ONE OF THEM IS HEADED FOR THE BRIDGE, TRYING TO MAKE AN ESCAPE.
OH, I SEE HIM.

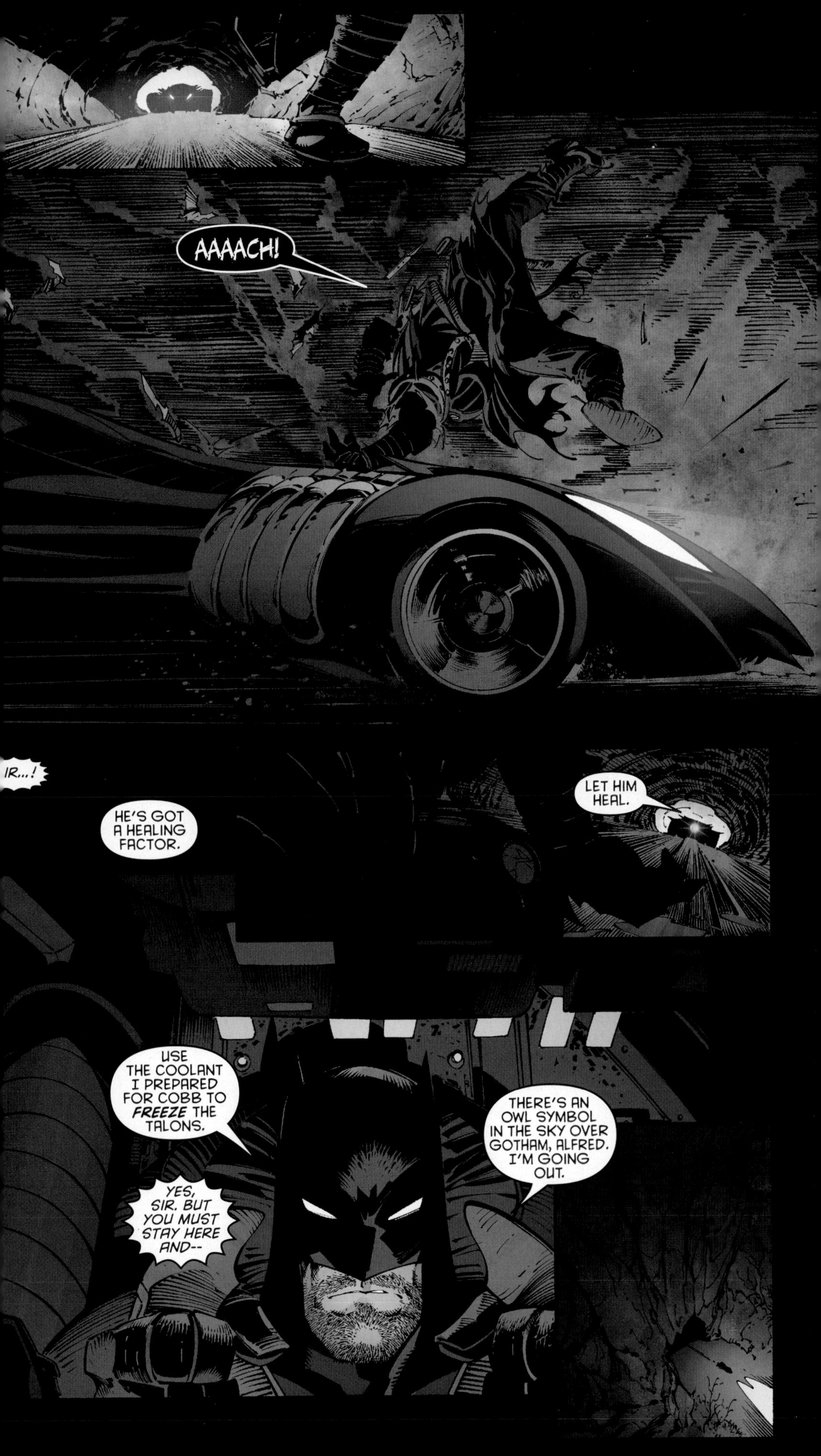
AAAACH!
IR...!
HE'S GOT A HEALING FACTOR.
LET HIM HEAL.
USE THE COOLANT I PREPARED FOR COBB TO *FREEZE* THE TALONS.
THERE'S AN OWL SYMBOL IN THE SKY OVER GOTHAM, ALFRED. I'M GOING OUT.
YES, SIR. BUT YOU MUST STAY HERE AND--

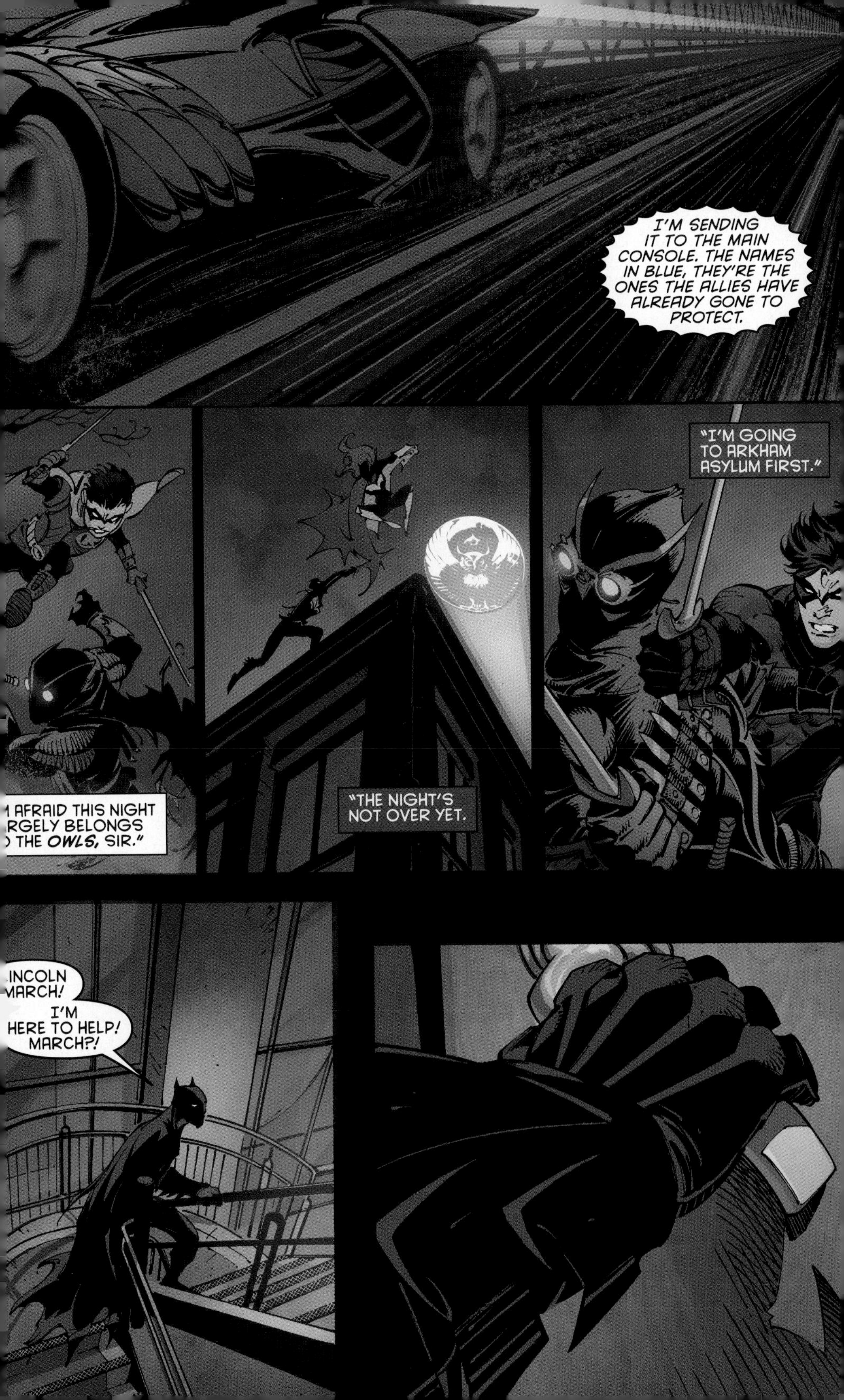
I'M SENDING IT TO THE MAIN CONSOLE. THE NAMES IN BLUE, THEY'RE THE ONES THE ALLIES HAVE ALREADY GONE TO PROTECT.
M AFRAID THIS NIGHT RGELY BELONGS THE *OWLS,* SIR."
"THE NIGHT'S NOT OVER YET.
"I'M GOING TO ARKHAM ASYLUM FIRST."
INCOLN MARCH!
I'M HERE TO HELP! MARCH?!

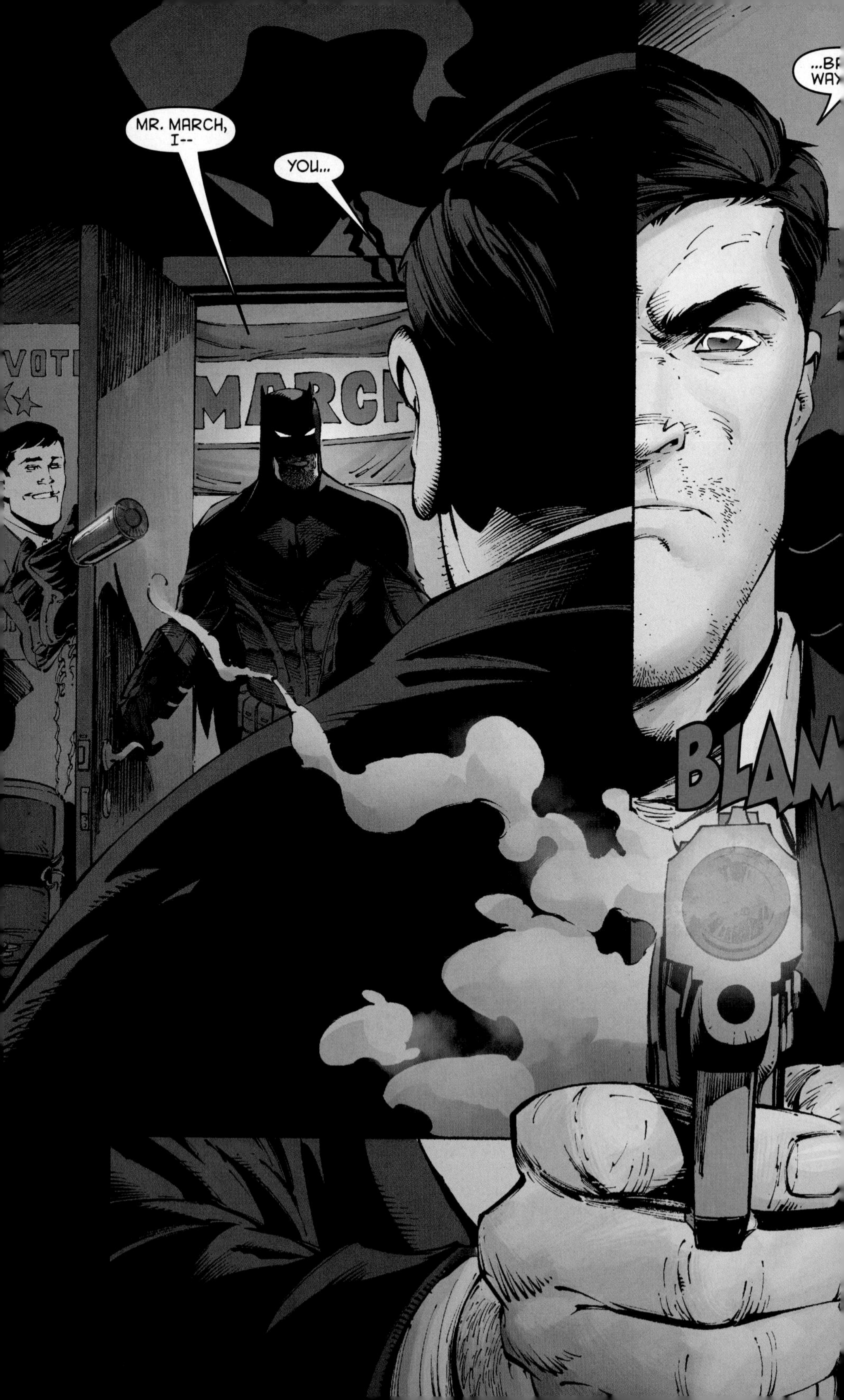
MR. MARCH, I--
YOU...
BLAM

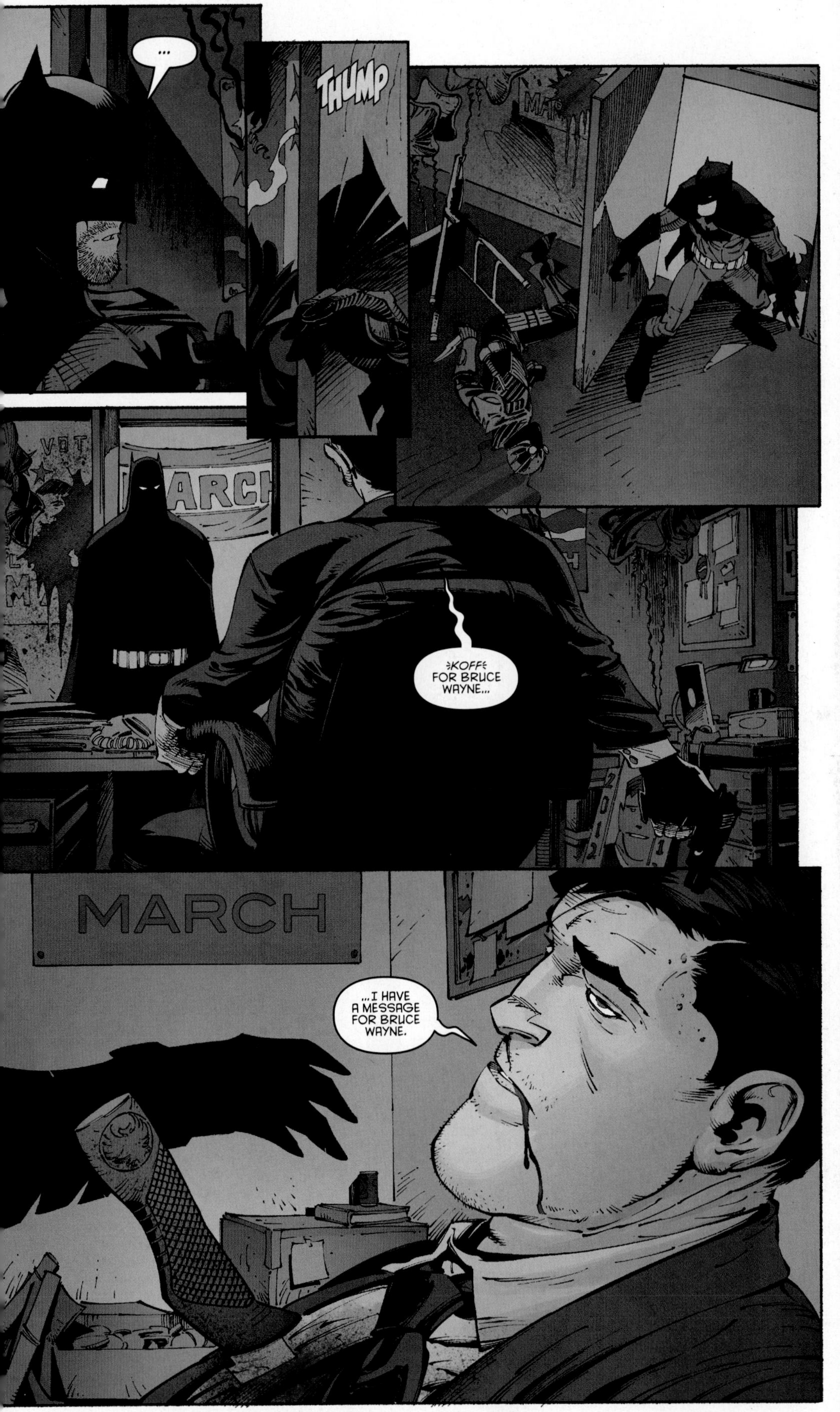
...
THUMP
MARCH
VOT
MARCH
KOFF FOR BRUCE WAYNE...
MARCH
...I HAVE A MESSAGE FOR BRUCE WAYNE.

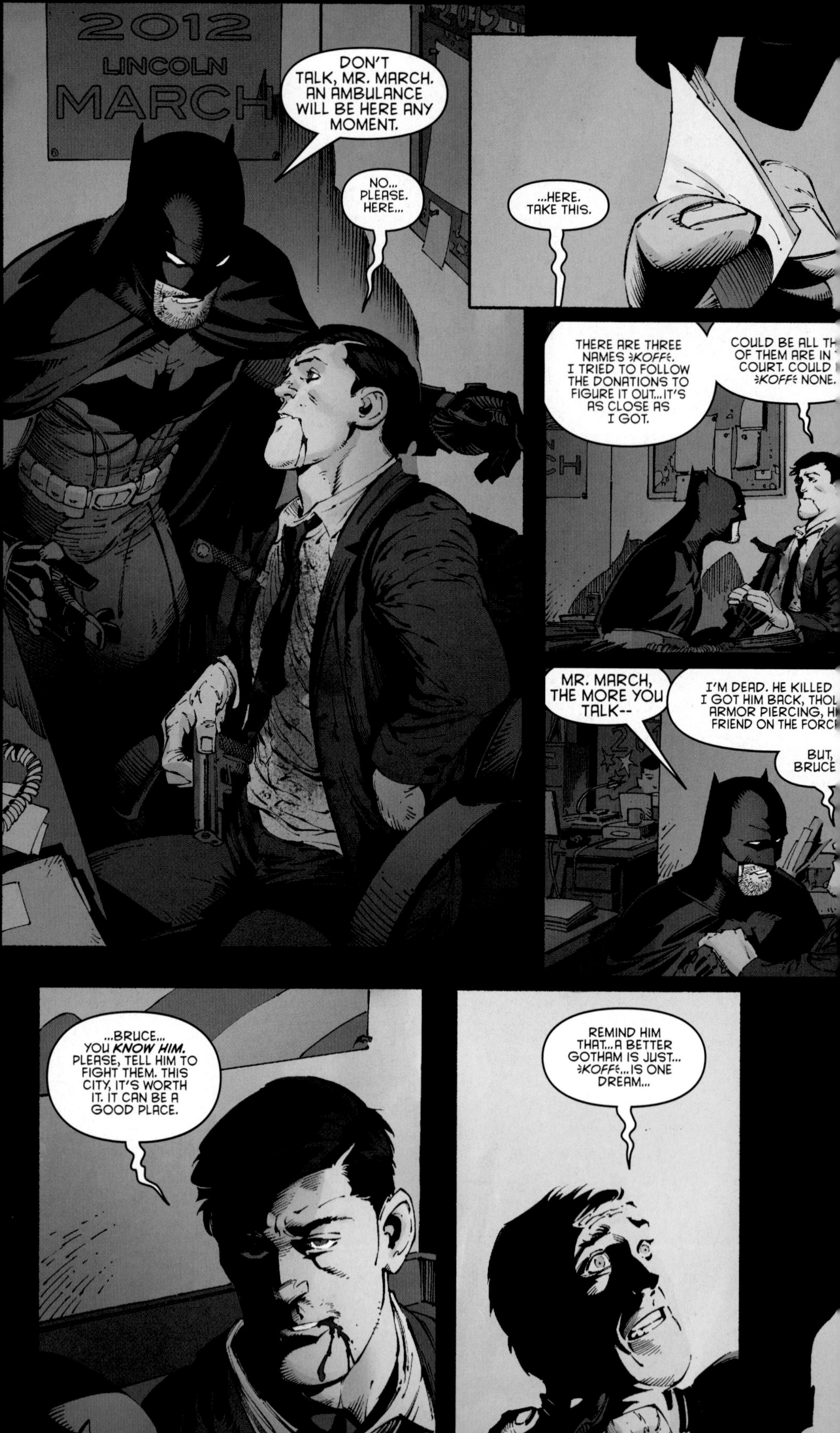
2012
LINCOLN
MARCH
DON'T TALK, MR. MARCH. AN AMBULANCE WILL BE HERE ANY MOMENT.
NO... PLEASE. HERE...
...HERE. TAKE THIS.
THERE ARE THREE NAMES ≈KOFF≈. I TRIED TO FOLLOW THE DONATIONS TO FIGURE IT OUT...IT'S AS CLOSE AS I GOT.
COULD BE ALL TH OF THEM ARE IN COURT. COULD ≈KOFF≈ NONE.
MR. MARCH, THE MORE YOU TALK--
I'M DEAD. HE KILLED I GOT HIM BACK, THOU ARMOR PIERCING, H FRIEND ON THE FORC
BUT, BRUCE
...BRUCE... YOU KNOW HIM. PLEASE, TELL HIM TO FIGHT THEM. THIS CITY, IT'S WORTH IT. IT CAN BE A GOOD PLACE.
REMIND HIM THAT...A BETTER GOTHAM IS JUST... ≈KOFF≈...IS ONE DREAM...

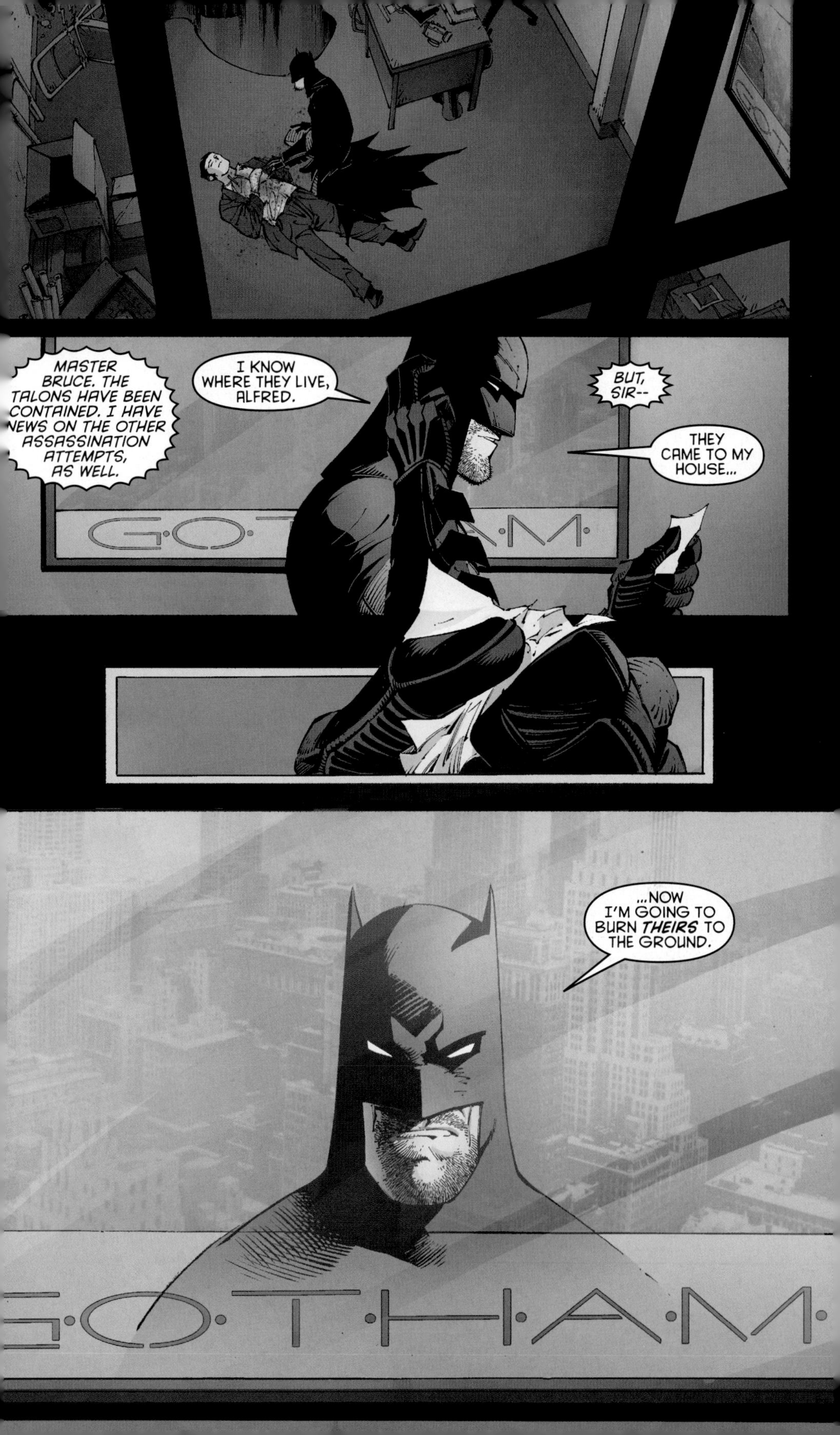
MASTER BRUCE. THE TALONS HAVE BEEN CONTAINED. I HAVE NEWS ON THE OTHER ASSASSINATION ATTEMPTS, AS WELL.
I KNOW WHERE THEY LIVE, ALFRED.
BUT, SIR--
THEY CAME TO MY HOUSE...
G·O·T·H·A·M
...NOW I'M GOING TO BURN *THEIRS* TO THE GROUND.
G·O·T·H·A·M

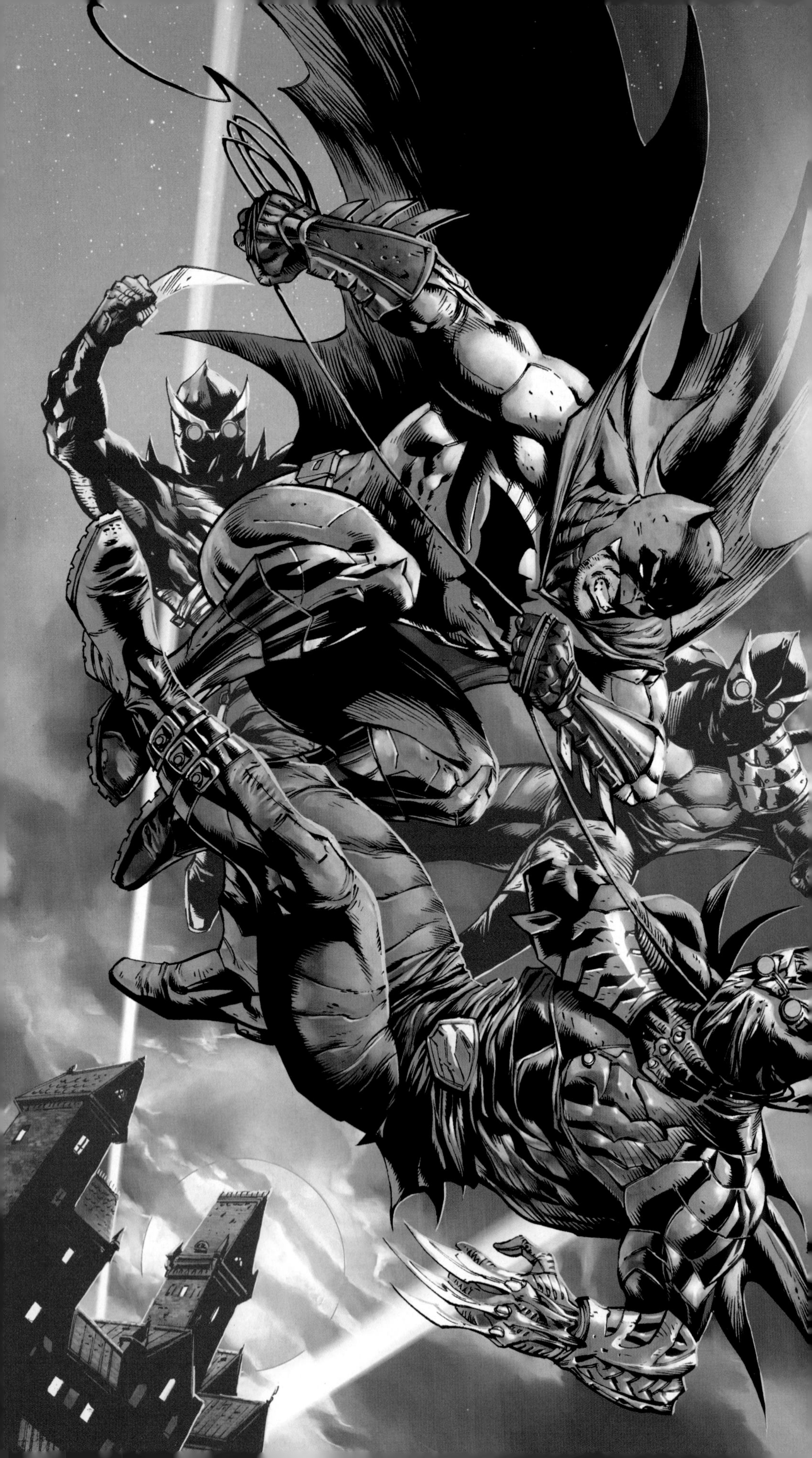

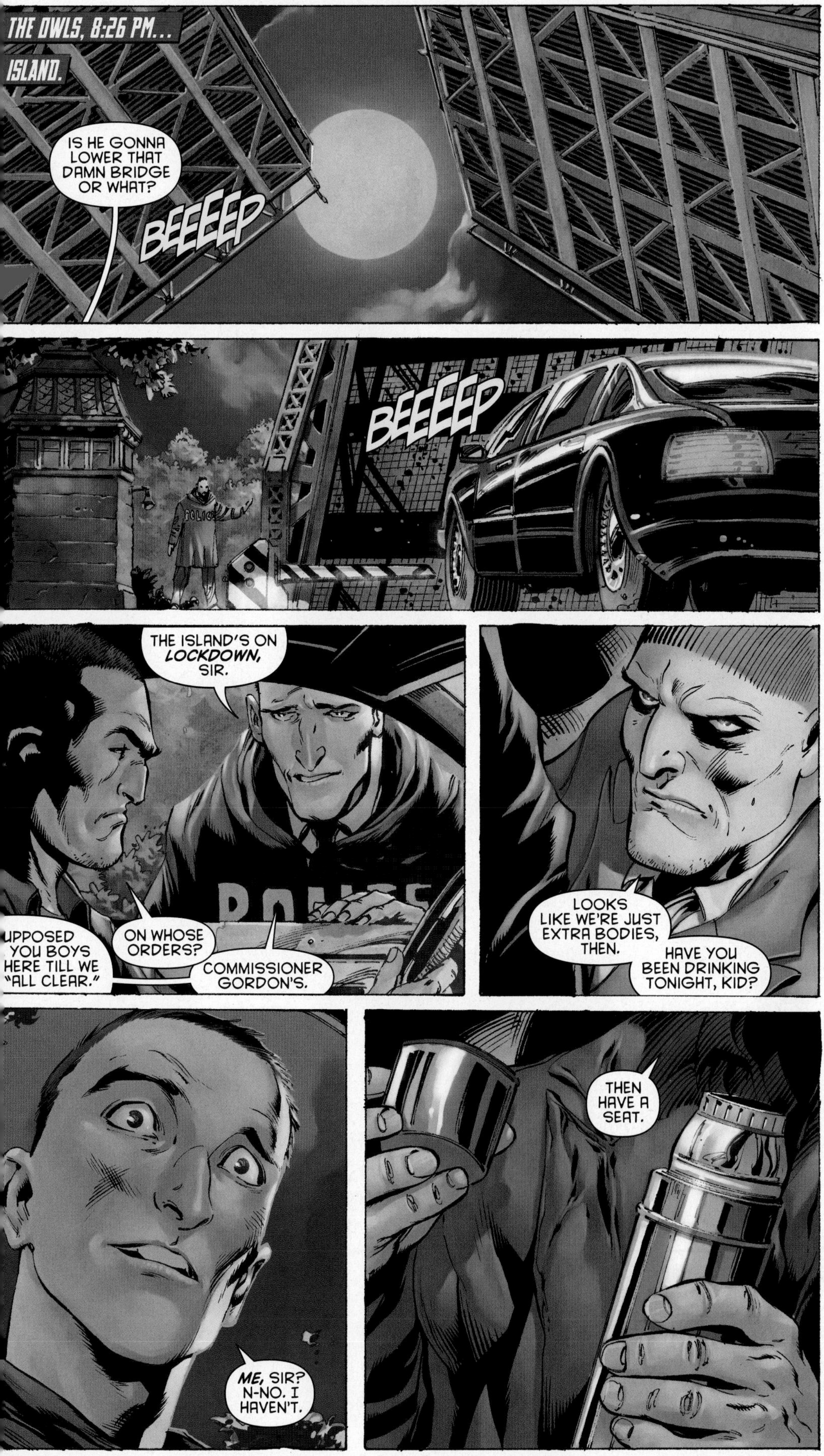
THE OWLS, 8:26 PM...
ISLAND.
IS HE GONNA LOWER THAT DAMN BRIDGE OR WHAT?
BEEEEP
BEEEEP
THE ISLAND'S ON *LOCKDOWN*, SIR.
ON WHOSE ORDERS?
COMMISSIONER GORDON'S.
UPPOSED YOU BOYS HERE TILL WE "ALL CLEAR."
LOOKS LIKE WE'RE JUST EXTRA BODIES, THEN.
HAVE YOU BEEN DRINKING TONIGHT, KID?
ME, SIR? N-NO. I HAVEN'T.
THEN HAVE A SEAT.

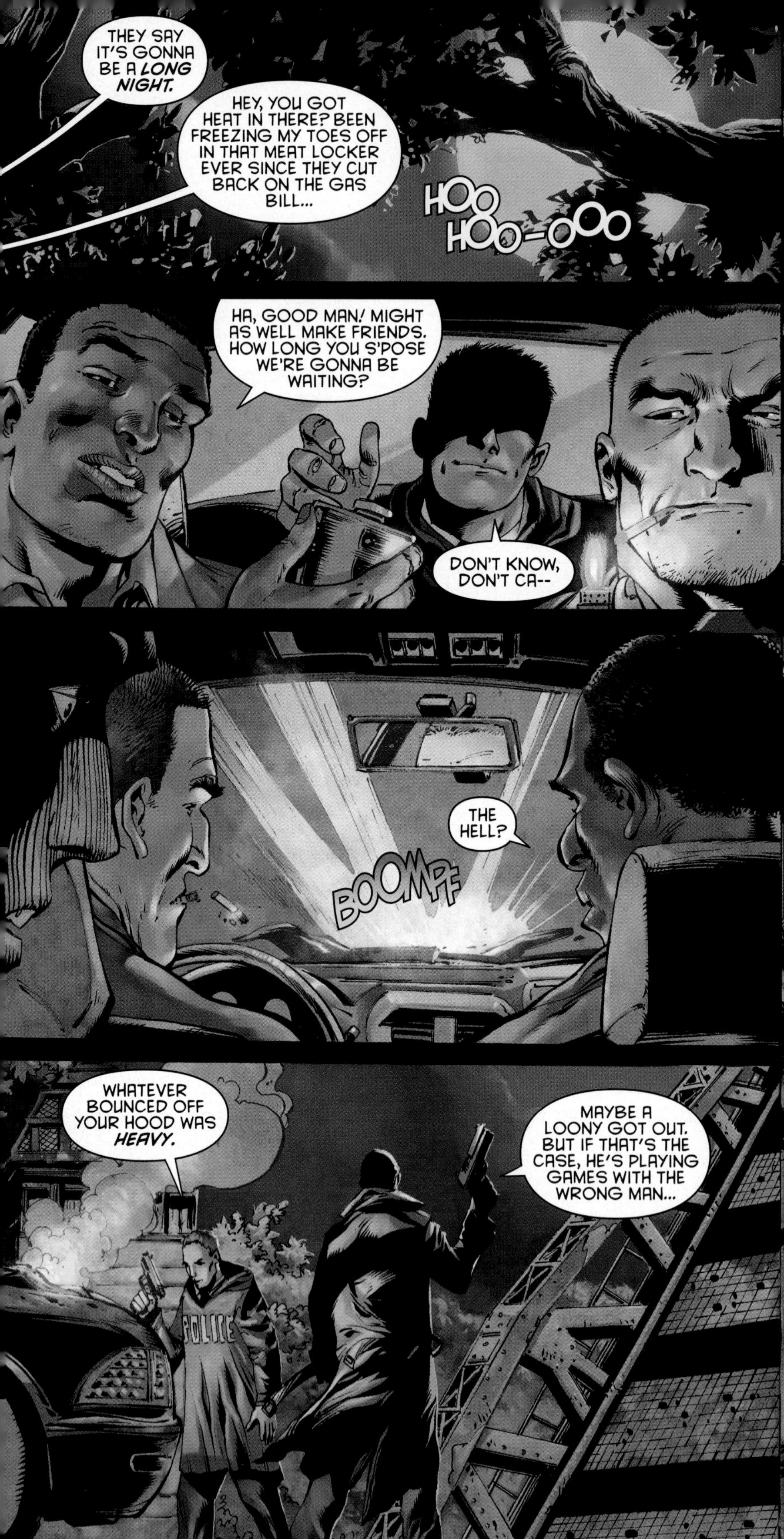
THEY SAY IT'S GONNA BE A *LONG NIGHT.*
HEY, YOU GOT HEAT IN THERE? BEEN FREEZING MY TOES OFF IN THAT MEAT LOCKER EVER SINCE THEY CUT BACK ON THE GAS BILL...
HOO HOO-OOO
HA, GOOD MAN! MIGHT AS WELL MAKE FRIENDS. HOW LONG YOU S'POSE WE'RE GONNA BE WAITING?
DON'T KNOW, DON'T CA--
BOOMPF
THE HELL?
WHATEVER BOUNCED OFF YOUR HOOD WAS *HEAVY.*
MAYBE A LOONY GOT OUT. BUT IF THAT'S THE CASE, HE'S PLAYING GAMES WITH THE WRONG MAN...
POLICE

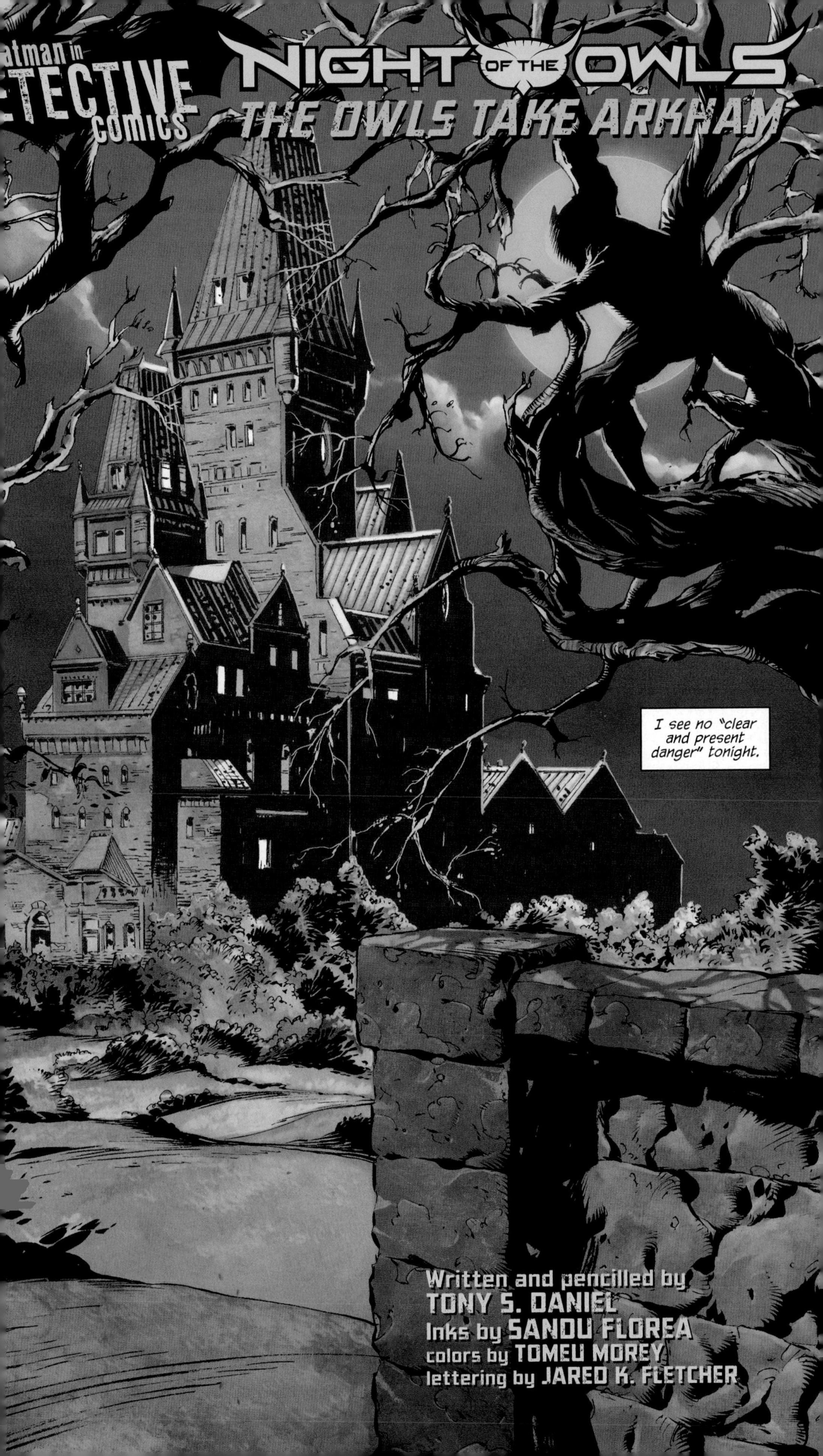
atman in
ETECTIVE
COMICS
NIGHT OF THE OWLS
THE OWLS TAKE ARKHAM
I see no "clear and present danger" tonight.
Written and pencilled by
TONY S. DANIEL
Inks by SANDU FLOREA
colors by TOMEU MOREY
lettering by JARED K. FLETCHER

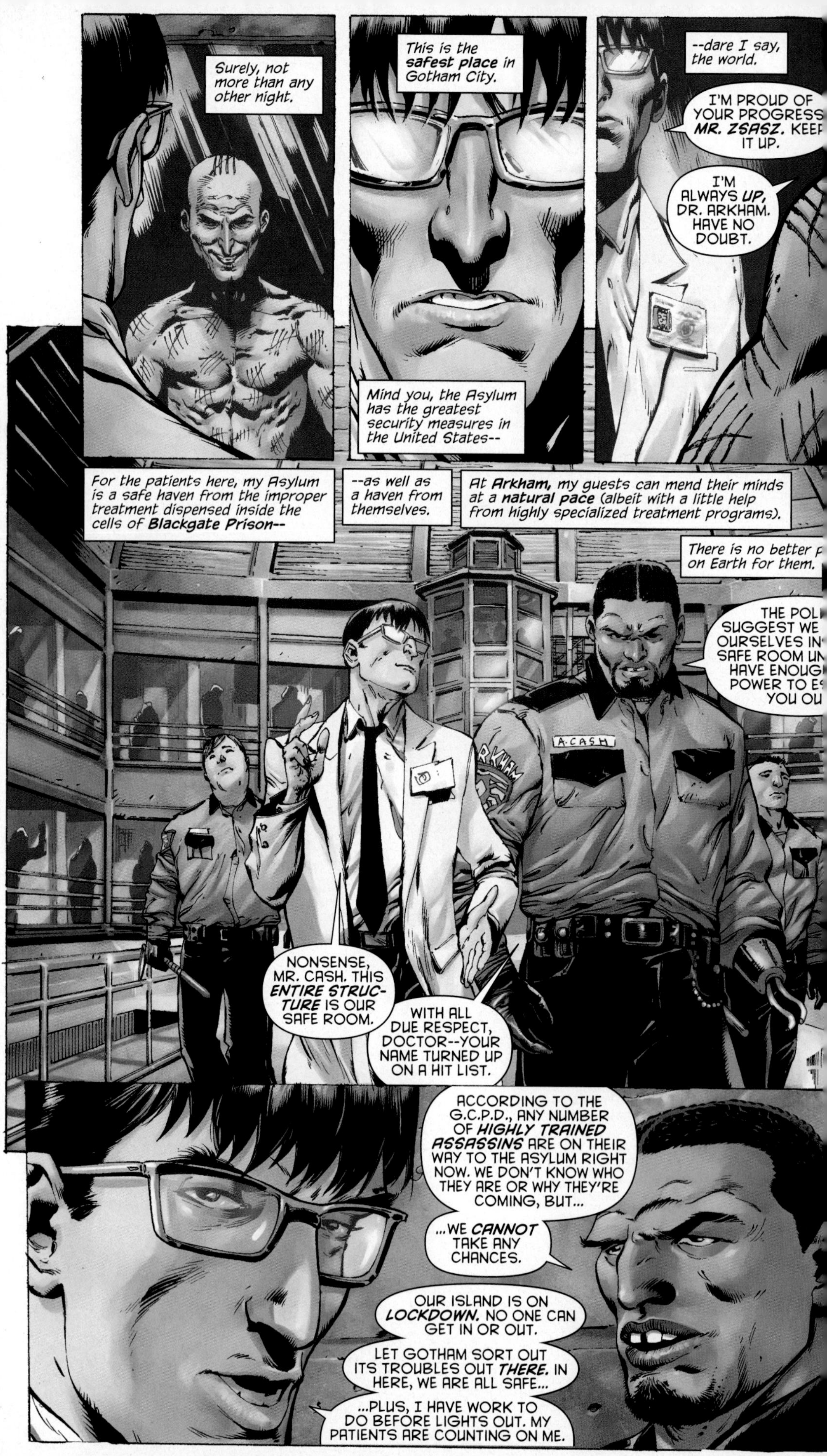
Surely, not more than any other night.
This is the safest place in Gotham City.
Mind you, the Asylum has the greatest security measures in the United States--
--dare I say, the world.
I'M PROUD OF YOUR PROGRESS MR. ZSASZ. KEE IT UP.
I'M ALWAYS UP, DR. ARKHAM. HAVE NO DOUBT.
For the patients here, my Asylum is a safe haven from the improper treatment dispensed inside the cells of Blackgate Prison--
--as well as a haven from themselves.
At Arkham, my guests can mend their minds at a natural pace (albeit with a little help from highly specialized treatment programs).
There is no better on Earth for them.
A.CASH
RKHAM
THE POL SUGGEST WE OURSELVES IN SAFE ROOM UN HAVE ENOUG POWER TO E YOU OU
NONSENSE, MR. CASH. THIS ENTIRE STRUCTURE IS OUR SAFE ROOM.
WITH ALL DUE RESPECT, DOCTOR--YOUR NAME TURNED UP ON A HIT LIST.
ACCORDING TO THE G.C.P.D., ANY NUMBER OF HIGHLY TRAINED ASSASSINS ARE ON THEIR WAY TO THE ASYLUM RIGHT NOW. WE DON'T KNOW WHO THEY ARE OR WHY THEY'RE COMING, BUT...
...WE CANNOT TAKE ANY CHANCES.
OUR ISLAND IS ON LOCKDOWN. NO ONE CAN GET IN OR OUT.
LET GOTHAM SORT OUT ITS TROUBLES OUT THERE. IN HERE, WE ARE ALL SAFE...
...PLUS, I HAVE WORK TO DO BEFORE LIGHTS OUT. MY PATIENTS ARE COUNTING ON ME.

nt A.
...et.

Like Linda Friitawa, or **Fright.**

Genetically manipulated, his bones are as hollow as his mind. He is a **victim**--as are the others I've come to know so well in recent months.

Victimized by both **Scarecrow** and the **Penguin.** Disfigured inside and out by illegal chemicals fused with her blood cells during so-called "medical studies."

s Basil Karlo, nously as **Clayface.**

d and betrayed by his own lust . A tragic set of events turned what he has now become...

Or take **Nocturna,** for example. Why, just the other day, she--

...an untouchable **behemoth** with an outer malleable membrane instead of flesh.

DR. ARKHAM, IT'S **ROMAN SIONIS.** HE'S **READY TO END** HIS HUNGER STRIKE--BUT HE WANTS TO TALK TO YOU FIRST.

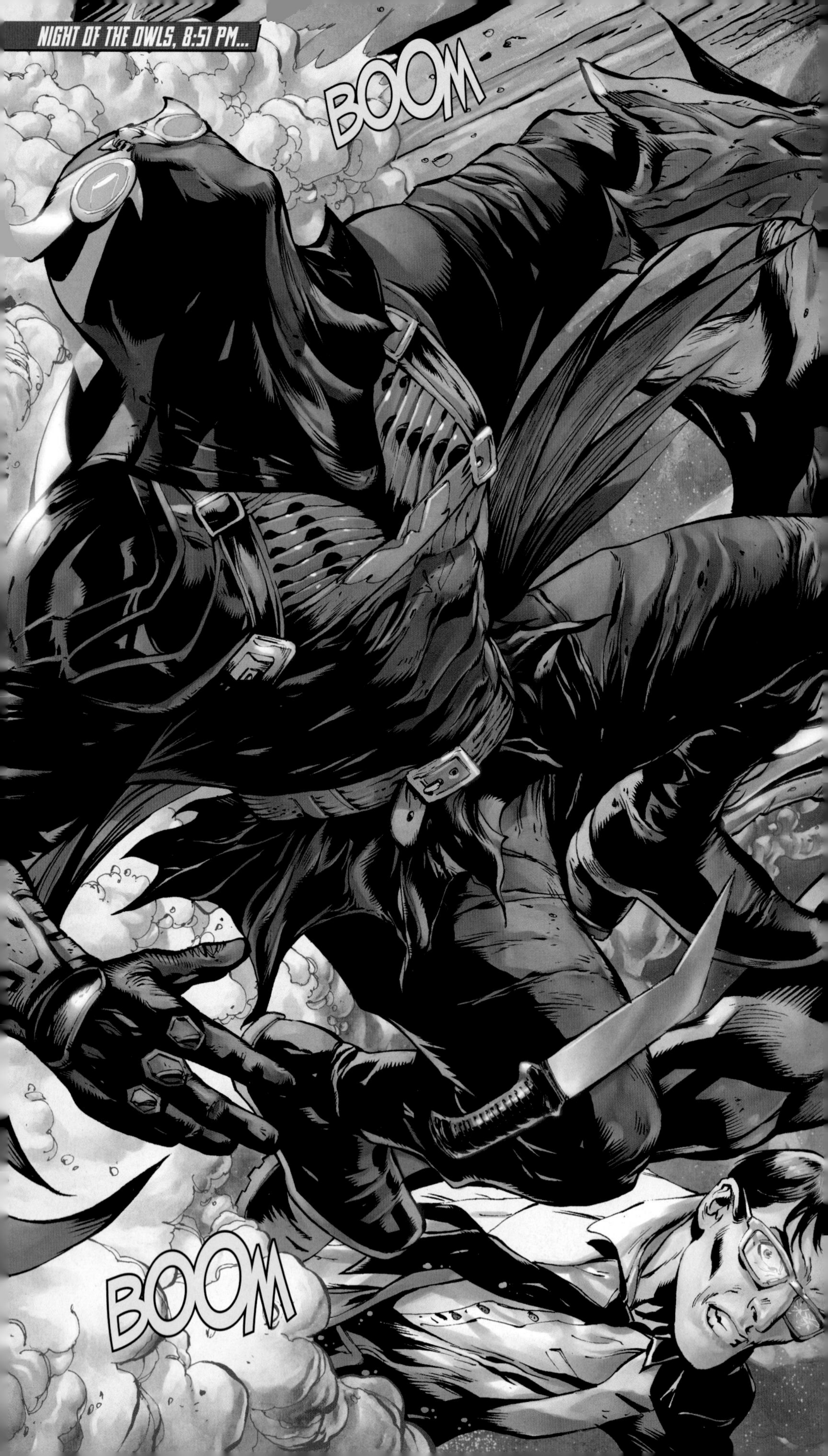
NIGHT OF THE OWLS, 8:51 PM...
BOOM
BOOM

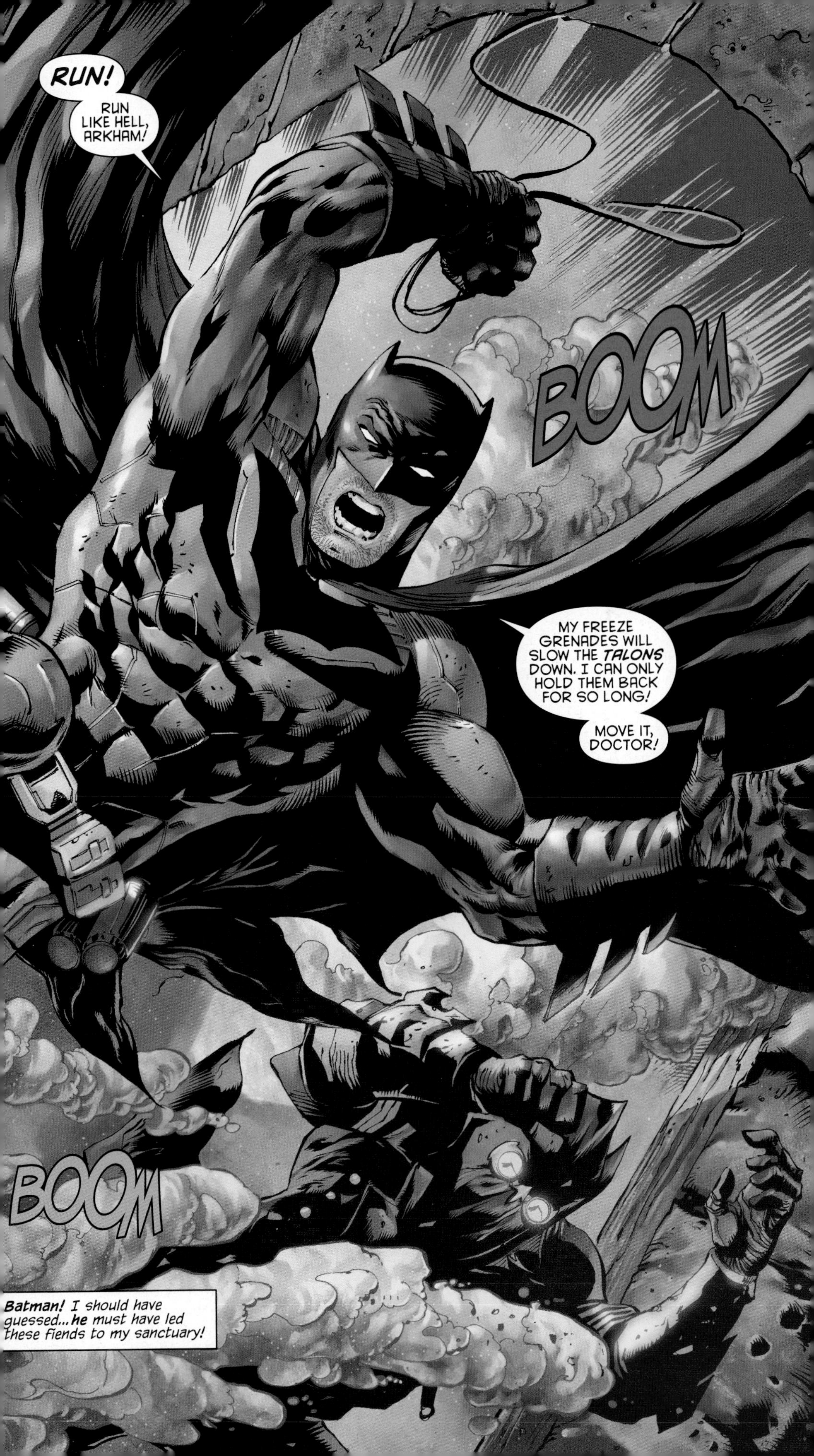
RUN!
RUN LIKE HELL, ARKHAM!
BOOM
MY FREEZE GRENADES WILL SLOW THE *TALONS* DOWN. I CAN ONLY HOLD THEM BACK FOR SO LONG!
MOVE IT, DOCTOR!
BOOM
Batman! I should have guessed... **he** must have led these fiends to my sanctuary!

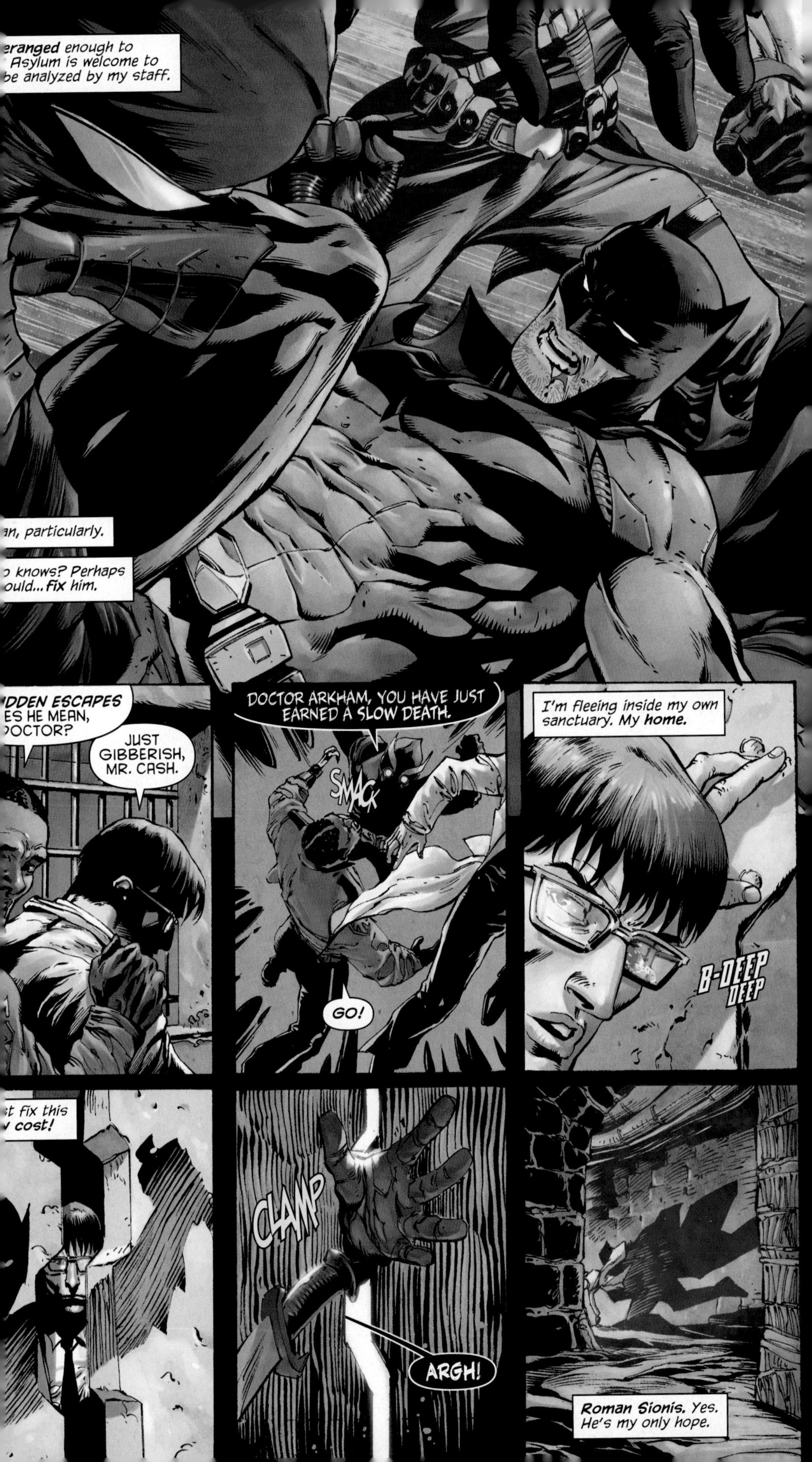

eranged enough to
Asylum is welcome to
be analyzed by my staff.
an, particularly.
o knows? Perhaps
ould... fix him.
DDEN ESCAPES
ES HE MEAN,
OCTOR?
JUST GIBBERISH, MR. CASH.
DOCTOR ARKHAM, YOU HAVE JUST EARNED A SLOW DEATH.
SMACK
GO!
I'm fleeing inside my own sanctuary. My home.
B-DEEP DEEP
t fix this
y cost!
CLAMP
ARGH!
Roman Sionis. Yes. He's my only hope.

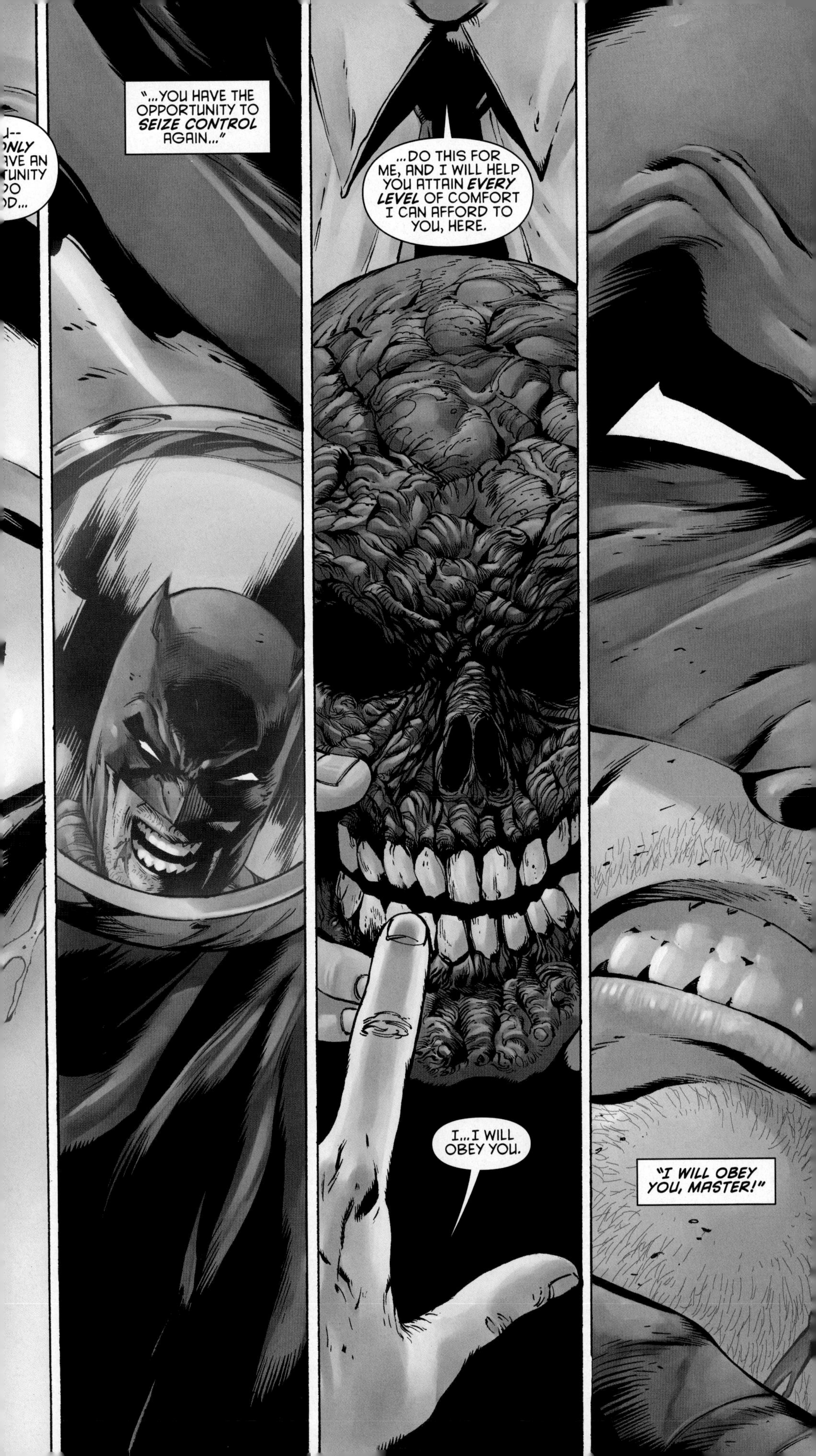
"...YOU HAVE THE OPPORTUNITY TO SEIZE CONTROL AGAIN..."
...DO THIS FOR ME, AND I WILL HELP YOU ATTAIN EVERY LEVEL OF COMFORT I CAN AFFORD TO YOU, HERE.
I...I WILL OBEY YOU.
"I WILL OBEY YOU, MASTER!"

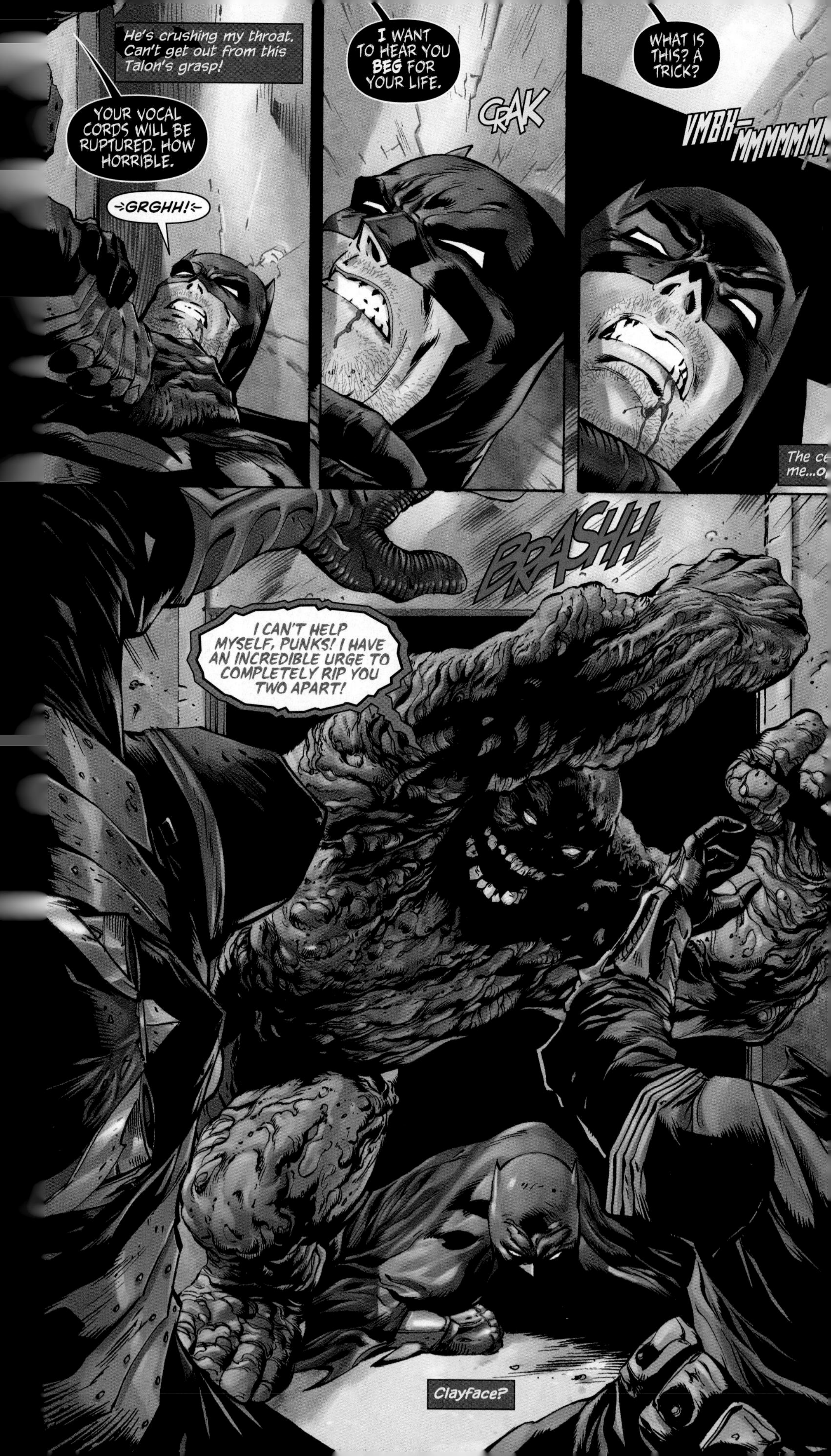
He's crushing my throat. Can't get out from this Talon's grasp!
YOUR VOCAL CORDS WILL BE RUPTURED. HOW HORRIBLE.
-GRGHH!-
I WANT TO HEAR YOU BEG FOR YOUR LIFE.
CRAK
WHAT IS THIS? A TRICK?
VMBH-MMMMMM
BRASHH
I CAN'T HELP MYSELF, PUNKS! I HAVE AN INCREDIBLE URGE TO COMPLETELY RIP YOU TWO APART!
Clayface?

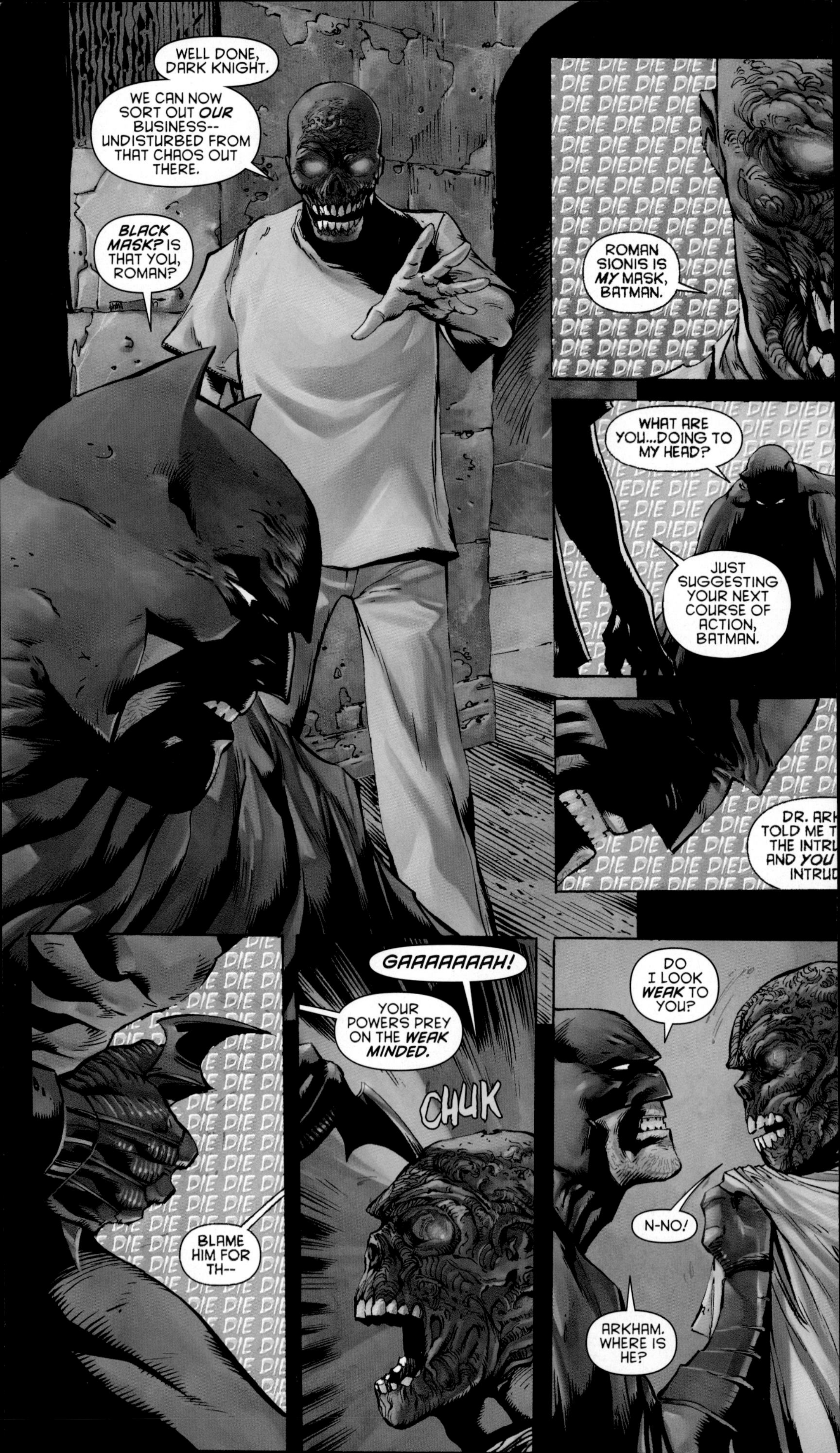
WELL DONE, DARK KNIGHT.
WE CAN NOW SORT OUT *OUR* BUSINESS-- UNDISTURBED FROM THAT CHAOS OUT THERE.
BLACK MASK? IS THAT YOU, ROMAN?
ROMAN SIONIS IS *MY* MASK, BATMAN.
WHAT ARE YOU...DOING TO MY HEAD?
JUST SUGGESTING YOUR NEXT COURSE OF ACTION, BATMAN.
DR. ARK TOLD ME T THE INTRU AND *YOU* INTRUD
BLAME HIM FOR TH--
GAAAAAAAH!
YOUR POWERS PREY ON THE *WEAK MINDED.*
CHUK
DO I LOOK *WEAK* TO YOU?
N-NO!
ARKHAM. WHERE IS HE?

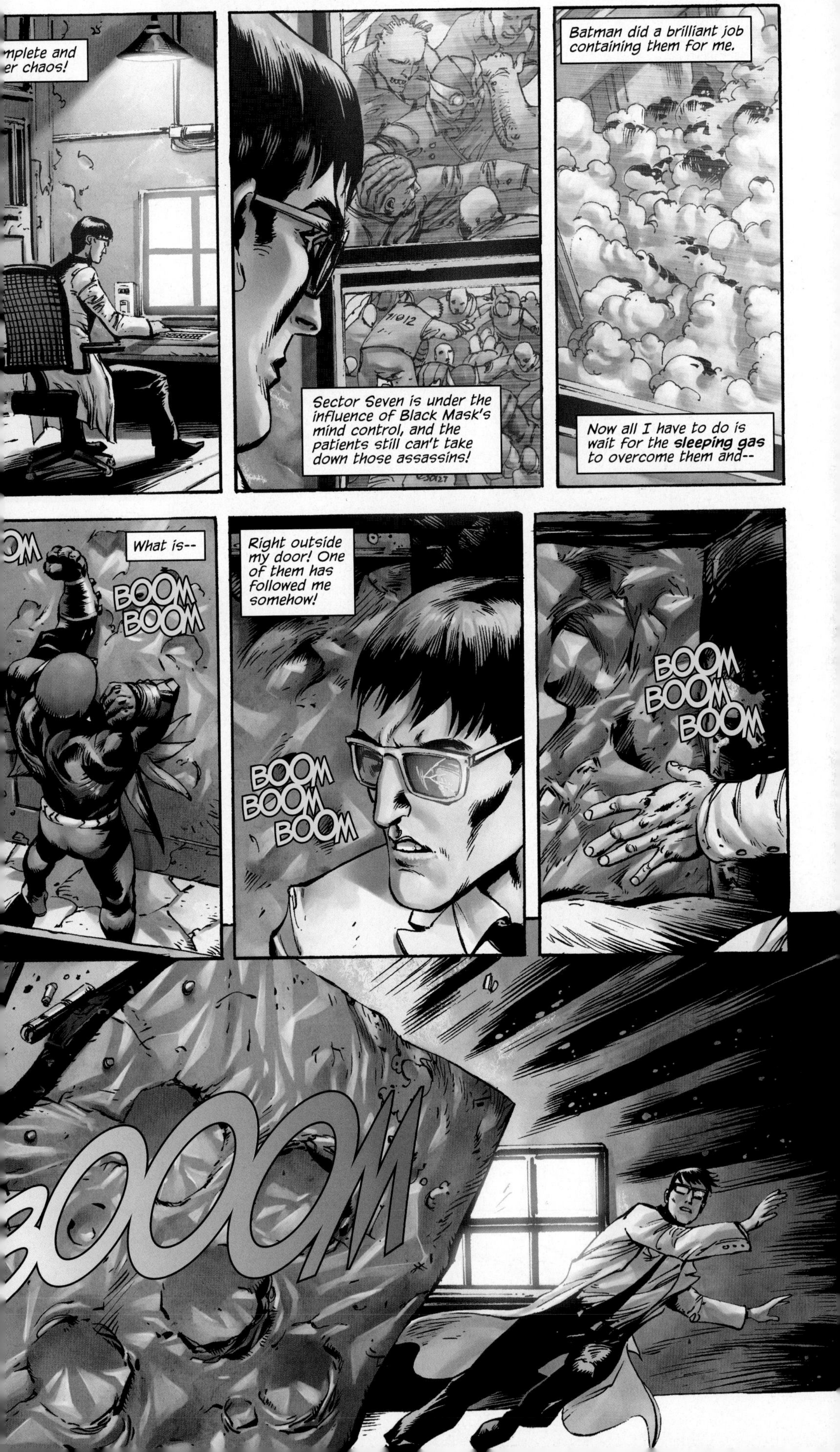

mplete and
er chaos!
Sector Seven is under the influence of Black Mask's mind control, and the patients still can't take down those assassins!
Batman did a brilliant job containing them for me.
Now all I have to do is wait for the **sleeping gas** to overcome them and--
What is--
BOOM BOOM
Right outside my door! One of them has followed me somehow!
BOOM BOOM BOOM
BOOM BOOM BOOM

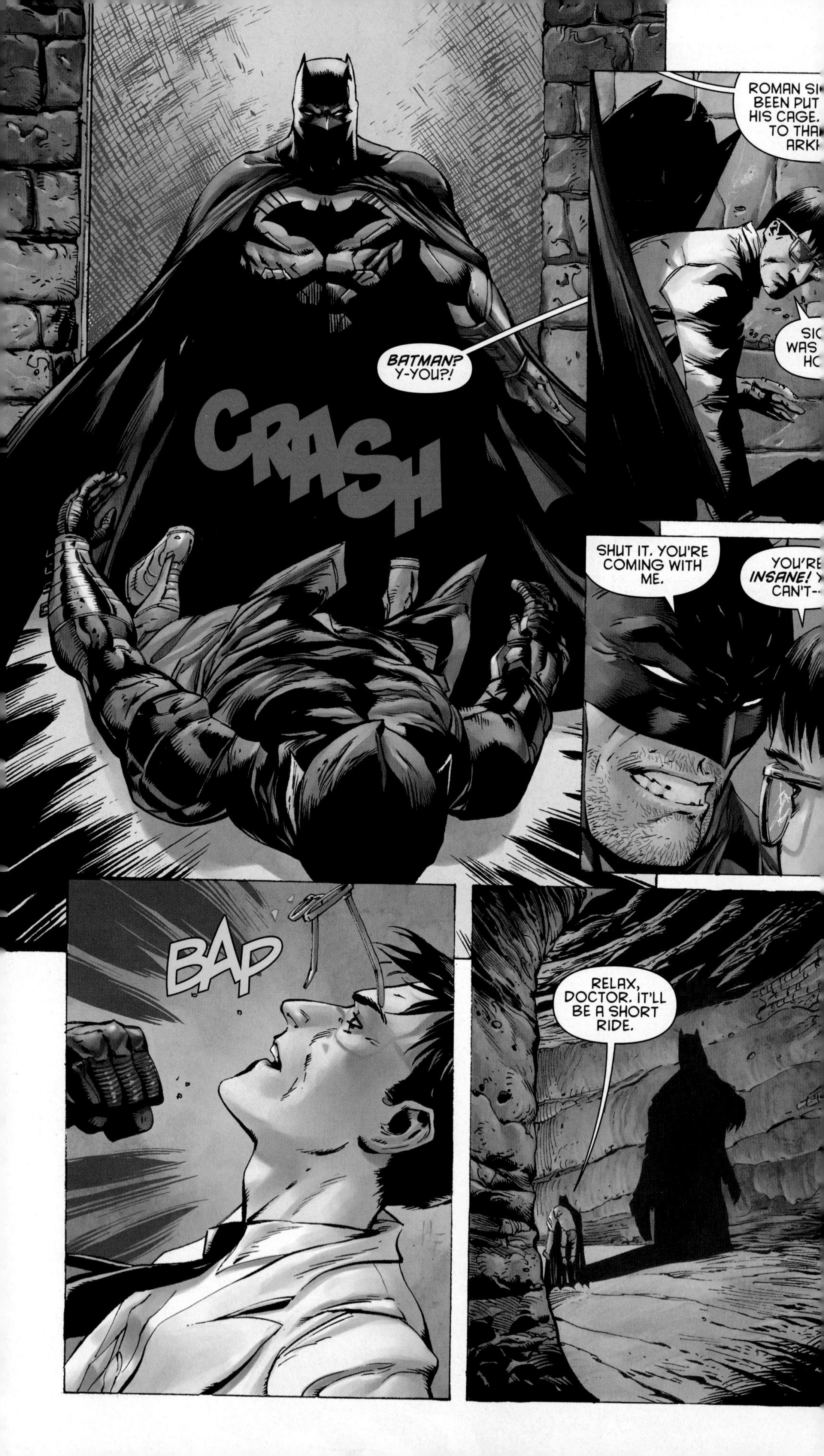
BATMAN? Y-YOU?!
CRASH
ROMAN SI
BEEN PUT
HIS CAGE.
TO THA
SI
WAS
SHUT IT. YOU'RE COMING WITH ME.
YOU'RE
INSANE!
CAN'T--
BAP
RELAX, DOCTOR. IT'LL BE A SHORT RIDE.

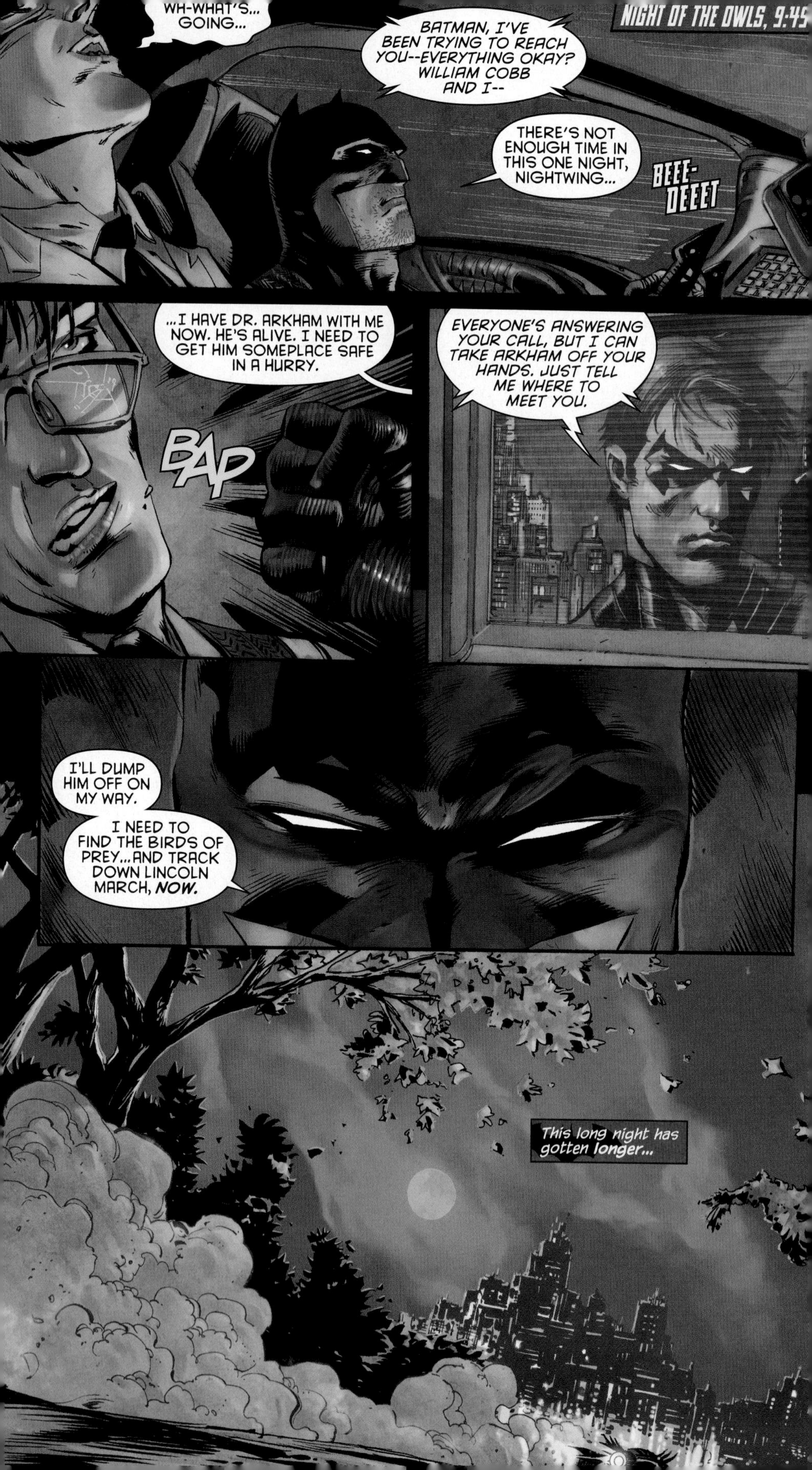
NIGHT OF THE OWLS, 9:45
WH-WHAT'S... GOING...
BATMAN, I'VE BEEN TRYING TO REACH YOU--EVERYTHING OKAY? WILLIAM COBB AND I--
THERE'S NOT ENOUGH TIME IN THIS ONE NIGHT, NIGHTWING...
BEEE-DEEET
...I HAVE DR. ARKHAM WITH ME NOW. HE'S ALIVE. I NEED TO GET HIM SOMEPLACE SAFE IN A HURRY.
BAP
EVERYONE'S ANSWERING YOUR CALL, BUT I CAN TAKE ARKHAM OFF YOUR HANDS. JUST TELL ME WHERE TO MEET YOU.
I'LL DUMP HIM OFF ON MY WAY.
I NEED TO FIND THE BIRDS OF PREY...AND TRACK DOWN LINCOLN MARCH, NOW.
This long night has gotten longer...

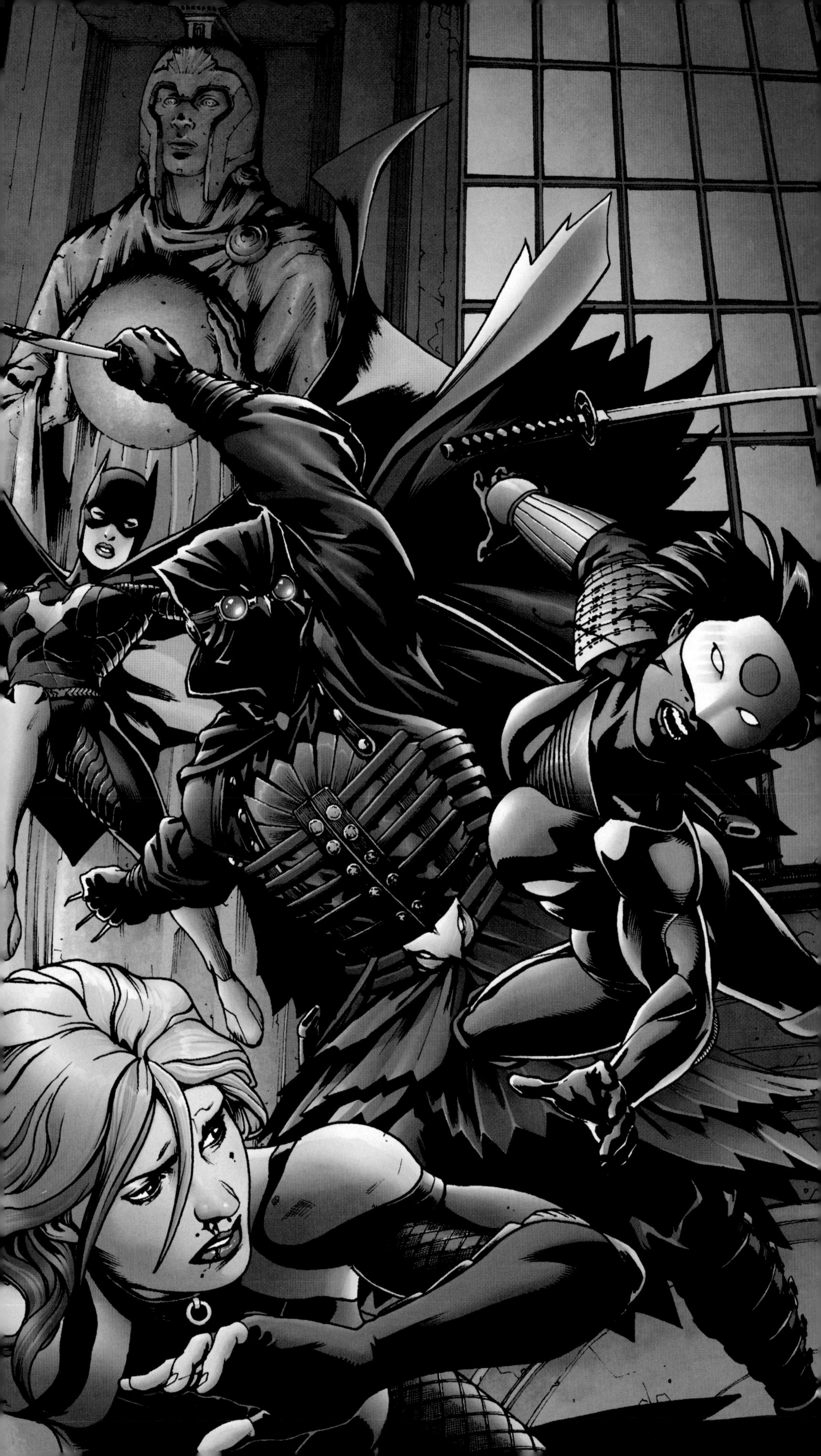

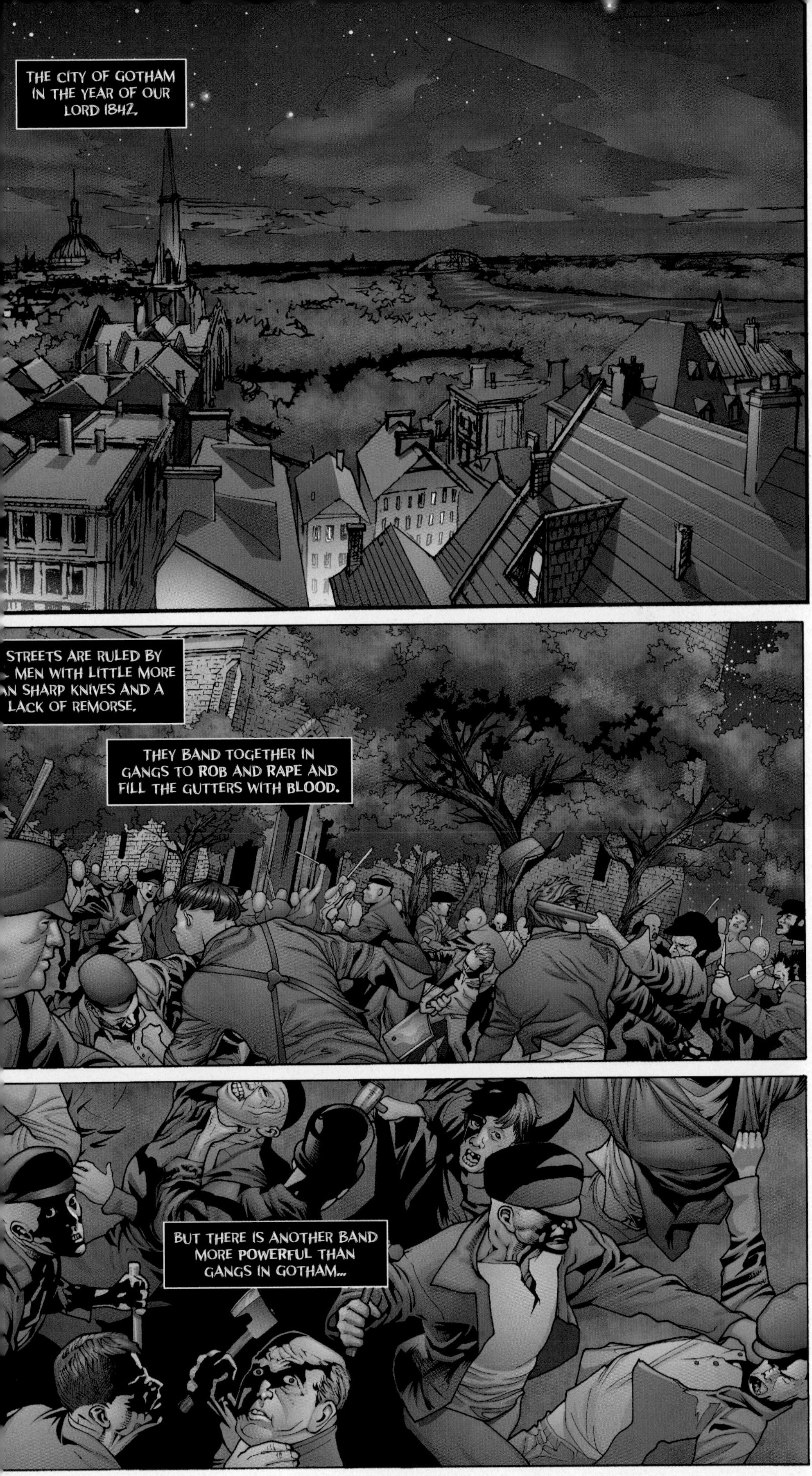
THE CITY OF GOTHAM IN THE YEAR OF OUR LORD 1842.
STREETS ARE RULED BY MEN WITH LITTLE MORE AN SHARP KNIVES AND A LACK OF REMORSE.
THEY BAND TOGETHER IN GANGS TO ROB AND RAPE AND FILL THE GUTTERS WITH BLOOD.
BUT THERE IS ANOTHER BAND MORE POWERFUL THAN GANGS IN GOTHAM...

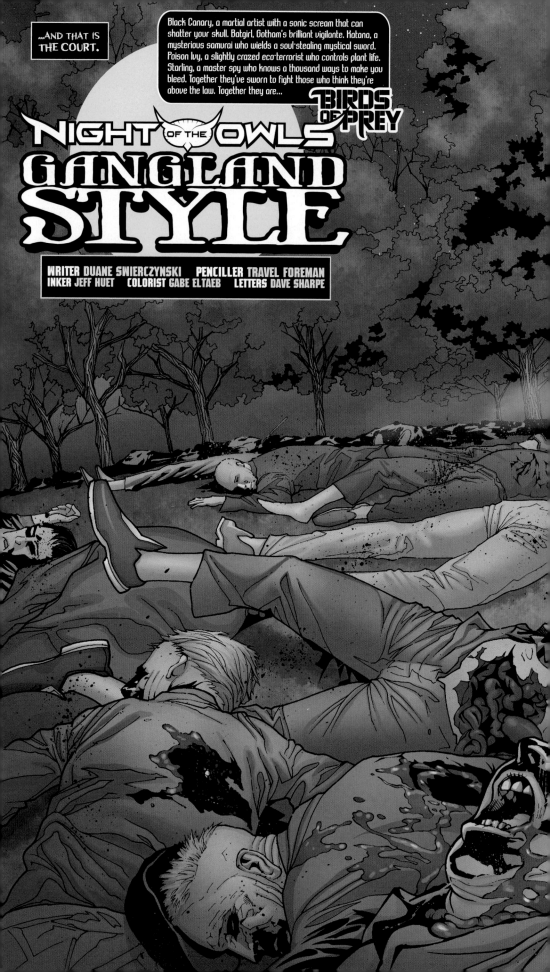

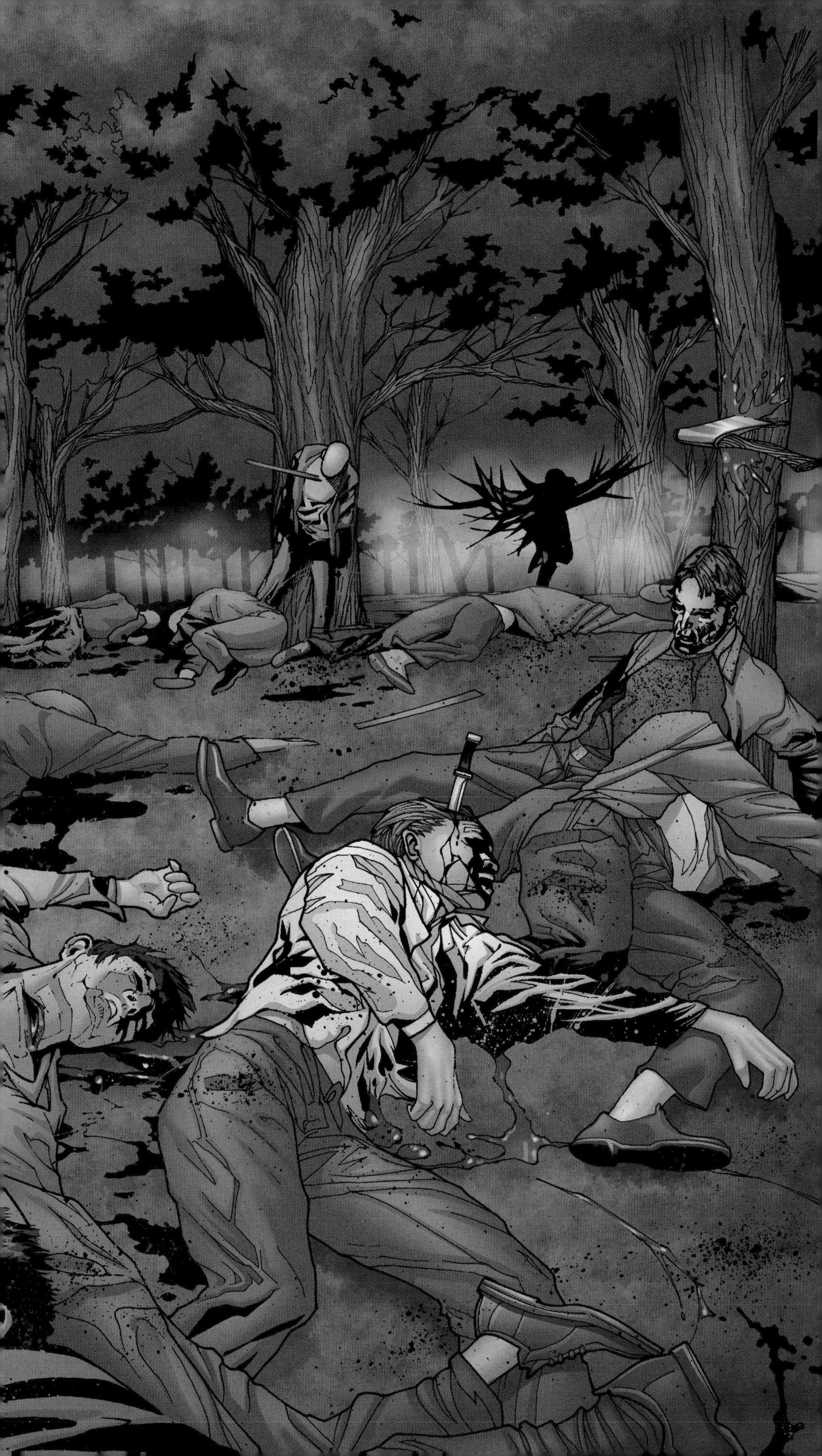

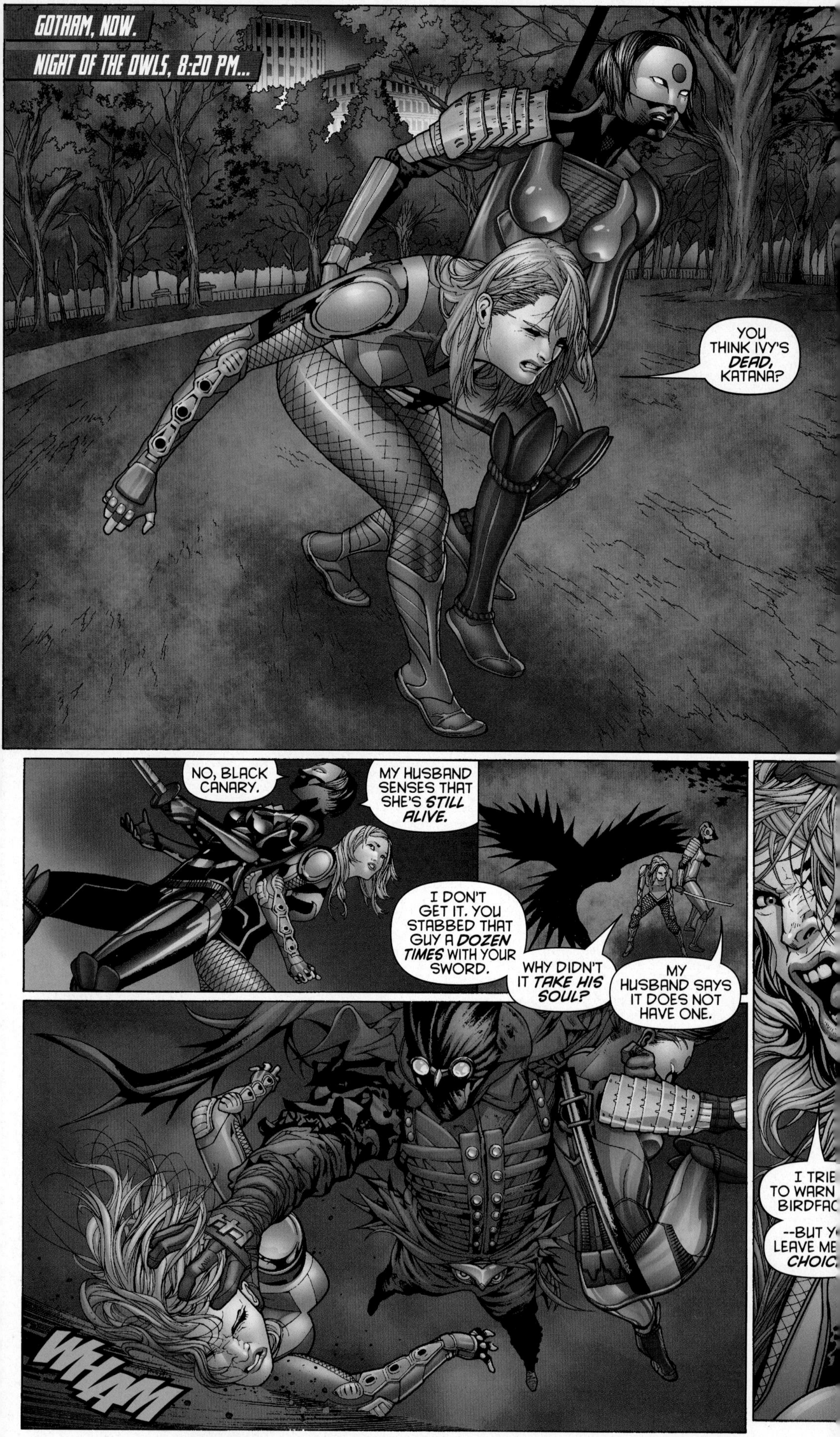
GOTHAM, NOW.
NIGHT OF THE OWLS, 8:20 PM...
YOU THINK IVY'S DEAD, KATANA?
NO, BLACK CANARY.
MY HUSBAND SENSES THAT SHE'S STILL ALIVE.
I DON'T GET IT. YOU STABBED THAT GUY A DOZEN TIMES WITH YOUR SWORD.
WHY DIDN'T IT TAKE HIS SOUL?
MY HUSBAND SAYS IT DOES NOT HAVE ONE.
WHAM
I TRIE TO WARN BIRDFAC
--BUT Y LEAVE ME CHOIC

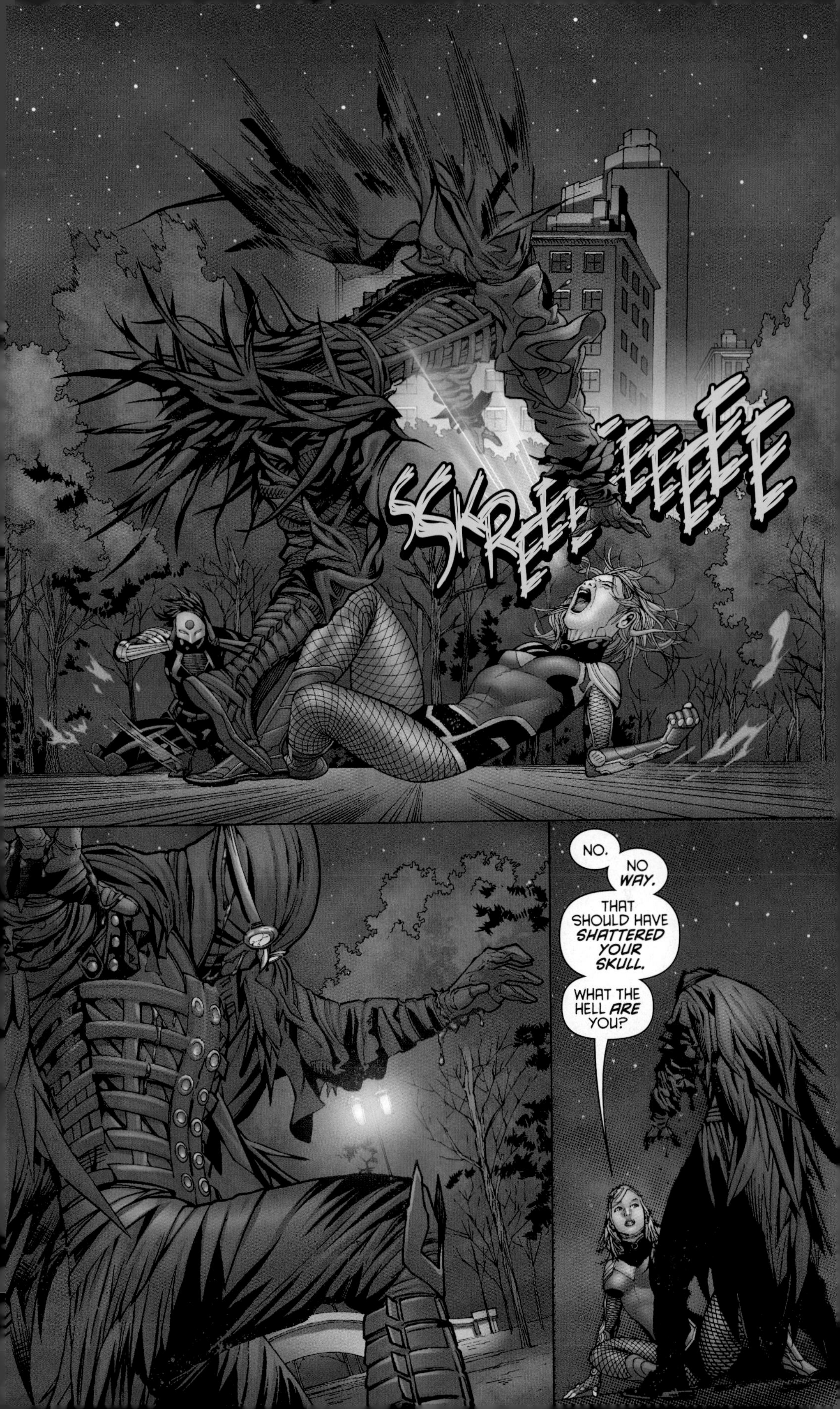
SSKREEEEEEEEEE
NO.
NO *WAY.*
THAT SHOULD HAVE *SHATTERED YOUR SKULL.*
WHAT THE HELL *ARE* YOU?

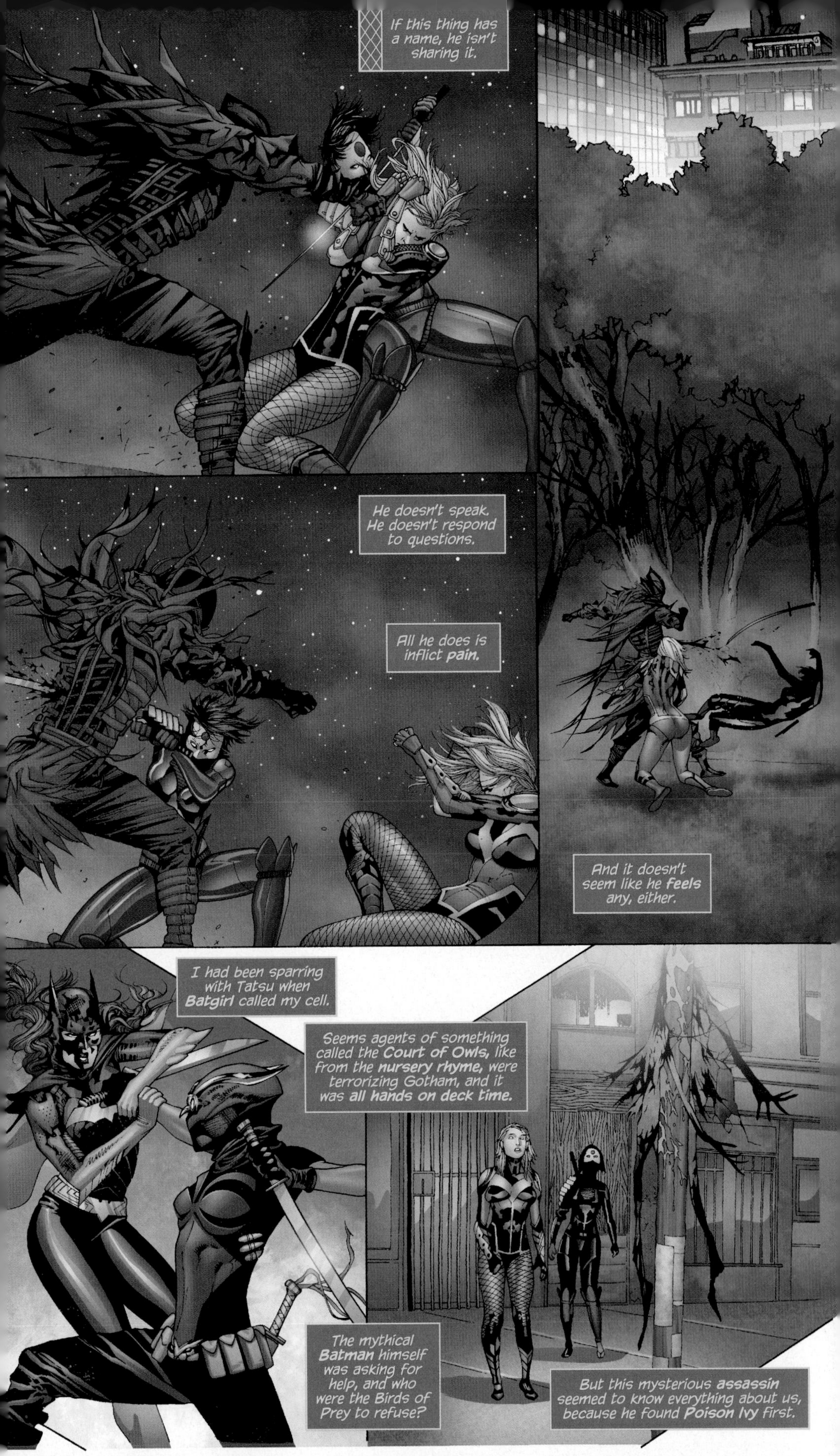
If this thing has a name, he isn't sharing it.
He doesn't speak. He doesn't respond to questions.
All he does is inflict pain.
And it doesn't seem like he feels any, either.
I had been sparring with Tatsu when Batgirl called my cell.
Seems agents of something called the Court of Owls, like from the nursery rhyme, were terrorizing Gotham, and it was all hands on deck time.
The mythical Batman himself was asking for help, and who were the Birds of Prey to refuse?
But this mysterious assassin seemed to know everything about us, because he found Poison Ivy first.

And tracked us down not long after.

KRNNK-H

No matter what kind of grievous injury we throw at him...and believe me, we've thrown *a lot* of grievous injuries his way...

...the c
bastard
even f

WE MUST FALL BACK, CANARY!

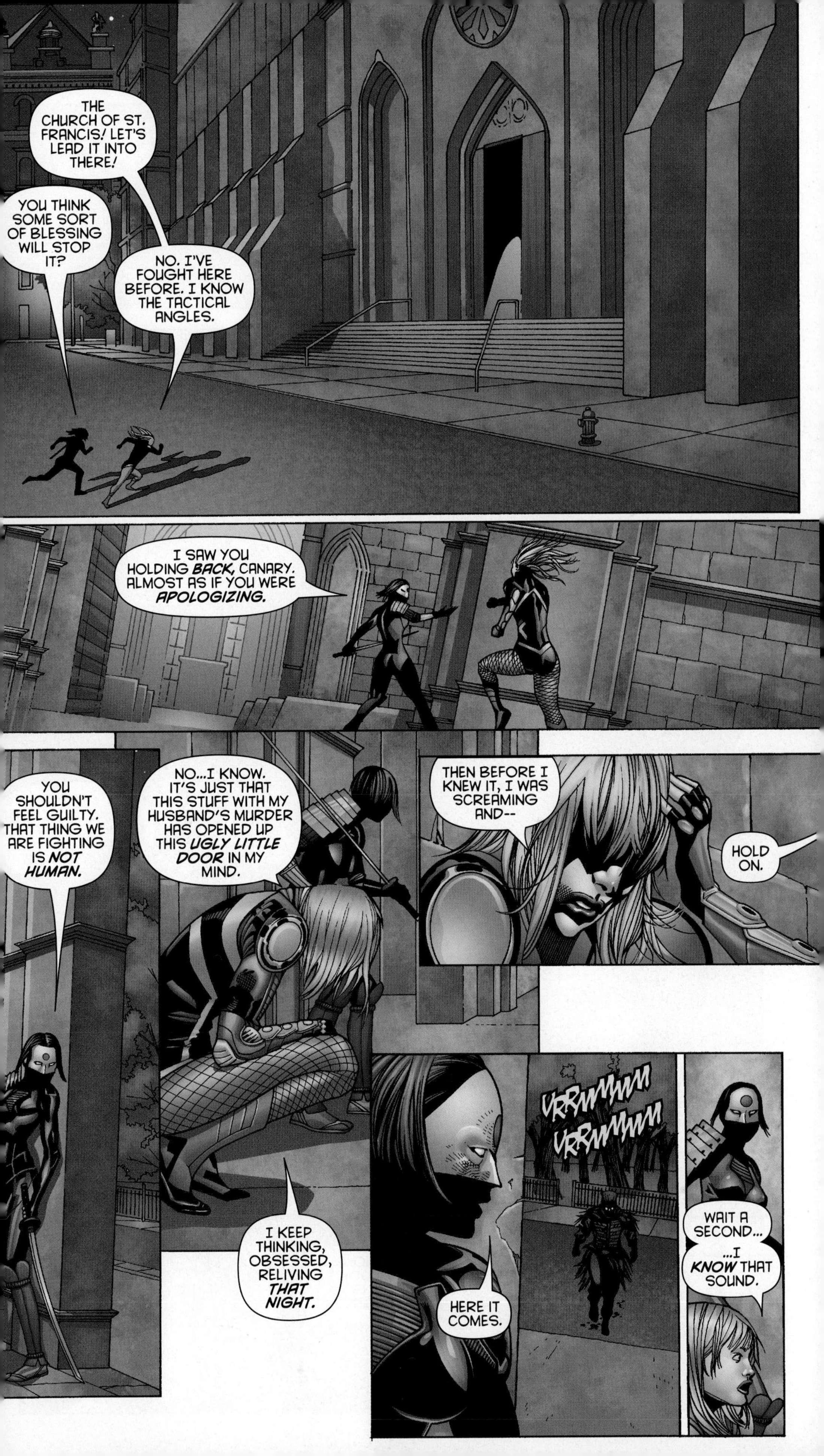
THE CHURCH OF ST. FRANCIS! LET'S LEAD IT INTO THERE!
YOU THINK SOME SORT OF BLESSING WILL STOP IT?
NO. I'VE FOUGHT HERE BEFORE. I KNOW THE TACTICAL ANGLES.
I SAW YOU HOLDING *BACK*, CANARY. ALMOST AS IF YOU WERE *APOLOGIZING.*
YOU SHOULDN'T FEEL GUILTY. THAT THING WE ARE FIGHTING IS *NOT HUMAN.*
NO...I KNOW. IT'S JUST THAT THIS STUFF WITH MY HUSBAND'S MURDER HAS OPENED UP THIS *UGLY LITTLE DOOR* IN MY MIND.
I KEEP THINKING, OBSESSED, RELIVING *THAT NIGHT.*
THEN BEFORE I KNEW IT, I WAS SCREAMING AND--
HOLD ON.
HERE IT COMES.
VRRMMM
VRRMMM
WAIT A SECOND...
...I *KNOW* THAT SOUND.

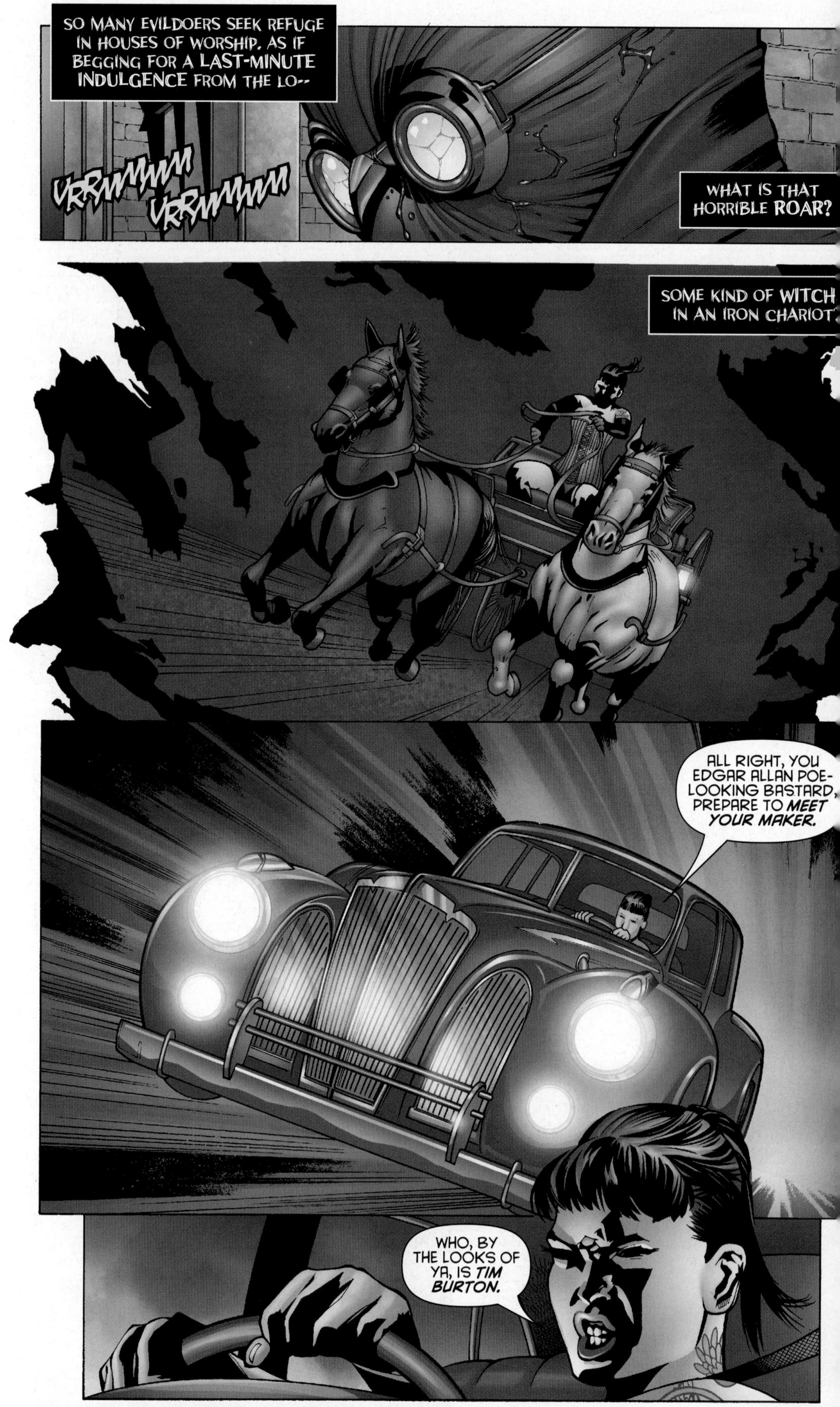
SO MANY EVILDOERS SEEK REFUGE IN HOUSES OF WORSHIP. AS IF BEGGING FOR A LAST-MINUTE INDULGENCE FROM THE LO--
VRRMMMM VRRMMMM
WHAT IS THAT HORRIBLE ROAR?
SOME KIND OF WITCH IN AN IRON CHARIOT?
ALL RIGHT, YOU EDGAR ALLAN POE-LOOKING BASTARD, PREPARE TO *MEET YOUR MAKER.*
WHO, BY THE LOOKS OF YA, IS *TIM BURTON.*

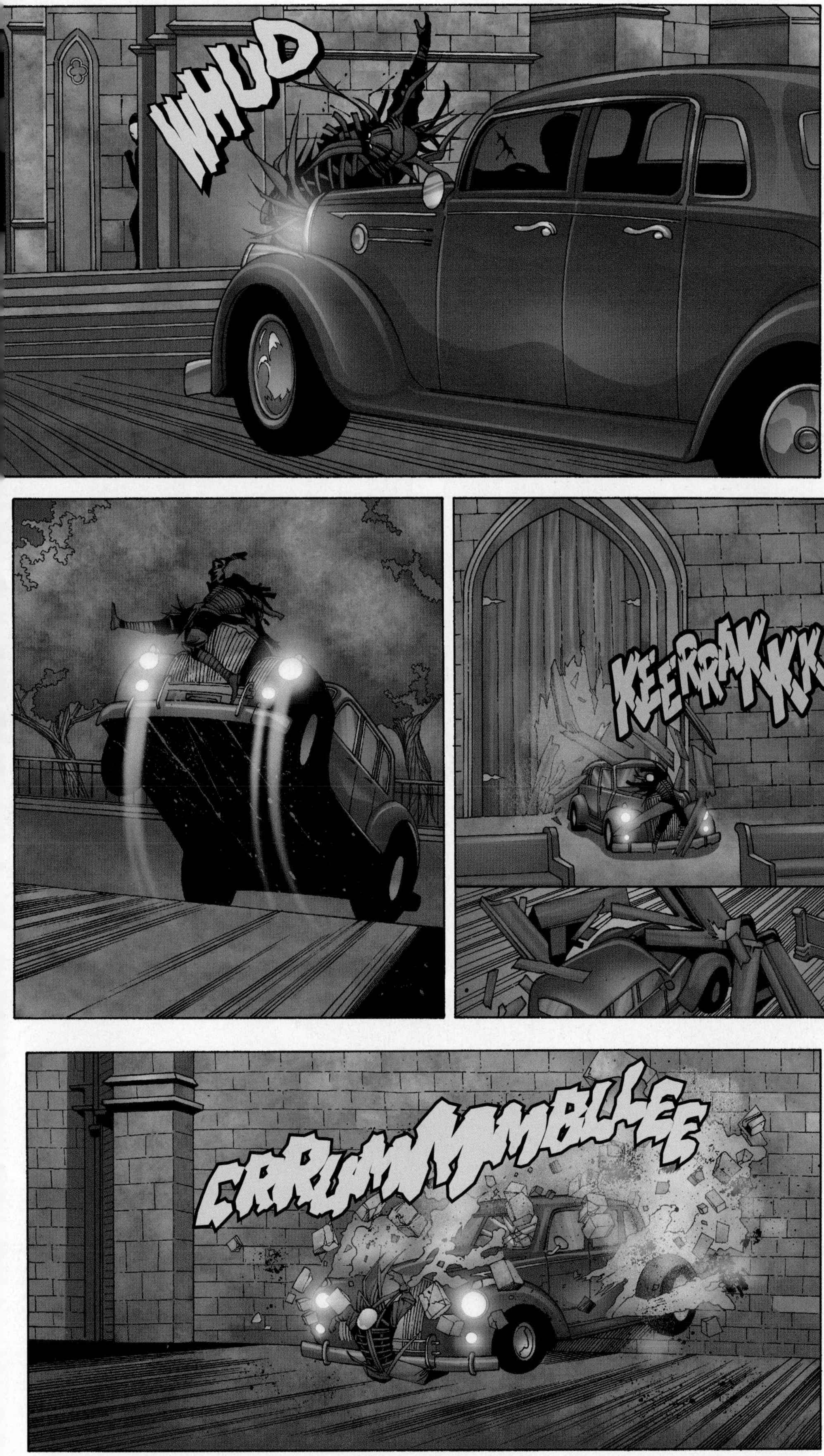
WHUD
KEERRAKKKK
CRRUMMMMBLLEE

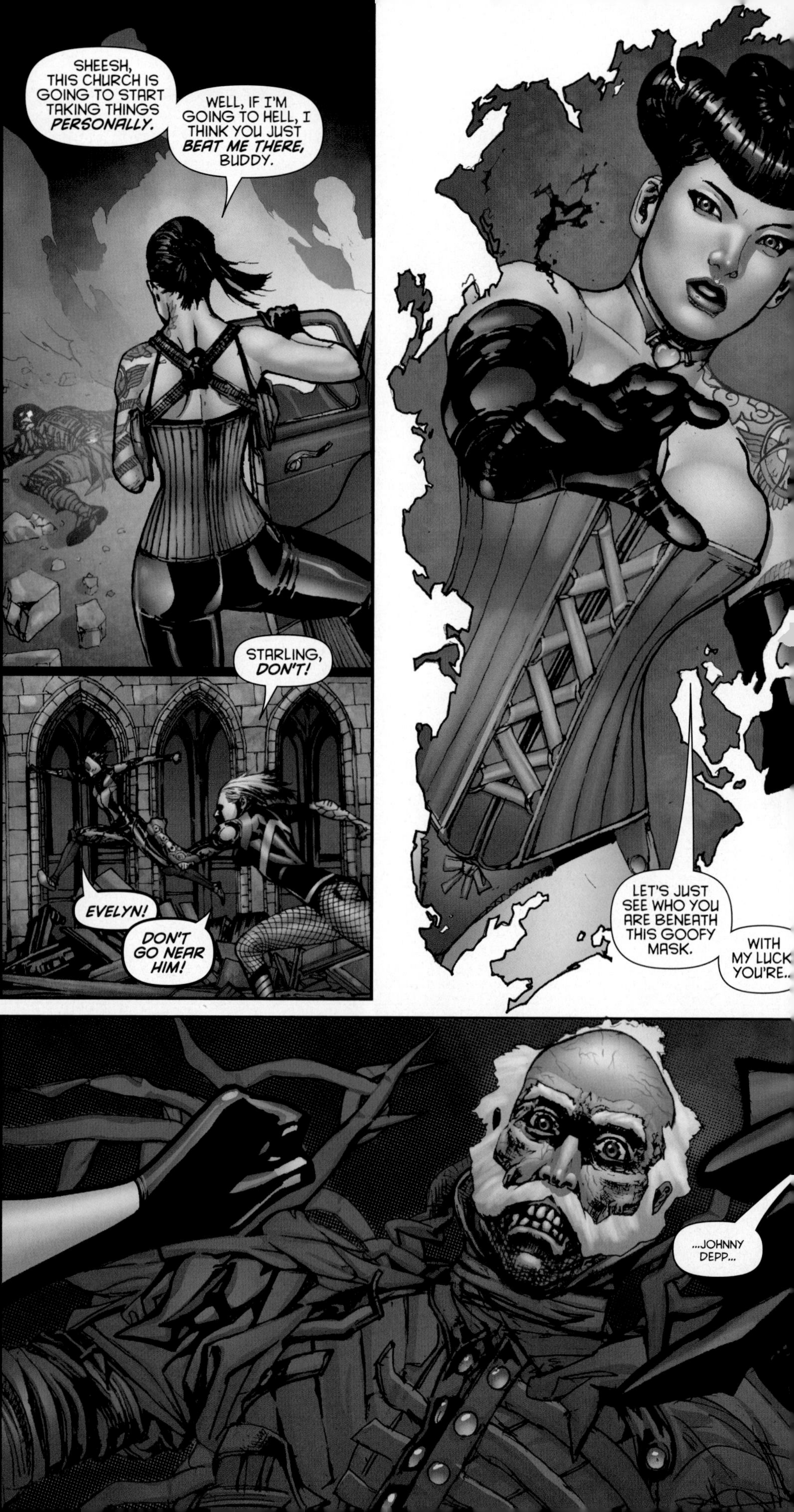

SHEESH, THIS CHURCH IS GOING TO START TAKING THINGS *PERSONALLY.*
WELL, IF I'M GOING TO HELL, I THINK YOU JUST *BEAT ME THERE,* BUDDY.
STARLING, *DON'T!*
EVELYN!
DON'T GO NEAR HIM!
LET'S JUST SEE WHO YOU ARE BENEATH THIS GOOFY MASK.
WITH MY LUCK YOU'RE...
...JOHNNY DEPP...

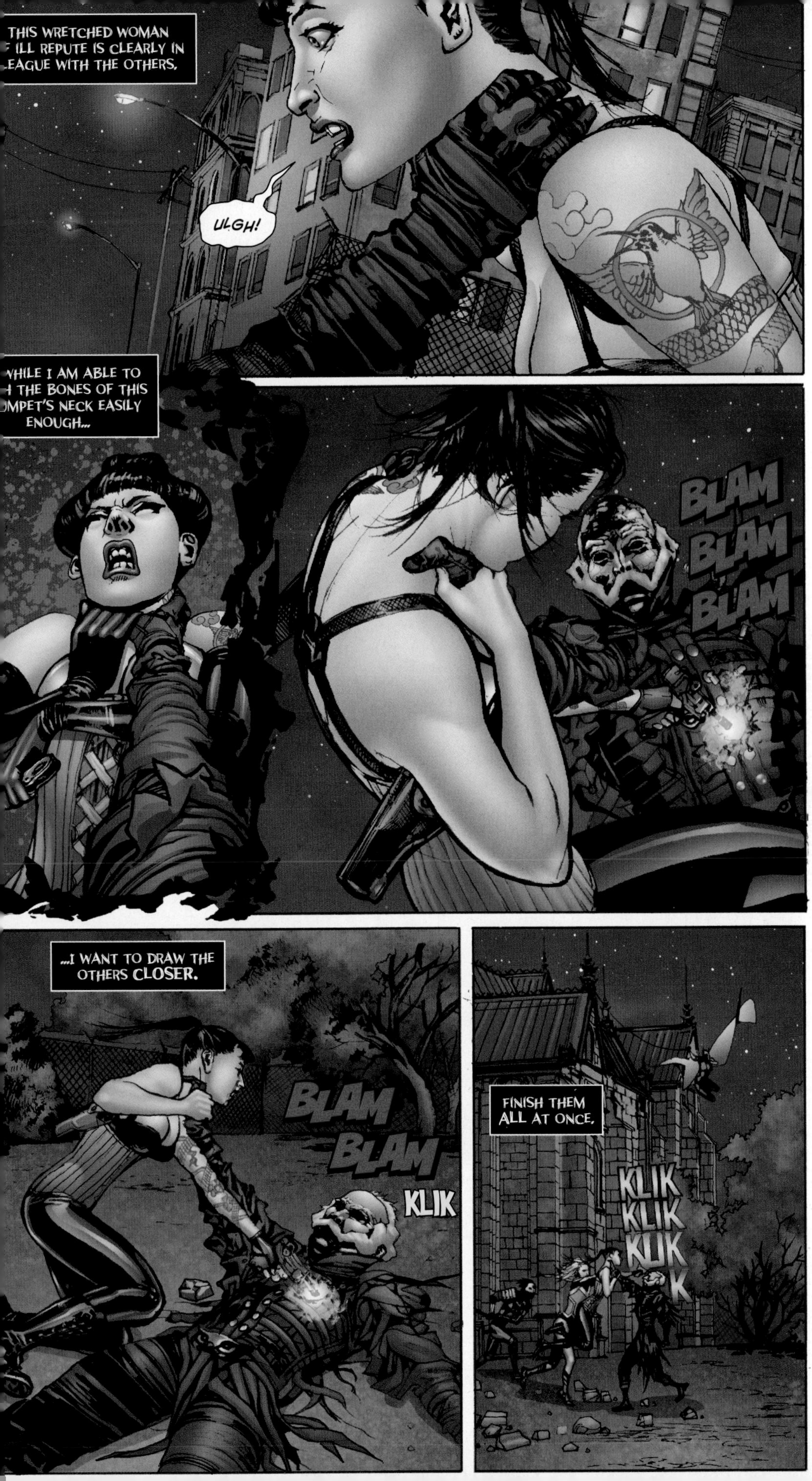
THIS WRETCHED WOMAN
F ILL REPUTE IS CLEARLY IN
EAGUE WITH THE OTHERS.
ULGH!
WHILE I AM ABLE TO
H THE BONES OF THIS
UMPET'S NECK EASILY
ENOUGH...
BLAM
BLAM
BLAM
...I WANT TO DRAW THE
OTHERS CLOSER.
BLAM
BLAM
KLIK
FINISH THEM
ALL AT ONCE.
KLIK
KLIK
KLIK
K

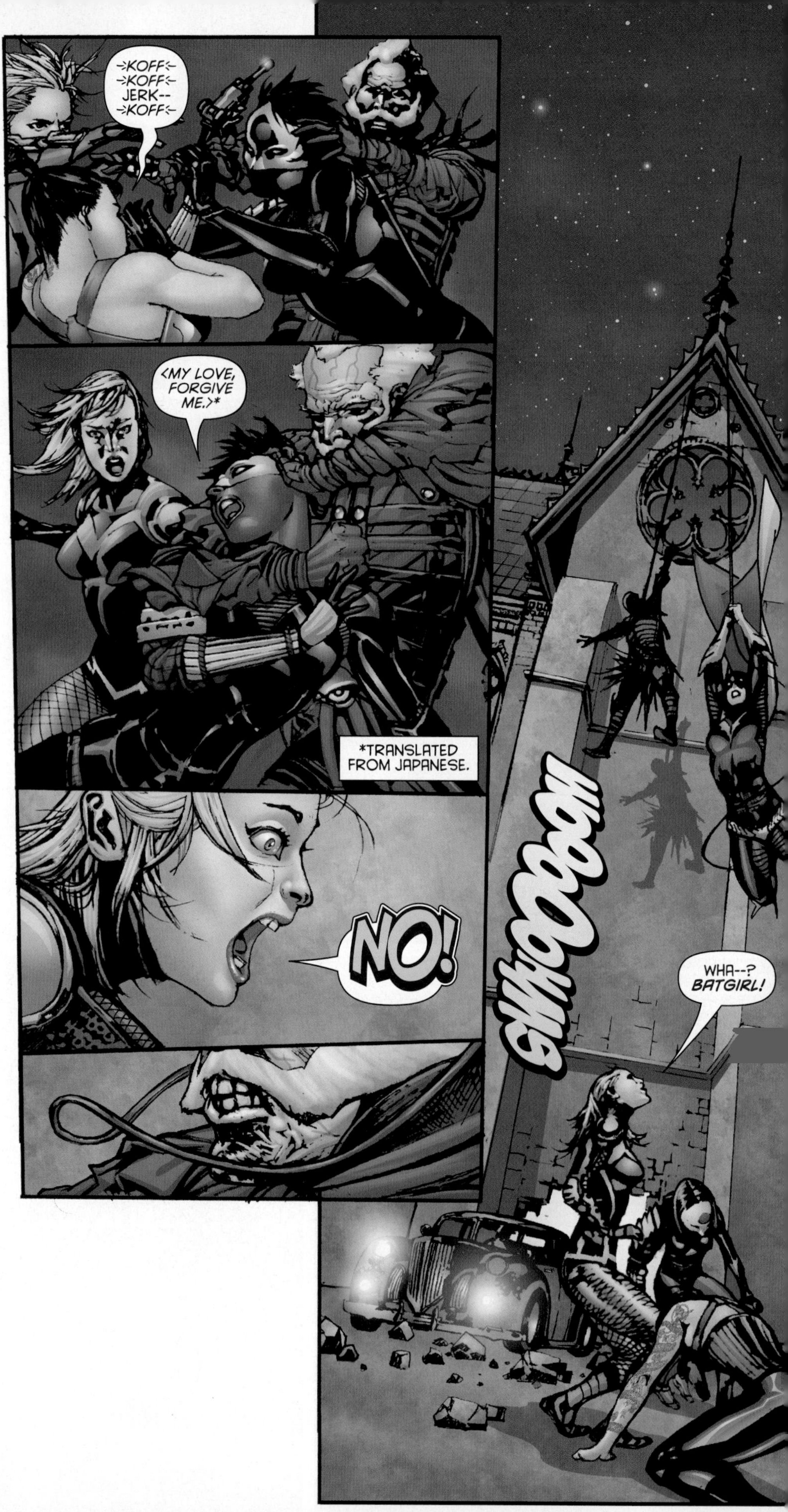

-KOFF-
-KOFF-
JERK--
-KOFF-
<MY LOVE, FORGIVE ME.>*
*TRANSLATED FROM JAPANESE.
NO!
SHWOOOOOP
WHA--? BATGIRL!

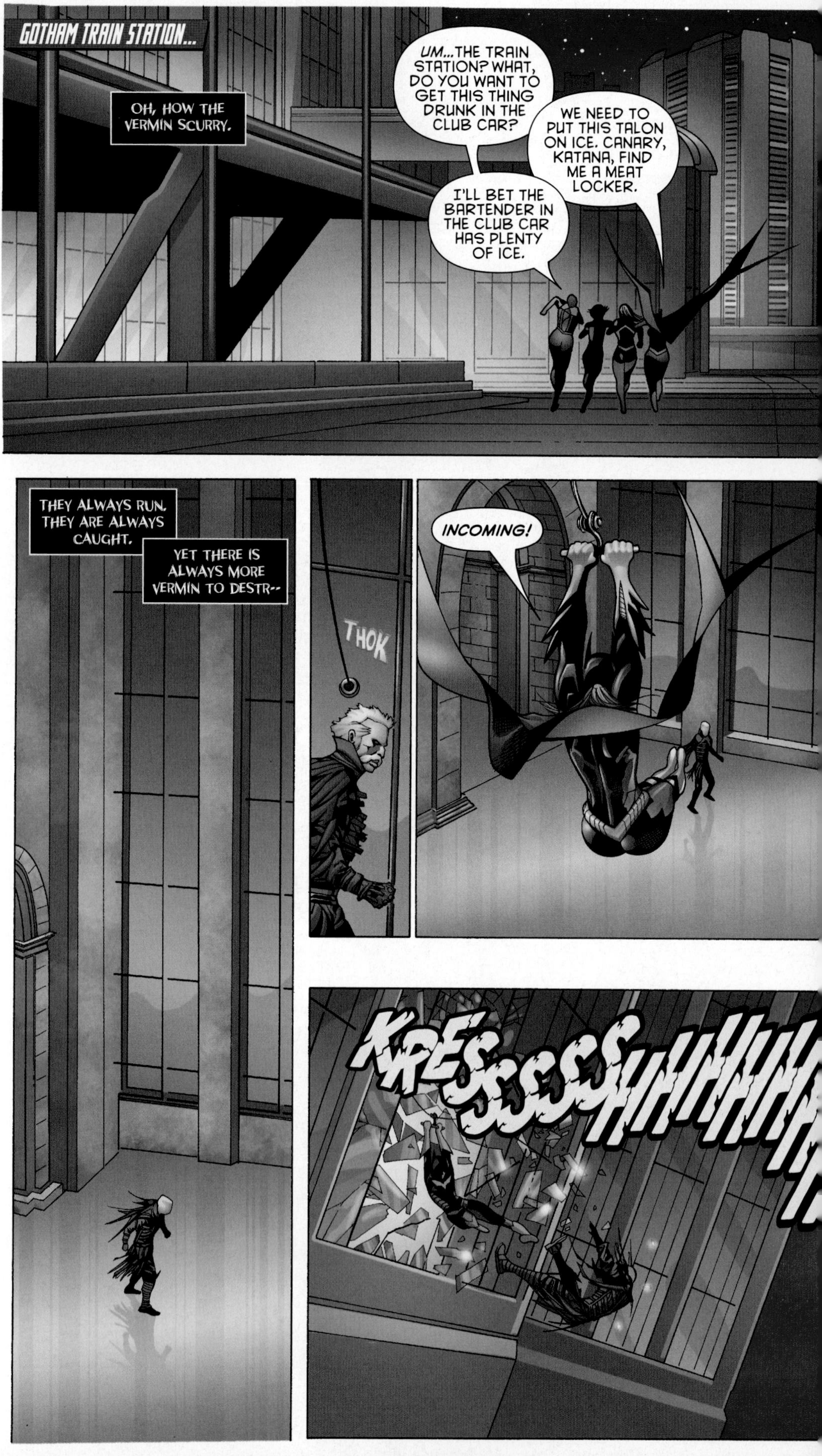
GOTHAM TRAIN STATION...
OH, HOW THE VERMIN SCURRY.
UM...THE TRAIN STATION? WHAT, DO YOU WANT TO GET THIS THING DRUNK IN THE CLUB CAR?
WE NEED TO PUT THIS TALON ON ICE. CANARY, KATANA, FIND ME A MEAT LOCKER.
I'LL BET THE BARTENDER IN THE CLUB CAR HAS PLENTY OF ICE.
THEY ALWAYS RUN. THEY ARE ALWAYS CAUGHT.
YET THERE IS ALWAYS MORE VERMIN TO DESTR--
THOK
INCOMING!
KRESSSSSSHHHHHH

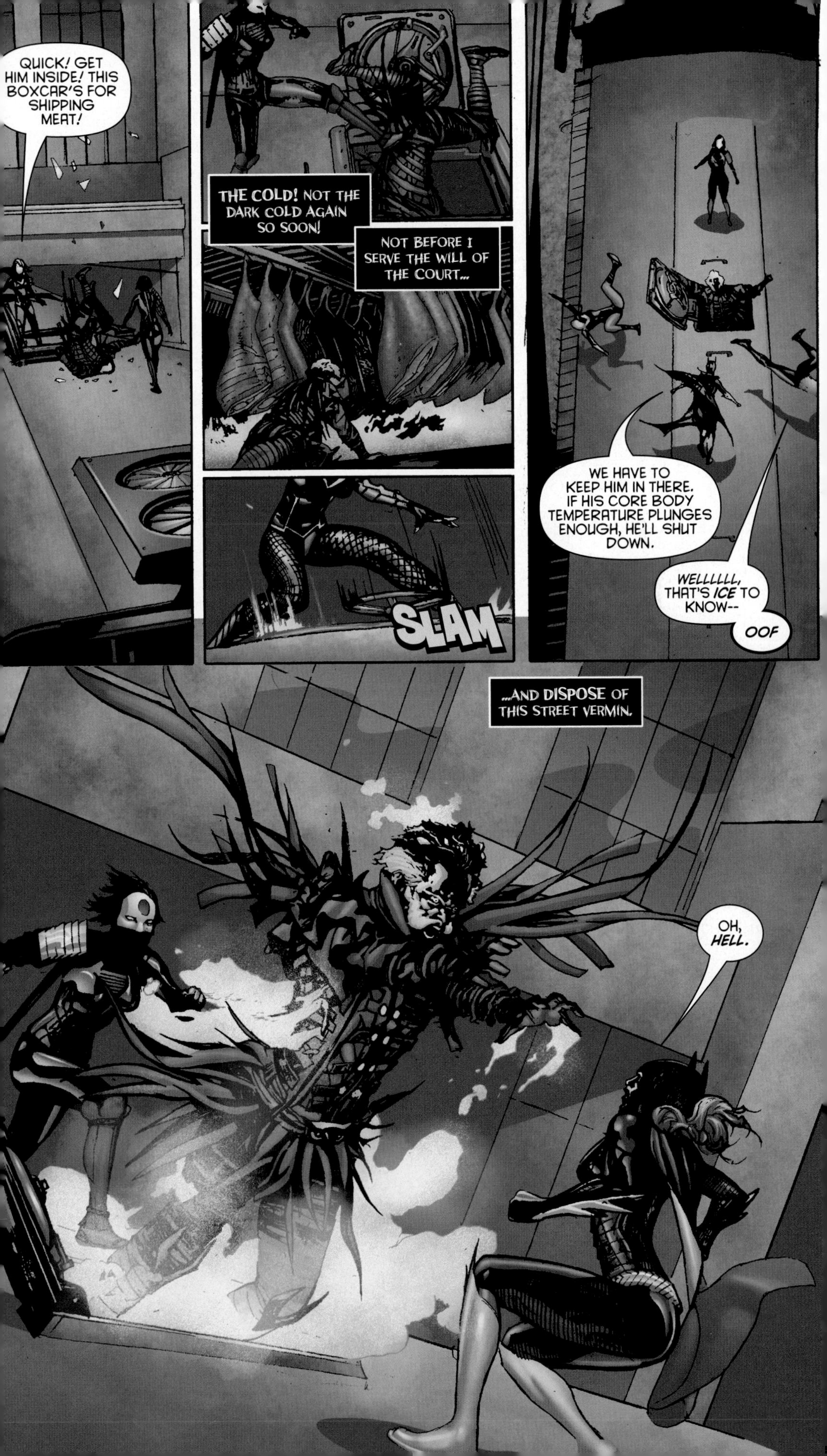
QUICK! GET HIM INSIDE! THIS BOXCAR'S FOR SHIPPING MEAT!
THE COLD! NOT THE DARK COLD AGAIN SO SOON!
NOT BEFORE I SERVE THE WILL OF THE COURT...
SLAM
WE HAVE TO KEEP HIM IN THERE. IF HIS CORE BODY TEMPERATURE PLUNGES ENOUGH, HE'LL SHUT DOWN.
WELLLLLLL, THAT'S *ICE* TO KNOW--
OOF
...AND DISPOSE OF THIS STREET VERMIN.
OH, *HELL.*

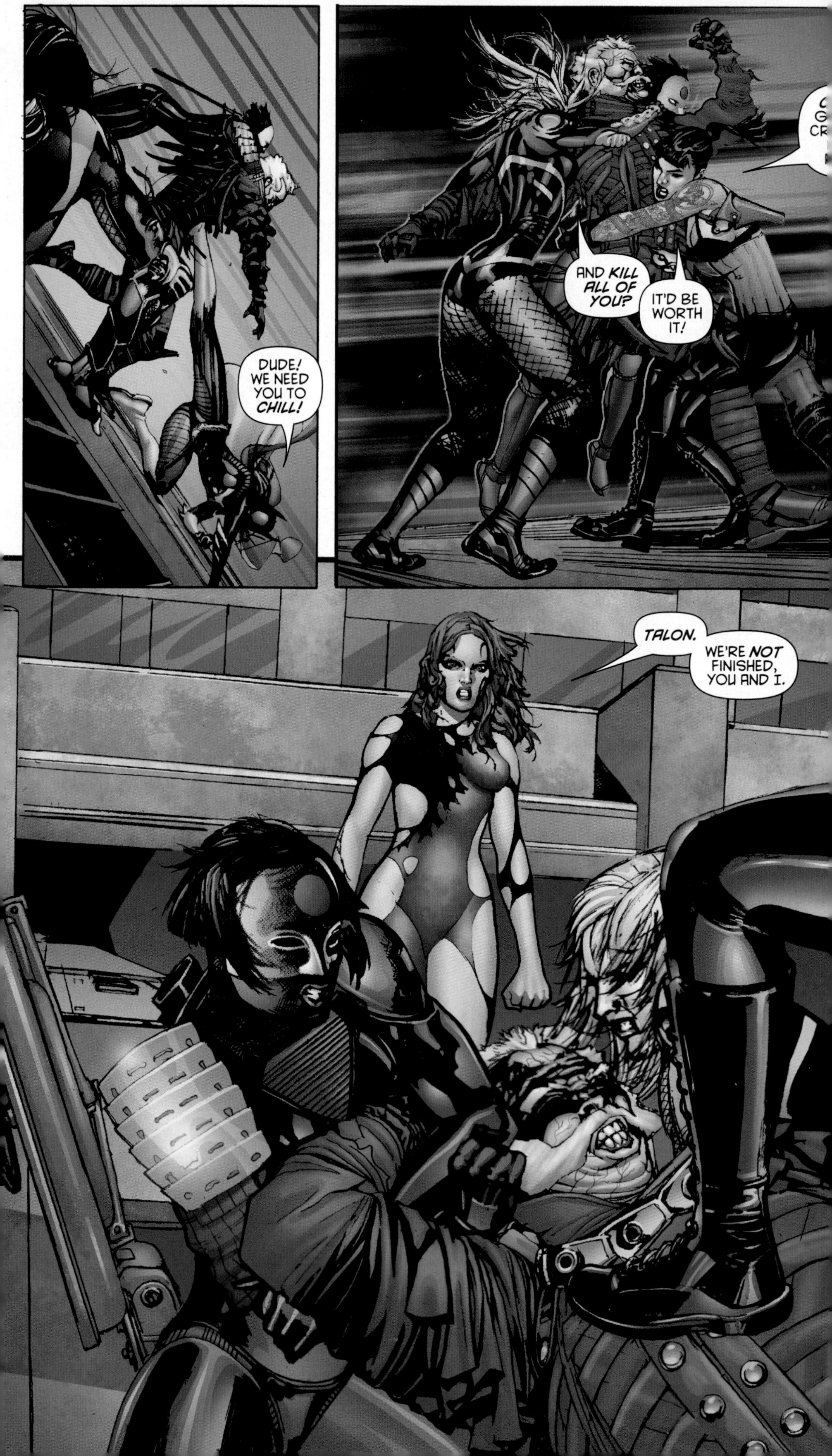
DUDE! WE NEED YOU TO *CHILL!*
AND *KILL ALL OF YOU?*
IT'D BE WORTH IT!
TALON.
WE'RE *NOT* FINISHED, YOU AND I.

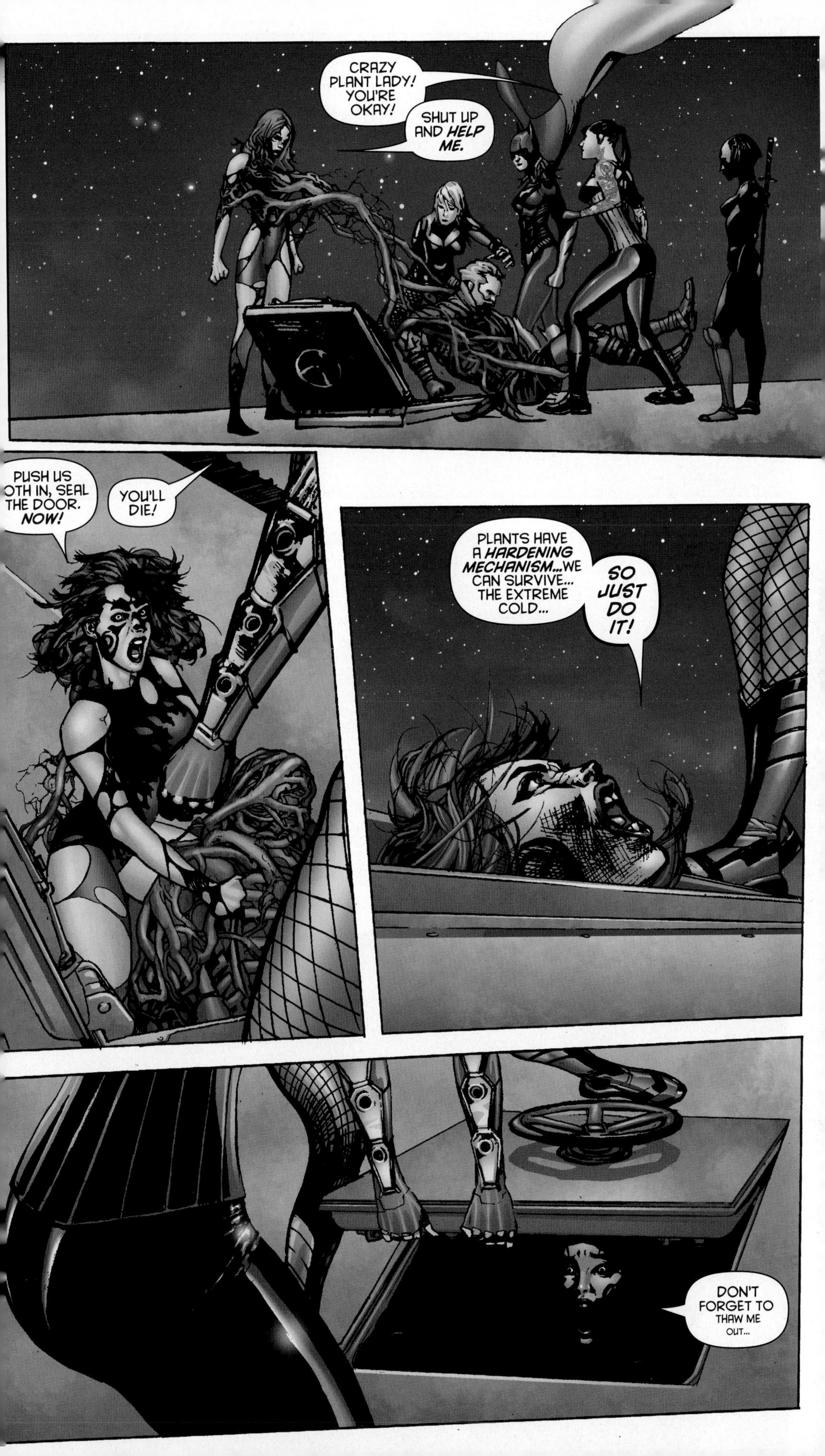

CRAZY PLANT LADY! YOU'RE OKAY!
SHUT UP AND HELP ME.
PUSH US OTH IN, SEAL THE DOOR. NOW!
YOU'LL DIE!
PLANTS HAVE A HARDENING MECHANISM...WE CAN SURVIVE... THE EXTREME COLD...
SO JUST DO IT!
DON'T FORGET TO THAW ME OUT...

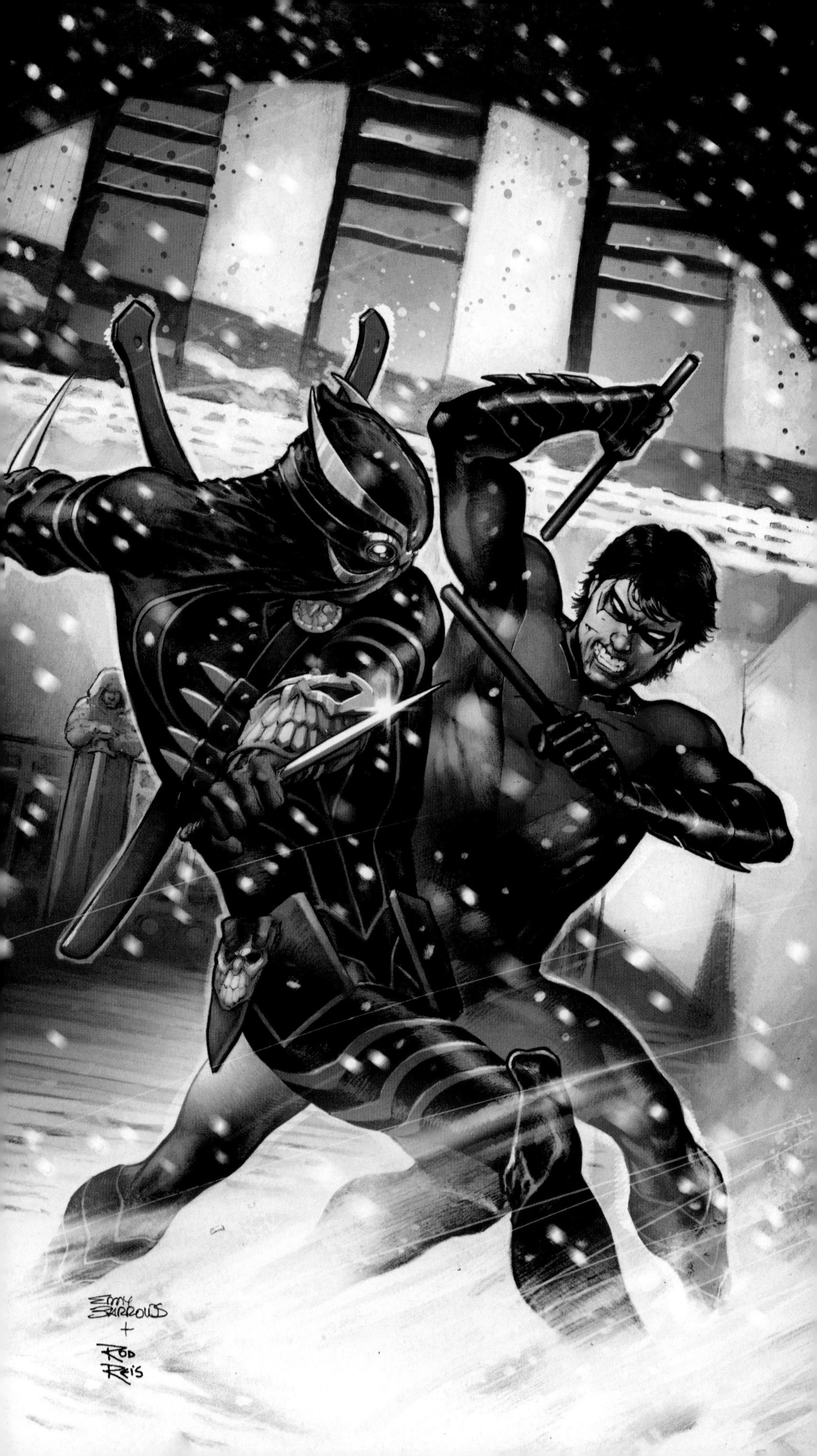

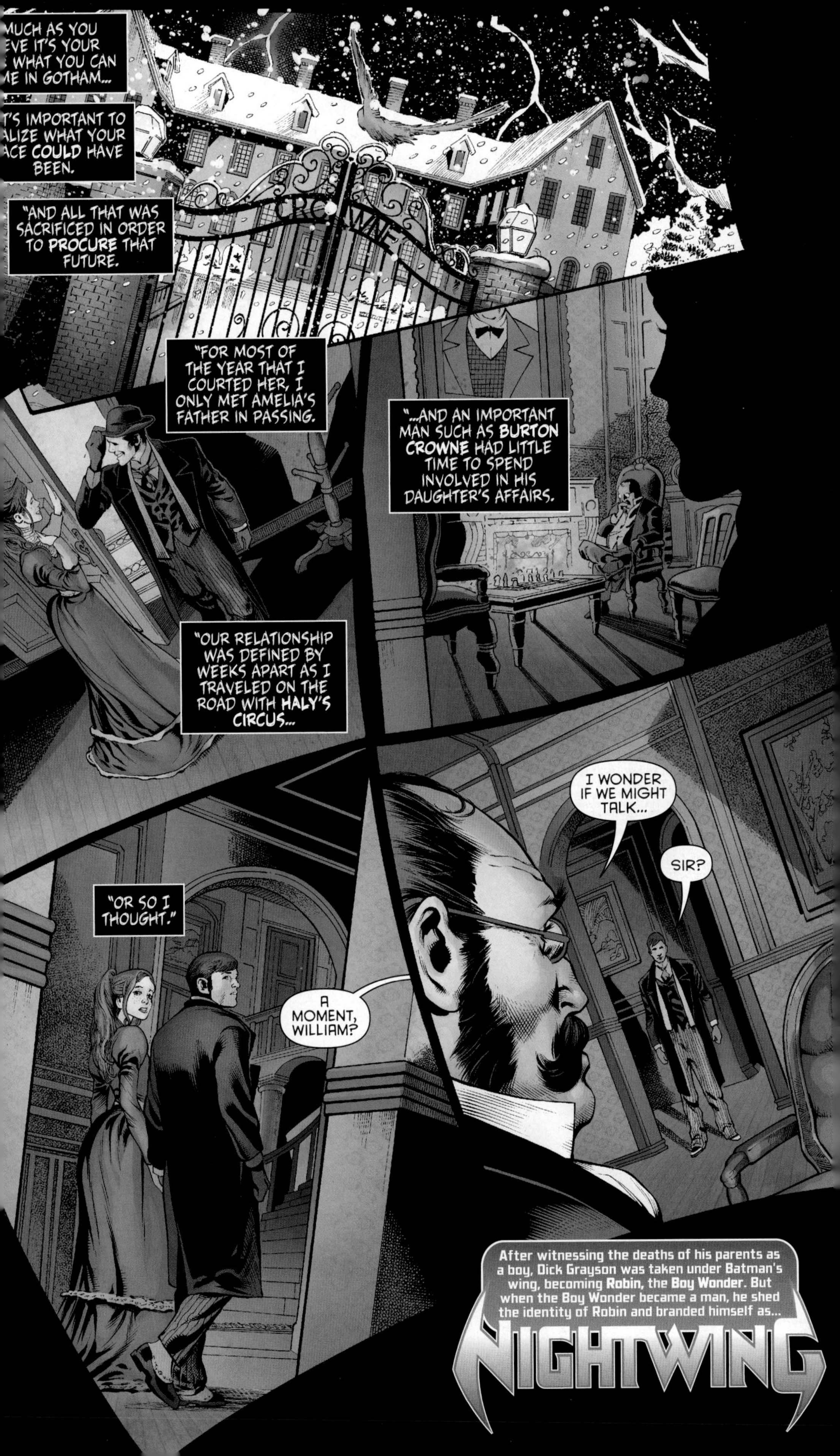

MUCH AS YOU
EVE IT'S YOUR
WHAT YOU CAN
E IN GOTHAM...
T'S IMPORTANT TO
ALIZE WHAT YOUR
ACE COULD HAVE
BEEN.
"AND ALL THAT WAS SACRIFICED IN ORDER TO PROCURE THAT FUTURE.
CROWNE
"FOR MOST OF THE YEAR THAT I COURTED HER, I ONLY MET AMELIA'S FATHER IN PASSING.
"...AND AN IMPORTANT MAN SUCH AS BURTON CROWNE HAD LITTLE TIME TO SPEND INVOLVED IN HIS DAUGHTER'S AFFAIRS.
"OUR RELATIONSHIP WAS DEFINED BY WEEKS APART AS I TRAVELED ON THE ROAD WITH HALY'S CIRCUS...
"OR SO I THOUGHT."
A MOMENT, WILLIAM?
I WONDER IF WE MIGHT TALK...
SIR?
After witnessing the deaths of his parents as a boy, Dick Grayson was taken under Batman's wing, becoming Robin, the Boy Wonder. But when the Boy Wonder became a man, he shed the identity of Robin and branded himself as...
NIGHTWING

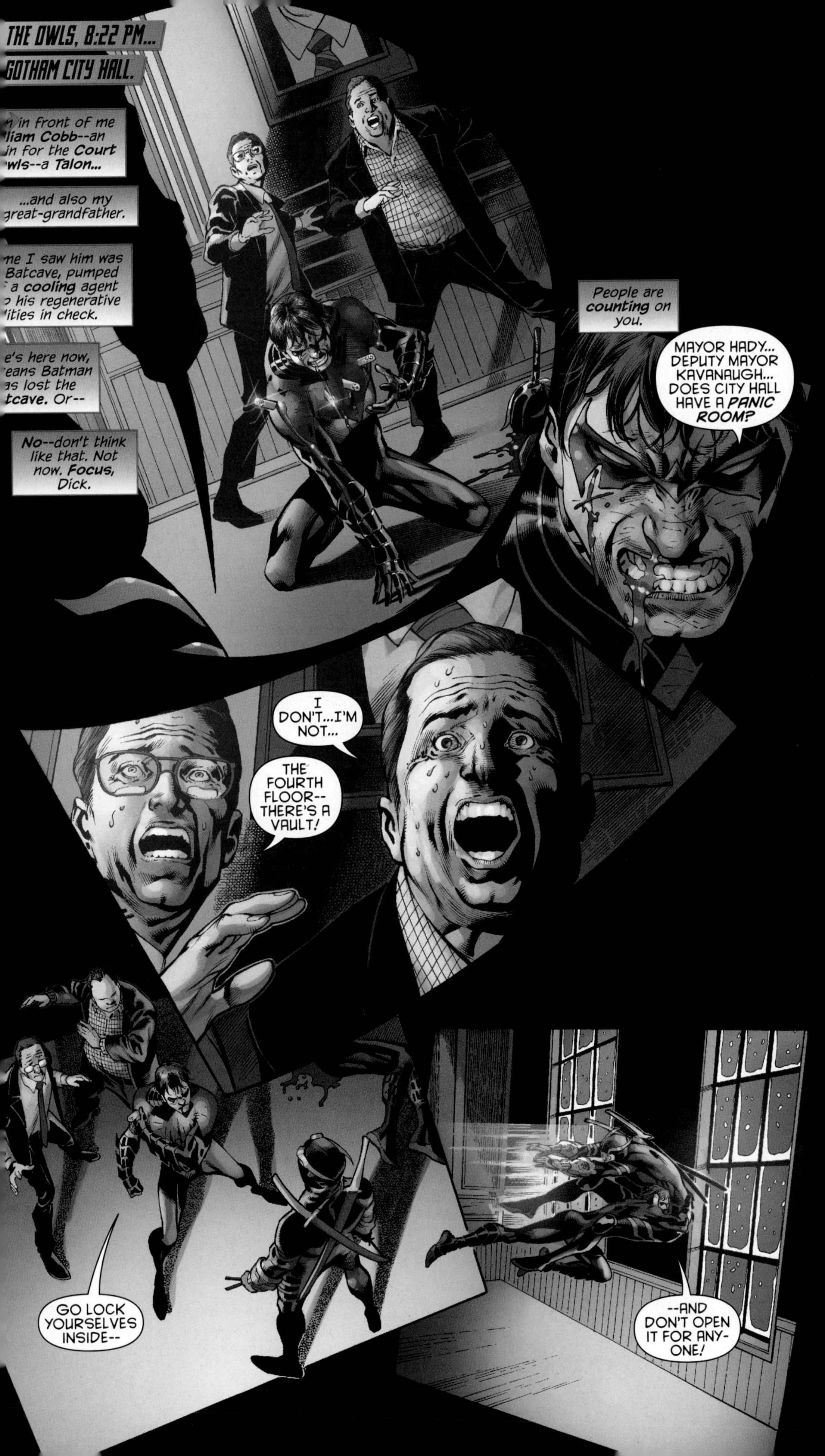

THE OWLS, 8:22 PM...
GOTHAM CITY HALL.
n in front of me lliam Cobb--an in for the Court wls--a Talon...
...and also my great-grandfather.
me I saw him was Batcave, pumped a cooling agent his regenerative lities in check.
e's here now, eans Batman as lost the tcave. Or--
No--don't think like that. Not now. Focus, Dick.
People are counting on you.
MAYOR HADY... DEPUTY MAYOR KAVANAUGH... DOES CITY HALL HAVE A PANIC ROOM?
I DON'T...I'M NOT...
THE FOURTH FLOOR-- THERE'S A VAULT!
GO LOCK YOURSELVES INSIDE--
--AND DON'T OPEN IT FOR ANY-ONE!

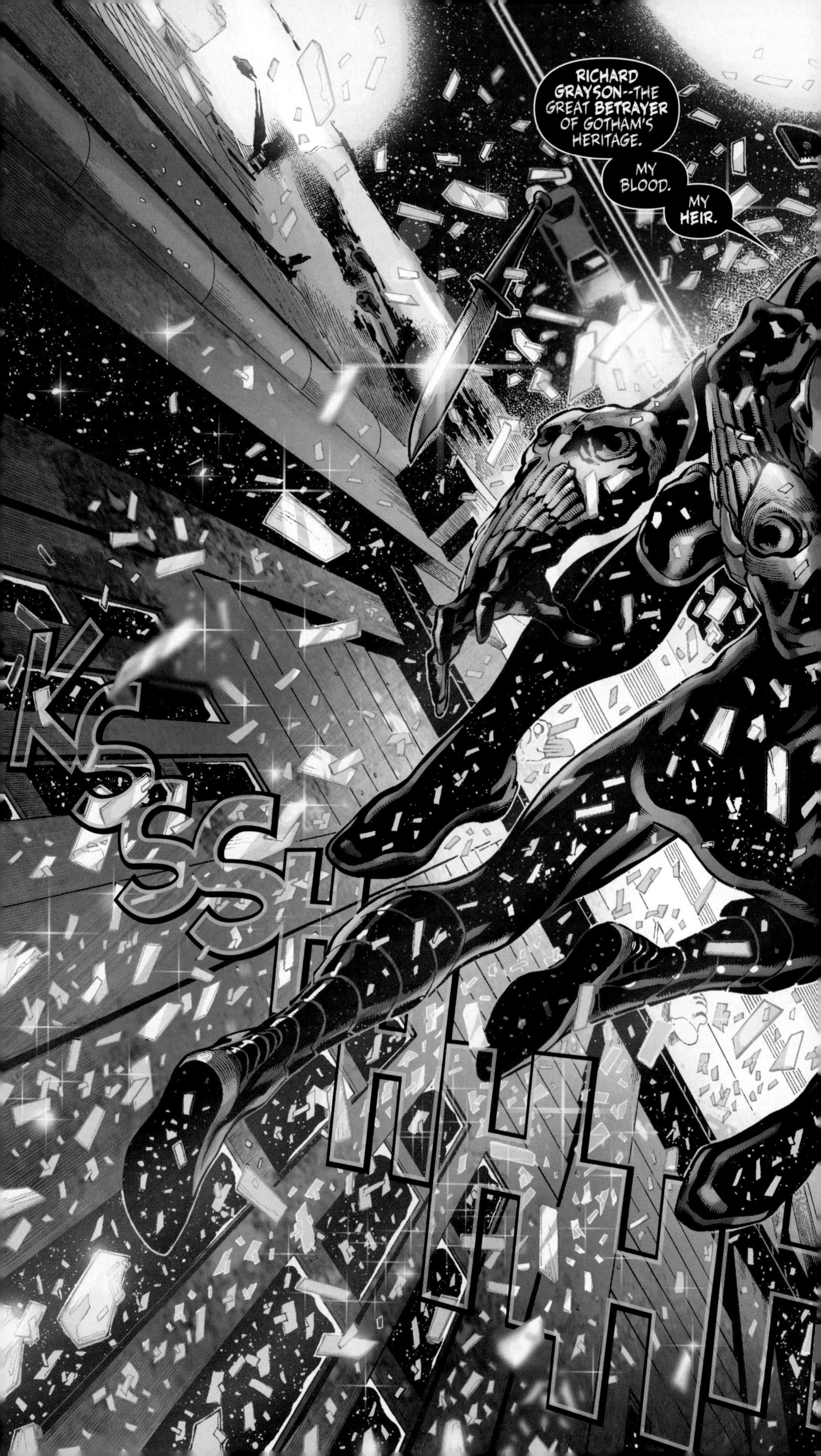
RICHARD GRAYSON--THE GREAT BETRAYER OF GOTHAM'S HERITAGE.
MY BLOOD.
MY HEIR.
KSSSHHHH

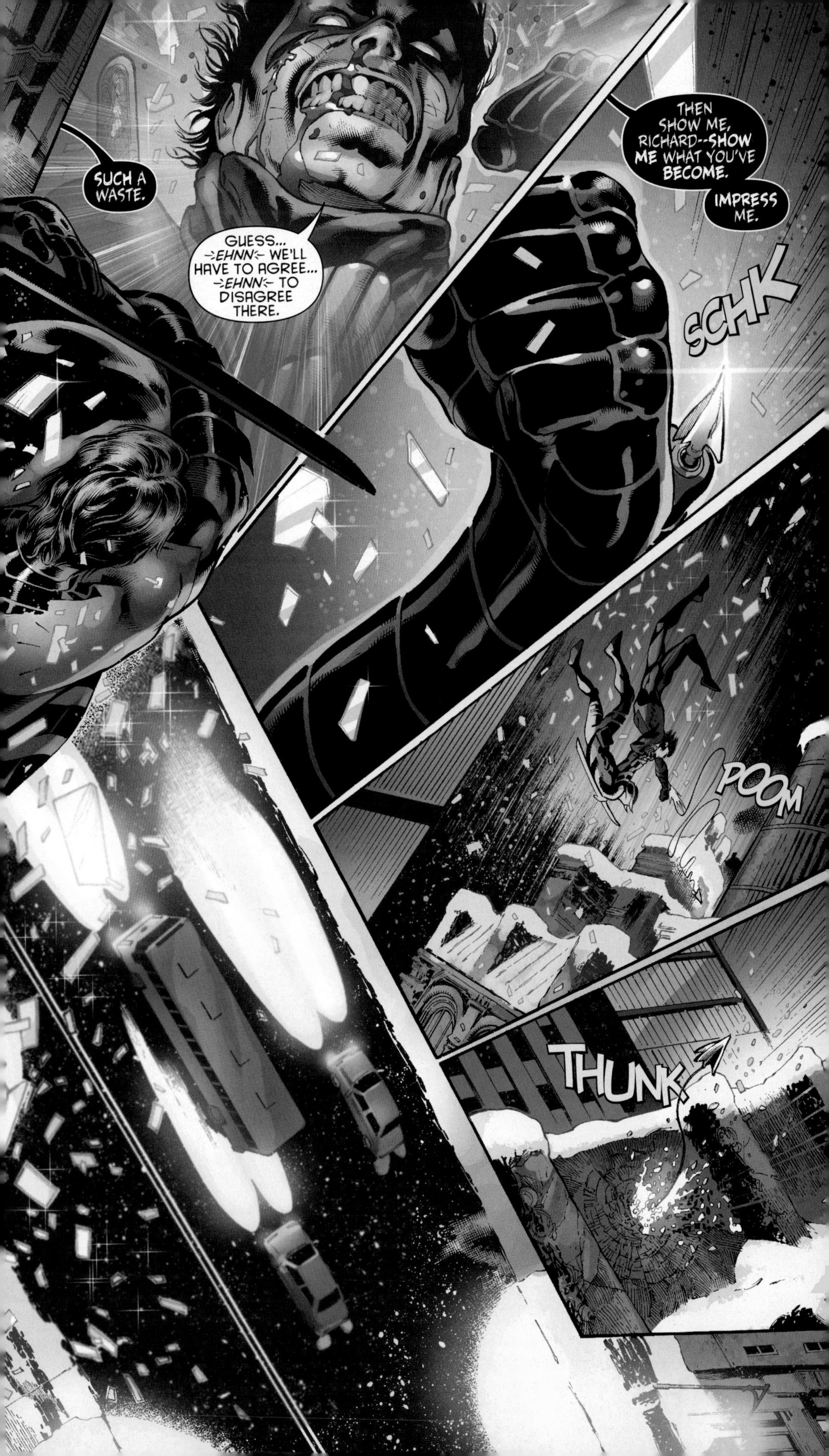
SUCH A WASTE.
GUESS... ~EHNN~ WE'LL HAVE TO AGREE... ~EHNN~ TO DISAGREE THERE.
THEN SHOW ME, RICHARD--SHOW ME WHAT YOU'VE BECOME.
IMPRESS ME.
SCHK
POOM
THUNK

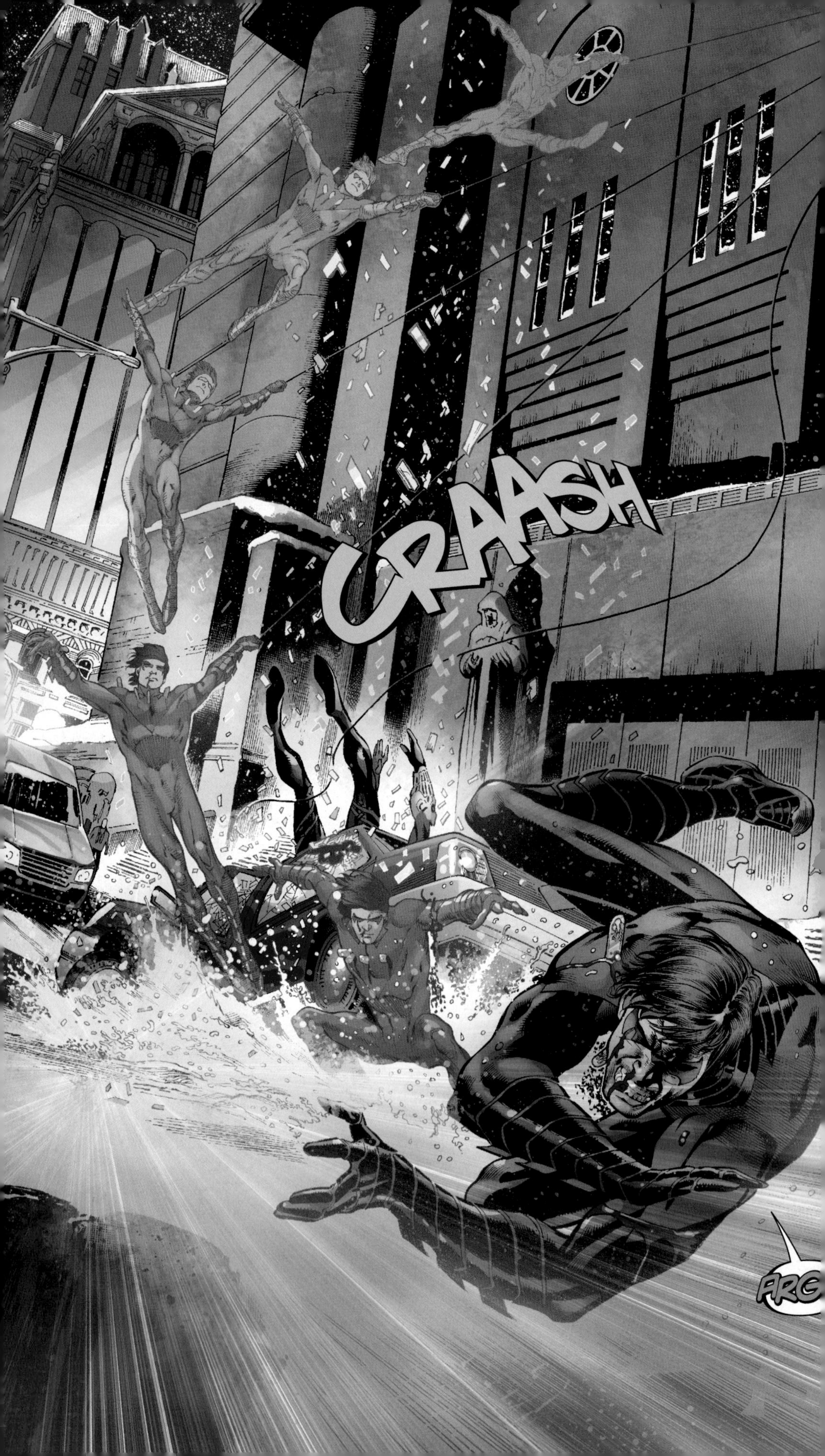
CRAASH
ARG

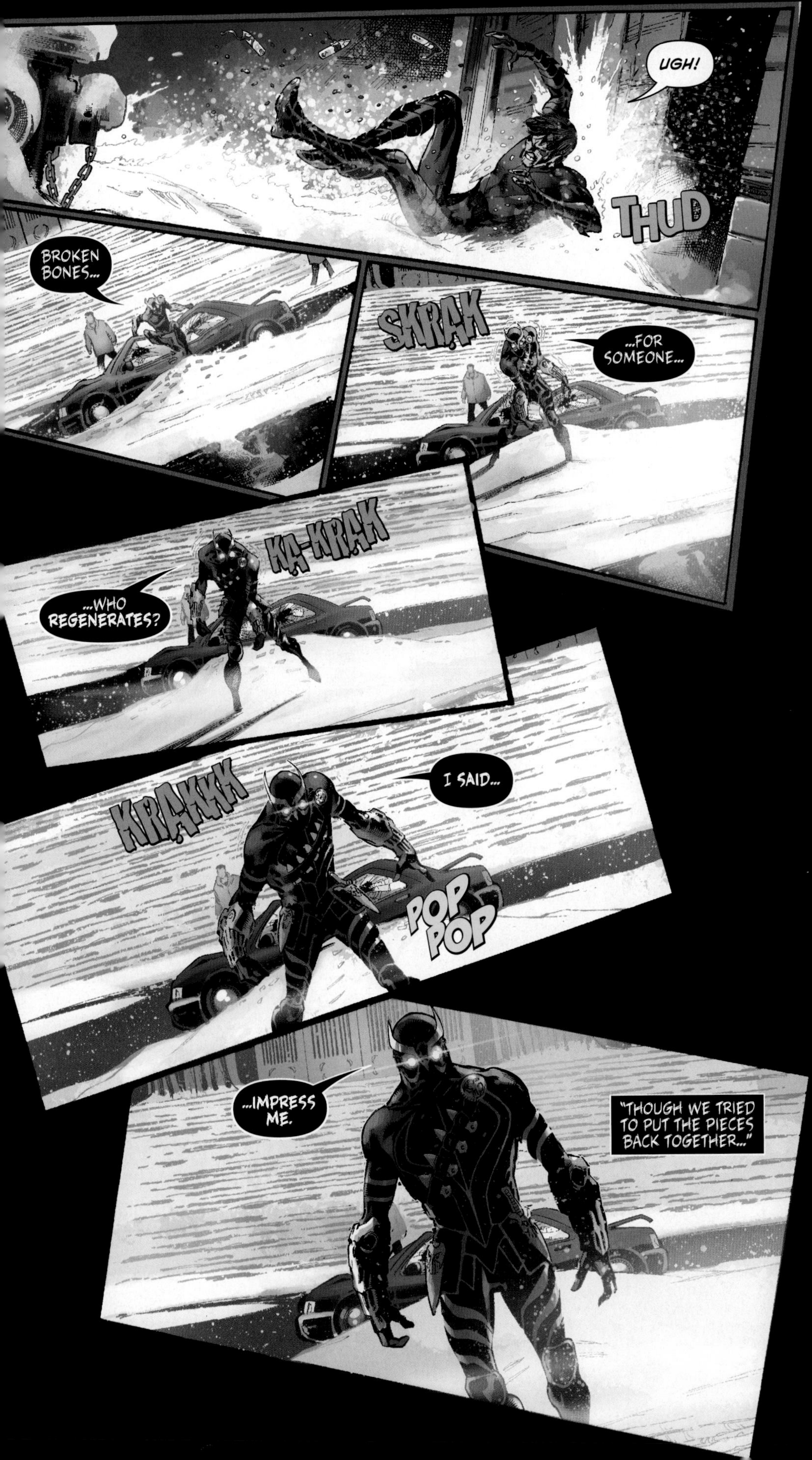
UGH!
THUD
BROKEN BONES...
SKRAK
...FOR SOMEONE...
KA-KRAK
...WHO REGENERATES?
KRAKKK
I SAID...
POP POP
...IMPRESS ME.
"THOUGH WE TRIED TO PUT THE PIECES BACK TOGETHER..."

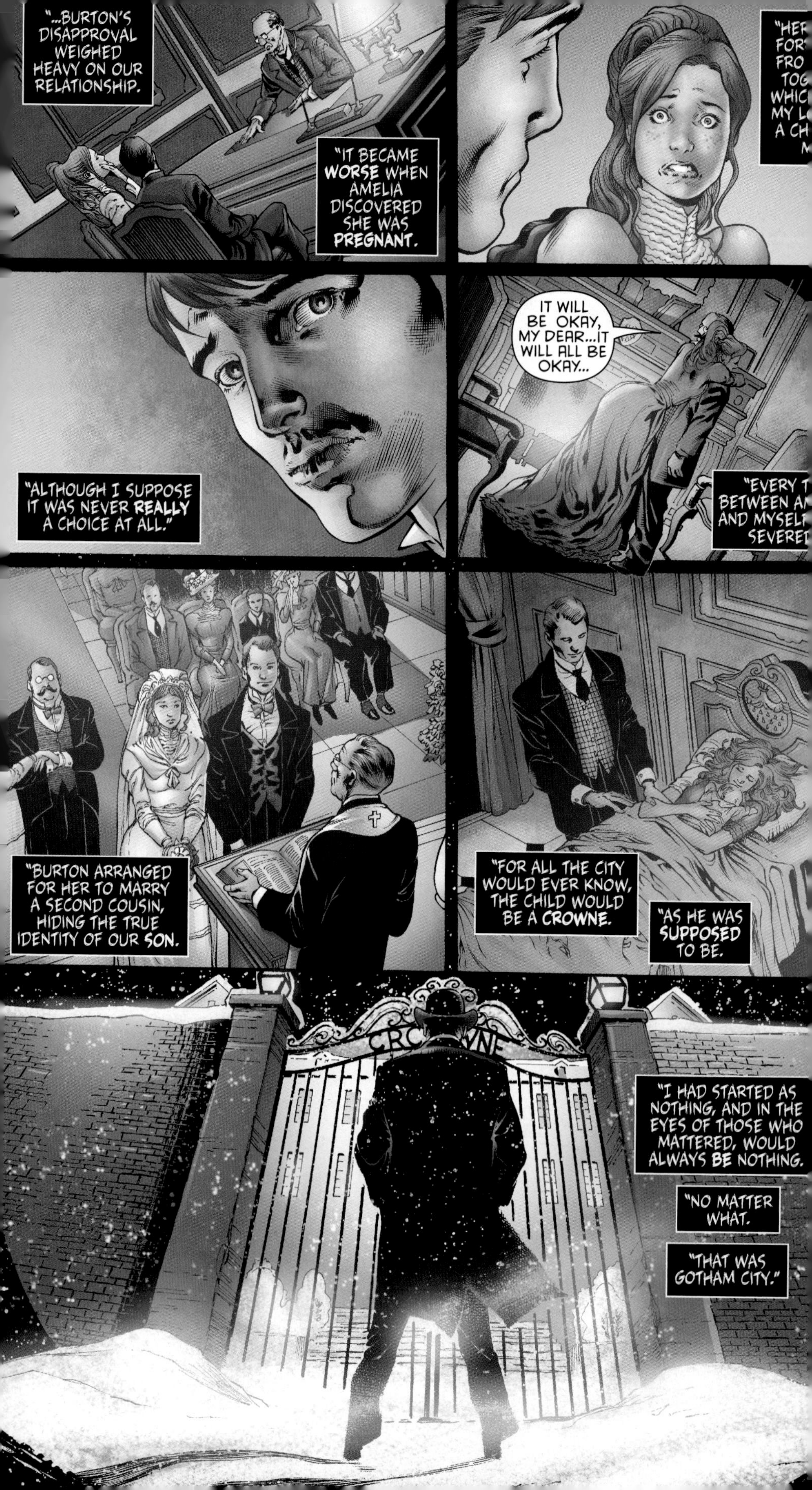
"...BURTON'S DISAPPROVAL WEIGHED HEAVY ON OUR RELATIONSHIP.
"IT BECAME WORSE WHEN AMELIA DISCOVERED SHE WAS PREGNANT.
"HER FOR FRO TOG WHIC MY L A CH M
"ALTHOUGH I SUPPOSE IT WAS NEVER REALLY A CHOICE AT ALL."
IT WILL BE OKAY, MY DEAR...IT WILL ALL BE OKAY...
"EVERY T BETWEEN A AND MYSEL SEVERE
"BURTON ARRANGED FOR HER TO MARRY A SECOND COUSIN, HIDING THE TRUE IDENTITY OF OUR SON.
"FOR ALL THE CITY WOULD EVER KNOW, THE CHILD WOULD BE A CROWNE.
"AS HE WAS SUPPOSED TO BE.
"I HAD STARTED AS NOTHING, AND IN THE EYES OF THOSE WHO MATTERED, WOULD ALWAYS BE NOTHING.
"NO MATTER WHAT.
"THAT WAS GOTHAM CITY."

THERE IS A REASON THE COURT WOKE ME FIRST, YOU KNOW.

EASON TRUST ME.

EST, --THE TALON EM

AND LAST I CHECKED, BATMAN *BEAT* YOU AND PUT YOU ON *ICE.* SO WHAT'S THAT SAY ABOUT--

ARGH!

YES--I RATHER JOYED MY TIME HIS LITTLE "CAVE." TELL ME--

--DID IT HURT WHEN HE HIT YOU? WHEN HE REJECTED YOU?

YOU COULD SEE US...?

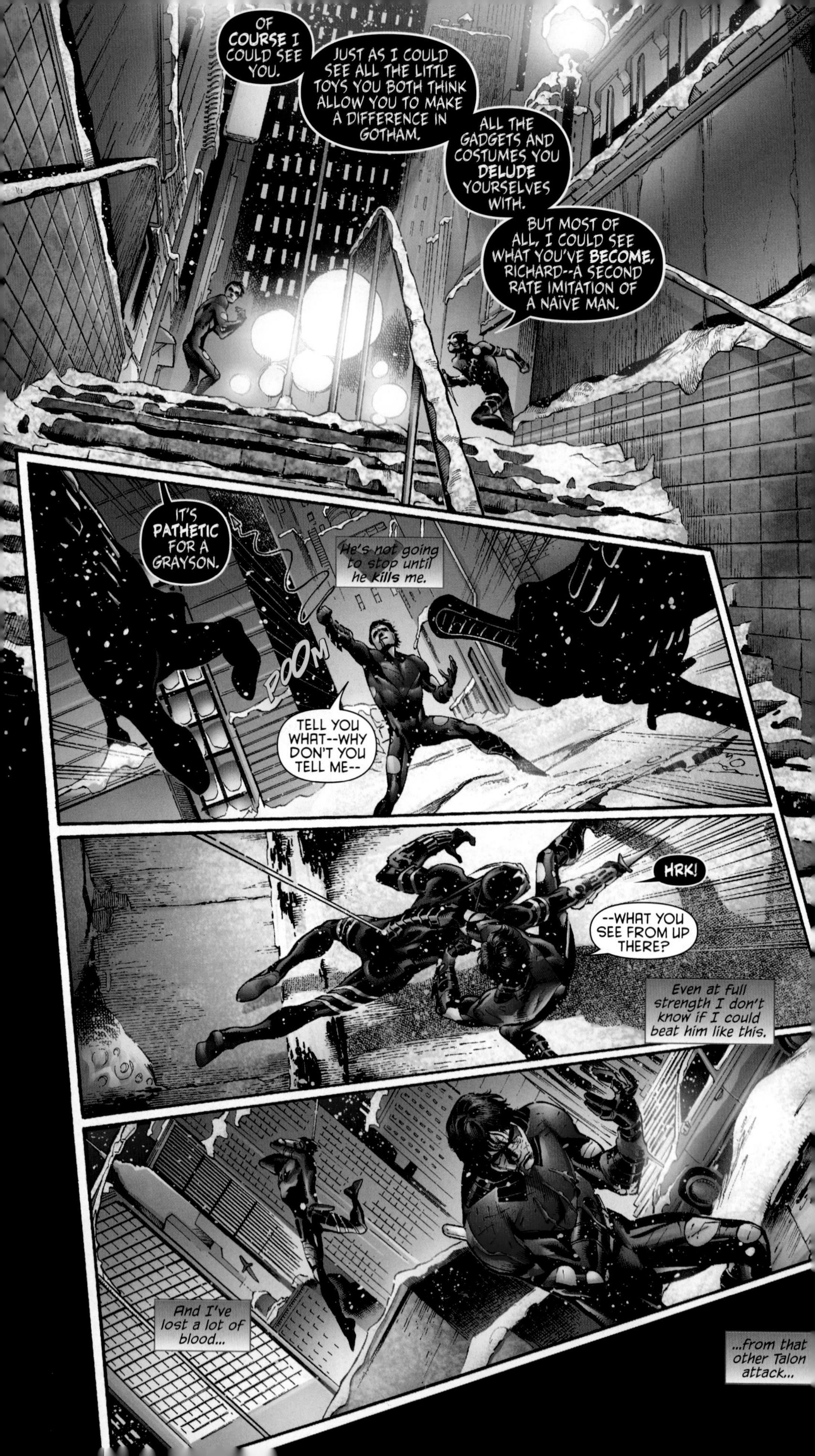

OF COURSE I COULD SEE YOU.
JUST AS I COULD SEE ALL THE LITTLE TOYS YOU BOTH THINK ALLOW YOU TO MAKE A DIFFERENCE IN GOTHAM.
ALL THE GADGETS AND COSTUMES YOU DELUDE YOURSELVES WITH.
BUT MOST OF ALL, I COULD SEE WHAT YOU'VE BECOME, RICHARD--A SECOND RATE IMITATION OF A NAÏVE MAN.
IT'S PATHETIC FOR A GRAYSON.
He's not going to stop until he kills me.
POOM
TELL YOU WHAT--WHY DON'T YOU TELL ME--
HRK!
--WHAT YOU SEE FROM UP THERE?
Even at full strength I don't know if I could beat him like this.
And I've lost a lot of blood...
...from that other Talon attack...

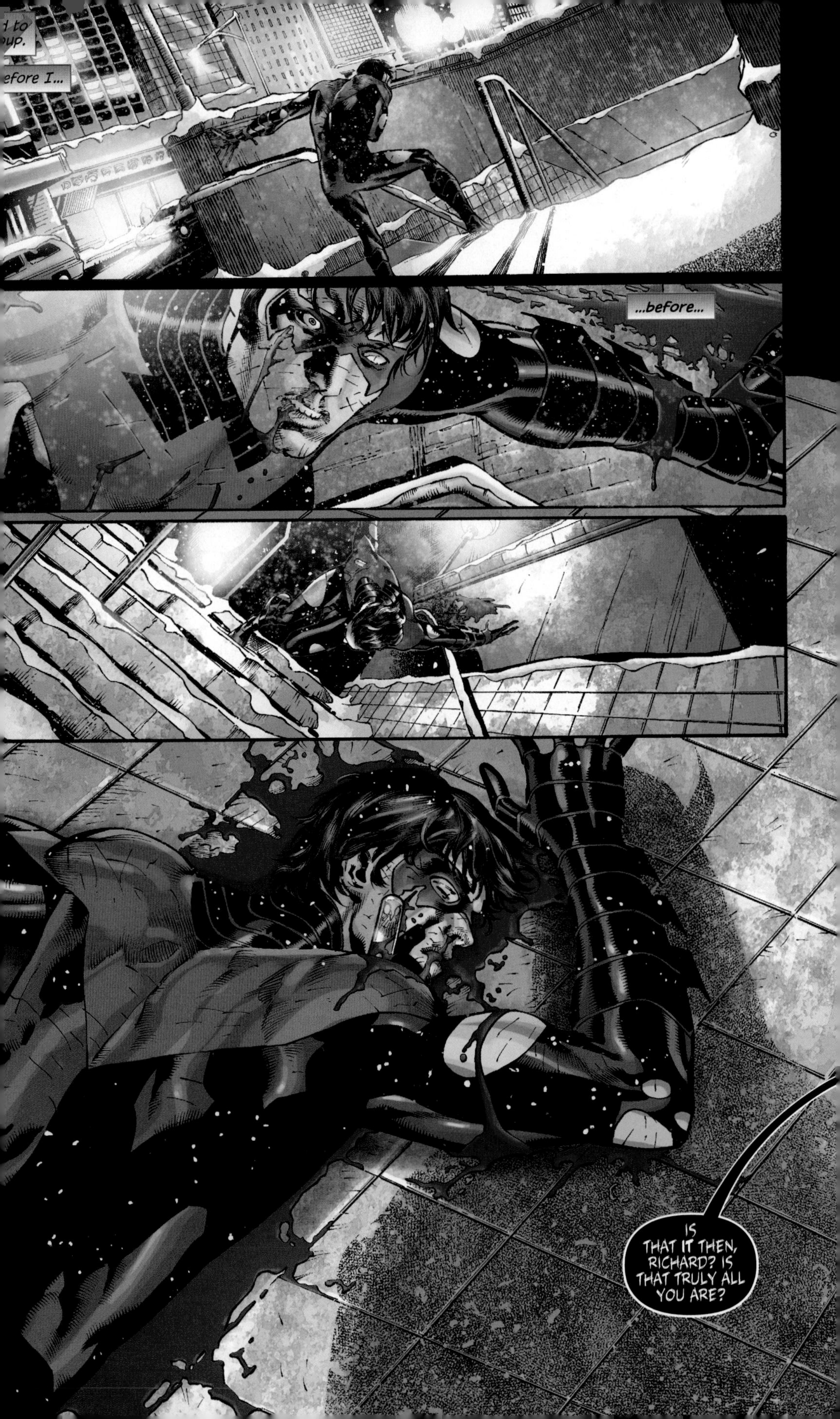
d to
oup.
efore I...
...before...
IS THAT IT THEN, RICHARD? IS THAT TRULY ALL YOU ARE?

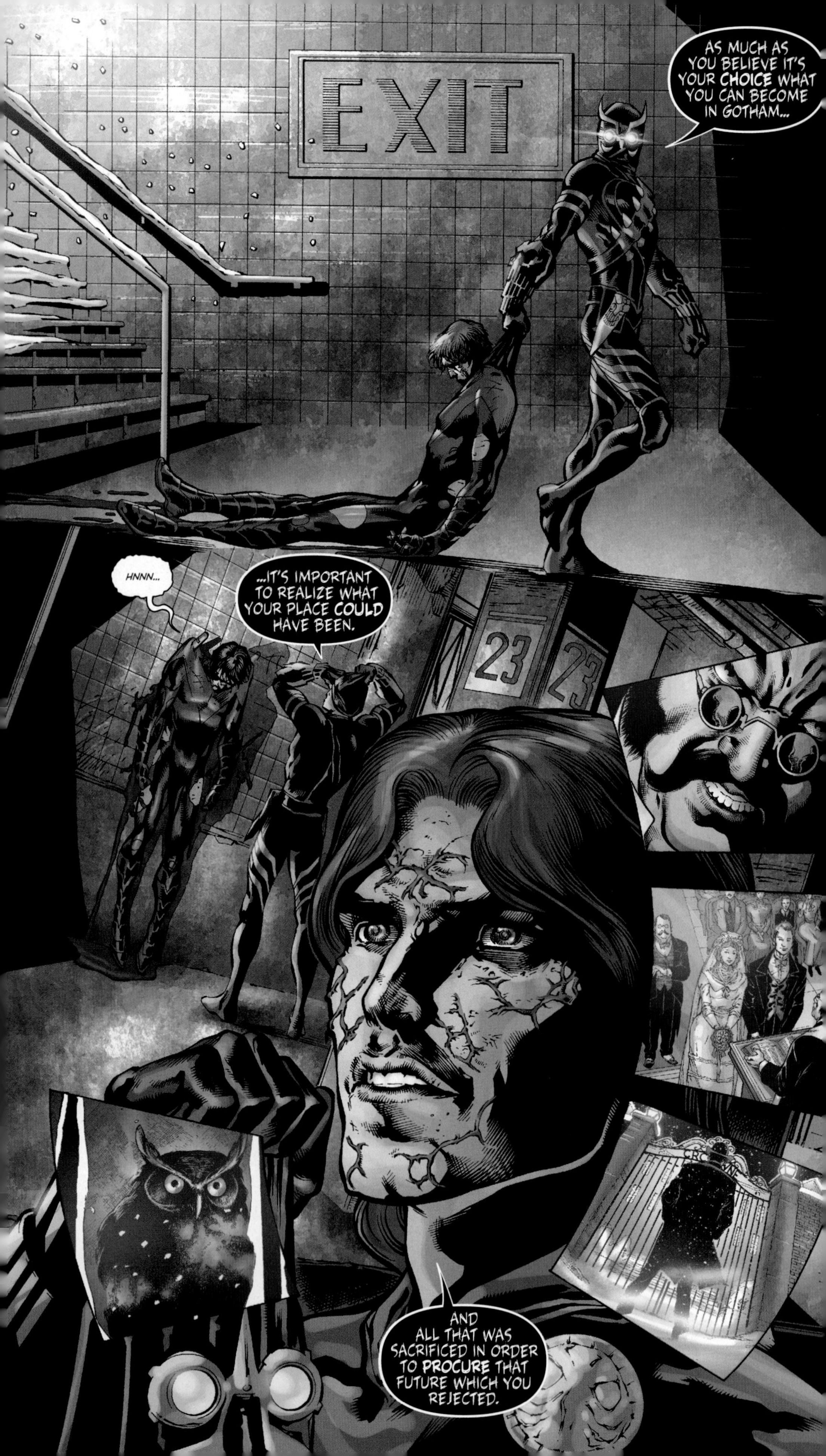
EXIT
AS MUCH AS YOU BELIEVE IT'S YOUR **CHOICE** WHAT YOU CAN BECOME IN GOTHAM...
HNNN...
...IT'S IMPORTANT TO REALIZE WHAT YOUR PLACE **COULD** HAVE BEEN.
23
23
AND ALL THAT WAS SACRIFICED IN ORDER TO **PROCURE** THAT FUTURE WHICH YOU REJECTED.

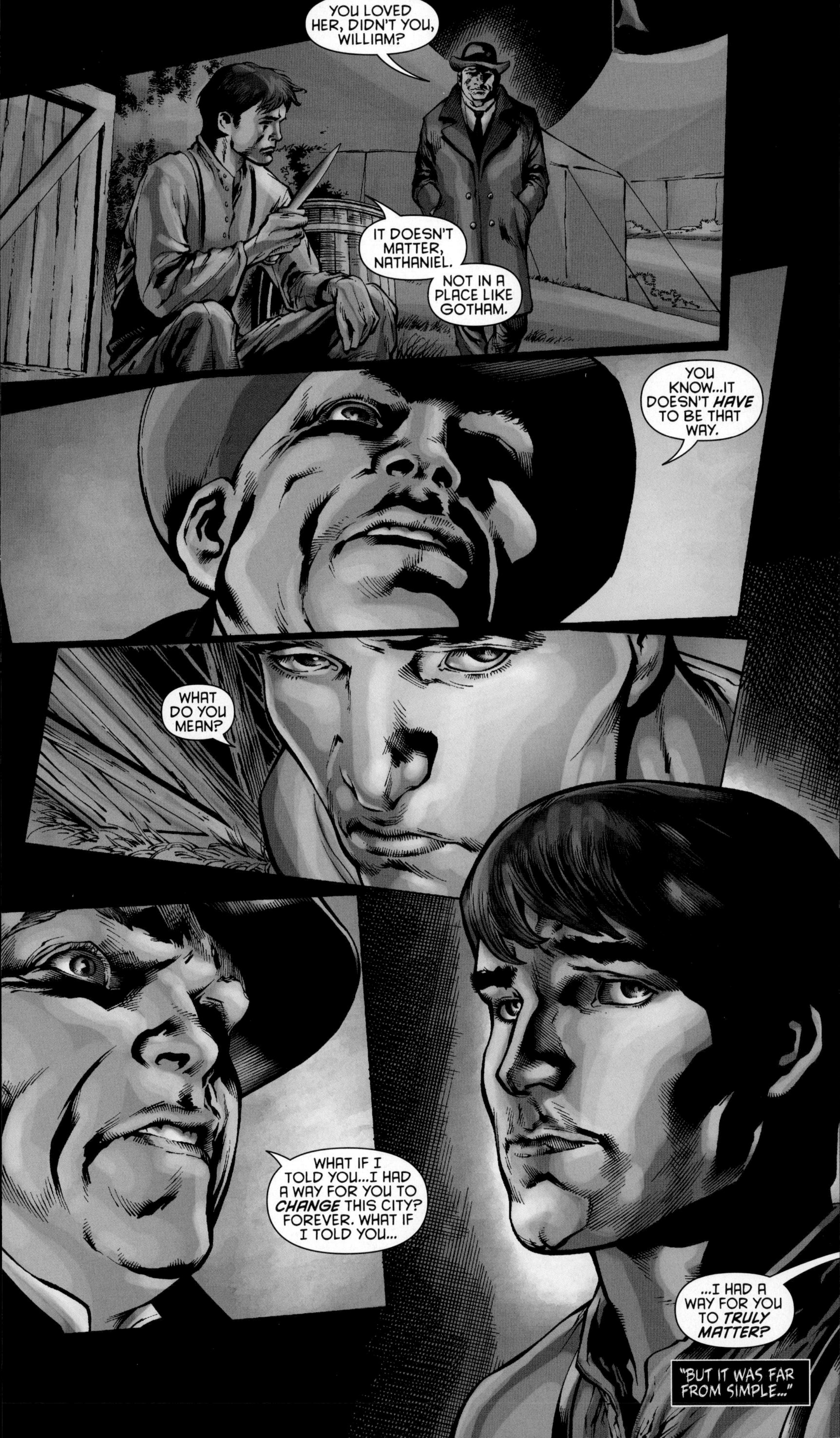
YOU LOVED HER, DIDN'T YOU, WILLIAM?
IT DOESN'T MATTER, NATHANIEL.
NOT IN A PLACE LIKE GOTHAM.
YOU KNOW...IT DOESN'T *HAVE* TO BE THAT WAY.
WHAT DO YOU MEAN?
WHAT IF I TOLD YOU...I HAD A WAY FOR YOU TO *CHANGE* THIS CITY? FOREVER. WHAT IF I TOLD YOU...
...I HAD A WAY FOR YOU TO *TRULY MATTER?*
"BUT IT WAS FAR FROM SIMPLE..."

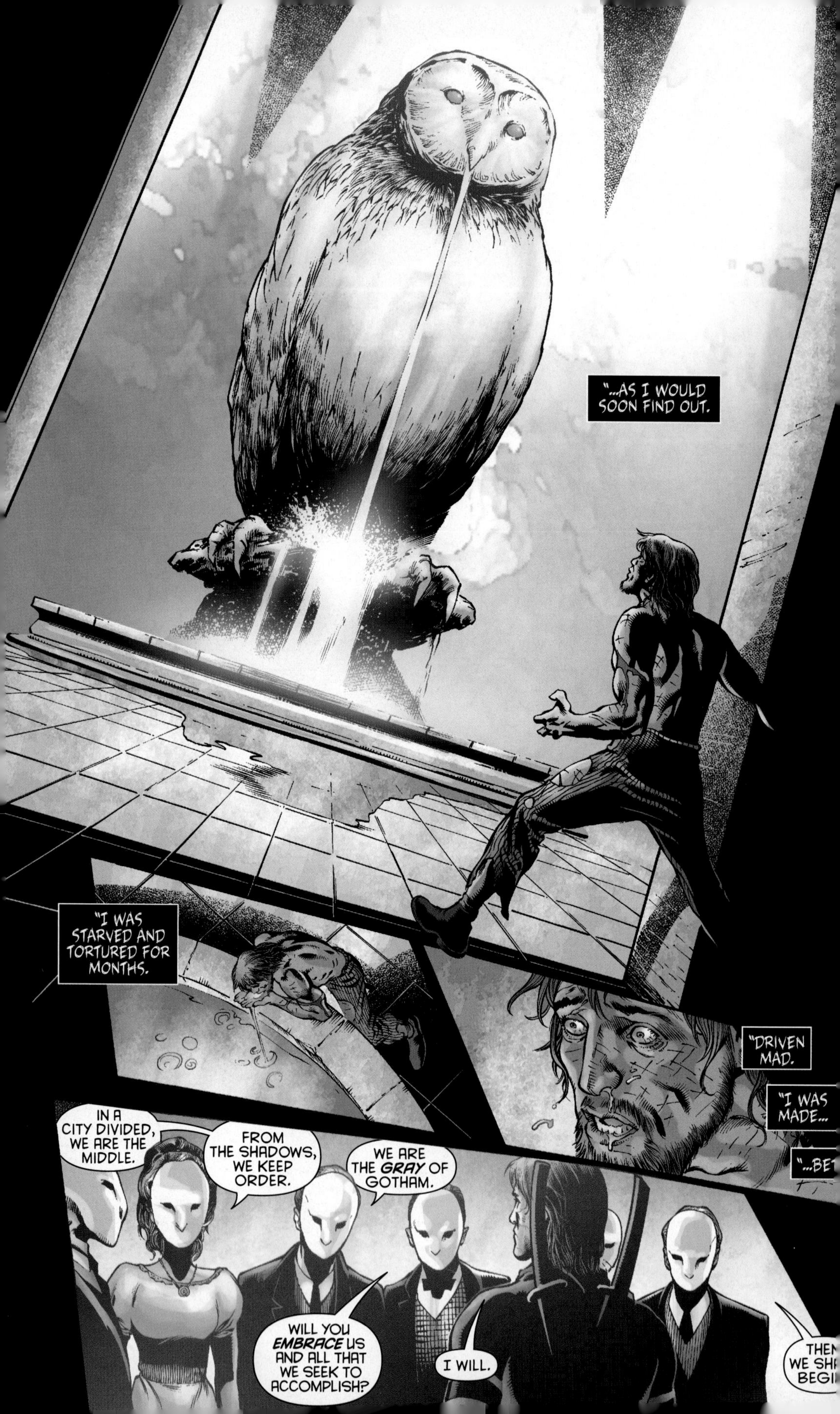
"...AS I WOULD SOON FIND OUT.
"I WAS STARVED AND TORTURED FOR MONTHS.
"DRIVEN MAD.
"I WAS MADE...
"...BE
IN A CITY DIVIDED, WE ARE THE MIDDLE.
FROM THE SHADOWS, WE KEEP ORDER.
WE ARE THE *GRAY* OF GOTHAM.
WILL YOU *EMBRACE* US AND ALL THAT WE SEEK TO ACCOMPLISH?
I WILL.
THEN WE SH BEGI

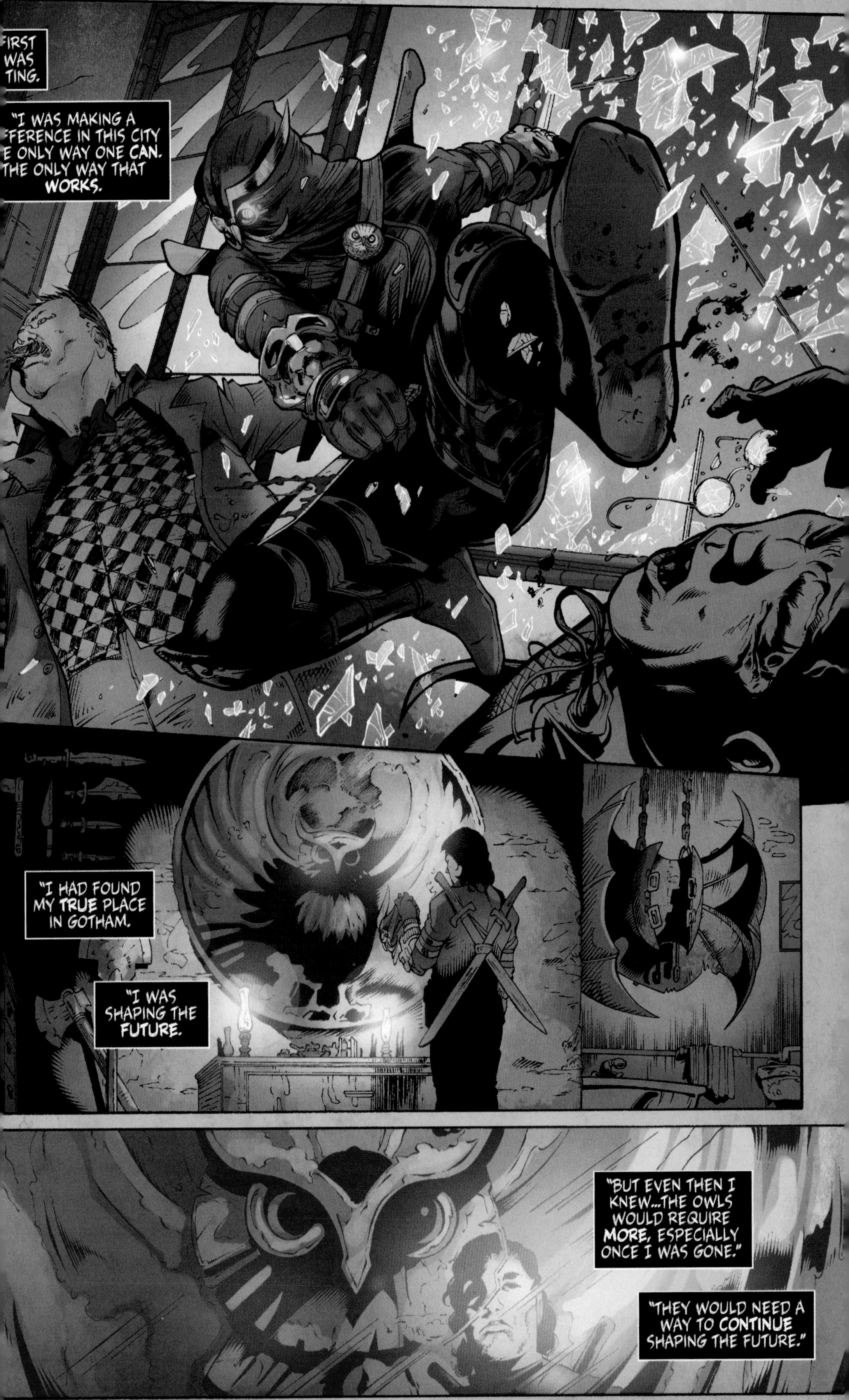
IRST
WAS
TING.
"I WAS MAKING A
FERENCE IN THIS CITY
E ONLY WAY ONE CAN.
THE ONLY WAY THAT
WORKS.
"I HAD FOUND
MY TRUE PLACE
IN GOTHAM.
"I WAS
SHAPING THE
FUTURE.
"BUT EVEN THEN I
KNEW...THE OWLS
WOULD REQUIRE
MORE, ESPECIALLY
ONCE I WAS GONE."
"THEY WOULD NEED A
WAY TO CONTINUE
SHAPING THE FUTURE."

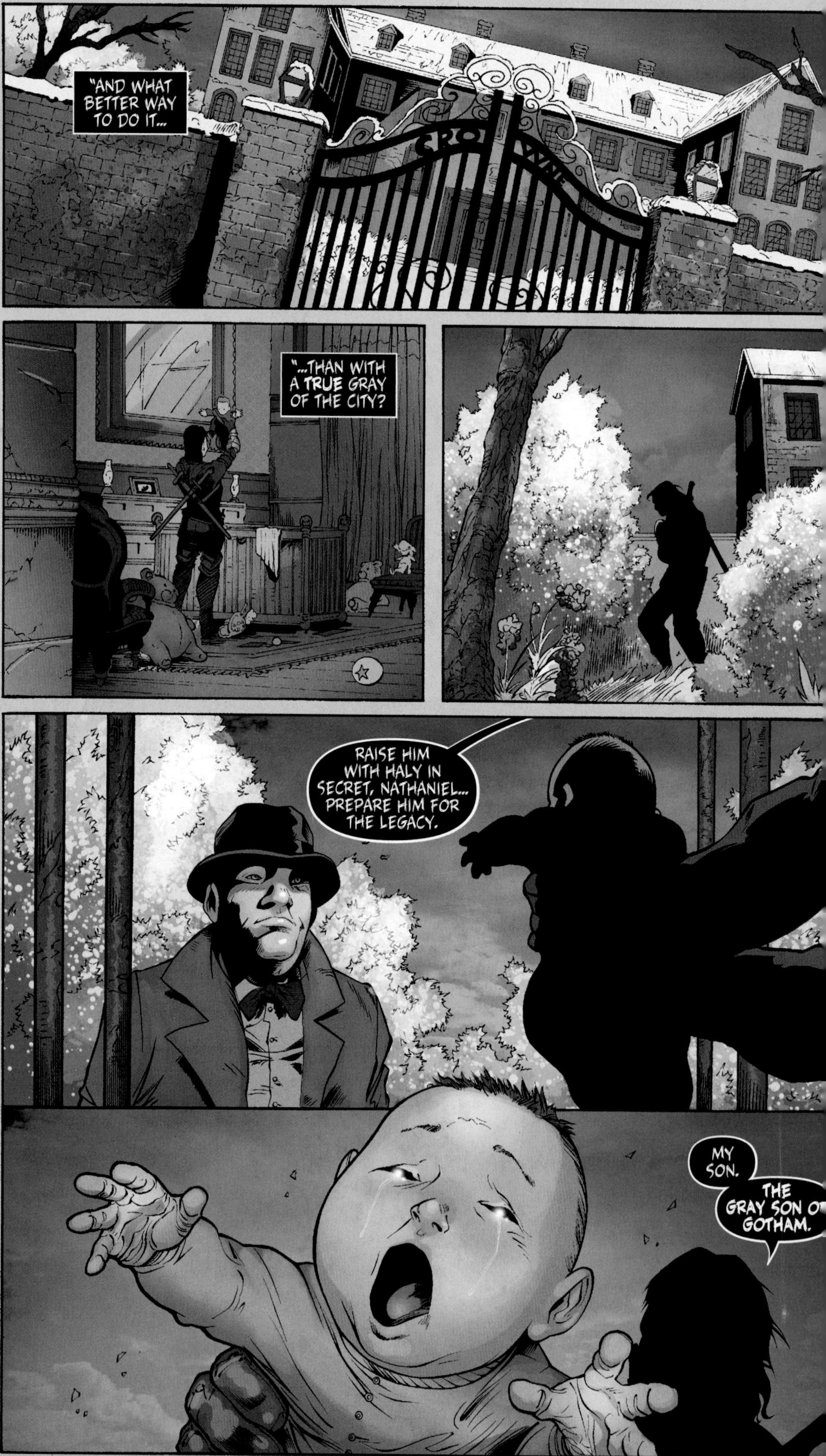
"AND WHAT BETTER WAY TO DO IT...
"...THAN WITH A TRUE GRAY OF THE CITY?
RAISE HIM WITH HALY IN SECRET, NATHANIEL... PREPARE HIM FOR THE LEGACY.
MY SON.
THE GRAY SON OF GOTHAM.

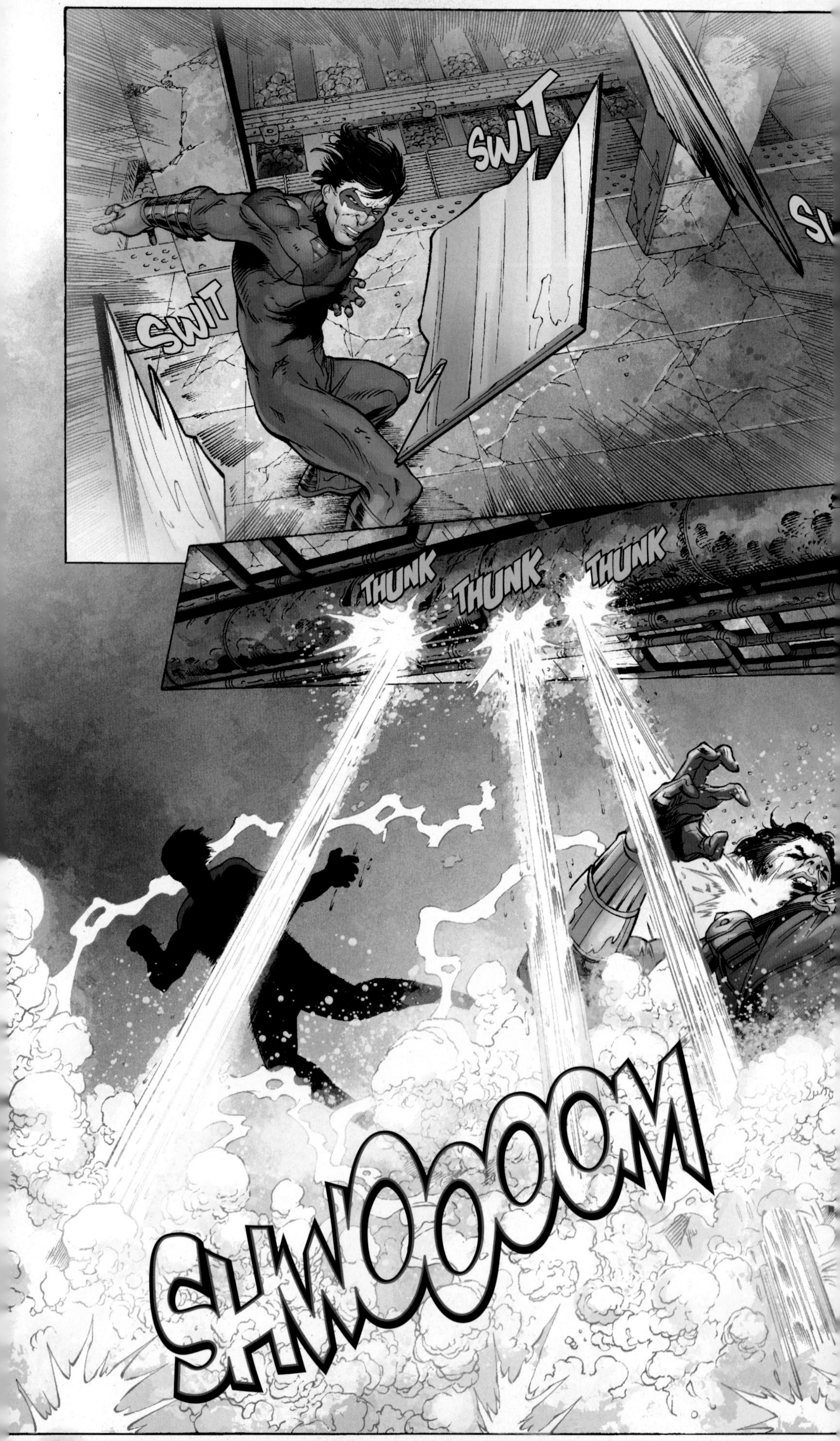
SWIT
SWIT
THUNK
THUNK
THUNK
SHWOOOOM

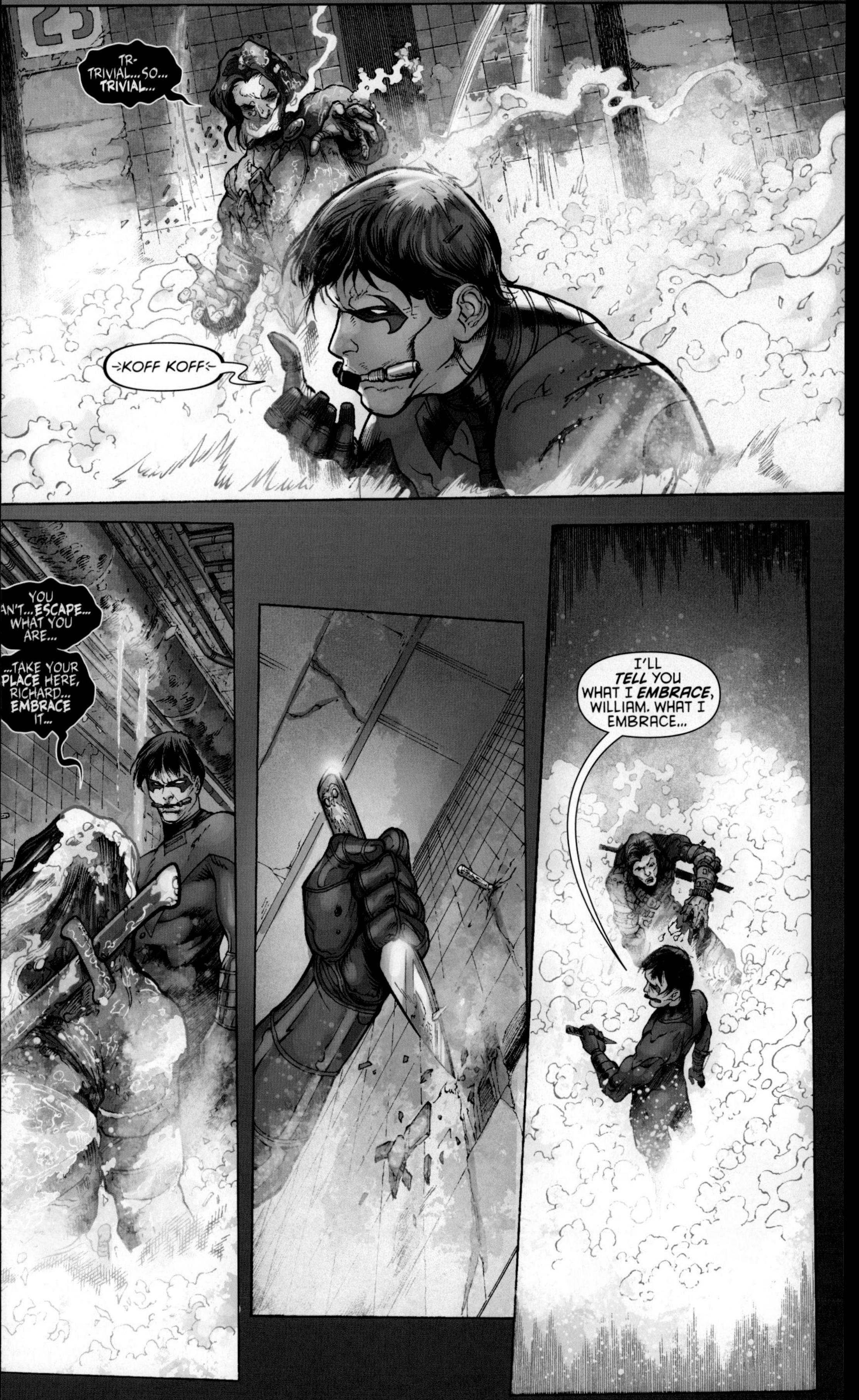
TR-TRIVIAL...SO... TRIVIAL...
KOFF KOFF
YOU CAN'T...ESCAPE... WHAT YOU ARE...
...TAKE YOUR PLACE HERE, RICHARD... EMBRACE IT...
I'LL TELL YOU WHAT I EMBRACE, WILLIAM. WHAT I EMBRACE...

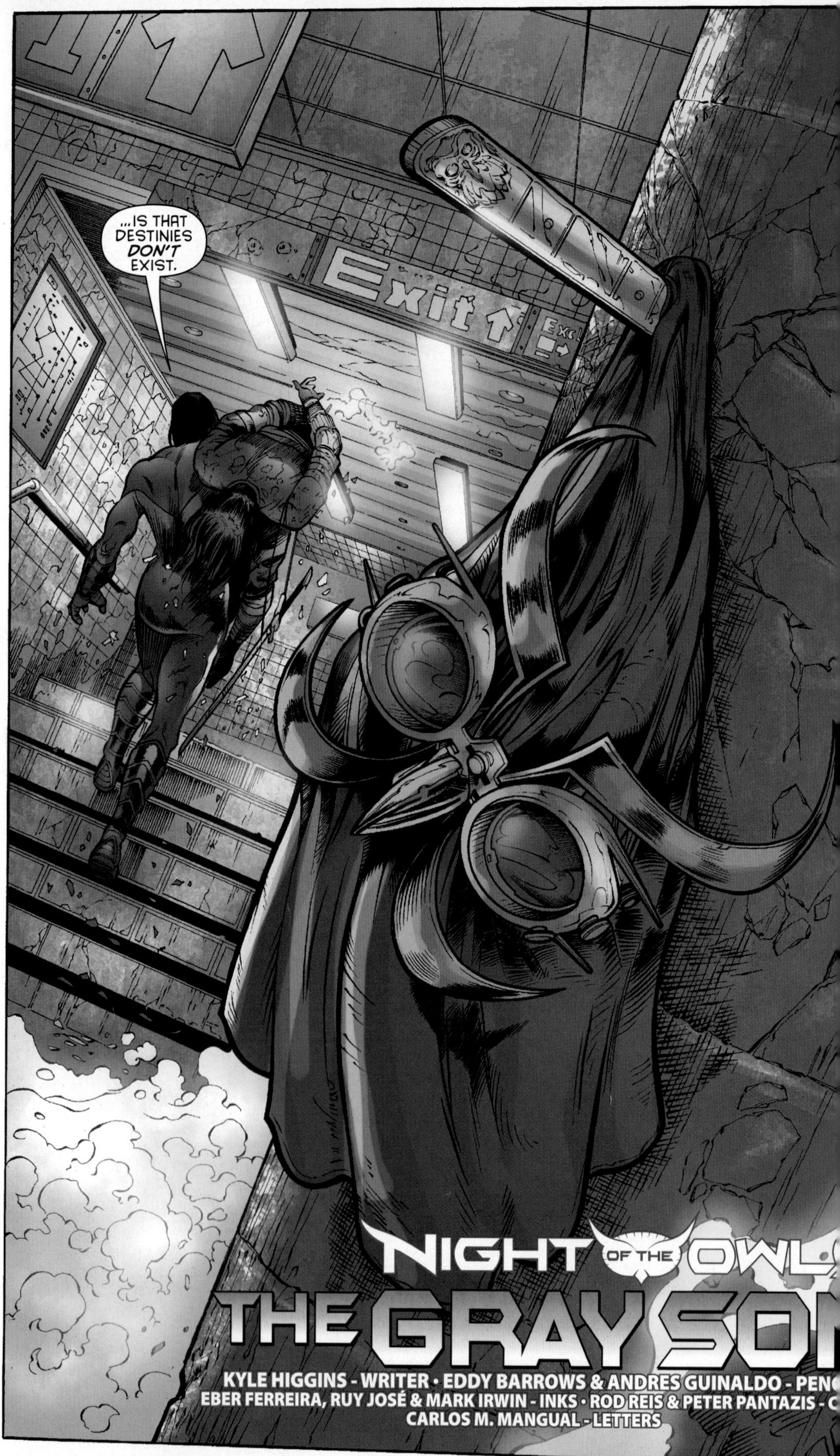
...IS THAT DESTINIES DON'T EXIST.
Exit
NIGHT OF THE OWL
THE GRAY SO
KYLE HIGGINS - WRITER · EDDY BARROWS & ANDRES GUINALDO - PEN
EBER FERREIRA, RUY JOSÉ & MARK IRWIN - INKS · ROD REIS & PETER PANTAZIS -
CARLOS M. MANGUAL - LETTERS

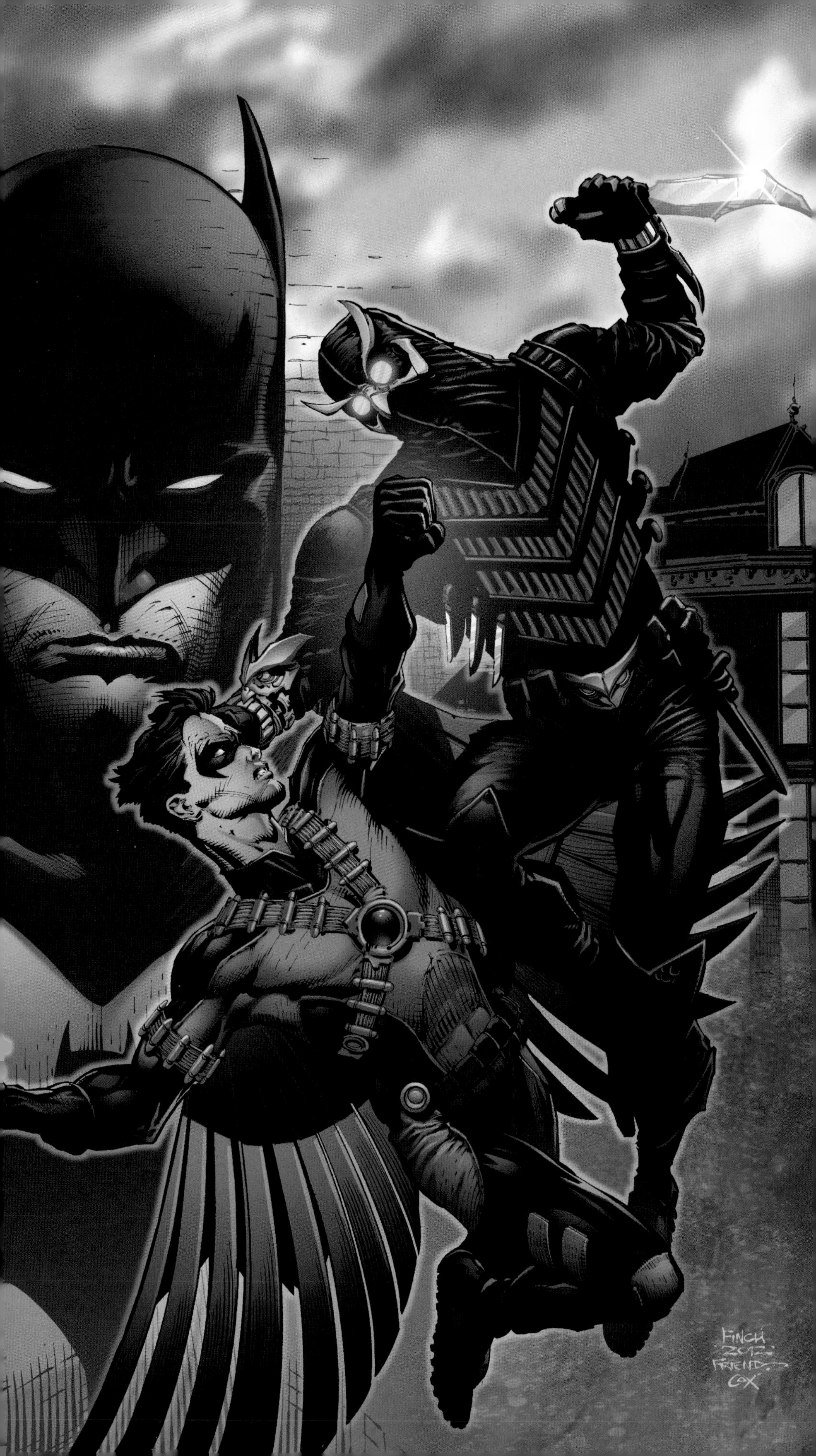
FINCH
2012
FRIEND
COX

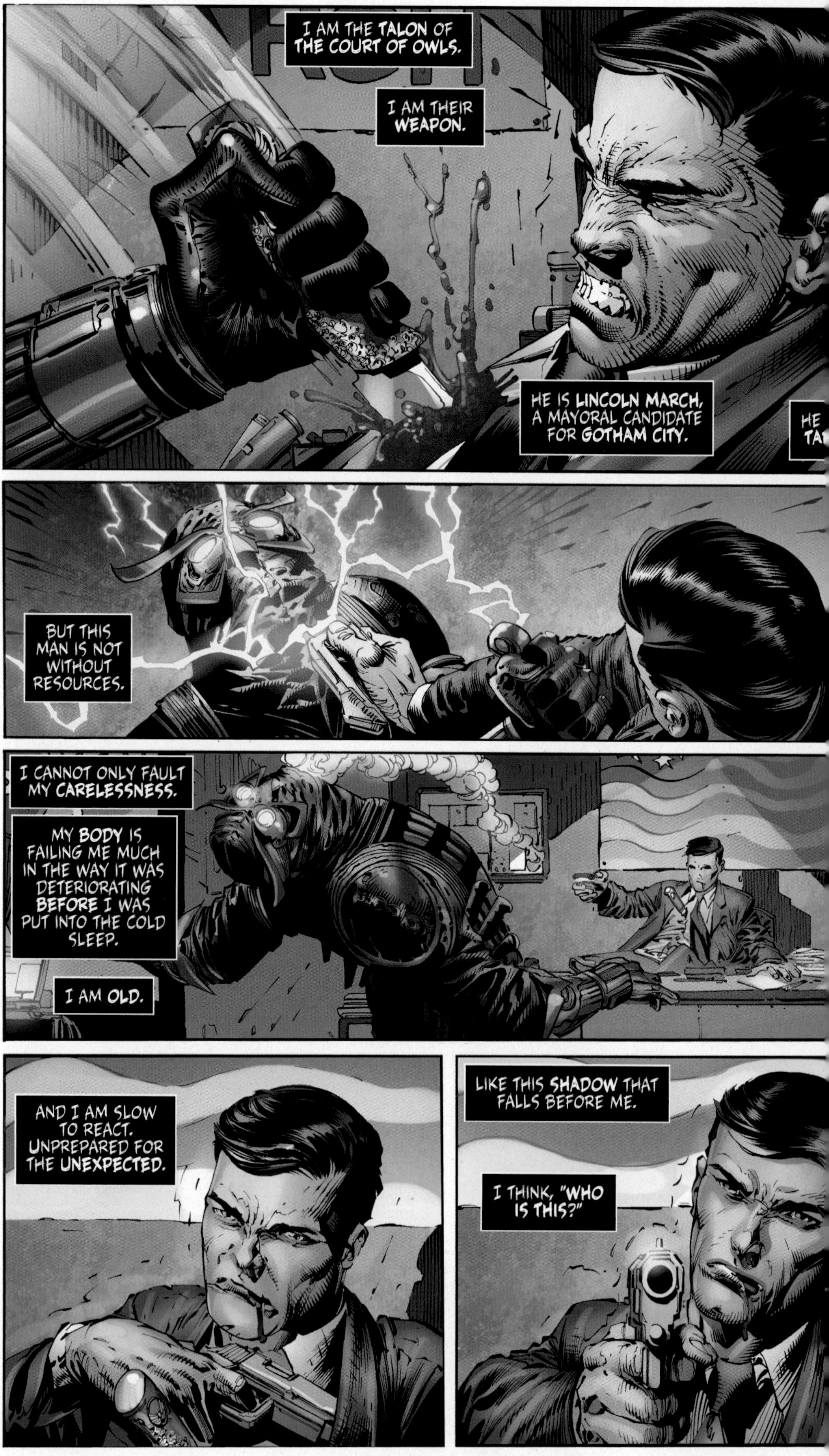

I AM THE TALON OF THE COURT OF OWLS.
I AM THEIR WEAPON.
HE IS LINCOLN MARCH, A MAYORAL CANDIDATE FOR GOTHAM CITY.
BUT THIS MAN IS NOT WITHOUT RESOURCES.
I CANNOT ONLY FAULT MY CARELESSNESS.
MY BODY IS FAILING ME MUCH IN THE WAY IT WAS DETERIORATING BEFORE I WAS PUT INTO THE COLD SLEEP.
I AM OLD.
AND I AM SLOW TO REACT. UNPREPARED FOR THE UNEXPECTED.
LIKE THIS SHADOW THAT FALLS BEFORE ME.
I THINK, "WHO IS THIS?"

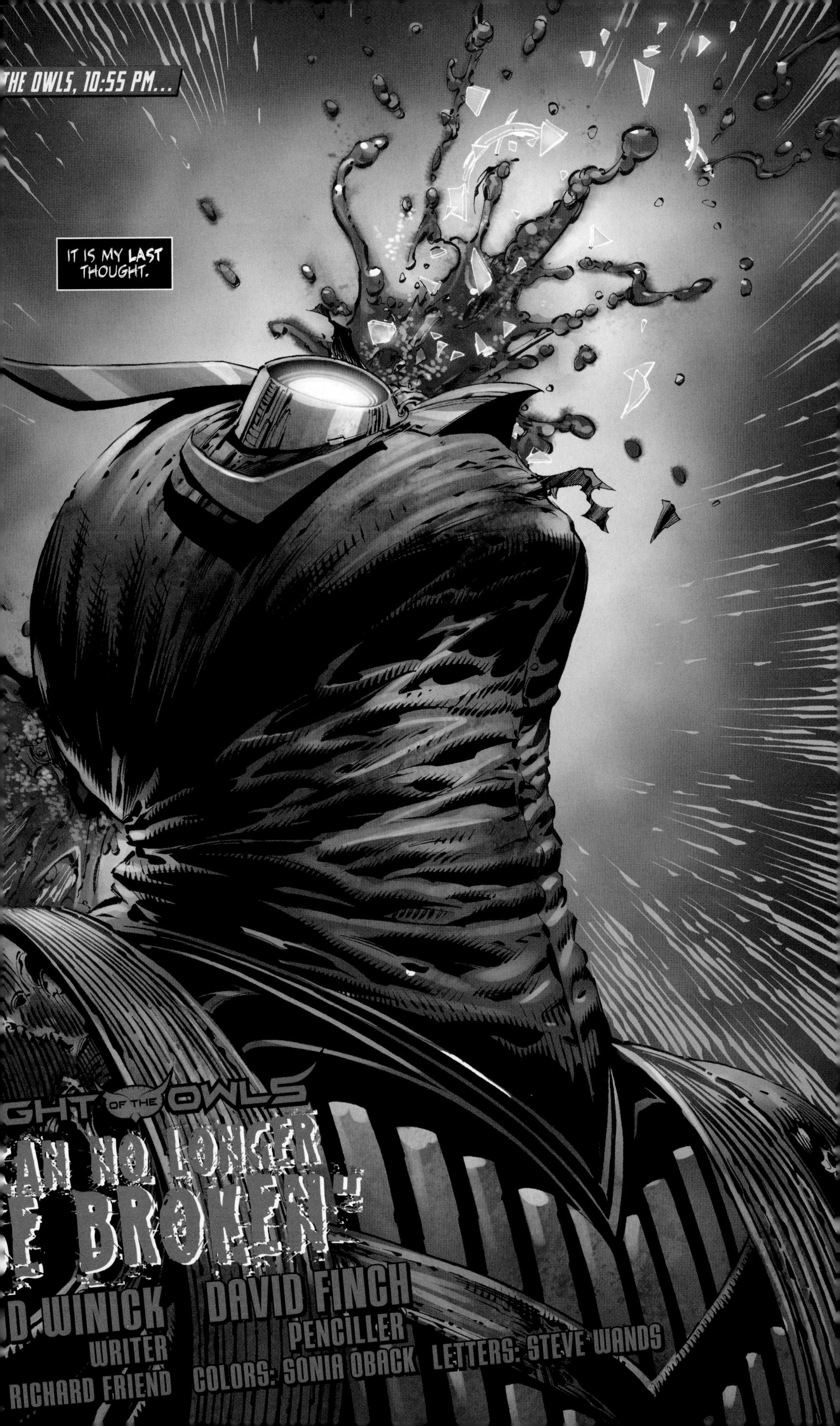

THE OWLS, 10:55 PM...
IT IS MY LAST THOUGHT.
GHT OF THE OWLS
AN NO LONGER
F BROKEN"
D WINICK WRITER
DAVID FINCH PENCILLER
RICHARD FRIEND
COLORS: SONIA OBACK
LETTERS: STEVE WANDS

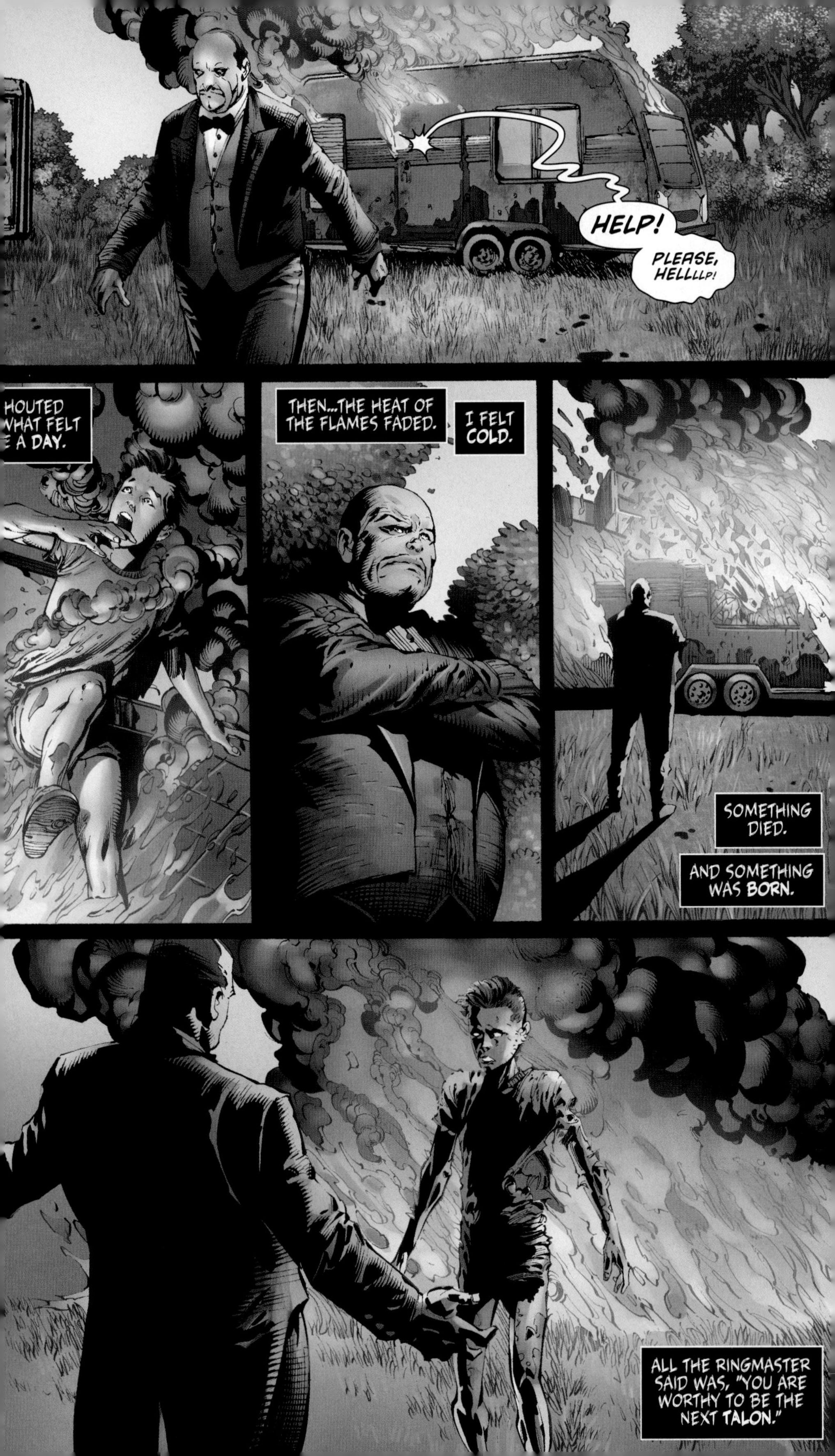
HELP!
PLEASE, HELLLLP!
HOUTED
WHAT FELT
E A DAY.
THEN...THE HEAT OF THE FLAMES FADED.
I FELT COLD.
SOMETHING DIED.
AND SOMETHING WAS BORN.
ALL THE RINGMASTER SAID WAS, "YOU ARE WORTHY TO BE THE NEXT TALON."

AND **THE TALON** IS WHAT I BECAME.

I SERVED **THE COURT OF OWLS**--THEY WHO HAVE CONTROLLED THE CITY SINCE BEFORE ITS FOUNDING.

I WAS A SILENT WEAPON.

DEATH ITSELF.

I HE
THE MA
LONGER
MOS

BUT MY SKILLS BECAME DULL.

"**THREE** POL
OFFICERS? D
YOU SWEEP
PERIMETER P
TO THE ATTA

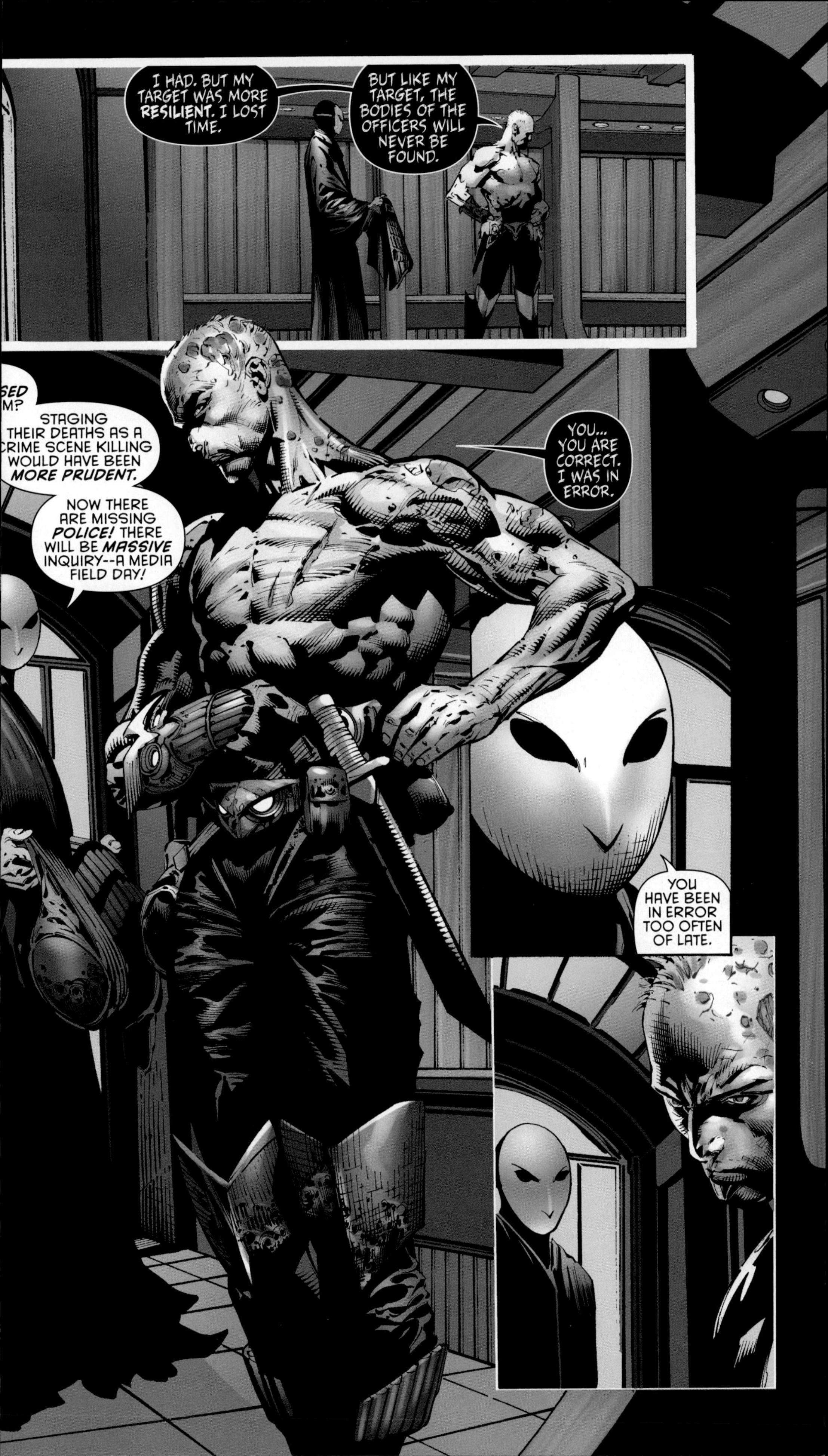
I HAD. BUT MY TARGET WAS MORE RESILIENT. I LOST TIME.
BUT LIKE MY TARGET, THE BODIES OF THE OFFICERS WILL NEVER BE FOUND.
STAGING THEIR DEATHS AS A CRIME SCENE KILLING WOULD HAVE BEEN MORE PRUDENT.
NOW THERE ARE MISSING POLICE! THERE WILL BE MASSIVE INQUIRY--A MEDIA FIELD DAY!
YOU... YOU ARE CORRECT. I WAS IN ERROR.
YOU HAVE BEEN IN ERROR TOO OFTEN OF LATE.

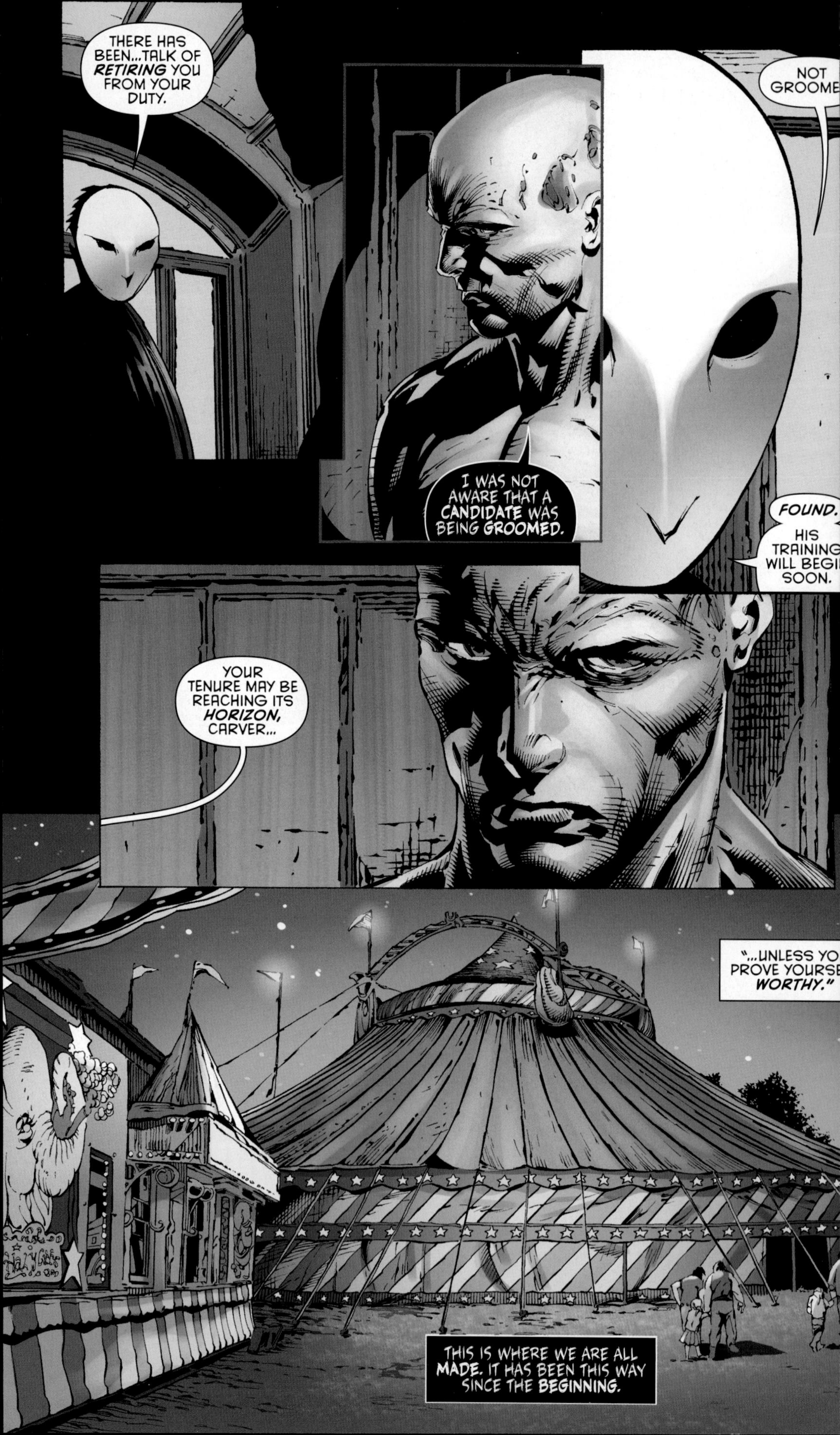
THERE HAS BEEN...TALK OF *RETIRING* YOU FROM YOUR DUTY.
I WAS NOT AWARE THAT A **CANDIDATE** WAS BEING **GROOMED**.
NOT GROOME
FOUND.
HIS TRAINING WILL BEGI SOON.
YOUR TENURE MAY BE REACHING ITS *HORIZON,* CARVER...
"...UNLESS YO PROVE YOURSE *WORTHY."*
THIS IS WHERE WE ARE ALL **MADE**. IT HAS BEEN THIS WAY SINCE THE **BEGINNING**.

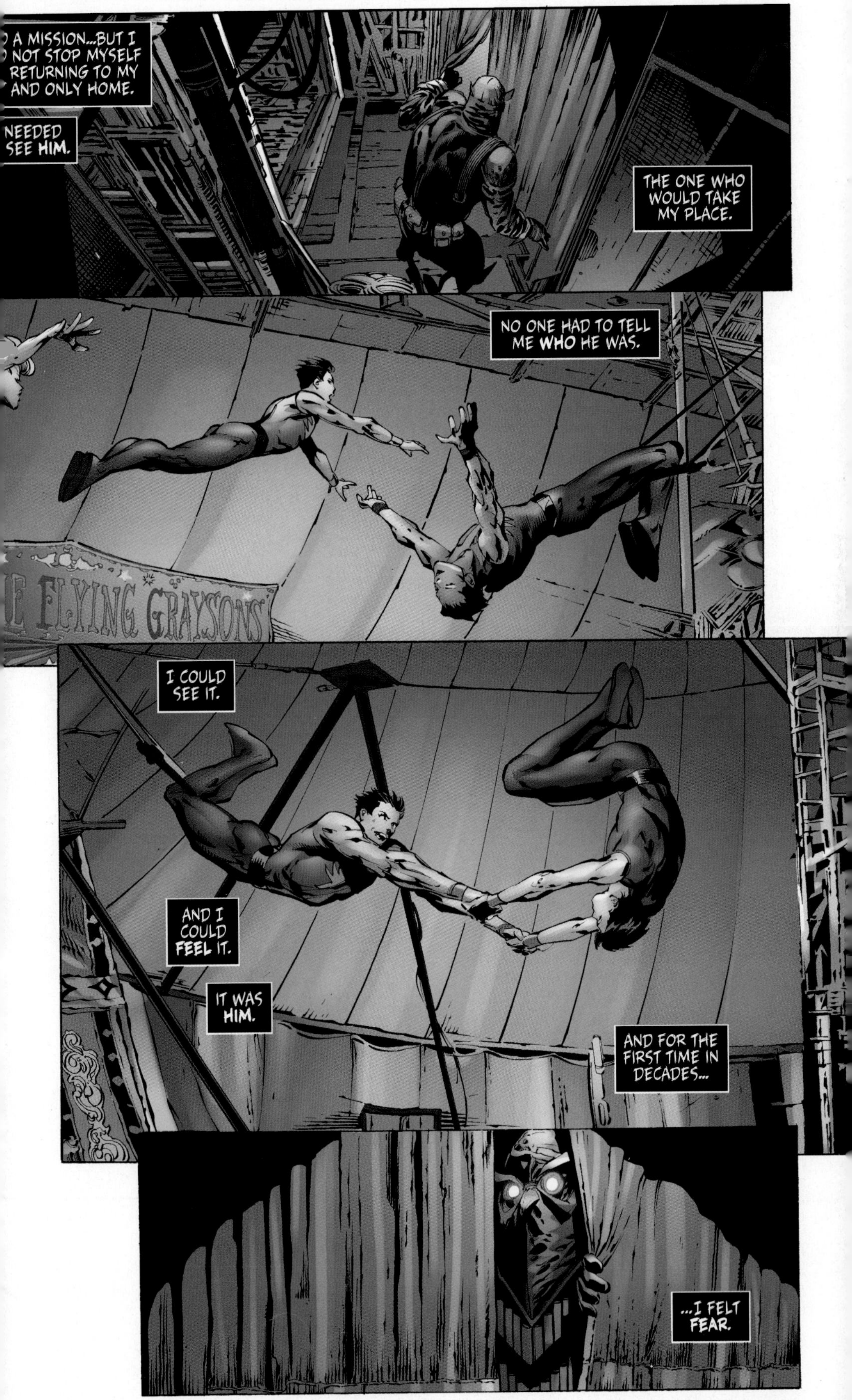
A MISSION...BUT I NOT STOP MYSELF RETURNING TO MY AND ONLY HOME.
NEEDED SEE HIM.
THE ONE WHO WOULD TAKE MY PLACE.
NO ONE HAD TO TELL ME WHO HE WAS.
FLYING GRAYSONS
I COULD SEE IT.
AND I COULD FEEL IT.
IT WAS HIM.
AND FOR THE FIRST TIME IN DECADES...
...I FELT FEAR.

BUT I WAS A **TALON**. AND I LIVED **WITHOUT FEAR**.

AND I WAS TO PERFOR[M] **WITHOUT FAILURE.**

HOWEVER, MY EXCURSION TO THE CIRCUS COST ME TIME AND FORCED ME TO CHANGE PLANS.

MY ATTACK WAS OUT ON THE STREETS.

IT WAS THERE THAT I MET SOMETHING **NEW** TO GOTHAM.

AND FOR THE SECOND TIME THAT NIGHT...

...I AF[

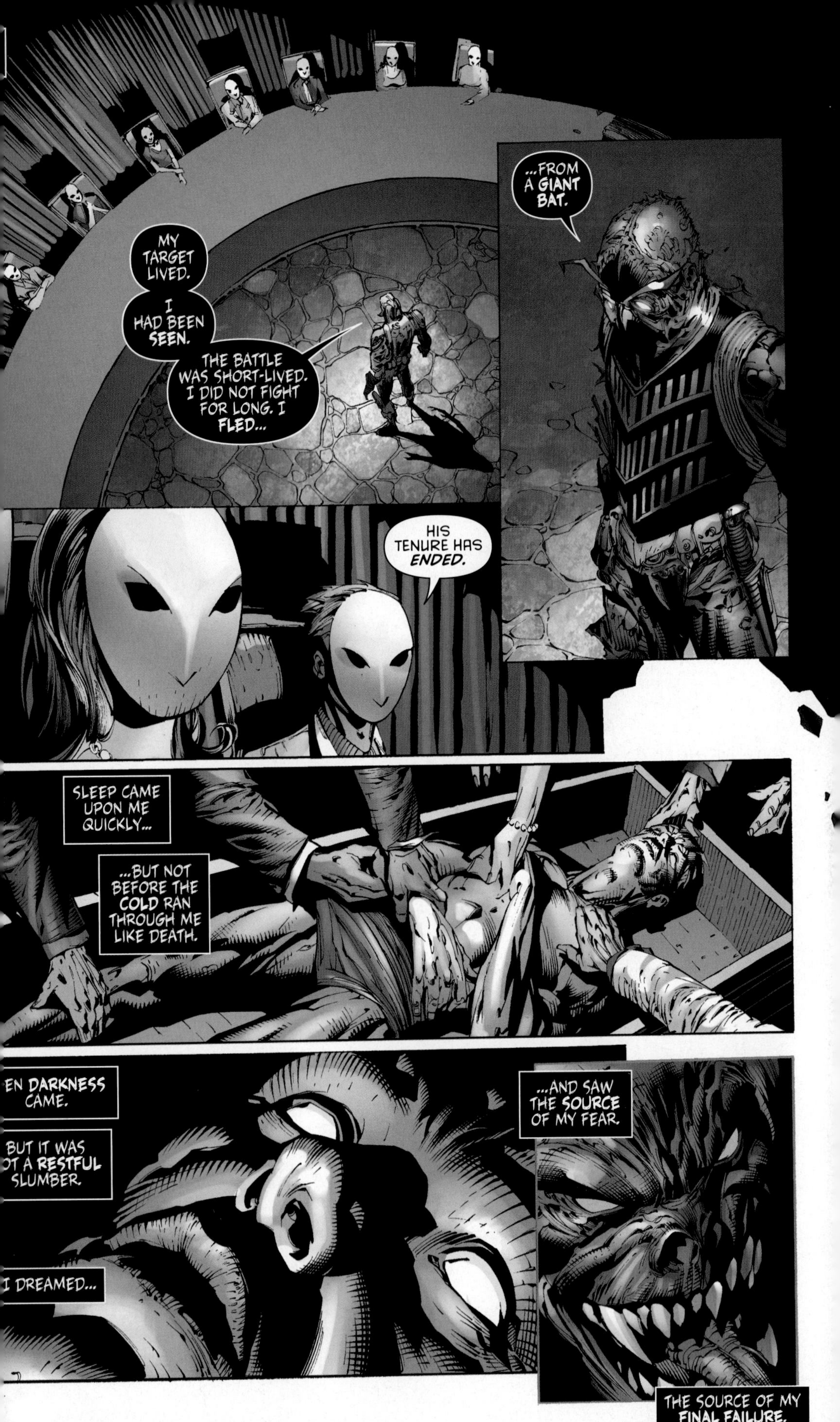
MY TARGET LIVED.
I HAD BEEN SEEN.
THE BATTLE WAS SHORT-LIVED. I DID NOT FIGHT FOR LONG. I FLED...
...FROM A GIANT BAT.
HIS TENURE HAS ENDED.
SLEEP CAME UPON ME QUICKLY...
...BUT NOT BEFORE THE COLD RAN THROUGH ME LIKE DEATH.
EN DARKNESS CAME.
BUT IT WAS OT A RESTFUL SLUMBER.
I DREAMED...
...AND SAW THE SOURCE OF MY FEAR.
THE SOURCE OF MY FINAL FAILURE.

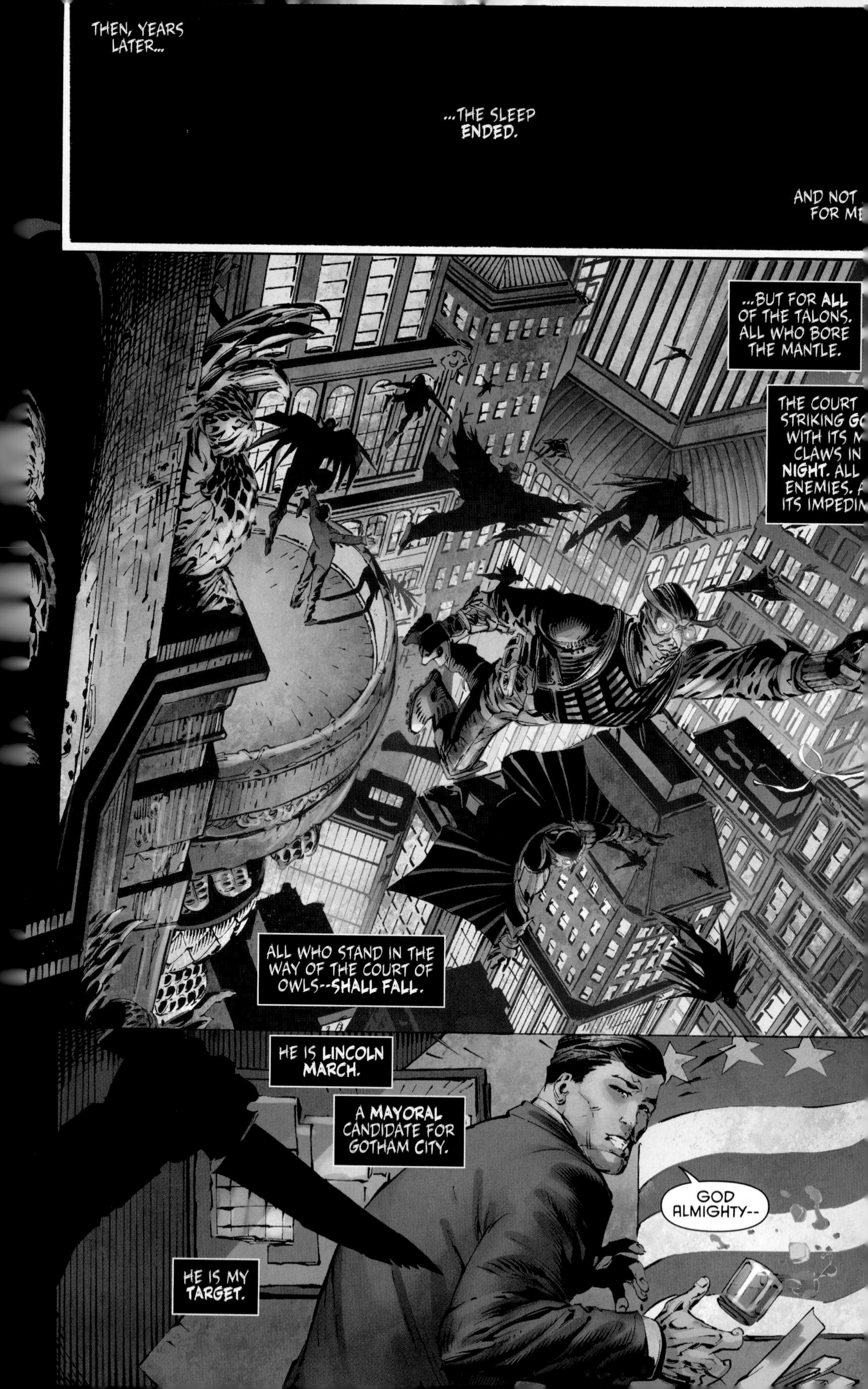
THEN, YEARS LATER...
...THE SLEEP ENDED.
AND NOT FOR ME
...BUT FOR ALL OF THE TALONS. ALL WHO BORE THE MANTLE.
THE COURT STRIKING GO WITH ITS M CLAWS IN NIGHT. ALL ENEMIES. ITS IMPEDIN
ALL WHO STAND IN THE WAY OF THE COURT OF OWLS--SHALL FALL.
HE IS LINCOLN MARCH.
A MAYORAL CANDIDATE FOR GOTHAM CITY.
GOD ALMIGHTY--
HE IS MY TARGET.

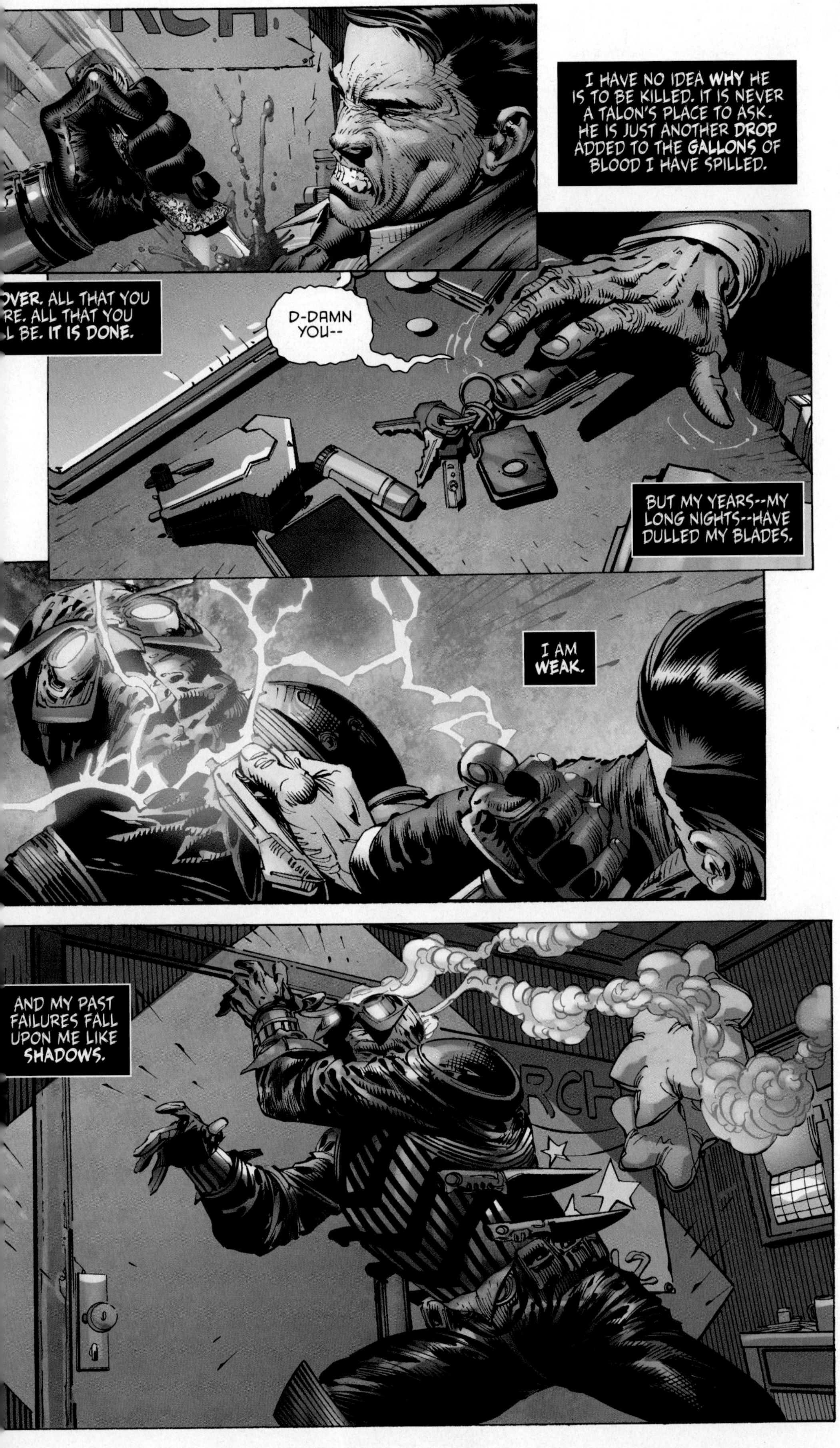

I HAVE NO IDEA WHY HE IS TO BE KILLED. IT IS NEVER A TALON'S PLACE TO ASK. HE IS JUST ANOTHER DROP ADDED TO THE GALLONS OF BLOOD I HAVE SPILLED.
OVER. ALL THAT YOU RE. ALL THAT YOU L BE. IT IS DONE.
D-DAMN YOU--
BUT MY YEARS--MY LONG NIGHTS--HAVE DULLED MY BLADES.
I AM WEAK.
AND MY PAST FAILURES FALL UPON ME LIKE SHADOWS.

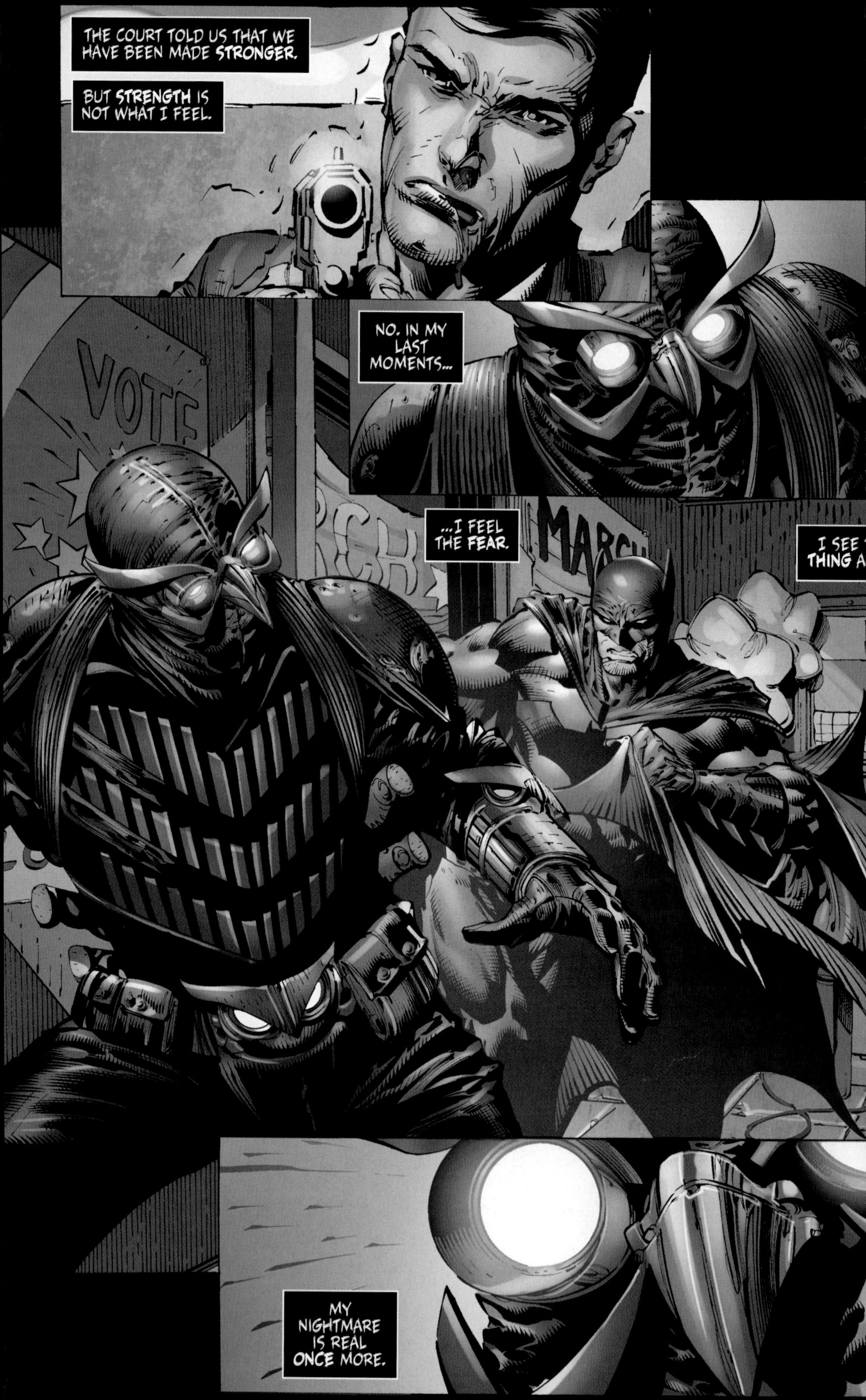

THE COURT TOLD US THAT WE HAVE BEEN MADE STRONGER.
BUT STRENGTH IS NOT WHAT I FEEL.
VOTE
NO. IN MY LAST MOMENTS...
...I FEEL THE FEAR.
MARCH
I SEE
THING
MY NIGHTMARE IS REAL ONCE MORE.

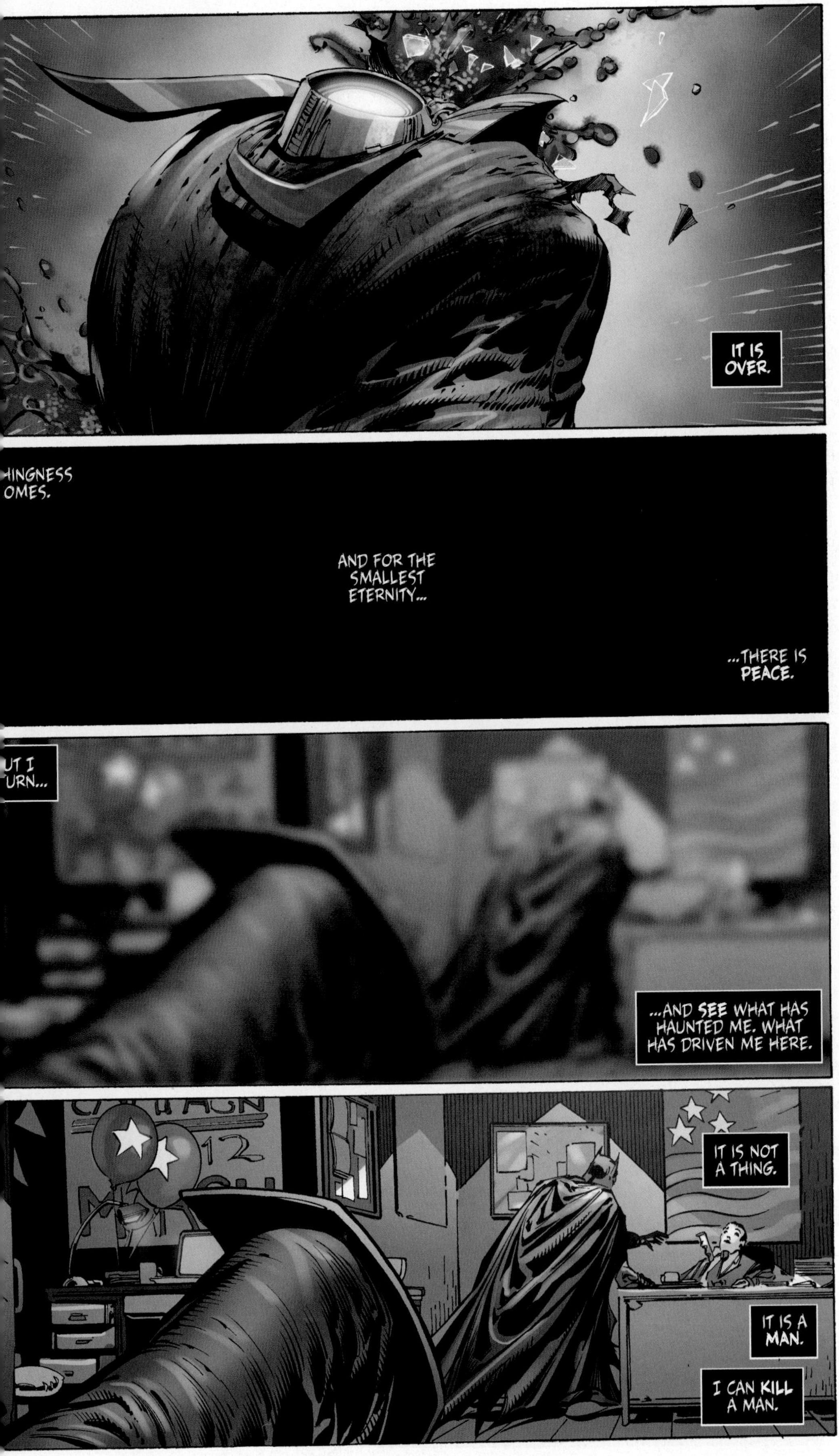
IT IS OVER.
HINGNESS
OMES.
AND FOR THE SMALLEST ETERNITY...
...THERE IS PEACE.
UT I
URN...
...AND SEE WHAT HAS HAUNTED ME. WHAT HAS DRIVEN ME HERE.
IT IS NOT A THING.
IT IS A MAN.
I CAN KILL A MAN.

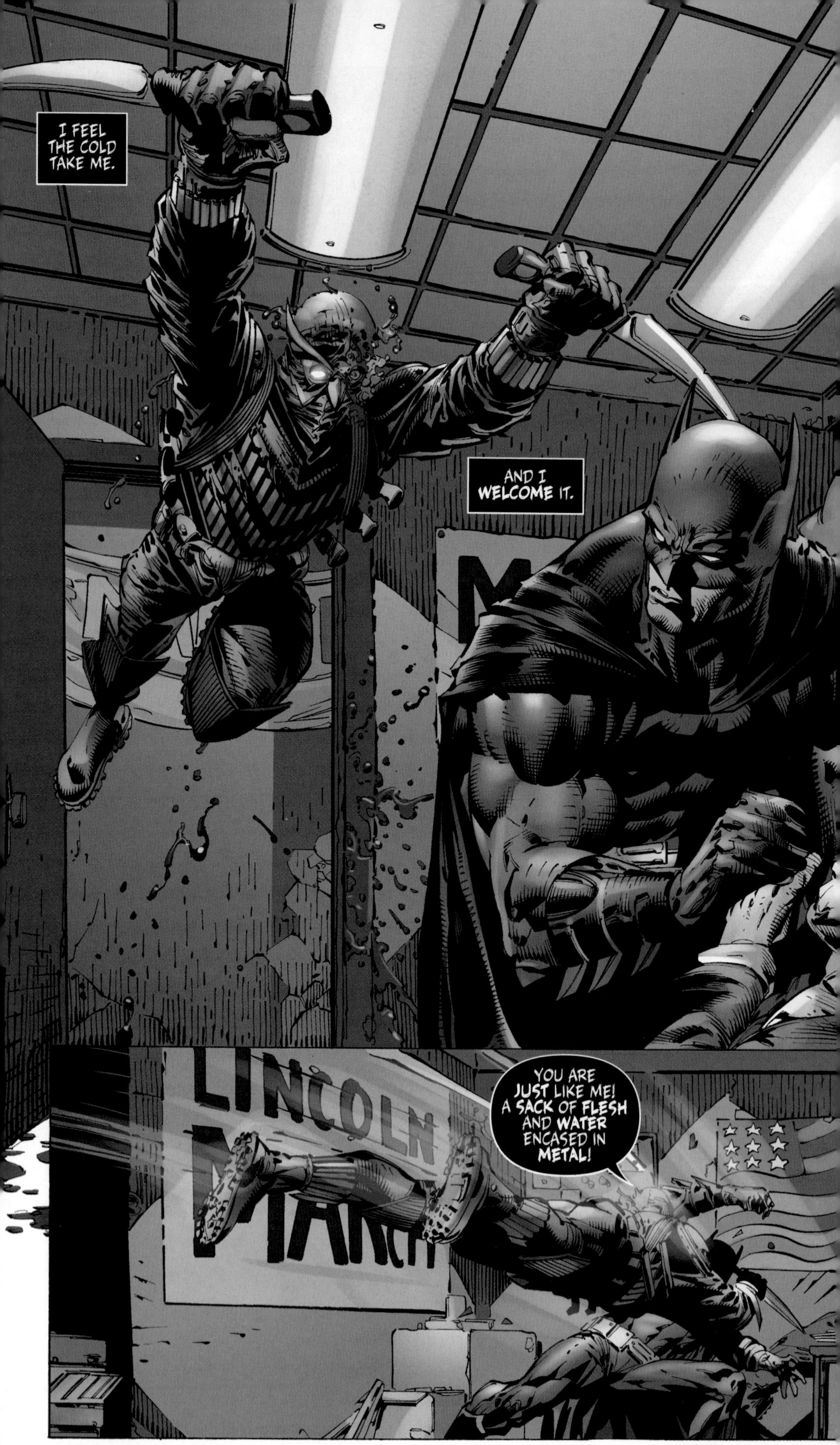

I FEEL THE COLD TAKE ME.
AND I WELCOME IT.
YOU ARE JUST LIKE ME! A SACK OF FLESH AND WATER ENCASED IN METAL!

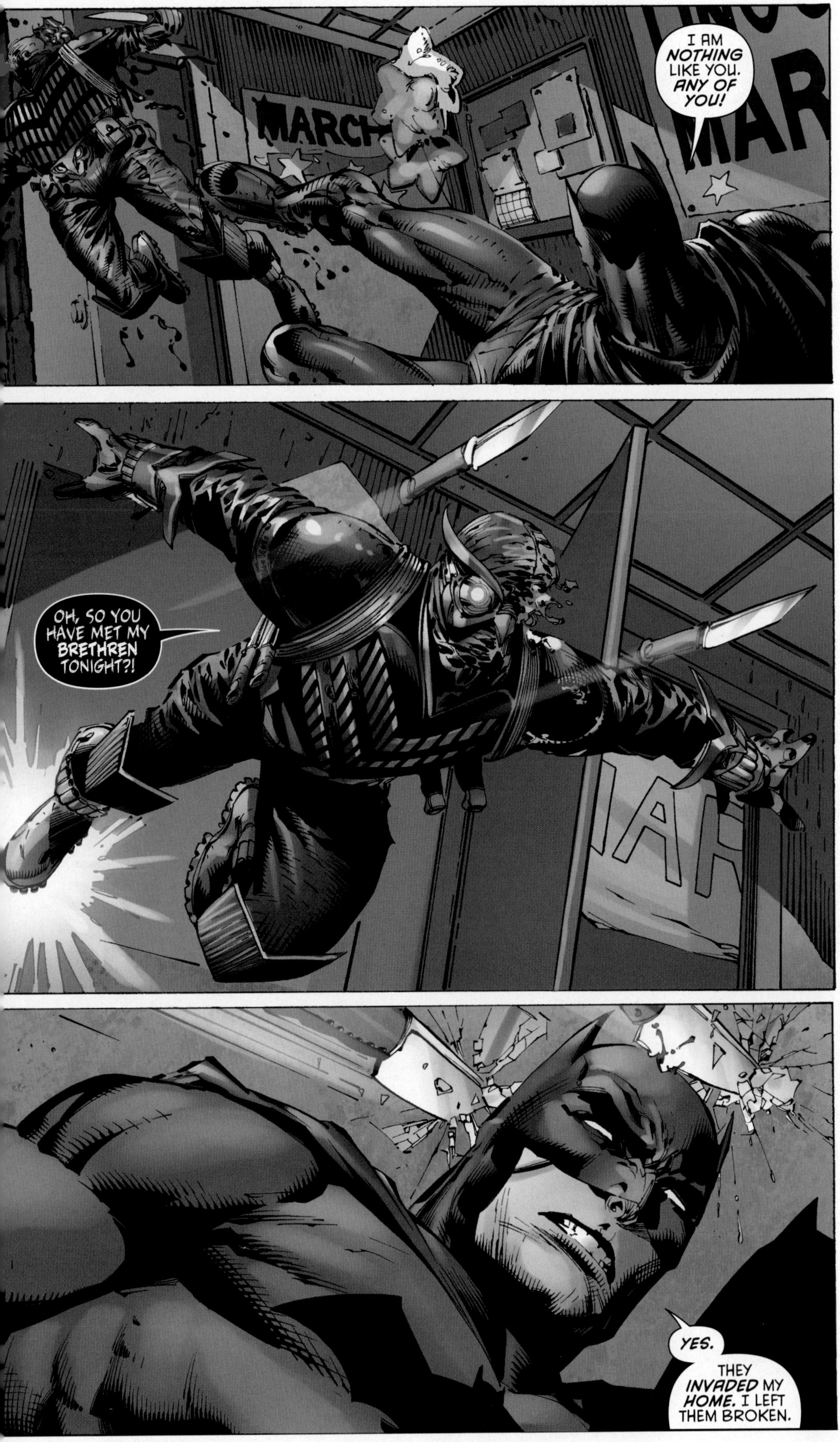
MARCH
I AM *NOTHING* LIKE YOU. *ANY OF YOU!*
OH, SO YOU HAVE MET MY **BRETHREN** TONIGHT?!
YES.
THEY *INVADED* MY *HOME.* I LEFT THEM BROKEN.

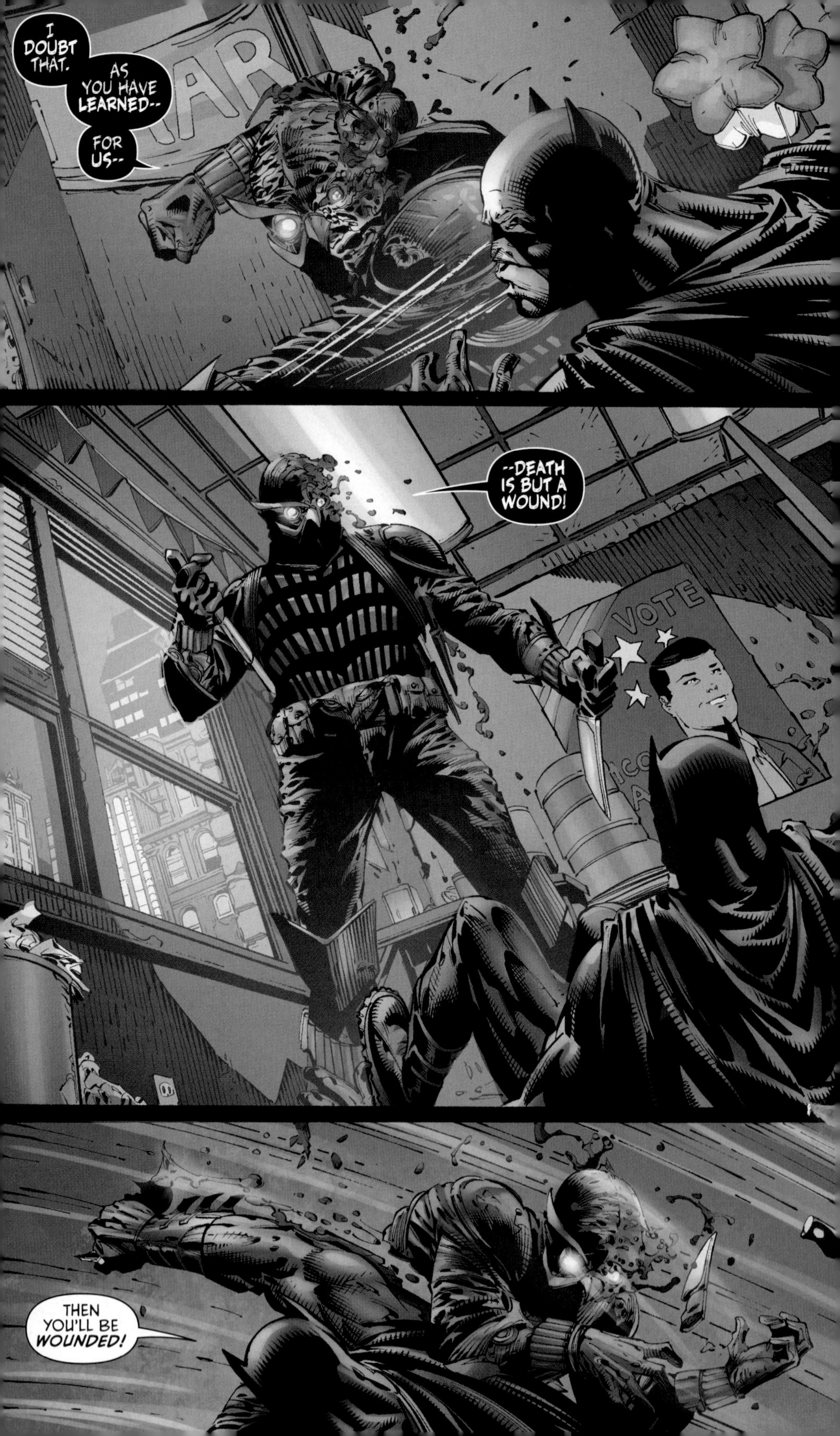
I DOUBT THAT.
AS YOU HAVE LEARNED--
FOR US--
VOTE
--DEATH IS BUT A WOUND!
THEN YOU'LL BE WOUNDED!

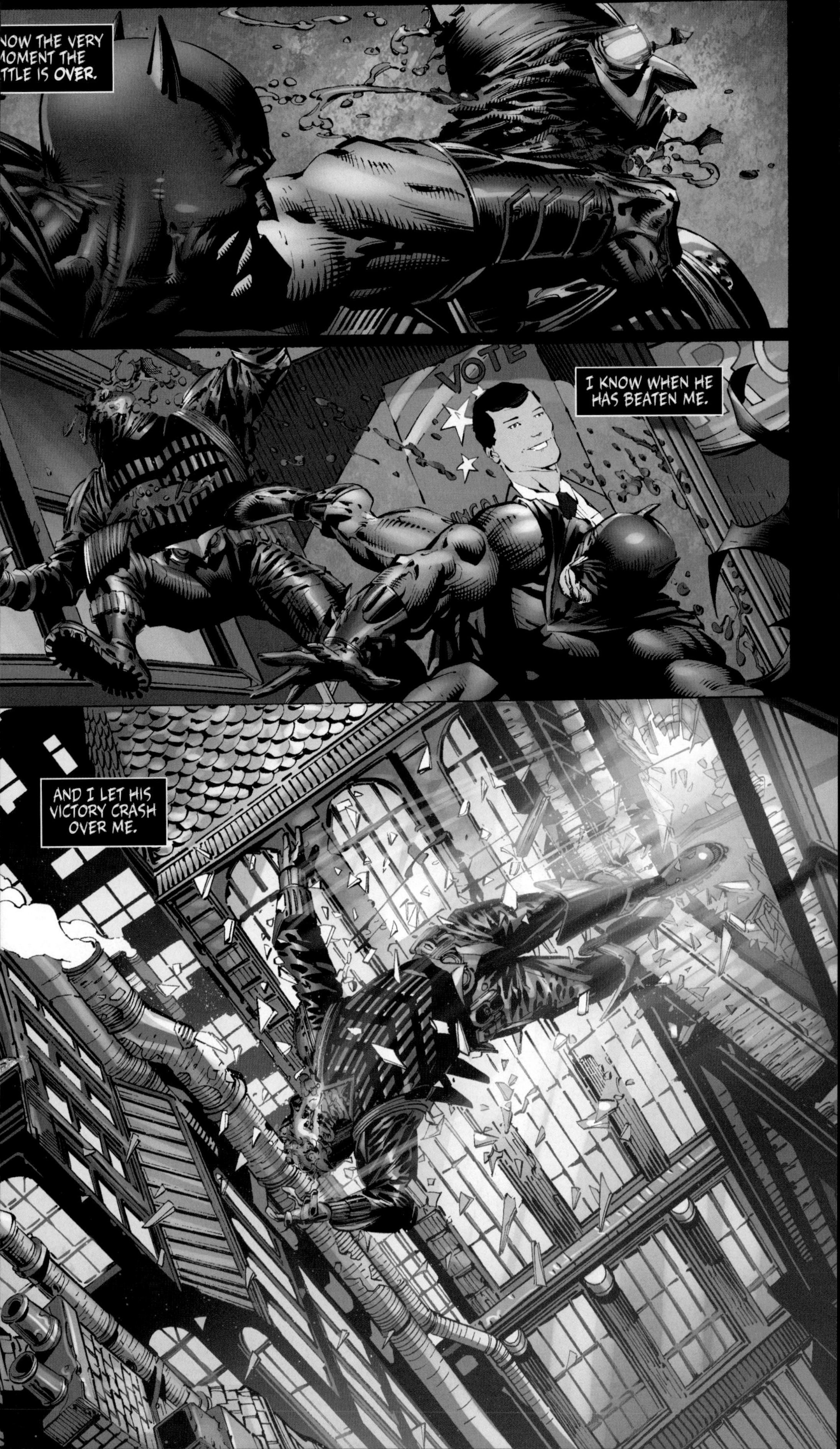
NOW THE VERY MOMENT THE TTLE IS OVER.
I KNOW WHEN HE HAS BEATEN ME.
VOTE
AND I LET HIS VICTORY CRASH OVER ME.

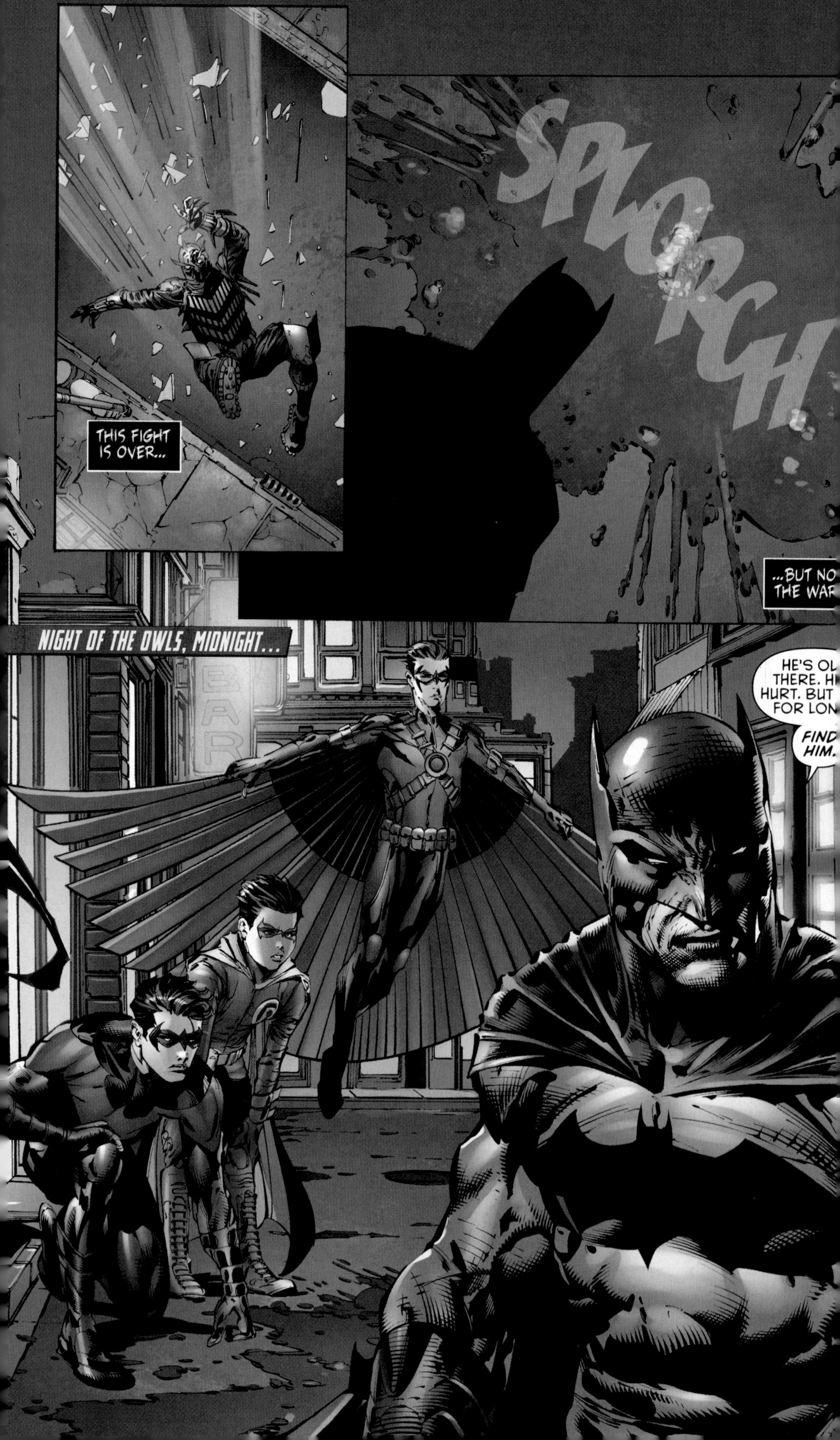
THIS FIGHT IS OVER...
SPLORCH
...BUT NO
THE WAR
NIGHT OF THE OWLS, MIDNIGHT...
BAR
HE'S OL
THERE. H
HURT. BUT
FOR LON
FIND
HIM.

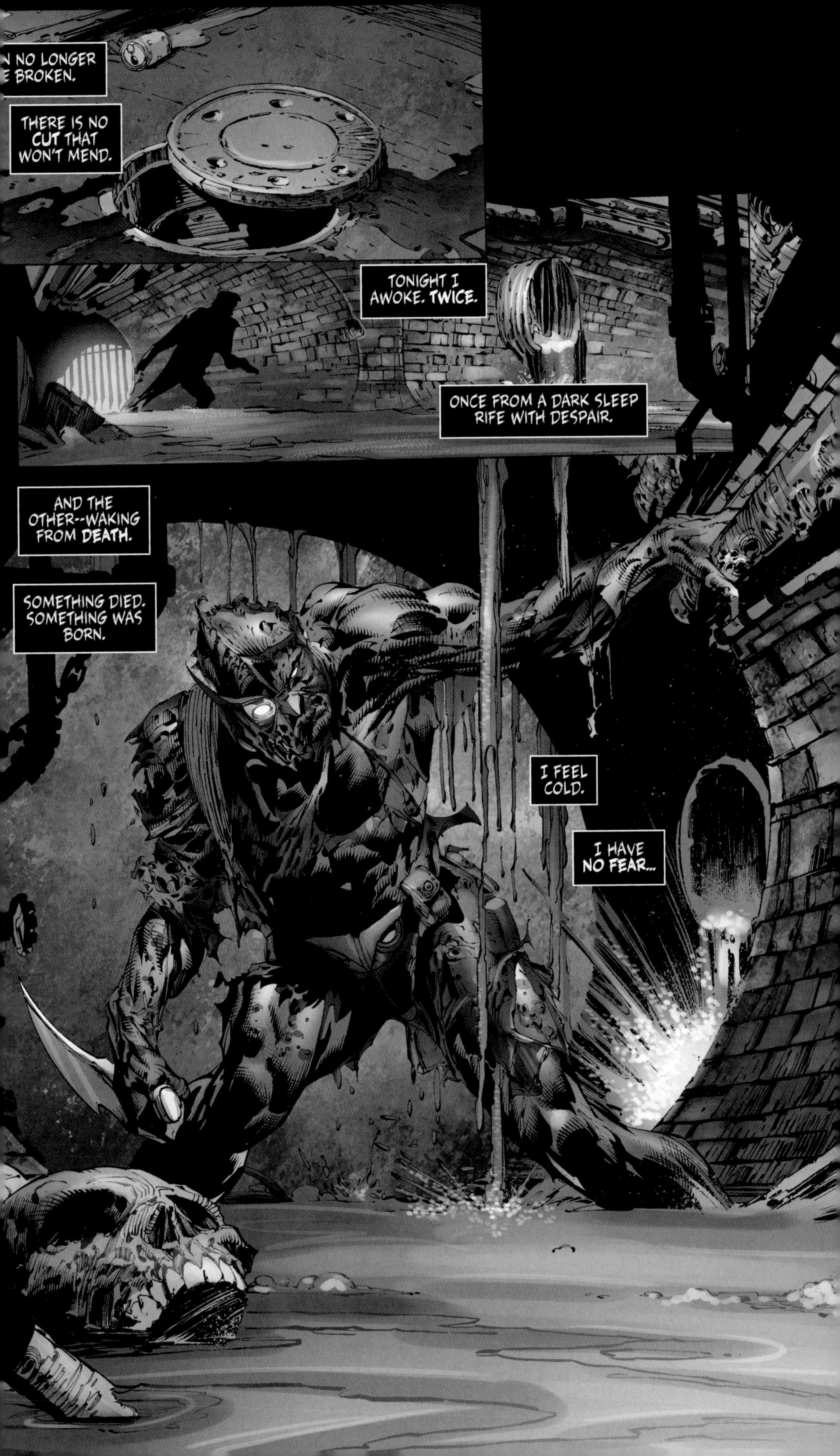
N NO LONGER
E BROKEN.
THERE IS NO CUT THAT WON'T MEND.
TONIGHT I AWOKE. TWICE.
ONCE FROM A DARK SLEEP RIFE WITH DESPAIR.
AND THE OTHER--WAKING FROM DEATH.
SOMETHING DIED. SOMETHING WAS BORN.
I FEEL COLD.
I HAVE NO FEAR...

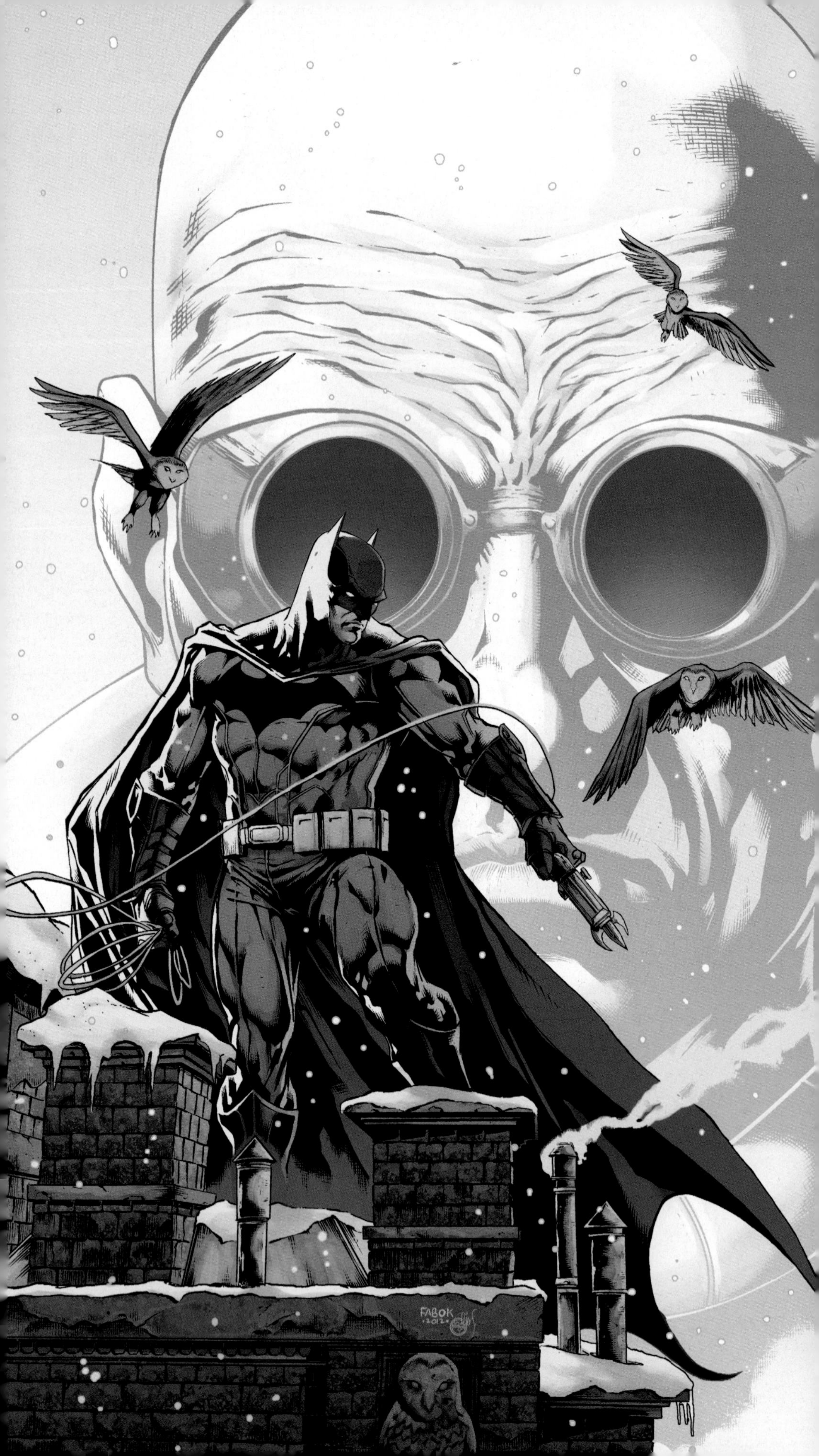
FABOK
2012

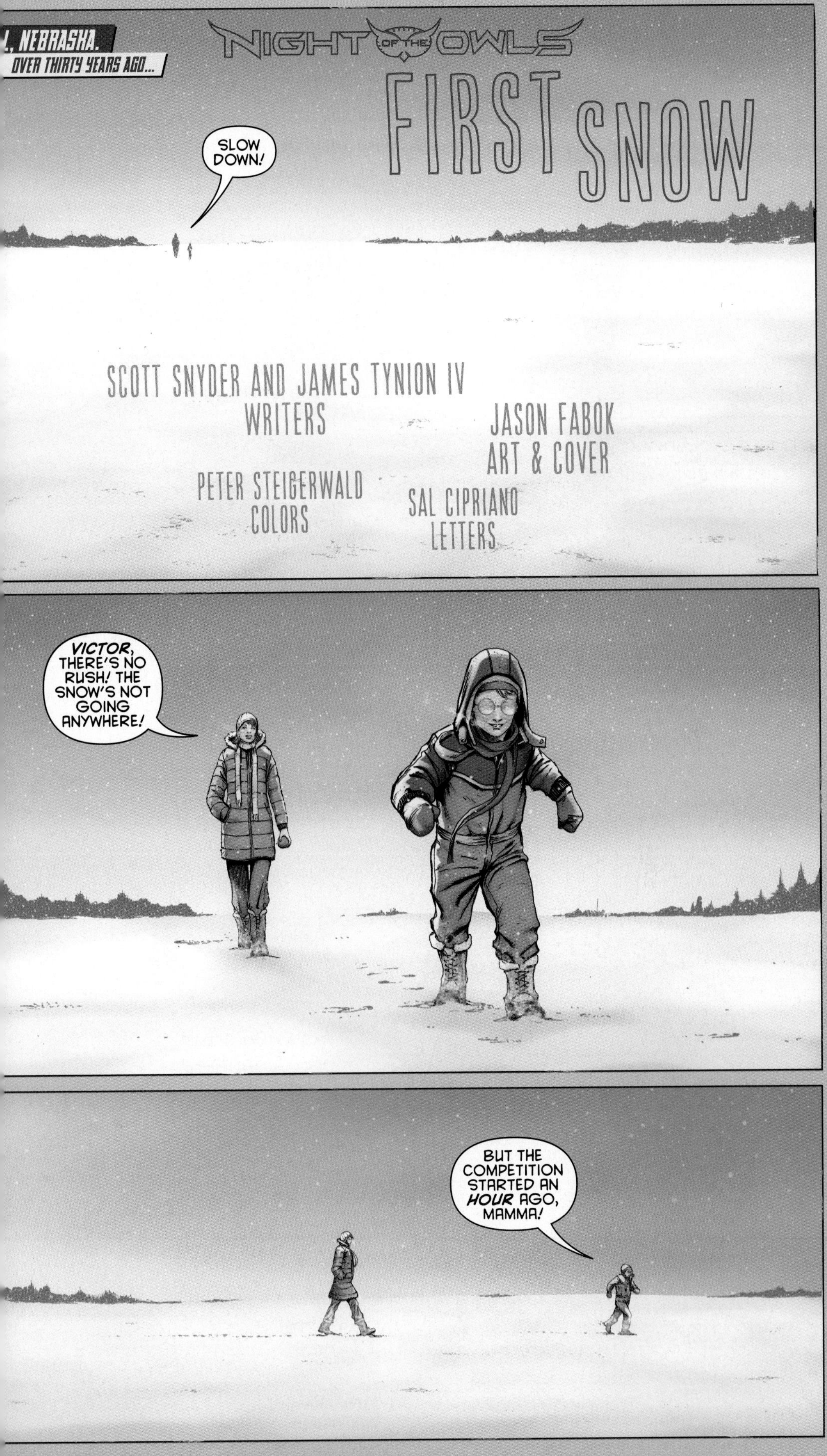

..., NEBRASKA.
OVER THIRTY YEARS AGO...
NIGHT OF THE OWLS
FIRST SNOW
SLOW DOWN!
SCOTT SNYDER AND JAMES TYNION IV
WRITERS
JASON FABOK
ART & COVER
PETER STEIGERWALD
COLORS
SAL CIPRIANO
LETTERS
VICTOR, THERE'S NO RUSH! THE SNOW'S NOT GOING ANYWHERE!
BUT THE COMPETITION STARTED AN HOUR AGO, MAMMA!

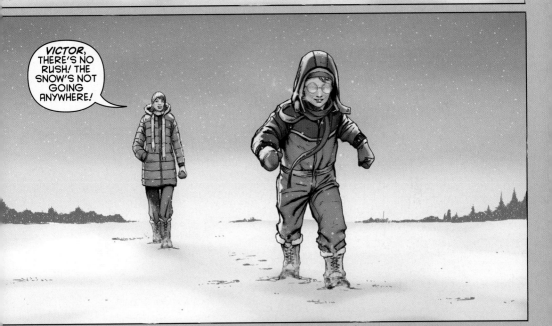

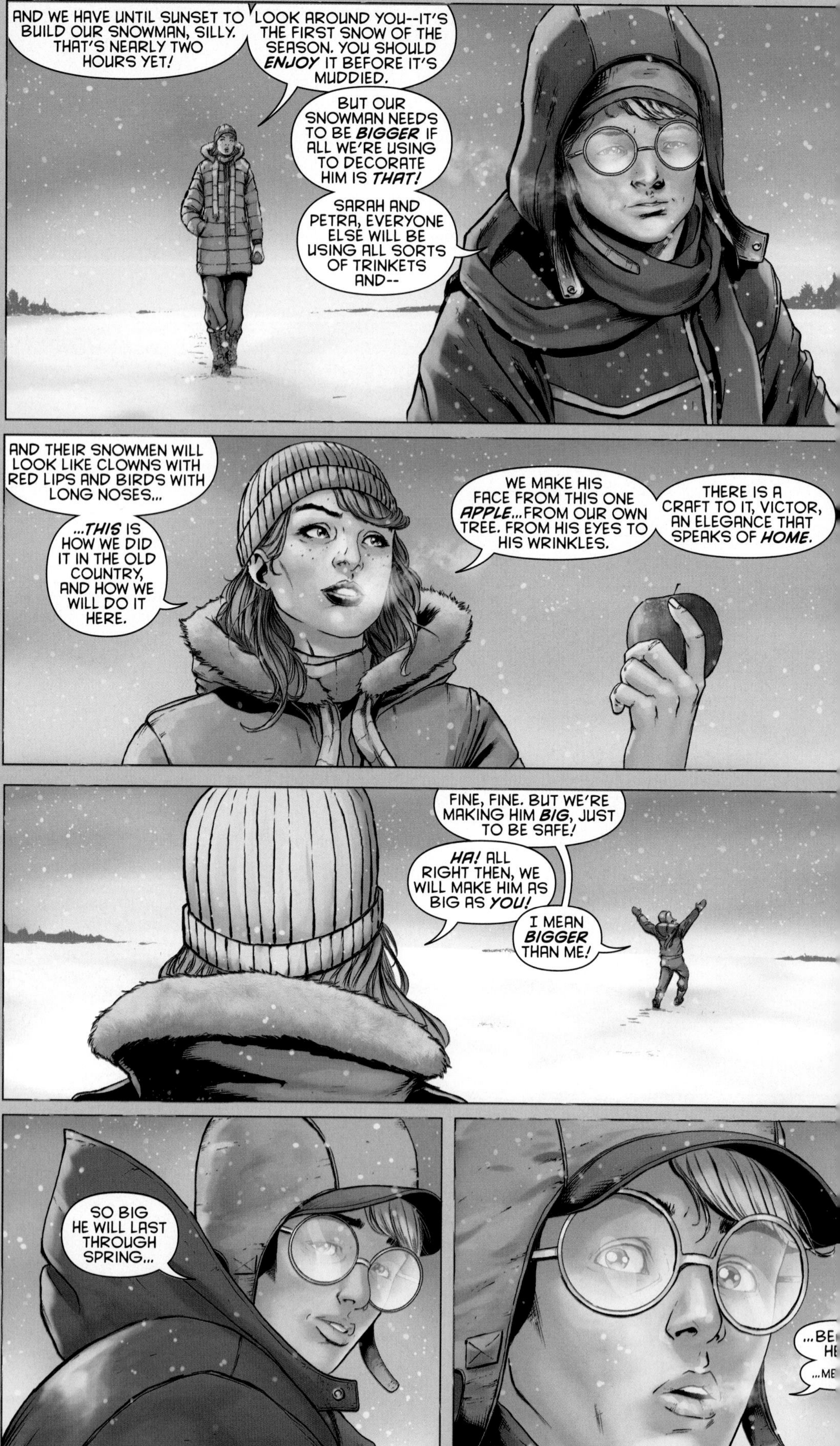
AND WE HAVE UNTIL SUNSET TO BUILD OUR SNOWMAN, SILLY. THAT'S NEARLY TWO HOURS YET!
LOOK AROUND YOU--IT'S THE FIRST SNOW OF THE SEASON. YOU SHOULD ENJOY IT BEFORE IT'S MUDDIED.
BUT OUR SNOWMAN NEEDS TO BE BIGGER IF ALL WE'RE USING TO DECORATE HIM IS THAT!
SARAH AND PETRA, EVERYONE ELSE WILL BE USING ALL SORTS OF TRINKETS AND--
AND THEIR SNOWMEN WILL LOOK LIKE CLOWNS WITH RED LIPS AND BIRDS WITH LONG NOSES...
...THIS IS HOW WE DID IT IN THE OLD COUNTRY, AND HOW WE WILL DO IT HERE.
WE MAKE HIS FACE FROM THIS ONE APPLE...FROM OUR OWN TREE. FROM HIS EYES TO HIS WRINKLES.
THERE IS A CRAFT TO IT, VICTOR, AN ELEGANCE THAT SPEAKS OF HOME.
FINE, FINE. BUT WE'RE MAKING HIM BIG, JUST TO BE SAFE!
HA! ALL RIGHT THEN, WE WILL MAKE HIM AS BIG AS YOU!
I MEAN BIGGER THAN ME!
SO BIG HE WILL LAST THROUGH SPRING...

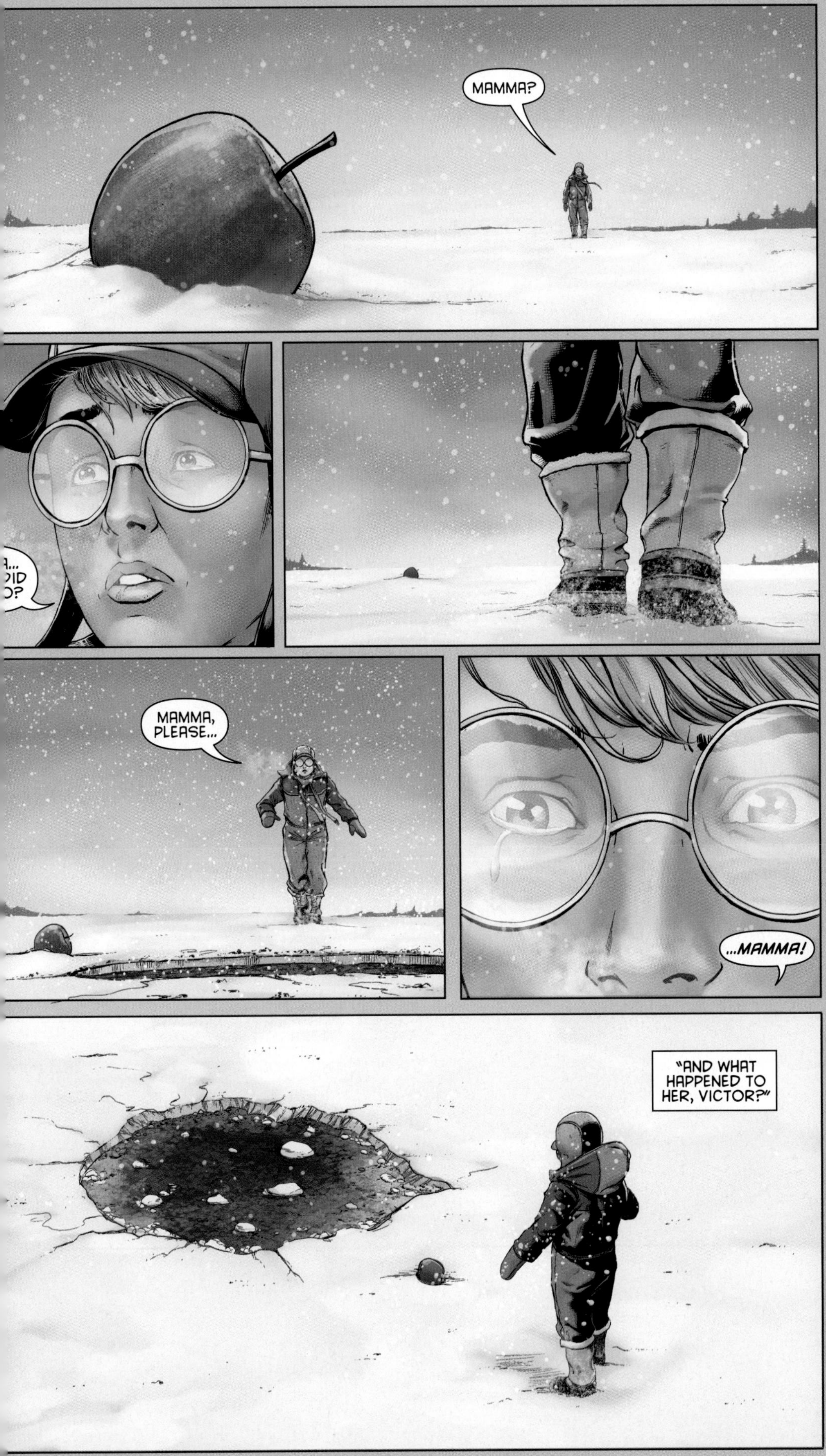
MAMMA?
MAMMA, PLEASE...
...MAMMA!
"AND WHAT HAPPENED TO HER, VICTOR?"

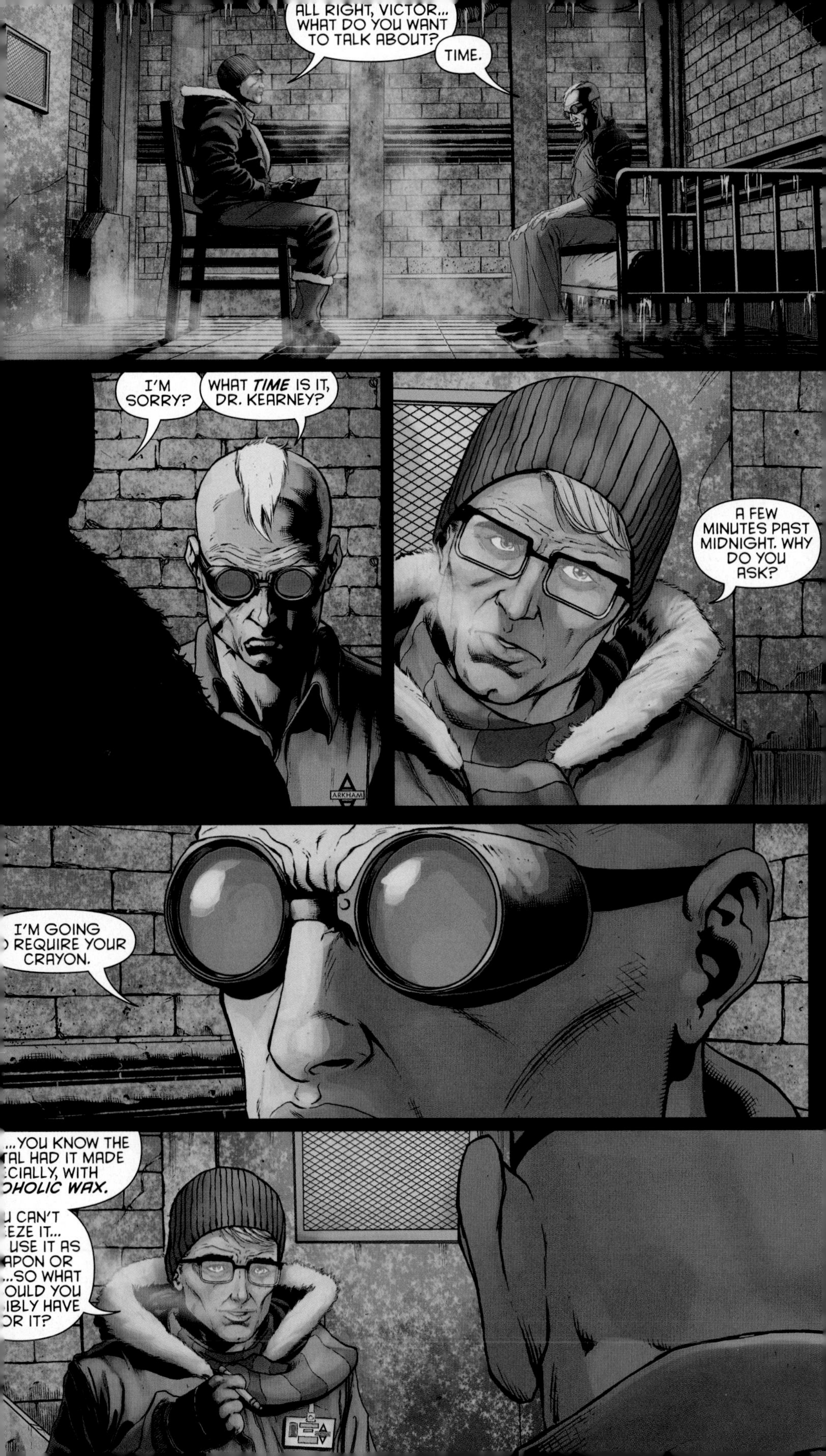

ALL RIGHT, VICTOR... WHAT DO YOU WANT TO TALK ABOUT?
TIME.
I'M SORRY?
WHAT *TIME* IS IT, DR. KEARNEY?
A FEW MINUTES PAST MIDNIGHT. WHY DO YOU ASK?
I'M GOING REQUIRE YOUR CRAYON.
...YOU KNOW THE TAL HAD IT MADE ECIALLY, WITH OHOLIC WAX.
U CAN'T EZE IT... USE IT AS APON OR ...SO WHAT OULD YOU IBLY HAVE OR IT?
ARKHAM

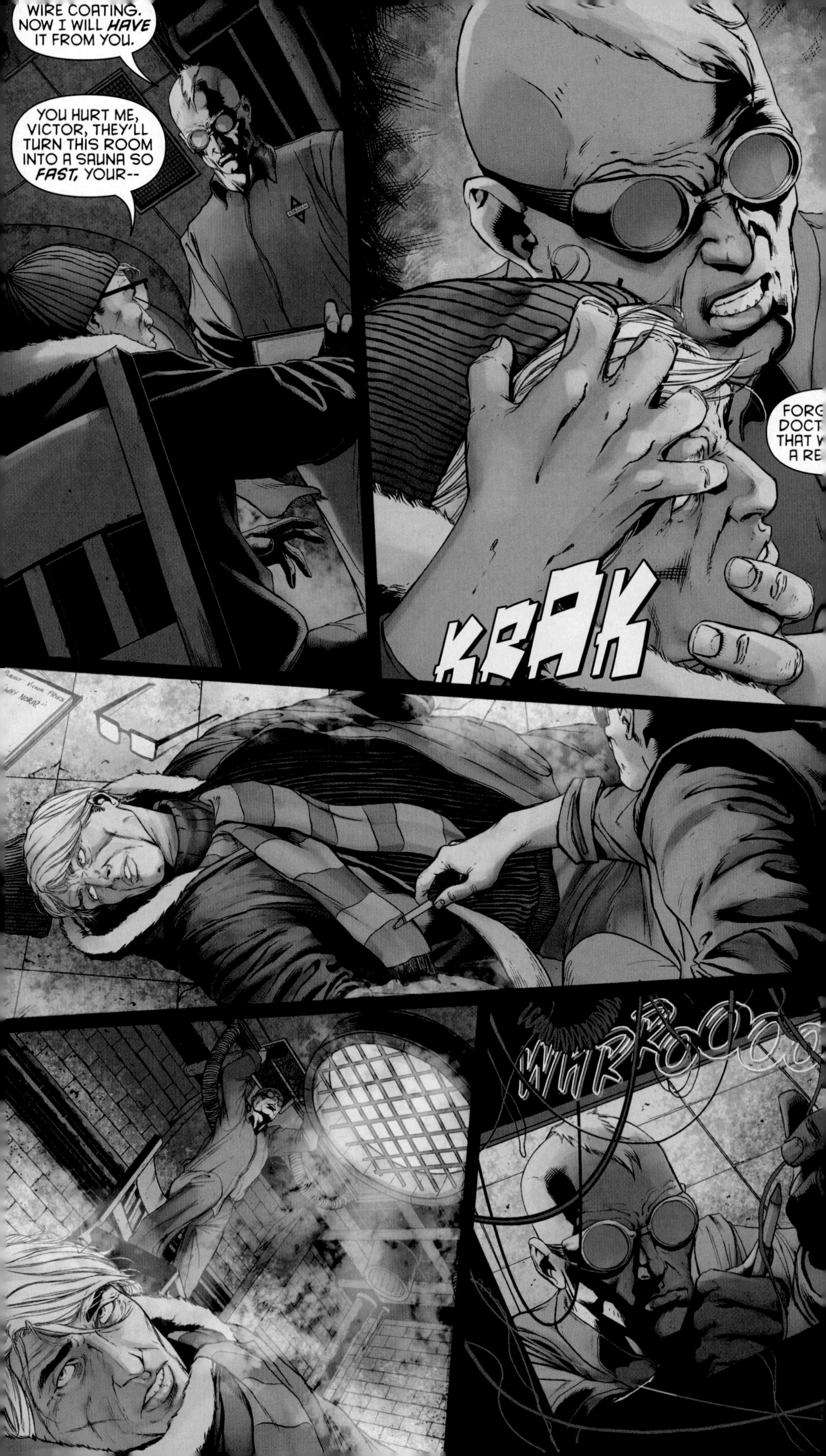

WIRE COATING. NOW I WILL *HAVE* IT FROM YOU.
YOU HURT ME, VICTOR, THEY'LL TURN THIS ROOM INTO A SAUNA SO *FAST,* YOUR--
FORG DOCT THAT W A RE
KRAK

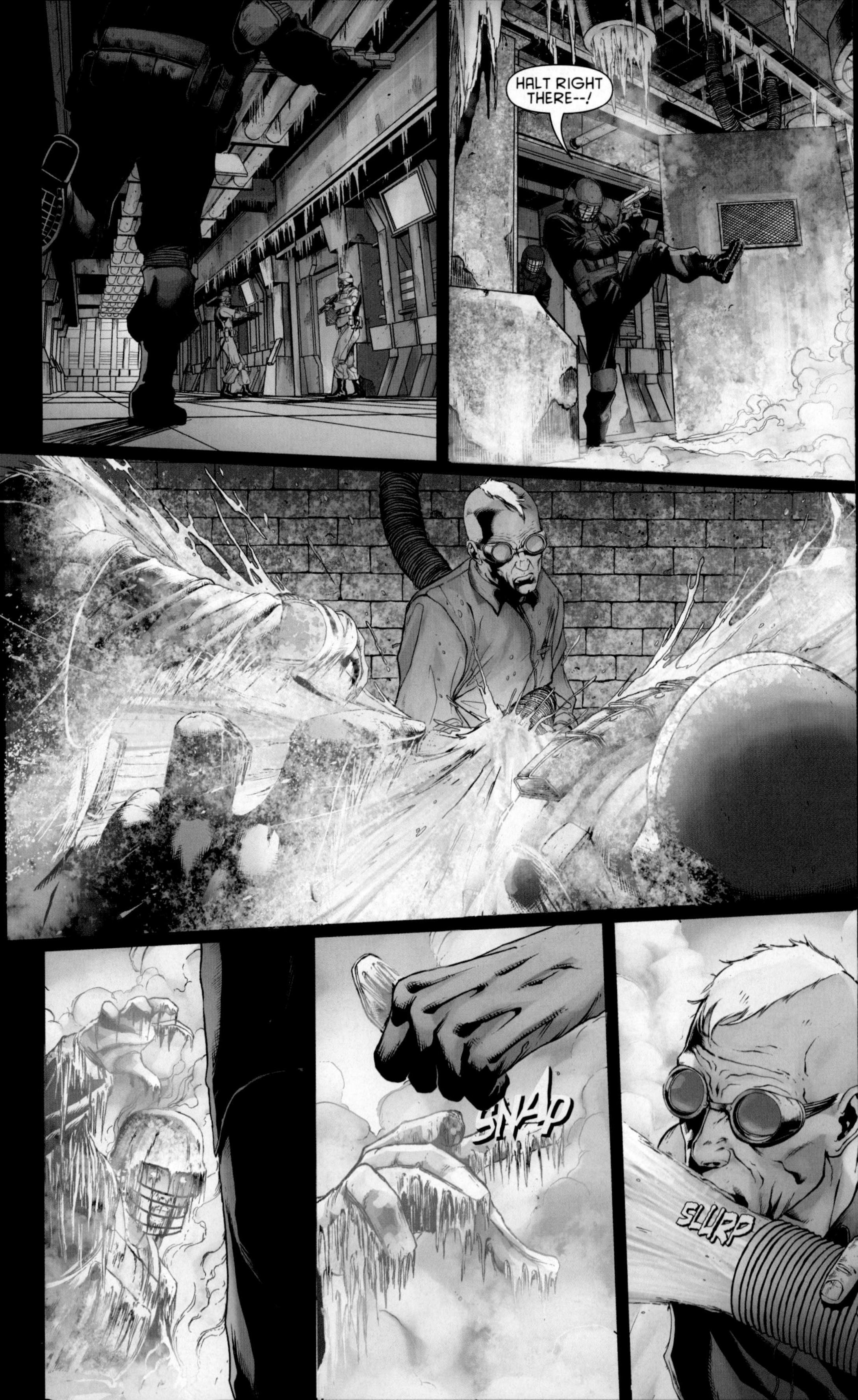
HALT RIGHT THERE--!
SNAP
SLURP

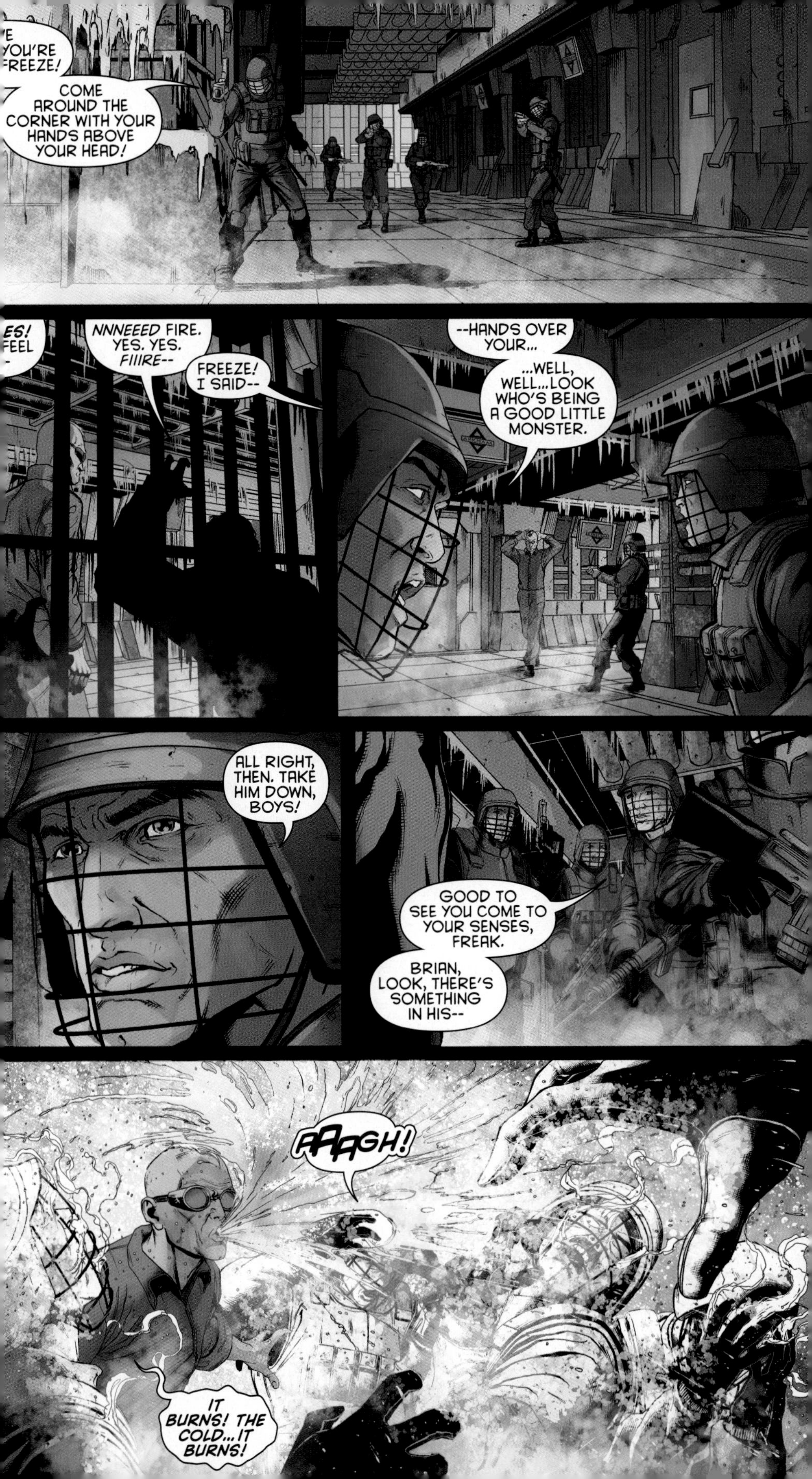

'E YOU'RE FREEZE!
COME AROUND THE CORNER WITH YOUR HANDS ABOVE YOUR HEAD!
ES! FEEL
NNNEEED FIRE. YES. YES. FIIIRE--
FREEZE! I SAID--
--HANDS OVER YOUR...
...WELL, WELL...LOOK WHO'S BEING A GOOD LITTLE MONSTER.
ALL RIGHT, THEN. TAKE HIM DOWN, BOYS!
GOOD TO SEE YOU COME TO YOUR SENSES, FREAK.
BRIAN, LOOK, THERE'S SOMETHING IN HIS--
AAAGH!
IT BURNS! THE COLD...IT BURNS!

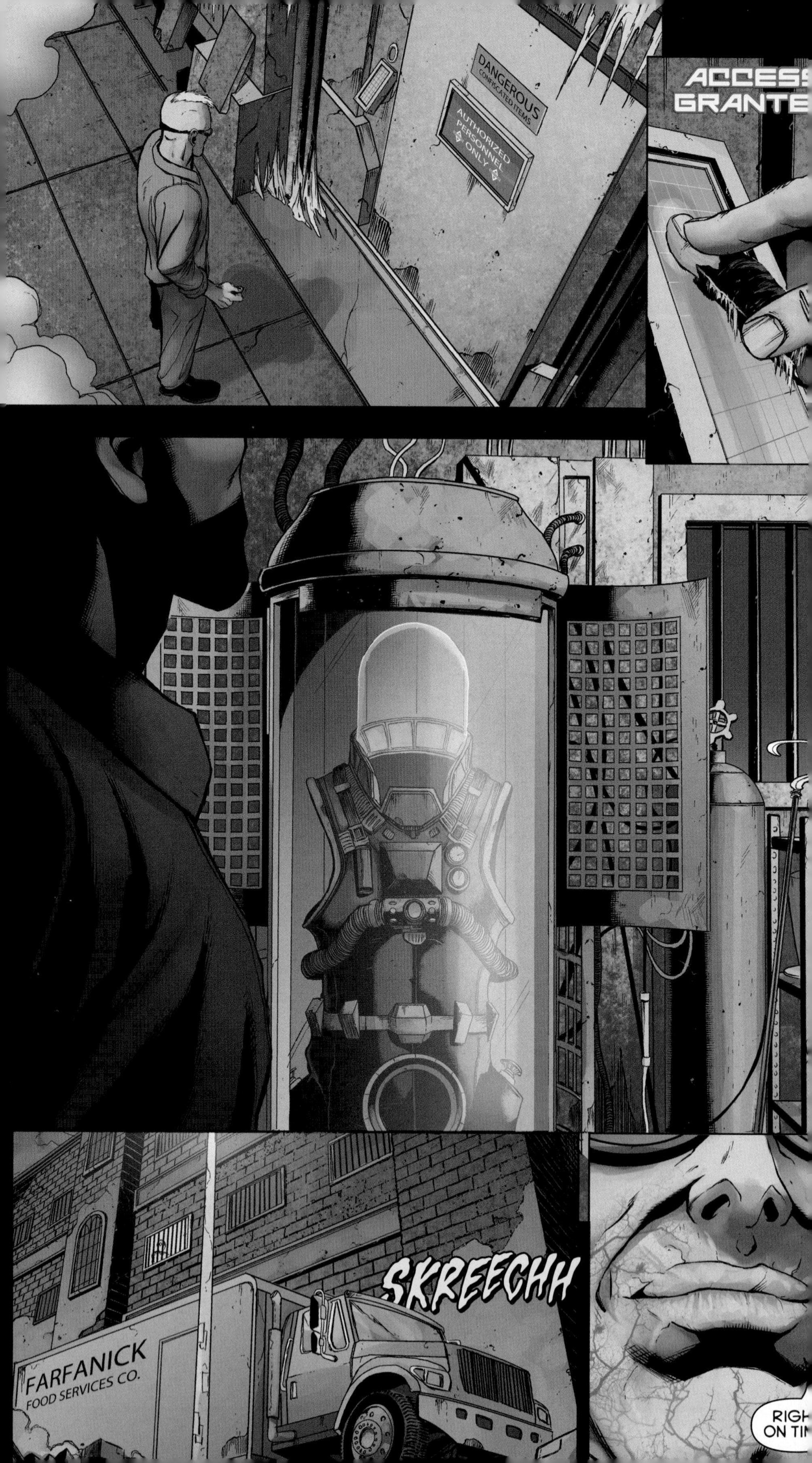
DANGEROUS
CONFISCATED ITEMS
AUTHORIZED PERSONNEL ONLY
ACCESS GRANTE
SKREECHH
FARFANICK
FOOD SERVICES CO.
RIGH ON TI

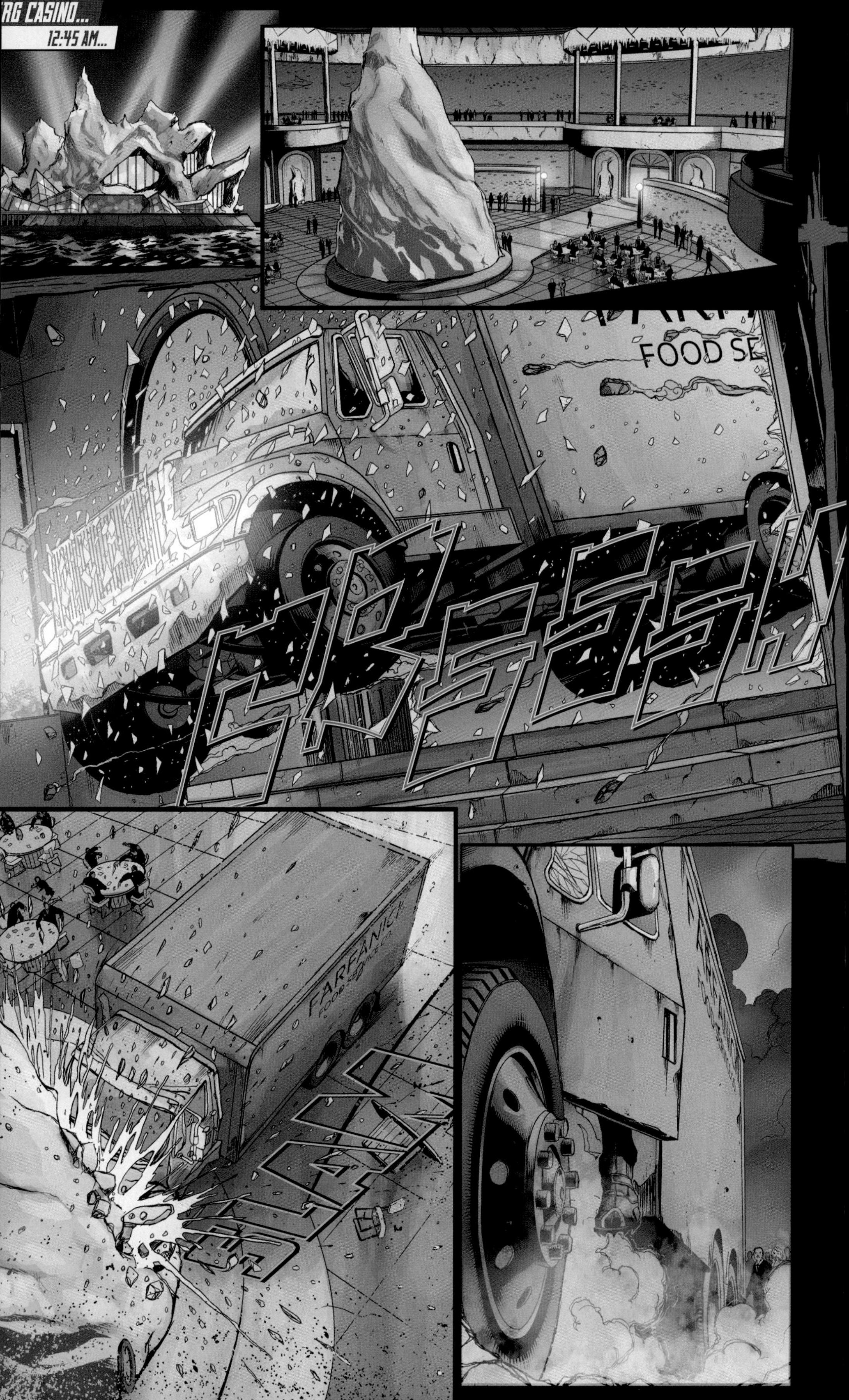
RG CASINO...
12:45 AM...
FOOD SE

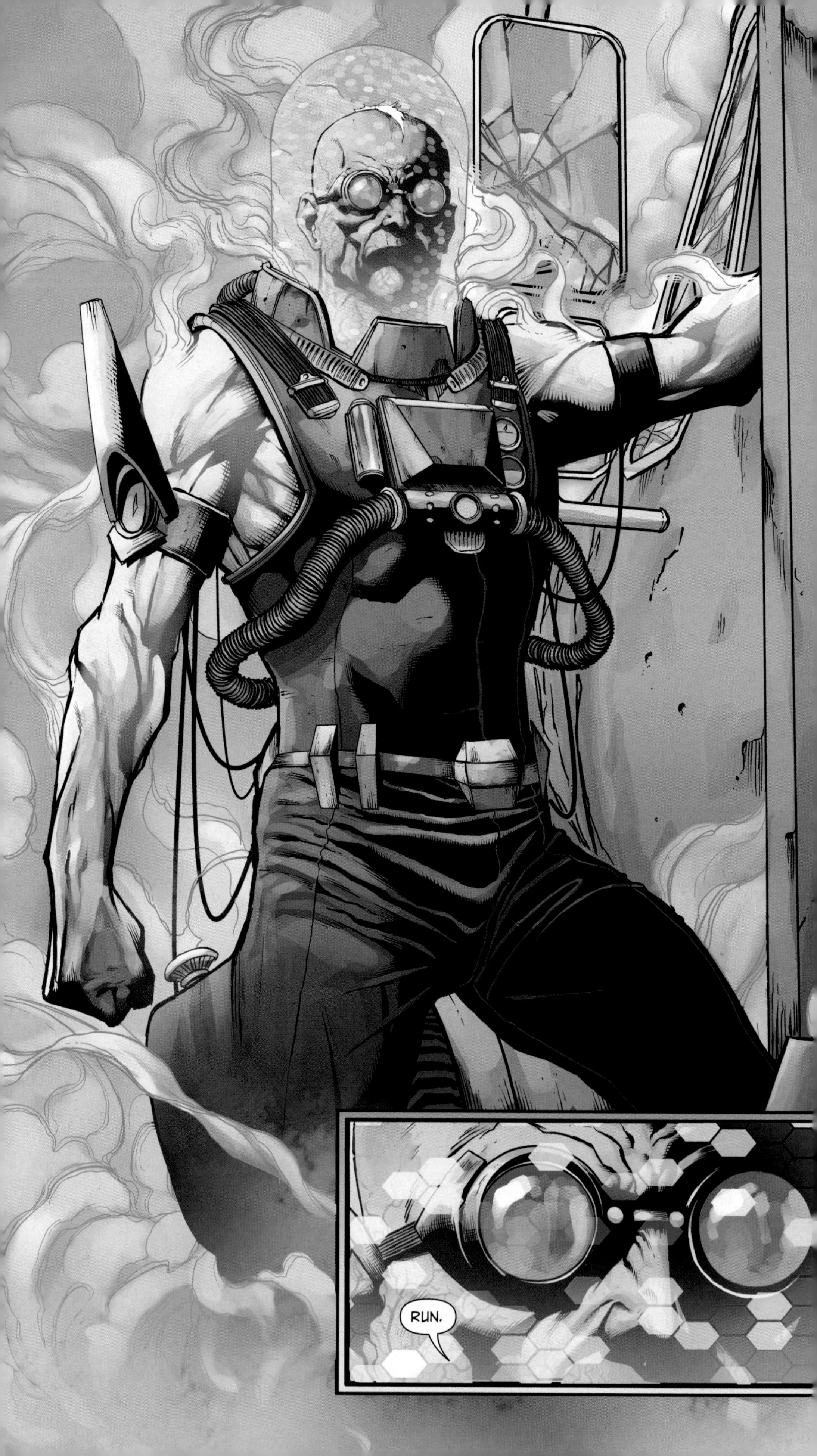
RUN.

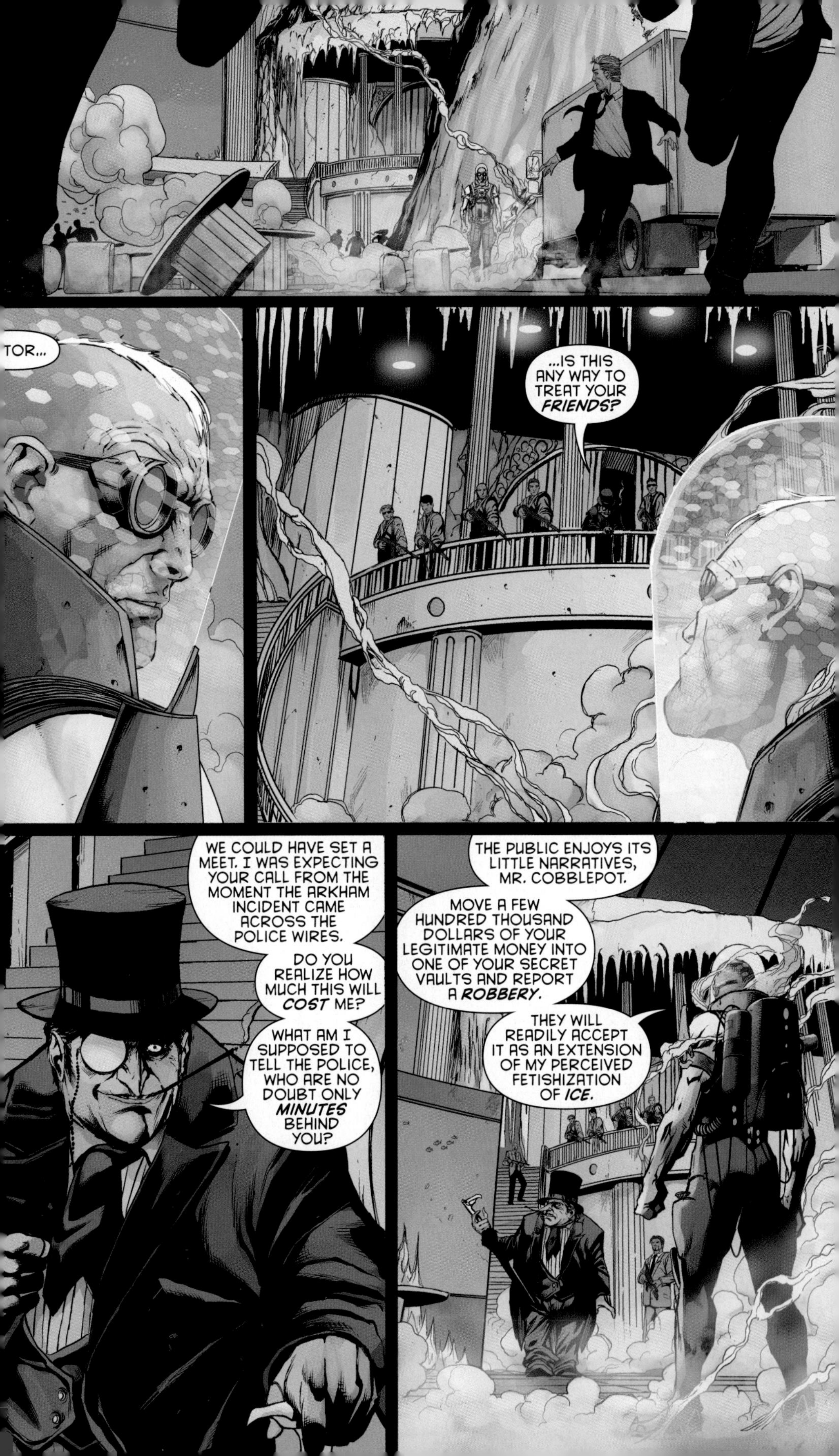

TOR...
...IS THIS ANY WAY TO TREAT YOUR FRIENDS?
WE COULD HAVE SET A MEET. I WAS EXPECTING YOUR CALL FROM THE MOMENT THE ARKHAM INCIDENT CAME ACROSS THE POLICE WIRES.
DO YOU REALIZE HOW MUCH THIS WILL COST ME?
WHAT AM I SUPPOSED TO TELL THE POLICE, WHO ARE NO DOUBT ONLY MINUTES BEHIND YOU?
THE PUBLIC ENJOYS ITS LITTLE NARRATIVES, MR. COBBLEPOT.
MOVE A FEW HUNDRED THOUSAND DOLLARS OF YOUR LEGITIMATE MONEY INTO ONE OF YOUR SECRET VAULTS AND REPORT A ROBBERY.
THEY WILL READILY ACCEPT IT AS AN EXTENSION OF MY PERCEIVED FETISHIZATION OF ICE.

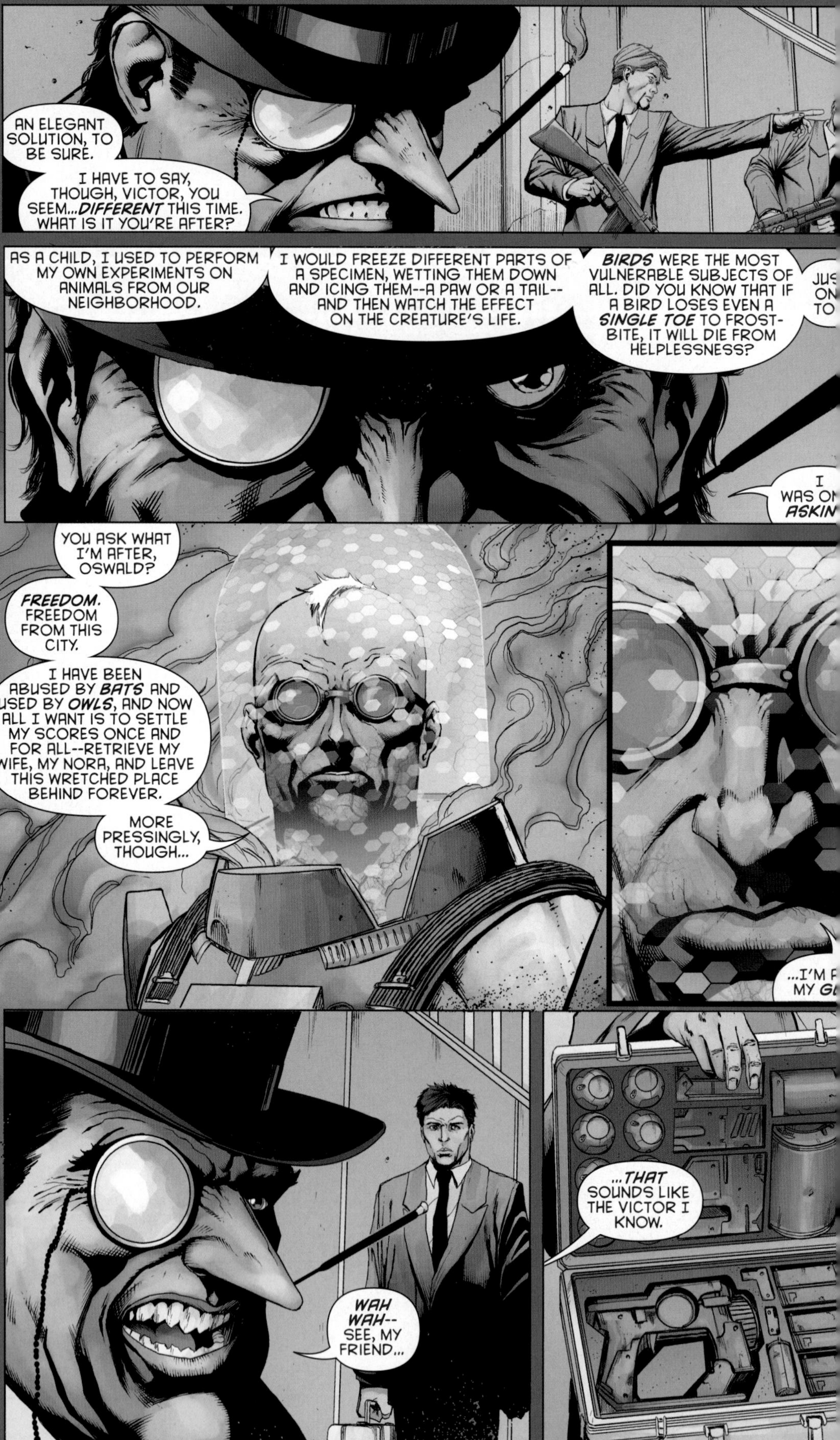
AN ELEGANT SOLUTION, TO BE SURE.
I HAVE TO SAY, THOUGH, VICTOR, YOU SEEM...*DIFFERENT* THIS TIME. WHAT IS IT YOU'RE AFTER?
AS A CHILD, I USED TO PERFORM MY OWN EXPERIMENTS ON ANIMALS FROM OUR NEIGHBORHOOD.
I WOULD FREEZE DIFFERENT PARTS OF A SPECIMEN, WETTING THEM DOWN AND ICING THEM--A PAW OR A TAIL--AND THEN WATCH THE EFFECT ON THE CREATURE'S LIFE.
BIRDS WERE THE MOST VULNERABLE SUBJECTS OF ALL. DID YOU KNOW THAT IF A BIRD LOSES EVEN A *SINGLE TOE* TO FROST-BITE, IT WILL DIE FROM HELPLESSNESS?
YOU ASK WHAT I'M AFTER, OSWALD?
FREEDOM. FREEDOM FROM THIS CITY.
I HAVE BEEN ABUSED BY *BATS* AND USED BY *OWLS*, AND NOW ALL I WANT IS TO SETTLE MY SCORES ONCE AND FOR ALL--RETRIEVE MY WIFE, MY NORA, AND LEAVE THIS WRETCHED PLACE BEHIND FOREVER.
MORE PRESSINGLY, THOUGH...
WAH WAH--SEE, MY FRIEND...
...*THAT* SOUNDS LIKE THE VICTOR I KNOW.

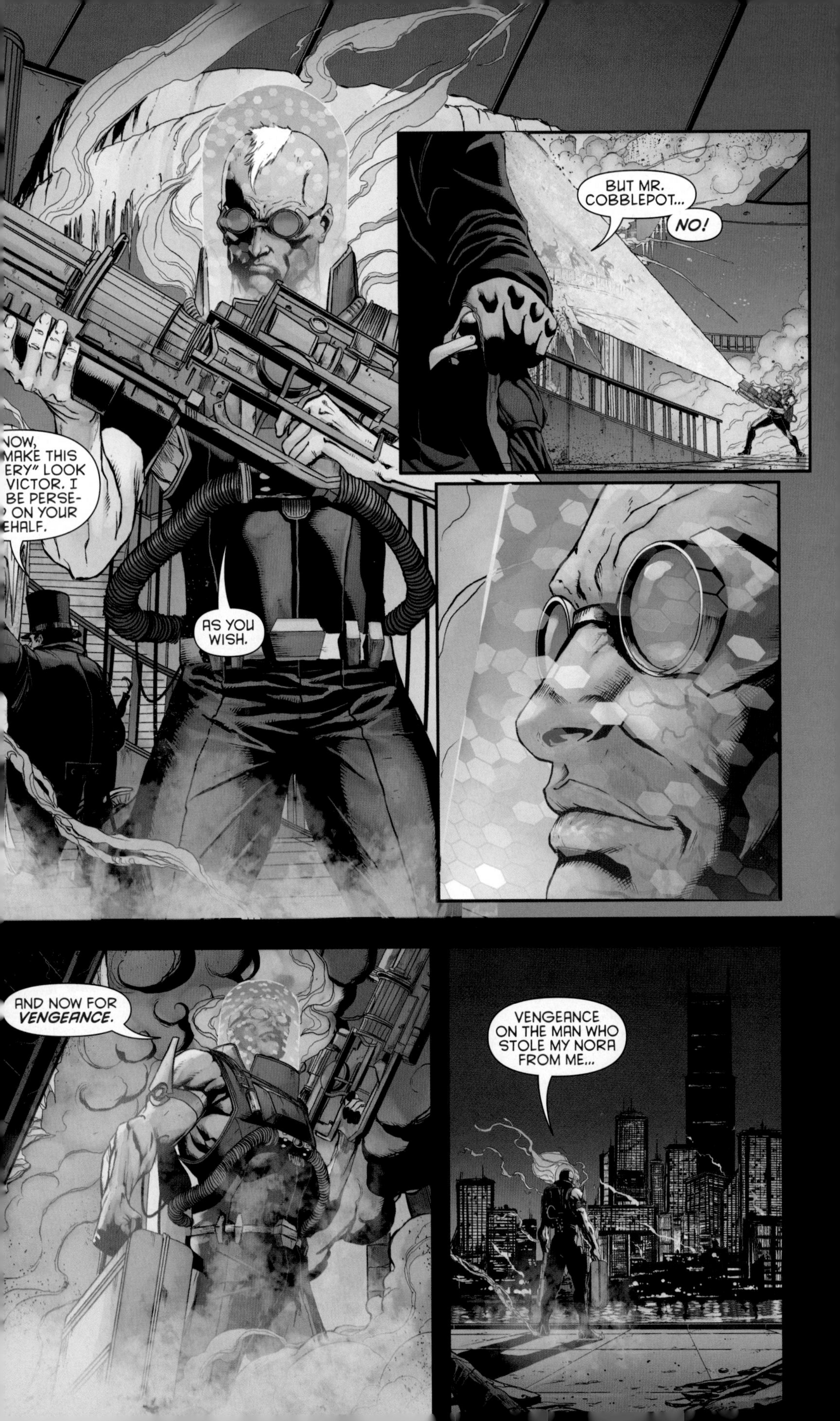

BUT MR. COBBLEPOT...
NO!
NOW, MAKE THIS ERY" LOOK VICTOR. I BE PERSE- ON YOUR EHALF.
AS YOU WISH.
AND NOW FOR VENGEANCE.
VENGEANCE ON THE MAN WHO STOLE MY NORA FROM ME...

"...VENGEANCE ON *BRUCE WAYNE*."

DR. VICTOR FRIES, I PRESENT TO YOU THE PRODIGAL SON, BRUCE WAYNE.

DR. FRIES RUNS THE SMALL CRYONICS LAB WE KEEP BENEATH THE LABORATORIES PROPER. FROZEN HEADS ABOUND.

DOCTOR, I'M GIVING MR. WAYNE A TOUR OF HIS KINGDOM, IF YOU WILL. HE ONLY RECENTLY *RETURNED* TO GOTHAM.

RIGHT. OF COURSE. YOU WERE VACATIONING, I TAKE IT?

THAT'S ONE WAY OF PUTTING IT. ISN'T THAT RIGHT, LUCIUS?

DR. FRIES, MR. WAYNE HAS BEEN OUT OF THE COUNTRY FOR QUITE SOME TIME.

FORGIVE ME. ADMITTEDLY, I DON'T GET OUT OF THE LABORATORY VERY OFTEN. I NOW RECALL SOMETHING IN THE LOCAL NEWS ABOUT IT. YOUR RETURN, I MEAN.

DON'T GIVE IT A SECOND THOUGHT, DOCTOR. FROM WHAT I HEAR, YOU'RE DOING IMPORTANT WORK DOWN HERE.

YES, YES WE ARE. THE ADVANCEMENTS WE'VE MADE IN THE *SLOW-HEATING PROCESS* OF CRYO-PRESERVED INDIVIDUALS--

SLOW-HEATING? LUCIUS, I THOUGHT THE LAB WAS SUPPOSED TO BE MOVING *AWAY* FR... CRYONICS, FROZEN MUMMIES AND ... THAT, TOWARDS NEWER, MORE SPECIA... FIELDS. LIKE ORGAN VITRIFICATIO...

IN FACT, WEREN'T WE SUPPOSED TO TRANSFER THE REST OF THESE OLD CRYO-PRESERVED BODIES HERE TO THE GOTHAM UNIVERSITY BIO-LAB?

I FEEL I WAS PRETTY DIRECT IN SAYING I WASN'T COMFORTABLE CONTINUING WITH THIS LINE OF RESEARCH.

MR. WAYN... WE CAN D... *BOTH!* WE ... PURSUE NEW ... LIKE VITRIFIC... WHILE STILL P... ING OUR OR... RESEARCH O... REANIMATIO... CRYO-PRESE... INDIVIDUA...

BOTH...WELL, BE CAREFUL, DOCTOR. AND KNOW THAT YOU'LL BE ... *CLOSE EXAMINATION* UNTIL WE DECID... TO DO WITH YOUR PROJECTS DOWN ...

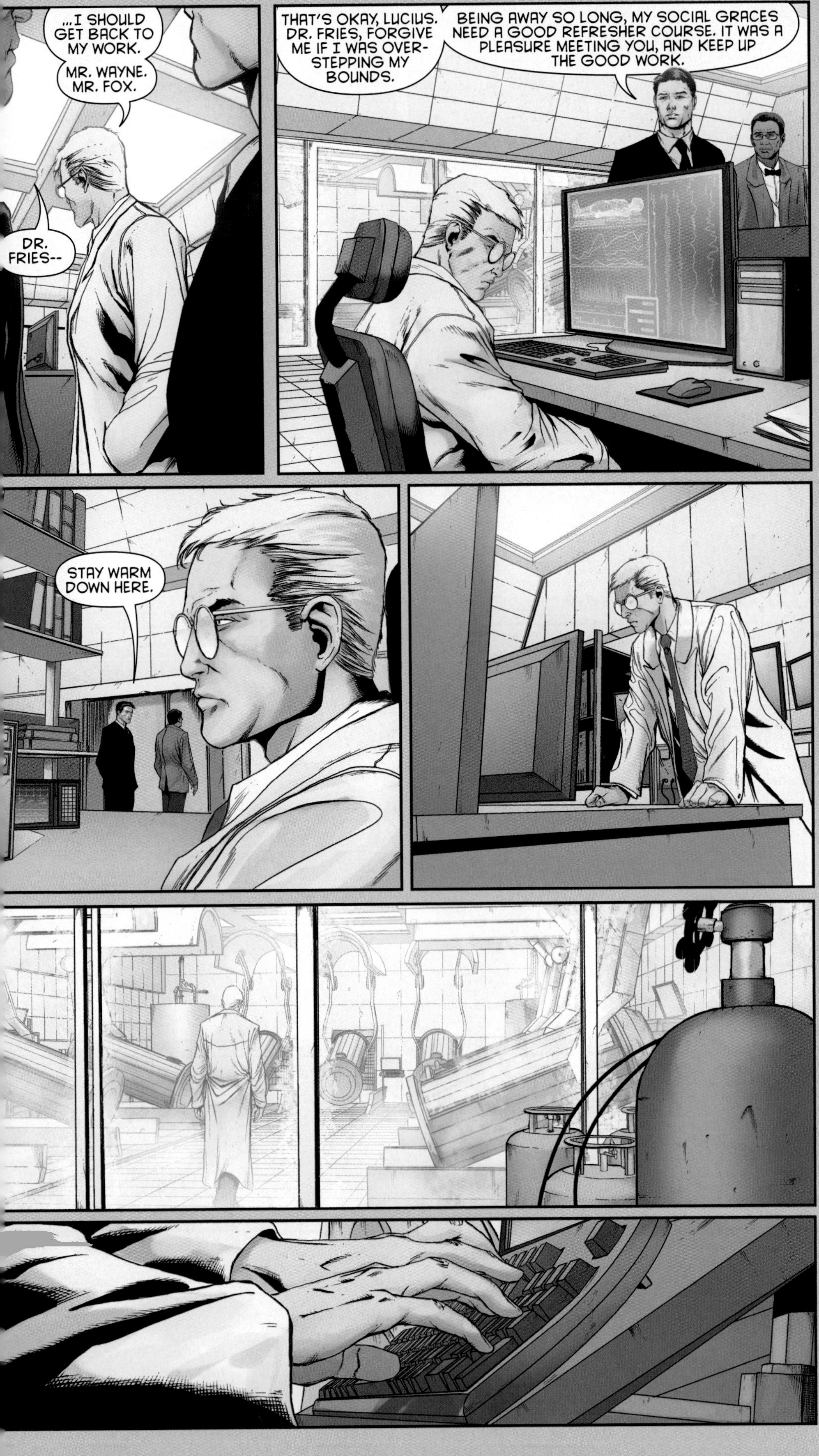
...I SHOULD GET BACK TO MY WORK.
MR. WAYNE. MR. FOX.
DR. FRIES--
THAT'S OKAY, LUCIUS. DR. FRIES, FORGIVE ME IF I WAS OVER-STEPPING MY BOUNDS.
BEING AWAY SO LONG, MY SOCIAL GRACES NEED A GOOD REFRESHER COURSE. IT WAS A PLEASURE MEETING YOU, AND KEEP UP THE GOOD WORK.
STAY WARM DOWN HERE.

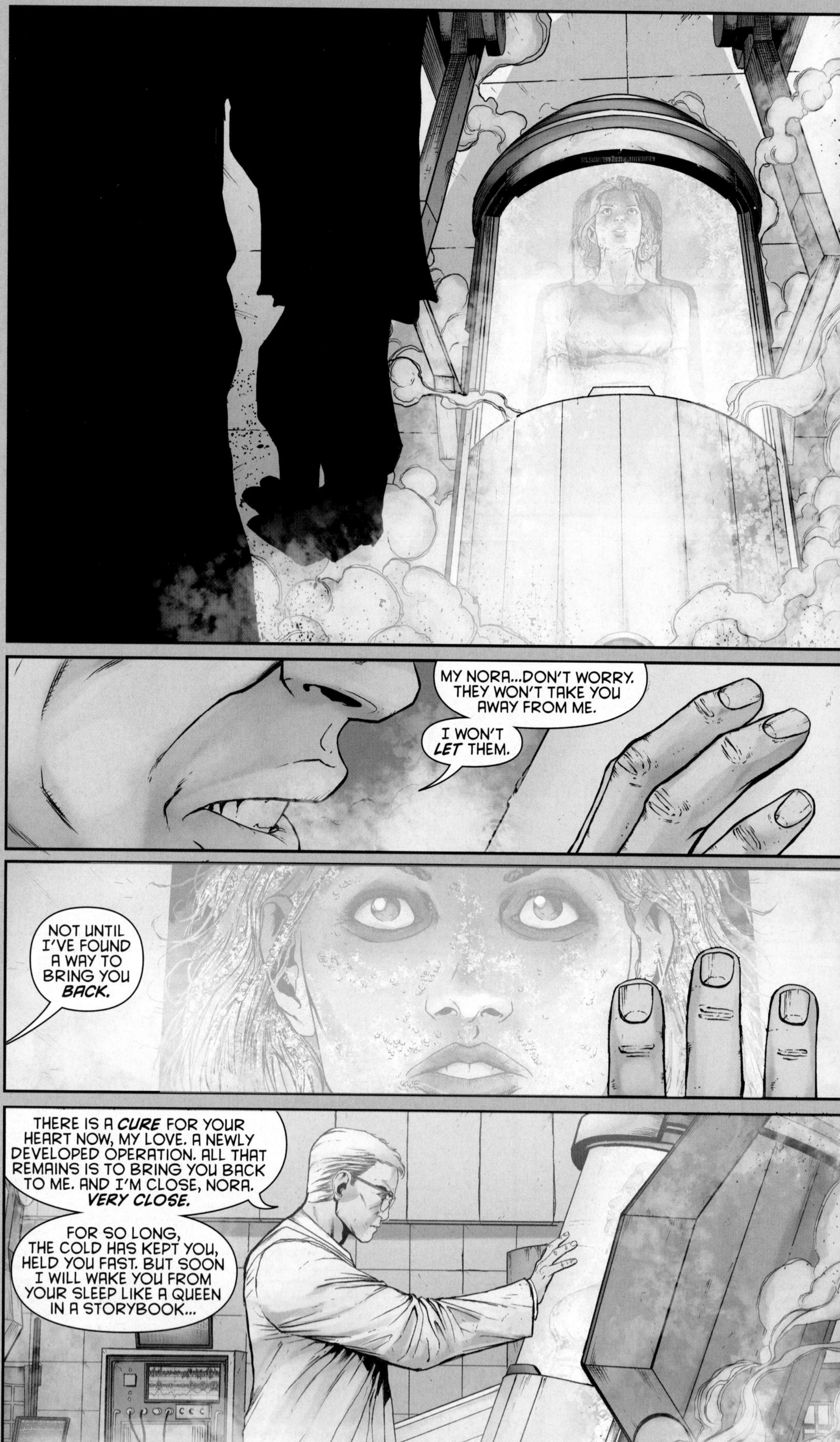
MY NORA...DON'T WORRY. THEY WON'T TAKE YOU AWAY FROM ME.
I WON'T *LET* THEM.
NOT UNTIL I'VE FOUND A WAY TO BRING YOU *BACK.*
THERE IS A *CURE* FOR YOUR HEART NOW, MY LOVE. A NEWLY DEVELOPED OPERATION. ALL THAT REMAINS IS TO BRING YOU BACK TO ME. AND I'M CLOSE, NORA. *VERY CLOSE.*
FOR SO LONG, THE COLD HAS KEPT YOU, HELD YOU FAST. BUT SOON I WILL WAKE YOU FROM YOUR SLEEP LIKE A QUEEN IN A STORYBOOK...

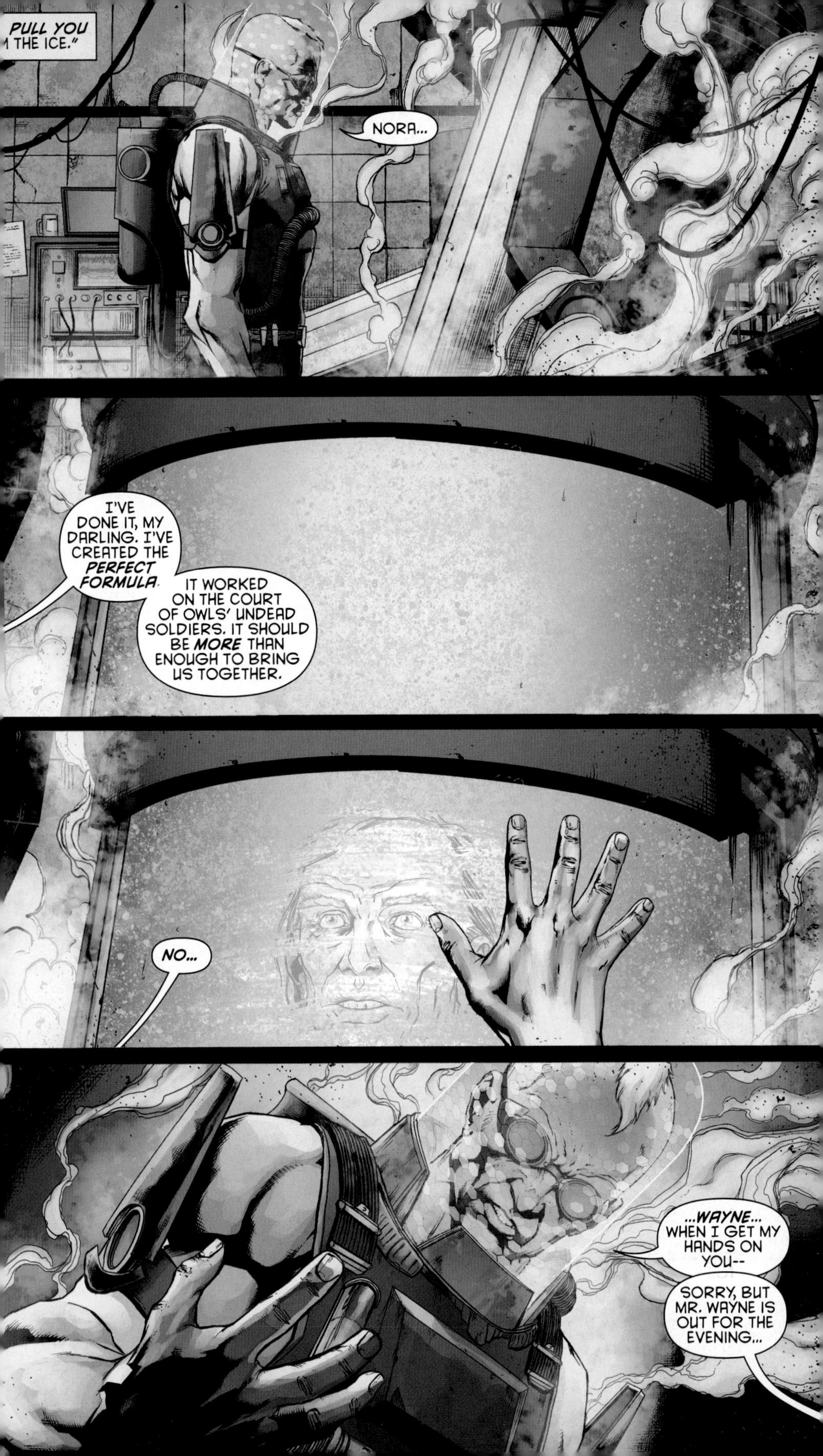
PULL YOU
THE ICE."
NORA...
I'VE DONE IT, MY DARLING. I'VE CREATED THE *PERFECT FORMULA*.
IT WORKED ON THE COURT OF OWLS' UNDEAD SOLDIERS. IT SHOULD BE *MORE* THAN ENOUGH TO BRING US TOGETHER.
NO...
...*WAYNE*... WHEN I GET MY HANDS ON YOU--
SORRY, BUT MR. WAYNE IS OUT FOR THE EVENING...

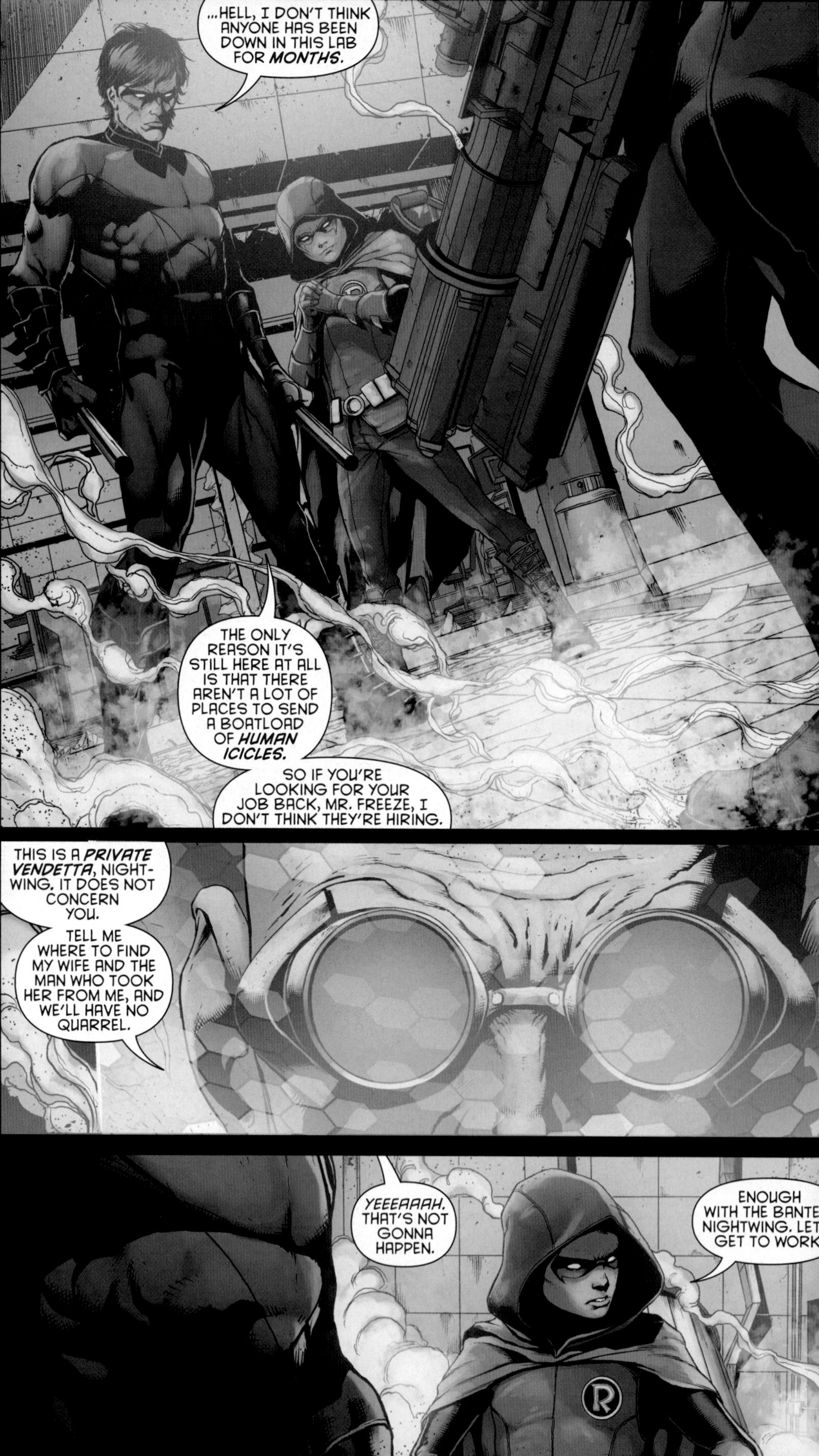

...HELL, I DON'T THINK ANYONE HAS BEEN DOWN IN THIS LAB FOR *MONTHS*.
THE ONLY REASON IT'S STILL HERE AT ALL IS THAT THERE AREN'T A LOT OF PLACES TO SEND A BOATLOAD OF *HUMAN ICICLES*.
SO IF YOU'RE LOOKING FOR YOUR JOB BACK, MR. FREEZE, I DON'T THINK THEY'RE HIRING.
THIS IS A *PRIVATE VENDETTA*, NIGHT-WING. IT DOES NOT CONCERN YOU.
TELL ME WHERE TO FIND MY WIFE AND THE MAN WHO TOOK HER FROM ME, AND WE'LL HAVE NO QUARREL.
YEEEAAAH. THAT'S NOT GONNA HAPPEN.
ENOUGH WITH THE BANTE NIGHTWING. LET GET TO WORK

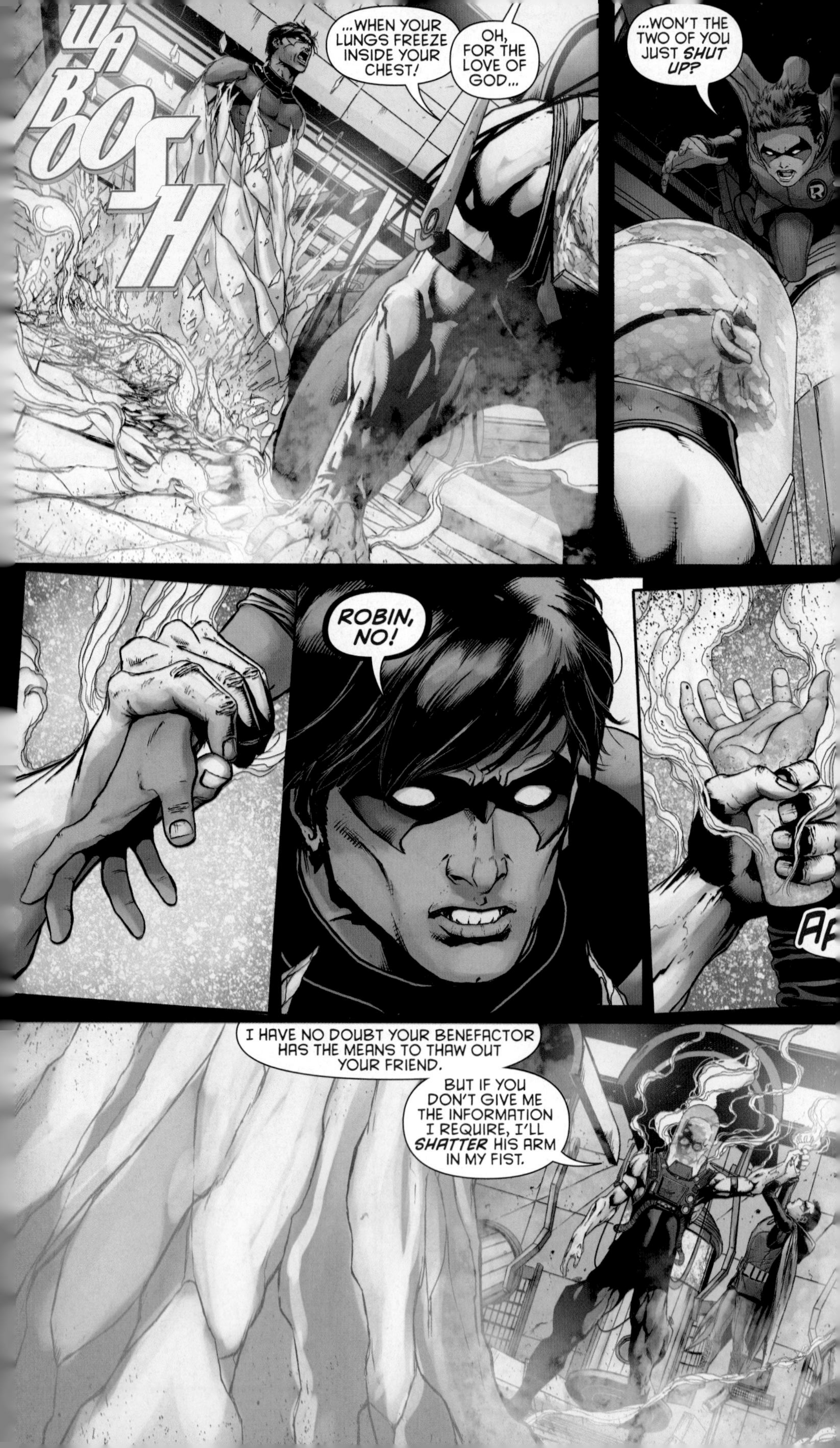
WABOOSH
...WHEN YOUR LUNGS FREEZE INSIDE YOUR CHEST!
OH, FOR THE LOVE OF GOD...
...WON'T THE TWO OF YOU JUST SHUT UP?
ROBIN, NO!
I HAVE NO DOUBT YOUR BENEFACTOR HAS THE MEANS TO THAW OUT YOUR FRIEND.
BUT IF YOU DON'T GIVE ME THE INFORMATION I REQUIRE, I'LL SHATTER HIS ARM IN MY FIST.

R, IT'S WAYNE. HE BOY GO.

WAYNE. SHOW YOUR FACE!

TAKE THE ELEVATOR UP TO THE PENTHOUSE, VICTOR. WE CAN STILL TALK THIS THROUGH. MAN TO MAN.

I GUARANTEE YOU, MR. WAYNE...

...TALKING IS NOT ON THE AGENDA.

WHAT ARE YOU DOING? GO AFTER HIM, YOU IDIOT!

CALM DOWN, ROBIN...BATMAN WANTS TO SETTLE THIS DIRECTLY. JUST THE TWO OF THEM.

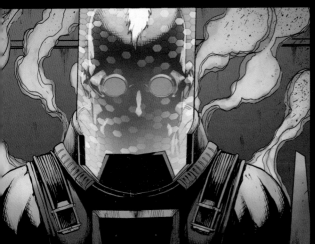

"IT'S TIME, NORA. TIME FOR US TO BE TOGETHER..."

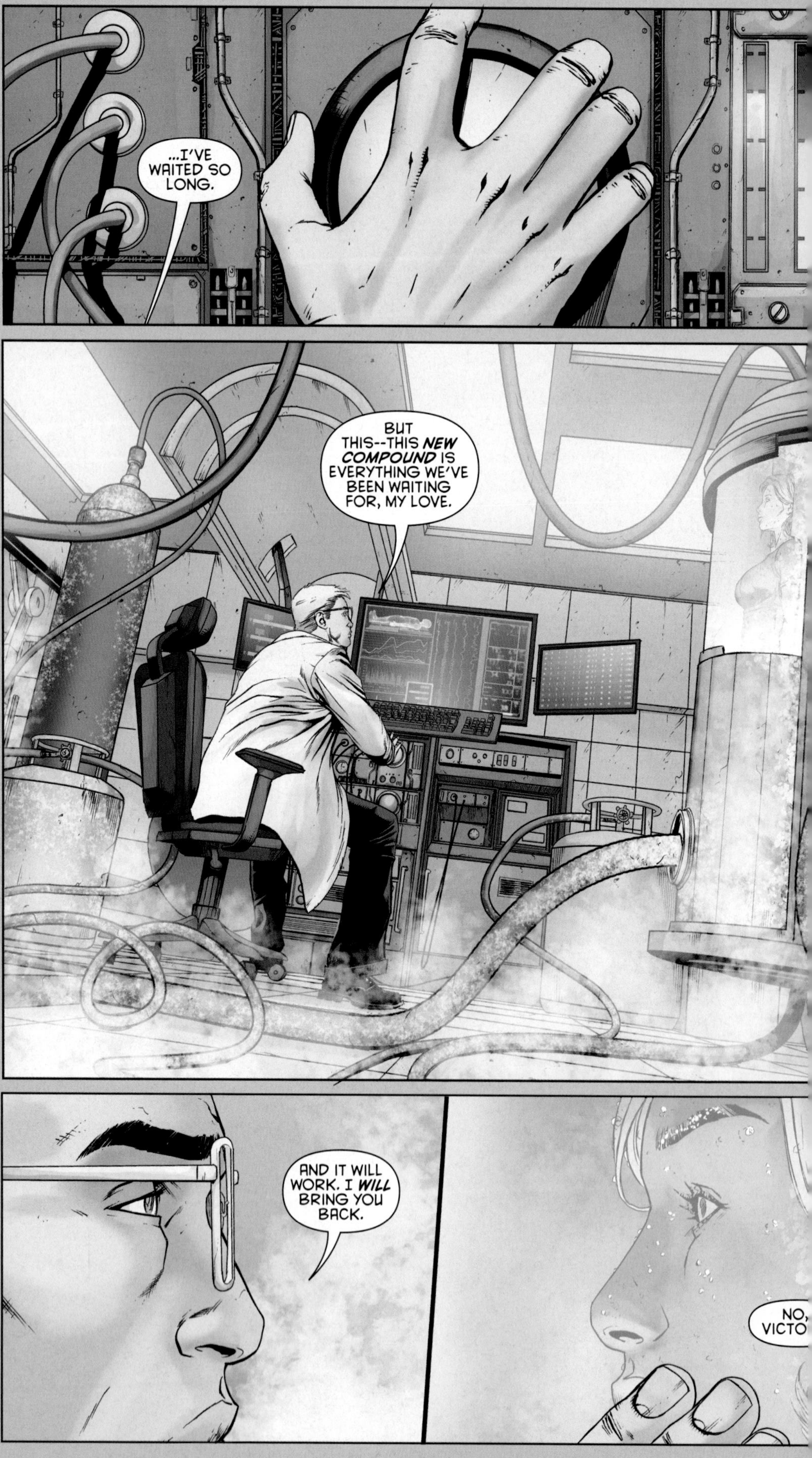
...I'VE WAITED SO LONG.
BUT THIS--THIS *NEW COMPOUND* IS EVERYTHING WE'VE BEEN WAITING FOR, MY LOVE.
AND IT WILL WORK. I *WILL* BRING YOU BACK.
NO,
VICTO

...YOU WON'T.

MR. WAYNE! YOU DON'T UNDERSTAND. THIS IS NORA, MY WIFE, AND--

I UNDERSTAND *PERFECTLY*, DR. FRIES. I SHUT THIS PROJECT DOWN MONTHS AGO, AND YET YOU'VE CONTINUED TO WORK ON YOUR OWN *PRIVATE EXPERIMENTS*.

YOUR METHODS HERE HAVEN'T BEEN REVIEWED OR TESTED, AND YOU'RE ABOUT TO ADMINISTER THEM ON A *PERSON* WHO HAS NO MEANS OF CONSENT.

I *CAN'T* ALLOW YOU TO CONTINUE PLAYING MAD SCIENTIST WHILE YOU NEGLECT THE RESEARCH YOU WERE HIRED TO DO.

PLEASE, YOU MUST UNDER-STAND. MY NORA...SHE'S THE ONLY WOMAN I HAVE EVER LOVED.

AND HER CONDITION, THERE ARE SURGERIES NOW... PROCEDURES DEVELOPED SINCE SHE WAS FROZEN THAT COULD REPAIR HER HEART.

IT'S ALL FOR *HER*, MR. WAYNE. *PLEASE* LET ME CONTINUE.

NO, VICTOR. I'VE CALLED THE AUTHORITIES.

BUT SHE'S...NO. YOU *CAN'T!* YOU CAN'T TAKE HER FROM ME!

I CAN, AND I *WILL*. SHE'S STAYING HERE. AND YOU'RE GOING.

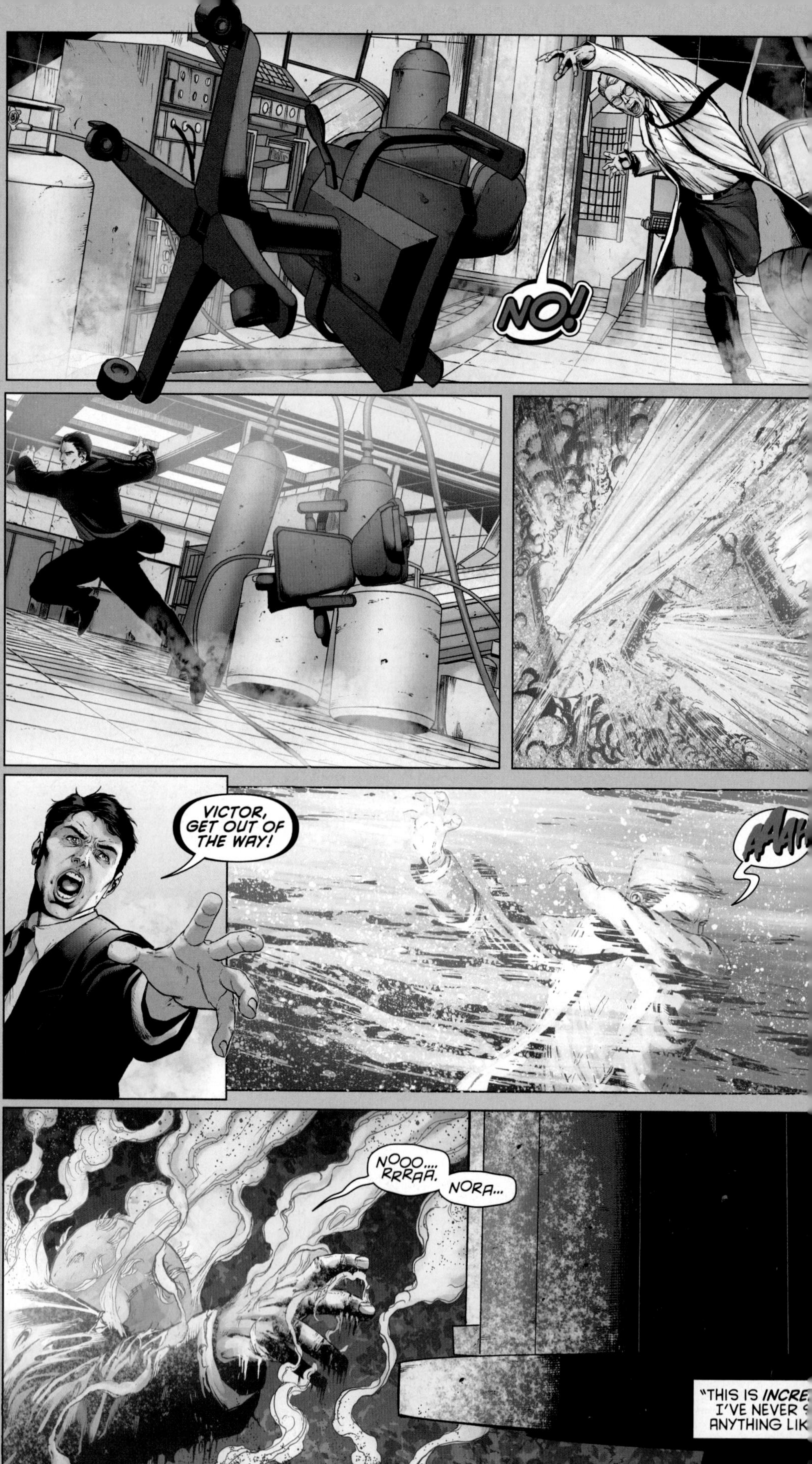
NO!
VICTOR, GET OUT OF THE WAY!
NOOO.... RRRAA.
NORA...
"THIS IS INCRE
I'VE NEVER
ANYTHING LIK

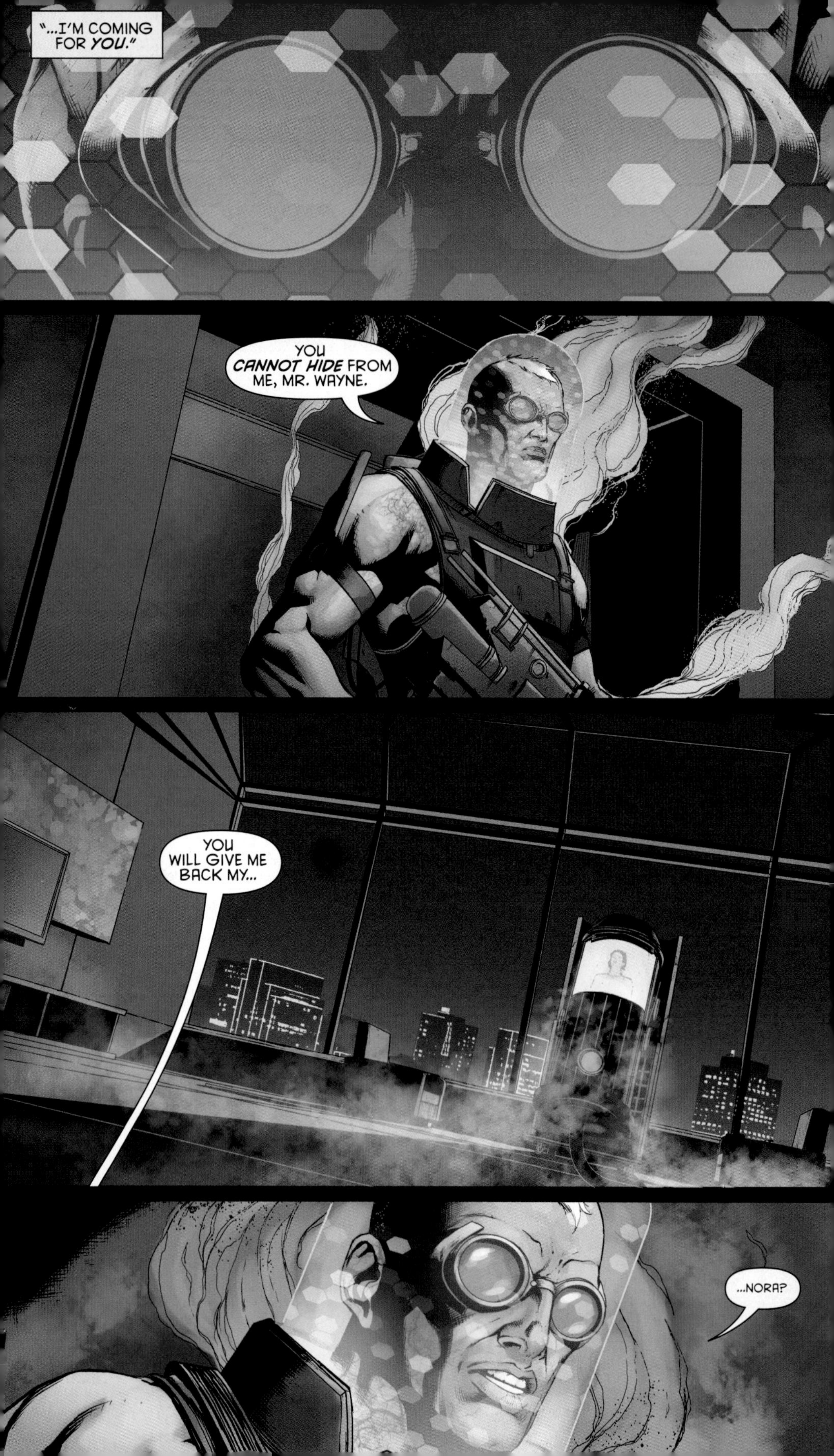
"...I'M COMING FOR *YOU*."
YOU *CANNOT HIDE* FROM ME, MR. WAYNE.
YOU WILL GIVE ME BACK MY...
...NORA?

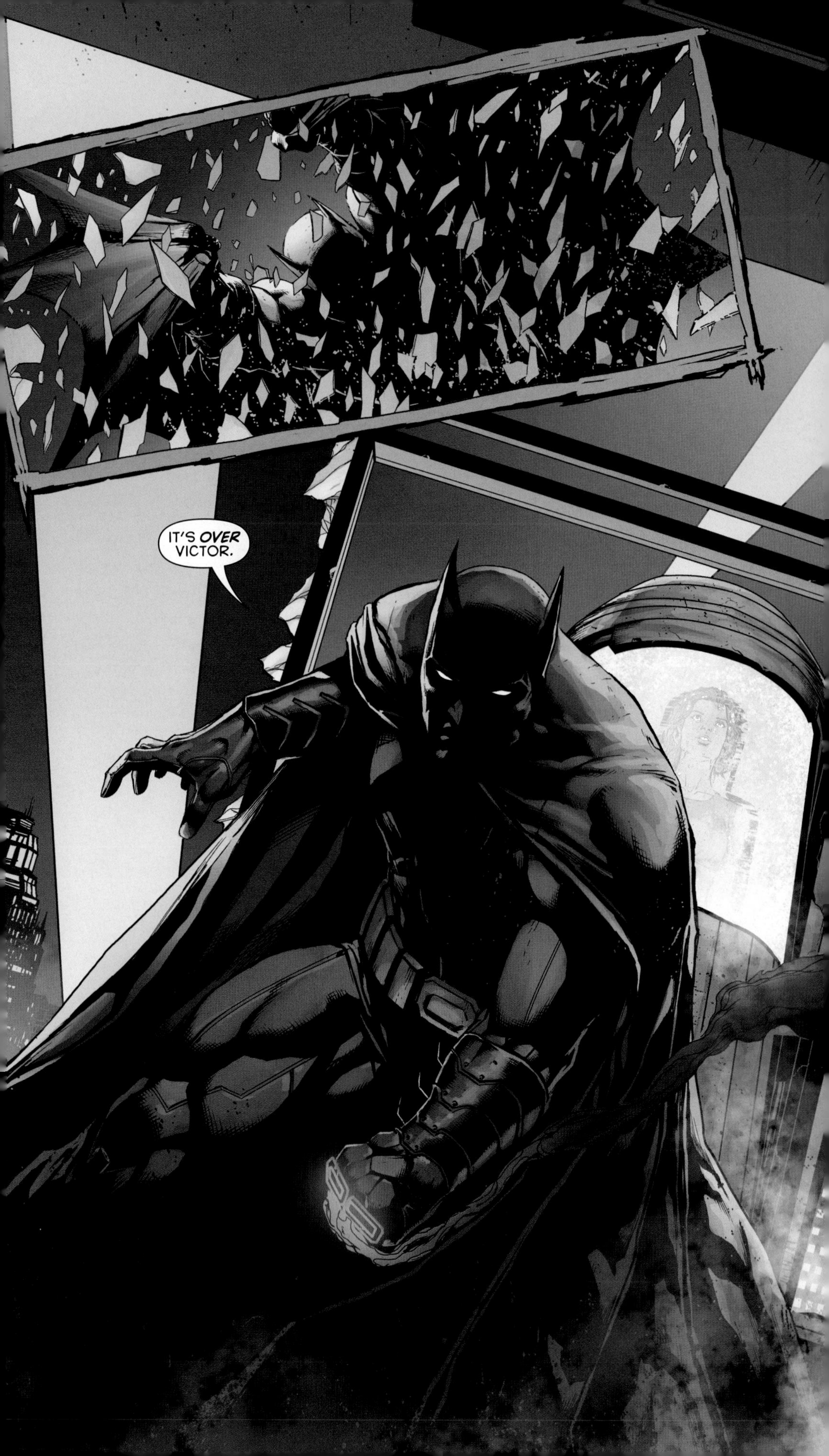
IT'S *OVER* VICTOR.

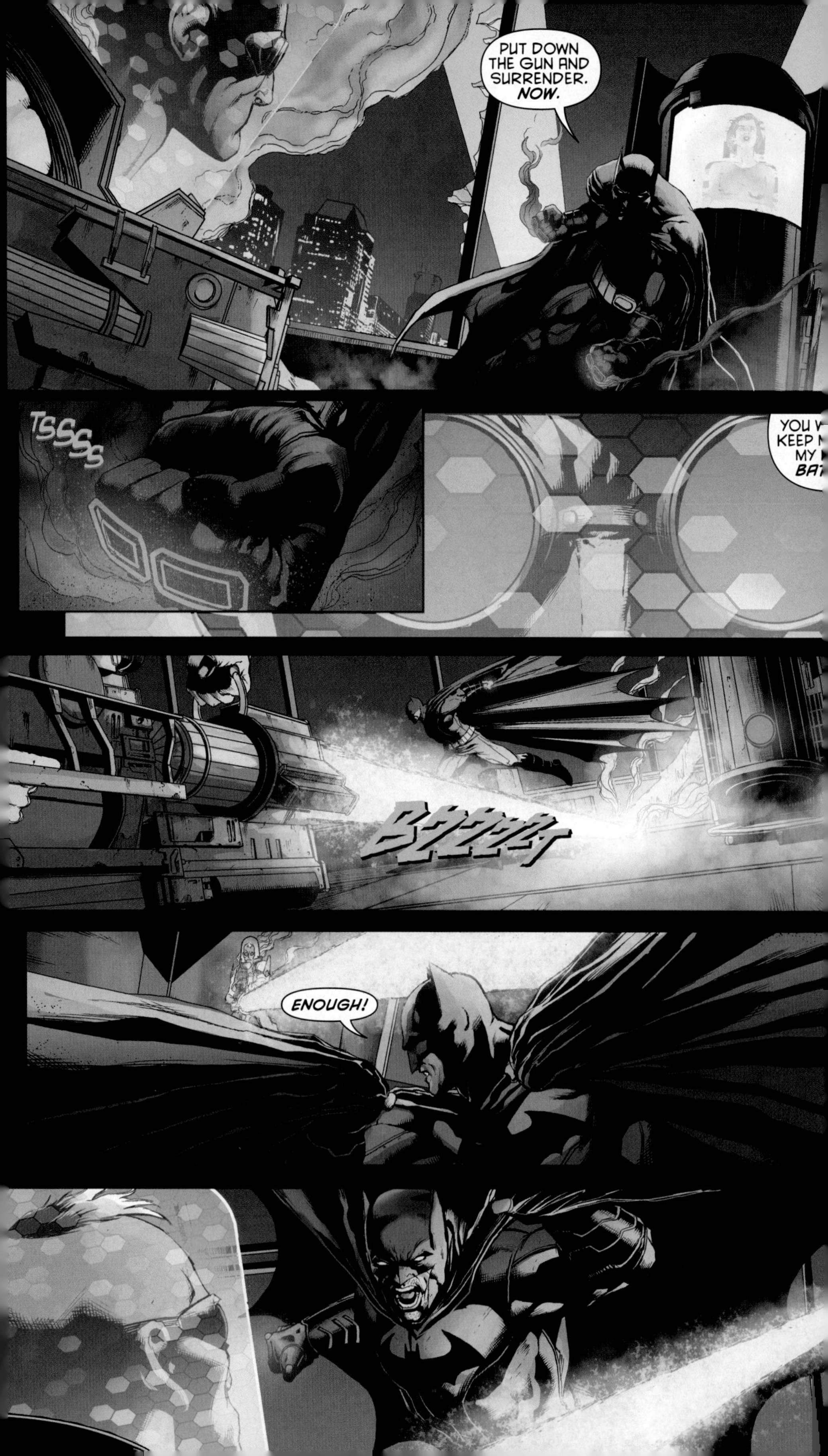
PUT DOWN THE GUN AND SURRENDER. NOW.
TSSSSS
ENOUGH!

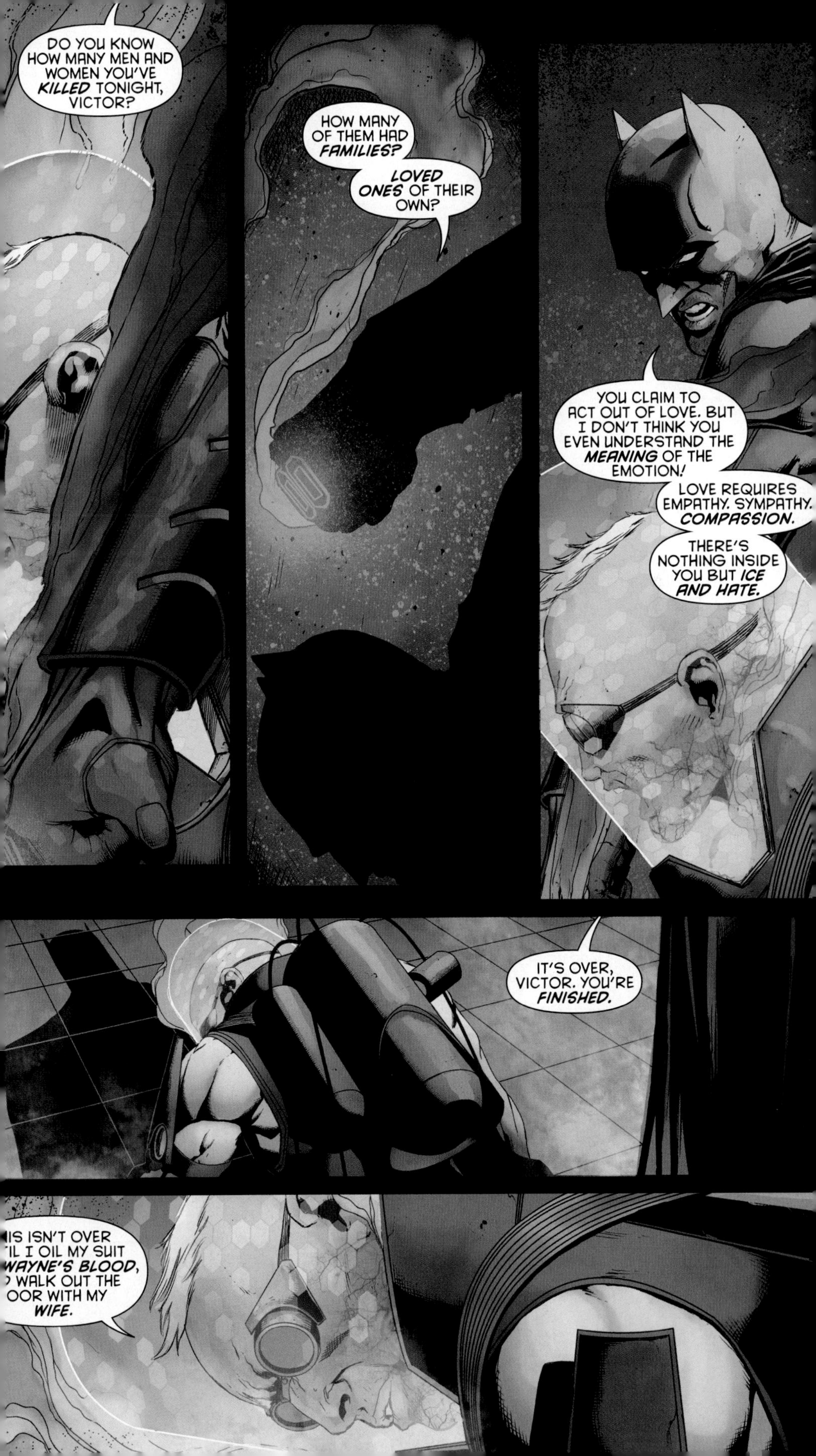
DO YOU KNOW HOW MANY MEN AND WOMEN YOU'VE *KILLED* TONIGHT, VICTOR?
HOW MANY OF THEM HAD *FAMILIES?*
LOVED ONES OF THEIR OWN?
YOU CLAIM TO ACT OUT OF LOVE. BUT I DON'T THINK YOU EVEN UNDERSTAND THE *MEANING* OF THE EMOTION!
LOVE REQUIRES EMPATHY. SYMPATHY. *COMPASSION.*
THERE'S NOTHING INSIDE YOU BUT *ICE AND HATE.*
IT'S OVER, VICTOR. YOU'RE *FINISHED.*
IS ISN'T OVER
IL I OIL MY SUIT
WAYNE'S BLOOD,
WALK OUT THE
OOR WITH MY
WIFE.

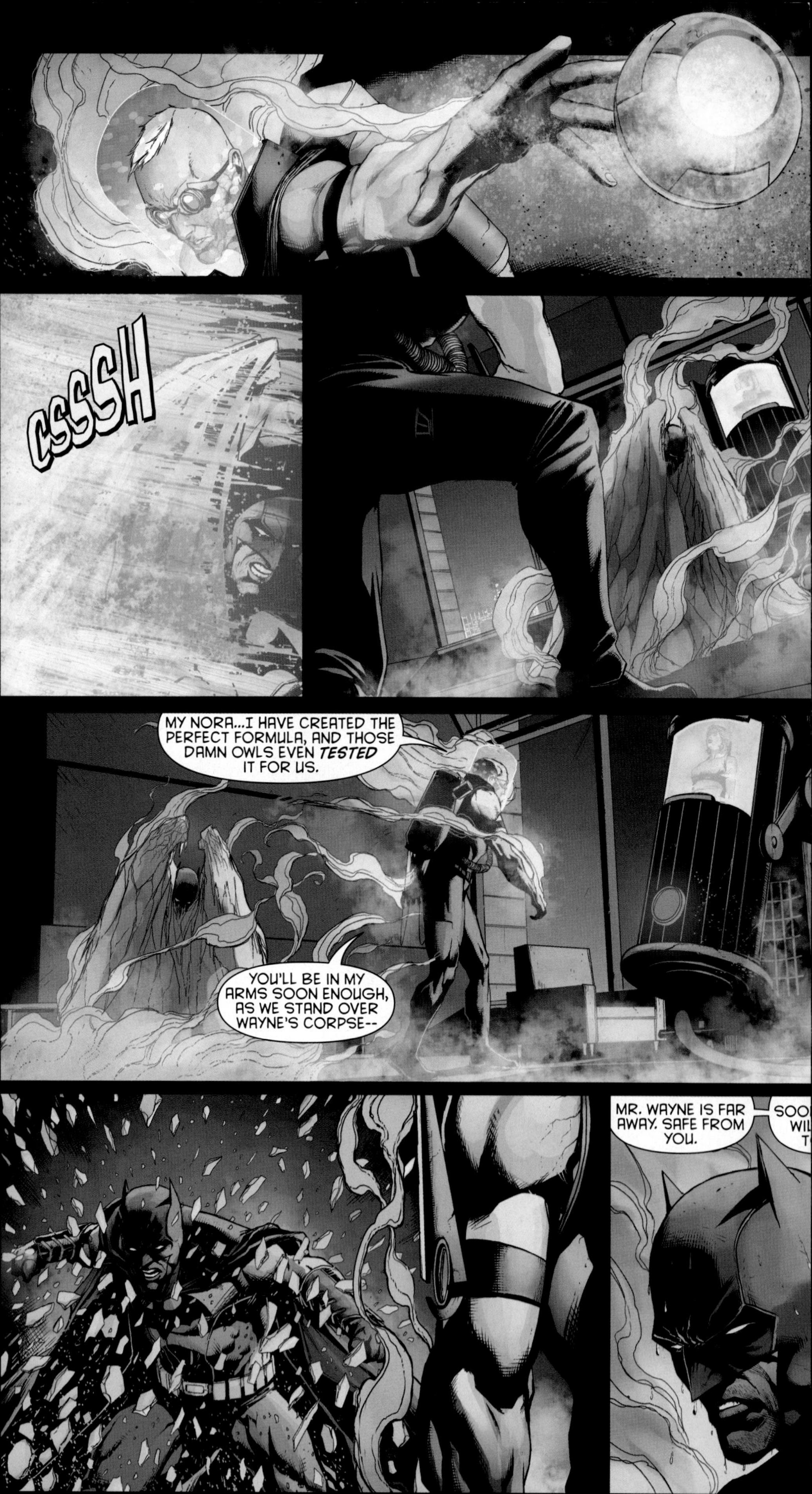
CSSSH
MY NORA...I HAVE CREATED THE PERFECT FORMULA, AND THOSE DAMN OWLS EVEN *TESTED* IT FOR US.
YOU'LL BE IN MY ARMS SOON ENOUGH, AS WE STAND OVER WAYNE'S CORPSE--
MR. WAYNE IS FAR AWAY. SAFE FROM YOU.

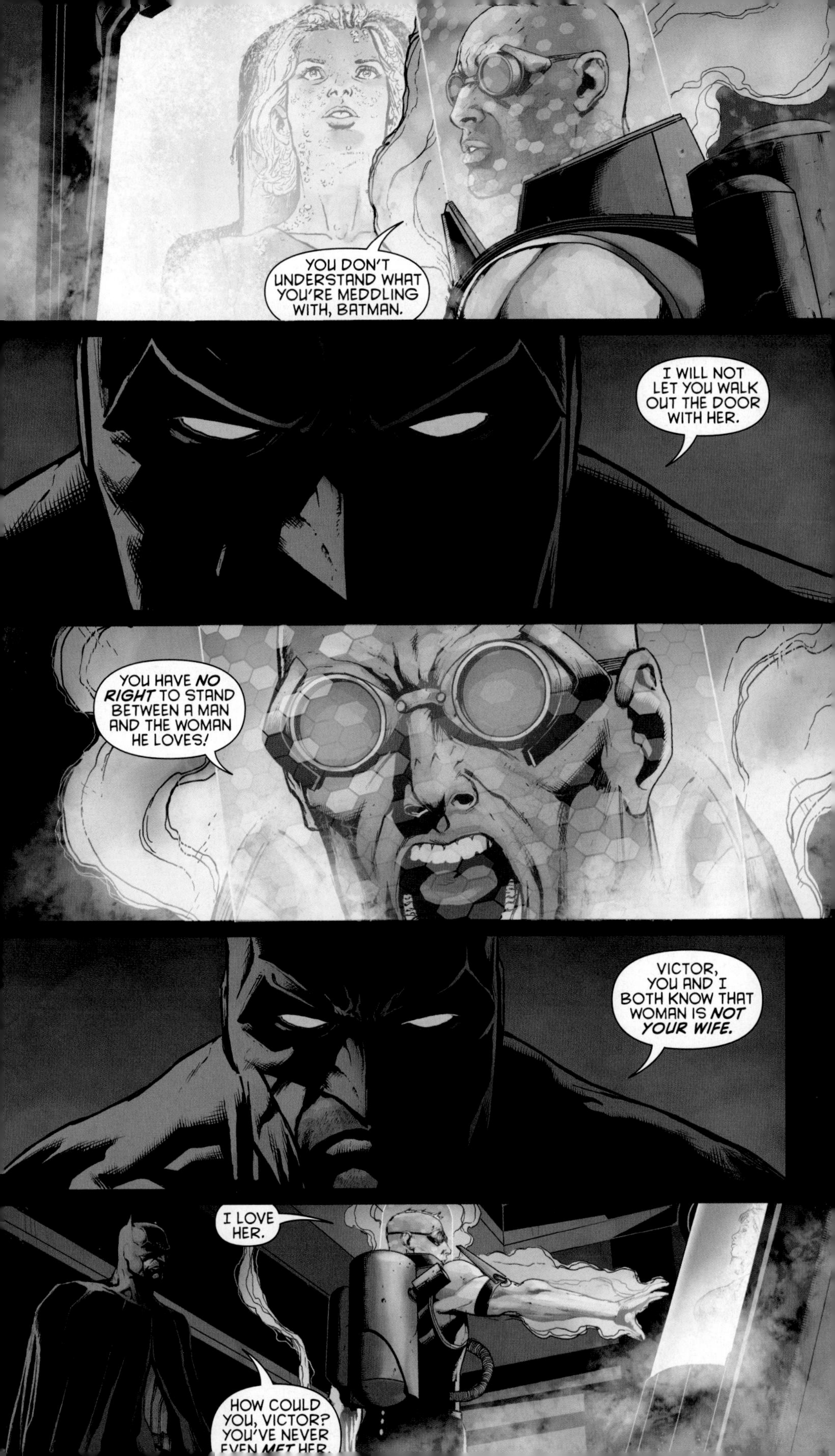
YOU DON'T UNDERSTAND WHAT YOU'RE MEDDLING WITH, BATMAN.
I WILL NOT LET YOU WALK OUT THE DOOR WITH HER.
YOU HAVE ***NO RIGHT*** TO STAND BETWEEN A MAN AND THE WOMAN HE LOVES!
VICTOR, YOU AND I BOTH KNOW THAT WOMAN IS ***NOT YOUR WIFE.***
I LOVE HER.
HOW COULD YOU, VICTOR? YOU'VE NEVER EVEN ***MET*** HER.

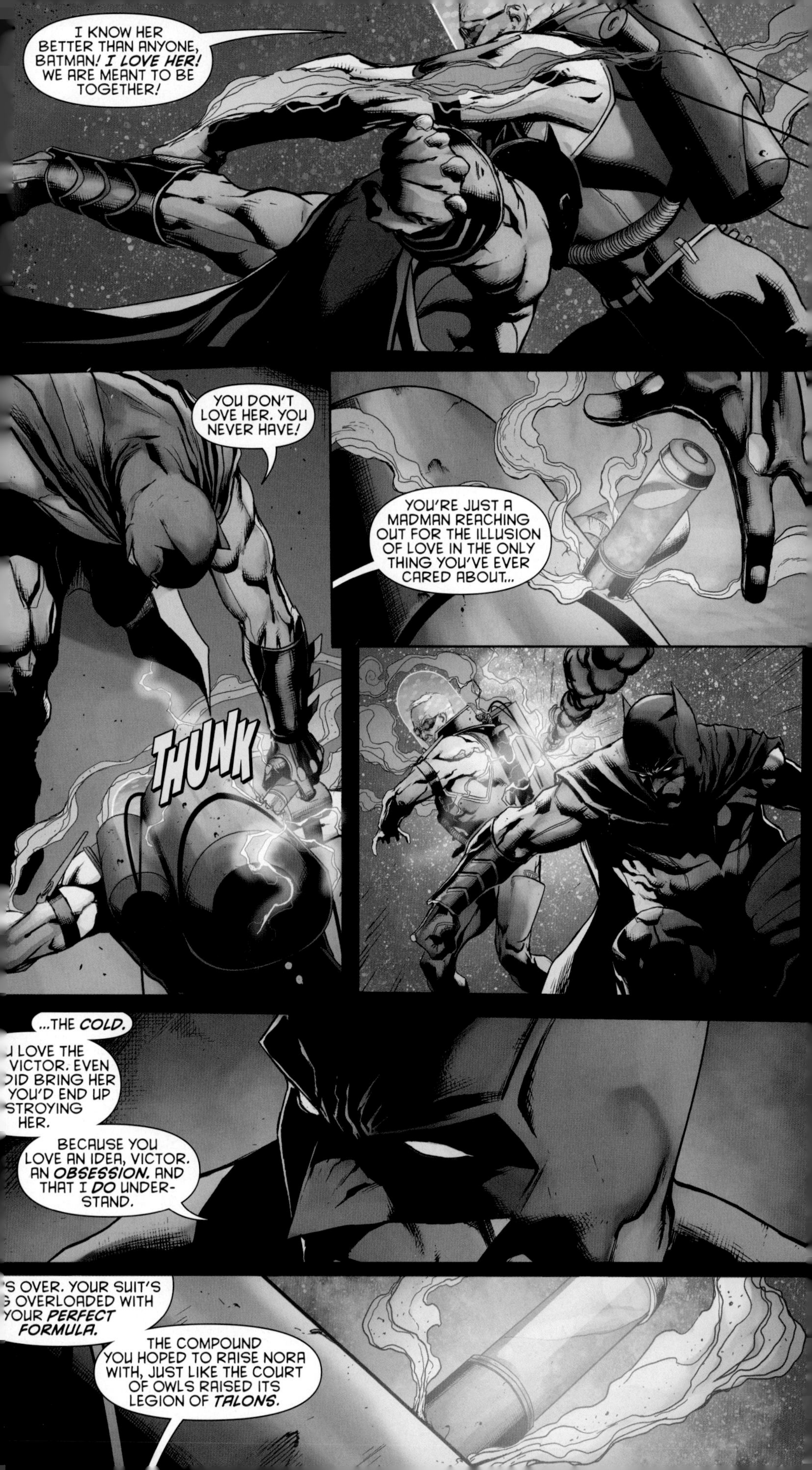
I KNOW HER BETTER THAN ANYONE, BATMAN! I LOVE HER! WE ARE MEANT TO BE TOGETHER!
YOU DON'T LOVE HER. YOU NEVER HAVE!
YOU'RE JUST A MADMAN REACHING OUT FOR THE ILLUSION OF LOVE IN THE ONLY THING YOU'VE EVER CARED ABOUT...
THUNK
...THE COLD.
U LOVE THE VICTOR. EVEN DID BRING HER YOU'D END UP STROYING HER.
BECAUSE YOU LOVE AN IDEA, VICTOR. AN OBSESSION. AND THAT I DO UNDER-STAND.
S OVER. YOUR SUIT'S G OVERLOADED WITH YOUR PERFECT FORMULA.
THE COMPOUND YOU HOPED TO RAISE NORA WITH, JUST LIKE THE COURT OF OWLS RAISED ITS LEGION OF TALONS.

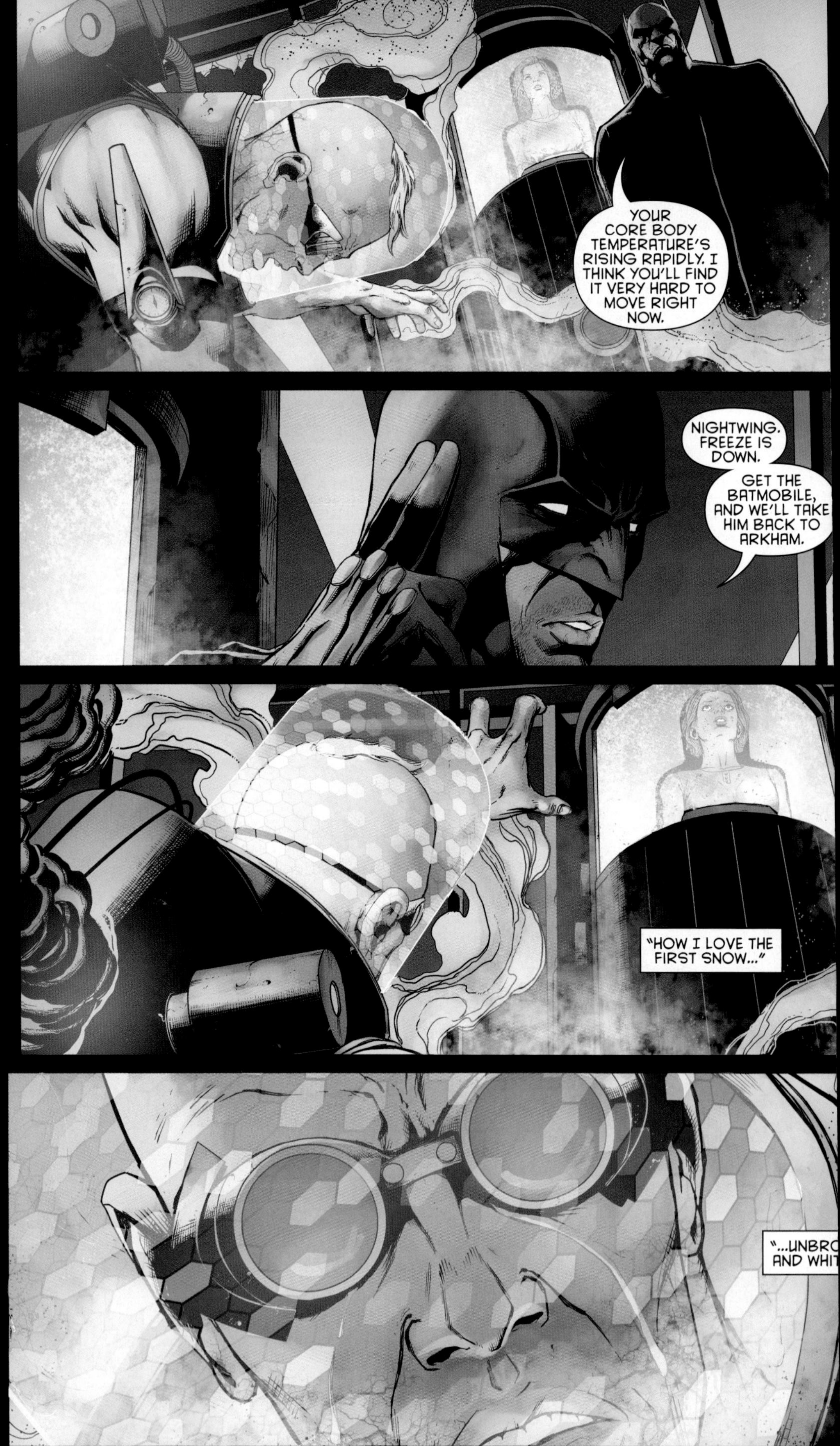
YOUR CORE BODY TEMPERATURE'S RISING RAPIDLY. I THINK YOU'LL FIND IT VERY HARD TO MOVE RIGHT NOW.
NIGHTWING. FREEZE IS DOWN.
GET THE BATMOBILE, AND WE'LL TAKE HIM BACK TO ARKHAM.
"HOW I LOVE THE FIRST SNOW..."

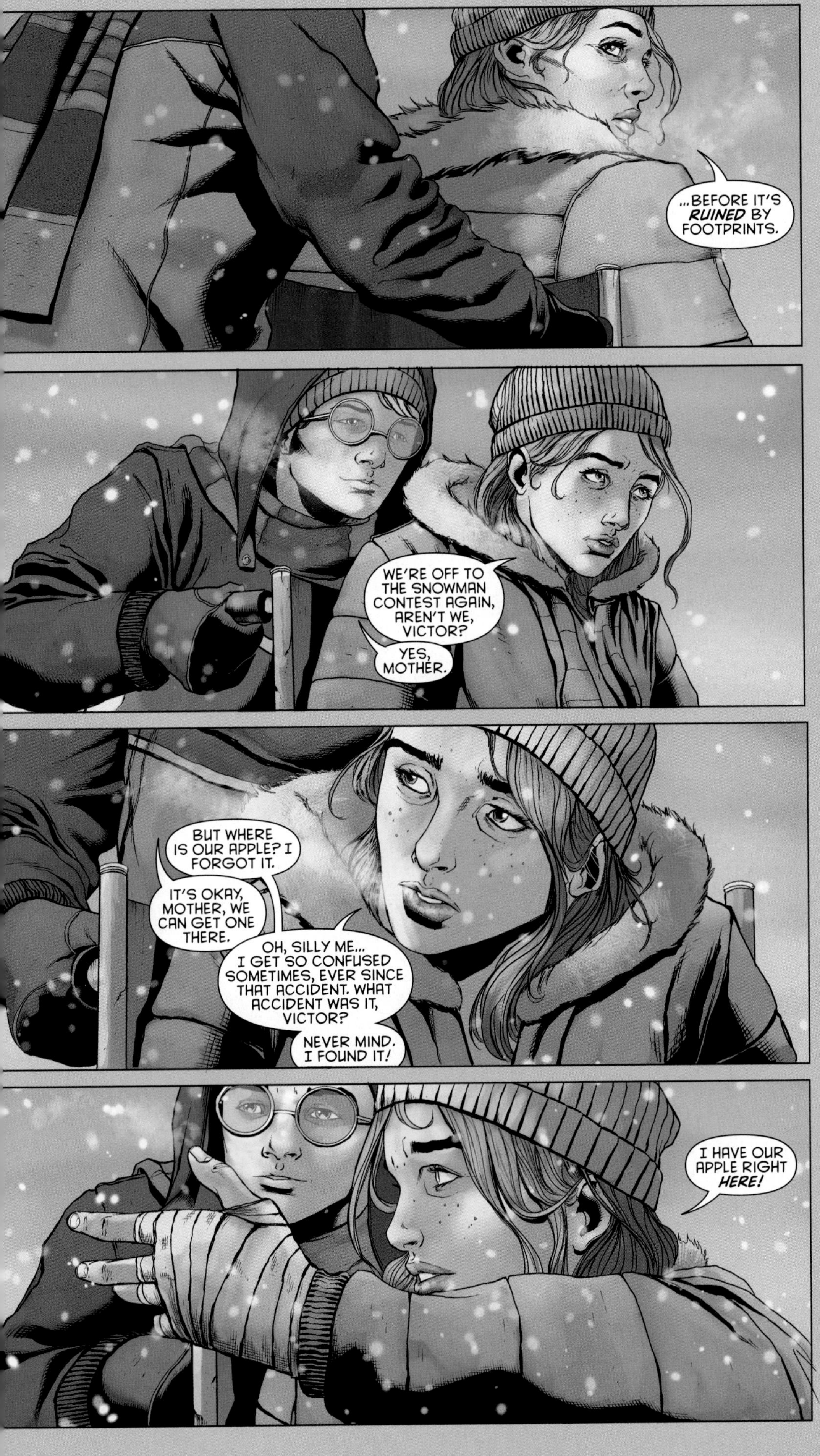
...BEFORE IT'S *RUINED* BY FOOTPRINTS.
WE'RE OFF TO THE SNOWMAN CONTEST AGAIN, AREN'T WE, VICTOR?
YES, MOTHER.
BUT WHERE IS OUR APPLE? I FORGOT IT.
IT'S OKAY, MOTHER, WE CAN GET ONE THERE.
OH, SILLY ME... I GET SO CONFUSED SOMETIMES, EVER SINCE THAT ACCIDENT. WHAT ACCIDENT WAS IT, VICTOR?
NEVER MIND. I FOUND IT!
I HAVE OUR APPLE RIGHT *HERE!*

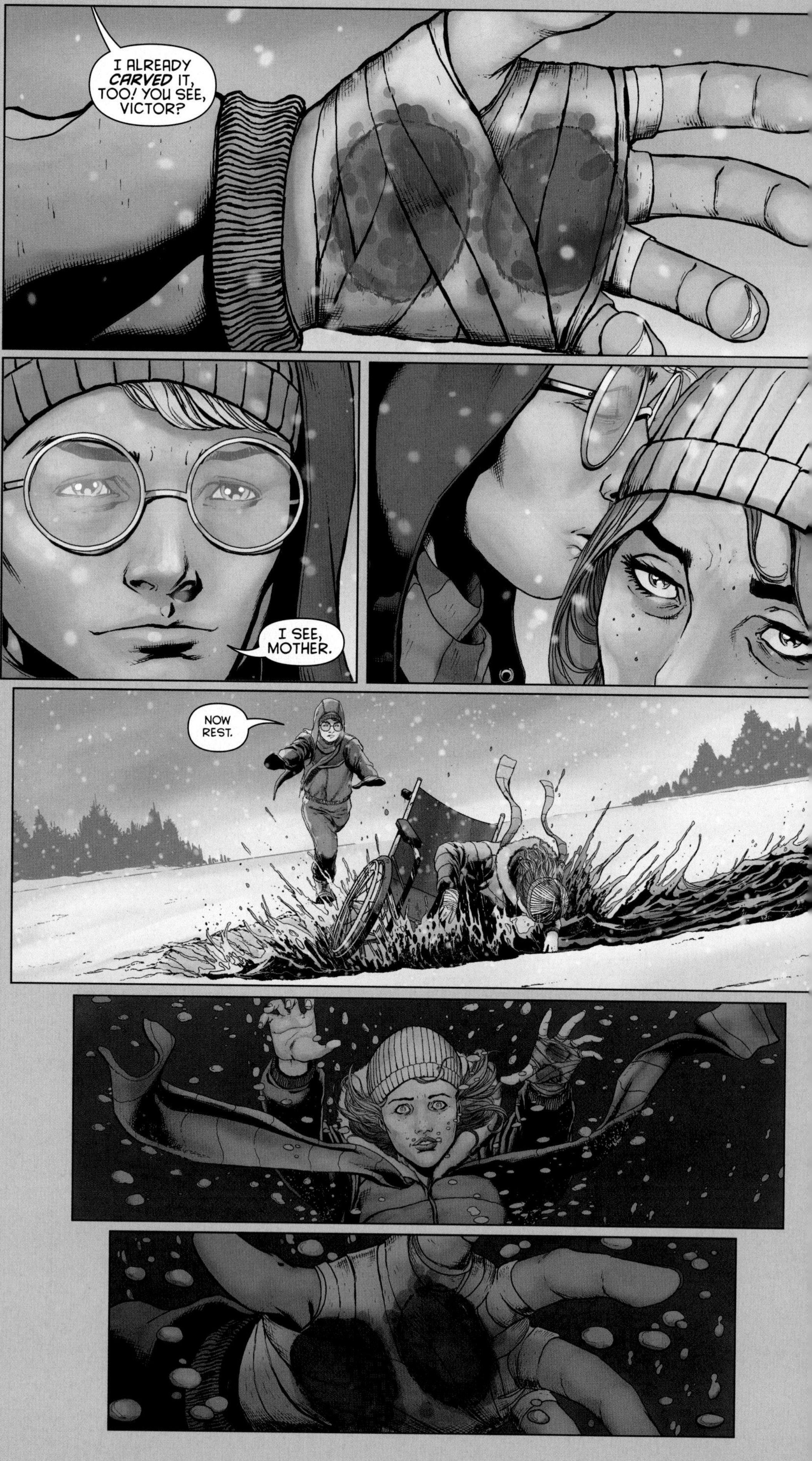
I ALREADY CARVED IT, TOO! YOU SEE, VICTOR?
I SEE, MOTHER.
NOW REST.

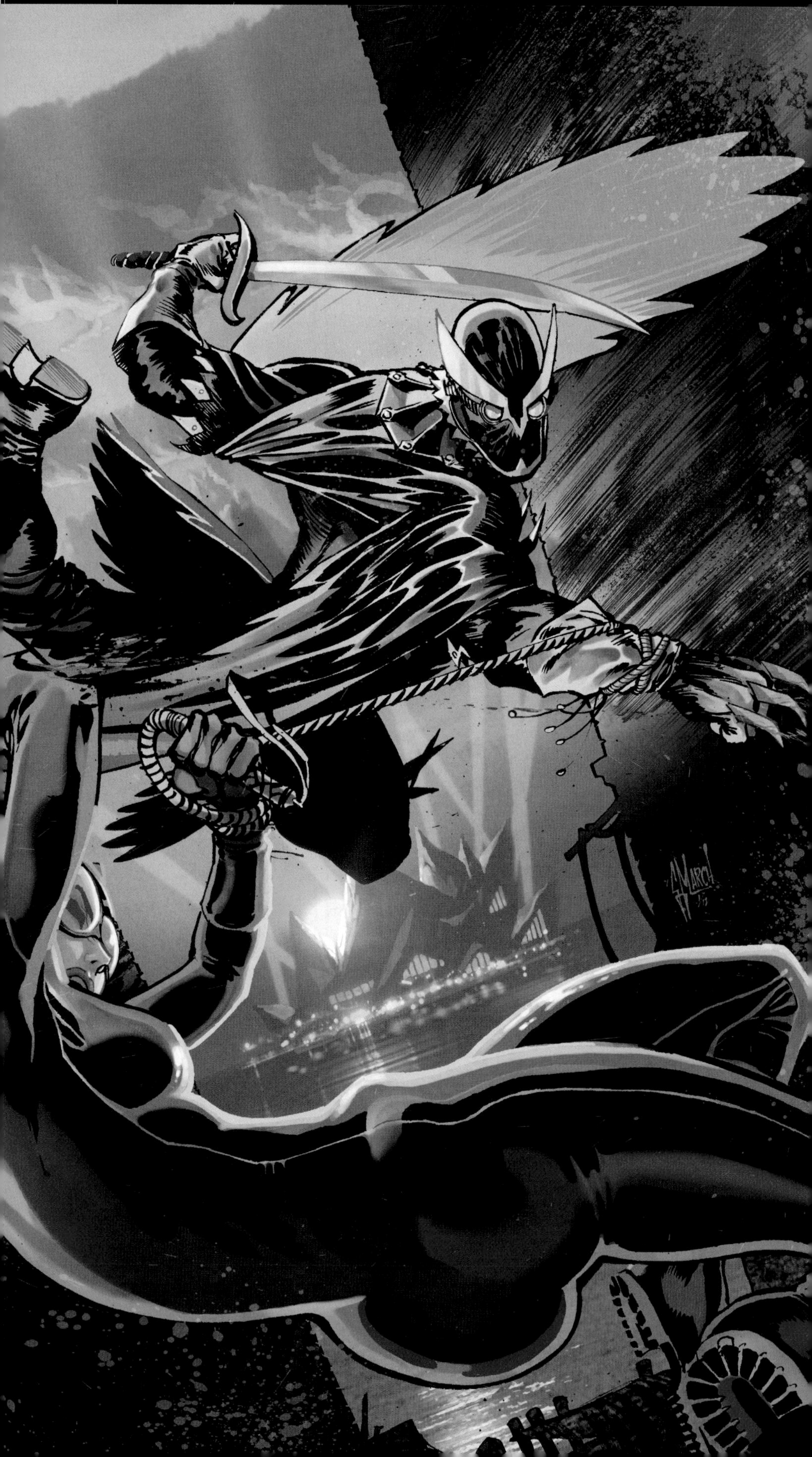

"HE HAS FAILED *THE COURT OF OWLS*."

"HOW SO? HAS *THE TALON* NOT COMPLETED HIS TASK?"

"NO. HE FOUND HIS PREY..."

"...BUT THERE WERE COMPLICATIONS."

"IS HIS QUARRY *DEAD* OR DOES HE STILL *BREATHE*?"

"NO. HIS CURSED SOUL HAS LEFT THIS EARTH.

"*BUT*, AS THE TALE HAS BEEN TOLD, THE T FOUND THE MAN DRESSING FOR BED, THE TARGET BEGGED FOR MERCY.

"THE TALON FELT IT 'LACKED HONOR' TO CUT HIM DOWN IN THIS MANNER. *SO*, HE ARMED THIS WHELP WITH A *DAGGER*, AND INSTRUCTED HIM TO BATTLE FOR HIS LIFE.

"BUT THE C SIMPLY RAN THE STRE BELLOW

"*AND TALON SEEN

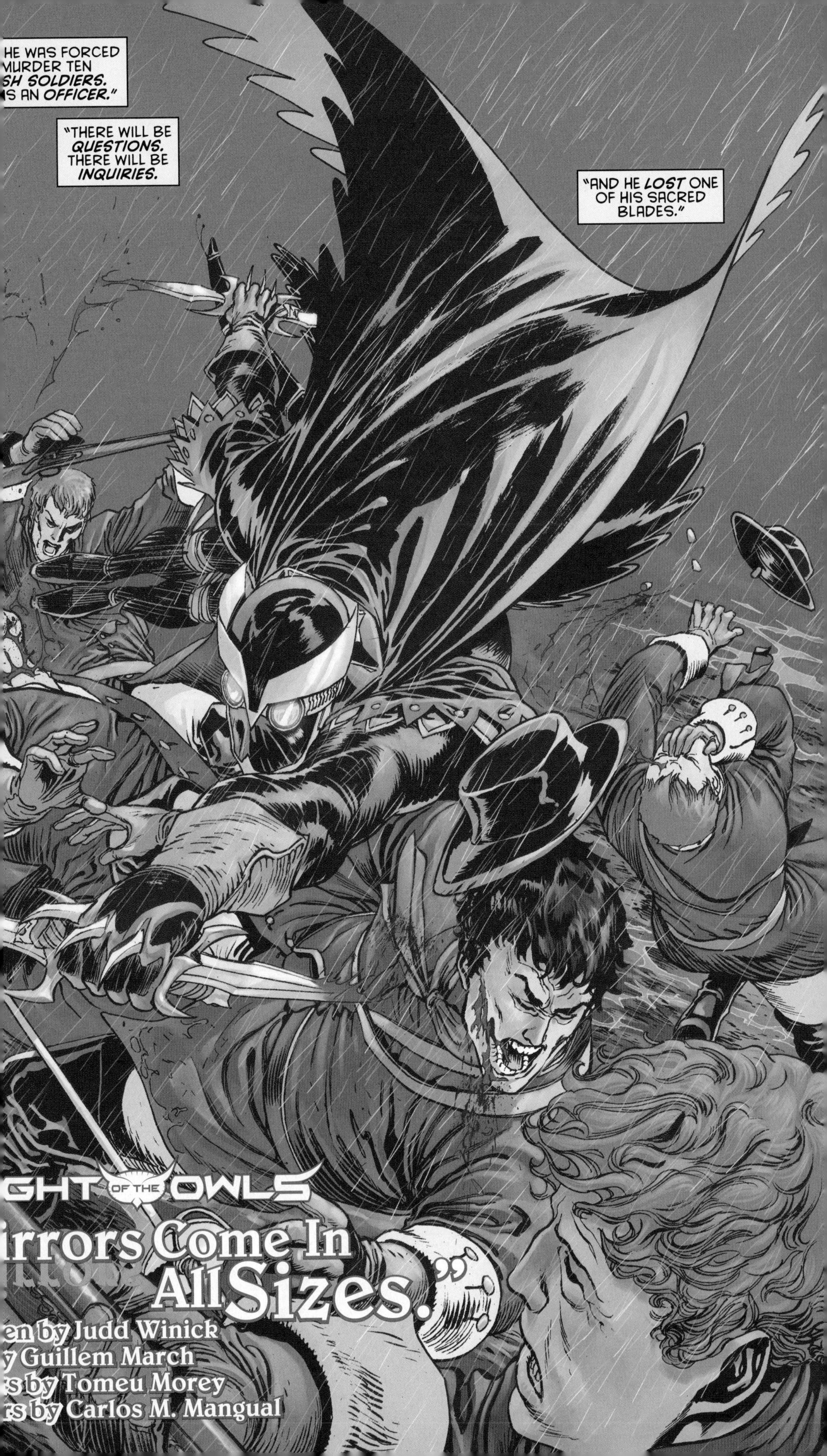
HE WAS FORCED
MURDER TEN
SH SOLDIERS.
S AN OFFICER."
"THERE WILL BE QUESTIONS. THERE WILL BE INQUIRIES.
"AND HE LOST ONE OF HIS SACRED BLADES."
GHT OF THE OWLS
irrors Come In All Sizes."
en by Judd Winick
y Guillem March
s by Tomeu Morey
s by Carlos M. Mangual

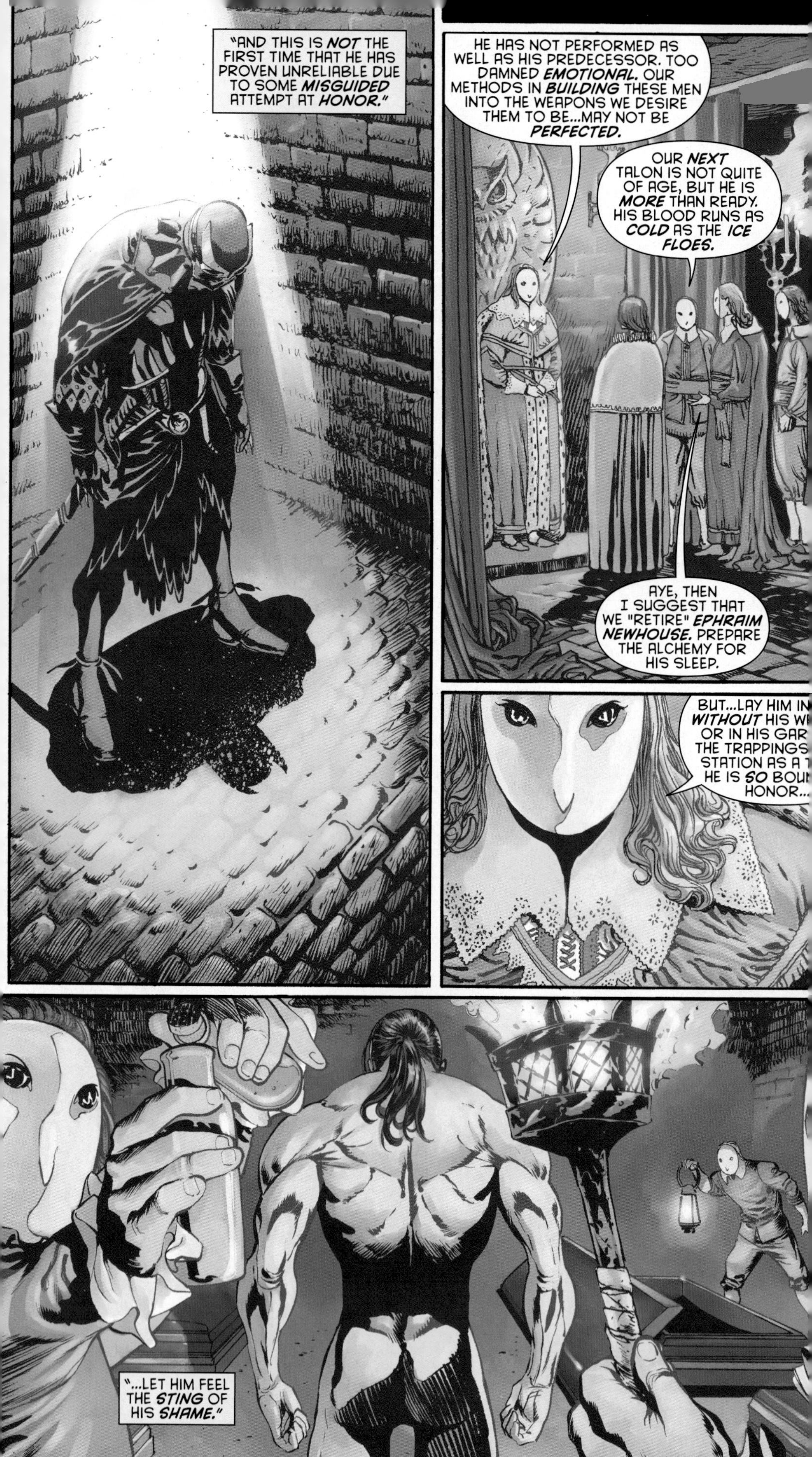
"AND THIS IS NOT THE FIRST TIME THAT HE HAS PROVEN UNRELIABLE DUE TO SOME MISGUIDED ATTEMPT AT HONOR."
HE HAS NOT PERFORMED AS WELL AS HIS PREDECESSOR. TOO DAMNED EMOTIONAL. OUR METHODS IN BUILDING THESE MEN INTO THE WEAPONS WE DESIRE THEM TO BE...MAY NOT BE PERFECTED.
OUR NEXT TALON IS NOT QUITE OF AGE, BUT HE IS MORE THAN READY. HIS BLOOD RUNS AS COLD AS THE ICE FLOES.
AYE, THEN I SUGGEST THAT WE "RETIRE" EPHRAIM NEWHOUSE. PREPARE THE ALCHEMY FOR HIS SLEEP.
BUT...LAY HIM IN WITHOUT HIS W OR IN HIS GAR THE TRAPPINGS STATION AS A HE IS SO BOU HONOR...
"...LET HIM FEEL THE STING OF HIS SHAME."

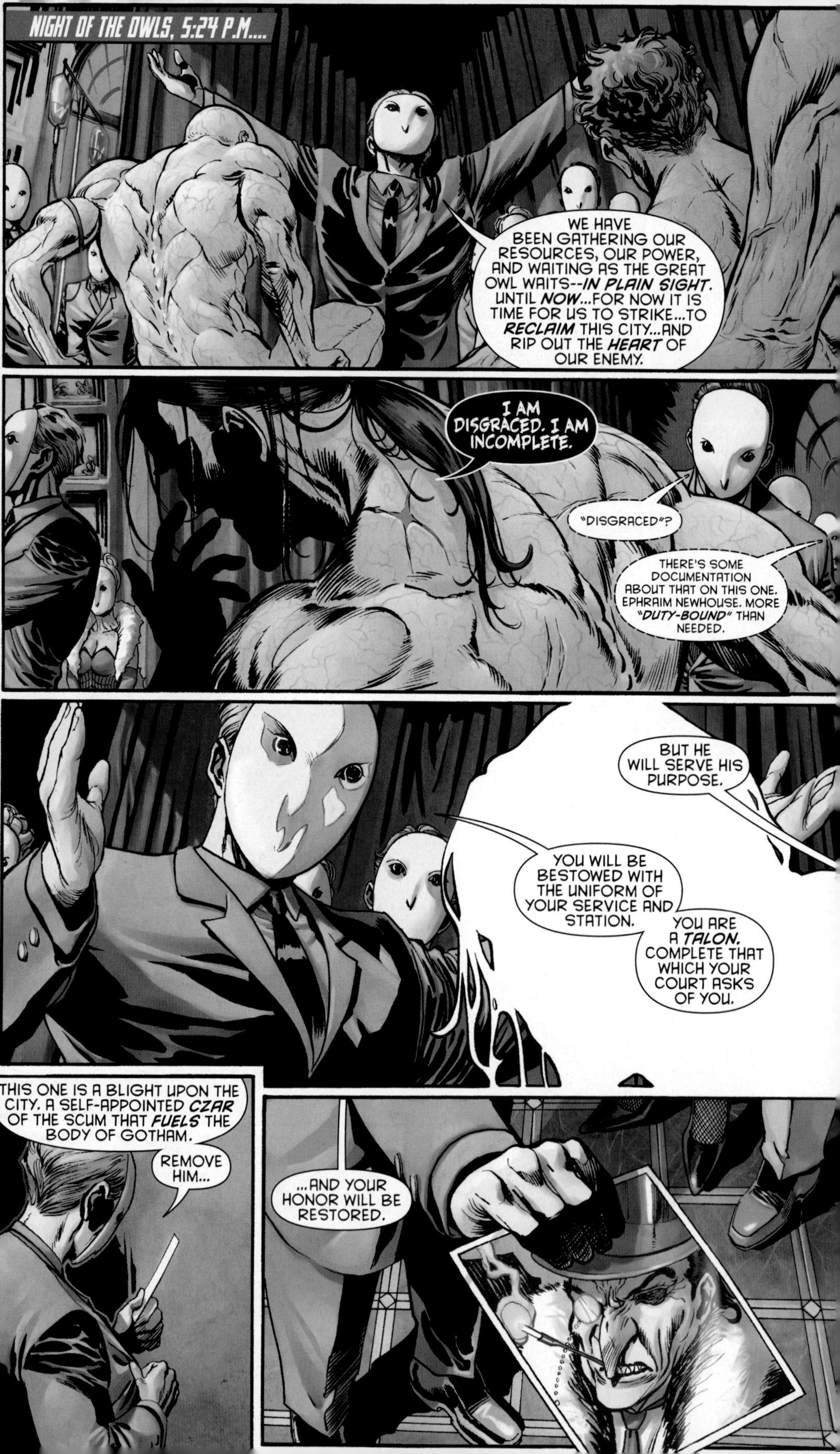
NIGHT OF THE OWLS, 5:24 P.M....
WE HAVE BEEN GATHERING OUR RESOURCES, OUR POWER, AND WAITING AS THE GREAT OWL WAITS--IN PLAIN SIGHT. UNTIL NOW...FOR NOW IT IS TIME FOR US TO STRIKE...TO RECLAIM THIS CITY...AND RIP OUT THE HEART OF OUR ENEMY.
I AM DISGRACED. I AM INCOMPLETE.
"DISGRACED"?
THERE'S SOME DOCUMENTATION ABOUT THAT ON THIS ONE. EPHRAIM NEWHOUSE. MORE "DUTY-BOUND" THAN NEEDED.
BUT HE WILL SERVE HIS PURPOSE.
YOU WILL BE BESTOWED WITH THE UNIFORM OF YOUR SERVICE AND STATION.
YOU ARE A TALON. COMPLETE THAT WHICH YOUR COURT ASKS OF YOU.
THIS ONE IS A BLIGHT UPON THE CITY. A SELF-APPOINTED CZAR OF THE SCUM THAT FUELS THE BODY OF GOTHAM.
REMOVE HIM...
...AND YOUR HONOR WILL BE RESTORED.

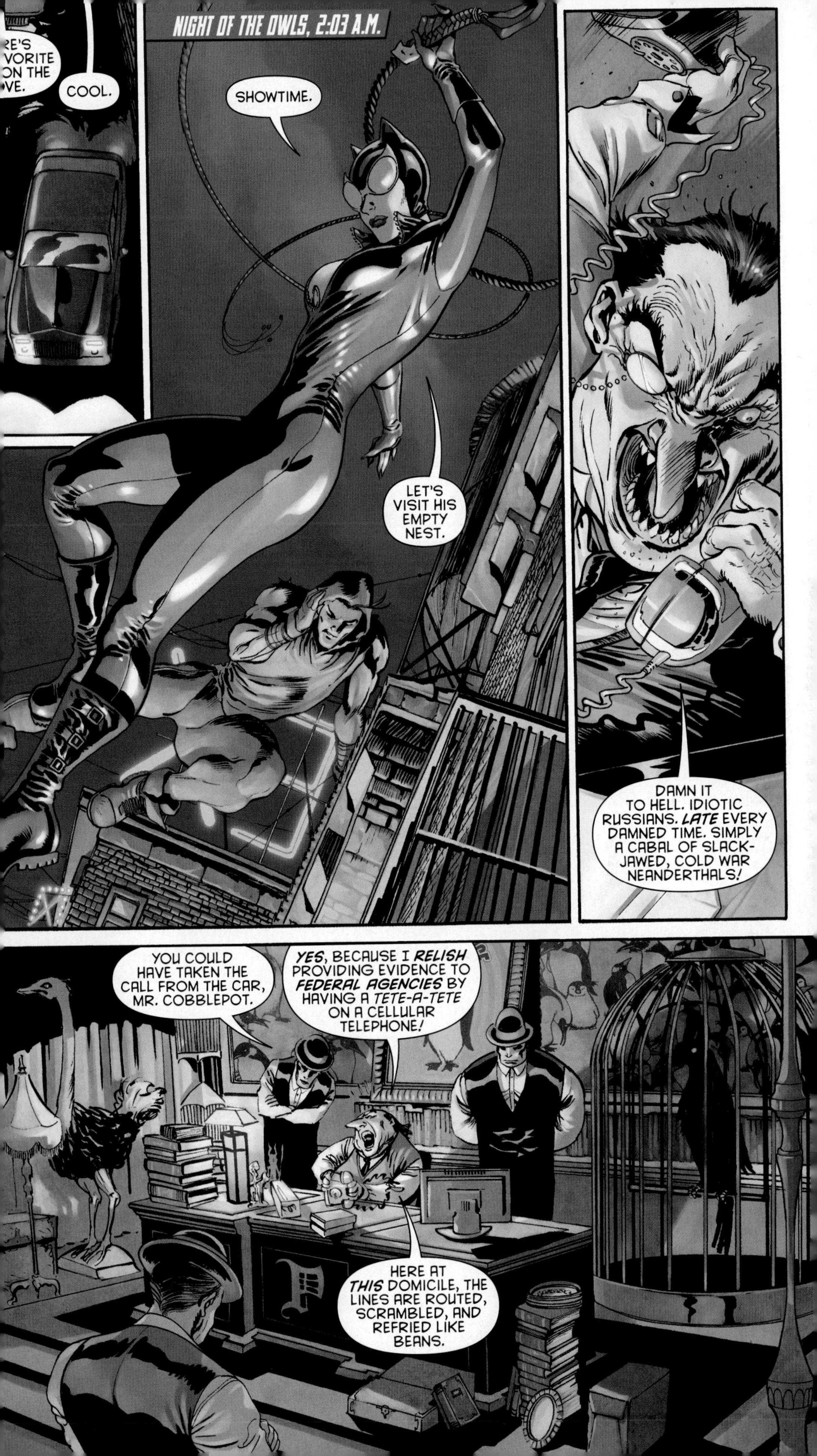

RE'S
VORITE
ON THE
VE.
COOL.
NIGHT OF THE OWLS, 2:03 A.M.
SHOWTIME.
LET'S VISIT HIS EMPTY NEST.
DAMN IT TO HELL. IDIOTIC RUSSIANS. LATE EVERY DAMNED TIME. SIMPLY A CABAL OF SLACK-JAWED, COLD WAR NEANDERTHALS!
YOU COULD HAVE TAKEN THE CALL FROM THE CAR, MR. COBBLEPOT.
YES, BECAUSE I RELISH PROVIDING EVIDENCE TO FEDERAL AGENCIES BY HAVING A TETE-A-TETE ON A CELLULAR TELEPHONE!
HERE AT THIS DOMICILE, THE LINES ARE ROUTED, SCRAMBLED, AND REFRIED LIKE BEANS.

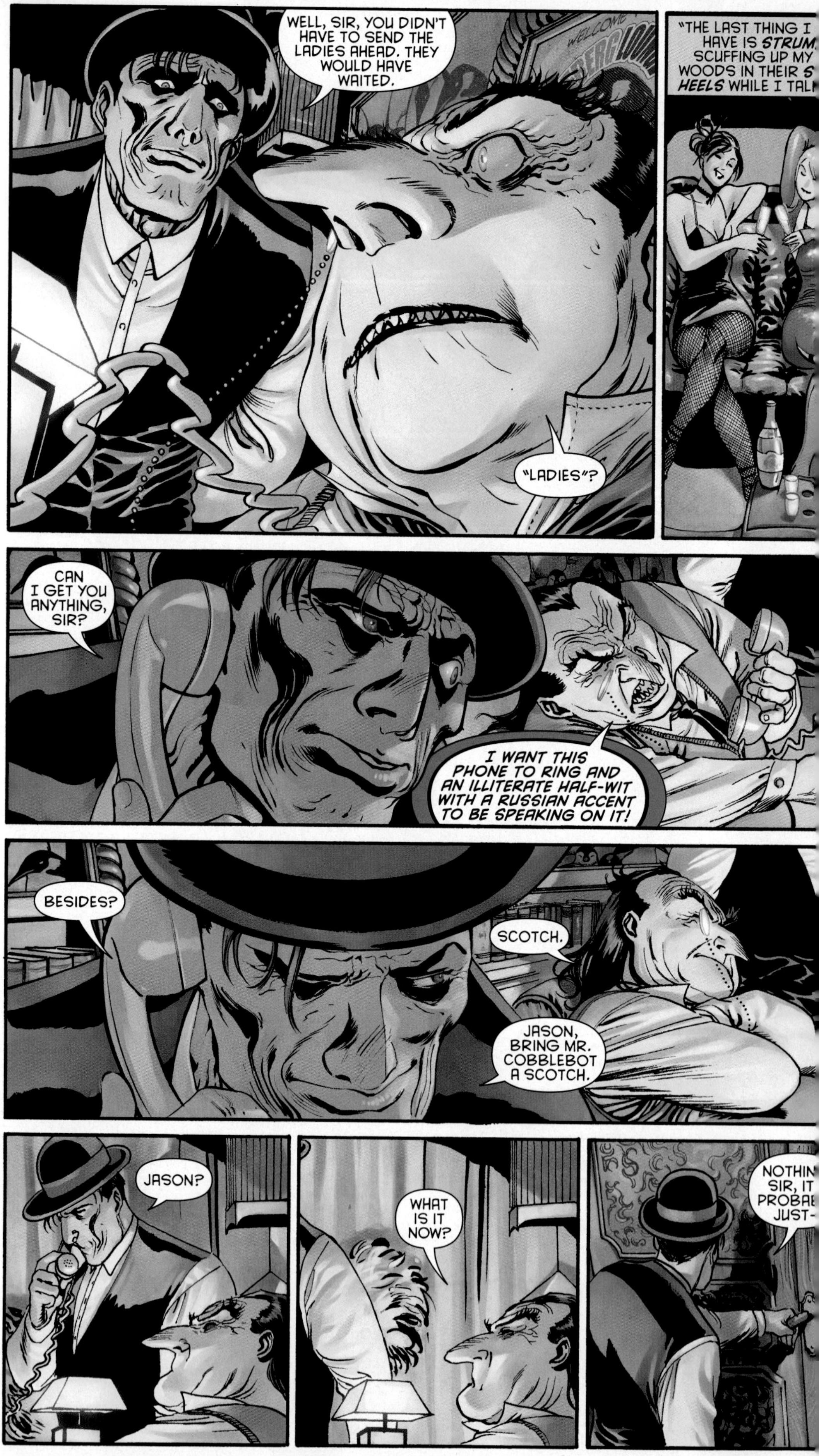
WELL, SIR, YOU DIDN'T HAVE TO SEND THE LADIES AHEAD. THEY WOULD HAVE WAITED.
"LADIES"?
"THE LAST THING I HAVE IS STRUM SCUFFING UP MY WOODS IN THEIR S HEELS WHILE I TAL
CAN I GET YOU ANYTHING, SIR?
I WANT THIS PHONE TO RING AND AN ILLITERATE HALF-WIT WITH A RUSSIAN ACCENT TO BE SPEAKING ON IT!
BESIDES?
SCOTCH.
JASON, BRING MR. COBBLEBOT A SCOTCH.
JASON?
WHAT IS IT NOW?
NOTHIN SIR, IT PROBAB JUST-

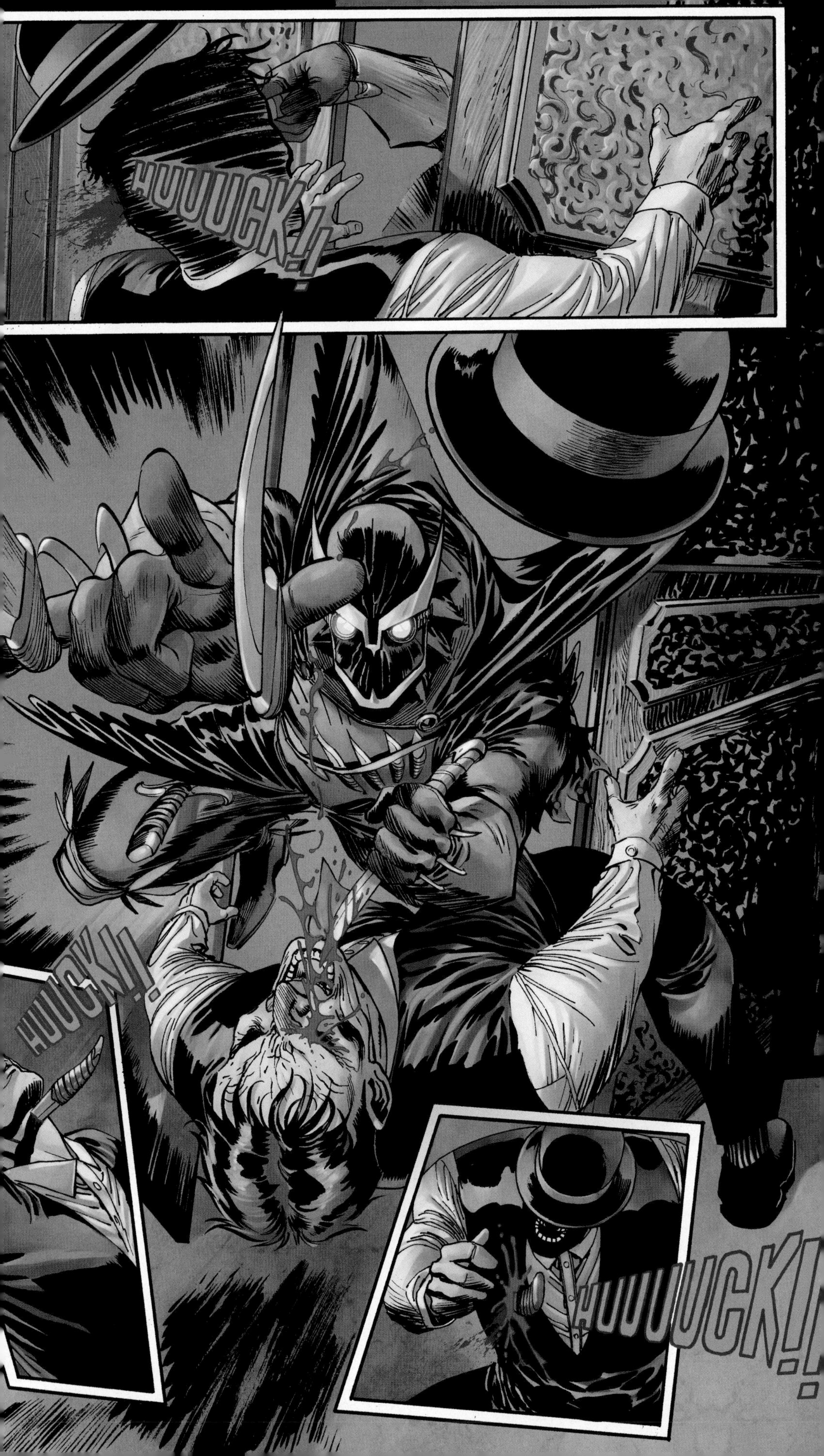
HUUUCK!!
HUUCK!!
HUUUUCK!!

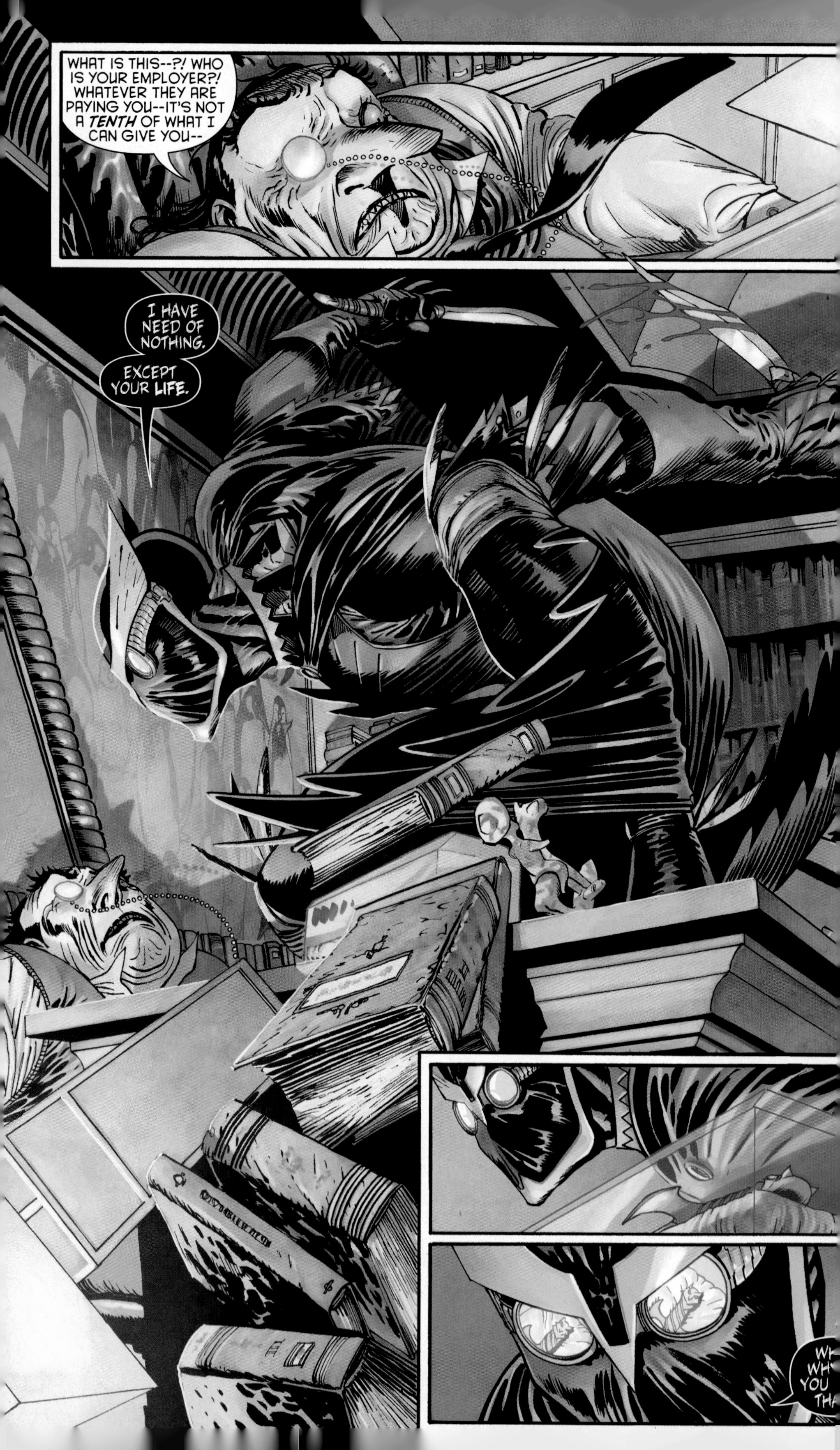
WHAT IS THIS--?! WHO IS YOUR EMPLOYER?! WHATEVER THEY ARE PAYING YOU--IT'S NOT A *TENTH* OF WHAT I CAN GIVE YOU--
I HAVE NEED OF NOTHING.
EXCEPT YOUR **LIFE.**

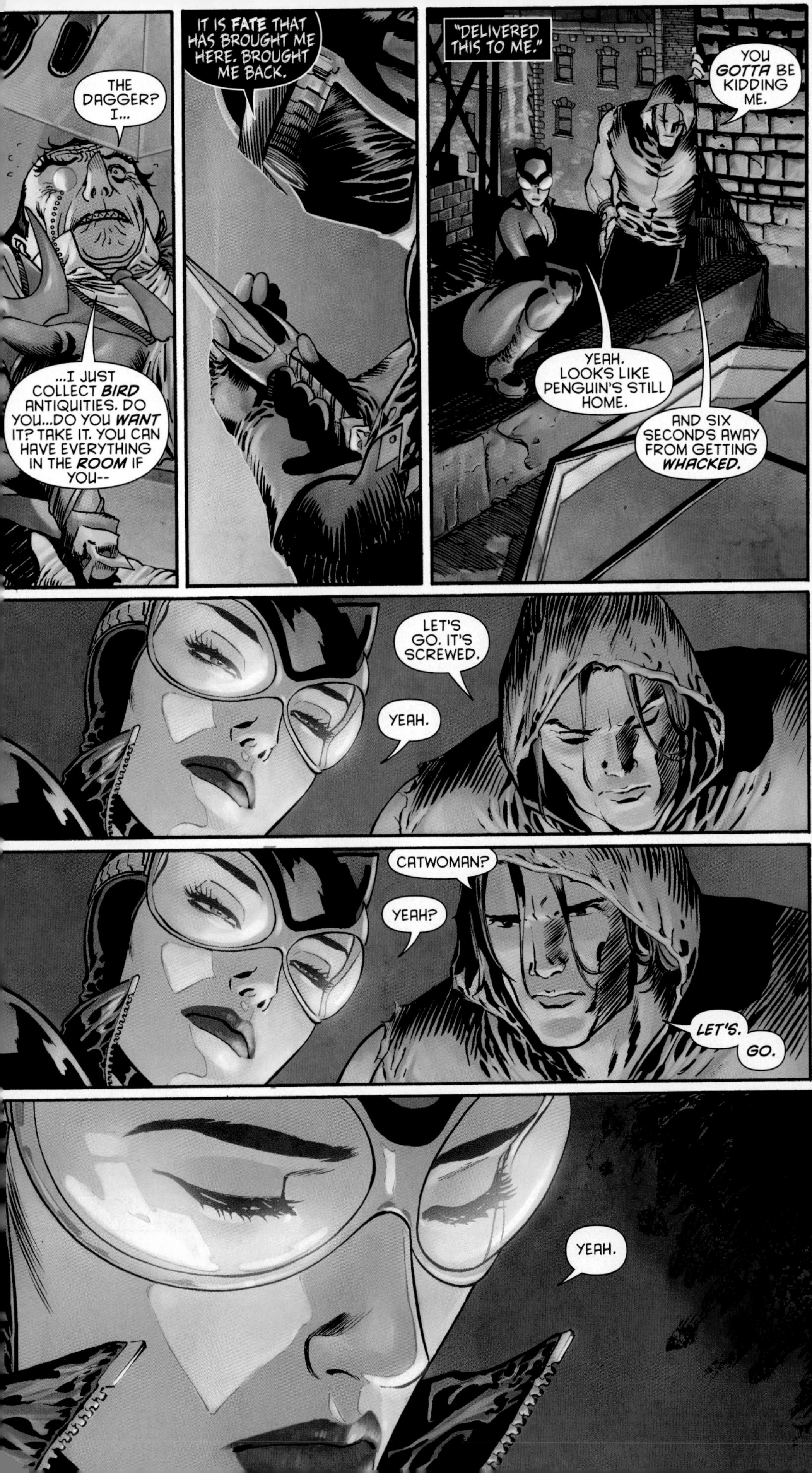
THE DAGGER? I...
...I JUST COLLECT BIRD ANTIQUITIES. DO YOU...DO YOU WANT IT? TAKE IT. YOU CAN HAVE EVERYTHING IN THE ROOM IF YOU--
IT IS FATE THAT HAS BROUGHT ME HERE. BROUGHT ME BACK.
"DELIVERED THIS TO ME."
YOU GOTTA BE KIDDING ME.
YEAH. LOOKS LIKE PENGUIN'S STILL HOME.
AND SIX SECONDS AWAY FROM GETTING WHACKED.
LET'S GO. IT'S SCREWED.
YEAH.
CATWOMAN?
YEAH?
LET'S. GO.
YEAH.

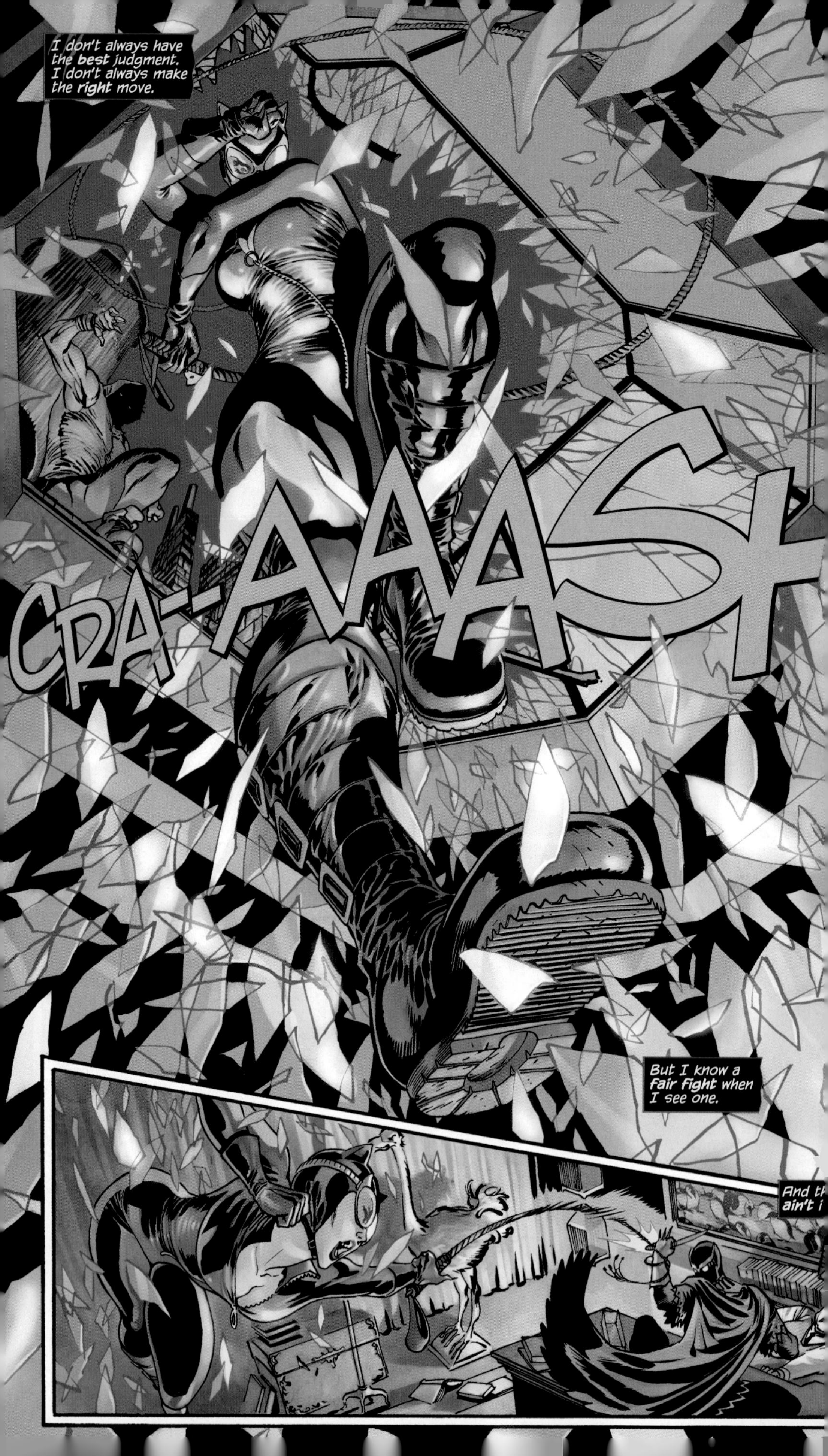
I don't always have the best judgment. I don't always make the right move.
CRA-AAASH
But I know a fair fight when I see one.
And th
ain't i

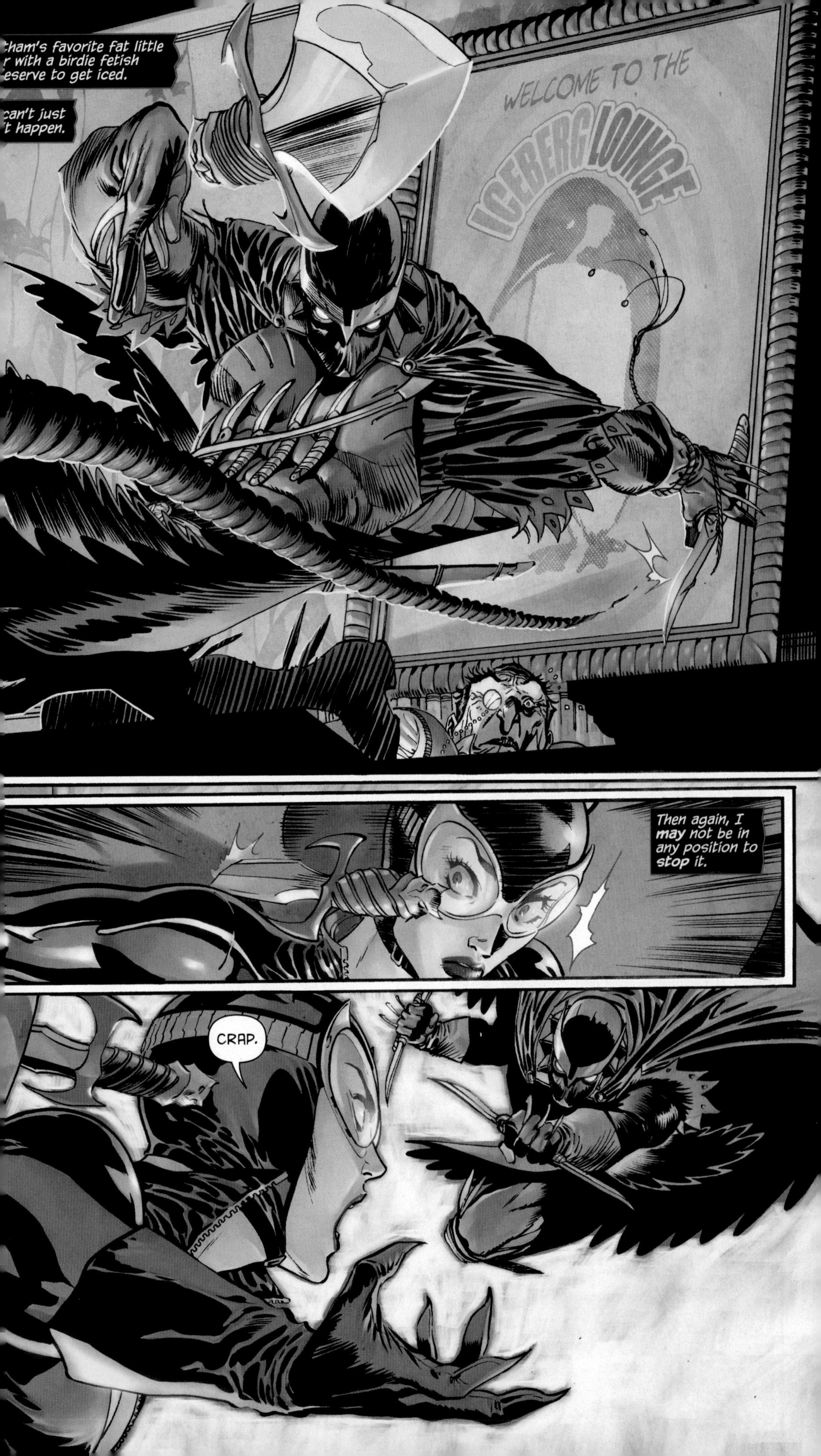
tham's favorite fat little
r with a birdie fetish
eserve to get iced.
can't just
t happen.
WELCOME TO THE
ICEBERG LOUNGE
Then again, I may not be in any position to stop it.
CRAP.

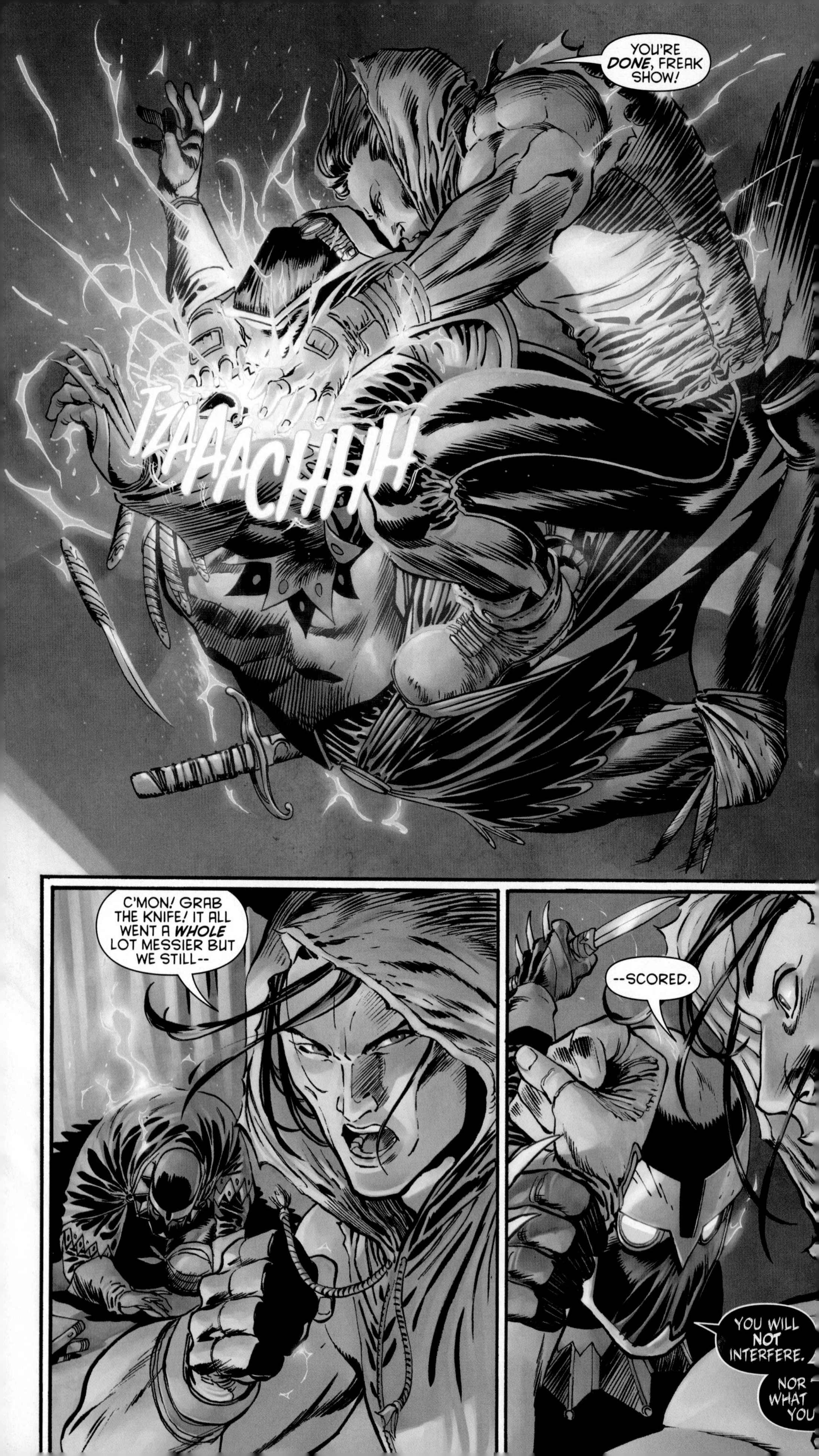
YOU'RE DONE, FREAK SHOW!
TZAAACHHH
C'MON! GRAB THE KNIFE! IT ALL WENT A WHOLE LOT MESSIER BUT WE STILL--
--SCORED.
YOU WILL NOT INTERFERE.
NOR WHAT YOU

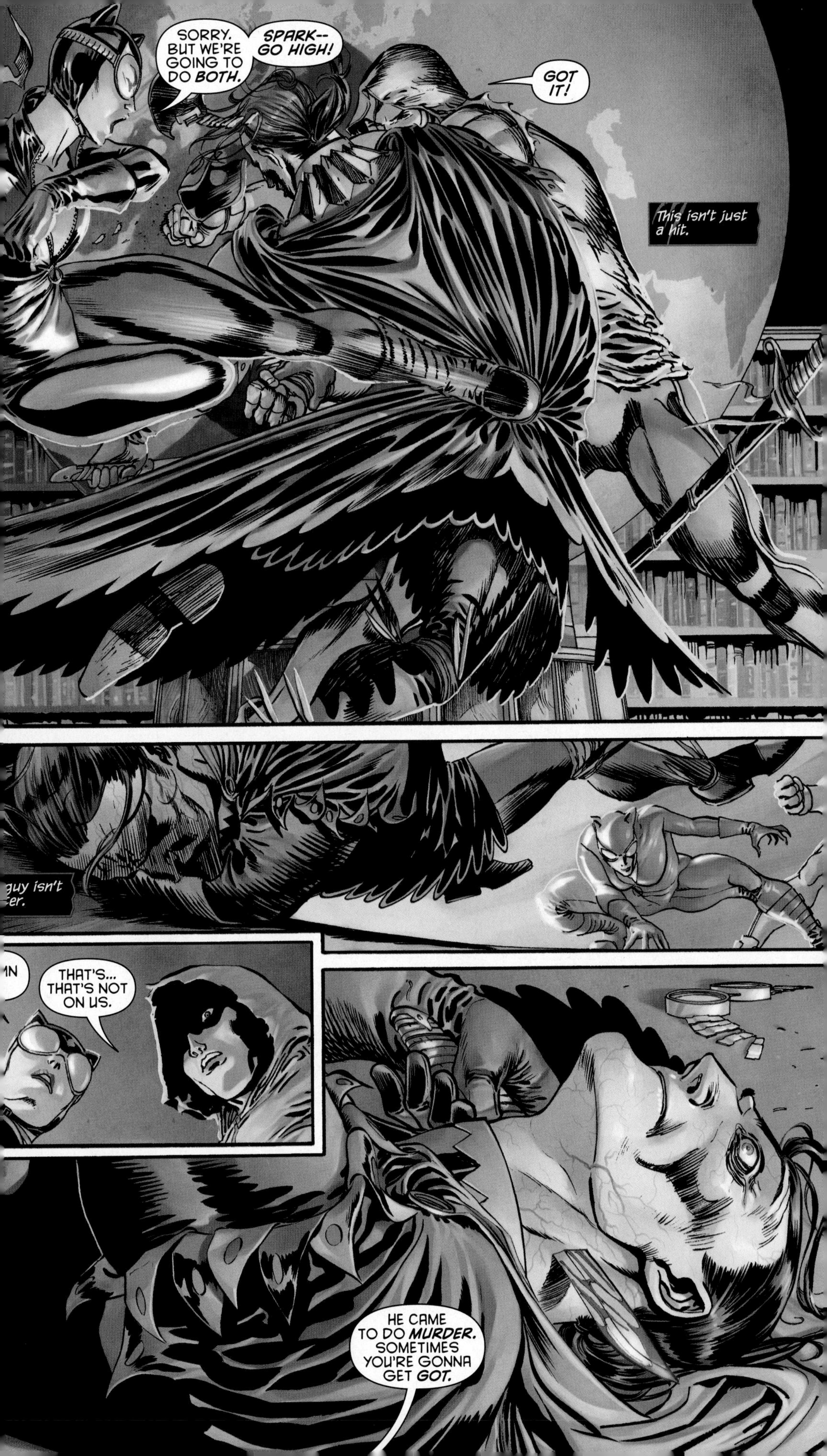
SORRY. BUT WE'RE GOING TO DO *BOTH.*
SPARK--
GO HIGH!
GOT IT!
This isn't just a hit.
guy isn't
er.
MN
THAT'S... THAT'S NOT ON US.
HE CAME TO DO *MURDER.* SOMETIMES YOU'RE GONNA GET *GOT.*

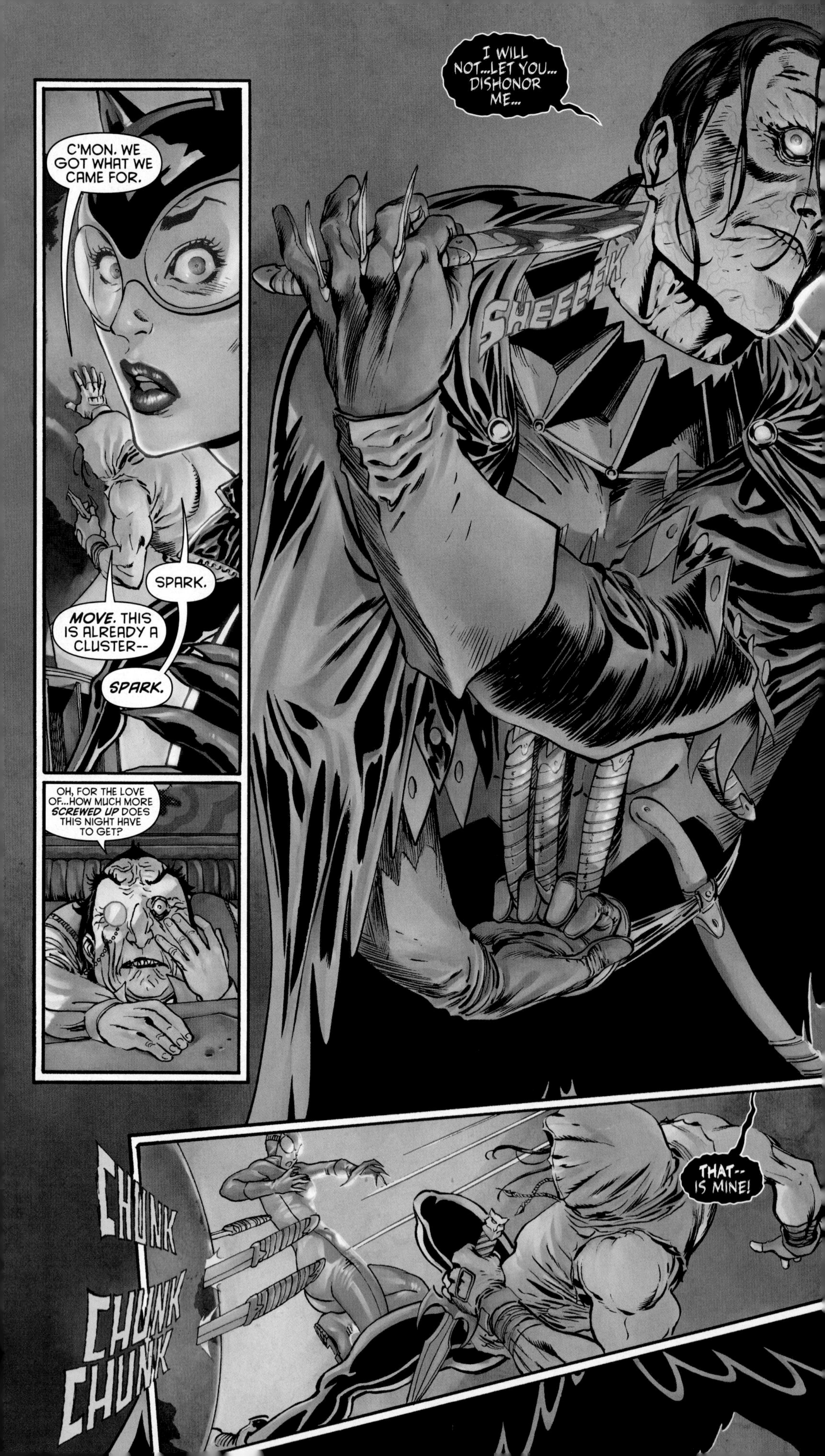

C'MON. WE GOT WHAT WE CAME FOR.
SPARK.
MOVE. THIS IS ALREADY A CLUSTER--
SPARK.
I WILL NOT...LET YOU... DISHONOR ME...
SHEEEEEK
OH, FOR THE LOVE OF...HOW MUCH MORE SCREWED UP DOES THIS NIGHT HAVE TO GET?
CHUNK
CHUNK
CHUNK
THAT-- IS MINE!

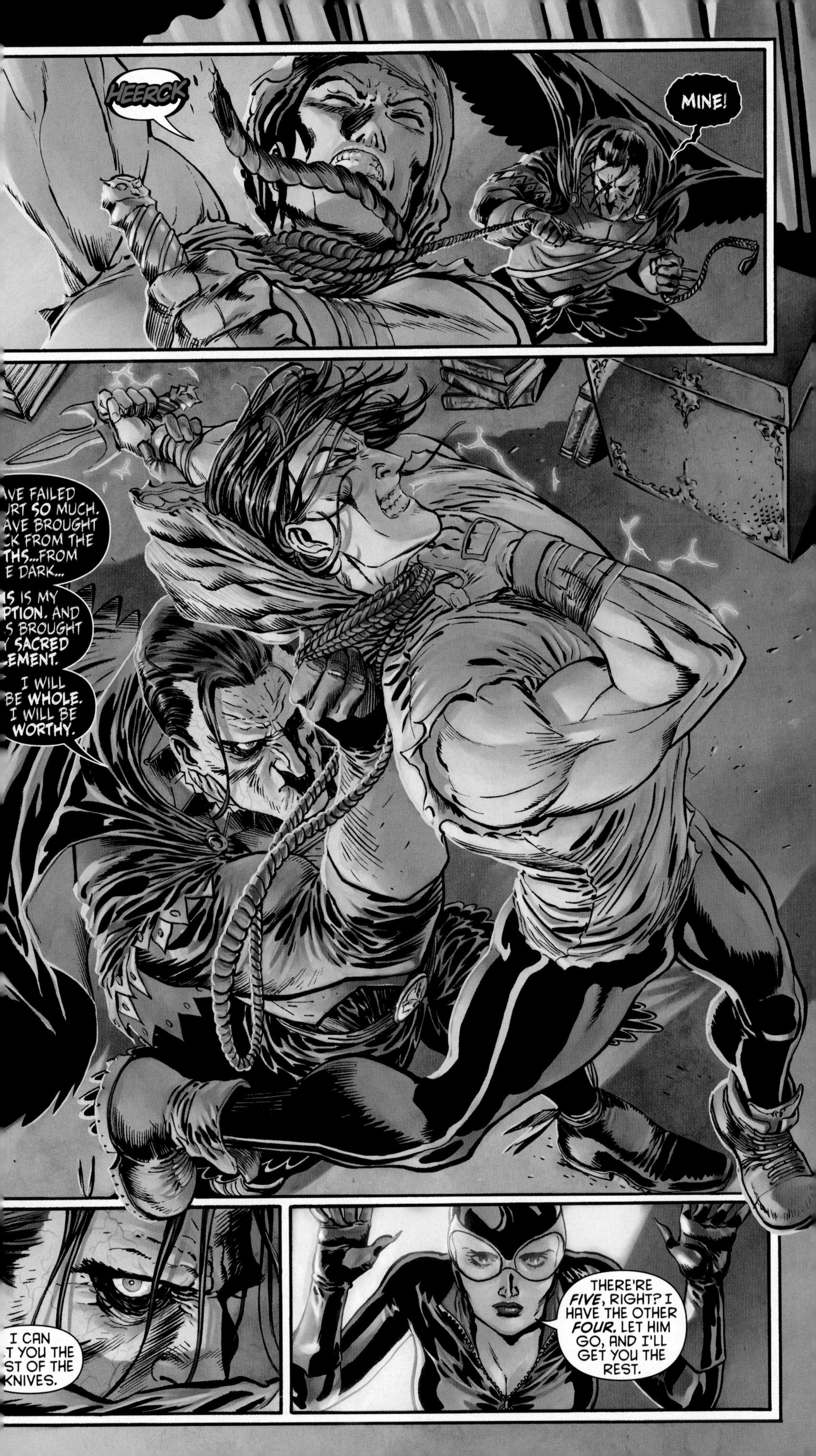
HEERCK
MINE!
AVE FAILED URT SO MUCH. AVE BROUGHT CK FROM THE THS...FROM E DARK...
IS IS MY PTION. AND S BROUGHT Y SACRED EMENT.
I WILL BE WHOLE. I WILL BE WORTHY.
I CAN T YOU THE ST OF THE KNIVES.
THERE'RE FIVE, RIGHT? I HAVE THE OTHER FOUR. LET HIM GO, AND I'LL GET YOU THE REST.

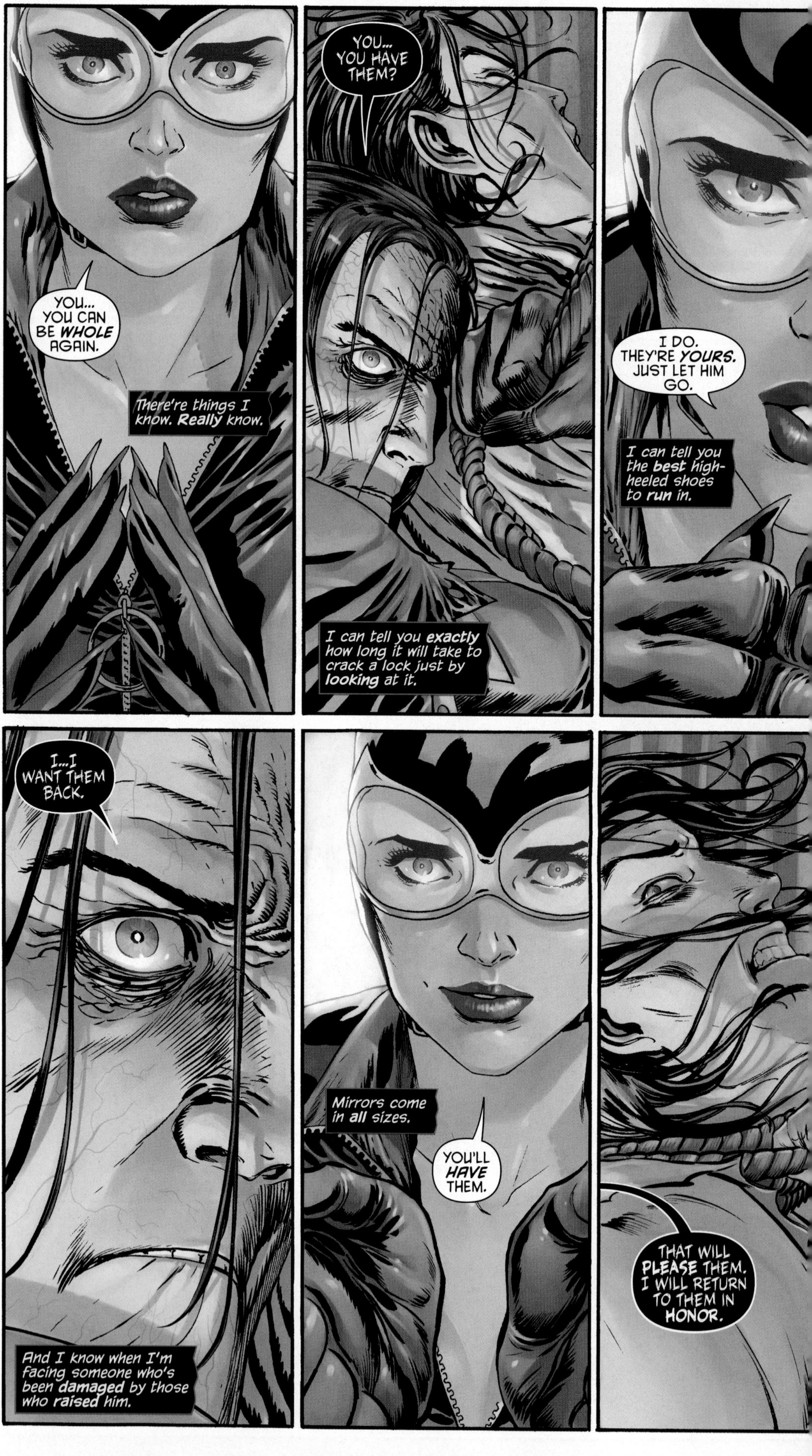
YOU... YOU CAN BE WHOLE AGAIN.
There're things I know. Really know.
YOU... YOU HAVE THEM?
I can tell you exactly how long it will take to crack a lock just by looking at it.
I DO. THEY'RE YOURS. JUST LET HIM GO.
I can tell you the best high-heeled shoes to run in.
I...I WANT THEM BACK.
And I know when I'm facing someone who's been damaged by those who raised him.
Mirrors come in all sizes.
YOU'LL HAVE THEM.
THAT WILL PLEASE THEM. I WILL RETURN TO THEM IN HONOR.

BANG

YOU'LL RETURN TO THEM WITHOUT A *FRICKIN'* HEAD!

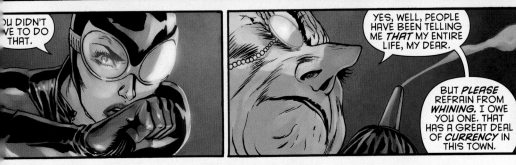

U DIDN'T VE TO DO THAT.

YES, WELL, PEOPLE HAVE BEEN TELLING ME *THAT* MY ENTIRE LIFE, MY DEAR.

BUT *PLEASE* REFRAIN FROM *WHINING.* I OWE YOU ONE. THAT HAS A GREAT DEAL OF *CURRENCY* IN THIS TOWN.

GODALMIGHTY... LET'S JUST GET THE HELL *OUT* OF HERE. WE'VE *GOT* THE *BLADE*--LET'S JUST GO.

CATWOMAN?

SPP
I'M G
TO NEE
BA

I don't exactly know what's happened tonight.

My gut tells me that this is all much bigger than *Penguin* and some old knives.

Those of
run arou
dark will
find our
face-to-
monster

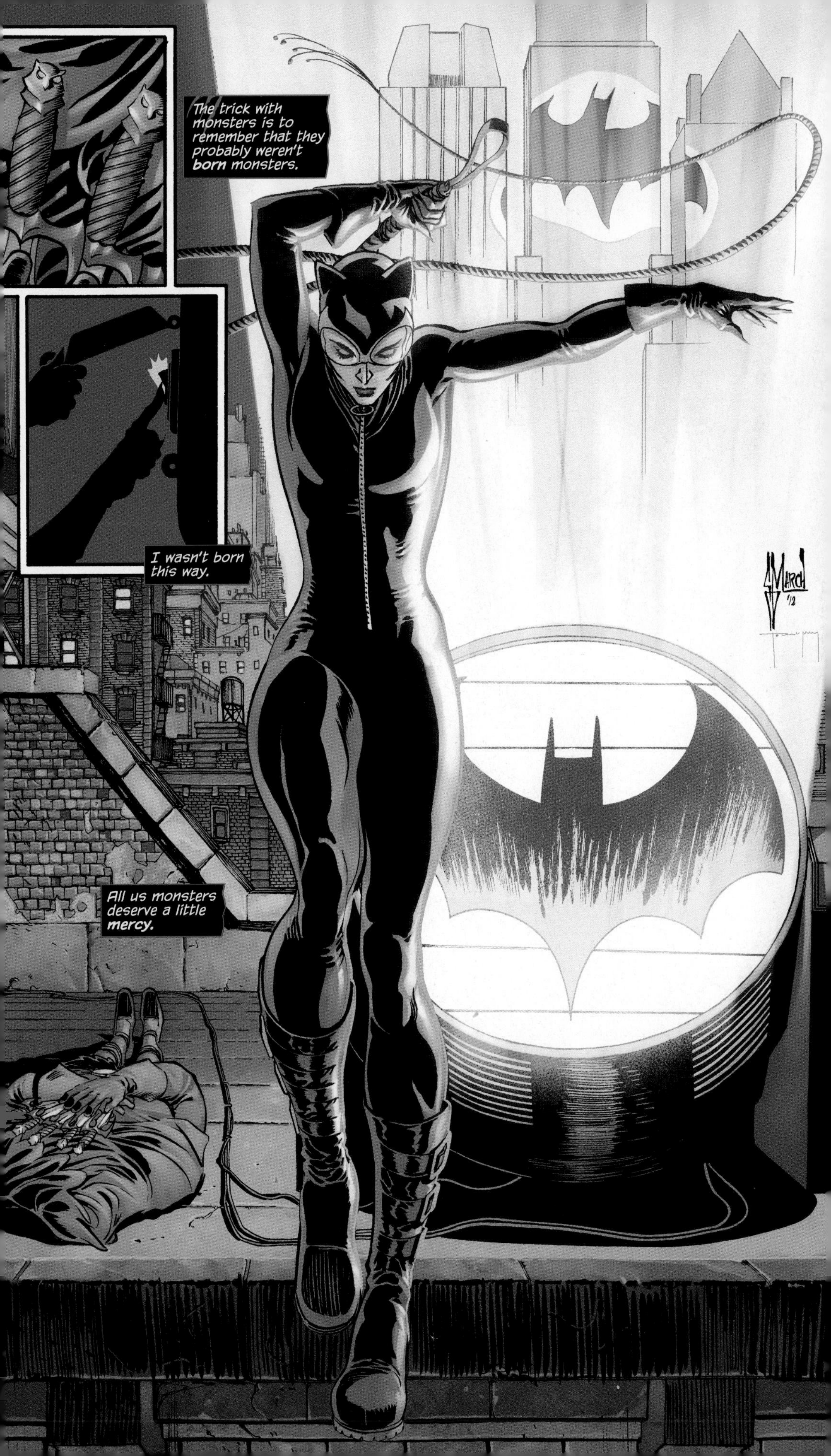

The trick with monsters is to remember that they probably weren't **born** monsters.
I wasn't born this way.
All us monsters deserve a little **mercy**.

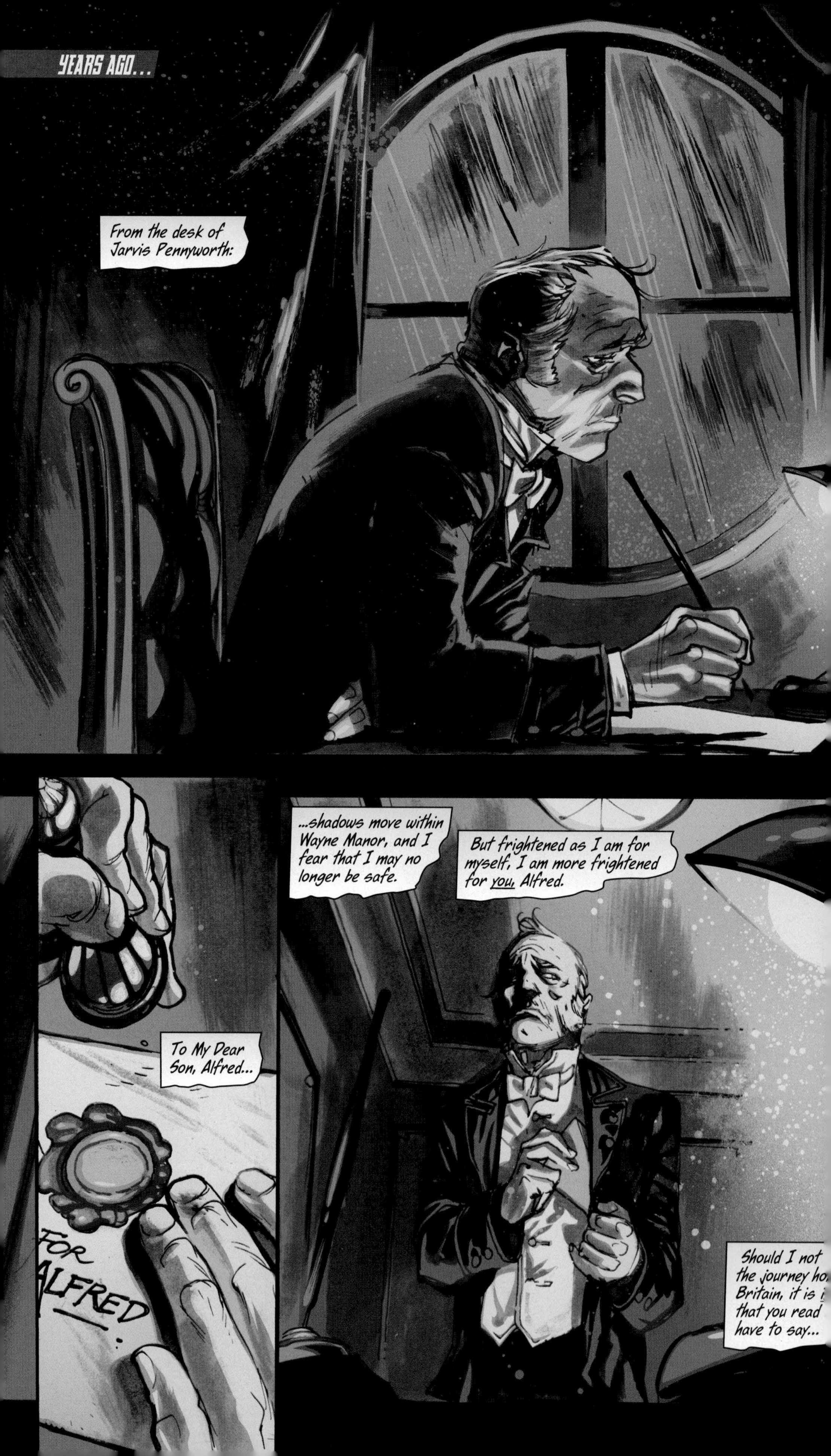
YEARS AGO...
From the desk of Jarvis Pennyworth:
To My Dear Son, Alfred...
FOR ALFRED
...shadows move within Wayne Manor, and I fear that I may no longer be safe.
But frightened as I am for myself, I am more frightened for you, Alfred.
Should I not the journey ho Britain, it is that you read have to say...

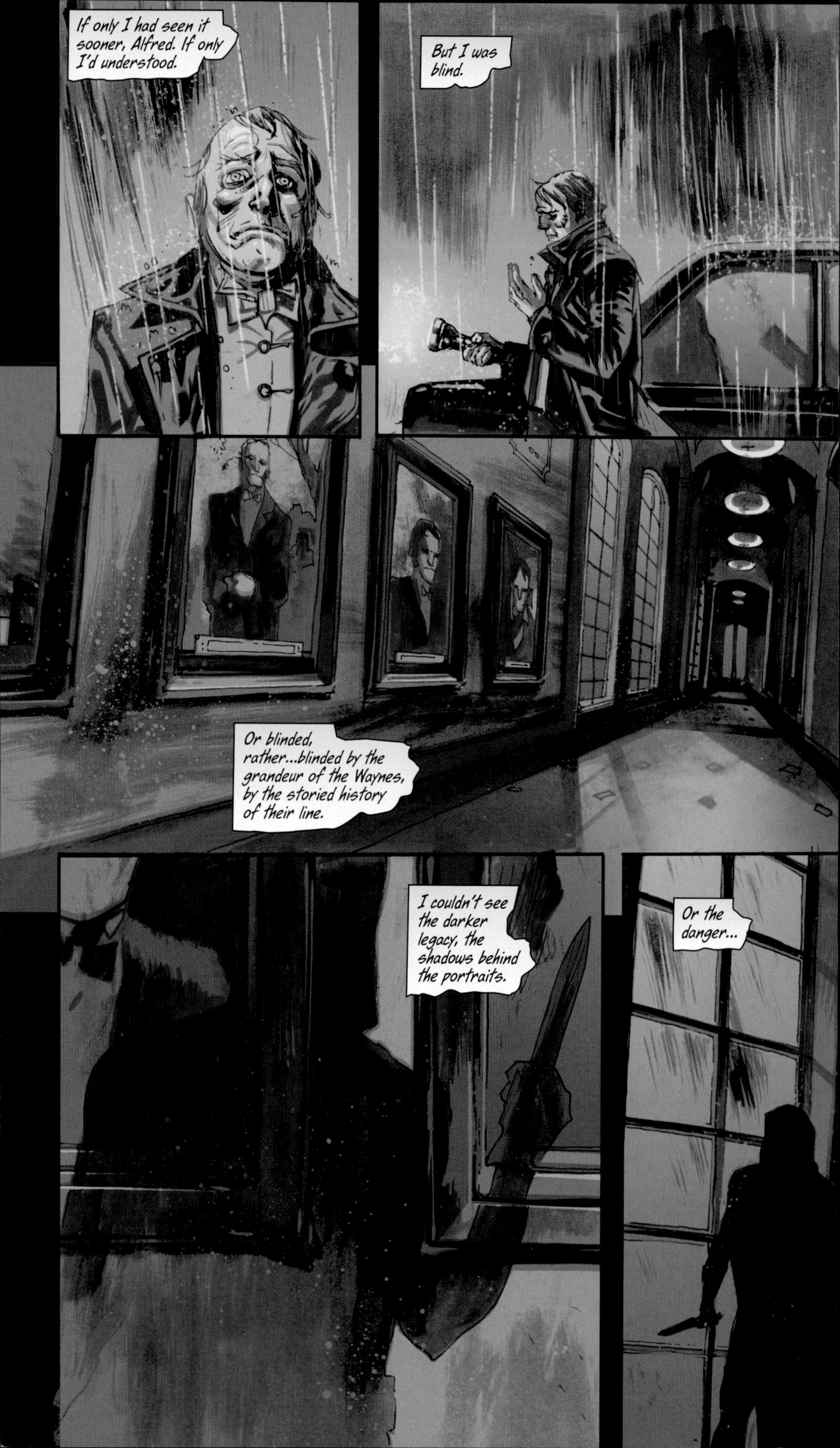

If only I had seen it sooner, Alfred. If only I'd understood.
But I was blind.
Or blinded, rather...blinded by the grandeur of the Waynes, by the storied history of their line.
I couldn't see the darker legacy, the shadows behind the portraits.
Or the danger...

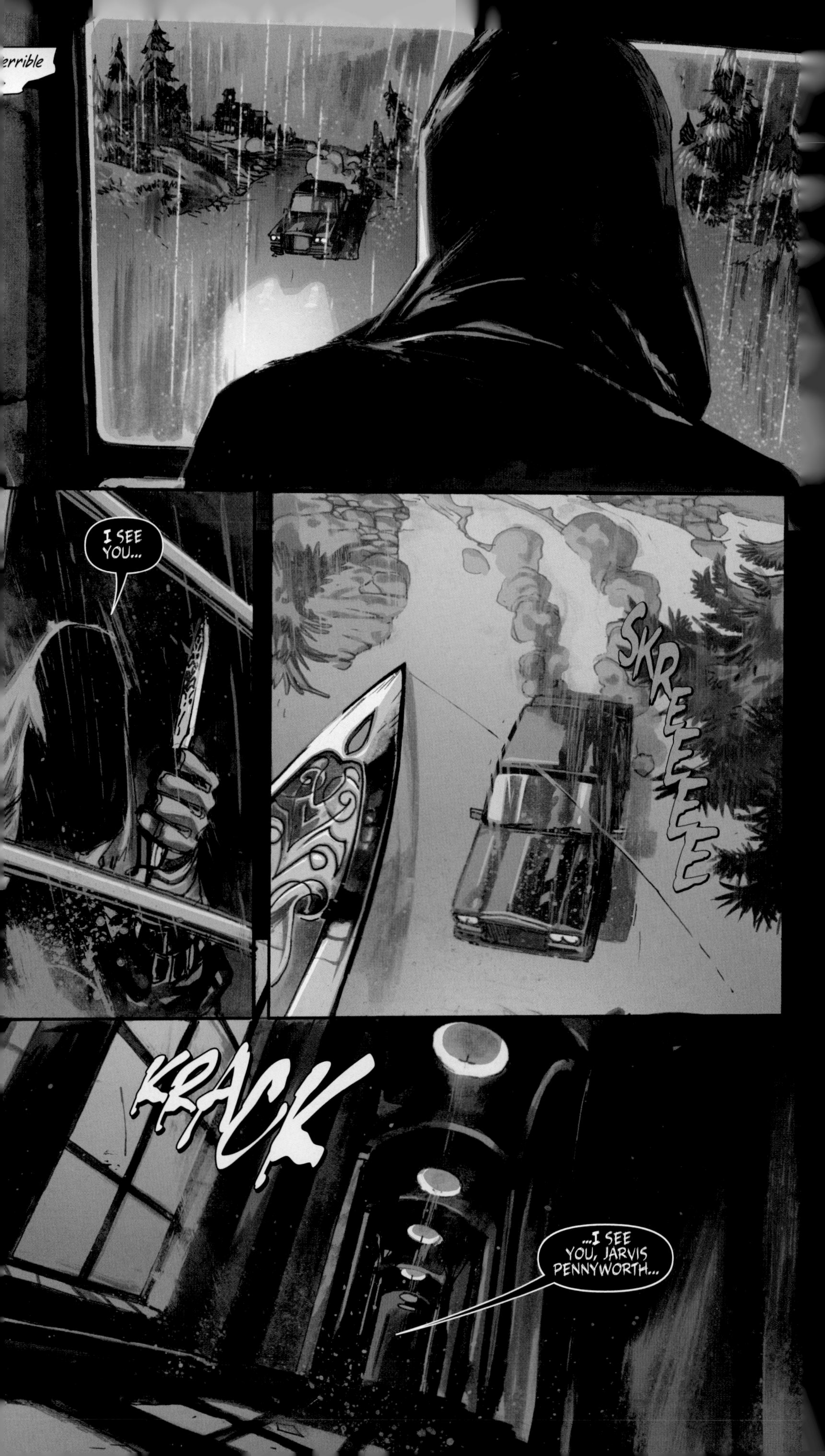
errible
I SEE YOU...
SKREEEEE
KRACK
...I SEE YOU, JARVIS PENNYWORTH...

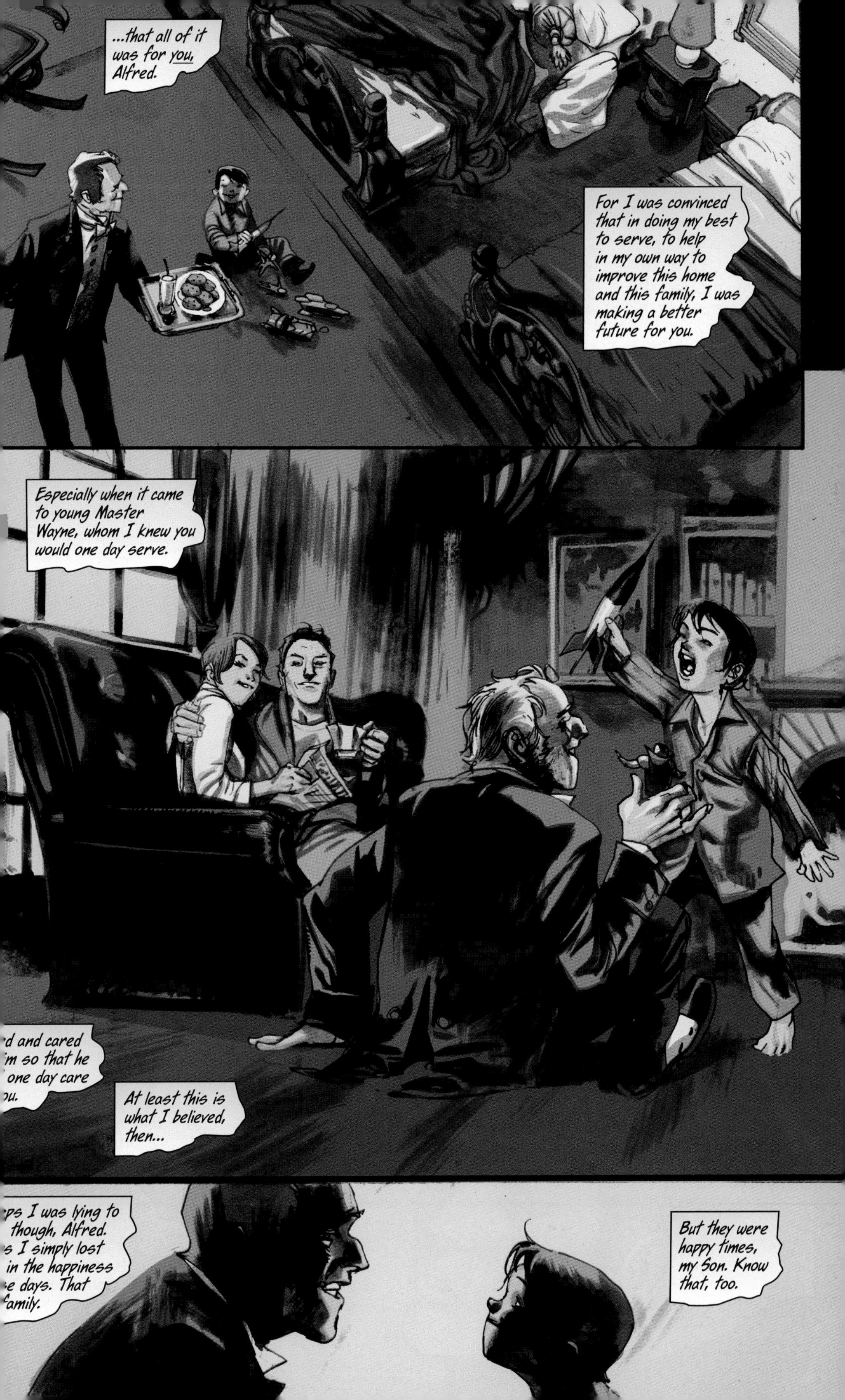
...that all of it was for you, Alfred.
For I was convinced that in doing my best to serve, to help in my own way to improve this home and this family, I was making a better future for you.
Especially when it came to young Master Wayne, whom I knew you would one day serve.
d and cared im so that he one day care ou.
At least this is what I believed, then...
ps I was lying to though, Alfred. s I simply lost in the happiness e days. That amily.
But they were happy times, my Son. Know that, too.

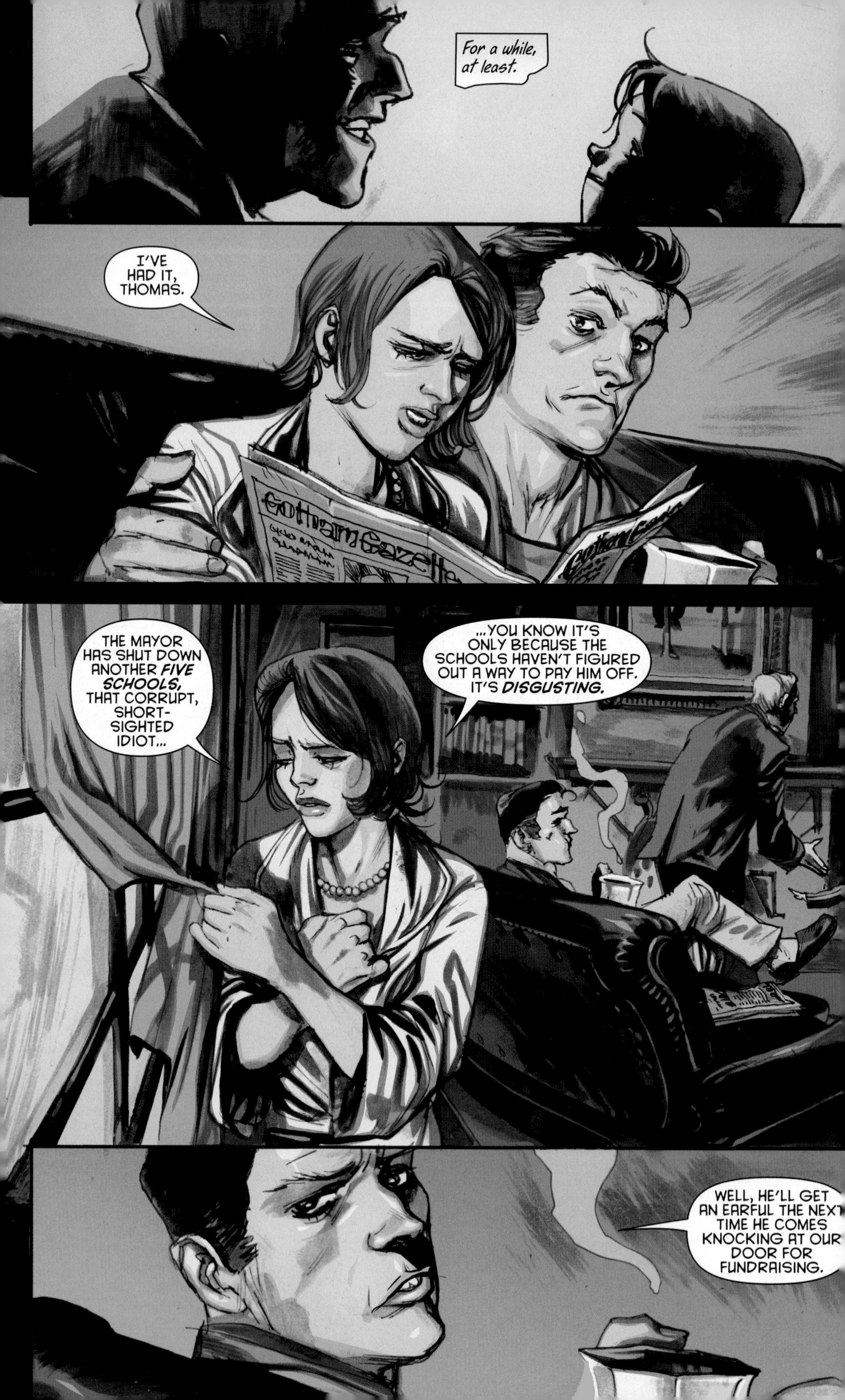
For a while, at least.
I'VE HAD IT, THOMAS.
THE MAYOR HAS SHUT DOWN ANOTHER FIVE SCHOOLS, THAT CORRUPT, SHORT-SIGHTED IDIOT...
...YOU KNOW IT'S ONLY BECAUSE THE SCHOOLS HAVEN'T FIGURED OUT A WAY TO PAY HIM OFF. IT'S DISGUSTING.
WELL, HE'LL GET AN EARFUL THE NEXT TIME HE COMES KNOCKING AT OUR DOOR FOR FUNDRAISING.

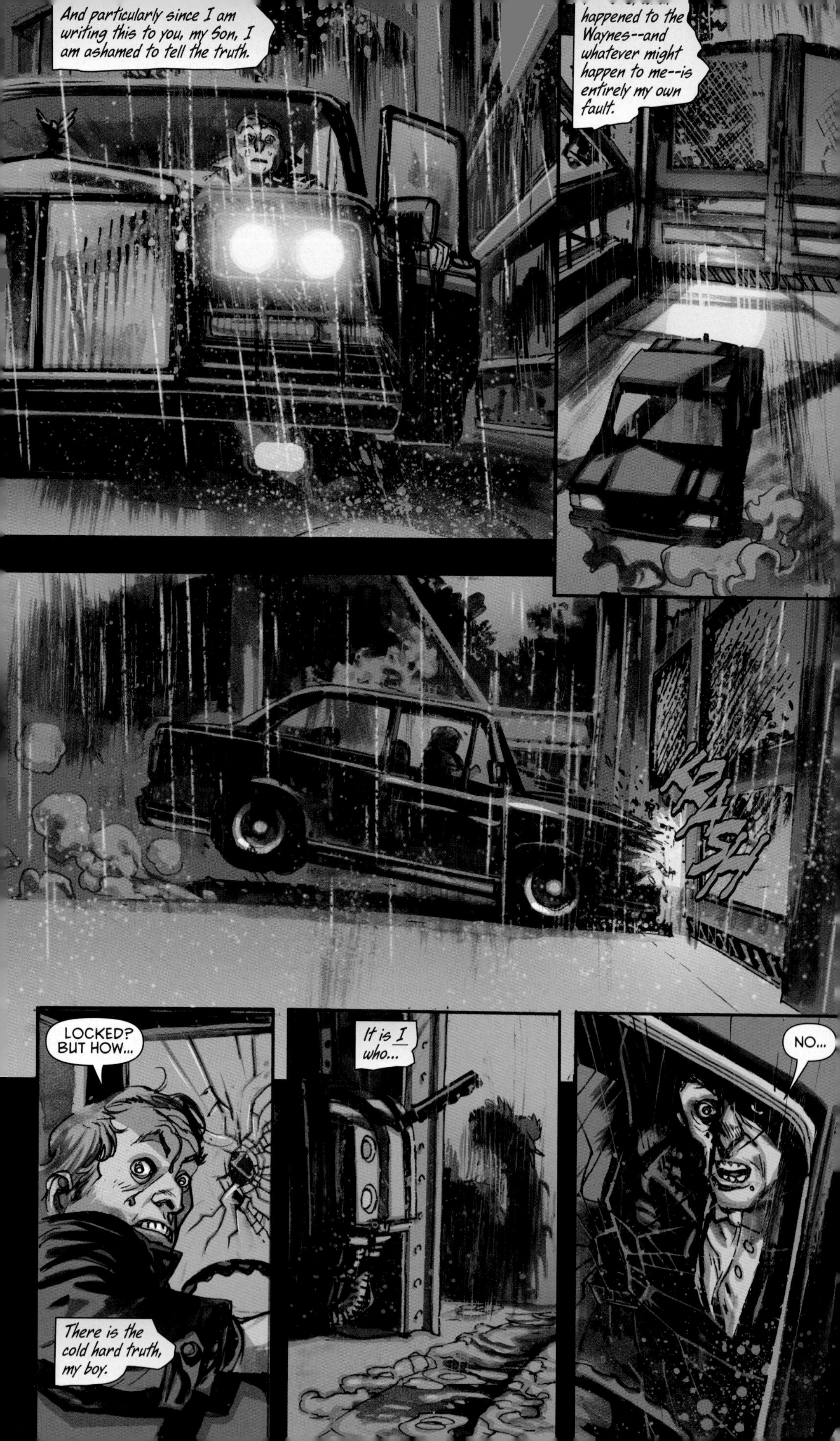
And particularly since I am writing this to you, my Son, I am ashamed to tell the truth.
happened to the Waynes--and whatever might happen to me--is entirely my own fault.
KRASH
LOCKED? BUT HOW...
There is the cold hard truth, my boy.
It is I who...
NO...

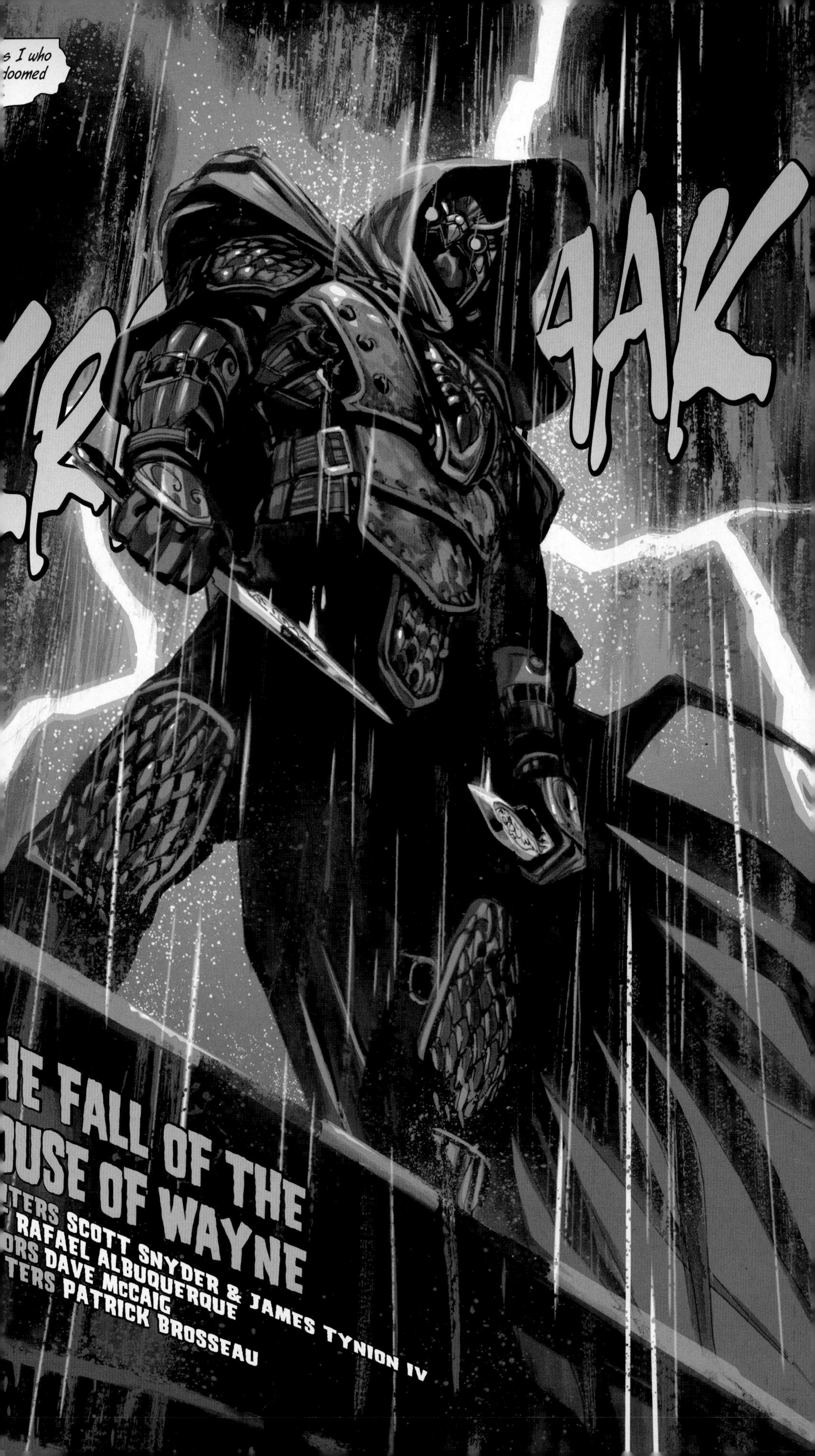

s I who
doomed
AAK
HE FALL OF THE
OUSE OF WAYNE
TERS SCOTT SNYDER & JAMES TYNION IV
RAFAEL ALBUQUERQUE
ORS DAVE McCAIG
TERS PATRICK BROSSEAU

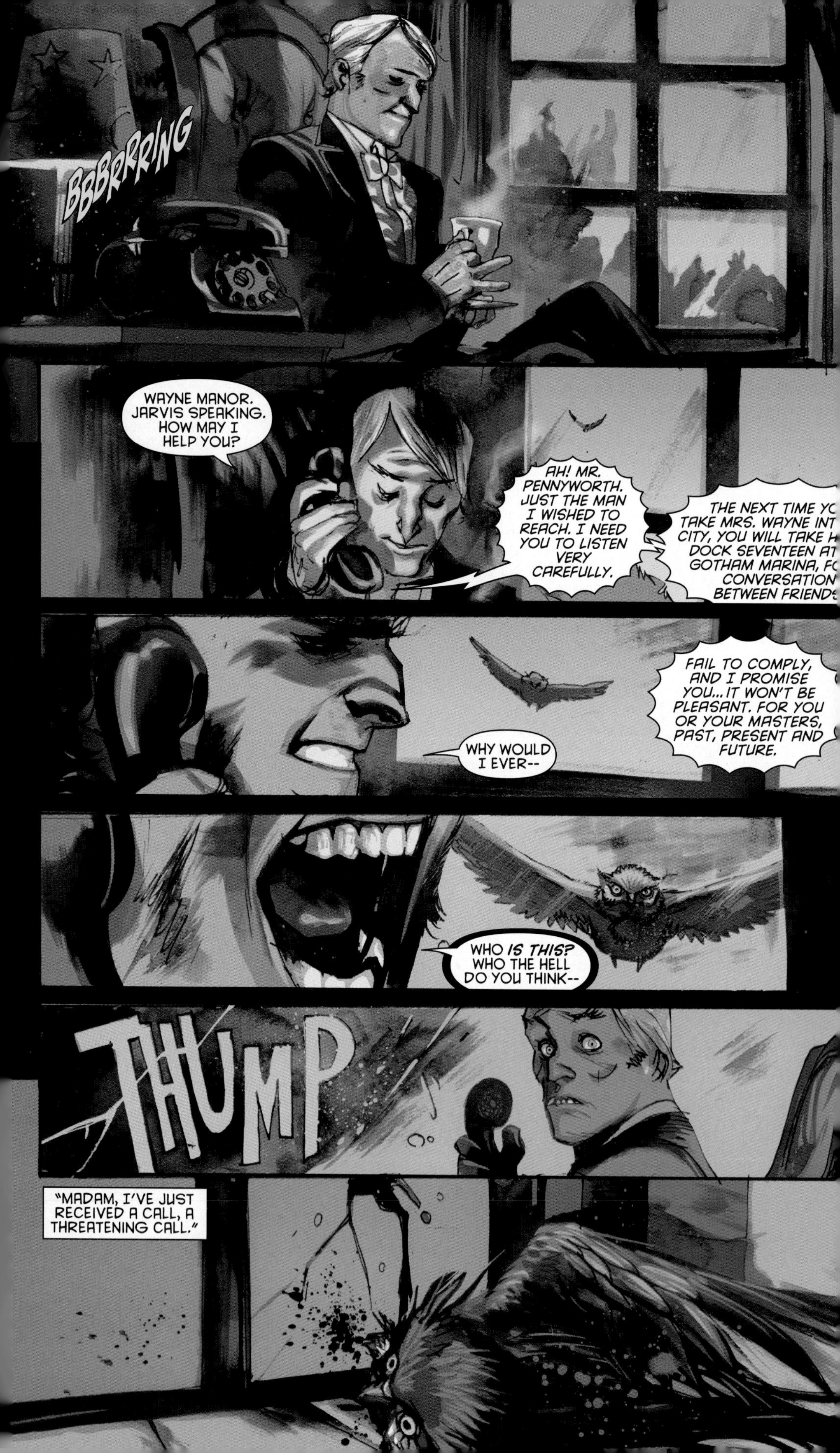
BBBRRRING
WAYNE MANOR. JARVIS SPEAKING. HOW MAY I HELP YOU?
AH! MR. PENNYWORTH. JUST THE MAN I WISHED TO REACH. I NEED YOU TO LISTEN VERY CAREFULLY.
THE NEXT TIME YO TAKE MRS. WAYNE INT CITY, YOU WILL TAKE H DOCK SEVENTEEN AT GOTHAM MARINA, FO CONVERSATION BETWEEN FRIENDS
FAIL TO COMPLY, AND I PROMISE YOU... IT WON'T BE PLEASANT. FOR YOU OR YOUR MASTERS, PAST, PRESENT AND FUTURE.
WHY WOULD I EVER--
WHO *IS THIS?* WHO THE HELL DO YOU THINK--
THUMP
"MADAM, I'VE JUST RECEIVED A CALL, A THREATENING CALL."

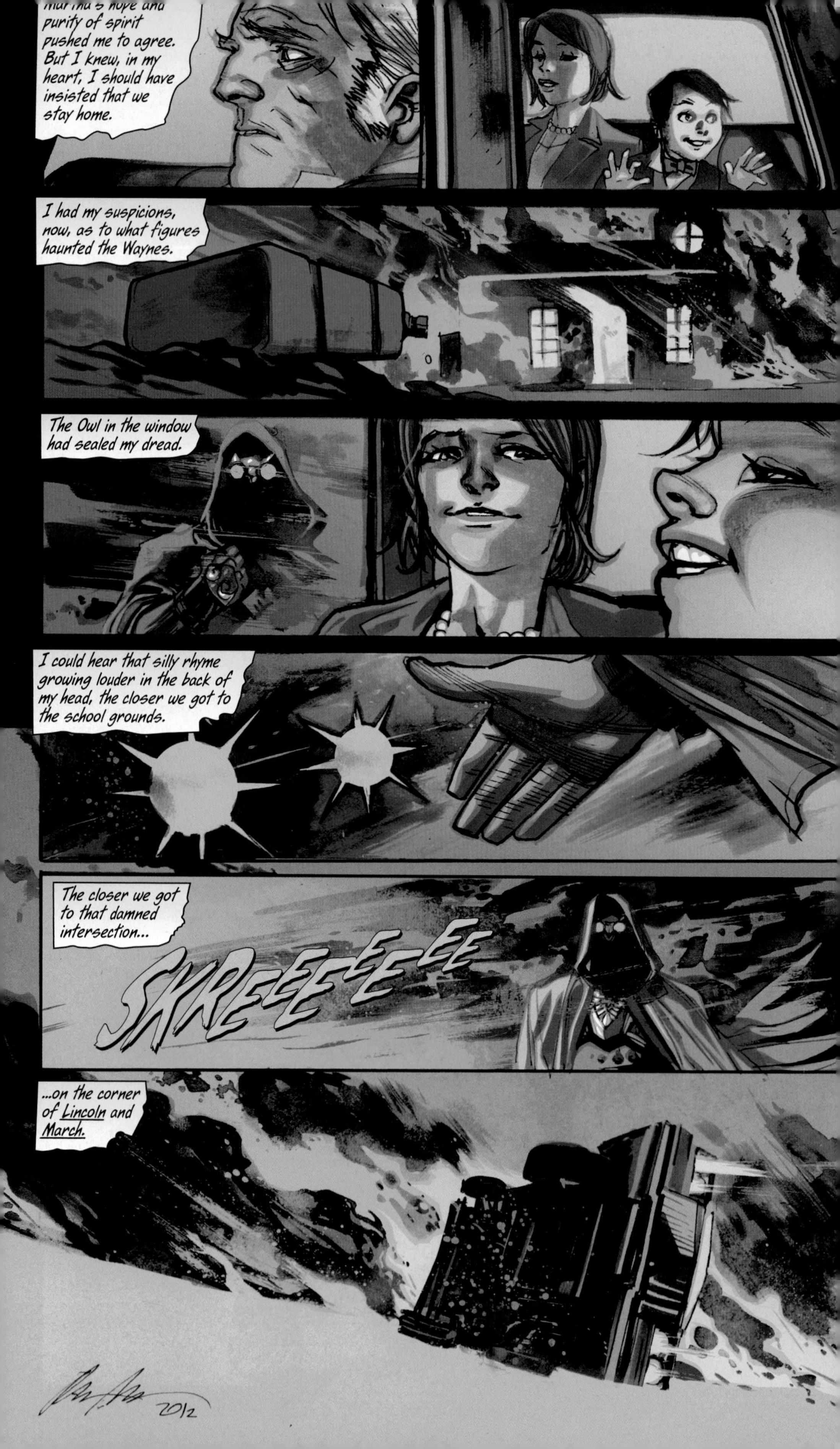
purity of spirit pushed me to agree. But I knew, in my heart, I should have insisted that we stay home.
I had my suspicions, now, as to what figures haunted the Waynes.
The Owl in the window had sealed my dread.
I could hear that silly rhyme growing louder in the back of my head, the closer we got to the school grounds.
The closer we got to that damned intersection...
SKREEEEEEE
...on the corner of Lincoln and March.
2012

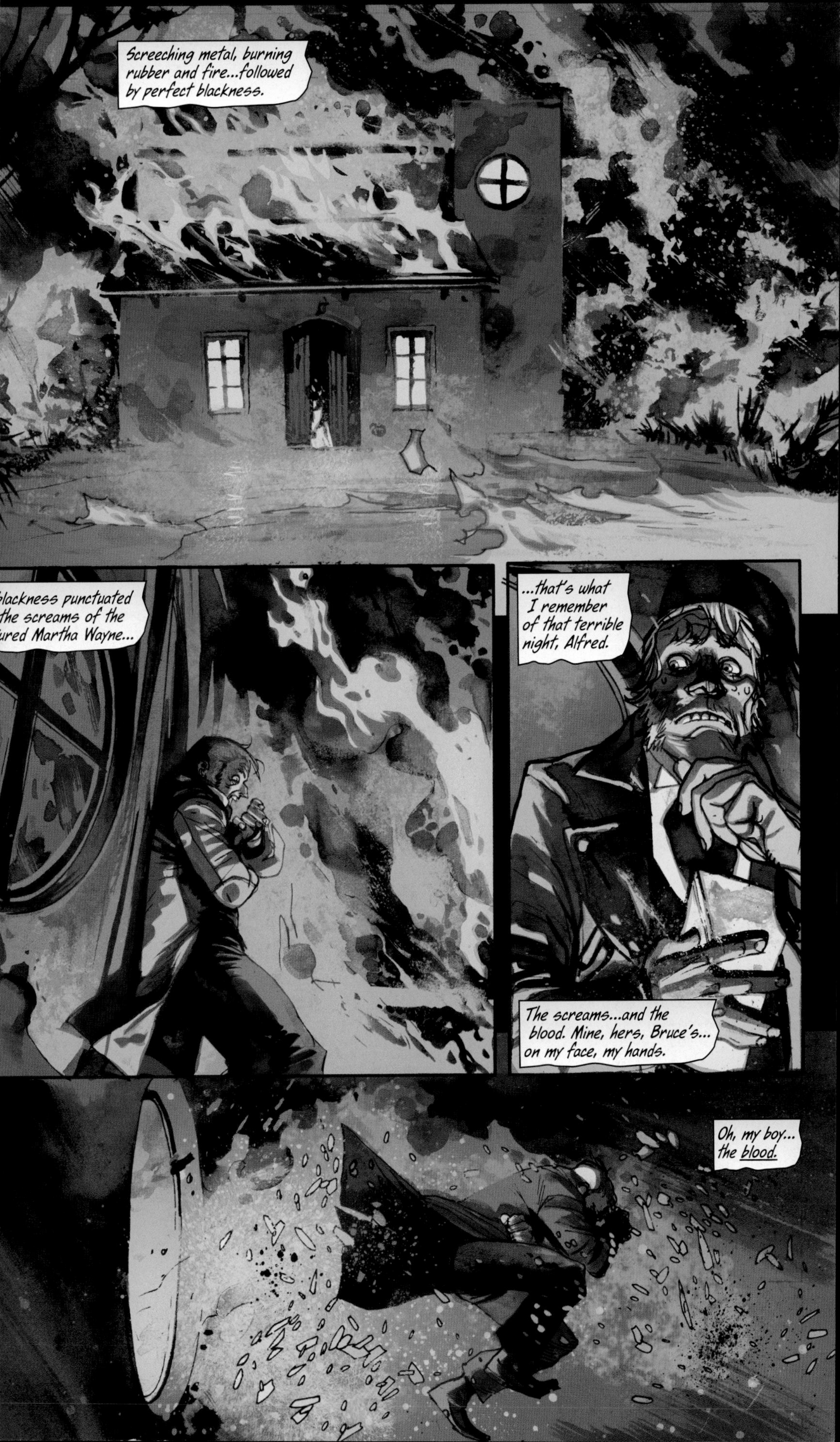
Screeching metal, burning rubber and fire...followed by perfect blackness.
Blackness punctuated
the screams of the
ured Martha Wayne...
...that's what I remember of that terrible night, Alfred.
The screams...and the blood. Mine, hers, Bruce's... on my face, my hands.
Oh, my boy... the blood.

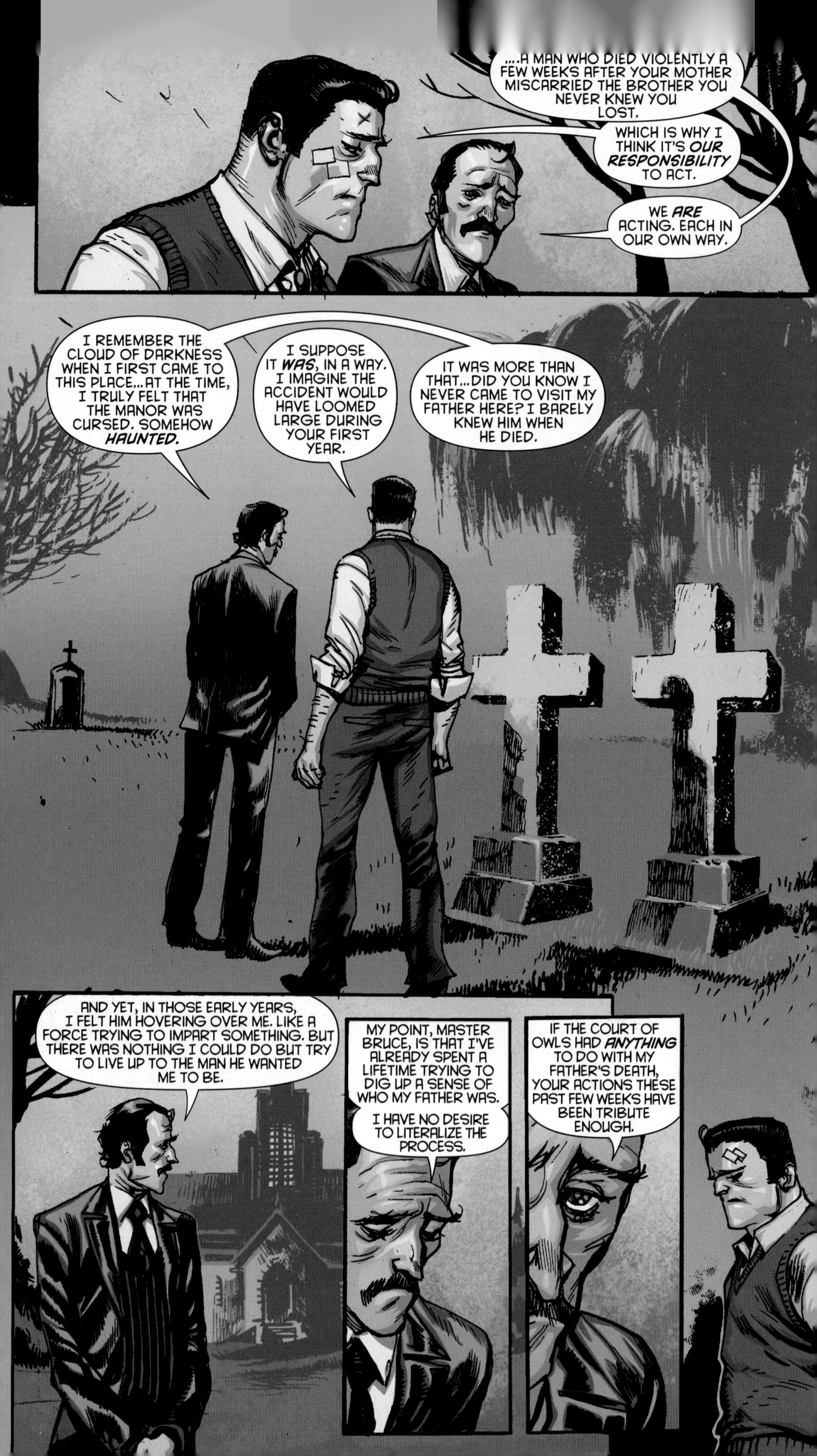
....A MAN WHO DIED VIOLENTLY A FEW WEEKS AFTER YOUR MOTHER MISCARRIED THE BROTHER YOU NEVER KNEW YOU LOST.
WHICH IS WHY I THINK IT'S OUR RESPONSIBILITY TO ACT.
WE ARE ACTING. EACH IN OUR OWN WAY.
I REMEMBER THE CLOUD OF DARKNESS WHEN I FIRST CAME TO THIS PLACE...AT THE TIME, I TRULY FELT THAT THE MANOR WAS CURSED. SOMEHOW HAUNTED.
I SUPPOSE IT WAS, IN A WAY. I IMAGINE THE ACCIDENT WOULD HAVE LOOMED LARGE DURING YOUR FIRST YEAR.
IT WAS MORE THAN THAT...DID YOU KNOW I NEVER CAME TO VISIT MY FATHER HERE? I BARELY KNEW HIM WHEN HE DIED.
AND YET, IN THOSE EARLY YEARS, I FELT HIM HOVERING OVER ME. LIKE A FORCE TRYING TO IMPART SOMETHING. BUT THERE WAS NOTHING I COULD DO BUT TRY TO LIVE UP TO THE MAN HE WANTED ME TO BE.
MY POINT, MASTER BRUCE, IS THAT I'VE ALREADY SPENT A LIFETIME TRYING TO DIG UP A SENSE OF WHO MY FATHER WAS.
I HAVE NO DESIRE TO LITERALIZE THE PROCESS.
IF THE COURT OF OWLS HAD ANYTHING TO DO WITH MY FATHER'S DEATH, YOUR ACTIONS THESE PAST FEW WEEKS HAVE BEEN TRIBUTE ENOUGH.

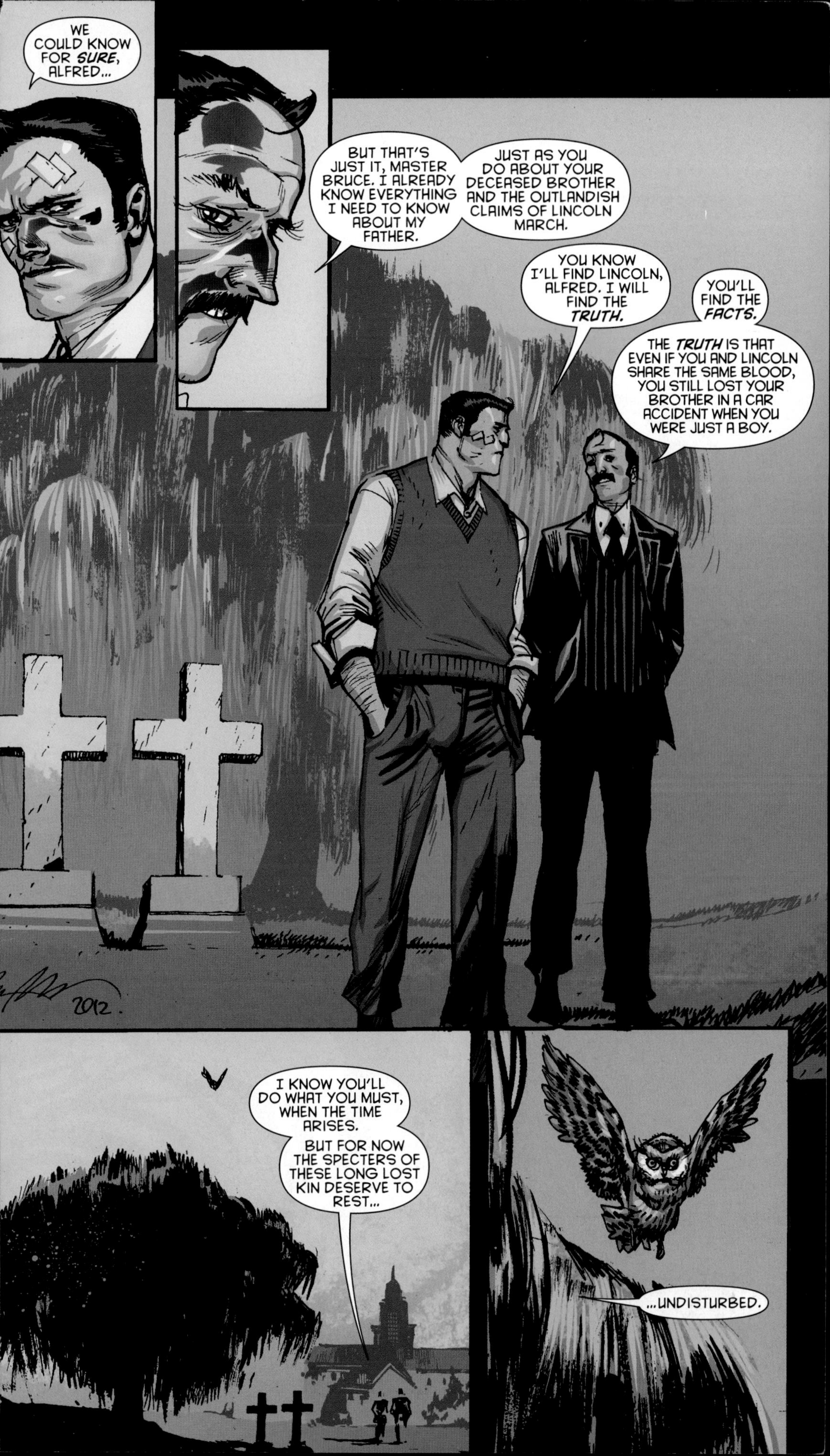
WE COULD KNOW FOR *SURE*, ALFRED...
BUT THAT'S JUST IT, MASTER BRUCE. I ALREADY KNOW EVERYTHING I NEED TO KNOW ABOUT MY FATHER.
JUST AS YOU DO ABOUT YOUR DECEASED BROTHER AND THE OUTLANDISH CLAIMS OF LINCOLN MARCH.
YOU KNOW I'LL FIND LINCOLN, ALFRED. I WILL FIND THE *TRUTH.*
YOU'LL FIND THE *FACTS.*
THE *TRUTH* IS THAT EVEN IF YOU AND LINCOLN SHARE THE SAME BLOOD, YOU STILL LOST YOUR BROTHER IN A CAR ACCIDENT WHEN YOU WERE JUST A BOY.
2012.
I KNOW YOU'LL DO WHAT YOU MUST, WHEN THE TIME ARISES.
BUT FOR NOW THE SPECTERS OF THESE LONG LOST KIN DESERVE TO REST...
...UNDISTURBED.

Batman battle suit armor design

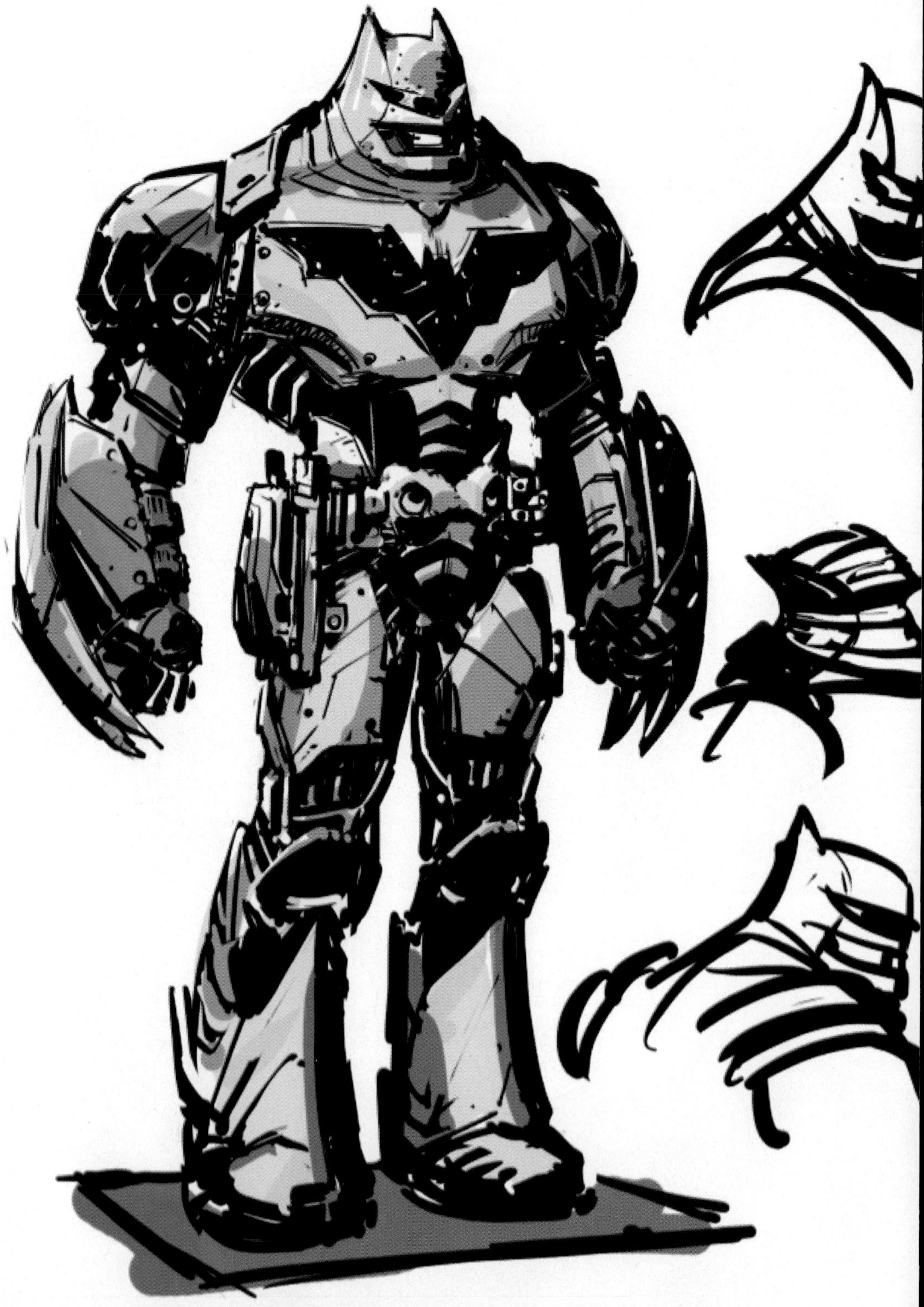

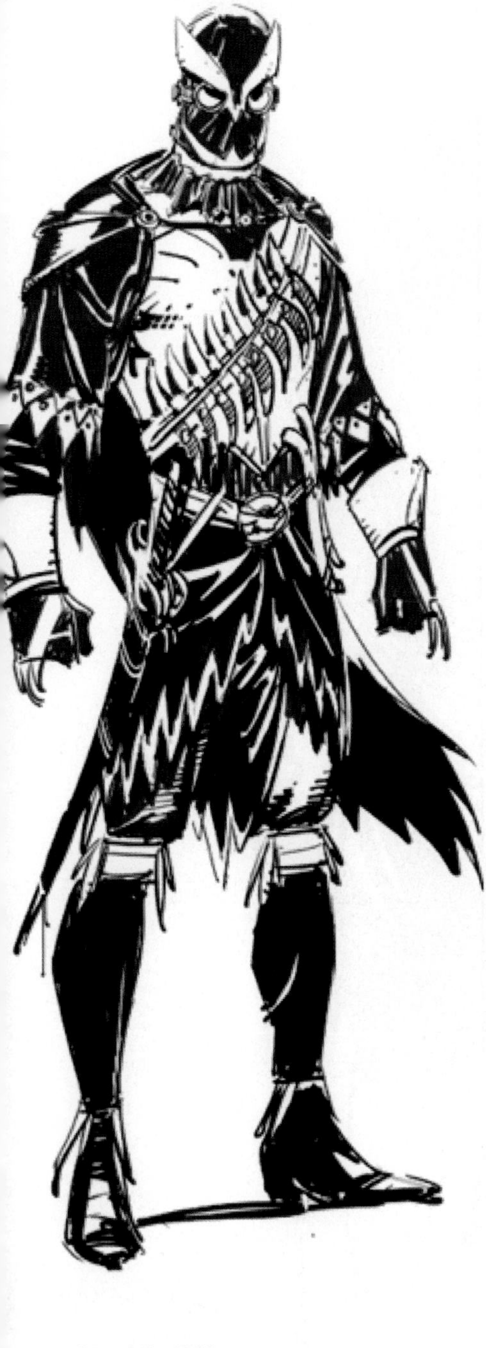

Talon of the 1660s

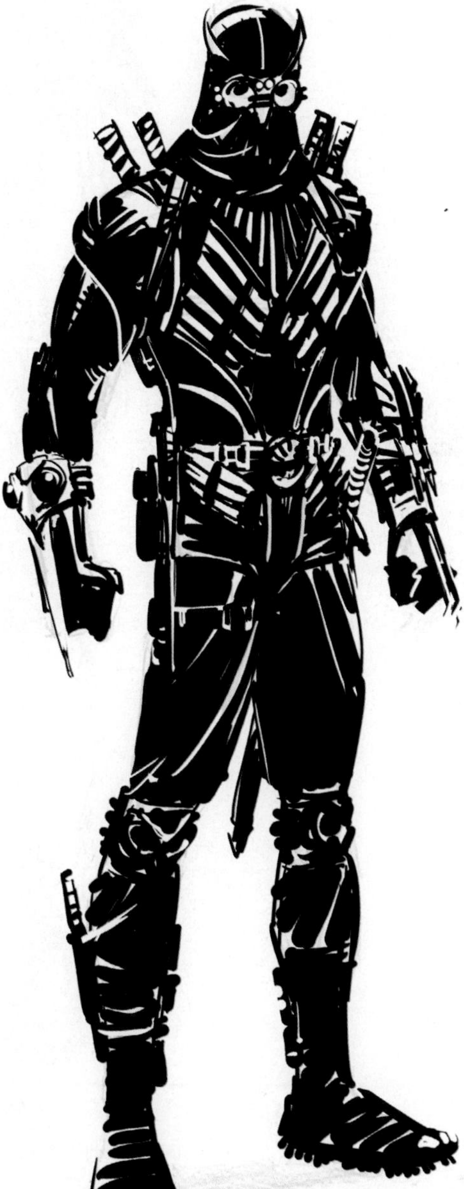

Talon of the 1980s

Talon of the 1700s

Talon of the 1840s

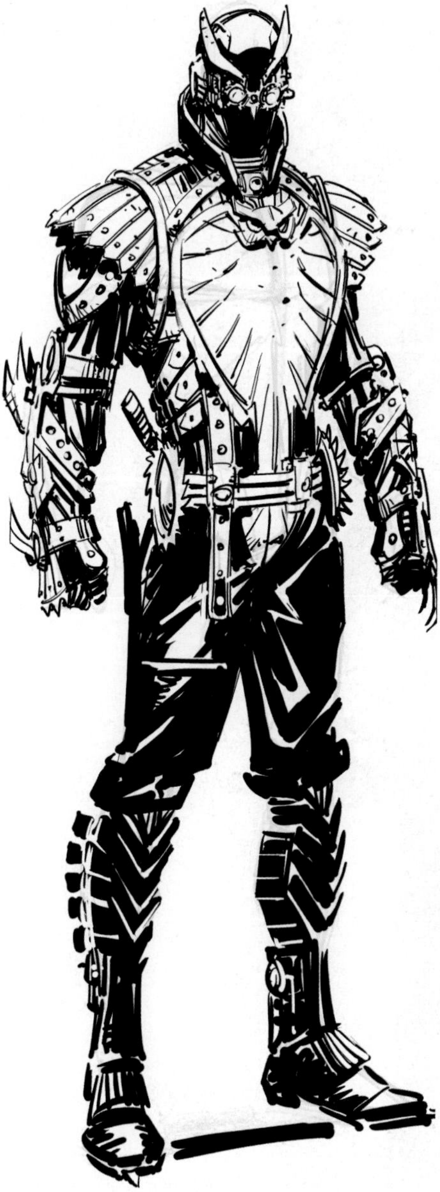

Talon of the 1870s

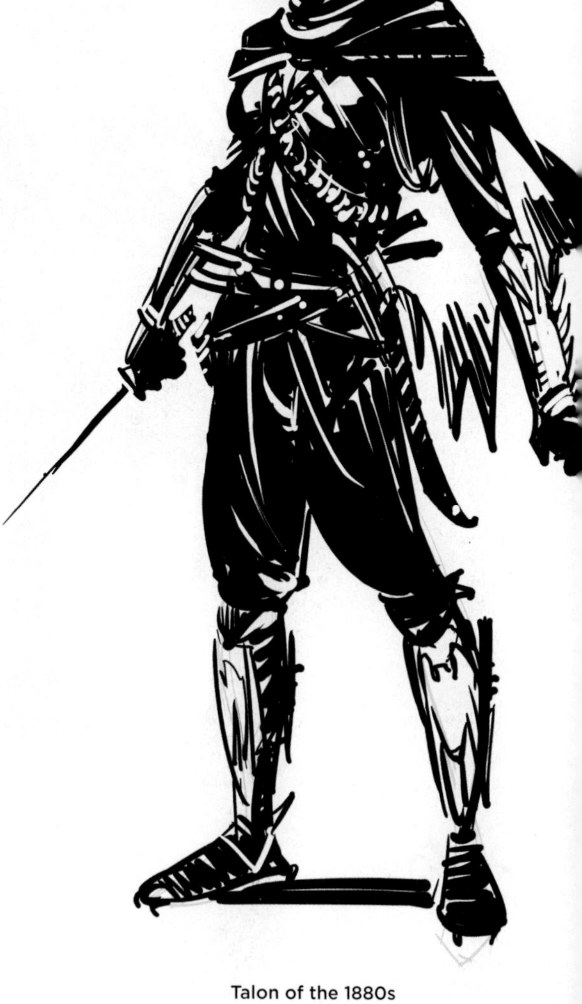

Talon of the 1880s

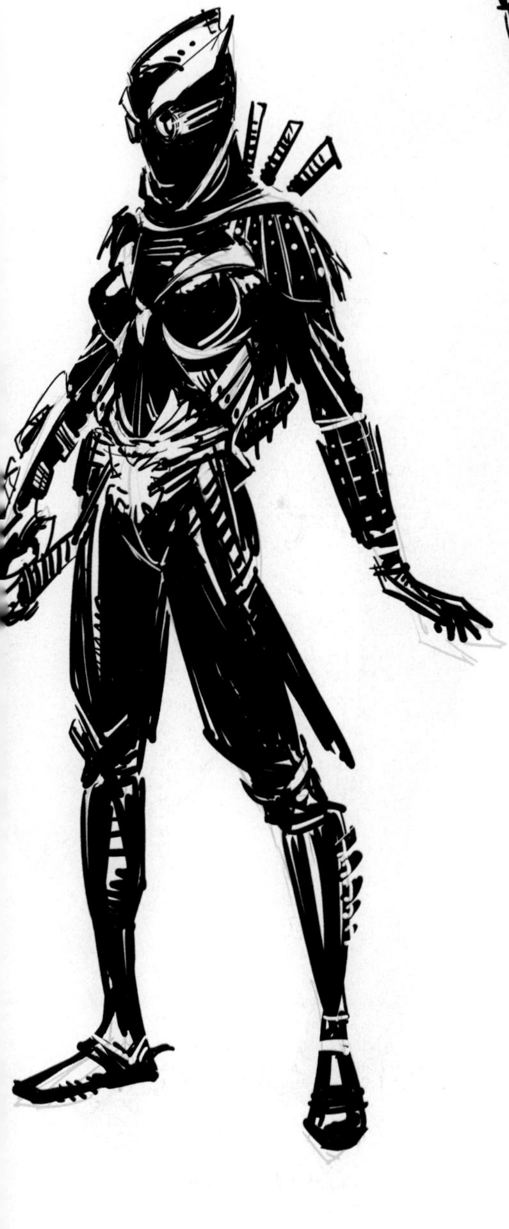

Talon of the 1940s

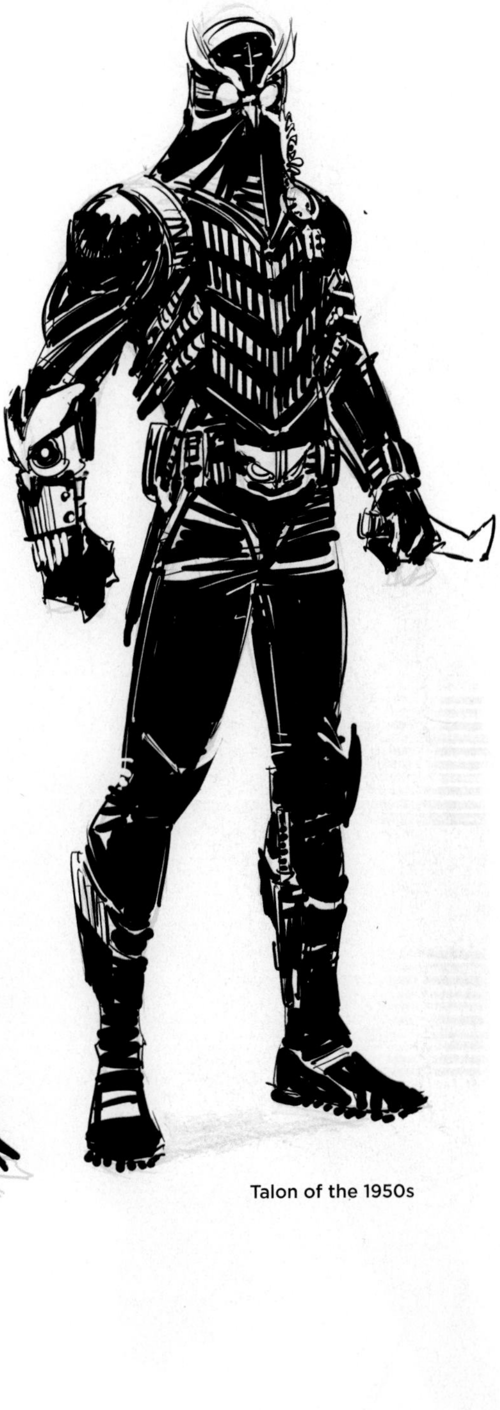

Talon of the 1950s

Talon of the 1880s
Design by MORITAT

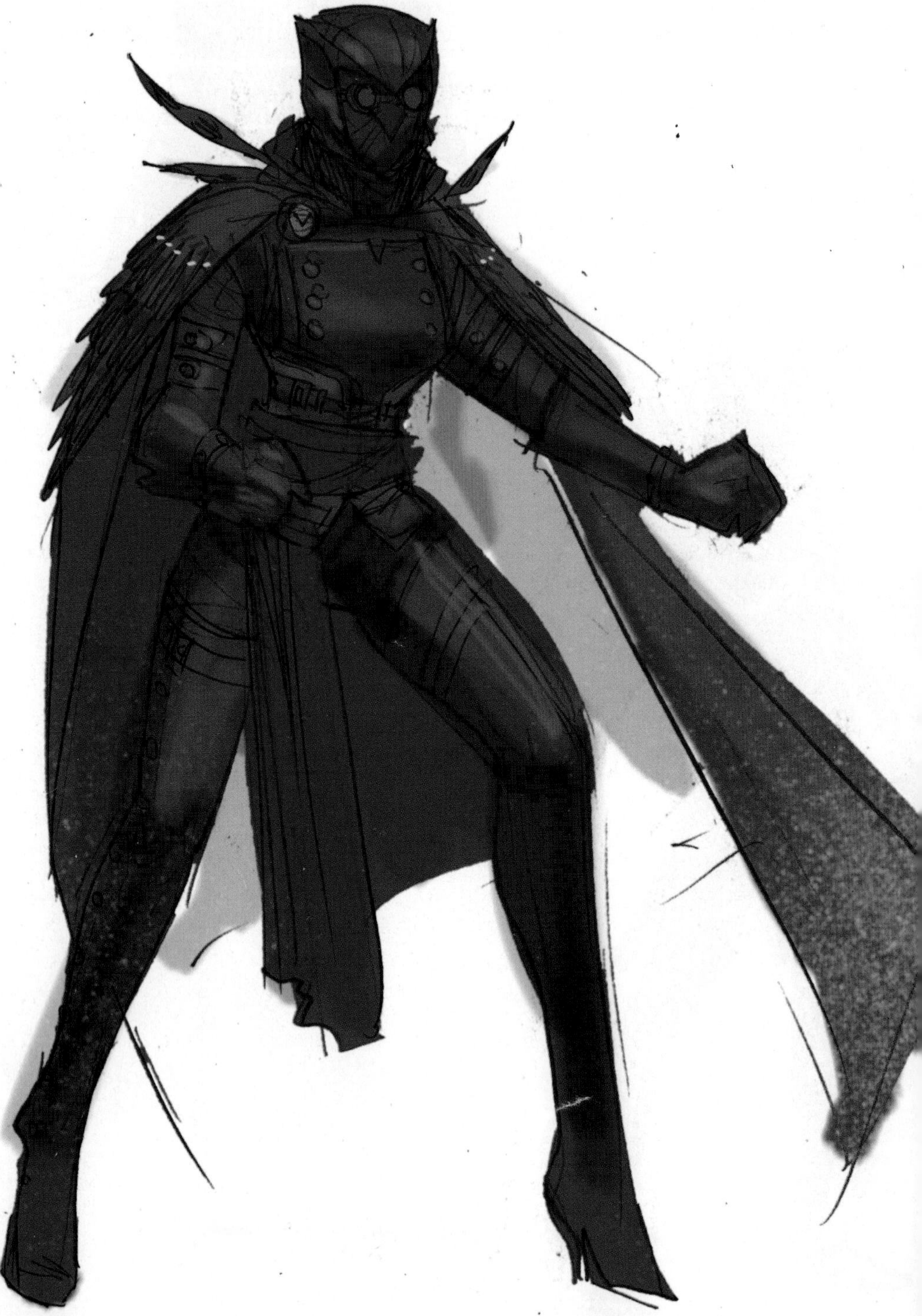